Methodological Issues & Strategies in Clinical Research

Methodological Issues & Strategies in Clinical Research

Edited by
Alan E. Kazdin

American Psychological Association
Washington, DC

First Printing   April 1992
Second Printing September 1992

Published by the
American Psychological Association
750 First Street, NE
Washington, DC 20002

Copies may be ordered from
APA Order Department
P.O. Box 2710
Hyattsville, MD 20784

This book was typeset in Goudy Old Style by Applied Graphics Technologies/Unicorn
Graphics, Washington, DC

Printer: BookCrafters, Chelsea, MI
Cover designer: Donya Melanson Associates
Technical editor and production coordinator: Deborah Segal

Library of Congress Cataloging-in-Publication Data

Methodological issues and strategies in clinical research/edited by Alan E. Kazdin.
    p. cm.
    Includes bibliographical references and index.
    ISBN 1-55798-154-X : $59.95 (list) : ($44.95 to members).—ISBN
    1-55798-167-1 (acid-free paper) : $39.95 (list & member)
    1. Clinical psychology—Research. I. Kazdin, Alan E.
    [DNLM: 1. Psychology, Clinical—methods. 2. Research Design. WM
      105 M5925]
    RC467.8.M48 1992 616.89'0072—dc20
    DNLM/DLC
    for Library of Congress   91-47118
                                                   CIP

Printed in the United States of America

CONTENTS

LIST OF CONTRIBUTORS

Robert L. Bangert-Drowns, Center for Research on Learning and Teaching, University of Michigan

John R. Bergan, Division of Educational Psychology, University of Arizona

Jenny L. Boyer, Department of Psychology, University of Oklahoma

Stephen J. Ceci, Human Development and Family Studies, Cornell University

Jacob Cohen, Department of Psychology, New York University

Michael Cowles, Department of Psychology, York University, Canada

Keven C. Davidson, Department of Psychology, University of Houston

Betsy Davis, Division of Counseling and Educational Psychology, University of Oregon

Caroline Davis, Department of Psychology, York University, Canada

René V. Dawis, Department of Psychology, University of Minnesota

Irene Elkin, School of Social Service, University of Chicago

Donald W. Fiske, Department of Psychology, University of Chicago

Jack M. Fletcher, Department of Pediatrics, University of Texas School of Medicine

Louis Fogg, Rush College of Nursing

Donelson R. Forsyth, Department of Psychology, Virginia Commonwealth University

David J. Francis, Department of Psychology, University of Houston

John V. Fulginiti, Division of Educational Psychology, University of Arizona

Gerd Gigerenzer, Institut für Psychologie, Universität Salzburg, Austria

Lawrence M. Glanz, Western Psychiatric Institute and Clinic and University of Pittsburgh School of Medicine

Roland H. Good III, Division of Counseling and Educational Psychology, University of Oregon

Bert F. Green, Department of Psychology, Johns Hopkins University

Anthony G. Greenwald, Department of Psychology, University of Washington

R. Karl Hanson, Department of Psychology, York University, Canada

Steven C. Hayes, Department of Psychology, University of Nevada

William P. Henry, Department of Psychology, Vanderbilt University

Louis M. Hsu, Department of Psychology, Fairleigh Dickinson University

Carl J. Huberty, Department of Educational Psychology, University of Georgia

John Hunsley, Center for Psychological Services, University of Ottawa, Canada

Stanley D. Imber, Western Psychiatric Institute and Clinic and University of Pittsburgh School of Medicine

Neil S. Jacobson, Department of Psychology, University of Washington

Alan E. Kazdin, Department of Psychology, Yale University

Gregory A. Kimble, Department of Psychology, Duke University

Helena Chmura Kraemer, Department of Psychiatry and Behavioral Sciences, Stanford University School of Medicine

William R. Leber, Psychological Services, Veterans Administration Medical Center, Oklahoma City

Brendan A. Maher, Department of Psychology, Harvard University

Alvin R. Mahrer, School of Psychology, University of Ottawa, Canada

Mary L. Miers, Office of Extramural Research and Training, National Institutes of Health, Bethesda, MD

Douglas G. Mook, Department of Psychology, University of Virginia

John D. Morris, Department of Human Services, Florida Atlantic University

Richard J. Morris, Department of Educational Psychology, University of Arizona

Eugene R. Oetting, Department of Psychology, Colorado State University

Kevin C. H. Parker, Child and Family Unit, Kingston General Hospital, Canada

Morris B. Parloff, Department of Psychology, American University

Douglas Peters, Department of Psychology, University of North Dakota

Jonathan Plotkin, Human Development and Family Studies, Cornell University

Robert Rosenthal, Department of Psychology, Harvard University

Ralph L. Rosnow, Department of Psychology, Temple University

Glenn L. Rowley, Department of Psychology, Monash University, Australia

Thomas E. Schacht, Department of Psychology, Vanderbilt University

Lee B. Sechrest, Department of Psychology, University of Arizona

Peter Sedlmeier, Institut für Psychologie, Universität Salzburg, Austria

Richard J. Shavelson, Graduate School of Education, University of California, Santa Barbara

Bradley Smith, Department of Psychology, University of Arizona

Stuart M. Sotsky, Department of Psychology, George Washington University

Stanley R. Strong, Department of Psychology, Virginia Commonwealth University

Hans H. Strupp, Department of Psychology, Vanderbilt University

Karla K. Stuebing, Department of Psychology, University of Houston

Nora M. Thompson, Southwest Neuropsychiatric Institute, San Antonio

Paula Truax, Department of Psychology, University of Washington

Bruce E. Wampold, Department of Counseling and Counselor Education, University of Wisconsin, Madison

Noreen M. Webb, Department of Psychology, University of California, Los Angeles

Allan W. Wicker, Department of Psychology, Claremont Graduate School

William H. Yeaton, Institute for Social Research, University of Michigan

PREFACE

This book provides readings designed to improve understanding of methodology and to enhance research practices in clinical psychology. The intended audience is persons who are in training or are actively involved in research. The primary focus of the readings is clinical psychology, but the issues and methods are relevant to other areas as well, such as counseling, educational and school psychology, psychiatry, and social work. The topics within each of these areas span theory, research, and application. Consequently, many of the methodological challenges are shared.

Several readings have been included to address a broad range of practices, procedures, and strategies for developing a sound knowledge base. The goal was to select, from a large literature on methodology and design, a special set of engaging articles of use to students and professionals alike. The articles address a wide range of topics within clinical research. At the same time, a number of the readings are related to psychological research in general and, hence, relate clinical psychology to the broader field of psychology.

The content of this book addresses experimental design, principles, procedures, and practices that govern research, assessment, sources of artifact and bias, data analyses and interpretation, ethical issues, and publication and communication of the results of research. The book is organized into sections that reflect the flow of the research process. The sections include the following:

- Background and Underpinnings of Research;
- Methods: Principles and Practices;
- Assessment;
- Data Analysis, Evaluation, and Interpretation;

- Special Topics in Clinical Research;
- Ethics in Research; and
- Publication and Communication of Research.

Within each area, the content cannot be exhaustive. Research design is a dynamic and active topic; novel methods of design, assessment, and evaluation continually emerge. Thus, a segment of available articles can only sample relevant domains to aid the researcher.

The organization of this book conveys features of research that follow in approximate logical and often temporal order as they arise in the flow of an investigation. Thus, underpinnings of research, development of the research idea, and procedures within the study obviously precede data analyses and write up of the study. However, underlying the book and the selection of articles is the view that diverse facets of design for a given study are integrally related at the outset, that is, when the study is conceived. For example, at the very outset during the planning stage of a study, the theory and rationale are, or at least should be, connected by the investigator to the statistical analyses and anticipated interpretations of the results. Similarly, an investigator's decisions about the experimental conditions, measures, and methods of administration are related to the final inferences and conclusions. Investigators developing a proposal might not be too concerned with analyses of the results or the discussion section. Yet, critical thought about how one is likely to analyze the data and the specific conclusions one wishes to draw from the study can greatly influence the design (e.g., experimental conditions, plan for their administration between or within subjects, measures, sample composition, and sample size). Although the topics of this book reflect and are organized according to the flow of research, articles were selected that transcended boundaries and discrete steps of research. The purpose was to convey the interdependence of all phases of research in relation to drawing valid conclusions.

A book of *readings* on the topic of *methodology* is not likely to make the best seller list, not to mention its poor prospects of being made into a movie. Edited books of readings are notoriously uneven in quality and level of the individual contributions. The topic of methodology adds to the risk because it is viewed as dry, technical, and difficult and cannot compete with alternatives for Saturday night entertainment. However, an effort was made to steer sharply away from the shoals of checkered quality and tedium.

To that end, three considerations guided the selection of articles. First, articles were designed to cover several steps or stages that emerge in planning and executing research. Key stages in the research process include developing the research idea; selecting methods, procedures, and assessment devices; analyzing and interpreting the data; and preparing a written report to communicate what was accomplished and why. Second, articles were selected not only to improve our understanding of research methods, but also to aid as often as possible in concrete recommendations and practices to guide the design of an investigation. Thus, many of the articles include recommendations that can be readily applied. Finally, an effort was made to identify highly readable articles. Hundreds of articles within the last several years were identified as relevant given their thrust and focus. From these, articles were selected that eschewed technical jargon, extensive formula, and similar features. Each of the articles has been published previously, which is an advantage because they have been reviewed for a prior publication process and, hence, their merit has been judged in advance of inclusion in this collection.

The rationale for selecting readable articles extends beyond the obvious. Technical writings and detailed entry into individual topics are critical to the development of research acumen. At the same time, such writings often require in-depth discussion and dialogue to establish the core concepts and to cull their implications. The process of selection in this book was designed to identify articles whose critical points could be readily gleaned from the articles themselves. Consequently, the book can be easily used on its own, particularly for graduate and advanced undergraduate courses or as a supplement to other texts.

Several persons have contributed to the development of this book. The contributors whose articles are included are gratefully acknowledged, not only for their specific articles, but also for the special contribution of their work to the field of psychology. Gary R. VandenBos and Julia Frank-McNeil of the American Psychological Association provided valuable support and guidance over the course of this project. Faculty and students in the Department of Psychology at Yale University provided a stimulating context for deliberating, discussing, and dissecting research issues and, hence, served as an important impetus for this book. I am especially grateful to the National Institute of Mental Health for the support of a Research Scientist Award (MH00353). That support has provided research, educational, and training opportunities directly related to assessment, methodology, and design. Finally, Michelle Kazdin, my daughter, helped in the final organization and evaluation of this book. I am, of course, grateful for her, not to mention her work on this book.

Alan E. Kazdin

INTRODUCTION

METHODOLOGY IN CLINICAL PSYCHOLOGY

Traditionally, clinical psychology has embraced a variety of topics including the study of personality; assessment and prediction of psychological functioning and adjustment; etiology, course, and outcome of various forms of clinical dysfunction; processes and outcomes of alternative treatment and preventive interventions, and cross-cultural differences in personality and behavior, to mention a few. Many issues of contemporary life have added to the range of topics as witnessed by the strong role that clinical psychology plays in medicine, psychiatry, and law; the study of violence, crime, homelessness, substance abuse, alternative family constellation patterns, child rearing, child care, and treatment of the elderly; and more generally, child and adult development. The complexity of current social living and the broad range of social and cultural issues are reflected in the richness of this field.

Clinical psychology includes the study of diverse populations, as illustrated by investigations of all age groups from infancy through old age. Indeed, the field extends beyond these age limits by studying processes before birth (e.g., prenatal characteristics of mothers and families) and in some ways, even after death (e.g., the impact of death on relatives and the treatment of bereavement). Also, research within the field of clinical psychology focuses on populations with unusual, stressful, or otherwise untoward experiences (e.g., the homeless and prisoners of wars), with psychological or psychiatric impairment (e.g., children, adolescents, or adults with depression, anxiety, posttraumatic stress disorder, autism, or schizophrenia), and with medical impairment and disease (e.g., cancer, acquired immune deficiency syndrome, spinal cord injury, or diabetes). Persons in contact with special populations are often studied themselves (e.g., children of alcoholics, spouses of depressed patients, and siblings of physically handicapped children). Examples of a few of the populations in clinical research can only begin to convey the breadth of focus. Consideration of the diverse settings in which clinical psychologists work (e.g., laboratories, clinics, hospitals, prisons, schools, and industries) and the multiple disciplines (e.g., medicine, psychiatry, neurology, pediatrics, and criminology) involved in this work would greatly broaden the scope.

The topical breadth of clinical psychology is accompanied by methodological diversity. Consider a few of the dimensions that characterize the field. Research in clinical psychology encompasses large-scale investigations as well as experiments with individual subjects, methods of data evaluation that include inferential statistical techniques as well as nonstatistical and clinical criteria to evaluate change, and laboratory experiments conducted in the course of a session or two at a given point in time or field studies that may assess and monitor changes over several years. The diversity of topics and types of research require coverage and appreciation of a broad range of methodological approaches, evaluative techniques, and research practices.

RESEARCH IN CLINICAL PSYCHOLOGY

General Goals

The general purpose of research in clinical psychology is to develop our understanding of human functioning. We wish to know the relations that exist among events and to understand the bases for such relations. Research is conducted to describe the relations and to reveal the mechanisms, processes, and reasons behind these relations. In the process of obtaining answers, further questions are invariably raised.

For example, a reasonably well-established finding is that harsh physical (corporal) punishment of children by their parents is often associated with elevated aggression in the children. (For purposes of this example, let us eschew the genuinely critical questions about what defines harsh punishment and what we mean by and how we measure aggression.) A statement about the relation, although based on research, conveys the need for additional research. Our goal in this case is to understand the relation of harsh child-rearing practices and child aggression. Among the tasks of research is to identify when the relation is and is not evident. After all, not all children who are punished harshly are highly aggressive. Also, we wish to know what characteristics other than aggression are evident among such children, what parents and families are like who engage in harsh practices, whether having two harsh parents is worse than one on severity of child aggression, and so on. Yet research is not conducted merely to fill in a table of "facts" or to demonstrate empirical relations among variables. We wish to understand the bases of these relations. Why do some parents engage in harsh discipline practices? Why are children punished severely? What mediates, accounts for, leads to, and causes parents to engage in harsh practices; what is the connection between such practices and related variables (e.g., stress, marital relations, or a history with their own parents)? Precisely how does the connection between harsh punishment and child aggression operate (e.g., does the child become aggressive because of seeing aggression in the parents, or is there some genetic predisposition toward aggression)? These examples only begin to identify lines of research required to elaborate on the relation of child rearing and aggression.

The agenda to describe and understand characterizes research generally. Within such areas as clinical psychology, applied research issues spawned by basic research are added to this because of our interest in extending and using the knowledge base for clinical and social benefit. Thus, given the earlier example, researchers in clinical psychology are interested in understanding and developing methods to alter those punishment practices suspected of promoting child maladjustment or other untoward consequences.

Theory and Methodology as Partners in Research

Research methods consist of careful observation and systematic evaluation of the subject matter. Diverse methods involve special arrangements and plans for observation that are designed to uncover relations between variables in a relatively unambiguous fashion. The relations may seem apparent in nature when a particular phenomenon is observed casually. Yet relations often are obscured by the complex interrelations and combinations of many variables as they normally appear. The task of identifying relations is compounded by the characteristics and limits of our perception. Among complex relations, it is easy and natural for us to connect variables perceptually and conceptually and then to integrate these relations into our belief systems. The relations can be firmly entrenched regardless of whether the variables are genuinely related to one another.

Scientific research attempts to simplify the complexity of nature and to isolate phenomena for careful scrutiny. The relation is often examined by manipulating the variables of interest while controlling extraneous factors that might otherwise influence the results. By controlling or holding constant sources of influence that might vary under ordinary circumstances, the relation between variables of interest can be studied. In addition to arranging features of nature, science also provides methods to aid perception. The methods consist of diverse practices, procedures, and decision rules to aid in drawing conclusions and in reaching a consensus about relations observed in research. Hence, methodology is an aid to understanding.

Theories, conceptual views, and ideas are also an aid to understanding and play a central role in the research process. Theories are posed to explain the relations and to connect the variables of interest that drive the research. Theory can refer to different levels of conceptualizing phenomena that vary in breadth and complexity. For example, a broad view can be derived from which several relations and predictions are made. At the other extreme, theory can refer to a tentative explanation of a specific relation. In a general sense, these explanations offer ideas about why or how variables operate together. Thus, a theory need not reflect a fully developed view of how the entire phenomenon operates, but rather refers to an explanation proposed to account for the specific relation of interest.

An idea or set of ideas provides a framework for understanding the possible bases or reasons for the connections among variables. There is an endless array of facts or data that could be generated by research; presumably, the interrelations among all conceivable variables of interest in clinical psychology might be studied. Theory helps to sort out those variables that may be of special interest, relevance, and importance. In the development of a research proposal, investigators occasionally argue that a particular study is important because the variables have not been studied before. However, this rationale as a primary or pivotal basis for research is weak; the goal is to understand—to advance theory and knowledge. The investigator must make the case that the variables of interest selected for study and the specific way they are to be studied serve to meet these ends.

Evaluation in Clinical Psychology

A central feature of psychology is training in assessment and evaluation. Methodology embraces systematic evaluation that includes multiple practices. These practices are designed to minimize ambiguity and to maximize replicability or repeated demonstration of a phenomenon. Although methodology is usually restricted to discussions of research, the principles and practices are directly relevant to clinical practice. For example, in the practice of therapy with an individual patient, we might say that treatment is proceeding well if the patient is experiencing critical processes—is reconceptualizing or "coming to terms" with the issues we are addressing. We could say this and often do based on our views of the events in therapy. These views would be greatly aided by introducing some systematic evaluation, perhaps in the form of audiotapes or videotapes of selected treatment sessions that someone else could rate or by standardized self-report measures of process and outcome. Introducing systematic methods into such situations raises other questions. Are the measures valid? Will the assessment process alter the phenomenon of interest? Potential problems themselves introduced by evaluation can be investigated, evaluated, and understood. It is the absence of systematic evaluation that raises serious problems. Without some systematic and documentable evaluation, it is not possible to infer, corroborate, or replicate what transpired. In clinical psychology, whether in research or practice, systematic evaluation is essential.

RESEARCH METHODS AND THEIR RAISON D'ETRE

Methodology refers to the diverse principles, procedures, and practices that govern research. The focus on concrete methods and practices draws attention to ingredients of research and perhaps conjures up an image of a cookbook for the design of experiments. Methodology is not a matter of including specific practices and ingredients. Even highly revered practices (e.g., random assignment of subjects and use of large samples) may be unnecessary to reach valid inferences in a given study. Understanding the rationale for methodological practices as well as the practices themselves are critically important. In general, methodology teaches us ways to think about the relations between variables, about causes and effects, and about conclusions drawn from theory, research, and experience. Methodology, as a way of thinking about phenomena, alerts us to the types of questions to ask and as importantly to the practices designed to obtain enlightened answers.

The purpose of research is to draw valid, sound, and well-based inferences about the relations between variables. Experiments are attempts to arrange the circumstances so as to minimize ambiguity in reaching these inferences. Fundamentals of experimentation are usually taught and conveyed in the context of laboratory research because opportunities for control, methodological elegance, and ideals of experimentation are optimal. Critically important practices such as randomly assigning subjects to conditions, selecting homogeneous samples of subjects, and carefully controlling manifold conditions to which subjects are exposed illustrate some of the central features that characterize laboratory studies. Clinical psychology often profits from these advantages of laboratory studies or studies that approximate the conditions of the laboratory. In clinical psychology, as well as in related areas, a great deal of research is conducted outside of the laboratory in such settings as hospitals, clinics, schools, and communities. Exigencies associated with recruitment of participants, the settings and conditions in which research is conducted, and the control over features that can affect the design present methodological challenges, to say the least. An in-depth understanding of methodology is particularly important because the range of influences that can obscure the relations among variables is vast. These influences cannot be used as an excuse for poorly designed research. On the contrary, the subject matter demands a grasp of the nuances of design and evaluation so that special experimental arrangements, novel control conditions, and statistical methods can be deployed to maximize clarity of results.

THE PRESENT BOOK

The research process includes a number of interrelated steps beginning with the development of the research idea through the communication of results. This book is organized into sections that are designed to reflect the flow of research issues and processes. Several articles have been selected to address methodological issues in clinical research.

The first section, "Background and Underpinnings of Research," provides an overview of psychological research in general as well as assumptions within clinical psychology. Assumptions, goals, and methods of research at a general level provide a point of departure for specific sections that follow. In addition, within this initial section are articles that cover the process of developing and discovering research ideas.

The second section, "Methods: Principles and Practices," includes articles that address several procedures, practices, and design options. Articles cover sampling issues and their relevance to drawing conclusions about research. Experimental manipulations or the conditions within an experiment are also discussed in this section. Finally, the strength and limitations of selected design options are presented.

The third section, "Assessment," presents scale evaluation and development. Basic concepts related to the development and validation of scales are discussed. Scale evaluation is illustrated by an example of research that examines reliability and validity of three of the most widely used measures within the field (Minnesota Multiphasic Personality Inventory, Rorschach Inkblot Test, and Wechsler Adult Intelligence Scale). Finally, the section ends with a discussion of generalizability theory and its conceptual and methodological contribution to assessment.

The fourth section, "Data Analysis, Evaluation, and Interpretation," contains several articles that relate data evaluation to other facets of research such as conceptualization of the study, decision making, and conclusions. Topics include the relation of hypotheses to statistical analyses, alternative methods of analysis, statistical power and data interpretation, and the interpretation of "negative results." Selected analyses often used within clinical psychology (multivariate analyses, meta-analysis, and structural equation modeling) and their role in building the knowledge base are presented.

In the fifth section, "Special Topics in Clinical Research," diverse topics of special interest in areas of clinical work are addressed. Articles discuss evaluation of individual cases both in the context of clinical practice and small sample research of clinical phenomena. Other topics include the search for client, therapist, and treatment influences in therapy research; placebo control groups and the conceptual and practical issues they raise; the evaluation of change; and clinical significance.

In the sixth section, "Ethics in Research," a broad range of ethical concerns is sampled. Two general categories of ethical issues are salient within the context of research. These are ethical issues related to the protection of research participants and obligations of the investigator to the field, colleagues, and, more generally, science.

The final section, "Publication and Communication of Research," addresses the preparation of manuscripts designed to communicate one's research. Communication is a logical conclusion to completion of research. From the standpoint of methodology, the rationale for research processes and practices are critically important to convey in the written report. The articles in this section are designed to convey the thought processes embraced by methodology that deserve attention in this critical phase of the research process.

Each of the sections of this book represents a broad domain of major topics. Indeed, each topic could easily serve as the basis of its own book. The sampling of papers within each domain raises central points. Many of the articles connect the research process by traversing different phases of research and, hence, serve a valuable role in conveying how theory, research design, assessment, and statistical evaluation act in concert. The articles do so in a way that I believe is engaging and, in general, user-friendly.

I

BACKGROUND AND UNDERPINNINGS OF RESEARCH

The conduct of research encompasses general issues as well as concrete practices. In this initial set of articles, general issues that need to be dealt with prior to the investigation itself are discussed. The first two articles discuss scientific research in psychology as well as in clinical work. Assumptions that underlie the research process in general as well as types of research are made explicit. Also in this section are articles discussing ideas, their sources, and the development of an investigation.

SCIENTIFIC METHOD

In the initial article, Gregory Kimble (1989) discusses the scientific underpinnings, tenets, and approaches of psychological research. Critical issues are examined including the role of theory, personal experience, and common sense in relation to the development of scientific research. The article provides a useful starting point by making explicit key assumptions about what we do in psychological research and how these assumptions relate to the research process and the accumulation of scientific knowledge.

Donelson Forsyth and Stanley Strong (1986) examine assumptions of research and the influences these have on the type of studies that are completed. In the context of psychotherapy research, Forsyth and Strong consider dualisms of research and the natural tensions between basic and applied research and science and technology. The need for diverse methods of study within clinical research, including both basic and applied research, is elaborated on. The role of theory is discussed as a way of linking research and practice and developing the knowledge base in clinical and counseling research.

DEVELOPING RESEARCH IDEAS

Research begins with the idea itself and the basis or question for investigation. In the article by Allan Wicker (1985), strategies are identified to stimulate new insights about phenomena and to translate these into research investigations. Specific suggestions to develop research hypotheses include alternative ways of selecting, developing, and playing with ideas, examining the context in which phenomena occur, challenging central assumptions, and scrutinizing key concepts. In developing the research idea, creativity is difficult to prescribe. Yet Wicker elaborates on concrete ways of reconsidering phenomena that can lead to novel ideas, a deeper understanding of phenomena, and alternative means of generating creative hypotheses for research.

Research involves the careful study of phenomena and testing of alternative hypotheses. Research is also the stage at which to develop ideas and hypotheses and to discover how variables relate to each other. In the article by Alvin Mahrer (1988), two different approaches to research are discussed, namely, hypothesis testing and discovery-oriented research. The article begins by discussing the more familiar hypothesis-testing approach that dominates psychological research in general. In the context of psychotherapy research, hypothesis testing is criticized for its intent, limited yield, and lack of impact on theory or clinical practice. Mahrer makes the case for the discovery-oriented approach as a basis for research. Discovery-oriented research seeks to examine the particulars in the area of interest (e.g., client–therapist interaction) and to isolate that which is novel, unexpected, and difficult to grasp or explain. The goal is not to confirm or disconfirm hypotheses, but to identify connections and relations and to collect data on these connections. Although the discovery-oriented approach is discussed in the context of psychotherapy, the approach can be extended more generally. This article discusses how to begin the process of identifying important relations and building an empirical and theoretical base of clinical work.

SCIENTIFIC METHOD

1

PSYCHOLOGY FROM THE STANDPOINT OF A GENERALIST

GREGORY A. KIMBLE

In recent years the question of whether psychology can be a single, general discipline has been the object of considerable discussion and controversy. Although some scholars have been able to see actual (e.g., Matarazzo, 1987) or potential (e.g., Staats, 1981) unity in the field, a greater number (e.g., Furedy & Furedy, 1982; Kendler, 1981; Koch, 1981) have found disunity and chaos. Discussions of this issue sometimes have taken on the quality of a methodological holy war because the disagreements are partly in the realm of values. Psychology is a house divided. One group of psychologists sees the field in terms of scientific values and accepts the concepts of objectivism, elementism, and nomothetic lawfulness. The group opposed sees psychology in terms of humanistic values and accepts the concepts of intuitionism, holism, and idiographic lawfulness. The positions seem irreconcilable, and the war goes on (Kimble, 1984).

Meanwhile, this epistemic jihad has encouraged the impression in

Reprinted from the *American Psychologist*, *44*, 491–499. Copyright 1989 by the American Psychological Association.

some quarters that our recent family squabbles are a scientific revolution of the type that Kuhn (1970) referred to as a "paradigm shift." The time has come, however, to put that myth to rest. There has been no revolution in psychology, just a series of tribal wars that have brought a new look to the battlefield. In particular, the concepts, methods, and subject matter of both cognitive and humanistic psychology, although very different, have gained legitimacy. As a result, the appearance of psychology now is not at all like what it was less than half a century ago. The major assertion of this article, however, is that the altered appearance of psychology is just a change in surface structure. At a deeper level, the structure of psychology is what it always was. The purpose of this article is to describe that structure in the belief that all psychologists may possibly find it acceptable because it will show that intuition, holism, and idiographic lawfulness are now included in the science of psychology and that this science operates within limits set by human values. In this article, I present a series of assertions that define what I take to be the major commitments and styles of thought that characterize scientific psychology. Each of these assertions is followed by explanatory text.

DETERMINISM, EMPIRICISM, AND THE DEFINITION OF PSYCHOLOGY

Two of the basic tenets of traditional science are those of determinism and empiricism. In psychology, those assumptions decide such fundamental issues as the definition of the field.

1. Behavior is determined by genetic endowment and environmental circumstances. The understanding, prediction, and control of behavior are reasonable scientific ambitions.

All psychologists accept these statements but in somewhat different ways. For the purely scientific psychologists, the emphasis is on abstract understanding. *Prediction* and *control* are terms that apply to theory and research. For the applied psychologists, the emphasis is on practical understanding. Prediction and control are concepts related to the goal of improving the lives of people. Although there are some psychologists who regard some human actions as otherwise uncaused voluntary expressions of "free will" (Kimble, 1984), I doubt that such a compromise is necessary.

For some time now it has been clear that voluntary acts are amenable to investigation by the methods of science. In an early article, Kimble and Perlmuter (1970) identified five hallmarks of volition. Voluntary behavior is learned, motivated, planned, attended to, and guided to completion by a comparator process. At one level, this analysis solves the problem of volition by reducing it to accepted scientific concepts. At another level, however, the solution creates problems of its own, because terms like *motivation, attention,* and *comparator process* require objective definition. Without it, they violate the second basic tenet of science, the principle of empiricism.

2. *The data of science are the publicly confirmable facts of observation. Psychology is the science of behavior.*

Although they are an important part of psychology, inner phenomena like thought, emotion, and ambition are not a part of the basic definition because they are not observable. They are concepts, inferences from behavior. They play a key role in the science of psychology, which I will describe after I develop the required foundation, beginning with a correction of some possible misunderstandings of the definition just presented.

Most important, perhaps, the definition does not exclude personal experience, common sense, or intuition from the science of psychology. Although private, they are important sources of hypotheses for the science. The principle of empiricism does not apply to the discovery of ideas but to the establishment of their validity. How one arrives at an idea has no bearing on its truth. It is its acceptance into science that requires objective evidence. Thus, if a man dreams that he was hiking in the mountains, and your intuition tells you that he had the dream because he unconsciously loves his mother, there is nothing in the tenet of empiricism to prevent your thinking that way. No one should take you very seriously, however, until you produce some type of evidence that the hypothesis is not false. If it turns out that such evidence is logically impossible to obtain, as is true of Marxist theory, "scientific" creationism, and some parts of psychoanalytic theory, the hypothesis is not part of science. Falsifiability is the criterion that marks the boundary line between science and nonscience.

Although personal experience plays the same legitimate role as intuition in psychology, it cannot provide the basic data of the science for reasons that become very clear in cases where the experiences of people differ. Suppose that my experience tells me that learning always is sudden and insightful, that men are more intelligent than women, and that people have dependable traits like honesty and sociability that appear in every situation. Suppose, by contrast, that your experience tells you that learning is always gradual, that women are more intelligent than men, and that traits like honesty and sociability are situation specific. Whose experience (if either) shall we accept as valid? You get the point: We cannot decide without a public test. The only alternatives appear to be (a) the creation of an epistemological elitist class whose personal experiences would define the truth for all the rest of us, or (b) the democratic decision that the experiences of everyone have been created equal. Neither of these alternatives is acceptable to science, however, because both of them violate the criterion of falsifiability.

The great problem with a reliance on common sense as evidence of psychological truths is that these truths are so defective (Kohn, 1988). Some of them are wrong ("Genius is closely related to insanity"). Some of them are contradictory ("Every individual human being is unique" versus "People are about the same the whole world over"). Most of the explanations appeal to essences ("People seek the company of others because they are gregarious by nature"). Probably without exception, the truths of common sense are oversimplifications.

COMPLEXITY AND ANALYSIS

Almost nothing important in behavior results from a single gene or from a single environmental influence. Behavior and its determinants are both complex. Multiple causes produce multiple psychological effects. Moreover, causes interact, and the influence of any single variable depends on the values of other variables in the situation. The need to unravel the threads of such complex causality has a fundamental implication.

3. Psychology must be analytic. A nonanalyzing science is an inarticulate science. Even to talk about a subject requires that it be analyzed into elements.

All science analyzes. Lewinian field theory (e.g., Lewin, 1931), which psychology now recognizes as possibly the most constructive holistic theory in its history (Jones, 1985), was very analytic. Lewin's fields contained boundaries, barriers, goals, and paths to goals, along with the individual. The individual was full of separate psychic regions, in various states of tension, separated by more or less permeable boundaries. Acted on by attracting and repelling vectors derived from objects with positive and negative valences, the individual moved within the field, sometimes reorganized it, and sometimes left it for the greener pastures of another level of reality. Lewinian theory was holistic in the sense that it treated behavior as dependent on the totality of many interacting variables, but that feature did not distinguish it from any other well-developed theory, for example that of Hull, one of Lewin's great rivals. The important difference between these theories was a difference in the level of analysis.

The products of analysis are the elements of a science. Because all science is analytic, it is also elementistic at some level. Different levels of analysis, and therefore different elements, are appropriate for different purposes. For example, the psycholinguists have been quite convincing on the point that the communicative functions of language involve overarching plans that control the production of sentences. It is impossible to understand the creation of an utterance in terms of strung-together linguistic units. Mistakes in language are another matter. They are only partly understandable in such holistic terms. I still write longhand, and every sentence that I write is the realization of a linguistic plan. The mistakes I make, however—the slips of the pen—almost always occur when some fragment of a word that should come later sneaks forward and occurs too early. The explanation of such linguistic behavior requires the use of elements that are smaller than a word.

In the history of psychology the elementist–holist argument centered on the question of whether the units of perception are attributes of sensations or organized perceptual patterns. The most important thing that has happened to that question is that it has become a question of fact rather than an item of faith. Research has now produced a blueprint of the answer to the question. The peripheral nervous system is equipped to handle only very elementary inputs: primary qualities, intensities, frequencies, durations, and extents of stimulation. By the time these neural messages reach the brain, however, they have given rise to organizations that endow such patterns of stimulation as those produced by phonemes, psychologically primary colors, visual angles, and the human face with the status of perceptual units. These particular organizing processes appear to be inborn, but experience also contributes to the creation of such units. Anyone who has tried the Stroop test (Stroop, 1935) has had a firsthand demonstration of the fact that words (learned organizations of letters) are extremely powerful perceptual units.

NATURE–NURTURE INTERACTION

Except in the minds of a few radical nativists and empiricists, the nature–nurture issue has long since been settled. The methods of behavioral genetics give quantitative meaning to the now-accepted statement that heredity and environment both contribute to human psychological characteristics but that they contribute to different degrees for different traits. Social attitudes and values are mostly learned (environmental), whereas height and weight are mostly inherited. Intelligence and introversion are somewhere in between. Whatever the proportions, however, the pattern of joint influence always seems to be the same.

4. For all psychological characteristics, inheritance sets limits on, or creates, a range of potentials for development. Environment determines how near the individual comes to developing the extremes of these potentials.

Inheritance provides different people with the intellect required to become a chess master, with a vulnerability to schizophrenia, or with the physical gifts required to compete in the Olympic Games. Environment determines whether these potential outcomes are realized. Questions about the relative importance of heredity and environment in the determination of such outcomes are questions for research, some of which is now available. For example, coefficients of heritability have been calculated for intelligence, various traits of personality, and the major forms of psychopathology. These coefficients usually ascribe less than half the variance in psychological traits to inheritance. Such data indicate that, although a biological basis for human diversity exists, the most powerful influences are environmental.

POTENTIAL VERSUS PERFORMANCE

Turning to the short-term dynamics of individual behavior, one encounters a similar pattern. Just as genetic factors put limits on the range of traits a person can develop, these developed traits define the limits of a person's behavior at the moment. Other factors determine whether this behavior reaches the limits of an individual's potential.

5. Individual behavior is the joint product of more or less permanent underlying potentials and more or less temporary internal and external conditions.

The distinction between trait- and state-anxiety shows how this idea works. A person may have a long-lasting potential for becoming anxious, a high level of trait-anxiety. The trait will lie dormant, however, until some threat occurs to throw this person into a state of anxiety. The distinctions in psychological theory between availability and accessibility of memories, linguistic competence and linguistic behavior, and sensitivity and bias provide additional examples. One may possess the memory of a certain person's name, but the memory may escape because of an interfering set. A little boy may know that the correct pronunciation of the word is "fish" although the best that he can do is "fis." Given the same sensory evidence, one subject in an experiment may report the presence of a signal and another may not because of their different criteria for making a positive response.

As in the case of nature and nurture, performance can never exceed the limits set by the underlying potential. Suppose that the anxious person described above has the potential to score 130 on an IQ test. In an anxious state, the person's performance may be much lower than that, but never higher. These statements are inherent in the definition of potential.

MENTALISTIC CONCEPTS

For the radical behaviorists, from Watson (1913) to Skinner (1987), all of this talk about anxiety, criteria, and potentials is offensive because these terms refer to phenomena that are subjective, mentalistic, and unobservable. They are not the raw materials that sciences are made of. In the final analysis, they hold (and I agree) that the only observables available to psychology are the behavior of organisms (responses) and the environmental circumstances (stimuli) in which behavior occurs. Everything else, they say, (but I do not agree) must be excluded if psychology is to be a science. The problem with this radical position is that it sacrifices everything of interest and importance in psychology by its exclusion of mentalistic concepts. Who can possibly care about a psychology that is silent on such topics as thinking, motivation, and volition? What has happened to human experience and the mind in this strangely unpsychological psychology? Do mentalistic concepts have no scientific role at all to play in a behavioristic world of facts? The answers to these questions take us back to a point that came up in connection with the definition of psychology.

6. *Mentalistic concepts enter psychology as inferences from behavior. The observations that define them often suggest causes.*

For as long as there has been a human species, people have noted that members of the species vary. All languages came to include such terms as "intelligence," "introversion," and "industriousness" to describe such variation. In the history of psychology, applications of this descriptive process have been important. They led Pavlov to the concept of the conditioned reflex, Piaget to the idea of developmental stages, and Selye to a recognition of the General Adaptation Syndrome.

In his very first classes in internal medicine as a young medical student, Selye (1976) was impressed with the fact that patients who were supposed to have different diseases shared many of the same symptoms: "They felt and looked ill, had a coated tongue, complained of more or less diffuse aches and pains in the joints, and of intestinal disturbances with loss of appetite" (p. 15). The symptoms that were supposed to help in differential diagnosis, "were absent or, at least, so inconspicuous that I could not distinguish them" (p. 16). This led Selye to the conception of a "general syndrome of disease," which later on became the "General Adaptation Syndrome" and then "stress." Selye hypothesized that the General Adaptation Syndrome was caused by any form of illness or injury to the body and that it was expressed in the symptoms common to all illness.

Selye was thinking in terms that came to be called "intervening variable theorizing." The construct, General Adaptation Syndrome, intervenes conceptually between a determining independent variable (any bodily injury) and a dependent variable (symptoms common to all illness). Figure 1 presents two diagrams of this kind of theorizing. The upper diagram based on the Selye example shows that processes of inference and hypothesis lead to the identification of psychological concepts and the postulation of possible lawful connections. The lower diagram presents the status of these connections as they were seen by Tolman (1938), the most important advocate of intervening variable theorizing. Tolman identified relationships among variables that are of different kinds, depending on whether the system includes intervening variables. Those that he called F-1 laws describe the direct dependence of behavioral phenomena on their determining antecedents. Those that he called F-2 and F-3 laws enter the picture with the introduction of intervening variables. The F-2 laws relate intervening variables to their antecedents. The F-3 laws describe the dependence of psychological phenomena on the intervening constructs.

THE GENERAL ADAPTATION SYNDROME

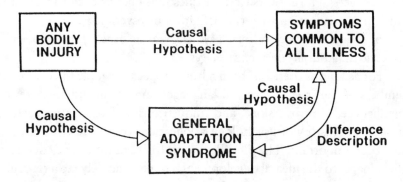

CONCEPTS AND TYPES OF LAWFULNESS

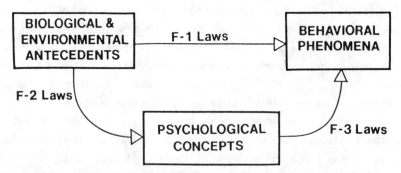

Figure 1: Intervening Variable Theorizing. Note: Psychological concepts are conceived as standing logically between independent variables on the left-hand side of the diagram and dependent variables on the right. The upper panel provides a concrete example and shows how inferences and causal hypotheses figure in the creation of intervening variables. The lower panel presents the more general case and shows how Tolman's (1938) F-1, F-2, and F-3 laws fit into the picture.

The great usefulness of the intervening variable approach is that it provides objectivity for unobservable mentalistic concepts. The F-2 and F-3 laws tie them to observable antecedents and behavioral consequences. This permits entry into psychology of the topics that the radical behaviorists would banish. It allows psychology to deal with such conceptions as "attitude," "plan," and "purpose," which most of us take to be important items in the subject matter of the science.

By now, of course, the cat is out of the bag. The approach that I am recommending is the logical-empiricist method that has received strong criticism from the philosophers of science (e.g., Spector, 1966). Public observability as the criterion of scientific truth is harder to pin down than first thoughts might suggest. What is observable to people with one type of physiology or personal history may not be observable to others. This criticism, however, only leads to another important point of understanding. Before abandoning any significant commitment, it is always a good idea to consider the options that would remain in the absence of what one is planning to give up. In this case, the most frequently offered alternatives are to accept personal experience or linguistic practice as the criterion of truth. These are alternatives that science must reject for reasons presented earlier in this article.

At the same time that we recognize the value of intervening variables, we must also recognize and avoid two abuses to which they are commonly subjected. First, concepts are reified too often. They are captured by the mistaken outlook that Stuart Chase (1938) once called "the tyranny of words." According to that misguided view, if there is a word for it in the dictionary, a corresponding item of physical or psychological reality must exist, and the major task of science is to discover the a priori meanings of these linguistic givens. On the current psychological scene, this foolish assumption gives rise to ill-conceived attempts to decide what motives, intelligence, personality, and cognition "really are." It also legitimates unproductive debates over such questions as whether alcoholism is a disease. Those involved in such disputes never seem to recognize that the controversies are always about definitions and not facts. This first misunderstanding is related to the second one.

Concepts are products of definition. They are merely descriptive and explain nothing. If someone says that a man has hallucinations, withdraws from society, lives in his own world, has extremely unusual associations, and reacts without emotion to imaginary catastrophes because he is schizophrenic, it is important to understand that the word *because* has been misused. The symptomatology defines (diagnoses) schizophrenia. The symptoms and the "cause" are identical. The "explanation" is circular and not an explanation at all.

It may be worth the few sentences that it takes to say that circular definitions are not a scientific sin. Definitions must be circular—by definition. They are verbal equations in which the quantity on the left-hand side of the equals sign must be the same as that on the right. The sin is the offering of definitions as though they were explanations, as one can catch the late-night talk show hosts doing almost any evening on the radio. The following are examples of such statements: "Your eight-year-old son is distractable in school and having trouble reading because he has an attention deficiency disorder"; and "The stock market crash of October 19, 1987, was caused by widespread economic panic." If I could make just one change in what the general public (and some psychologists) understand about psychology, it would be to give them an immunity to such misuses of definitions.

SCIENTIFIC STRUCTURE OF PSYCHOLOGY

Figure 2 summarizes much of the previous content of this article. The top part of the figure, labeled "Psychology Without Concepts," makes two points: (a) Defined in terms of observable dependent variables, psychology is the science of behavior; and (b) this science operates on the assumption that behavior is determined. Explanation, prediction, and control are possible. The bottom part of the figure, labeled "Psychology With Concepts," reviews two further points: (a) In the determination of behavior, nature places limits on potentials for development, and environment determines the extent to which these potentials are realized; and (b) the behavior of an individual at any moment is the joint outcome of realized potential interacting with a temporary state.

In its entirety, Figure 2 is a review of the intervening variable approach and the meaning of Tolman's F-1, F-2, and F-3 laws. As an aid to the further development of these ideas, I return now to the concept of stress. Figure 3 presents the current situation of this concept in the general framework shown in Figure 2 and in enough detail to support several interpretative points.

First, the collection of independent and dependent variables has become quite large. Moreover, they *are* variables. Each of them has an infinite number of possible values, and people's positions on these many different dimensions are largely uncorrelated. Such complexity surrounds every important psychological concept. It provides a way for bringing common sense and science together on an important point: Individual uniqueness is no problem for psychology.

7. *Every individual is a unique expression of the joint influence of a host of*

PSYCHOLOGY WITHOUT CONCEPTS

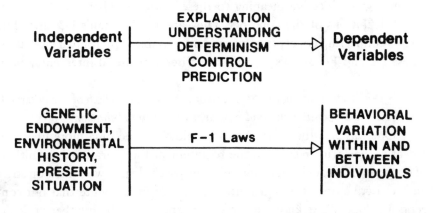

| Independent Variables | EXPLANATION UNDERSTANDING DETERMINISM CONTROL PREDICTION | Dependent Variables |

GENETIC ENDOWMENT, ENVIRONMENTAL HISTORY, PRESENT SITUATION — F-1 Laws → BEHAVIORAL VARIATION WITHIN AND BETWEEN INDIVIDUALS

PSYCHOLOGY WITH CONCEPTS

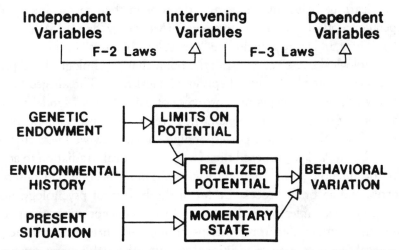

Independent Variables — F-2 Laws — Intervening Variables — F-3 Laws — Dependent Variables

GENETIC ENDOWMENT → LIMITS ON POTENTIAL

ENVIRONMENTAL HISTORY → REALIZED POTENTIAL → BEHAVIORAL VARIATION

PRESENT SITUATION → MOMENTARY STATE

Figure 2: Summary of the Argument. *Note:* The upper panel reviews the contributions of the empiricistic and deterministic tenets. The lower panel shows how three major classes of independent variables interact to define intervening variables and how the intervening variables interact in the production of behavior.

variables. Such uniqueness results from the specific (idiographic) effects on individuals of general (nomothetic) laws.

The contradictory truths of common sense that "every individual is unique" but that "people are the same the whole world over" are really not contradictory. People are the same in that they represent the outcome of the same laws operating on the same variables. They differ in degree and not in kind. People are unique in that the details of those operations differ from person to person.

Second, in Figure 2, the arrows connecting independent variables to concepts give objective meaning to these concepts. They are the operational definitions of the concepts. They are also Tolman's F-2 laws. The arrows connecting concepts to dependent variables are Tolman's F-3 laws. These F-2 and F-3 arrows identify the criteria of useful intervening variables.

8. *A concept is acceptable to psychology only if it meets both of two criteria. It must be defined operationally and have a relationship to behavior.*

One way in which scientific psychology has become more liberal in recent years is with respect to the requirement for operational definitions of concepts. Although there are still some psychologists who insist on strict and restrictive operational definitions, most of us recognize that our concepts are "open." As knowledge of a concept grows, the number of determining (therefore, defining) variables also increases, as happened with the concept of stress. This state of affairs creates great problems for psychology in the operational realization of its concepts. Such problems do not justify the abandonment of the operational approach, however. "Psychologists must learn to be sophisticated and rigorous in their metathinking about open concepts at the substantive level" (Meehl, 1978, p. 815).

Third, in Figure 3, including "physiology of stress" in the same box as "psychological stress" emphasizes the point that psychological and physiological concepts play identical epistemological roles. The alleged "reality" of physiological concepts may or may not exist. When Mendel proposed the concept of the gene to explain the hereditary transmission of traits, no one had yet observed any corresponding entity. Now we know that genes exist. When Pavlov proposed the concept of cortical irradiation to account for the phenomenon of stimulus generalization, no one had observed a corresponding brain process. So far in the history of psychology, no one has. These examples show that psychological concepts with physiological sounding names differ from other psychological concepts only if the physiological concepts acquire additional meaning through separate operations carried out at the level of physiology. Calling them physiological does not give them physical reality, only surplus meaning. As Donald Hebb (1955) once noted, CNS stands for "conceptual nervous system" until such independent observations have been made.

Finally, the appearance of "response defined individual characteristics" as well as "stressors" on the independent variable side of Figure 3 represents the relevance to the study of stress of both of the two sciences of psychology described by Cronbach (1957). The first science is stimulus–response (S–R) psychology, whose independent variables are situational events. The second science is response–response (R–R) psychology, whose independent variables are the behavior of individuals.

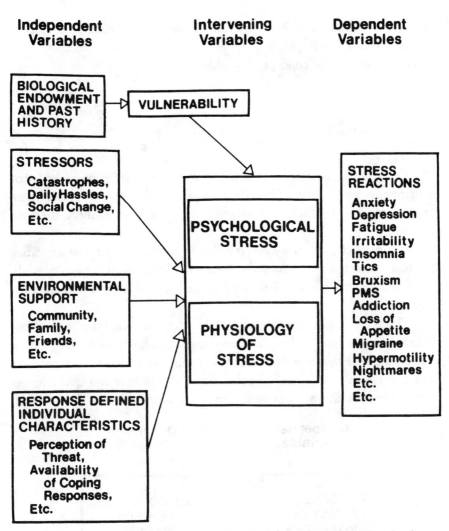

Independent Variables　　　**Intervening Variables**　　　**Dependent Variables**

BIOLOGICAL ENDOWMENT AND PAST HISTORY → VULNERABILITY

STRESSORS

Catastrophes, Daily Hassles, Social Change, Etc.

ENVIRONMENTAL SUPPORT

Community, Family, Friends, Etc.

RESPONSE DEFINED INDIVIDUAL CHARACTERISTICS

Perception of Threat, Availability of Coping Responses, Etc.

PSYCHOLOGICAL STRESS

PHYSIOLOGY OF STRESS

STRESS REACTIONS

Anxiety
Depression
Fatigue
Irritability
Insomnia
Tics
Bruxism
PMS
Addiction
Loss of Appetite
Migraine
Hypermotility
Nightmares
Etc.
Etc.

Figure 3: Current Status of the Concept of Stress. *Note:* This figure spells out the details and analyzes the argument of Figure 2. This figure is an explication of concepts in Selye (1976).

The independent variables of both sciences are independent in the sense that they are the variables from which the scientist makes predictions about behavior. The independent variables of the two sciences differ in that those of stimulus–response psychology can, in principle, be defined without reference to organisms and manipulated directly. Those of response–response psychology lack those properties. Experimental psychology typifies the S–R approach. The effort is to find the laws that relate behavior to environmental variables, for example, amount learned (R) as a function of distribution of practice (S). Psychometric psychology typifies the R–R approach. The effort is to find the laws that relate behavior in one situation to behavior in some other situation, most commonly a test, for example, college grades (R-2) as a function of SAT scores (R-1). The independent variables of R–R psychology sometimes become the dependent variables of S–R psychology. Figure 4 makes this point, using an example based on the concept of intelligence.

PSYCHOLOGICAL THEORY

Networks of the type laid out in Figure 3 represent the present state of theorizing in psychology. They define theoretical concepts, relate these concepts to one another, and identify the laws that connect them to behavior.

9. *A psychological theory puts a collection of concepts and their associated laws into a structure that allows the deduction of behavioral consequences. To show that a fact of behavior is deducible from such a theory is what it means to explain that fact.*

This is the method that Hull (1935) sometimes called the "hypothetico-deductive method." Although that designation has gone out of fashion, it is the method that scientists continue to use whenever they argue that their theories lead to specified predictions. Psychology has made recognizable progress in the sophistication with which it uses the method.

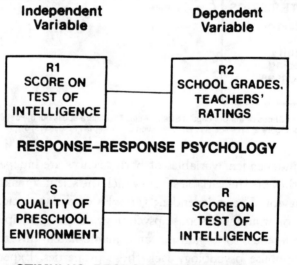

Figure 4: Psychology's Two Scientific Disciplines. *Note:* The psychometric (R–R) and experimental (S–R) sciences of psychology differ in their choice of independent variables. The first uses previous behavior to predict performance, and the second uses stimulus events for that purpose. Depending on their functions, performance measures such as scores on tests can be independent variables (upper panel) or dependent variables (lower panel). Neither of the disciplines is more important than the other (Cronbach, 1957).

Theoretical structures are often expressed in terms of formal logic or mathematics. Many of our concepts have acquired legitimate physiological meaning. The basic method remains unchanged, however.

The only alternative to hypothetico-deductive theorizing that I can think of is the radical empiricistic approach, sometimes advocated by the Skinnerians. This alternative would rule out intervening variables, replacing them with an assemblage of F-1 laws like those identified at the top of Figure 2. In this view, theory would arise (if at all) inductively as the individual laws accumulated. Knowledge would provide its own theoretical organization.

One problem with this extreme view is that theory-free investigation is impossible. The choice of empirical questions to study and the selection of dependent and independent variables always entail theoretical assumptions. A second problem is that this approach encourages the delusion that facts somehow give unaided rise to scientific theories. In actuality, theories are creative products of scientific minds. Finally, for many of us the most unattractive aspect of the radical empiricistic view is that it takes the joy out of science. The process of making predictions, testing them, and finding out that they are right is the most exciting part of science. The radical empiricistic approach would rob the scientist of this excitement. In addition, that approach would leave the scientist unable to see the forest through the impenetrable tangle of F-1 trees. For all of those reasons it seems unlikely that theorizing will soon go out of style.

Because behavior is so complex and because it is amenable to treatment at so many different levels, an essentially unlimited array of theories is possible. Is there any way to choose among them? Obviously there is. The best theory is the one that survives the fires of logical and empirical testing. An evolutionary metaphor appears to be applicable. Scientific progress will be most rapid when a large pool of theoretical variants exists along with heavy selective pressure in the form of criticism and empirical tests. In the ideal scientific world, psychologists could preach and publish whatever they wanted to, no matter how unpopular, unorthodox, or unlikely to be correct. Physiological, mathematical, behavioristic, and humanistic theories would all participate in the struggle for survival. Freely published criticism would quickly lead to the extinction of the most maladaptive theoretical mutations. Empirical investigations would decide the fate of all the rest. The theories that survived and continued to evolve would be those that were best able to generate and validate behavioral deductions. The great diversity in psychology means that there is a niche for many different theoretical species.

THE QUESTION OF VALUES

I have now done most of what I set out to do in this article in showing that the science of psychology is not inimical to the conceptions that characterize the new look in psychology. Intuition and common sense are major sources of ideas for this science. Mental states are concepts without which an acceptable science of behavior cannot exist. The elementism–holism issue disappears because research has shown that what is whole and what is elementary depends on the level of analysis. Human uniqueness is a factual consequence of the complexity of the determination of behavior. Idiographic and nomothetic lawfulness both make their contributions. Every type of theorizing is allowed its day in court. This leaves the question of values. Should scientific or humanistic values control the science of psychology? What should psychology be doing to solve the human problems of our age?

10. The values that govern the science of psychology are scientific values. Humanistic values govern the behavior of psychological scientists and of psychologists who apply the knowledge gained by science.

As a science, psychology is dedicated to discovering facts about behavior and creating theories to explain these facts. In this abstract conception, questions of human values do not arise. The scientific value system requires only that psychology discover the most dependable facts and produce the best theories that it can. Reality is more complex than that, however, because the science of psychology deals with living organisms. Research may require deprivation, concealment, deception, threat, punishment, or the invasion of privacy, and such procedures put scientific values into conflict with human values. For every psychological investigation this conflict raises a question: Is it worth it? Do the potential benefits to science and eventually to animal and human lives justify the costs to be extracted here and now? Psychology has wrestled with this issue for years, and guidelines now exist that protect the welfare of animal and human participants in psychological research. In these guidelines, humanistic values take precedence and form the basis for decisions regarding the acceptability of scientific research. In psychology today most research is in conformity with these codes of ethics.

The ethical acceptability of psychological research does not mean that it will answer the great moral questions of our age or decide which social policy is best. Such questions include the right to bear arms versus handgun control, bans on dirty books versus freedom of literary expression, the public's right to know versus the individual's right to privacy, retribution versus rehabilitation as the aim of criminal codes, affirmative action versus traditional indexes of merit, a verdict of "not guilty by reason of insanity" versus one of "guilty but insane," and freedom of choice versus right to life. Much of what scientific psychology knows is relevant to these important questions, but it cannot supply the answers. They must come from decisions that are made beyond the reach of science, in the court of human values.

The distinction that is implied here is one that should be guarded jealously. If psychology is to have a future as a science, it must obey the scientific rules. These rules define the limits of scientific authority. Science gains its strength and credibility by operating within these limits and understanding that, in other realms, it has no special power or status. Already in its short history, psychology has made important scientific contributions. The credibility acquired by reason of those accomplishments must not be mistaken for moral authority, however. It is a misuse of the credibility of psychology to use it as a basis to promote social prejudices or political goals, and the use of our status as psychologists for such purposes is an even worse misuse. The potential cost of these misuses is loss of the very credibility and status that allowed the misuse in the first place (Gould, 1987).

REFERENCES

Chase, S. (1938). *The tyranny of words*. New York: Harcourt, Brace.

Cronbach, L. J. (1957). Two disciplines of scientific psychology. *American Psychologist, 12*, 671-684.

Furedy, J. J., & Furedy, C. (1982). Socratic versus sophistic strains in the teaching of undergraduate psychology: Implicit conflicts made explicit. *Teaching of Psychology, 9*, 14-20.

Gould, S. J. (1987). William Jennings Bryan's last campaign. *Natural History, 96*(11), 16-26.

Hebb, D. O. (1955). Drives and the C. N. S. (conceptual nervous system). *Psychological Review, 62*, 243-254.

Hull, C. L. (1935). The conflicting psychologies of learning—A way out. *Psychological Review, 42*, 491-516.

Jones, E. E. (1985). History of social psychology. In G. A. Kimble & K. Schlesinger (Eds.), *Topics in the history of psychology* (Vol. 2, pp. 371-407). Hillsdale, NJ: Erlbaum.

Kendler, H. H. (1981). *Psychology: A science in conflict*. New York: Oxford University Press.

Kimble, G. A. (1984). Psychology's two cultures. *American Psychologist, 39*, 833-839.

Kimble, G. A., & Perlmuter, L. C. (1970). The problem of volition. *Psychological Review, 77*, 361-384.

Koch, S. (1981). The nature and limits of psychological knowledge. *American Psychologist, 36,* 257-269.

Kohn, A. (1988, April). You know what they say. *Psychology Today,* pp. 36-41.

Kuhn, T. S. (1970). *The structure of scientific revolutions.* Chicago: University of Chicago Press.

Lewin, K. (1931). Environmental forces in child behavior and development. In C. Murchison (Ed.), *A handbook of child psychology* (pp. 94-127). Worcester, MA: Clark University Press.

Matarazzo, J. D. (1987). There is only one psychology, no specialties, but many applications. *American Psychologist, 42,* 893-903.

Meehl, P. E. (1978). Theoretical risks and tabular asterisks: Sir Karl, Sir Ronald and the slow progress of soft psychology. *Journal of Consulting and Clinical Psychology, 46,* 806-834.

Selye, H. (1976). *The stress of life.* New York: McGraw-Hill.

Skinner, B. F. (1987). Whatever happened to psychology as the science of behavior? *American Psychologist, 42,* 780-786.

Spector, M. (1966). Theory and observation (I). *British Journal of the Philosophy of Science, 17,* 1-20.

Staats, A. W. (1981). Paradigmatic behaviorism, unified theory, unified theory construction methods, and the zeitgeist of separatism. *American Psychologist, 36,* 239-256.

Stroop, J. R. (1935). Studies of interference in serial verbal reactions. *Journal of Experimental Psychology, 18,* 643-662.

Tolman, E. C. (1938). The determiners of behavior at a choice point. *Psychological Review, 45,* 1-41.

Watson, J. B. (1913). Psychology as a behaviorist views it. *Psychological Review, 20,* 158-177.

2

THE SCIENTIFIC STUDY OF COUNSELING AND PSYCHOTHERAPY: A UNIFICATIONIST VIEW

DONELSON R. FORSYTH AND STANLEY R. STRONG

Although psychologists have been investigating the process of counseling and psychotherapy for many years, a number of critical methodological issues remain unresolved: Should research in counseling and clinical psychology be directly relevant to psychotherapy? Are findings obtained in other fields of psychology—such as social or developmental psychology— relevant to psychotherapy? Can studies conducted in laboratory settings have any bearing on psychotherapy? Should correlational findings based on nonexperimental designs be taken seriously? Are subjective conclusions reached during the course of psychotherapy scientifically sound data? What is the role of theory in guiding psychotherapy research?

These complex issues undoubtedly arise from a number of interrelated sources. However, Kuhn's (1962) approach to science suggests that these issues remain unanswered because psychologists disagree about the goals of science, psychology, and clinical and counseling (or, more simply,

Reprinted from the *American Psychologist, 41*, 113–119. Copyright 1986 by the American Psychological Association.

psychotherapy) research. We lack a *disciplinary matrix*, or *paradigm* (Kuhn, 1970)—a shared set of fundamental beliefs, exemplars, and symbolic generalizations. Therefore, disagreements about what makes for good research and what should be done to advance the field are inevitable.

Kuhn's concept of paradigm suggests that one path to the resolution of the current methodological and epistemological debate requires a careful and open examination of psychology's undergirding, if implicit, paradigmatic assumptions. As a first step toward this goal, we wish to nominate three propositions about psychotherapy research and science as candidates for psychology's paradigm. The three potential shared beliefs are: (a) Psychotherapy research is science; (b) psychotherapy research is part of a larger effort aimed at understanding human behavior; and (c) all scientific tools are acceptable in the drive to better understand the process of psychotherapy. Although we strive to defend these three statements, it must be stressed that—in the logical and rhetorical sense—they remain propositions: statements or arguments that can be accepted, doubted, or rejected. Thus, we admit from the outset that these statements must be treated as propositions (conjectures, suppositions, or assumptions), rather than as taken-for-granted givens, axioms, or truths. After examining these three propositions, a number of contemporary questions concerning research in psychotherapy are then raised, and possible answers suggested by the three propositions are offered. Again, the issues involved are complex and highly debatable, and so our proposition-based conclusions should be viewed as stimulating suggestions rather than solutions to long-debated questions. Last, the three propositions are used to derive possible guidelines for improving psychological research.

THREE PROPOSITIONS

Psychotherapy Research Is Science

Philosophers of science often note that basic science is not the same thing as applied science (e.g., Bunge, 1974; Ziman, 1974). For example, Bunge (1974) emphasized their divergent goals; he noted that systematic knowledge is the essential goal of basic researchers, whereas the applied scientist seeks information that will increase knowledge while also proving itself to be relevant to some particular problem. Bunge also proposed that research questions originate from different sources in basic and applied research. The basic researcher, according to Bunge, is interested in investigating some puzzle or problem that is suggested by theory. He or she asks

"Let's compare 'what is' with 'what should be' to see if the theory is adequate." In applied science, the research may spring from practical concerns as much as from theoretically relevant hypotheses. In essence, the applied researcher asks "Let's understand the nature of this problem so we can do something to resolve it."

Although similar distinctions between basic and applied research have also been noted in the psychological literature (e.g., Azrin, 1977; Bevan, 1980; Fishman & Neigher, 1982; Morell, 1979), our first proposition suggests that basic and applied research are more similar than different, for both are science rather than technology. Both accept the long-term goal of increasing knowledge and understanding. Both involve relating observations back to theoretical constructs that provide the framework for interpreting data and generating predictions. Both insist that the test of theory lies in objective, empirical methods rather than logical claims or subjective feelings. Both involve a striving for consensus among members of the discipline concerning acceptable, unacceptable, and to-be-evaluated explanations of empirical observations.

Our first proposition states that psychotherapy research, although characterized by both basic and applied concerns, is science rather than "technology," "social engineering," or "developmental research." Problems relevant to the therapeutic process are the initial source of research questions, but these applied concerns are ultimately placed into a theoretical context, and the long-term goal of such research includes testing the adequacy of assumptions and hypotheses that make up the theory. The theory is therefore not solely used to develop some product, such as a diagnostic instrument that can be sold for profit, an intake procedure that will satisfy the needs of some treatment agency, or a cost-effective structured training workshop. Rather, the theory is examined by gathering information relevant to predictions derived from that theory. Furthermore, the adequacy of the theory—and the value of any products or practical, useful information that are obtained through psychotherapy research—must be determined by methods recognized as acceptable by other researchers in the field. With technological research, the employer is sometimes the only regulator of methods and evaluator of conclusions. Finally, psychotherapy research involves a free exchange of information and findings among researchers in the hope of finding answers to key questions with psychotherapeutic relevance. The consumers of the products created by researchers are not just clients or employers, but other researchers as well.

Psychotherapy Research Is Part of a Larger Effort
to Understand Human Behavior

Just as our first proposition argued for the scientific unity of basic and applied research, our second proposition recommends the unification of psychotherapy research and other branches of psychology. Although the unique characteristics of psychotherapeutic settings pose special problems for researchers, the unification perspective argues that psychotherapy researchers and investigators in other areas of psychology share the superordinate goal of increasing our understanding of human behavior.

In contrast to a unificationist viewpoint, other investigators have advocated a *dualistic* approach to psychotherapy research. Due to their circumscribed interest in (a) the psychotherapy process and/or (b) problems related to psychological adjustment and functioning, proponents of dualism suggest that psychotherapy is so unique that its processes cannot be explained using principles of human behavior derived from other branches of psychology. One proponent of this view stated that, "as counseling researchers we are interested in developing principles of human behavior only inasmuch as they tap principles of counseling" (Gelso, 1979, p. 14). According to this perspective, Gelso stated that investigators must keep "actual counseling in central focus" (p. 14) with methodologies that closely approximate ongoing psychotherapy. To the staunch dualist, basing explanations of psychotherapeutic processes on theoretical propositions drawn from other areas of psychology (or on conclusions drawn from studies specifically designed to test psychotherapy-relevant theories but conducted in nontherapy settings) is misguided (cf. Garfield, 1979, 1980; Gibbs, 1979; see Bandura, 1978, for a discussion of the dualistic approach).

In arguing against dualism, the second proposition emphasizes the shared goal of psychological scientists: to develop and test generalizable principles of human behavior. If these "laws" of behavior make reference to specific settings, then the inevitable changes in these settings that take place over time and across situations undermine the generalizability of the laws themselves. For example, a proposition such as "Black clients respond best when given tangible rewards rather than verbal rewards" may fade in importance when racial differences in socialization and socioeconomic status are erased in 30 years time. However, the more general the statement— for example, "The impact of verbal rewards as reinforcers is directly related to socioeconomic background" (Zigler & Kanzer, 1962)—the more likely the hypothesis will stand the test of time. Similarly, a proposition such as "Gestalt group therapy is more effective than sensitivity training" seems trivial in a time when few therapists use unstructured group methods, but a more lawlike statement such as "Groups with centralized rather than decentralized communication networks stimulate more rapid member change" is less temporally limited.

Because researchers should strive to explain clients' actions in terms of general statements that hold across many situations and times, findings obtained in other branches of psychology that bear on these general statements are necessarily relevant in evaluating the adequacy of these propositions. For example, if a therapist suggests that behavior modification represents an effective means of dealing with social skills deficits, she or he can buttress this argument by drawing on supporting evidence for operant conditioning obtained in experimental research settings. If, however, basic researchers discovered that the law of effect does not hold for the acquisition of social behaviors, then this finding would warn the therapist that the behavior modification of social skills may fail. Evidence concerning the adequacy of a general principle of human behavior should be drawn from all available sources, including both basic research and applied research within and outside clinical and counseling psychology. As Merton (1949) noted long ago, applied researchers cannot afford to adopt a myopic, single-discipline focus because practical problems often involve variables that do not fall within the scope of any particular subfield of psychology. From this perspective, psychotherapy research must draw on the findings of other fields to be successful.

All Scientific Tools Are Acceptable in the Effort
to Understand the Process of Psychotherapy

Homans emphasized the importance of empirical evidence when judging sciences. To Homans (1967), "When the test of truth of a relationship lies finally in the data themselves, and the data are not wholly manufactured—when nature, however stretched out on the rack, still has a chance to say 'no!'—then the subject is a science" (p. 4). This viewpoint, although a simplification of science, nonetheless underscores the importance of some type of data in scientific research. In addition, the proposition also suggests that—like eclectic therapists who integrate many theories of psychological functioning when interacting with clients—psychological scientists must also remain eclectic by drawing on findings generated in fields other than their own. That is, researchers should use any and all scientific means possible to gather information concerning the theoretical system under investigation. Whether experimental, correlational, field, laboratory, role-play, or analog, no opportunity to further our understanding of psychotherapy should be bypassed. As Hilgard (1971) noted, in order to "satisfy the criteria of 'good science'" the researcher "must cover the whole spectrum of basic and applied science by doing sound (and conclusive) work all along the line" (p. 4).

IMPLICATIONS

The three propositions form the foundation for what can be termed a *unificationist* view of psychological science. To the unificationist, researchers working in the many and varied subfields of psychology are united in their professional identity (they are all scientists), their goals (they seek to extend our understanding of behavior), and their empirical outlook (they all strive to collect data relevant to the research questions at hand). In consequence, unificationism (which is an admittedly prescriptive viewpoint arguing how psychology *should be*) advocates the integration and synthesis of theory and research dealing with psychological topics. The position also offers potential answers to the currently debated methodological issues in psychotherapy research examined below.

Applied Versus Basic Science

Glasser (1982) and Sommer (1982) each commented on the problematic consequences of separating applied and basic research. According to Glasser, as early as 1900 John Dewey recommended unificationism in the study of learning; that is, linking theory and educational practice with each pursuit stimulating the other. However, for many decades experimental learning theorists worked on their own questions in psychology departments, whereas educational researchers examined practical problems from positions in education programs. Glasser suggested that the slow progress of educational psychology stemmed from this artificial separation and recommended integration under the rubric "instructional psychology."

Sommer (1982) focused on basic research gone awry in his analysis of historical trends in Prisoner's Dilemma (PD) research. As he noted, the laboratory simulations became further and further removed from the original questions concerning bargaining and negotiation. In consequence, "PD research has tended to be drawn from previous PD research, thus creating a hermetic laboratory system without the validity checks and enrichment of experimental conditions that could come from the study of actual cases" (Sommer, 1982, p. 531). Sommer therefore stated that "a blending of laboratory and field methods rather than an exclusive preoccupation with either will be of most value to both psychological science and to society" (p. 531).

Supporting Glasser and Sommer, the unificationist view suggests that psychotherapy research should be as basic as it is applied. Basic research provides the initial evidence concerning theoretical propositions and hence represents the first hurdle that any explanation of human action must pass. The second hurdle, however, is the successful application of the theory to psychotherapy. As in medicine, basic research should be inextricably linked with applied research to guard against the limitations of each pursuit. If too applied, research can become theoretically simplistic, situationally restricted, and technologically oriented. In contrast, basic researchers sometimes develop elaborate theoretical conceptualizations that have little relationship to reality or lose sight of the social value of their findings. As Lewin (1951) stated long ago, psychologists can reach their goal of helping others only if applied researchers make use of theories *and* basic researchers develop theories that can be applied to important social problems.

Fact Finding

Science is based on the accumulation of evidence and fact, but such an accumulation is not the only goal of science. Facts are used to spin theoretical systems or support existing frameworks, but because of their mutability and situational specificity, facts are of little long-lasting value in science. Unfortunately, many psychotherapy researchers consider themselves to be finders of facts, striving to answer such questions as: What impact does extensive eye contact have on client behavior? Is therapist effectiveness related to client race? Does therapy X work better than therapy Y? Is an elevated score on a certain subscale of the Minnesota Multiphasic Personality Inventory (MMPI) an indicator of psychopathology? Are therapists' religious values related to their clinical style? Although all raise important issues, such studies cannot advance our understanding of psychotherapy unless the obtained findings are relevant to transitional statements dealing with behavior. Specific facts—or, as in this case, empirical findings—are not themselves generalizable, but the hypotheses they either support or disconfirm are. For example, the investigator who finds that therapists who maintain eye contact 60% of the time are more effective than therapists who maintain eye contact 30% of the time may be tempted to tell practitioners to maintain a good deal of eye contact. Unfortunately, the specifics of the setting—the attractiveness of the therapists, the type of clients, the content of the therapists' statements during eye contact—all limit the generalizability of the "fact" that high eye contact makes counselors and clinicians more effective. If, however, the researcher had been studying a higher order theoretical proposition—such as (a) the greater the client's trust in the therapist, the more effective the therapy, (b) ceteris paribus, eye contact implies honesty and openness, and therefore (c)

eye contact will create greater client–therapist trust and facilitate therapy—
then the study has implications beyond the obtained data. In this case the
researcher would be scientifically justified in suggesting that therapists
establish a deep level of trust with clients and that this trust can be created
by appropriate nonverbal behaviors.

Although the three propositions advocate the development of higher
order hypotheses to guide and summarize research, the researcher must
always remember Hempel's (1966) requirement of testability: "the statements constituting a scientific explanation must be capable of empirical
test" (p. 49). Seeking broad, generalizable explanations of behavior is a
laudable goal, but these explanations must not be so general that they are
untestable or so empirically bound that they are merely accidental generalizations (Goodman, 1973). The investigator must therefore strike a balance
between generality and specificity in his or her theoretical thinking. (For a
philosophical discussion of the difference between generalizable, lawlike
statements and accidental generalizations see Goodman's {1973} theory of
"projectability.")

The Generalizability Quandary

The question "Do laboratory findings have any relevance for understanding 'real' behavior?" has been a topic of recent debate in many areas of
psychology (e.g., Berkowitz & Donnerstein, 1982; Bronfenbrenner, 1977;
Dipboye & Flanagan, 1978; Gelso, 1979; Gibbs, 1979; Harré & Secord,
1972; Herrnstein, 1977; Jenkins, 1974; McCall, 1977; McGuire, 1973;
Mook, 1983; Rakover, 1980). In terms of application to psychotherapy
research, several discussants have suggested that laboratory studies that
simulate psychotherapy or examine only one particular aspect of the psychotherapeutic setting in detail are only tangentially relevant to clinical
and counseling practices (e.g., Gibbs, 1979; Goldman, 1978). They suggest
that the nature of clinical and counseling psychology requires field studies
conducted in real therapy settings, with real clients and real therapists, and
that only findings that can be easily generalized to real-life psychotherapy
are data worth discussing.

Although the issues are complex and defy any simple solution, the
second and third propositions of a unificationist position advocate an
empirical eclecticism that is inconsistent with the wholesale rejection of any
research method or theory. To elaborate, a unificationist approach argues
that the generalizability question (a) should be settled empirically and (b)
may be a moot issue from an epistemological perspective. Focusing first on
the empiricism argument, the third assumption suggests that the context

must be thought of as only one more variable or dimension that must be interpreted within the larger theoretical scheme. Kazdin (1978) stated,

> Research in psychotherapy and behavior therapy can differ from clinical application of treatment along several dimensions such as the target problem, the clients and the manner in which they are recruited, the therapists, the selection treatment, the client's set, and the setting in which treatment is conducted. (p. 684)

However, Kazdin argued that increasing the "similarity of an investigation to the clinical situation . . . does not necessarily argue for greater generality of the results" (p. 684). In essence, the importance of the setting must be established empirically (Bass & Firestone, 1980; Berkowitz & Donnerstein, 1982; Flanagan & Dipboye, 1980).

Second, as Mook (1983) and Rakover (1980) have noted recently, many laboratory studies certainly involve highly artificial situations. However, they may still be relevant to practical problems if they examine theoretical generalizations that are relevant to these applied problems (Stone, 1984). For example, say a therapist is asked to choose between two therapies. The first, therapy X, has never been applied to a clinical population, but in over two dozen laboratory studies the theory has perfectly predicted behavior change. Therapy Y, in contrast, has never been tested in the laboratory, but in one study conducted with clients at a Veterans Administration hospital several of the curative factors emphasized in the approach were positively correlated with improvement. Which therapy should be used?

To many psychotherapists, therapy Y may seem to be the more appropriate choice because it was supported by field research. However, what if the therapist's clients are verbally skilled female teenagers, and the subjects in the study of therapy Y were World War II combat veterans with only limited verbal abilities? In contrast, what if the laboratory studies examined the effects of dietary factors on behavior and found that the behavior the therapist wished to increase could be reliably obtained by modifying the client's diet?

The generalizability of a theory from one situation to another depends more on the theory than on the results that support it. Although therapy Y was corroborated in a field setting, if its theoretical structure cannot explain what effect gender, age, and verbal skill have on the therapy outcome, then it does not generalize to the new situation. If, however, therapy X is based on a physiological explanation of behavior that applies to a wide range of individuals, then its generalizability is far greater. In sum, generalizability is determined more by the structure of the theory—its scope, specificity, and universality—than by location of the supporting research.

The Value of Theory

Implicit in all three propositions making up the unificationist view is the belief that science depends upon theory as much as it depends upon data. Although the role of theory in psychotherapy research and practice has been questioned by some (e.g., Rogers, 1973; see Sarason, 1981; Strupp, 1975; Wachtel, 1980), theory provides the organizing framework for conceptualizing problems, organizing knowledge, and suggesting solutions. Supporting this view, when decision makers in mental health fields (federal and state administrators of psychological services programs) were asked "What makes research useful?" (Weiss & Weiss, 1981), the most frequently mentioned attribute was the theoretical conceptualization of the problem.

This implication contrasts sharply with the recommendation to avoid theory because it biases the researcher's observations. In contrast to this argument, a pro-theory perspective suggests that research is always guided by some assumptions and that theories are the means by which these assumptions can be clearly articulated and explicitly determined. According to Jacob (1977),

> The scientific process does not consist simply in observing, in collecting data, and in deducing from them a theory. One can watch an object for years and never produce any observation of scientific interest. To produce a valuable observation, one has first to have an idea of what to observe, a preconception of what is possible. (p. 1161)

These theoretical propositions need not be the formal, elegant models once prescribed by deductive–nomological approaches to science (e.g., Hempel, 1966), but at minimum some theoretical ideas are required to structure our knowledge and provide direction for future efforts. According to Sidman (1960), "observations must be brought into some kind of order before they can be said to contribute to a science of behavior" (p. 12).

The Value of Information Obtained During Practice

Although we hold that basic and applied research share scientific unity, wholly problem-solving activities are best described as technology rather than science. Even though the distinction is not always clear, attempts to solve a specific problem in a specific situation without concern for increasing our general understanding of human behavior are more akin to technological research or social engineering than to science. Technological researchers may borrow the theories of science to guide their problem solving, but their efforts are not designed to test generalizable propositions derived from these theories. Technological research may generate information that is useful in science—such as providing an indication of what variables are important in a given setting, stimulating research, or refining methodological tools and innovations—but the research is so problem and situation specific that generalizations to other settings are limited.

Another distinction between science and technology has been noted by Ziman (1974). Although he prefaced his analysis by stating that the two areas are "now so intimately mingled that the distinction can become rather pedantic" (p. 24), he pointed out that scientists strive for a "consensus of rational opinion over the widest possible field" (p. 11). Technology, Ziman continued, does not attempt to gain this consensus, for it is focused on solving a specific problem; it provides the "means to do a definite job—bridge this river, cure this disease, make better beer" (p. 23). In consequence, the technological researcher owes primary responsibility to his or her employer rather than peers.

Although the actual practice of psychotherapy may involve a "scientific attitude," it is not science per se. However, the close correspondence between science and practice cannot be overstated. For example, although a good theory of psychological adjustment may state that increases in factors A, B, and C will benefit clients with D, E, and F characteristics, technological research may be needed to determine the optimal levels of A, B, and C, techniques to use in varying these factors, and ways to assess D, E, and F. Few theories in psychology are so precise that they yield mathematical statements describing the magnitude of important variables, and so practitioners must be prepared to turn to situation-specific and client-specific research to obtain the precision they require.

BEYOND THE THREE PROPOSITIONS

The three propositions suggest that the scientific study of psychotherapy cannot succeed without an interweaving of theory and research. The widespread outcry over the apparent sterility and lack of relevance of research to practice (Goldman, 1976; 1978) as well as the current controversy over the generalizability of research results (Gelso, 1979; Osipow, Walsh, & Tosi, 1980; Strong, 1971) are inevitable consequences of inadequate attention to the role of theory in scientific endeavors. Graduate training in clinical and counseling psychology focuses on the technology of collecting and analyzing data, with a special emphasis on applying findings to therapy, whereas the vital and creative steps of generating transituational propositions from observed relationships are bypassed. The result is the reduction of the scientific study of psychotherapy to technological inquiry. Technicians are being trained rather than scientists, and the products of their situationally limited work are of little value to practitioners.

A solution to these limitations of training and research lies in more fully developing the theoretical side of psychological science and integrating research and theory. Although the logic and methods of science can be described in many ways (e.g., Hempel, 1966; Lakatos & Musgrave, 1970; Manicas & Secord, 1983; Platt, 1964; Popper, 1959), descriptions of the scientific inference process often make reference to the dual importance of theory construction and theory testing. Unfortunately, researchers tend to be so preoccupied with theory testing that they overlook the critical role played by theory construction. Granted, investigators are highly proficient in finding hypotheses to test, operationalizing concepts in the specific settings examined in the study, determining the statistical significance of the results, and even relating the evidence back to the initial hypotheses, but too often researchers fail to go the additional steps needed to develop strong, applicable theoretical systems. In consequence, very few theories capable of explaining psychotherapeutic processes possess many of the characteristics of good theories: simplicity, interpretability, usefulness, generality, testability, disconfirmability, and logical internal consistency.

As to integrating theory and research, how often do researchers conduct research programs that facilitate "strong inference" (Platt, 1964, p. 347) by devising alternative hypotheses, pitting rival hypotheses against one another in carefully designed studies, and refining the theory through the development of subhypotheses? Likewise, how many researchers follow the scientific steps recommended by Popper's "sophisticated methodological falsifictionism" (Lakatos & Musgrave, 1970; Popper, 1959) approach to science by focusing more on unexpected, disconfirming findings rather than on confirming evidence? Although we are often more gratified by supporting rather than disconfirming evidence, failures to corroborate hypotheses invite us to abandon our preconceived notions and creatively reconstruct our perspective to better account for observed relationships. Popper and other philosophers of science suggest that the greatest advances in science occur when researchers focus on unexpected irregularities in their data, seemingly trivial observations, and even subjective impressions that are inconsistent with the best theories they can construct. From these disconfirmations the scientist artfully reconstructs a broader, more all-encompassing system that not only accounts for findings that supported the previous theory but also explains the newly obtained disconfirming data. Granted, such research practices may require creativity, the abandonment of firmly held beliefs, a propensity toward risk taking, speculation, and commitment to goals of research, but the growth of knowledge requires theoretical refinements and revolutions as much as it requires empiricism.

At core, the major roadblock to advancement in the scientific study of psychotherapy is inadequate attention to discovery (McGuire, 1973; Wachtel, 1980). Concern for directly applicable research has short-circuited the scientific process and inhibited rather than encouraged the creative use of evidence from both field and laboratory settings. According to Stone (1984), this obsession with "relevance" has led to a "knee-jerk mentality" in research consumers who "automatically dismiss meaningful research solely on artificiality grounds" (p. 108). Rather than focusing exclusively on application, we should also take care to generate theoretical statements that link together therapeutic and interpersonal variables. Instead of being concerned about how similar a specific time/space event of a study is to a specific time/space event of therapy, we should creatively reconstruct how the relations among events differ in various settings and induce transituational statements about these differences. Rather than limiting our focus to only therapeutic settings, we should generate theories of such wide scope that they apply to a host of interpersonal situations.

Psychotherapy will not be better understood by overvaluing generalizability of settings, but by the energetic application of the scientific model to generate a theory of biological, social, interpersonal, and psychological relationships that specifies how the dynamics of therapeutic and nontherapeutic settings differ (Sarason, 1981). In addition, increased effectiveness of psychotherapy will not come from direct application of research results to practice, but from the application of theory to practice (Shakow, 1976; Strupp, 1975). Events generated for research purposes are applications of theories to a specific time and place, just as psychotherapy is an application of a theory to a particular client with a particular therapist in a specific treatment location. Theories that explain psychotherapeutic outcomes must, in many ways, be capable of explaining outcomes in many other types of interpersonal settings.

REFERENCES

Azrin, N. H. (1977). A strategy for applied research: Learning based but outcome oriented. *American Psychologist, 32,* 140–149.

Bandura, A. (1978). On paradigms and recycled ideologies. *Cognitive Therapy and Research, 2,* 79–103.

Bass, A. R., & Firestone, I. J. (1980). Implications of representativeness for generalizability of field and laboratory research findings. *American Psychologist, 35*, 463–464.

Berkowitz, L., & Donnerstein, E. (1982). External validity is more than skin deep. *American Psychologist, 37*, 245–257.

Bevan, W. (1980). On getting in bed with a lion. *American Psychologist, 35*, 779–789.

Bronfenbrenner, U. (1977). Toward an experimental ecology of human development. *American Psychologist, 32*, 513–531.

Bunge, M. (1974). Towards a philosophy of technology. In A. C. Michalos (Ed.), *Philosophical problems of science and technology* (pp. 28–46). Boston: Allyn & Bacon.

Dipboye, R. L., & Flanagan, M. R. (1978). Research settings in industrial and organizational psychology: Are findings in the field more generalizable than in the laboratory? *American Psychologist, 34*, 141–150.

Fishman, D. B., & Neigher, W. D. (1982). American psychology in the eighties: Who will buy? *American Psychologist, 37*, 533–546.

Flanagan, M. R., & Dipboye, R. L. (1980). Representativeness does have implications for the generalizability of laboratory and field research findings. *American Psychologist, 35*, 464–466.

Garfield, S. L. (1979). Editorial. *Journal of Consulting and Clinical Psychology, 47*, 1–4.

Garfield, S. L. (1980). *Psychotherapy: An eclectic approach.* New York: Wiley.

Gelso, C. J. (1979). Research in counseling: Methodological and professional issues. *The Counseling Psychologist, 8*, 7–36.

Gibbs, J. C. (1979). The meaning of ecologically oriented inquiry in contemporary psychology. *American Psychologist, 34*, 127–140.

Glasser, R. (1982). Instructional psychology. *American Psychologist, 37*, 292–305.

Goldman, L. (1976). A revolution in counseling research. *Journal of Counseling Psychology, 23*, 543–552.

Goldman, L. (Ed.). (1978). *Research methods for counselors.* New York: Wiley.

Goodman, N. (1973). *Fact, fiction, and forecast* (3rd ed.). New York: Bobbs-Merrill.

Harré, R., & Secord, P. F. (1972) *The explanation of social behavior.* Oxford, England: Blackwell.

Hempel, C. G. (1966). *Philosophy of natural science.* Englewood Cliffs, NJ: Prentice-Hall.

Hernstein, R. J. (1977). The evolution of behaviorism. *American Psychologist, 32*, 593–603.

Hilgard, E. R. (1971). Toward a responsible social science. *Journal of Applied Social Psychology, 1*. 1–6.

Homans, G. C. (1967). *The nature of social science.* New York: Harcourt, Brace, & World.

Jacob, F. (1977). Evolution and tinkering. *Science, 196*, 1161–1167.

Jenkins, J. J. (1974). Remember that old theory of memory? Well, forget it! *American Psychologist, 29*, 785–795.

Kazdin, D. E. (1978). Evaluating the generality of findings in analogue therapy research. *Journal of Consulting and Clinical Psychology, 46,* 673–686.

Kuhn, T. S. (1962). *The structure of scientific revolutions.* Chicago: University of Chicago Press.

Kuhn, T. S. (1970). *The structure of scientific revolutions* (2nd ed.). Chicago: University of Chicago Press.

Lakatos, I., & Musgrave, A. (Eds.). (1970). *Criticism and the growth of knowledge.* New York: Cambridge University Press.

Lewin, K. (1951). *Field theory in social science.* New York: Harper.

Manicas, P. T., & Secord, P. F. (1983). Implications for psychology of the new philosophy of science. *American Psychologist, 38,* 399–413.

McCall, R. B. (1977). Challenges to a science of developmental psychology. *Child Development, 48,* 333–344.

McGuire, W. J. (1973). The yin and yang of progress in social psychology: Seven koan. *Journal of Personality and Social Psychology, 26,* 446–456.

Merton, R. K. (1949). *Social theory and social structure.* Glencoe, IL: Free Press.

Mook, D. G. (1983). In defense of external invalidity. *American Psychologist, 38,* 379–387.

Morell, J. A. (1979). *Program evaluation in social research.* New York: Pergamon.

Osipow, S. H., Walsh, W. B., & Tosi, D. J. (1980). *A survey of counseling methods.* Homewood, IL: Dorsey Press.

Platt, J. R. (1964). Strong inference. *Science, 146,* 347–353.

Popper, K. R. (1959). *The logic of scientific discovery.* New York: Basic Books.

Rakover, S. S. (1980). Generalization from analogue therapy to the clinical situation: The paradox and the dilemma of generality. *Journal of Consulting and Clinical Psychology, 48,* 770–771.

Rogers, C. R. (1973). Some new challenges. *American Psychologist, 28,* 379–387.

Sarason, S. B. (1981). An asocial psychology and a misdirected clinical psychology. *American Psychologist, 36,* 827–836.

Shakow, D. (1976). What is clinical psychology? *American Psychologist, 31,* 553–360.

Sidman, M. (1960). *Tactics of scientific research.* New York: Basic Books.

Sommer, R. (1982). The district attorney's dilemma: Experimental games and the real world of plea bargaining. *American Psychologist, 37,* 526–532.

Stone, G. L. (1984). Reaction: In defense of the "artificial." *Journal of Counseling Psychology, 31,* 108–110.

Strong, S. R. (1971). Experimental laboratory research in counseling. *Journal of Counseling Psychology, 18,* 106–110.

Strupp, H. H. (1975). Clinical psychology, irrationalism, and the erosion of excellence. *American Psychologist, 31,* 561–571.

Wachtel, P. J. (1980). Investigation and its discontents: Some constraints on progress in psychological research. *American Psychologist, 35,* 399–408.

Weiss, J. A., & Weiss, C. H. (1981). Social scientists and decision makers look at the usefulness of mental health research. *American Psychologist, 36,* 837–847.

Zigler, E., & Kanzer, P. (1962). The effectiveness of two classes of verbal reinforcers on the performance of middle- and lower-class children. *Journal of Personality, 30,* 157–163.

Ziman, J. (1974). What is science? In A. C. Michalos (Ed.), *Philosophical problems of science and technology* (pp. 5–27). Boston: Allyn & Bacon.

DEVELOPING RESEARCH IDEAS

3

GETTING OUT OF OUR CONCEPTUAL RUTS: STRATEGIES FOR EXPANDING CONCEPTUAL FRAMEWORKS

ALLAN W. WICKER

In 1879, Sir Francis Galton published an article describing a leisurely stroll he took in the interests of science—specifically to explore how the mind works. In the article, Galton told of walking down a London street and scrutinizing every object that came into his view. He recorded the first thought or two that occurred to him as he focused on each of about 300 objects. Galton reported that this method produced a great variety of associations, including memories of events that had occurred years earlier.

After several days, Galton repeated the walk and the recording procedure and again found a variety of associations. He also discovered a great deal of repetition or overlap in his thoughts on the two occasions. Galton likened his thoughts to actors in theater processions in which the players march off one side of the stage and reappear on the other. This recurrence of ideas piqued Galton's curiosity. He next devised some word association tasks that led him to the same conclusion as his walks, namely, that "the

Reprinted from the *American Psychologist, 40*, 1094–1103. Copyright 1985 by the American Psychological Association.

roadways of our minds are worn into very deep ruts" (Galton, 1879, cited by Crovitz, 1970, p. 35).

Although Galton's methods may have been faulty by present standards, he seems to have discovered a stable psychological principle: the recurrence of ideas (Crovitz, 1970). My comments here assume that Galton was right—that our thoughts flow in a limited number of channels and that our research efforts are thereby constrained.

This article sketches a variety of approaches for stimulating new insights on familiar research problems. Four sets of strategies, phrased as advice to researchers, are discussed as follows:

1. Researchers should play with ideas through a process of selecting and applying metaphors, representing ideas graphically, changing the scale, and attending to process.

2. Researchers should consider contexts. They can place specific problems in a larger domain, make comparisons outside the problem domain, examine processes in the settings in which they naturally occur, consider the practical implications of research, and probe library resources.

3. It is important for researchers to probe and tinker with assumptions through such techniques as exposing hidden assumptions, making the opposite assumption, and simultaneously trusting and doubting the same assumption.

4. Finally, it is vital that researchers clarify and systematize their conceptual frameworks. They should scrutinize the meanings of key concepts, specify relationships among concepts, and write a concept paper.

The need for psychologists to attend to conceptual framing processes has been widely acknowledged (see, for example, Brinberg & McGrath, 1985; Campbell, Daft, & Hulin, 1982; Caplan & Nelson, 1973; Gergen, 1978, 1982; Jones, 1983; McGuire, 1973, in press; Tyler, 1983; Wachtel, 1980; Weick, 1979).

Several caveats are in order before we proceed:

1. Some readers may already be familiar with certain strategies and find them obvious. I have tried to include a diversity of heuristics in the hope that even seasoned investigators will find something of value.

2. Given the goal of presenting a range of strategies, only limited space is available for describing and illustrating each procedure. There is a risk that important and complex topics have been oversimplified—possibly even trivialized. I strongly recommend further reading on any strategy that seems promising; references are provided in the text.

3. These strategies are offered as heuristics. Most have not been

systematically evaluated, although they have been useful to the scholars who proposed them and to others who have used them.

4. The substantial and important psychological literature on problem solving and critical and creative thinking has not been reviewed or even cited here. Much of that research addresses problems for which there are consensual solutions derived from mathematical or other logical systems. And some of that literature presumes that thinking habits developed from work on abstract puzzles or exercises are readily transferable to a wide range of other problems. The present concern is how to generate useful ideas whose "accuracy" cannot immediately be assessed. The following strategies draw upon, and in some cases expand, the researcher's existing knowledge structures (cf. Glaser, 1984). They are directly applicable to research problems in all areas of psychology.

PLAY WITH IDEAS

A playful, even whimsical, attitude toward exploring ideas is appropriate for the first set of strategies. These strategies include working with metaphors, drawing sketches, imagining extremes, and recasting entities as processes.

Select and Apply Metaphors

Playing with metaphors can evoke new perspectives on a problem. One strategy for exploiting metaphors is to identify some features from the research domain that are also discernible in another domain—perhaps another discipline or area of activity. Attention is shifted to this new area (the metaphor), which is then closely examined. From this examination, the researcher may discover some variables, relationships, or patterns that can usefully be translated back to the research problem.

A productive metaphor in social psychology is McGuire's inoculation theory of resistance to persuasion. The metaphor used was the medical procedure of stimulating bodily defenses against massive viral attacks by inoculating individuals with weakened forms of the virus. This procedure suggested the possibility of increasing resistance to persuasion by presenting weak arguments before strong arguments are encountered (McGuire, 1964). (The heuristic value of metaphors is discussed in Gowin, 1981b; Smith, 1981; and Weick, 1979. Leary, 1983, has analyzed the role of metaphor in the history of psychology. See Lakoff & Johnson, 1980, for a readable philosophical/linguistic analysis of metaphors.)

Exploring multiple, unusual metaphors may lead researchers to a greater awareness of the complexities and subtleties inherent in their domains (Weick, 1979). For example, likening interpersonal attraction to magnetic fields, a performance of Swan Lake, symbiosis, and hypnotism may reveal significant aspects of personal relationships that are not considered by such established perspectives as social exchange and equity theories.

Represent Ideas Graphically

A casual scan of such journals as *Science, American Scientist*, and *Scientific American* suggests that researchers in the physical and biological sciences make greater use of graphic presentations than do psychologists. We may be overlooking a powerful tool. In the developmental stages of a research problem, a pad of large drawing paper and a set of multicolored pens may be more useful than a typewriter. Visual images and sketches of problems can be liberating to researchers accustomed to representing their ideas only in linear arrangements of words, sentences, and paragraphs. Kurt Lewin, who used diagrams extensively, reportedly was ecstatic upon discovering a three-colored automatic pencil, which he carried everywhere to sketch his ideas (R. G. Barker, personal communication, April 10, 1983).

Many kinds of graphic schemes can be used to explore ideas and communicate them to others. Tabular grids, organization charts, flow diagrams, topological regions, and schematics are examples of abstract graphic languages. They have their own grammar and syntax and can be used to portray a variety of contents (McKim, 1972; Nelms, 1981). Figure 1 illustrates the flow diagram; it simply and clearly presents the three main approaches researchers have taken in studying relations between behavioral and somatic variables.

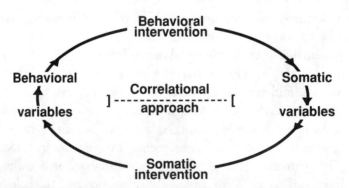

Figure 1: A Graphic Representation of Three Approaches to Research on the Relation Between Behavioral and Somatic Variables. *Note:* From "Experience, Memory, and the Brain" by M. R. Rosenzweig, 1984, *American Psychologist, 39*, p. 366. Copyright 1984 by American Psychological Association. Reprinted by permission.

In freehand idea sketching, there are no rules to be followed. With practice, researchers can fluently represent and explore their ideas and boldly experiment with relationships just as artists, composers, and urban planners have profitably done (McKim, 1972).

Change the Scale

Imagining extreme changes in proportion can stimulate our thinking. Mills (1959) gave this advice: "If something seems very minute, imagine it to be simply enormous, and ask yourself: What difference might that make? And vice versa, for gigantic phenomena" (p. 215). He then asked readers to imagine what preliterate villages might have been like with 30 million inhabitants. Or, to take another example, consider how child-rearing would be different if at birth children had the motor ability and strength of adults. And if there were no memory loss, how would human information processing be different?

A variation of this procedure is to imagine what would be required for a perfect relationship to exist between two variables presumed to be linked. For example, psychologists have often assumed that a person's expressed attitudes determine how he or she will behave in daily affairs (Cohen, 1964). However, for people to act in complete accordance with their attitudes, they would have to be independently wealthy, to have unlimited time at their disposal, to have no regard for the opinions of others, to be unaffected by unforeseen chance occurrences, to have a wide range of high-level skills, and even to be in several places at once (Wicker, 1969). Reflections on such factors can lead to more realistic theories and expectations.

Attend to Process

Research psychologists typically favor concepts that represent stable entities, perhaps because such concepts are easier to measure and to incorporate into theories than are processes. Yet it can be fruitful to view presumably stable concepts in dynamic terms. One systematic approach that can help us focus on process is the tagmemic method from the field of rhetoric: The same unit of experience is regarded alternatively as a "particle" (a thing in itself), a "wave" (a thing changing over time), and as part of a field (a thing in context; Young, Becker, & Pike, 1970).

A related strategy is changing nouns into verbs, or as Weick (1979) advised, "think'ing.'" Many concepts in our research vocabularies are nouns: perception, organization, social norm. Weick suggested imagining such concepts not as stable entities but as dynamic processes, constantly in flux, continually being reconstructed through accretion and erosion. Changing nouns to verbs may promote process imagery. Thus, one would speak of perceiving, organizing, and "norming."

In a recent application of this strategy, Wicker (in press) has recast the behavior setting concept from a relatively stable "given" to a more dynamic entity that develops over a series of life stages and in response to changing internal and external conditions.

CONSIDER CONTEXTS

The strategies in this section direct researchers' attention to the extended social world in which psychological events occur. These strategies are not theoretically neutral. They advance a viewpoint that has been expressed in ecological and environmental psychology (e.g., Barker, 1968; Stokols, 1982; Wicker, in press) and that has been stated more generally in terms of the implications for psychology of the new "realist" philosophy of science (e.g., Georgoudi & Rosnow, 1985; Manicas & Secord, 1983). The style of thought promoted here contrasts with much that is typical in psychology, but it can broaden our perspectives and suggest alternatives to traditional practices and ways of thinking.

Place Specific Problems in a Larger Domain

Researchers can use this strategy to decide where to begin work in a new area and to plan new research directions. The goal is to map out the broader domain of which an existing or contemplated study is only a part. Once the boundaries and features of a conceptual territory have been charted, judgments can be made about which areas are most promising for further exploration.

Such mapping of a research problem depends upon the researcher's current conceptual frame and upon a variety of information sources, such as intuition, theory, and research findings. An early step is to specify the boundaries of the broader domain at an appropriate level of abstraction. For example, in one of several case studies cited by McGrath (1968) to illustrate this strategy, the domain was bounded by criteria for the mental health of emotionally disturbed patients.

Once the domain has been defined, the next step is to identify the major factors or influences that bear on the topic. Each of the major factors can then be analyzed into its components or attributes, and a systematic classification scheme can be developed. By examining all logical combinations of attributes, investigators can plan research to cover appropriate—

perhaps neglected—aspects of the problem. In McGrath's (1968) example, three main factors were identified and analyzed into components: (a) sources of data on patients' mental health, whose components included self-reports, ratings by staff, and observations in standard and uncontrived situations; (b) modes of behavior, including motor, cognitive, emotional, and social; and (c) temporal frame of measurement, including measures of immediate treatments, overall hospital stay, and posthospital adjustment. This conceptual framework helped guide a study of how patients were affected by their move to a new hospital building.

A set of components applicable to most research domains consists of actors, behaviors, and contexts (Runkel & McGrath, 1972). Actors may be individuals, groups, organizations, or entire communities. Behaviors are actions that actors undertake toward objects. Contexts are immediate surroundings of actors and their behaviors, including time, place, and condition. Each component would be further subdivided into aspects appropriate to the research domain. Laying out the components and their subdivisions in a grid produces a domain "map" on which any particular investigation can be located. For example, the following factors could be used in a classification scheme for group problem solving: members' abilities and motives, type of tasks performed, relationships among members, group staffing levels, and type of settings in which groups perform.

Developing a comprehensive framework for a research domain contrasts with the more prevalent "up and out" strategy, in which investigators link their work on relatively narrow, focused topics with events outside their domain and then transpose their framework and findings to this new area. For example, research on students' verbal reactions to brief intervals of crowding has been extrapolated to prisons, homes, and transportation systems. An analysis of crowding using the three components mentioned above would reveal many additional factors that could be considered and incorporated into subsequent research. Actors could be expanded to include prisoners and homemakers; behaviors could include social interaction and task performance; contexts could include living quarters, worksites, recreational settings, and time frames of months or years. Some research on crowding reflects these broader considerations (e.g., Cox, Paulus, & McCain, 1984).

Make Comparisons Outside the Problem Domain

We are familiar with the principle that knowledge is an awareness of differences—it is our rationale for using control groups. This principle can be invoked to generate new ideas: Comparisons can be made with actors, behaviors, or settings outside one's current problem domain. For example,

Piotrkowski (1978) has provided insights into family interaction patterns by examining the nature of the work that family members perform both inside and outside the home. The emotional availability of family members to one another may depend less on their personalities than on the quality and timing of their work experiences, such as how stressful and fatiguing the work is and whether overtime and late shift work is involved.

More remote comparisons may also be fruitful. What we regard as basic social and cognitive processes are conditioned by cultural and historical factors (Gergen, 1982; Mills, 1959; Segall, Campbell, & Herskovitz, 1966). Researchers who focus on contemporary events in Western culture can profitably examine similar events in other periods and cultures. Guttentag and Secord's (1983) recent elaboration of social exchange theory to include social structural variables provides an illustration: Social exchange theorists have regarded participants in dyadic interactions as free agents capable of negotiating the the most favorable outcomes for themselves. Using data from several cultures and historical periods, the investigators demonstrated that the demographic condition of disproportionate sex ratios (substantially more men than women in a particular population, or vice versa) directly affected the exchange process between man and women. For example, when men outnumbered women, men were less likely to enter or stay in a monogamous heterosexual relationship. Women might either cater to men or withdraw from them to express female independence (Guttentag & Secord, 1983; Secord, 1984). (More general treatments of theoretical and methodological issues in historical and cross-cultural research are found in Gergen & Gergen, 1984, and Malpass, 1977.)

We can also probe the structure of contemporary society for subtle influences on how we frame research topics. Sampson (1981) was concerned that psychologists interpret and present socially and historically limited events as fundamental properties of the human mind. He argued that the predominant psychological world view portrays people as independent agents whose primary functions are ruminations—cognitive activities such as planning, wishing, thinking, organizing, and problem solving—with little regard for the objective social world. Furthermore, he contended that such a view may not only be time bound, but may also serve to reaffirm present societal arrangements and values. Sampson's advocacy of a "critical study of psychology and society, a study that is self-conscious about its context, its values, and its relationship to human freedom (p. 741)" has numerous and profound implications for many specific research domains. Theories of work motivation, for example, may need to consider the worker's psychological state *and* the organizational, legal, economic, cultural, and even nutritional conditions under which work is performed (cf. Barrett & Bass, 1976).

Parenthetically, it is worth noting that academic disciplines and research specialties may also benefit from "outside" influences; for example, requirements in graduate programs for coursework outside the major field (Lawson, 1984), cross-disciplinary collaboration, and serious efforts to include perspectives of women, ethnic minorities, gays, and scholars from developing countries.

Examine Processes in the Settings in Which They Naturally Occur

Most psychological and behavioral processes unfold in behavior settings (taken-for-granted configurations of time, place, and objects where routine patterns of behavior occur) such as offices, workshops, hospital waiting rooms, parks, and worship services (Barker, 1968). These small-scale, commonsense units of social organization variously promote, afford, permit, encourage, and require behaviors that are part of or are compatible with the main activity, and they discourage or prohibit behaviors that interfere with it.

By contrast, much psychological research is conducted in contrived environments that lack the characteristics of behavior settings. Table 1

TABLE 1
Contrast Between a Typical Small Group Study and Behavior Setting Features

Typical small group study	Behavior setting features
Fixed duration, 1 hour or less	Indefinite duration, typically months or years
Group composed of college students	Staff composed of community members
No prior interaction among group members	Extensive prior interaction among staff members
Imposed task, often an intellectual problem to be solved	Endogenous tasks, typically involving behavior objects such as equipment and supplies
Casual interactions	Meaningful interactions
No enduring local culture	Established local culture
No hierarchical relationships among members	Hierarchical relationships among members
Closed system: no personnel changes, not part of a system network including suppliers, external information sources, and recipients of products	Open system: changes in personnel, part of a system network that includes suppliers, external information sources, and recipients of products

illustrates some differences between features of a typical laboratory study of small groups (see Miller, 1971) and a behavior setting.

In some psychological specialties, theories are formulated and may be revised on the basis of generations of studies conducted exclusively in the laboratory. Recognized experts may lack firsthand experience with the events and subjects that produce their data (cf. Jones, 1983). Yet the work of such seminal figures as Piaget and Lewin illustrates the benefits of direct observation of behaviors in context. (Observational strategies are discussed by Lofland, 1976, and Weick, 1968).

Ideally, researchers who wish to consider contextual factors would first identify and then representatively sample settings where the behaviors of interest regularly occur (cf. Brunswik, 1947; Petrinovich, 1979). But such an extensive effort may not be necessary to gain insights from behavioral contexts. Investigators might observe people in a few settings where the behaviors or processes of interest are a significant part of the program. For example, workers' adjustments to stress can be studied in police dispatcher worksites (Kirmeyer, 1984).

Ventures out of the laboratory can reveal neglected but significant influences on a behavior or process. For example, an environmental psychologist interested in personal space might, by observing people in medical office waiting rooms, discover that people's sense of what is a comfortable distance from others depends on how ill they feel, on whether the others may have contagious diseases, and on furniture arrangements and design, including whether chairs have armrests.

Consider Practical Implications of Research

Reflections on how research might be applied also can lead to expanded views of basic psychological processes. For example, theories and findings on human learning and memory can be used to design instructional materials. Through such efforts, previously unseen gaps in existing frameworks might become evident and could lead to broadened research procedures. Stimulus materials could be made more complex and more natural, response alternatives increased and made more meaningful, time frames expanded, and tasks and environments made more realistic (Mackie, 1974). Designed applications could be discussed with practitioners and then be implemented and evaluated.

Probe Library Resources

One of the most accessible vehicles for transcending narrow conceptual frames is the research library, whose extensive resources are scarcely considered by many researchers. As psychologists, we may limit our literature searches to work listed in the *Psychological Abstracts* or even to a few select journals. If so, we are ignoring enormous amounts of potentially useful information and sources of ideas from the larger social world.

The resources include both quantitative and qualitative data. Baseline data and other statistics relevant to most research topics can usually be found. For example, the *Statistical Abstract of the United States* (1985), published annually by the Bureau of the Census, includes national data on health, education, housing, social services, the labor force, energy, transportation, and many other topics. It also contains a guide to other statistical publications.

Statistics such as these can provide perspectives not generally available in the psychological literature. They can, for example, show trends in the frequency and distribution of events. Such data can suggest new research directions: A researcher might choose to give greater emphasis to cases that are more frequent, use more resources, have more beneficial or detrimental consequences, affect more people, or are on the leading edge of an important trend or development. Researchers of legal decision making might, for example, be influenced by the following facts: (a) In each of the past several years, less than 7% of civil cases before U.S. District Courts came to trial, and (b) from 1965 to 1983, the percentage of cases (civil and criminal cases combined) tried by jury in these courts declined from 51% to 40% (*Statistical Abstract of the United States*, 1985, pp. 178–179). Researchers of mock juries might profitably expand their work to include other aspects of legal decision making such as pretrial negotiations and the ways that judges consider and weigh evidence. (Bibliographies of useful statistical sources are found in Bart & Frankel, 1981; and Cottam & Pelton, 1977.)

Libraries are also a bountiful source of qualitative information on the range of human experience and behavior. These data take many forms: newspapers and magazines, popular nonfiction, oral histories, legal cases, ethnographies, diaries and letters, atlases, novels, and photographs, as well as the scholarly literature. Such materials can be sampled and analyzed much as a sociological field worker selects and studies people and events in a community. Qualitative information in libraries can be perused at the researcher's convenience, and it often covers extended time periods, allowing for analyses of trends. (The use of library data in theory building is discussed by Glaser & Strauss, 1967, chapter 7.)

The benefits of consulting a broad range of sources are evident in Heider's (1958/1983) influential book, *The Psychology of Interpersonal Relations*. In an attempt to document and systematize the layperson's knowledge of social relationships, Heider drew upon the works of philosophers, economists, novelists, humorists—and social scientists. For example, he credited the 17th century philosopher Spinoza for the insights that led to his statement of cognitive balance.

An illustration of the creative use of qualitative data in a psychological specialty where laboratory investigations predominate is Neisser's (1981) study of the memory of former presidential counsel John Dean. Neisser compared Dean's testimony before the Senate Watergate Investigating Committee with subsequently revealed transcripts of the conversations Dean had testified about. Neisser's analysis drew upon memory theories and recent laboratory-based research to suggest a new term (*repisodic*) for memories that are accurate in general substance but inaccurate in their detail (Neisser, 1981).

PROBE AND TINKER WITH ASSUMPTIONS

Virtually any conceptual framework, methodology, or perspective on a problem incorporates judgments that are accepted as true, even though they may not have been confirmed. Probing and tinkering with these assumptions can stimulate thinking in productive directions. Strategies considered here include making hidden assumptions explicit, making opposing assumptions, and simultaneously trusting and discrediting the same assumption.

Expose Hidden Assumptions

The task of revealing our own implicit assumptions is inherently difficult and can never be fully accomplished. Some assumptions may be imbedded in everyday or technical language, and others may be tied into our sensory and nervous systems. About all we can hope for is an increased awareness of a small portion of the assumptive network. And to probe any assumption, we must trust many others (Campbell, 1974).

The contrastive strategy—juxtaposing dissimilar elements from alternative or competing perspectives—is one way to uncover hidden assumptions. The juxtaposition can also lead to more precise statements of one or both conceptual frameworks. The conditions under which the alternative perspectives are most applicable may thus be clarified (McGuire, in press). To illustrate, two theories make contradictory predictions about how staff members respond when service settings such as child day care facilities and emergency medical services are understaffed. One theory (Barker, 1968) predicted a positive response: The staff will work harder, will assume additional responsibilities, and will have increased feelings of self-worth and competence. Another theory (Milgram, 1970) predicted such negative responses as disaffection with the work and disregard for clients' individual needs and low-priority claims for attention. Both theories are likely to be correct in certain circumstances. Positive responses may occur in settings where understaffing is infrequent and known to be temporary, whereas negative responses may characterize settings where there is a chronic shortage of staff members (Wicker, 1979/1983). In this case, the theorists apparently made different implicit assumptions about the frequency and duration of understaffing.

Allison's (1971) analysis of governmental decision making during the 1962 Cuban Missile Crisis illustrates the benefits of applying different conceptual perspectives to the same set of events. He demonstrated that certain actions were best explained by assuming that the various branches of the American and Soviet governments (such as the U.S. Navy and the Soviet KGB) followed their standard operating procedures. Other actions were better understood as "resultants" of pulling and hauling by political players within the governments. Both perspectives were contrasted with the more commonly accepted "rational actor model," which presumes that governmental actions are chosen after reviews of the costs and benefits of alternatives (Allison, 1971).

Make the Opposite Assumption

A more playful strategy is to recast an explicit assumption into its opposite and then to explore the implications of the reversal. A general procedure for recasting theoretical assumptions has been suggested by Davis (1971), who contended that theories are judged interesting when they challenge the assumption ground of an audience. He identified 12 general ways of recasting theoretical statements (see Table 2).

The following example illustrates the general-local contrast from Davis's list. Many research psychologists assume that if they empirically test a hypothesized relationship and the predicted result is obtained, they confirm not only that particular relationship but also the higher level conceptual hypothesis and general theory from which it was derived. An opposing assumption is that demonstrated effects are conceptually local, that is, limited to a subset of populations and/or conditions similar to those in the investigation. Researchers who seriously consider this latter assumption may become more sensitive to differences in populations and conditions and may even become interested in developing taxonomies that would be useful for specifying limits of generality.

An argument along these lines has been advanced by McKelvey (1982). He stated that management theorists and academic social scientists (notably social psychologists and sociologists) routinely advance principles

TABLE 2
Ways of Recasting Theoretical Statements

What something seems to be	What it is in reality (or vice versa)
Disorganized	Organized
Heterogeneous	Composed of a single element
A property of persons	A property of a larger social system
Local	General
Stable and unchanging	Unstable and changing
Ineffective	Effective
Bad	Good
Unrelated	Correlated
Coexisting	Incompatible
Positively correlated	Negatively correlated
Similar	Opposite
Cause	Effect

Note: Adapted from "That's Interesting: Toward a Phenomenology of Sociology and a Sociology of Phenomenology" by M. S. Davis, 1971, *Philosophy of the Social Sciences, 1,* pp. 309–314. Copyright 1971 by Wilfred Laurier University Press. Adapted by permission.

that they assume are applicable to organizations in general. In a provocative challenge to this assumption, McKelvey drew upon evolutionary theory to propose an "organizational species" concept, "dominant competence," that he believed could be used to build a taxonomy of organizations.

Numerous recognized theoretical contributions in psychology can be viewed as articulated denials of existing assumptions. For example, Barker's (1963) classic article introducing behavior settings was essentially a rejection of the view that human environments are disordered, unstable, and without obvious boundaries. And Zajonc's (1965) analysis of social facilitation was a demonstration that seemingly incompatible research findings can coexist in a framework that distinguishes between responses that are high and low in the subject's response hierarchy.

Simultaneously Trust and Doubt the Same Assumption

Our thinking becomes more complicated when we devalue what we believe:

> Any person who has a view of the world and who also discredits part of that view winds up with two ways to examine a situation. Discrediting is a way to enhance requisite variety and a way to register more of the variety that's present in the world. (Weick, 1979, p. 228)

Researchers can use this device to introduce flexibility and ambivalence into their conceptual framework—they can trust an assumption for some purposes and distrust it for others. The strategy has both theoretical and methodological applications. For example, when attempting to explain the behavior of people over their life span, a personality theorist might presume that actions are guided by a few enduring behavioral dispositions (traits), but when considering how people act on a specific occasion the theorist might doubt that traits are useful. Or a researcher might devise and administer a questionnaire or interview schedule on the assumption that people respond openly and freely, but interpret the responses in a way that assumes people respond primarily in guarded and self-serving ways.

CLARIFY AND SYSTEMATIZE THE CONCEPTUAL FRAMEWORK

Most of the above strategies will expand the researcher's conceptual framework. At some point the enlarged set of ideas should be reviewed to select the most provocative thoughts for further, more intensive analysis. The following procedures can be helpful in this sifting process as well as earlier in the conceptual framing process.

Scrutinize the Meanings of Key Concepts

Researchers should have and communicate a clear understanding of the concepts they use. One way to clarify meanings of key terms is to explore their roots, synonyms, and earliest known uses. Numerous sources are available, including dictionaries (etymological, unabridged, reverse, technical), technical books, handbooks, and encyclopedias. The nuances in meaning revealed by these sources can help researchers choose terms that precisely express their ideas. Consider, for example, the nuances implicit in the root meanings of these related words: *educate* (to rear or bring up), *instruct* (to construct or arrange), *teach* (to show, guide, or direct), and *train* (to pull, draw, or drag) (*Webster's Third New International Dictionary of the English Language, Unabridged*, 1969).

Theorists need to be sensitive to the different levels of generality that are implied by their concepts. Often it is advisable to examine terms at more than one level. Abstract terms can often be broken into components whose various meanings are worth exploring. For example, *health-promoting behavior* may include several types of actions, including habits like tooth brushing and infrequent voluntary activities like scheduling and taking a physical examination. More general terms may be sought for theoretical concepts currently defined in a limited domain. More abstract terms also may suggest other domains where the theory might be applied (Mills, 1959, pp. 212–213). For example, the concept "social loss of dying patients" can be expanded to "the social value of people" (Glaser & Strauss, 1967).

Concept analysis, a procedure developed by philosophers, can be used to clarify our thinking about terms we use in research. The first step is to identify cases or examples that clearly fit the intended meaning of the concept being analyzed. To illustrate, a clear example of my concept of job involvement might be working extra hours without pay when there is no external pressure to do so. Other examples—ones that are clearly outside the intended meaning and others that are borderline—are then evoked. From a careful review of such cases, the researcher can draw out the essential properties of the concept as he or she uses it. (Concept analysis is described and illustrated in Wilson, 1963, and in Gowin, 1981b, pp. 199–205.)

Specify Relationships Among Concepts

The most rigorous ways of expressing relationships among concepts, such as mathematical modeling and hypothetico-deductive systems, are well known to psychologists. Other procedures such as concept mapping can also be used to simplify and clarify a research domain. Figure 2 illustrates a concept map; it represents Gowin's (1981a) theory of educating.

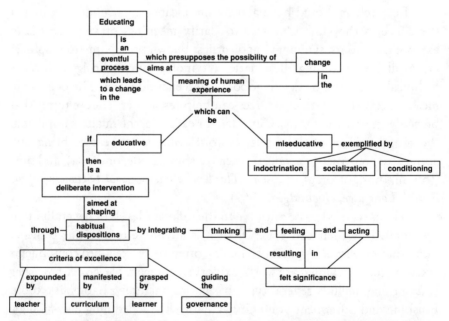

Figure 2: A Concept Map of Gowin's Theory of Educating. *Note:* From *Educating* (p. 94) by D. B. Gowin, 1981, Ithaca, NY: Cornell University Press. Copyright 1981 by Cornell University Press. Reprinted by permission.

The first step in producing such a map is to list the major concepts that are part of a developing framework or theory. The concepts are then ranked in order of importance. This order is preserved in the concept map, with the most important concept at the top, and so on. Concepts are placed in boxes, and relationships among concepts are indicated by lines and brief verbal descriptions (Gowin, 1981a, pp. 93–95).

In another variation of concept mapping, arrows are used to show a presumed direction of causality, and signs (+, −) are used to show whether the influence is positive or negative. From the pattern of such relationships, inferences can be drawn about the domain being considered; for example, whether a system is amenable to change, and if so, where change efforts might be directed (Maruyama, 1963; Weick, 1979, 68–88).

Write a Concept Paper

Perhaps the most powerful tool for ordering and clarifying thinking is putting one's ideas into words. Writing is so familiar and often so burden-some that we often overlook or avoid it until we feel ready to communicate with an audience. Writing should be brought into play much earlier; it is an excellent medium for experimenting with conceptual meanings and rela-tionships. Working papers can help researchers explore their thoughts and reveal gaps, inconsistencies, and faulty reasoning (Flower, 1981). In such papers researchers should address questions such as these: What is the core issue or question here? Why is it important? What key concepts are imbed-ded in this topic and how are they related? What alternative methods can be used to answer the central question? What types of answers are desirable and feasible? (cf. Gowin, 1981a, pp. 86–107).

HOW TO BEGIN

Researchers who wish to explore these techniques should choose several strategies that seem appropriate to their problem and then consult the cited references for further details on each strategy. Any strategy explored should be given at least several hours of the researcher's "best time"—a period when he or she is alert, relaxed, and free from distractions and interruptions. Not every strategy attempted will prove fruitful for a given person or problem.

Devoting time to expanding and ordering one's conceptual frame can seem like a frivolous diversion from more pressing tasks. Yet the potential payoffs are substantial. A single new insight can go a long way, particularly in specialties in which theoretical and methodological traditions are strong and in which most published contributions are variations on familiar themes. Properly developed, a fresh idea can have a lasting impact.

REFERENCES

Allison, G. T. (1971). *Essence of decision*. Boston: Little, Brown.

Barker, R. G. (1963). On the nature of the environment. *Journal of Social Issues*. 19(4), 17–38.

Barker, R. G. (1968). *Ecological psychology: Concepts and methods for studying the environment of human behavior*. Stanford, CA: Stanford University Press.

Barrett, G. V., & Bass, B. M. (1976). Cross-cultural issues in industrial and organizational psychology. In M. D. Dunnette, (Ed.), *Handbook of industrial and organizational psychology* (pp. 1639–1686). Chicago: Rand-McNally.

Bart, P., & Frankel, L. (1981). *The student sociologist's handbook* (3rd ed.). Glenview, IL: Scott, Foresman.

Brinberg, D., & McGrath, J. E. (1985). *Validity and the research process*. Beverly Hills, CA: Sage.

Brunswik, E. (1947). *Systematic and representative design on psychological experiments*. Berkeley: University of California Press.

Campbell, D. T., (1974, September). *Qualitative knowing in action research*. Paper presented at the meeting of the American Psychological Association, New Orleans.

Campbell, J. P., Daft, R. L. & Hulin, C. L. (1982). *What to study: Generating and developing research questions*. Beverly Hills, CA: Sage.

Caplan, N., & Nelson, S. D. (1973). On being useful: The nature and consequences of psychological research on social problems. *American Psychologist*, 28, 199–211.

Cohen, A. R. (1964). *Attitude change and social influence*. New York: Basic Books.

Cottam, K. M., & Pelton, R. W. (1977). *Writer's research handbook*. New York: Barnes & Noble.

Cox, V. C., Paulus, P. B., & McCain, G. (1984). Prison crowding research: The relevance for prison housing standards and a general approach regarding crowding phenomena. *American Psychologist*, 39, 1148–1160.

Crovitz, H. F. (1970). *Galton's walk*. New York: Harper & Row.

Davis, M. S. (1971). That's interesting: Toward a phenomenology of sociology and a sociology of phenomenology. *Philosophy of the Social Sciences*, 1, 309–314.

Flower, L. (1981). *Problem-solving strategies for writing*. New York: Harcourt Brace Jovanovich.

Galton, F. (1879). Psychometric experiments. *Brain*, 2. 148–162.

Georgoudi, M., & Rosnow, R. L. (1985). Notes toward a contextualist understanding of social psychology. *Personality and Social Psychology Bulletin*, 11, 5–22.

Gergen, K. J. (1978). Toward generative theory. *Journal of Personality and Social Psychology, 36*, 1344–1360.

Gergen, K. J. (1982). *Toward transformation in social knowledge.* New York: Springer.

Gergen, K. J., & Gergen, M. M. (Eds.). (1984). *Historical social psychology.* Hillsdale, NJ: Erlbaum.

Glaser, B. G., & Strauss, A. L. (1967). *The discovery of grounded theory.* Hawthorne, NY: Aldine.

Glaser, R. (1984). Education and thinking: The role of knowledge. *American Psychologist, 39*, 93–104.

Gowin, D. B. (1981a). *Educating.* Ithaca, NY: Cornell University Press.

Gowin, D. B. (1981b). Philosophy. In N. L. Smith (Ed.), *Metaphors for evaluation* (pp. 181–209). Beverly Hills, CA: Sage.

Guttentag, M., & Secord, P. F. (1983). *Too many women? The sex ratio question.* Beverly Hills, CA: Sage.

Heider, F. (1983). *The psychology of interpersonal relations.* Hillsdale, NJ: Erlbaum. (Original work published 1958)

Jones, R. A. (1983, December). Academic insularity and the failure to integrate social and clinical psychology. *Society for the Advancement of Social Psychology Newsletter,* pp. 10–13.

Kirmeyer, S. L. (1984). Observing the work of police dispatchers: Work overload in service organizations. In S. Oskamp (Ed.), *Applied social psychology annual* (Vol. 5, pp. 45–66). Beverly Hills, CA: Sage.

Lakoff, G., & Johnson, M. (1980). *Metaphors we live by.* Chicago: University of Chicago Press.

Lawson, R. B. (1984). The graduate curriculum. *Science, 225*, 675.

Leary, D. E. (1983, April). *Psyche's muse: The role of metaphor in psychology.* Paper presented at the meeting of the Western Psychological Association, San Francisco.

Lofland, J. (1976). *Doing social life: The qualitative study of human interaction in natural settings.* New York: Wiley.

Mackie, R. R. (1974, August). *Chuckholes in the bumpy road from research to application.* Paper presented at the meeting of the American Psychological Association, New Orleans.

Malpass, R. S. (1977). Theory and method in cross-cultural psychology. *American Psychologist. 32*, 1069–1079.

Manicas, P. T., & Secord, P. F. (1983). Implications for psychology of the new philosophy of science. *American Psychologist, 38*, 399–413.

Maruyama, A. J. (1963). The second cybernetics: Deviation-amplifying mutual causal processes. *American Scientist, 51*, 164–179.

McGrath, J. E. (1968). A multifacet approach to classification of individual, group, and organization concepts. In B. P. Indik & F. K. Berrien (Eds.), *People, groups, and organizations* (pp. 192–215). New York: Teachers College Press.

McGuire, W. J. (1964). Inducing resistance to persuasion. In L. Berkowitz (Ed.), *Advances in experimental social psychology* (Vol. 1, pp. 192–229). New York: Academic Press.

McGuire, W. J. (1973). The yin and yang of progress in social psychology: Seven koan. *Journal of Personality and Social Psychology, 26,* 446–456.

McGuire, W. J. (in press). Toward psychology's second century. In S. Koch & D. E. Leary (Eds.), *A century of psychology as science.* New York: McGraw-Hill.

McKelvey, B. (1982). *Organizational systematics.* Berkeley: University of California Press.

McKim, R. H. (1972). *Experiences in visual thinking.* Monterey, CA: Brooks/Cole.

Milgram, S. (1970). The experience of living in cities. *Science, 167,* 1461–1468.

Miller, J. G. (1971). Living systems: The Group. *Behavioral Science, 16,* 302–398.

Mills, C. W. (1959). *The sociological imagination.* New York: Oxford University Press.

Neisser, U. (1981). John Dean's memory: A case study. *Cognition, 9,* 1–22.

Nelms, N. (1981). *Thinking with a pencil.* Berkeley: Ten Speed Press.

Petrinovich, L. (1979). Probabilistic functionalism: A conception of research method. *American Psychologist, 34,* 373–390.

Piotrkowski, C. S. (1978). *Work and the family system.* New York: Free Press.

Rosenzweig, M. R. (1984). Experience, memory, and the brain. *American Psychologist, 39,* 365–376.

Runkel, P. J., & McGrath, J. E. (1972). *Research on human behavior: A systematic guide to method.* New York: Holt, Rinehart & Winston.

Sampson, E. E. (1981). Cognitive psychology as ideology. *American Psychologist, 36,* 730–743.

Secord, P. F. (1984). Love, misogyny, and feminism in selected historical periods. In K. J. Gergen & M. M. Gergen (Eds.), *Historical social psychology* (pp. 259–280). Hillsdale, NJ: Erlbaum.

Segall, M. H., Campbell, D. T., & Herskovitz, M. J. (1966). *The influence of culture on visual perception.* Indianapolis, IN: Bobbs-Merrill.

Smith, N. L. (1981). Metaphors for evaluation. In N. L. Smith (Ed.), *Metaphors for evaluation* (pp. 51–65). Beverly Hills, CA: Sage.

Statistical abstract of the United States. (1985). Washington, DC: U.S. Government Printing Office.

Stokols, D. (1982). Environmental psychology: A coming of age. In A. Kraut (Ed.), *G. Stanley Hall lecture series* (Vol. 2, pp. 155–205). Washington, DC: American Psychological Association.

Tyler, L. E. (1983). *Thinking creatively.* San Francisco: Jossey-Bass.

Wachtel, P. L. (1980). Investigation and its discontents: Some constraints on progress in psychological research. *American Psychologist, 35,* 399–408.

Webster's third new international dictionary of the English language, unabridged. (1969). Springfield, MA: Merriam.

Weick, K. E. (1968). Systematic observational methods. In G. Lindzey & E. Aronson (Eds.), *The handbook of social psychology* (2nd ed., pp. 357–451). Reading, MA: Addison-Wesley.

Weick, K. E. (1979). *The social psychology of organizing* (2nd ed.). Reading, MA: Addison-Wesley.

Wicker, A. W. (1969). Attitudes versus actions: The relationship of verbal and overt behavioral responses to attitude objects. *Journal of Social Issues, 25*(4), 41–78.

Wicker, A. W. (1983). *An introduction to ecological psychology.* New York: Cambridge University Press. (Original work published 1979).

Wicker, A. W. (in press). Behavior settings reconsidered: Temporal stages, resources, internal dynamics, context. In D. Stokols & I. Altman (Eds.), *Handbook of environmental psychology.* New York: Wiley.

Wilson, J. B. (1963). *Thinking with concepts.* Cambridge, England: Cambridge University Press.

Young, R. E., Becker, A. L., & Pike, K. L. (1970). *Rhetoric: Discovery and change.* New York: Harcourt Brace Jovanovich.

Zajonc, R. B. (1965). Social facilitation. *Science, 149,* 269–274.

4

DISCOVERY-ORIENTED PSYCHOTHERAPY RESEARCH: RATIONALE, AIMS, AND METHODS

ALVIN R. MAHRER

In their companion introductions to the special issues on psychotherapy research for the *American Psychologist* and the *Journal of Consulting and Clinical Psychology,* both VandenBos (1986) and Kazdin (1986a) flagged the accelerating breadth of development in this research field over the past four decades. One of these developments, mentioned both inside and outside these special issues, is a small but vigorous interest in what is coming to be known as discovery-oriented psychotherapy research (Elliott, 1983a, 1983b, 1984; Gendlin, 1986; Glaser, 1978; Glaser & Strauss, 1967; Greenberg, 1986; Kazdin, 1986b; Mahrer, 1985, 1988; Rennie, Phillips, & Quartaro, 1988; Rice & Greenberg, 1984; Stiles, Shapiro, & Elliott, 1986; Strupp, 1986).

In this kind of research, the pivotal question is how to study psychotherapy to discover the discoverable, to learn the secrets of psychotherapy. If this question is kept centered, what begins to emerge is an increasing

Reprinted from the *American Psychologist,* 43, 694–702. Copyright 1988 by the American Psychological Association.

differentiation between research that is discovery-oriented and research that is oriented toward the testing of hypotheses. The differentiation is across the board, from the opening intent to do the research to the design and methodology of the study, and from the framing of the research question to the sense that is made of the findings. The purpose of this article is to introduce discovery-oriented psychotherapy research as an alternative to hypothesis-testing research; to present the rationale, aims, and goals of this approach; to outline the methods in sufficient detail for adoption by psychotherapy researchers; and thereby to stimulate research that is genuinely enthusiastic, interesting, practical, and conceptually challenging and that allows us to discover what is there to be discovered.

HYPOTHESIS-TESTING RESEARCH

The preponderance of mainstream psychotherapy research is designed to test hypotheses. In the field of psychotherapy, there are at least two main aims of this kind of research, and my thesis is that hypothesis-testing is disappointingly ineffective for both.

The Confirmation or Disconfirmation of Theoretical Propositions

One of the major aims of hypothesis-testing research is to confirm or disconfirm theoretical propositions. The rationale is that a network of theoretical assumptions is logically bound to a set of propositions that provides the empirical basis for the testing of hypotheses (cf. Brodbeck & Feigl, 1968). If the proposition is confirmed, the theory is a little more secure. If the proposition is disconfirmed or refuted (Popper, 1968), the theory may be in trouble.

A serious problem lies in going from the findings to the theoretical proposition and from there to the network of theoretical assumptions, that is, the theory of psychotherapy. Although theoretical propositions may bear some degree of consistency or inconsistency with the findings, rarely if ever does logical necessity include significant modification or abandonment of the theoretical proposition. It is even rarer to find it necessary to significantly modify or abandon the network of theoretical assumptions (Armstrong, 1982; Brush, 1974; Danziger, 1985; Feyerabend, 1975; Gould, 1981; Kuhn, 1962; Lakatos, 1976; Orne, 1969; Popper, 1968; Rosenthal, 1966). "No theory can be proven true by empirical data. And, just as it is impossible to prove a theory, so also is it impossible to prove one false" (Greenwald, Pratkanis, Leippe, & Baumgardner, 1986, p. 226). I know of no established theory of psychotherapy that declared bankruptcy because of research that failed to confirm, disconfirmed, or falsified its theoretical propositions and network of theoretical assumptions; nor is there a logical necessity for that to occur.

Theories of psychotherapy wax and wane because of considerations that have virtually nothing to do with the testing of hypotheses bearing on their theoretical propositions. "It is simply a sad fact that in soft psychology theories rise and decline, come and go, more as a function of baffled boredom than anything else" (Meehl, 1978, p. 807; cf. Feyerabend, 1975; Kuhn, 1962; Mahrer, 1978; Polanyi, 1958). The careers of theories of psychotherapy are under no logical necessity of being seriously affected by the results of hypothesis-testing research.

Indeed, there are solid reasons why no theory of psychotherapy need be in any genuinely grave danger from hypothesis-testing research. "One reason is that the usual use of null hypothesis testing in soft psychology as a means of 'corroborating' substantive theories does not subject the theory to grave risk of refutation *modus tollens*, but only to a rather feeble danger" (Meehl, 1978, p. 821, cf. Greenwald, 1975; Weimer, 1979). Meehl argued convincingly that the use of null hypotheses and significance tests leave the theoretical propositions in a state of virtual imperviousness to the findings.

Second, the space between a theory of psychotherapy and a derived or deduced testable hypothesis is so extensive, loose, and filled with implicit and explicit clauses and conditions that the theory is in no grave danger from whatever findings are obtained. Especially in the field of psychotherapy,

> no theory on its own ever gives rise to predictions of a testable sort. A theory itself is a set of general postulates together with their deductive consequences, and to obtain a testable prediction about a system we need to feed in both statements of the initial conditions of the system and auxiliary hypotheses. (Newton-Smith, 1981, p. 80)

When the findings are in, the theory of psychotherapy is in little danger.

Third, such research is rarely targeted on core theoretical propositions so that the theory of psychotherapy is in any real danger from the findings. Instead, the research is almost inevitably constrained to propositions that the theory of psychotherapy could easily live without.

Fourth, the propositions of theories of psychotherapy are generally so loose, floppy, and rarely, if ever, framed in explicit terms that they are safely immune from any attempts by researchers to disconfirm or refute what is not there to be disconfirmed or refuted (Grünbaum, 1979; Nagel, 1959). Furthermore, the case may be made that whereas there may be some qualified theories in the behavioral and social sciences, in the field of psychotherapy so-called theories are little more than loose collections of beliefs, ideologies, and second rate mythologies whose qualifications as scientific theories are amateur at best (Feyerabend, 1975; Mahrer, 1987, in press).

Fifth, it has probably never happened that the proponents of a theory of psychotherapy have spelled out the research grounds under which they would publicly foreswear their theory or renounce an important theoretical proposition (cf. Newton-Smith, 1981).

Sixth, rival theories are in no genuinely grave danger when pitted against one another by a researcher because it is rare that the rival theories agree that the contestants selected by the researcher are legitimate representatives of the theory. It is also rare that the proponents of rival theories accept the rules of the contest, that the theories agree on the consequences of losing, and especially that the theorists accept the referees and judges. The net result is that the contest is legitimate mainly in the eyes of the researcher while placing the losing theories at little risk.

Seventh, not only are firm believers easily able to refute and discount unfriendly findings of hypothesis-testing research, always managing to stay safely out of range, but their research lieutenants can inevitably be counted on to generate counterbalancing friendly studies.

Indeed, any theory that sponsors research can develop a methodology that ensures friendly results and pronounces alien research as dismissibly and discountably unscientific. The theory is "protected from the effects of contrary evidence because no evidence from outside the charmed methodological circle is accepted as valid . . . methods based on assumptions about the nature of the subject matter only produce observations which must confirm these assumptions" (Danziger, 1985, p. 10). Not only does the theory set the rules for what is to be accepted and rejected as scientific or unscientific, but the theory also can guarantee findings that are hypothesis-friendly by appropriate adjustments and readjustments of the research procedures, by continual reanalyses of the findings until they are friendly, and by persistent redoing of the study until it produces the right results (Armstrong, 1982; Brush, 1974; Gould, 1981; Greenwald et al., 1986; Lakatos, 1976; Orne, 1969; Rosenthal, 1966). "Putting it crudely, if you have enough cases and your measures are not totally unreliable, the null hypothesis will always be falsified, regardless of the truth of the substantive theory" (Meehl, 1978, p. 822). The net result is an increasingly successful partnership between theories of psychotherapy and the confirmatory empirical findings that their research produces. According to Feyerabend (1975), the theory

> is successful not because it agrees so well with the facts; it is success-
> ful because no facts have been specified that could constitute a test,
> and because some such facts have even been removed. Its "success" *is*

entirely man-made. . . . This is how empirical "evidence" may be *created* by a procedure which quotes as its justification the very same evidence it has produced. (p. 44)

Behavioral theories of psychotherapy can justifiably claim to be supported by empirical research because they set their own rules for doing theory-friendly studies and for ensuring that they are in no danger from alien hypothesis-testing research.

To make matters even worse, reviewers engage in the confounding game of counting up the number of studies that are in favor and against, adding appropriate weights for carefulness and rigor, and then arriving at pronouncements about the research-supported status of the theoretical proposition.

> The writings of behavioral scientists often read as though they assumed—what is hard to believe anyone would explicitly assert if challenged—that successful and unsuccessful predictions are practically on all fours in arguing for and against a substantive theory . . . as if one could, so to speak, "Count noses," so that if a theory has somewhat more confirming than disconfirming instances, it is in pretty good shape evidentially. . . . We know that this is already grossly incorrect on purely formal grounds, it is a mistake a fortiori. (Meehl, 1967, p. 112; cf. Edelson, 1984; Smith & Glass, 1977)

All in all, theories of psychotherapy are safely impervious from the findings of hypothesis-testing research. Psychoanalysis is in no grave danger from the analysis of variance. I suggest that hypothesis testing is essentially unable to fulfill its self-assigned mission of confirming or disconfirming psychotherapeutic propositions or theories. Indeed, in the field of psychotherapy, the mission itself is fruitless. What is left for hypothesis-testing research in psychotherapy?

Contribution to the Cumulative Body of Knowledge in Psychotherapy

Hypothesis-testing research is justified as contributing to a supposed cumulative body of knowledge in psychotherapy. Picture a scientific body of knowledge containing at least two admissible classes of psychotherapeutic knowledge. One consists of scientifically stamped facts, hard and objective, empirical and tested, the tough data base of psychotherapeutic knowledge. The other class consists of psychotherapeutic laws and principles, canons and tenets. Hypothesis-testing research is apotheosized as the royal gatekeeper, guardian, and contributor to this cumulative body of psychotherapeutic knowledge. My thesis is that hypothesis-testing research is an inadequate means of contributing to an essentially nonexistent and mythical body of psychotherapeutic knowledge. The whole mission is both groundless and fruitless.

One of the problems is that precious little from outside the accepted body of knowledge is granted entry by hypothesis-testing research. Hypothesis testing contributes virtually nothing because most of the hypotheses are already in the body of knowledge, given their legitimacy by one lobby group or another. Nor is the hypothesis in any danger of exclusion by the findings of hypothesis-testing research provided that it is protected by a strong enough lobby.

Kiesler (1971) identified two major classes of hypotheses for psychotherapy researchers, both of which are already part and parcel of the cumulative body of knowledge because of powerful support groups. One class consists of the articulated clinical wisdom of the great thinkers in psychotherapy. "Here we find Freud, Sullivan, Rogers, Wolpe and the like—all originally practitioners of the art—attempting via explicit formulations to bring order out of chaos" (Kiesler, 1971, p. 39). Their followers already accept their formulations as entrenched landmarks in the body of knowledge. In contrast, the self-appointed role of psychotherapy researchers is to lend their weight of research confirmation or disconfirmation to the pieces of accepted knowledge and thereby to show that they either belong or do not belong. The problem is that proponents of these great clinical thinkers will continue to retain their formulated clinical wisdom in the body of psychotherapeutic knowledge, with the findings of hypothesis-testing research as lightweight irrelevancies.

The second class consists of the accepted knowledge base of such traditional academic fields as learning, perception, motivation, cognition, personality, biology, physiology, neurology, and social psychology (Kiesler, 1971). The problem here is that the factual knowledge and theories in these fields are already stamped as a legitimate part of the body of knowledge by powerful scientific lobbies. "The history of the social sciences reveals that whenever a theory showed itself to be promising, a conceptual leap was made from the empirical to the epistemological and the ontological" (Stigliano, 1986, p. 42). The aim of hypothesis-testing researchers is to convince psychotherapists to accept, cherish, respect, and apply to psychotherapy what is already firmly entrenched in the body of knowledge by the powerful lobbies of academic proponents of learning, perception, motivation, cognition, personality, biology, physiology, neurology, and social psychology. All in all, hypothesis-testing research does little more than confirm or fail to confirm the knowledge we already firmly believe we have, as supported by powerful lobby groups.

In fact, if hypothesis-testing research confirms the piece of knowledge, it is perhaps more firmly entrenched in the body of knowledge. If hypothesis-testing research fails to confirm the piece of knowledge, it should be on its way out of the body of knowledge, according to the research catechism, but it is typically unaffected as far as its proponents are concerned. The net result is that hypothesis-testing research either has no serious effect on the body of knowledge in psychotherapy, or far from contributing to a supposed cumulative body of knowledge, the research contributes to a shrinking body of knowledge that we hold with greater confidence. On the basis of hypothesis-testing research, we know less and less, but with higher and higher confidence.

The proof of the pudding is to take a look at the body of knowledge that all our hypothesis-testing has produced. If we look at the larger body of knowledge in the social and behavioral sciences, the pantry is embarrassingly bare (Deutsch, Platt, & Senghors, 1971; Hesse, 1980; Kristol & Bell, 1981; MacIntyre, 1981; Stigliano, 1986); "The National Science Foundation was considering terminating funding for the social and behavioral sciences because no data base has emerged from the decades of studies which have been carried out" (Stigliano, 1986, p. 37).

When one takes a look at the corner of the cumulative body of knowledge that relates to psychotherapy, one finds a loosely conglomerated mixed bag. There are pieces of knowledge authoritatively contributed by the fields of learning, perception, motivation, cognition, personality, biology, physiology, neurology, and social psychology. There is also an even looser bag of psychotherapeutic truths, axioms, lore, tenets, laws, principles, canons, dictates, constructs, and firmly held beliefs. These vary all the way from the "law of effect" to the psychoanalytic "unconscious" and to such axiomatic truths as "in paranoia there are unconscious conflicts involving homosexual impulses." Even a moderately critical appraisal indicates that the body of scientific psychotherapeutic knowledge is bordering on nonexistent.

Instead of a single grand body of scientific psychotherapeutic knowledge, it is inviting to picture that each psychotherapeutic approach has its own package of cherished truths, dignified as a body of knowledge, with grossly varying weights attached to the findings of hypothesis-testing research, which stands relatively helpless in its assigned task of contributing to any cumulative body of knowledge in psychotherapy.

My conclusion is that hypothesis-testing research is poorly equipped for and disappointingly ineffective either in confirming or disconfirming theoretical propositions or in contributing to the supposed cumulative body of knowledge in psychotherapy. Yet hypothesis-testing is just about all we do. My recommendation is that hypothesis testing be left in the hands of those who can see no alternative and that the balance of researchers adopt the rationale, aims, and methods of discovery-oriented psychotherapy research.

AN ALTERNATIVE APPROACH TO PSYCHOTHERAPY RESEARCH

In the field of psychotherapy, the discovery-oriented approach is only a gleam in the eye of a few psychotherapy researchers (e.g., Elliott, 1983a, 1983b, 1984; Gendlin, 1986; Glaser, 1978; Glaser & Strauss, 1967; Mahrer, 1985; Rennie et al., 1988; Rice & Greenberg, 1984). Indeed, if one looks at the field of psychotherapy through the eyes of devout hypothesis-testers there is no such thing as discovery-oriented research as a distinctly viable alternative, for all good research can only be hypothesis-testing in one form or another. When hypothesis-testing is done properly it includes discovery. It can include discovery in the form of correlational investigations that may even study multidimensional and factorial relations among variables (Cronbach, 1957; Kiesler, 1971). Hypothesis testing graciously grants a measure of respectability to coming up with (i.e., discovery of) useful hypotheses from naturalistic or single case studies.

> Intensive study of the single case (either controlled or uncontrolled, with or without measurements) is a valuable *source of hypotheses*. . . . Discovery of hypotheses is a legitimate and essential scientific activity. But idiographic study has little place in the confirmatory aspect of scientific activity, which looks for laws applying to individuals generally. (Kiesler, 1971, p. 66)

Hypothesis-testing researchers tend to regard discovery-oriented methods as a somewhat useful secondary tool for the serious work of scientific hypothesis testing. In contrast, my aim is to nominate the discovery-oriented approach as a distinctly viable alternative for psychotherapy researchers, with its own rationale, aims, and methods. I submit that there are at least two aims and purposes of discovery-oriented research that are different from those of hypothesis-testing research (cf. Polkinghorne, 1983). One of these is to provide a closer, discovery-oriented look at psychotherapeutic phenomena, and the other is to discover the relations among psychotherapeutic conditions, operations, and consequences. The aims and purposes of discovery-oriented research thereby are distinct from the confirmation or disconfirmation of theoretical propositions or from contribution to a cumulative body of psychotherapeutic knowledge. Indeed, this "approach does not strive to contribute to any version of a bank of human data containing the cumulative record of eternal verities" (Kremer, 1986, p. 66). The whole basis for designing hypothesis-testing studies revolves around some predetermined, formulated idea or expectation or prediction or hypothesis that one then proceeds to test. "To design an experiment, one must first have an idea which he wishes to test" (Lathrop, 1969, p. 28). In contrast, the whole basis for designing discovery-oriented studies is the intention to learn more; to be surprised; to find out what one does not already expect, predict, or hypothesize; to answer a question whose answer provides something one wants to know but might not have expected, predicted, or hypothesized. To design a discovery-oriented investigation, one must first have a motivating interest in discovering what may be discovered by taking a closer look into psychotherapy or by inquiring into the interconnections among psychotherapeutic conditions, operations, and consequences. Accordingly, the purpose of the balance of this article is to show why and how to carry out this alternative approach to psychotherapy research.

TAKING A CLOSER, DISCOVERY-ORIENTED LOOK

The aim is to take a closer, in-depth look at psychotherapy and to discover what is there to be discovered. There are five steps to be followed by the researcher.

Selecting the Target of the Investigation

The first step is to select some area in psychotherapy into which you want to take a closer look. What psychotherapeutic event or phenomenon excites you, piques your interest, or invites your taking a closer look? What is it that you would like to see in more detail, that you would like to investigate by getting down into it? Think of all the phenomena of psychotherapy, no matter how big and loose or small and tight. Think in terms of simple words rather than technical jargon constructs (such as locus of control, transference, self-efficacy, or ego alienness). Set aside general psychotherapeutic laws or principles or hypotheses. Just let yourself concentrate on whatever interests you enough so that you are drawn to taking a closer look into it.

Would you be interested in taking a closer look at what actually happened in Sigmund Freud's work with patients? If there were recordings of those sessions, I would be fascinated to discover what transpired. I am also interested in taking a closer look at what is going on when patients are in an extremely intense state of feeling and emotion or when patients are in the throes of genuinely impressive change or when patients are recounting incidents from very early childhood. Some of the targets may be big, such as an entire session by Freud. Some of the targets may be small, such as a patient's erupting into a spontaneous outburst of strong, hearty laughter. In any case, the aim is to take a closer look in order to discover what may be there to be discovered.

Obtaining Instances of the Target of the Investigation

The second step is to obtain instances of the target of your investigation, of that area into which you want to take a closer look. Usually this means audiotapes or videotapes of your target. Try to obtain a large number of these tapes, particularly high-grade, fine instances of the target. Sometimes you are limited to one or only a few instances of your target. It would be fortunate to have even a single precious recording of one of Freud's sessions. Some targets are themselves rare or very hard to produce, such as instances of patients undergoing profoundly significant personality change. It is not easy to obtain 50 instances of patients erupting into sudden spontaneous outbursts of strong, hearty laughter. It might be easier to obtain a large number of instances of patients being in an extremely intense state of feeling and emotion, or of patients recounting incidents from very early childhood. Whatever the selected target into which you want to take a closer look, it is helpful to obtain as many and as good instances as you can.

Obtaining an Instrument for Taking a Closer Look

The third step is to obtain (select or develop) an instrument that allows you to take a closer look at whatever target you selected. Some instruments may consist of a procedure. For example, you may get a closer look at moments in which patients have attained high levels of feeling and emotion by the procedure of interviewing the patients and therapists to find out more about those moments (e.g., Elliott, 1984). The instrument might be a tape recorder. Wouldn't it be wonderful to have audiotapes and videotapes of Freud's sessions? Audiotapes and videotapes are useful instruments for taking closer looks. You can use all sorts of technical instruments to get closer looks. For example, you need an instrument that records dreams so that you can get a closer look at the dreams by means of the video dream recorder. You need instruments to measure the exact body location and intensity of a feeling as it occurs in both therapist and patient in the ongoing session.

I rely on category systems that are custom designed to provide a closer look at the selected target of investigation. Suppose that you wanted to take a closer look at what patients are saying and doing during spontaneous outbursts of strong, hearty laughter. Start with a search of the research and clinical literatures to provide some provisional hypotheses. Then obtain a large and representative number of audiotaped excerpts of such instances. With a group of judges, go through each of the excerpts one by one, slowly and carefully describing what the patient is saying and doing in each instance. Use terms that are close to the data and are simple, rather than using high-level constructs wrapped in the jargon of any therapeutic approach. With each succeeding instance, frame provisional categories, refine the categories you have already obtained, reorganize the system on the basis of each new instance against the backdrop of the developing category system complemented by the provisional hypotheses from the literature. In this serially progressive procedure, by the time you and the judges have completed your analysis of a large number of instances, you will have developed a category system that is generated from actual data and is increasingly rigorous and comprehensive. It is a category system of what patients are judged to be saying and doing during moments of spontaneous outbursts of strong, hearty laughter. My colleagues and I have followed this same procedure in developing category systems for taking closer looks at other targets of investigation. For example, one of the more robustly useful is a category system of good moments in psychotherapy—moments of patient change, progress, improvement, movement, and process—that are valued and prized from the perspectives of a broad range of therapeutic approaches (Mahrer, 1985, 1988; Mahrer & Nadler, 1986).

The instrument (e.g., category system) is the means for taking the closer look. It is careful and rigorous enough to keep the researcher honest, and it provides a better quality of data than trying to look into the target without the instrument. Nor is the instrument to be opposed to simple clinical study and analysis because it was born out of clinical study and analysis in the very process of its development.

On the other hand, the kind of instrument you use opens up a particular kind of closer look and reveals a particular class of data. A category system of what patients are saying and doing in moments of strong, hearty laughter will likely reveal nothing about changes in galvanic skin responses or heart rates. A category system of the good moments in psychotherapy sessions provides that kind of data and little else. Whatever instrument you use to take a closer look is limited to its own class of data.

Gathering the Data

The fourth step is to gather the data. Apply the instrument to all the instances of your selected target. If you have plenty of instances, apply the category system to instances that were not used in developing the category system. If you have only a limited number of instances, use a different set of judges and apply the category system to the instances used in constructing the category system. In any case, the application of the category system in a careful and rigorous way will yield the data for taking the closer look. Now you must make discovery-oriented sense of the data.

Making Discovery-Oriented Sense of the Data

It takes a particular attitude or perspective to see what there is to be discovered in the data. All the instrument can do is to organize and display the data in as hard and objective a manner as the instrument is able. Making discovery-oriented sense of the data is the job of the researcher. It calls for some helpful guidelines.

Welcoming receptivity to the discoverable. The clinical researcher is to be exceedingly open to what is new in the data, to what is out of the ordinary, different, unexpected, exceptional, surprising, challenging, disconcerting. The researcher must be vigilant to what does not seem to fit, to what is hard to grasp, organize, explain. By taking this stance, the clinical researcher will be sensitive to the discoverable.

This way of seeing and listening to the data means that the investigator is to be a clinical researcher, with sufficient knowledge of what is ordinary, mainstream, or expected. Indeed, it helps to have a group of independent clinical researchers. The clinical researcher should also be passively naive in taking plenty of time to allow the data to show what is there to be discovered. This process involves a blend of passive naiveté and knowledgeable understanding in being sensitive to what is new, different, unexpected, exceptional, surprising, and discoverable.

You must scan the data, be open to cues and leads, try out various patternings, attend to repeated instances, organize and reorganize the data, and go back to the data again and again until you receive the discoverable.

Declining traps that mask the discoverable. There are several traps that tend to obfuscate the discoverable. Researchers should decline to mask the discoverable with easy explanations and rushed understandings, especially from their favorite psychotherapeutic approach. Another trap is to lose the discoverable by rising to higher levels of generalization that fit, make sense of, and manage to assimilate the discoverable. A third trap is to bypass the discoverable under central tendencies and normative schemas; statistical means and common themes easily hide the discoverable. Fourth, the researcher should decline the rush toward general laws, truths, and principles. All of these traps are easy and appealing, but they obfuscate the discoverable and are to be declined in the task of making discovery-oriented sense of the data.

By following these five steps, the clinical researcher can take a closer look into psychotherapy, a look that offers a good chance to discover something new. Researchers can take a closer, discovery-oriented look at Freud's actual work with patients, at what may be going on when patients are in an extremely intense state of feeling and emotion or are undergoing profoundly significant personality change, at what patients are saying and doing during spontaneous outbursts of strong, hearty laughter, or at any other events that are of genuine interest to researchers who want to see what may be discovered by taking a closer look into psychotherapy. However, this is only one way of doing discovery-oriented psychotherapy research.

DISCOVERING INTERCONNECTIONS AMONG CONDITIONS, OPERATIONS, AND CONSEQUENCES

There are lots of ways of carving up or imposing a schema or perspective on psychotherapy. The way that is selected in this research approach is to organize psychotherapy into conditions, operations, and consequences (Mahrer, 1985, in press). Furthermore, each of these three terms is taken as referring to more or less specific and concrete events rather than abstractions that are loose and general, and to events that occur in psychotherapy sessions rather than to anything occurring outside of these sessions.

Accordingly, *conditions* refer to the patient in the session, to what the patient is doing and to how the patient is being. The condition is when the patient is on the verge of tears, says that his or her headache is starting to pound, begins to protest and complain in a loud voice, starts the session with a deep sigh, puts the therapist on the spot with a few well-aimed questions, or sinks into a conspicuous silence. Discovery-oriented researchers describe conditions in this way rather than identifying the patient as a borderline, phobic, or incest survivor or as being in the termination phase of treatment.

Operations refer to what the therapist does right here in these statements. The therapist gives an interpretation, tells the patient to say it with more feeling, or provides an empathic reflection. Operations do not refer to supportive therapy, assertion training, or desensitization.

Consequences refer to what the patient does and how the patient is subsequent to the therapist operation. Consequences refer to the patient's outburst of hearty laughter, expression of insightful understanding, or recounting of his or her first day at school. Consequences do not refer to Minnesota Multiphasic Personality Inventory (MMPI) profile or a post-therapy symptom checklist.

The aim of this research is to discover the interconnections among in-therapy conditions, operations, and consequences. In a way, this sounds somewhat like the bellwether question of psychotherapy research, which was nicely articulated by Paul (1967): "*What* treatment, by *whom*, is most effective for *this* individual with *that* specific problem, and under *which* set of circumstances" (p. 111; cf. Kiesler, 1971). This question is widely accepted as the solid foundation of what psychotherapy researchers should be investigating (Parloff, 1979). However, it is not the question asked by discovery-oriented researchers. The smaller difference is that discovery-oriented researchers are examining specifically concrete meanings of conditions, operations, and consequences whose referential meanings are in-session events. The larger difference is that they are engaged in a discovery-oriented search for the interconnections. If one begins with the more or less accepted psychotherapy research question, tightens it to include specifically concrete in-session referential meanings, and encases the modified traditional question in a discovery-oriented framework, one emerges with three general questions for discovering the interconnections among psychotherapeutic conditions, operations, and consequences.

1. Given this *operation*, carried out under this condition, what are the consequences? That is, if the therapist does this operation, when the patient is being this way, what will happen?

2. Given this *consequence*, what operations under what conditions can achieve this consequence? That is, what can the therapist do to effect this desired consequence?

3. Given this *condition*, what operation can achieve this consequence? That is, when the patient is this way, what does the therapist want to achieve, and what does the therapist do to achieve this consequence?

There are three steps in carrying out this research approach: (a) specifying the question, (b) obtaining data, and (c) examining the data.

Specifying the Discovery-Oriented Research Question

The first step is to start with one of the general research questions and to frame a specific discovery-oriented research question.

Given this operation, carried out under this condition, what are the consequences? This is B. F. Skinner's favorite discovery-oriented research question. Skinner "had little use for making hypotheses or predictions about what the effect of a manipulation *ought* to be. You can just make the manipulation and *see* what its effect is" (Mook, 1982, p. 410).

How does the psychotherapy researcher select a manipulation (operation), carried out under some condition, to see what its effect (consequence) is? One way is to begin with cherished therapeutic axioms and convert them into discovery-oriented research questions. Consider this axiom, "When the client focuses on meaningful material, and the therapist provides an empathic reflection, the consequence is enhanced self-exploration." This yields the following research question: When the client focuses on meaningful material, and the therapist provides an empathic reflection, what are the consequences—including enhanced self-exploration? The axiom that "when the patient talks about himself or herself, and the therapist self-discloses, the consequence is enhanced self-disclosure" becomes the following research question: "When the patient talks about himself or herself, and the therapist self-discloses, what are the consequences—including enhanced self-disclosure?" Another axiom is that when there is an appropriate therapeutic relationship, and the therapist offers interpretations, the cumulative consequence is increased insight and understanding. As a research question, this becomes "When there is an appropriate therapeutic relationship, and the therapist offers interpretations, what are the consequences—including increased insight and understanding?"

Another way of framing discovery-oriented research questions is by asking reasonably appealing "what ifs." When a therapist is exasperated with a patient, what if the therapist gives vent to his or her exasperation? When the patient is perched on the scary edge of falling apart, what would the consequences be if the therapist encouraged the patient to go ahead? When the therapist has private thoughts, what would the consequences be if the therapist disclosed them openly and freely?

Given this consequence, what operations under what conditions can achieve this consequence? Proceeding from this general research question to a particular and specific one calls for the researcher's selecting in-session consequences that are impressive, welcomed, desired, and significant, especially those that are taken as indicating therapeutic change, process, movement, progress, or improvement. Given that a patient's persistent headache has now cleared and is gone, what therapist operations under what conditions appear to have been instrumental in achieving this consequence? Given a patient's welcomed increase in self-assuredness, energy and enthusiasm, feeling level, or strength and toughness, what therapist operations under what conditions led to this desirable consequence? The researcher merely specifies a particular consequence, something the patient is or does that is welcomed and desired, and the discovery-oriented research question is in place.

Given this condition, what operation can achieve this consequence? The researcher turns this into a specific research question by identifying some concrete condition (or problem), figuring out the related consequence that is welcomed and desired, and looking for the right operations that can effect that consequence. For example, in the beginning of a session (condition), what therapist operations enable the patient to achieve a state of strong experiencing and feeling (consequence)? When the patient withdraws into an enveloping silence (condition), what therapist operations succeed in lifting the patient out of the silence and into providing useful therapeutic material (consequence)? Greenberg and his colleagues

(Greenberg, 1984a) translated this general question into the following specific research question: When a client is in a condition regarded in gestalt therapy as a conflict split, what therapist–client operations are effective in achieving the desired consequence of a resolution of the conflict? Answering this question exemplifies the task analysis method (Greenberg, 1984b) wherein the discovery-oriented target is to identify therapist–client operations for moving from a designated in-therapy condition to a designated in-therapy consequence.

Obtaining the Data

Once the general research question is refined and put into a specific discovery-oriented question, the second step is to obtain the relevant data. Perhaps the best way of obtaining the data is from actual tapes and transcripts of therapists and patients. It is this step that punctuates the need for rich tape libraries in that each of the three general research questions yields specific discovery-oriented research questions whose answers are best provided by a rich tape library (cf. Gendlin, 1986; Mahrer, in press).

Consider three specific questions, each taken from one of the three general questions: (a) When the client focuses on meaningful material, and the therapist provides an empathic reflection, what are the consequences? (b) Given that the patient's persistent headache was extinguished at this point in the session, what therapist operations under what conditions were instrumental in achieving this consequence? (c) In the beginning of a session, what therapist operations enable the patient to achieve a state of strong experiencing and feeling? It seems clear that the most appropriate data for each of the three questions call for a rich library of tapes, yet it is the rare researcher who has access to tapes offering ample instances of the right conditions, operations, and consequences.

One of the three general questions, however, lends itself to manufacturing the data by experimental manipulation. This is the first general question; that is, given this operation, carried out under this condition, what are the consequences? It is feasible, for example, to instruct therapists that when the patient focuses on meaningful material, the therapist is to provide an empathic reflection, or when the therapist is exasperated with the patient, the therapist is to give vent to his or her exasperation. Although data for this first general question may be obtained either by experimental manipulation or through selection from a research tape library, data for the other two questions are beyond experimental manipulation and are best obtained through a research tape library.

In this research, much of the carefulness and rigor lie in specifying the meanings of the terms used in defining the conditions, operations, and consequences. The researcher must be reasonably precise in defining conditions such as "when there is an appropriate therapeutic relationship" or "when a client is in a gestalt conflict split," in defining therapist operations such as self-disclosure or empathic reflections, and in defining consequences such as the extinguishing of a persistent headache or the achievement of a state of strong experiencing and feeling.

Examining the Data to Obtain a Discovery-Oriented Answer

The method of examining the data varies with the general research question. Consider the general research question: Given this consequence, what operations under what conditions can achieve this consequence? For each instance of the target consequence, the method is to examine the antecedent therapist and patient statements, opening the window progressively larger and larger. It is helpful to use a number of independent clinical researchers to examine the antecedent operations and conditions.

A different method is called for in examining the data for the second general question: Given this operation, carried out under this condition, what are the consequences? With a large number of instances, it is helpful to use a category system tailor-made for those consequences according to the guidelines described earlier. The third general question is: Given this condition, what operation can achieve this consequence? Once again, it is useful to have a large number of instances and to use another category system tailor-made from, and for, the therapist (and patient) operations intervening between the conditions and the consequences.

Each of these three methods enables the clinical researcher to examine the data to answer the research question. However, as is required when the researcher takes a closer look into the psychotherapeutic phenomenon, it is important to examine the data so as to be exceedingly open to the discoverable, to what is new, out of the ordinary, different, unexpected, exceptional, or surprising. It is also important for the researcher to be sensitive to and avoid the common traps that bypass, hide, and lose the discoverable. By means of this third step, the clinical researcher examines the data to obtain a discovery-oriented answer to the research question and thereby to discover the interconnections among psychotherapeutic conditions, operations, and consequences.

CONCLUDING IMPLICATIONS

Hypothesis-testing research is essentially inadequate and unproductive for serious confirmation or disconfirmation of the propositions that make up theories of psychotherapy and also for contributing to a purportedly cumulative body of psychotherapeutic knowledge. Nor is hypothesis-testing research useful in discovering what is to be discovered in the field of psychotherapy. Hypothesis testing should be left in the hands of those who see no alternative way of doing psychotherapeutic research; otherwise, it should be abandoned.

Discovery-oriented research is a distinctive alternative whose rationale, aims, and methods contrast sharply with those of hypothesis-testing research. There are two approaches to this research. One consists of providing a closer, discovery-oriented look into psychotherapeutic events and phenomena, and the other consists of the discovery of the interconnections among psychotherapeutic conditions, operations, and consequences. Each of these two kinds of discovery-oriented research has its own characteristic methodology and procedural steps. The challenge is that the development of the field of psychotherapy will benefit more from discovery-oriented than from hypothesis-testing research, and that rigorous and productive discovery-oriented research will unseat hypothesis testing as the scientific means of inquiry in the field of psychotherapy research.

The findings of discovery-oriented research are of prime quality for (a) rigorously scientific theory building in the field of psychotherapeutic conceptualization, (b) generating advances throughout the field of psychotherapeutic practice, (c) opening up new avenues of psychotherapeutic research, and (d) integratively blending theory, practice, and research in the field of psychotherapy. Psychotherapy researchers are encouraged to develop the methodologies and procedures of discovery-oriented psychotherapy research and to adopt this way of discovering what is to be discovered in the field of psychotherapy.

These are the two kinds of research that comprise the discovery-oriented approach to psychotherapy research. Although they both differ from the rationale, aims, and methods of hypothesis-testing research, each has its own characteristic rationale, aims, and steps. Some psychotherapy researchers will remain steadfast in their allegiance to hypothesis testing. Others may assert that discovery-oriented aims and methods are already in place in the larger program of hypothesis testing. Still others may hold that they already do discovery-oriented psychotherapy research, although it may be described in different words. However, for those who are willing to consider discovery-oriented research as a distinctly viable alternative to hypothesis testing, I submit that we are headed toward a new period of discovering what is discoverable in the field of psychotherapy.

REFERENCES

Armstrong, J. S. (1982). Research on scientific journals: Implications for editors and authors. *Journal of Forecasting, 1*, 83–104.

Brodbeck, M., & Feigl, H. (1968). *Readings in the philosophy of the social sciences.* New York: MacMillan.

Brush, S. G. (1974). Should the history of science be rated X? *Science, 183*, 1164–1172.

Cronbach, L. J. (1957). The two disciplines of scientific psychology. *American Psychologist, 12.* 671–684.

Danziger, K. (1985). The methodological imperative in psychology. *Philosophy of the Social Sciences, 15*, 1–13.

Deutsch, K., Platt, J., & Senghors, D. (1971). Predictability in the social sciences. *Science, 107*, 1113–1116.

Edelson, M. (1984). *Hypothesis and evidence in psychoanalysis.* Chicago: University of Chicago Press.

Elliott, R. (1983a). Fitting process research to the practicing psychotherapist. *Psychotherapy: Theory, Research, and Practice, 20*, 47–55.

Elliott, R. (1983b). "That in your hands": A comprehensive process analysis of a significant event in psychotherapy. *Psychiatry, 46*, 113–129.

Elliott, R. (1984). A discovery-oriented approach to significant change events in psychotherapy: Interpersonal Process Recall and Comprehensive Process Analysis. In L. N. Rice & L. S. Greenberg (Eds.), *Patterns of change* (pp. 249–286). New York: Guilford.

Feyerabend, P. (1975). *Against method.* London: Verso.

Gendlin, E. T. (1986). What comes after traditional psychotherapy research? *American Psychologist, 41*, 131–136.

Glaser, B. G. (1978). *Theoretical sensitivity: Advances in the methodology of grounded theory.* Mill Valley, CA: The Sociology Press.

Glaser, B. G., & Strauss, A. (1967). *The discovery of grounded theory: Strategies for qualitative research.* Chicago: Aldine.

Gould, S. J. (1981). *The mismeasure of man.* New York: Norton.

Greenberg, L. S. (1984a). A task analysis of interpersonal conflict resolution. In L. N. Rice & L. S. Greenberg (Eds.), *Patterns of change* (pp. 67–123). New York: Guilford.

Greenberg, L. S. (1984b). Task analysis: The general approach. In L. N. Rice & L. S. Greenberg (Eds.), *Patterns of change* (pp. 124–148). New York: Guilford.

Greenberg, L. S. (1986). Change process research. *Journal of Consulting and Clinical Psychology, 54*, 4–9.

Greenwald, A. G. (1975). Consequences of prejudice against the null hypothesis. *Psychological Bulletin, 82*, 1–20.

Greenwald, A. G., Pratkanis, A. R., Leippe, M. R., & Baumgardner, M. H. (1986). Under what conditions does theory obstruct research progress? *Psychological Review, 93*, 216–229.

Grünbaum, A. (1979). Is Freudian psychoanalytic theory pseudo-scientific by Karl Popper's criterion of demarcation? *American Philosophical Quarterly, 16,* 131–141.

Hesse, M. (1980). Theory and value in the social sciences. In P. Pettit & C. Hookway (Eds.), *Action and interpretation* (pp. 1–16). New York: Cambridge University Press.

Kazdin, A. E. (1986a). Editor's introduction to the special issue. *Journal of Consulting and Clinical Psychology, 54,* 3.

Kazdin, A. E. (1986b). Comparative outcome studies of psychotherapy: Methodological issues and strategies. *Journal of Consulting and Clinical Psychology, 54,* 95–105.

Kiesler, D. J. (1971). Experimental designs in psychotherapy research. In A. E. Bergin & S. L. Garfield (Eds.), *Handbook of psychotherapy and behavior change: An empirical analysis* (pp. 36–74). New York: Wiley.

Kremer, J. W. (1986). The human science approach as discourse. *Saybrook Review, 6,* 65–105.

Kristol, I., & Bell, D. (1981). *The crisis in economic theory.* New York: Basic Books.

Kuhn, T. (1962). *The structure of scientific revolutions.* Chicago: University of Chicago Press.

Lakatos, I. (1976). *Proofs and refutations.* London, England: Cambridge University Press.

Lathrop, R. G. (1969). *Introduction to psychological research: Logic, design, analysis.* New York: Harper & Row.

MacIntyre, A. (1981). *After virtue.* Notre Dame, IN: University of Notre Dame Press.

Mahrer, A. R. (1978). *Experiencing: A humanistic theory of psychology and psychiatry.* New York: Brunner/Mazel.

Mahrer, A. R. (1985). *Psychotherapeutic change: An alternative approach to meaning and measurement.* New York: Norton.

Mahrer, A. R. (1987). These are the components of any theory of psychotherapy. *Journal of Integrative and Eclectic Psychotherapy, 6,* 28–31.

Mahrer, A. R. (1988). Research and clinical applications of "good moments" in psychotherapy. *Journal of Integrative and Eclectic Psychotherapy, 1,* 81–93.

Mahrer, A. R. (in press). *The integration of psychotherapies: A guide for practicing psychotherapists.* New York: Human Sciences Press.

Mahrer, A. R., & Nadler, W. P. (1986). Good moments in psychotherapy: A preliminary review, a list, and some promising research avenues. *Journal of Consulting and Clinical Psychology, 54,* 10–16.

Meehl, P. E. (1967). Theory-testing in psychology and physics: A methodological paradox. *Philosophy of Science, 34,* 103–115.

Meehl, P. E. (1978). Theoretical risks and tabular asterisks: Sir Karl, Sir Ronald, and the slow progress of soft psychology. *Journal of Consulting and Clinical Psychology, 46,* 806–834.

Mook, D. G. (1982). *Psychological research: Strategy and tactics.* New York: Harper & Row.

Nagel, E. (1959). Methodological issues in psychoanalytic theory. In S. Hook (Ed.), *Psychoanalysis, scientific method, and philosophy* (pp. 38–56). New York: Grove Press.

Newton-Smith, W. H. (1981). *The rationality of science.* London: Routledge & Kegan Paul.

Orne, M. T. (1969). Demand characteristics and the concept of quasi-controls. In R. Rosenthal & R. L. Rosnow (Eds.), *Artifact in behavioral research* (pp. 97–128). New York: Academic Press.

Parloff, M. B. (1979). Can psychotherapy research guide the policy-maker? *American Psychologist, 34,* 296–306.

Paul, G. L. (1967). Strategy of outcome research in psychotherapy. *Journal of Consulting Psychology, 31,* 109–118.

Polanyi, M. (1958). *Personal knowledge: Towards a post-critical philosophy.* Chicago: University of Chicago Press.

Polkinghorne, D. (1983). *Methodology for the human sciences.* Albany, NY: State University of New York Press.

Popper, K. (1968). *The logic of scientific discovery.* London: Hutchinson.

Rennie, D. L., Phillips, J. R., & Quartaro, G. K. (1988). Grounded theory: A promising approach to conceptualization in psychology? *Canadian Psychology, 29,* 139–150.

Rice, L. N., & Greenberg, L. S. (1984). *Patterns of change.* New York: Guilford.

Rosenthal, R. (1966). *Experimenter effects in behavioral research.* New York: Appleton.

Smith, M. L., & Glass, G. V. (1977). Meta-analysis of psychotherapy outcome studies. *American Psychologist, 32,* 752–760.

Stigliano, A. (1986). An ontology for the human sciences. *Saybrook Review, 6,* 33–63.

Stiles, W. A., Shapiro, D. A., & Elliott, R. (1986). "Are all psychotherapies equivalent?" *American Psychologist, 41,* 165–180.

Strupp, H. H. (1986). Psychotherapy: Research, practice, and public policy (How to avoid dead ends). *American Psychologist, 41,* 120–130.

VandenBos, G. R. (1986). Psychotherapy research: A special issue. *American Psychologist, 41,* 111–112.

Weimer, E. B. (1979). *Notes on the methodology of scientific research.* Hillsdale, NJ: Erlbaum.

II

METHODS: PRINCIPLES
AND PRACTICES

The theories, hypotheses, predictions, and ideas behind studies are obviously critical. Methodological issues emerge concretely at the stage where the idea is to be tested. Several decisions are required that affect the inferences that can be drawn. The conditions under which research is conducted can vary widely in clinical and other areas such as counseling and educational psychology where laboratory and applied settings are evaluated. The articles in this section address several research conditions that emerge upon moving from the idea to implementation of research.

SAMPLING: SUBJECTS AND CONDITIONS

The selection and assignment of research participants (subjects) to conditions are central to experimentation. Among the many issues is the concern over biases that can arise when subjects are identified and placed into alternative groups. Obviously, an initial goal is to form groups (e.g., experimental and control) with no preexisting difference that could ultimately interfere with the conclusions that are to be drawn. Before groups are exposed to their conditions, experimental interventions, and other tasks, we would like the groups to be equivalent. Investigators usually ascribe to the view that unbiased methods of selecting cases from an available subject pool and assigning these cases to conditions produce equivalent groups. Equivalent means that there are no differences on a host of *nuisance variables*—those variables that are not of interest to the investigator (e.g., social class, intelligence, and various personality traits). Louis Hsu (1989) discusses pivotal concepts of randomization and identifies situations in which misleading conclusions about the intervention might be drawn. Specifically, he elaborates on how groups may differ if samples are small and groups are formed by random assignment. Psychotherapy research is used as a basis to illustrate several of the points and to make recommendations for sample sizes in research. Because small samples (e.g., $n < 20$ per group) characterize a great deal of clinical research, the present evaluation warrants careful consideration in the design of studies.

Researchers are concerned with the generality of results from one set of subjects (e.g., college students) to another (e.g., clinic cases). A neglected feature of generality of results pertains to the stimulus conditions included in the investigation. The conditions presented to the subject reflect such features as the range, number, and characteristics of the experimenters, therapists, and vignettes or stories presented to the subject. Experimenters often include a narrow range of stimulus conditions (e.g., one therapist, one vignette) with the intention of controlling or holding constant the stimulus presented to the subject. Brendan Maher (1978) notes the importance of representing a broader range of stimulus conditions within an experiment. He discusses the concept of *representative design*, which refers to sampling the range of stimulus conditions from which the investigator wishes to generalize. Sampling of stimulus conditions is critically important as the basis for deciding the generality of results of a study and, more fundamentally, for separating the influence of the intervention or experimental manipulation from a restricted or single stimulus condition with which it may be confounded.

DESIGN OPTIONS AND PROCEDURES

In the present set of articles, specific design considerations and options are developed. Among those are issues related to the conditions under which research is conducted, the implementation and evaluation of experimental manipulations, and selected research design strategies.

Conducting research in the laboratory is often viewed as limited in clinical psychology because of the inferential leap required to persons, situations, and circumstances in the "real world." In fact, much research in clinical psychology is conducted in laboratory settings. This section begins with an article by Douglas Mook (1983) who discusses the purposes and importance of laboratory research. A central point is that research in the laboratory is often designed to convey what can happen and, in so doing, contributes significantly to understanding human functioning. Generality and applicability of the results are not always important or relevant. Mook elaborates on the role of laboratory research and its unique contribution to understanding.

The investigator is interested in evaluating the impact of some variable. The extent to which the impact is demonstrated depends in part on whether that variable or intervention is actually related to or has an effect on the dependent variables. Assuming that the variables are in fact related, whether or not an effect will be demonstrated within a particular investigation depends on a variety of conditions. William Yeaton and Lee Sechrest (1981) discuss the strength and integrity of the intervention within an experiment and how these influence the conclusions that the investigator wishes to draw. They discuss these points in the context of intervention research in psychotherapy, health, and related areas. However, the lessons can be extended to situations in which investigators seek to examine group differences. The question for the investigator in designing research is whether the experimental manipulation or condition represents a potent test, dose, or level of the conditions. At the design stage, it is critical to consider the strength of the independent variable and the different levels of the variable that are provided among groups. During the study itself, it is critical to assess and monitor conditions to ensure that they were implemented as intended.

Experimental designs refer to the arrangement or plan to evaluate the condition or intervention of interest. Among the many options is the decision of how to present the different conditions to the subjects. Anthony Greenwald (1976) writes about strategies in which subjects are assessed repeatedly and exposed to two or more experimental conditions (within-subject designs) or in which subjects are exposed to only one of the conditions (between-subject designs). The benefits and limitations of different design approaches are discussed. In this context, artifacts and influences that emerge in the designs are described. The special advantages of within-subject designs are presented. In a given experiment, the benefits of both within- and between-subject strategies can be obtained by a combined design in which measures are administered on more than one occasion to the same subjects (e.g., pre-, mid-, and posttreatment) to assess performance of subjects in each group.

SAMPLING: SUBJECTS AND CONDITIONS

5

RANDOM SAMPLING, RANDOMIZATION, AND EQUIVALENCE OF CONTRASTED GROUPS IN PSYCHOTHERAPY OUTCOME RESEARCH

LOUIS M. HSU

Simple random sampling and random assignment (randomization) are some of the best and most popular methods of attaining the pretreatment equivalence of contrasted groups in psychological research (see Cook & Campbell, 1979), in medical research (see O'Fallon et al., 1978), and in the specialized area of psychotherapy efficacy studies (Huesmann, 1982; Kendall & Norton-Ford, 1982; D. A. Shapiro & Shapiro, 1983). In fact, in a recent meta-analysis of comparative psychotherapy outcome research that focused on some of the best studies in this area, D. A. Shapiro and Shapiro (1982, 1983) noted that unconstrained randomization was used in 57% of the client groups.

One of the most appealing characteristics of random sampling and randomization is that these methods can equate groups on several nuisance variables simultaneously and that these methods do not require the researcher to be aware of (a) how the important nuisance variables are related

Reprinted from the *Journal of Consulting and Clinical Psychology, 57,* 131–137. Copyright 1989 by the American Psychological Association.

to the response measure, (b) the identities of the important nuisance variables, or even (c) the number of important nuisance variables (see Efron, 1971). These are, perhaps, the principal advantages of simple randomization and random sampling over alternative methods of controlling the effects of nuisance variables such as matching, stratification, analysis of covariance, analysis of covariance with reliability corrections, change score analysis, and standardized change score analysis. In all of these alternatives, the efficacy of control of the nuisance variables is contingent on the researcher's ability to identify the important nuisance variables or to develop a realistic model of how the contrasted groups would differ in the absence of different treatment effects (see Boruch, 1976; Kenny, 1975, 1979; Lord, 1967, 1969; McKinlay, 1977). Several authors have noted that, when sufficient information is available, these as well as other alternatives may be clearly preferable to simple random sampling and randomization (e.g., Fleiss, 1981, 1986; Pocock & Simon, 1975; Simon, 1979). Unfortunately, this information is often not available. (See Boruch, 1976, for an excellent discussion of this topic and for numerous real-world illustrations of problems associated with various alternatives to randomization.) Simple random sampling and randomization appear to be the methods of choice for controlling the effects of nuisance variables, especially the internal validity threats of maturation and selection and the selection–maturation interaction (see Cook & Campbell, 1979; Kirk, 1982), when information about the importance, the identities, and the number of variables is lacking.

However, as noted by Efron (1971), "complete randomization ... suffers from the disadvantage that in experiments which are limited to a small number of subjects, the final distributions of treatments and controls {on the nuisance variables} can be very unbalanced" (p. 403). Similarly, Cook and Campbell (1979) warned that the "equivalence achieved by random assignment is probabilistic" (p. 341) and that it may not work with small samples. A related point was made by Keppel (1973): "Random assignment of subjects to treatments will ensure in the long run that there will be an equivalence of subjects across the different treatments" (p. 24). All of these statements indicate that random sampling and randomization can be expected to result in the equivalence of large samples but need not result in the equivalence of small samples.

It is generally recognized that clinical studies often involve small samples. Kraemer (1981), for example, pointed out that "a minority of clinical research studies report {as many as} 30–40 subjects" (p. 311). She further noted that "in recent psychiatric clinical research, 20 seems a generally acceptable sample size" (p. 311) but that "many studies with fewer than 20 subjects are published" (p. 311). The situation appears to be even worse in the specialized area of comparative therapy outcome studies (see Kazdin, 1986). More specifically, D. A. Shapiro and Shapiro (1983), whose meta-analysis focused on "an unbiased sample of relatively well-designed, recently published comparative outcome studies" (p. 43) in this area, reported that "the 414 treated groups in our meta-analysis contained a mean of 11.98 (SD = 7.12) clients; the 143 control groups contained a mean of 12.12 (SD = 6.64) clients" (p. 44). They further indicated (a) that "forty-two (10%) of the treated groups contained six or fewer clients" (p. 44), (b) that 109 (26%) of these groups contained 7 to 9 clients, (c) that 148 (36%) contained between 10 and 12 clients, and (d) that only 115 (28%) contained 13 or more clients.

This article has five objectives related to the equivalence of contrasted groups in psychotherapy efficacy studies. The first objective is to investigate the relation of sample size and number of nuisance variables to the equivalence of groups in two popular models, a simple randomization model and a simple random sampling model. The second objective is to discuss the specific implications of these relations concerning the equivalence of groups described in D. A. Shapiro and Shapiro's (1982, 1983) recent meta-analyses of psychotherapy efficacy studies. The third objective is to illustrate how nonequivalence of contrasted groups can result in Simpson's paradox: The less beneficial treatment is estimated to be more beneficial. The fourth objective is to discuss the implications of Tversky and Kahneman's findings (1971) about belief in the law of small numbers concerning the interpretation of estimates of the relative efficacy of treatments in small psychotherapy efficacy studies. And the fifth objective is to compare the minimum sample sizes required for equivalence with the minimum sample sizes that have been recommended by Kraemer (1981) on the basis of other criteria.

FACTORS DETERMINING THE EQUIVALENCE OF GROUPS

Randomization

The efficacy of randomization as a method of equating groups on nuisance variables can be investigated in a variety of research designs. The single-factor independent-groups design was selected here because of the popularity of this design in comparative psychotherapy outcome research (see D. A. Shapiro & Shapiro, 1982). More specifically, this section focuses on a randomization (also called random assignment or permutation) version of this design. The next section focuses on a random sampling version of the same design.

Consider that N subjects are available for an experiment in which a treatment is to be contrasted with a control condition. Half of the subjects are randomly selected from the pool of N and are assigned to the treatment condition, whereas the remaining half are assigned to the control condition (the term *control* is a convenient term used, in this note, to refer to any condition other than the treatment condition, including other forms of treatment). Consider that the N subjects differ on K independent dichotomous variables and that the same fraction of the N subjects fall in one category of the dichotomy as in the other. It should be noted that this last characteristic does not exclude studies in which nuisance variables are continuous because continuous nuisance variables can be dichotomized at the median of the combined groups. For example, if a pool of 60 subjects is available for a study, we may think of 30 as scoring above (and 30 as scoring below) the median of the combined groups on a social desirability scale. In this example, we might define the treatment and control groups as nonequivalent in social desirability if the proportion of subjects who exceed the combined groups' median is at least twice as large in one group (say the treatment group) as it is in the other (the control group). More generally, in this section we will define the groups as nonequivalent on any nuisance variable (including pretreatment values of the dependent variable) if the proportion of subjects who fall in one category of the dichotomous nuisance variable in one group is at least twice that of the other group.[1]

The general term of the hypergeometric distribution was used to determine, for the class of experiments described previously, the probability of the nonequivalence of groups on any one nuisance variable for subject pool sizes ranging from 8 to 100 (see Table 1). The general term of the binomial expansion was then used to estimate the probability that the groups would be nonequivalent on at least one of the K nuisance variables (for K = 2 and K = 3) for the same subject pool sizes.

Table 1 shows that the probability the equal-sized treatment and control groups will be nonequivalent (a) increases with an increase in the number of nuisance variables and (b) generally decreases, with one excep-

---

[1]An anonymous reviewer noted that my definition of nonequivalence does not take into account nonequivalence with respect to interactions of nuisance variables. I acknowledge that this is an important limitation of my definition. It should be noted that a definition that takes interactions of nuisance variables into account would generally imply that larger sample sizes would be required for equivalence than the sample sizes implied by my definition. This makes sense, in the context of this article, if we conceive of interactions as additional dichotomous nuisance variables defined in terms of combinations of levels of the original nuisance variables. The same reviewer suggested that nonequivalence for interactions could be defined in terms of imbalance across treatment and control groups, within any combination of levels of the original dichotomous variables. This is a very interesting idea but, in my opinion, it would typically result in a very conservative view of equivalence because it would require labeling entire groups as nonequivalent if imbalance occurred in what would typically be a small fraction (related to the number of combinations of levels of the original dichotomous variables) of these groups.

TABLE 1

Estimated Probabilities That Groups Constructed by Random Assignment Will Be Nonequivalent on at Least One Nuisance Variable as a Function of the Number of Nuisance Variables and the Total Sample Size (N)

N	Number of nuisance variables		
	1	2	3
8	.4857	.7355	.8640
12	.5671	.8126	.9189
18	.3469	.5735	.7214
24	.2203	.3921	.5260
32	.0756	.1455	.2101
40	.0256	.0505	.0749
64	.0055	.0110	.0164
80	.0034	.0068	.0102
100	.0006	.0012	.0018

Note: Nonequivalence was considered to occur for one nuisance variable in the randomization model if the proportion of subjects who belonged to one category of the dichotomous variable was at least twice as large in one group as in the other.

tion, with an increase in the size of the total subject pool. The exception reflects the fact that the minimum imbalance for the presence of nonequivalence, as defined in this article, cannot be obtained for all Ns: Note, more specifically, that when the total pool size is 12, it is possible for the proportion of above-median subjects (on the nuisance variable) in the treatment group (viz., 4/6) to be exactly twice that of the control group (2/4). But if $N = 8$, the smallest imbalance that fits the definition of nonequivalence is 3/4 for one group and 1/4 for the other. In that case, the ratio of the proportions is not 2.0 but rather 3.0.

The following example may be used to illustrate the meaning of the entries in Table 1. Suppose that a pool of 18 subjects is available for a comparative outcome study. Nine subjects randomly drawn from this pool are assigned to the treatment condition, whereas the remaining 9 are assigned to the control condition. Now consider that these 18 subjects are evenly split on two independent dichotomous nuisance variables. Note that it is not necessary to have measurements of these nuisance variables, nor is it necessary even to know what these variables are, in order to use Table 1. The entry of .5735 corresponding to a row entry of 18 (the total pool size) and a column entry of 2 (the number of nuisance variables) indicates a probability of about .57 that the two groups are nonequivalent (as previously defined) on at least one of the two nuisance variables. Thus, in this situation, it is likely that randomization will not result in groups that can be considered equivalent on the nuisance variables.

Random Sampling

The random sampling version of the two independent groups design, considered in this article, differs from the randomization version in the following way. Instead of having a fixed number of subjects available for the study, the researcher has a very large pool of potential subjects. A random sample of $(N/2)$ subjects is drawn from this pool and exposed to the treatment condition; another independent random sample of $(N/2)$ subjects is drawn from the same pool and is exposed to the control condition. Thus, in the random sampling model, the samples used in the study are viewed as independent random samples drawn from a very large pool of subjects. In the randomization model, all available subjects are used, and the two samples are not viewed as random samples from a large population. As in the case of the randomization model, we will assume in the random sampling model that subjects can be dichotomized into two equal-sized categories on each of K independent nuisance variables.[2] These categories may once more be defined in terms of median splits, but these splits are made in the population rather than in the combined samples. Nonequivalence in the random sampling model will be defined in a manner that is comparable to the definition of nonequivalence adopted in the randomization model: The groups will be viewed as nonequivalent on one nuisance variable if the proportion of one group falling in one category of the dichotomized variable differs from the corresponding proportion in the second group by at least 0.33333. For example, if 68% of one group is above the population median and only 33% of the second group is above the population median, then the groups would differ by .68 − .33 = .35 and, therefore, would be viewed as nonequivalent.

The exact probabilities of nonequivalence on at least one nuisance variable were determined for similar combinations of total sample sizes as those considered in the randomization model and for 1–10 nuisance variables. The algorithms used to determine these probabilities were similar to the algorithms that may be used to calculate exact probabilities in ridit analysis (see Fleiss, 1981, 1986). Figure 1 summarizes the findings for total sample sizes ranging from 6 to 84 and for numbers of nuisance variables

---

[2]An anonymous reviewer noted that the possible lack of independence of nuisance variables and the implications of nonindependence of nuisance variables should be mentioned. This reviewer indicated that if nuisance variables are nonindependent, then "the number of nuisance variables one has to worry about may not be as large as one thinks, because control of one variable may indirectly result in control of another." Consistent with this reviewer's comment, it should be noted that certain types of dependence between nuisance variables would imply that, as the number of nuisance variables increases, the probability of nonequivalence on at least one will not be as large as expected if these variables were independent. It should also be noted that other types of dependence imply the opposite: That is, that increasing the number of these nuisance variables would result in a greater increase in the probability of nonequivalence on at least one nuisance variable than would be expected if these variables were independent.

ranging from 1 to 10. It is clear that these results, for the random sampling model, are very similar to the results obtained for the randomization model.

EQUIVALENCE OF GROUPS IN PSYCHOTHERAPY EFFICACY STUDIES

It may be recalled that in D. A. Shapiro and Shapiro's (1982, 1983) meta-analysis, (a) 10% of the treated groups contained 6 or fewer clients, (b) 26% contained 7–9 clients, (c) 36% contained 10–12 clients, and (d) only 28% contained 13 or more clients. An examination of the Table 1 entries relevant to groups with 6 or fewer clients indicates that if two contrasted groups in a design involving randomization each contained 6 clients, the probability would be greater than .5 that the groups would be nonequivalent following random assignment, even if the clients differed on only one nuisance variable. Figure 1 yields comparable findings if the clients differed on two nuisance variables. Similarly, entries relevant to groups with 7–9 clients suggest that groups containing 9 clients would probably be non-equivalent (i.e., the probability of nonequivalence would be greater than

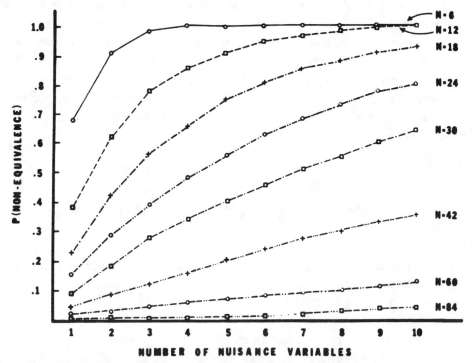

Figure 1: The probability of nonequivalence of randomly selected groups on at least one nuisance variable as a function of number of nuisance variables and total sample size.

.5) if subjects in the pool differed on as few as two independent nuisance variables for the randomization model and on three nuisance variables for the random sampling model. Entries relevant to groups with 10–12 clients indicate a better than even chance of nonequivalence of two randomly assigned groups containing 12 subjects each if subjects in the pool of 24 subjects differed on as few as three independent nuisance variables in the randomization model and on four or more independent nuisance variables in the random sampling model. It should be recalled, in relation to this finding, that the average sizes of client and control groups in D. A. Shapiro and Shapiro's (1982, 1983) meta-analyses were 11.98 and 12.12, respectively, and that only 28% of client groups were larger than 12. (The realism of considering that several important nuisance variables may be present in a variety of research settings has been clearly demonstrated by Boruch, 1976.) Thus, it appears that in more than half of the comparative therapy outcome studies examined by D. A. Shapiro and Shapiro (1983), the samples were of small enough size to suggest (assuming that the models used in this article are realistic) a better than even chance of nonequivalence of the contrasted groups constructed by random assignment or random sampling.

It must be emphasized that the object of this article is not to argue against the use of simple randomization or random sampling in psychotherapy efficacy studies. Nor is the object to argue against the use of these methods for the purpose of creating equivalent contrasted groups (for that argument, see Luborsky, Singer, & Luborsky, 1975). Instead, the object is to draw attention to specific conditions under which it may be unrealistic (and to other conditions under which it may be realistic) to expect that these methods will result in the equivalence of contrasted groups and to point out some possible harmful consequences of nonequivalence on the estimation of the relative efficacy of different psychotherapeutic treatments.

CONSEQUENCES OF NONEQUIVALENCE: SIMPSON'S PARADOX

The major consequence of any specific degree of nonequivalence between contrasted groups is bias in the estimates of relative efficacy of treatment effects: That is, the difference in the effects of the treatments (or of the treatment versus the control condition) on the therapy outcome measure may be either overestimated or underestimated because of the nonequivalence of the contrasted groups on the nuisance variables (see Pocock & Simon, 1975, for a more detailed discussion of this topic).

Only the most serious type of bias will be described in this section: In the presence of nonequivalence on a dichotomous nuisance variable, it is possible that the control condition will result in a greater mean on the outcome measure than will the treatment condition, even though the treatment mean is greater than the control mean within each level of the nuisance variable. That is, the efficacy of the treatment is underestimated to the point that it is wrongly estimated to be less effective than the control condition. It is, of course, also possible for the opposite to happen—that the treatment mean will be greater than the control mean even though the control mean is greater than the treatment mean within each of the two levels of the nuisance variable. Occurrences of this type may be viewed as manifestations of what has been described, in somewhat different contexts, as the reversal paradox (e.g., Messick & van de Geer, 1981) or as Simpson's paradox (e.g., S. H. Shapiro, 1982; Simpson, 1951; Wagner, 1982). (See Messick and van de Geer, 1981, for an excellent discussion of the potential universality of the reversal paradox.)

Graphic methods proposed by Paik (1985) may be used to illustrate how the reversal paradox can be caused by the nonequivalence of the psychotherapy treatment and control groups on a dichotomous nuisance variable (see Figure 2). Figure 2 is divided into three parts (2a, 2b, and 2c). Each part represents a different degree of nonequivalence.

Each ellipse in each part corresponds to a subgroup of patients defined by a level of the dichotomous nuisance variable (e.g., say, the presence or absence of some condition) and a level of the independent variable (i.e., treatment or control). The sizes of the ellipses are proportional to subgroup sizes. The six ellipses in the upper portion of Figure 2 correspond to the presence of the nuisance variable, and the six ellipses in the lower portion correspond to the absence of the nuisance variable. Let us view the outcome measure as dichotomous for each patient: The patient manifests or does not manifest improvement. Each circle at the center of an ellipse represents the proportion of patients in the subgroup who show improvement.

It should be noted that this descriptive statistic (the proportion of members of a group who manifest improvement) appears to be consistent with several measures of clinical significance of the results of psychotherapy outcome studies (see Jacobson, Follette, & Revenstorf, 1984). This proportion may be viewed as a mean outcome measure for that subgroup if we assign a dummy variable value of 1 for improvement and of 0 for no improvement. We choose to do this in order to emphasize the generality of the reversal paradox with respect to psychotherapy response measures: That is, the reversal paradox is not limited to dichotomous response measures but is also observable with continuous response measures. Group (i.e.,

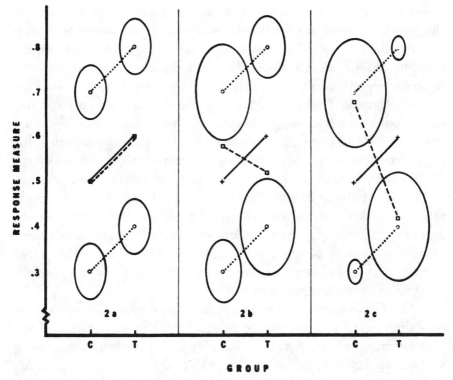

Figure 2: The biasing effects of three degrees of nonequivalence of groups (Figures 2a, 2b, 2c) on the estimate of differences between group means.

treatment and control) means are represented by the two small squares connected by the broken line in each part of Figure 2. It is clear that the slope of each broken line carries information about the relative efficacy of the treatment and control conditions. The solid straight lines are used to represent the relation of treatment and control means in a balanced design (i.e., the same fraction of control subjects show the presence of the nuisance variable as of the treatment subjects). Similarly, the slope of each dotted line carries information about the relative efficacy of the treatment and control conditions within a level of the nuisance variable.

It is apparent that only when the slope of the broken line is identical to the slope of both dotted lines in a part of Figure 2 is the estimate of the relative efficacy of the treatment and control conditions the same within levels of the nuisance variable as it is when we ignore the nuisance variable. Note that this happens only in Figure 2a, where the proportion of the control group that manifests the presence of the nuisance variable is equal to that of the treatment group (as reflected in the sizes of the ellipses). Figure 2b shows the effect of the minimum degree of imbalance that was considered to yield nonequivalence in both the randomization and the random sampling models discussed previously: The proportion of control

100   LOUIS M. HSU

subjects who show the presence of the nuisance variables (.67) is more than twice that of treatment subjects, or the difference between these proportions is at least .33. Note the influence of relative sizes of subgroups (reflected in the relative sizes of corresponding ellipses) within each group on the position of the group mean: In Figure 2a, the group mean is halfway between the subgroup means, reflecting the fact that these subgroups are of equal size. In Figure 2c, the group mean is 95% of the distance between the two subgroup means, reflecting the fact that one subgroup is 95% of the size of the group. In Figure 2b, the group mean is two thirds of the distance between subgroup means, reflecting the fact that one subgroup is twice as large as the other within that group.

An examination of Figure 2b indicates that, even when this minimum degree of imbalance is present, estimates of the relative efficacy of treatment and control not only will be different from the estimates obtained within levels of the nuisance variable but also will be reversed. That is, the mean outcome score (viz., 0 = *no improvement*, 1 = *improvement*) of all control subjects is greater than that of all treatment subjects even though the treatment mean is greater than the control mean within each level of the nuisance variable.

Figure 2c shows the effect of increasing the degree of imbalance: Now we consider that 95% of the control subjects and only 5% of the treatment subjects show the presence of the nuisance variable. The difference in the slopes of the dotted and broken lines illustrate a very large reversal: The means of outcome measures of treatment subjects are greater than those of control subjects within each level of the nuisance variable, whereas the mean of all control subjects is much larger than that of all treatment subjects. Note more specifically that 68% of control patients show improvement, whereas only 42% of treatment patients show improvement but that, within each level of the nuisance variable, a greater proportion of treatment patients show improvement than of control patients (80% vs. 70% for the presence of the nuisance variable and 40% vs. 30% for absence of that variable). There are two principal reasons for the large reversal in Figure 2c: First, the nuisance variable has a strong effect on the response measure, and, second, the degree of imbalance (or nonequivalence) is large. Researchers typically have little control over the first reason but can control the second reason by using sufficiently large samples.

NONEQUIVALENCE AND NONSIGNIFICANCE

Tversky and Kahneman (1971) found that both naive subjects and trained scientists tend to "view a sample randomly drawn from a population as highly representative, that is, similar to the population in all essential characteristics. Consequently, they expect any two samples drawn from a particular population to be more similar to one another . . . than sampling theory would predict, at least for small samples" (p. 105). Tversky and Kahneman (1971) described this expectation as a belief in the law of small numbers.

This belief, which is an unrealistic expectation of the equivalence of small groups constructed by random sampling, can result in misinterpretations of estimates of treatment efficacy obtained in individual studies. As was observed in Figure 2a, the equivalence of groups implies a lack of bias of the estimate of the relative efficacy of treatments. Consequently, one who believes in the law of small numbers is likely to consider the observed difference between group means a valid index of the relative efficacy of the treatments. As noted by Tversky and Kahneman (1971), "if {a scientist} believes in the law of small numbers, {she or he} will have exaggerated confidence in the validity of conclusions based on small samples" (p. 106).

Those who believe in the law of small numbers tend to ignore or downplay the influence of sampling error on estimates of treatment effects and, therefore, tend to downplay the importance of statistical significance tests, which evaluate estimates of treatment effects in relation to estimates of sampling error (see Tversky & Kahneman, 1971). However, these tests yield valid significance levels when groups have been constructed by randomization (see Efron, 1971, p. 404) or random sampling (Winer, 1971). The failure to obtain a statistically significant difference should be interpreted to mean that the difference can be conservatively explained in terms of sampling error rather than in terms of the effects of treatments.[3] As noted by Tversky and Kahneman (1971), "the computation of significance levels . . . forces the scientist to evaluate the obtained effect in terms of a valid estimate of sampling variance rather than in terms of his subjective biased estimate" (p. 106).

Tversky and Kahneman's (1971) points appear worth repeating because of the numerous criticisms of significance tests that have recently appeared in psychological journals (see Kupfersmid, 1988, for a summary). Cohen and Hyman (1979), for example, stated that "even if . . . results are not statistically significant, the magnitude or direction of the effect is often (more than just occasionally) most significant" (p. 14). Cohen and Hyman

---

[3]An anonymous reviewer noted that randomization and random sampling are sufficient to ensure the validity of statistical significance tests and that failure to use these methods raises questions about the validity of these tests. This reviewer also noted that "the probability of a significant result includes the probability of a false positive result arising from random variation (nonequivalence) between the two groups." An important implication of this statement is that the nonsignificance of a statistical test should be interpreted to mean that the observed difference between group means can reasonably be attributed to sampling error (which includes nonequivalence of groups).

(1979) illustrated their point by noting that a statistically nonsignificant sample effect size of 1 (in a situation in which the predicted effect size was .5) obtained from small samples is a "dramatically significant difference" (p. 14). They also noted that "a researcher can not find that difference and then not accept it because of high alpha" (p. 14). Similarly, Carver (1978) argued that estimates of treatment effects "should be interpreted with respect to the research hypothesis regardless of its statistical significance" (p. 394). It is clear that following Cohen and Hyman's (1979) and Carver's (1978) advice, in the area of psychotherapy efficacy studies in which samples are small and nonequivalence is therefore highly probable (see Table 1 and Figure 1), could easily result in the misinterpretation of biased andand misleading estimates of treatment efficacy. Clearly, the worst situations of this type occur with the reversal paradox in which the wrong treatment could be estimated to yield the better outcome.

MINIMUM SAMPLE SIZES: AGREEMENT OF DIFFERENT CRITERIA

That there are certain combinations of total subject pool sizes and numbers of nuisance variables for which random sampling and randomization should not be expected to result in the equivalence of treatment and control groups is clearly demonstrated in Table 1 (for the randomization model) and in Figure 1 (for the random sampling model). Also demonstrated in Table 1 and Figure 1 is the fact that, when samples are large (40 per group), randomization and random sampling appear to be effective methods of creating groups that are equivalent on the maximum number of nuisance variables examined in this article. Even when samples are of moderate size (20–40 per group), randomization and random sampling appear to work well provided the number of nuisance variables is small.

Kraemer (1981) noted that "a sample size of 20 [per group] which seems acceptable and feasible and which yields reasonable power in well-designed research (based on our own experience as well as evidence in published research ...) ... seems a reasonable base level for sample size" (p. 312). She also argued against using sample sizes less than 10 (p. 311). Her recommendations are based on criteria of "acceptability, feasibility, [statistical] power, and cost" (p. 311). The information in Table 1 and Figure 1 clearly supports her argument against using samples smaller than 10 and conditionally supports her recommendation of sample sizes of 20. The condition for recommendation of samples as small as 20, based on Table 1 and Figure 1 information, is that the number of important nuisance variables be small. Recommendations that sample size equal 20 or more, based on Kraemer's criteria and on the criterion of equivalence of this note, appear to be relevant to research in the area of comparative psychotherapy outcome studies because sample sizes of past studies in this area have generally been below 20 (Kazdin, 1986; D. A. Shapiro & Shapiro, 1982, 1983). It is an interesting coincidence that sample sizes that appear to be consistent with the criteria of acceptability, feasibility, statistical power, and cost (Kraemer's criteria) are about the same as the minimum sample sizes that appear to be consistent with the criteria of the equivalence (as defined in this article) of contrasted groups on nuisance variables and on pre-existing values of the psychotherapy response variable.

REFERENCES

Boruch, R. F. (1976). On common contentions about randomized field experiments. In G. Glass (Ed.), *Evaluation studies: Review annual* (Vol. 1, pp. 158-194). Beverly Hills, CA: Sage.

Carver, R. P. (1978). The case against statistical significance testing. *Harvard Educational Review, 48,* 378-399.

Cohen, S. A., & Hyman, J. S. (1979). How come so many hypotheses in educational research are supported? *Educational Researcher, 8,* 12-16.

Cook, T. D., & Campbell, D. T. (1979). *Quasi-experimentation: Design and analysis issues for field settings.* Chicago: Rand McNally.

Efron, B. (1971). Forcing a sequential experiment to be balanced. *Biometrics, 58,* 403-417.

Fleiss, J. L. (1981). *Statistical analysis for rates and proportions.* New York: Wiley.

Fleiss, J. L. (1986). *The design and analysis of clinical experiments.* New York: Wiley.

Huesmann, L. R. (1982). Experimental methods in research in psychopathology. In P. C. Kendall & J. N. Butcher (Eds.), *Handbook of research methods in clinical psychology* (pp. 223-248). New York: Wiley.

Jacobson, N. S., Follette, W. C., & Revenstorf, D. (1984). Psychotherapy outcome research: Methods for reporting variability and evaluating clinical significance. *Behavior Therapy, 15,* 336-352.

Kazdin, A. E. (1986). Comparative outcome studies in psychotherapy: Methodological issues and strategies. *Journal of Consulting and Clinical Psychology, 54,* 95-105.

Kendall, P. C., & Norton-Ford, J. D. (1982). Therapy outcome research methods. In P. C. Kendall & J. N. Butcher (Eds.), *Handbook of research methods in clinical psychology* (pp. 429-460). New York: Wiley.

Kenny, D. A. (1975). A quasi-experimental approach to assessing treatment effects in the nonequivalent control group design. *Psychological Bulletin, 82,* 887-903.

Kenny, D. A. (1979). *Correlation and causality.* New York: Wiley.

Keppel, G. (1973). *Design and analysis: A researcher's handbook*. Englewood Cliffs, NJ: Prentice-Hall.

Kirk, R. (1982). *Experimental design* (2nd ed.). Belmont, CA: Brooks/Cole.

Kraemer, H. C. (1981). Coping strategies in psychiatric clinical research. *Journal of Consulting and Clinical Psychology, 49*, 309–319.

Kupfersmid, J. (1988). Improving what is published. *American Psychologist, 43*, 635–642.

Lord, F. M. (1967). A paradox in the interpretation of group comparisons. *Psychological Bulletin, 68*, 304–305.

Lord, F. M. (1969). Statistical adjustments when comparing pre-existing groups. *Psychological Bulletin, 72*, 336–337.

Luborsky, L., Singer, B., & Luborsky, L. (1975). Comparative studies of psychotherapies. *Archives of General Psychiatry, 32*, 995–1008.

McKinlay, S. (1977). Pair-matching—A reappraisal of a popular technique. *Biometrics, 33*, 725–735.

Messick, D. A., & van de Geer, J. P. (1981). A reversal paradox. *Psychological Bulletin, 90*, 582–593.

O'Fallon, J. R., Dubey, S. D., Salsburg, D. S., Edmonson, J. H., Soffer, A., & Colton, T. (1978). Should there be statistical guidelines for medical research papers? *Biometrics, 34*, 687–695.

Paik, M. (1985). A graphic representation of a three-way contingency table: Simpson's paradox and correlation. *American Statistician, 39*, 53–54.

Pocock, S. J., & Simon, R. (1975). Sequential treatment assignment with balancing for prognostic vactors in the controlled clinical trial. *Biometrics, 31*, 103–115.

Shapiro, D. A., & Shapiro, D. (1982). Meta-analysis of comparative therapy outcome studies: A replication and refinement. *Psychological Bulletin, 92*, 581–604.

Shapiro, D. A., & Shapiro, D. (1983). Comparative therapy outcome research: Methodological implications of meta-analysis. *Journal of Consulting and Clinical Psychology, 51*, 42–53.

Shapiro, S. H. (1982). Collapsing contingency tables—A geometric approach. *The American Statistician, 36*, 43–46.

Simon, R. (1979). Restricted randomization designs in clinical trials. *Biometrics, 35*, 503–512.

Simpson, E. H. (1951). The interpretation of interaction in contingency tables. *Journal of the Royal Statistical Society, 13*, 238–241.

Strube, M. J., & Hartmann, D. P. (1982). A critical appraisal of meta-analysis. *British Journal of Psychology, 21*, 129–139.

Tversky, A., & Kahneman, D. (1971). Belief in the law of small numbers. *Psychological Bulletin, 76*, 105–110.

Wagner, C. H. (1982). Simpson's paradox in real life. *The American Statistician, 36*, 46–48.

Winer, B. J. (1971). *Statistical principles in experimental design*. New York: McGraw-Hill.

6

STIMULUS SAMPLING IN CLINICAL RESEARCH: REPRESENTATIVE DESIGN REVIEWED

BRENDAN A. MAHER

More than 30 years ago, Egon Brunswik (1947) pointed out that if we wish to generalize the results of a psychological experiment to populations of subjects and to populations of stimuli, we must sample from both populations. This argument was elaborated by him in other articles and was summarized cogently in a short article by Hammond (1948). The purpose of this article is to review the issues that Brunswik raised and to examine some of their implications for contemporary research in clinical psychology.

Brunswik's thesis is very simple. When we conduct an experiment intended to investigate the effect of different values of an independent variable on a population, we always take care to draw a sample of subjects that is representative of the population in question. We do so, naturally, because we recognize the range of variation that exists in populations of individuals. We wish to make sure that deviant individual values do not

Reprinted from the *Journal of Consulting and Clinical Psychology, 46*, 643–647. Copyright 1978 by the American Psychological Association.

distort our estimate of the parameters of the population. If the stimuli that we use are defined in physical units, we are (or should be) careful to confine our generalizations to the range of values actually included in the study. When physical units are involved, we have relative confidence that the stimulus can be replicated by another investigator, provided that the detailed description of the stimulus is followed carefully. Should a subsequent investigator change one or more of these attributes, we are not surprised if there is a concomitant change in the responses that are made to the stimulus.

When the stimuli to which the subjects respond cannot be defined in physical units and are likely to vary within a population, a different situation arises. Outstanding examples are to be seen in research directed to the investigation of the effects of human beings as stimuli that elicit behavior from other human beings. Consider some instances drawn from recent volumes of this journal. Acosta and Sheehan (1976) reported that Mexican American subjects viewed an Anglo American professional therapist as more competent than a Mexican American professional when all other variables were matched. Babad, Mann, and Mar-Hayim (1975) reported that trainee clinicians who were told that a testee was a high-achieving upper-middle class child assigned higher scores to Wechsler Intelligence Scale for Children (WISC) responses than did another sample of clinicians who were led to believe that the same responses had been made by an underachieving deprived child. Research of this kind is generally cast in terms of a hypothesis that members of a specified population respond in discriminatory fashion to members of certain other populations. Thus, for example, we encounter such questions as, Do physicians give less adequate medical care to ex-mental patients than they do to normal medical patients? (Farina, Hagelauer, & Holzberg, 1976) and Are therapists with a behavioral orientation less affected by the label *patient* when evaluating observed behavior than are therapists of psychodynamic persuasion? (Langer & Abelson, 1974).

SINGLE-STIMULUS DESIGN

Human attributes are generally distributed in such a fashion that any one of them is likely to be found in conjunction with a wide variety of others. Let us consider an investigation of bias toward ex-mental patients. To belabor the obvious a little, we can note that the attribute *ex-mental patient* can be associated with any measure of intelligence, age, sex, education, socioeconomic status, physical attractiveness, and so forth. It is true that some of these attributes may have significant correlations with each other; a patient of upper socioeconomic status is quite likely to have had substantial education, for example. Nonetheless, even the largest of these correlations is quite modest, and the population of ex-mental patients to which we wish to generalize will have a wide range of values on these attributes.

When we employ only one person as a stimulus, we are faced with the fact that the specific values of some of the other attributes possessed by this person will also have stimulus value that will be unknown and uncontrolled. Responses made by a sample of the normal population to an ex-mental patient who is female, young, attractive, articulate, and intelligent may well be different from those made to a normal control who is male, old, ugly, incoherent, and dull. These differences cannot be assigned to the patient/nonpatient status of the two stimulus persons, as many other unidentified differences were uncontrolled. At first sight it may appear that this problem is solved by the simple expedient of matching the patient and the control on all variables other than that of patient status. Unfortunately, this can only be achieved at the cost of further difficulties. We do not know the full range of variables that should be matched, and hence this solution necessarily involves resort to an actor and a script, barring the unlikely availability of discordant monozygotic twins for research purposes! Scripts bring with them some special problems, of which more will be said later. The main point to note here is that the use of a *single* human stimulus acting as his or her own control fails to deal with the problem of the *interaction* of the attribute under investigation with those that have been controlled by matching. Pursuing for a moment the example of responses to the label *ex-mental patient*, let us consider a hypothetical study using a male actor with athletic physique and vigorous movements. The willingness of a normal subject to accept this individual as a fellow worker, neighbor, or friend may well be influenced by the perception that the ex-patient, if violent, could be dangerous. Had the actor been older and visibly frail, the reaction might well be different. Under the first set of circumstances, the bias hypothesis would probably be confirmed, and under the second set, the null hypothesis might fail to be rejected.

An additional difficulty is incurred by the single-stimulus own-control strategy. We cannot determine whether a finding of no difference between group means is due to the weakness of the hypothesis, errors of method, or the inadvertent selection of an atypical stimulus person to represent one or both conditions. An example of the complexities of interpretation with this design can be found in Farina et al. (1976). These investigators hypothesized that physicians would provide less adequate medical care to former mental patients than to normal medical students. To test this hypothesis one stimulus person, a 23-year-old male graduate student, approached 32 medical practitioners. In each case he entered the doctor's office

> carrying a motorcycle helmet and a small knapsack. . . . The same symptoms were reported to all doctors. Stomach pains suggestive of ulcers were selected to be neither clearly psychiatric nor unrelated to the mind. . . . Every other practitioner was told the pains had first occurred 9 months earlier while the patient was traveling around the country. The remaining 16 doctors were also informed that the pain had appeared 9 months earlier, but at that time the patient reported being in a mental hospital. (Farina et al., 1976, p. 499)

No significant difference of any relevance was found in the kind of medical care given by the practitioners under either condition. In conclusion, the authors stated that "a former mental patient seems to receive the same medical treatment as anyone else" (p. 499).

Logically, several conclusions are compatible with this finding. One obviously valid conclusion is that a young male motorcyclist with the symptoms of ulcers receives a certain class of treatment whether or not he describes himself as a former mental patient. We cannot tell whether this treatment is the same, better, or worse than that typically given to a random sample of the normal population of patients who seek treatment for stomach pains, as no such sample was obtained. A substantial number of physicians may have had opinions about motorcyclists as unfavorable as those that they were hypothesized to have about former mental patients, and hence both conditions produced equally inadequate medical care. Alternatively, the physicians may have felt the necessity to be unusually careful in providing care to individuals who might be assumed to be irresponsible (such as motorcyclists and mental patients), and hence they provided better than average care. Finally, medical practice may be sufficiently precise about the adequate procedures to follow with patients who complain of stomach pains that no real room for bias exists, the treatment provided being the same as would be given to any sample of patients.

We can summarize the limitations of the single-stimulus design as follows:

1. Obtained differences may be due to the validity of the tested hypothesis or to the effect of uncontrolled stimulus variables in critical interaction with the intended independent variable. No method of distinguishing between these two explanations is possible.

2. Lack of difference may be due to the invalidity of the hypothesis, undiscovered methodological factors such as subject sampling error, or the presence of an uncontrolled stimulus variable operating to either counteract the effect of the intended independent variable or to raise this effect to a ceiling value in both experimental and control situations.

It is readily apparent that the problem of uncontrolled attributes occurring in a single stimulus person can only be solved by the provision of an adequate sample of stimulus persons, since they will tend to cancel each other out. No satisfactory solution is possible within the single-stimulus design.

SCRIPTS AND MANTICORES

Some investigators have attempted to solve the problems of the single-subject stimulus by fabricating scripts without the use of a human actor to present them. Case histories, dossiers, vignettes, audiotapes, or other devices have been used to reduce the effects of the uncontrolled aspects of a human stimulus. Thus, in a study by Babad et al. (1975), the trainee clinicians were given only the WISC protocol and did not see the child who was alleged to have been tested. These manufactured materials may be termed *scripts*. Scripts may be taken from existing sources of genuine material, such as clinical files; they may be created de novo in accordance with prior theoretical guidelines or in an attempt to present an ideal "typical" case.

When the script is drawn from original clinical files, the investigator is assured that at least one such case exists in nature. The limitations on the results obtained from such scripts are, in principle, the same as those that plague any single-stimulus design. Some minor advantage accrues to the method, however, in that the number of uncontrolled accidental attributes has been reduced by the elimination of those attributes associated with physical appearance, dress, and so forth. When the script is fabricated for research purposes, a new problem develops—namely that in devising material according to theoretical guidelines, a case is created that like the manticore, may never have existed in nature. We can imagine a hypothetical investigation of the attitudes of males toward females of varying degrees of power. Varying naval ranks with male and female gender of the occupant of each rank, we create the dossier of an imaginary female Fleet Admiral. Whatever our male subject's response to this dossier may be, we have no way of knowing whether it is due to the theoretically important combination of high rank with female gender or to the singularity of a combination that is, as yet, unknown to human experience.

For a recent illustration of this problem, we can turn to Acosta and Sheehan (1976). They presented groups of Mexican American and Anglo American undergraduates with a videotaped excerpt of enacted psychotherapy. Each group saw an identical tape, except that in one version the therapist spoke English with a slight Spanish accent and in the other version the accent was standard American English. Some subjects were told that the therapist was a highly trained professional; the others were told that the therapist was a para-professional of limited experience. There were thus four experimental conditions and two kinds of subjects. The Spanish-accent tape of a trained professional was introduced with a background vignette describing the therapist as American born of Mexican parentage and as having a Harvard doctorate in his field and a distinguished professional record. For the American-English-accent tape, the therapist was introduced with the same vignette but with an Anglo-Saxon name and parentage identified as Northern European. Anglo American ratings of the therapist's competence were uninfluenced by the ethnic identification, whereas Mexican Americans rated the Mexican American therapist less favorably than the Anglo American therapist.

In their discussion of this somewhat surprising result, the authors noted that the number of Mexican American therapists actually in practice in the United States shortly before the study was done was 48 (28 psychologists and 20 psychiatrists). We do not know what characteristics would be typical of this population, and no attempt seems to have been made to ascertain them before preparing the script. There is, therefore, no way to be sure that the therapeutic style, choice of words, gesture, and so forth, were authentically typical of actual Mexican American therapists. Given that essentially the same script was used for both ethnic conditions, we must conclude that either one or the other version of the script was ethnically inaccurate or, less likely, that the only actual difference that would be seen in the comparative behaviors of Mexican American and Anglo American therapists would be their accent. In brief, we cannot ignore the possibility that the Mexican American subjects disapproved of the Mexican American therapist not because he was Mexican American but because his behavior was not representative of that of actual Mexican Americans. Like the woman admiral, he may have presented a combination of characteristics that is theoretically possible but unknown in the experience of the subjects responding to it. The only guarantee that a script is free from impossible or improbable combinations of variables is when it is directly drawn from an actual clinical case or other human transaction. We cannot produce a fictional script of a psychotherapeutic session with any confidence that it is as representative as a transcript of an actual session. The ideal or typical therapeutic interview may be as rare as the perfect textbook case of conversion hysteria or as a stereotypical Mexican American. This rarity or implausibility may well determine a subject's response far more than the attributes that were planned to make it appear typical. Our hesitation in generalizing from a single stimulus case to a population of cases is increased substantially by the prospect of generalizing from a case that is not known to have existed at all.

REPRESENTATIVE DESIGN

The moral to the foregoing review is simple. If we wish to generalize to populations of stimuli, we must sample from them. Only in this way can we be confident that the various attributes that are found in the population will be properly represented in the sample. Those attributes that are significantly correlated with membership in the population will appear in appropriate and better-than-chance proportions; those attributes that are uncorrelated with population membership will appear in chance proportions but will not affect the outcomes. If we intend to draw conclusions about the way in which physicians treat former mental patients, we must sample physicians and former mental patients. If we wish to know what Mexican American students think of Mexican American therapists, we must sample students and therapists. This is the essence of Brunswik's (1947) concept of representative design. There is no satisfactory alternative to it. Nonetheless, the use of representative design is rarely, if ever, seen in reported research. There are, in my opinion, three reasons for this. First, many clinical psychologists are unaware of Brunswik's work. The remedy for this is obvious and easy to apply. Second, there is a common failure to understand that the replication of single-stimulus studies with additional single-stimulus studies cannot create accumulated representative design unless the selection of single-stimulus persons was achieved by sampling.

Let us consider a hypothetical series of studies of the effect of examiner gender on children's test responses. In the population of examiners, there are likely to be attributes that distinguish males from females in addition to those that are inseparable from gender. Thus the proportions of married and single persons, prior experience with children, knowledge of various hobbies, mean age, prior locale of undergraduate education, and so forth, may differ between the two groups. In the first study we use one male examiner and one female examiner, each with 1 year of experience. Using samples of male and female children, we find differences in test responses attributable to examiner gender. Conscious of the fact that we included inexperienced examines, we replicate the study with one male examiner and one female examiner each with 3 years of experience. Now we find no difference. Our series ends when we have made gender comparisons for examiners with 1, 3, 5, 7, 9, 11, 13, 15, 17, and 19 years of experience. We found significant examiner effects at every level of experience except 3 and 5 years. As 8 of our 10 students have found significant differences due to gender, we conclude that there is a generalizable finding. We might even treat the entire series as a single experiment comparing the group of 10 male examiners with the group of 10 female examiners and find a statistically significant difference between the mean test responses elicited by one group versus the other.

To accept this conclusion it is first necessary to know what the true proportion of the total population of examiners at each level of experience is. If the experience range of 3–5 years includes 65% of all examiners, our best conclusion is that gender differences have not been established. The reason is, of course, that the "sample" of examiners was not representative of the population to which it is intended to generalize, being underrepresented in the 3- to 5-year experience range. Note that we cannot handle this by some proportional weighing of the data obtained from the examiners with 3–5 years of experience, as the results obtained from those comparisons suffer from the limitations of single-stimulus design and might well be due to the effects of uncontrolled differences between examiners other than gender.

A third reason for the failure to use representative design is that it is laborious and expensive. Providing an adequate sample of stimulus persons, each of whom is to be observed by an adequate sample of subjects, necessarily involves large numbers and long hours. For some investigators it is, as one of my correspondents put it, "too hard to do it right."

There is however, no satisfactory alternative to doing it right. Clinical psychology is concerned with real people and not with hypothetical collections of attributes. Our research into the behavior of patients, therapists, diagnosticians, normal persons, and the like, must produce generalizations that are valid for actual populations of these people. Conclusions based on inadequate sampling may be worse than no conclusions at all if we decide to base our clinical decisions on them. If the patience and time that it takes to do it right create better science, our gratitude should not be diminished by the probability that fewer publications will be produced.

REFERENCES

Acosta, F. X., & Sheehan, J. G. (1976). Preferences toward Mexican American and Anglo American psychotherapists. *Journal of Consulting and Clinical Psychology, 44,* 272–279.

Babad, E. Y., Mann, M., & Mar-Hayim, M. (1975). Bias in scoring WISC subtests. *Journal of Consulting and Clinical Psychology, 43,* 268.

Brunswik, E. (1947). *Systematic and representative design of psychological experiments.* Berkeley: University of California Press.

Farina, A., Hagelauer, H. D., & Holzberg, J. D. (1976). Influence of psychiatric history on physician's response to a new patient. *Journal of Consulting and Clinical Psychology, 44,* 499.

Hammond, K. (1948). Subject and object sampling—A note. *Psychological Bulletin,* *45,* 530–533.

Langer, E. J., & Abelson, R. P. (1974). A patient by an other name . . . : Clinician group differences in labeling bias. *Journal of Consulting and Clinical Psychology,* *42,* 4–9.

DESIGN OPTIONS AND PROCEDURES

7

IN DEFENSE OF EXTERNAL
INVALIDITY

DOUGLAS G. MOOK

The greatest weakness of laboratory experiments lies in their artificiality. Social processes observed to occur within a laboratory setting
might not necessarily occur within more natural social settings.
—Babbie, 1975, p. 254

In order to behave like scientists we must construct situations in
which our subjects . . . can behave as little like human beings as possible and we do this in order to allow ourselves to make statements about
the nature of their humanity.
—Bannister, 1966, p. 24

Experimental psychologists frequently have to listen to remarks like
these. And one who has taught courses in research methods and experimental psychology, as I have for the past several years, has probably had no
problem in alerting students to the "artificiality" of research settings. Students, like laypersons (and not a few social scientists for that matter), come

Reprinted from the American Psychologist, 38, 379–387. Copyright 1983 by the American Psychological Association.

to us quite prepared to point out the remoteness of our experimental chambers, our preoccupation with rats and college sophomores, and the comic-opera "reactivity" of our shock generators, electrode paste, and judgments of lengths of line segments on white paper.

They see all this. My problem has been not to alert them to these considerations, but to break their habit of dismissing well-done, meaningful, informative research on grounds of "artificiality."

The task has become a bit harder over the last few years because a full-fledged "purr" word has gained currency: *external validity*. Articles and monographs have been written about its proper nurture, and checklists of specific threats to its well-being are now appearing in textbooks. Studies unescorted by it are afflicted by—what else?—*external invalidity*. That phrase has a lovely mouth-filling resonance to it, and there is, to be sure, a certain poetic justice in our being attacked with our own jargon.

WARM FUZZIES AND COLD CREEPIES

The trouble is that, like most "purr" and "snarl" words, the phrases *external validity* and *external invalidity* can serve as serious barriers to thought. Obviously, any kind of validity is a warm, fuzzy Good Thing; and just as obviously, any kind of invalidity must be a cold, creepy Bad Thing. Who could doubt it?

It seems to me that these phrases trapped even their originators, in just that way. Campbell and Stanley (1967) introduce the concept thus: "*External validity* asks the question of *generalizability*: To what populations, settings, treatment variables, and measurement variables can this effect be generalized?" (p. 5). Fair enough. External validity is not an automatic desideratum; it *asks a question*. It invites us to think about the prior questions: To what populations, settings, and so on, do we *want* the effect to be generalized? Do we want to generalize it at all?

But their next sentence is: "Both types of criteria are obviously important . . ." And ". . . the selection of designs strong in both types of validity is obviously our ideal" (Campbell & Stanley, 1967, p. 5).

I intend to argue that this is simply wrong. If it sounds plausible, it is because the word *validity* has given it a warm coat of downy fuzz. Who wants to be invalid—internally, externally, or in any other way? One might as well ask for acne. In a way, I wish the authors had stayed with the term *generalizability*, precisely because it does not sound nearly so good. It would then be easier to remember that we are not dealing with a criterion, like clear skin, but with a question, like "How can we get this sofa down the stairs?" One asks that question if, and only if, moving the sofa is what one wants to do.

But *generalizability* is not quite right either. The question of external validity is not the same as the question of generalizability. Even an experiment that is clearly "applicable to the real world," perhaps because it was conducted there (e.g., Bickman's, 1974, studies of obedience on the street corner), will have *some* limits to its generalizability. Cultural, historical, and age-group limits will surely be present; but these are unknown and no single study can discover them all. Their determination is empirical.

The external-validity question is a special case. It comes to this: Are the sample, the setting, and the manipulation so artificial that the class of "target" real-life situations to which the results can be generalized is likely to be trivially small? If so, the experiment lacks external validity. But that argument still begs the question I wish to raise here: Is such generalization our intent? Is it what we want to do? Not always.

THE AGRICULTURAL MODEL

These baleful remarks about external validity (EV) are not quite fair to its originators. In defining the concept, they had a particular kind of research in mind, and it was the kind in which the problem of EV is meaningful and important.

These are the applied experiments. Campbell and Stanley (1967) had in mind the kind of investigation that is designed to evaluate a new teaching procedure or the effects of an "enrichment" program on the culturally deprived. For that matter, the research context in which sampling theory was developed in its modern form—agricultural research—has a similar purpose. The experimental setting resembles, or is a special case of, a real-life setting in which one wants to know what to do. Does this fertilizer (or this pedagogical device) promote growth in this kind of crop (or this kind of child)? If one finds a significant improvement in the experimental subjects as compared with the controls, one predicts that implementation of a similar manipulation, in a similar setting with similar subjects, will be of benefit on a larger scale.

That kind of argument does assume that one's experimental manipulation represents the broader-scale implementation and that one's subjects and settings represent their target populations. Indeed, part of the thrust of the EV concept is that we have been concerned only with subject representativeness and not enough with representativeness of the settings and manipulations we have sampled in doing experiments.

Deese (1972), for example, has taken us to task for this neglect:

Some particular set of conditions in an experiment is generally taken to be representative of all possible conditions of a similar type. . . . In the investigation of altruism, situations are devised to permit people to make altruistic choices. Usually a single situation provides the setting for the experimental testing. . . . {the experimenter} will allow that one particular situation to stand for the unspecified circumstances in which an individual could be altruistic. . . . the social psychologist as experimenter is content to let a particular situation stand for an indefinite range of possible testing situations in a vague and unspecified way. (pp. 59–60)

It comes down to this: The experimenter is generalizing on the basis of a small and biased sample, not of subjects (though probably those too), but of settings and manipulations.[1]

The entire argument rests, however, on an applied, or what I call an "agricultural," conception of the aims of research. The assumption is that the experiment is *intended* to be generalized to similar subjects, manipulations, and settings. If this is so, then the broader the generalizations one can make, the more real-world occurrences one can predict from one's findings and the more one has learned about the real world from them. However, it may not be so. There are experiments—very many of them—that do not have such generalization as their aim.

This is not to deny that we have talked nonsense on occasion. We have. Sweeping generalizations about "altruism," or "anxiety," or "honesty" have been made on evidence that does not begin to support them, and for the reasons Deese gives. But let it also be said that in many such cases, we have seemed to talk nonsense only because our critics, or we ourselves, have assumed that the "agricultural" goal of generalization is part of our intent.

But in many (perhaps most) of the experiments Deese has in mind, the logic goes in a different direction. We are not *making* generalizations, but *testing* them. To show what a difference this makes, let me turn to an example.

A CASE STUDY OF A FLAT FLUNK

Surely one of the experiments that has had permanent impact on our thinking is the study of "mother love" in rhesus monkeys, elegantly con-

---

[1] In fairness, Deese goes on to make a distinction much like the one I intend here. "If the theory and observations are explicitly related to one another through some rigorous logical process, then the sampling of conditions may become completely unnecessary" (p. 60). I agree. "But a theory having such power is almost never found in psychology" (p. 61). I disagree, not because I think our theories are all that powerful, but because I do not think all that much power is required for what we are usually trying to do.

ducted by Harlow. His wire mothers and terry-cloth mothers are permanent additions to our vocabulary of classic manipulations. And his finding that contact comfort was a powerful determinant of "attachment," whereas nutrition was small potatoes, was a massive spike in the coffin of the moribund, but still wriggling, drive-reduction theories of the 1950s.

As a case study, let us see how the Harlow wire- and cloth-mother experiment stands up to the criteria of EV.

The original discussion of EV by Campbell and Stanley (1967) reveals that the experimental investigation they had in mind was a rather complex mixed design with pretests, a treatment imposed or withheld (the independent variable), and a posttest. Since Harlow's experiment does not fit this mold, the first two of their "threats to external validity" do not arise at all: pretest effects on responsiveness and multiple-treatment interference.

The other two threats on their list do arise in Harlow's case. First, "there remains the possibility that the effects . . . hold only for that unique population from which the . . . {subjects were} selected" (Campbell & Stanley, 1967, p. 19). More generally, this is the problem of sampling bias, and it raises the spectre of an unrepresentative sample. Of course, as every student knows, the way to combat the problem (and never mind that nobody does it) is to select a random sample from the population of interest.

Were Harlow's baby monkeys representative of the population of monkeys in general? Obviously not; they were born in captivity and then orphaned besides. Well, were they a representative sample of the population of lab-born, orphaned monkeys? There was no attempt at all to make them so. It must be concluded that Harlow's sampling procedures fell far short of the ideal.

Second, we have the undeniable fact of the "patent artificiality of the experimental setting" (Campbell & Stanley, 1967, p. 20). Campbell and Stanley go on to discuss the problems posed by the subjects' knowledge that they are in an experiment and by what we now call "demand characteristics." But the problem can be generalized again: How do we know that what the subjects do in this artificial setting is what they would do in a more natural one? Solutions have involved hiding from the subjects the fact that they are subjects; moving from a laboratory to a field setting; and, going further, trying for a "representative sample" of the field settings themselves (e.g., Brunswik, 1955).

What then of Harlow's work? One does not know whether his subjects knew they were in an experiment; certainly there is every chance that they experienced "expectations of the unusual, with wonder and active puzzling" (Campbell & Stanley, 1967, p. 21). In short, they must have been cautious, bewildered, reactive baby monkeys indeed. And what of the representativeness of the setting? Real monkeys do not live within walls. They do not encounter mother figures made of wire mesh, with rubber nipples; nor is the advent of a terry-cloth cylinder, warmed by a light bulb, a part of their natural life-style. What can this contrived situation possibly tell us about how monkeys with natural upbringing would behave in a natural setting?

On the face of it, the verdict must be a flat flunk. On every criterion of EV that applies at all, we find Harlow's experiment either manifestly deficient or simply unevaluable. And yet our tendency is to respond to this critique with a resounding "So what?" And I think we are quite right to so respond.

Why? Because using the lab results to make generalizations about real-world behavior was no part of Harlow's intention. It was not what he was trying to do. That being the case, the concept of EV simply does not arise— except in an indirect and remote sense to be clarified shortly.

Harlow did not conclude, "Wild monkeys in the jungle probably would choose terry-cloth over wire mothers, too, if offered the choice." First, it would be a moot conclusion, since that simply is not going to happen. Second, who cares whether they would or not? The generalization would be trivial even if true. What Harlow did conclude was that the hunger-reduction interpretation of mother love would not work. If anything about his experiment has external validity, it is this theoretical point, not the findings themselves. And to see whether the theoretical conclusion is valid, we extend the experiments or test predictions based on theory.[2] We do not dismiss the findings and go back to do the experiment "properly," in the jungle with a random sample of baby monkeys.

The distinction between generality of findings and generality of theoretical conclusions underscores what seems to me the most important source of confusion in all this, which is the assumption that the purpose of collecting data in the laboratory is to *predict real-life behavior in the real world*. Of course, there are times when that is what we are trying to do, and there are times when it is not. When it is, then the problem of EV confronts us, full force. When it is not, then the problem of EV is either meaningless or trivial, and a misplaced preoccupation with it can seriously distort our evaluation of the research.

But if we are not using our experiments to predict real-life behavior, what are we using them for? Why else do an experiment?

There are a number of other things we may be doing. First, we may be

---

[2] The term *theory* is used loosely to mean, not a strict deductive system, but a conclusion on which different findings converge. Harlow's demonstration draws much of its force from the context of other findings (by Ainsworth, Bowlby, Spitz, and others) with which it articulates.

asking whether something *can* happen, rather than whether it typically *does* happen. Second, our prediction may be in the other direction; it may specify something that ought to happen *in the lab*, and so we go to the lab to see whether it does. Third, we may demonstrate the power of a phenomenon by showing what it happens even under unnatural conditions that ought to preclude it. Finally, we may use the lab to produce conditions that have no counterpart in real life at all, so that the concept of "generalizing to the real world" has no meaning. But even where findings cannot possibly generalize and are not supposed to, they can contribute to an understanding of the processes going on. Once again, it is that understanding which has external validity (if it does)—not the findings themselves, much less the setting and the sample. And this implies in turn that we cannot assess that kind of validity by examining the experiment itself.

ALTERNATIVES TO GENERALIZATION

"What Can" Versus "What Does"

"Person perception studies using photographs or brief exposure of the stimulus person have commonly found that spectacles, lipstick and untidy hair have a great effect on judgments of intelligence and other traits. It is suggested . . . that these results are probably exaggerations of any effect that might occur when more information about a person is available" (Argyle, 1969, p. 19). Later in the same text, Argyle gives a specific example: "Argyle and McHenry found that targeted persons were judged as 13 points of IQ more intelligent when wearing spectacles and when seen for 15 seconds; however, if they were seen during 5 minutes of conversation spectacles made no difference" (p. 135).

Argyle (1969) offers these data as an example of how "the results [of an independent variable studied in isolation] may be exaggerated" (p. 19). Exaggerated with respect to what? With respect to what "really" goes on in the world of affairs. It is clear that on these grounds, Argyle takes the 5-minute study, in which glasses made no difference, more seriously than the 15-second study, in which they did.

Now from an "applied" perspective, there is no question that Argyle is right. Suppose that only the 15-second results were known; and suppose that on the basis of them, employment counselors began advising their students to wear glasses or sales executives began requiring their salespeople to do so. The result would be a great deal of wasted time, and all because of an "exaggerated effect," or what I have called an "inflated variable" (Mook, 1982). Powerful in the laboratory (13 IQ points is a lot!), eyeglasses are a trivial guide to a person's intelligence and are treated as such when more information is available.

On the other hand, is it not worth knowing that such a bias *can* occur, even under restricted conditions? Does it imply an implicit "theory" or set of "heuristics" that we carry about with us? If so, where do they come from?

There are some intriguing issues here. Why should the person's wearing eyeglasses affect our judgments of his or her intelligence under any conditions whatever? As a pure guess, I would hazard the following: Maybe we believe that (a) intelligent people read more than less intelligent ones, and (b) that reading leads to visual problems, wherefore (c) the more intelligent are more likely to need glasses. If that is how the argument runs, then it is an instance of how our person perceptions are influenced by causal "schemata" (Nisbett & Ross, 1980)—even where at least one step in the theoretical sequence ({b} above) is, as far as we know, simply false.

Looked at in that way, the difference between the 15-second and the 5-minute condition is itself worth investigating further (as it would not be if the latter simply "invalidated" the former). If we are so ready to abandon a rather silly causal theory in the light of more data, why are some other causal theories, many of them even sillier, so fiercely resistant to change?

The point is that in thinking about the matter this way, we are taking the results strictly as we find them. The fact that eyeglasses *can* influence our judgments of intelligence, though it may be quite devoid of real-world application, surely says something about us as judges. If we look just at that, then the issue of external validity does not arise. We are no longer concerned with generalizing from the lab to the real world. The lab (qua lab) has led us to ask questions that might not otherwise occur to us. Surely that alone makes the research more than a sterile intellectual exercise.

Predicting From and Predicting To

The next case study has a special place in my heart. It is one of the things that led directly to this article, which I wrote fresh from a delightful roaring argument with my students about the issues at hand.

The study is a test of the tension-reduction view of alcohol consumption, conducted by Higgins and Marlatt (1973). Briefly, the subjects were made either highly anxious or not so anxious by the threat of electric shock, and were permitted access to alcohol as desired. If alcohol reduces tension and if people drink it because it does so (Cappell & Herman, 1972), then the anxious subjects should have drunk more. They did not.

Writing about this experiment, one of my better students gave it short shrift: "Surely not many alcoholics are presented with such a threat under normal conditions."

Indeed. The threat of electric shock can hardly be "representative" of the dangers faced by anyone except electricians, hi-fi builders, and Psychology 101 students. What then? It depends! It depends on what kind of conclusion one draws and what one's purpose is in doing the study.

Higgins and Marlatt could have drawn this conclusion: "Threat of shock did not cause our subjects to drink in these circumstances. Therefore, it probably would not cause similar subjects to drink in similar circumstances either." A properly cautions conclusion, and manifestly trivial.

Or they could have drawn this conclusion: "Threat of shock did not cause our subjects to drink in these circumstances. Therefore, tension or anxiety probably does not cause people to drink in normal, real-world situations." That conclusion would be manifestly risky, not to say foolish; and it is that kind of conclusion which raises the issue of EV. Such a conclusion does assume that we can generalize from the simple and protected lab setting to the complex and dangerous real-life one and that the fear of shock can represent the general case of tension and anxiety. And let me admit again that we have been guilty of just this kind of foolishness on more than one occasion.

But that is not the conclusion Higgins and Marlatt drew. Their argument had an entirely different shape, one that changes everything. Paraphrased, it went thus: "Threat of shock did not cause our subjects to drink in these circumstances. Therefore, the tension-reduction hypothesis, which predicts that it should have done so, either is false or is in need of qualification." This is our old friend, the hypothetico-deductive method, in action. The important point to see is that the generalizability of the results, from lab to real life, is not claimed. It plays no part in the argument at all.

Of course, these findings may not require *much* modification of the tension-reduction hypothesis. It is possible—indeed it is highly likely— that there are tensions and tensions; and perhaps the nagging fears and self-doubts of the everyday have a quite different status from the acute fear of electric shock. Maybe alcohol does reduce these chronic fears and is taken, sometimes abusively, because it does so.[3] If these possibilities can be shown to be true, then we could sharpen the tension-reduction hypothesis, restricting it (as it is not restricted now) to certain kinds of tension and,

---

[3] I should note, however, that there is considerable doubt about that as a statement of the general case. Like Harlow's experiment, the Higgins and Marlatt (1973) study articulates with a growing body of data from very different sources and settings, but all, in this case, calling the tension-reduction theory into question (cf. Mello & Mendelson, 1978).

perhaps, to certain settings. In short, we could advance our understanding. And the "artificial" laboratory findings would have contributed to that advance. Surely we cannot reasonably ask for more.

It seems to me that this kind of argument characterizes much of our research—much more of it than our critics recognize. In very many cases, we are not using what happens in the laboratory to "predict" the real world. Prediction goes the other way: Our theory specifies what subjects should do *in the laboratory*. Then we go to the laboratory to ask, Do they do it? And we modify our theory, or hang onto it for the time being, as results dictate. Thus we improve our theories, and—to say it again—it is these that generalize to the real world if anything does.

Let me turn to an example of another kind. To this point, it is artificiality of *setting* that has been the focus. Analogous considerations can arise, however, when one thinks through the implications of artificiality of, or bias in, the *sample*. Consider a case study.

A great deal of folklore, supported by some powerful psychological theories, would have it that children acquire speech of the forms approved by their culture—that is, grammatical speech—through the impact of parents' reactions to what they say. If a child emits a properly formed sentence (so the argument goes), the parent responds with approval or attention. If the utterance is ungrammatical, the parent corrects it or, at the least, withholds approval.

Direct observation of parent–child interactions, however, reveals that this need not happen. Brown and Hanlon (1970) report that parents react to the content of a child's speech, not to its form. If the sentence emitted is factually correct, it is likely to be approved by the parent; if false, disapproved. But whether the utterance embodies correct grammatical form has surprisingly little to do with the parent's reaction to it.

What kind of sample were Brown and Hanlon dealing with here? Families that (a) lived in Boston, (b) were well educated, and (c) were willing to have squadrons of psychologists camped in their living rooms, taping their conversations. It is virtually certain that the sample was biased even with respect to the already limited "population" of upper-class-Bostonian-parents-of-young-children.

Surely a sample like that is a poor basis from which to generalize to any interesting population. But what if we turn it around? We start with the theoretical proposition: Parents respond to the grammar of their children's utterances (as by making approval contingent or by correcting mistakes). Now we make the prediction: Therefore, the *parents we observe* ought to do that. And the prediction is disconfirmed.

Going further, if we find that the children Brown and Hanlon studied went on to acquire Bostonian-approved syntax, as seems likely, then we can draw a further prediction and see it disconfirmed. If the theory is true, and if *these* parents do not react to grammaticality or its absence, then *these* children should not pick up grammatical speech. If they do so anyway, then parental approval is not necessary for the acquisition of grammar. And that is shown not by generalizing from sample to population, but by what happened *in the sample.*

It is of course legitimate to wonder whether the same contingencies would appear in Kansas City working-class families or in slum dwellers in the Argentine. Maybe parental approval/disapproval is a much more potent influence on children's speech in some cultures or subcultures than in others. Nevertheless, the fact would remain that the parental approval theory holds only in some instances and must be qualified appropriately. Again, that would be well worth knowing, and *this* sample of families would have played a part in establishing it.

The confusion here may reflect simple historical accident. Considerations of sampling from populations were brought to our attention largely by survey researchers, for whom the procedure of "generalizing to a population" is of vital concern. If we want to estimate the proportion of the electorate intending to vote for Candidate X, and if Y% of our sample intends to do so, then we want to be able to say something like this: "We can be 95% confident that Y% of the voters, plus or minus Z, intend to vote for X." Then the issue of representativeness is squarely before us, and the horror stories of biased sampling and wildly wrong predictions, from the *Literary Digest* poll on down, have every right to keep us awake at night.

But what has to be thought through, case by case, is whether that is the kind of conclusion we intend to draw. In the Brown and Hanlon (1970) case, nothing could be more unjustified than a statement of the kind, "We can be W% certain that X% of the utterances of Boston children, plus or minus Y, are true and are approved." The biased sample rules such a conclusion out of court at the outset. But it was never intended. The intended conclusion was not about a population but about a theory. That parental approval tracks content rather than form, in *these children,* means that the parental approval theory of grammar acquisition either is simply false or interacts in unsuspected ways with some attribute(s) of the home.

In yet other cases, the subjects are of interest precisely because of their unrepresentativeness. Washoe, Sarah, and our other special students are of interest because they are not representative of a language-using species. And with all the quarrels their accomplishments have given rise to, I have not seen them challenged as "unrepresentative chimps," except by students on examinations (I am not making that up). The achievements of mnemonists (which show us what *can* happen, rather than what typically *does*) are of interest because mnemonists are not representative of the rest of us. And when one comes across a mnemonist one studies that mnemonist, without much concern for his or her representativeness even as a mnemonist.

But what do students read? "Samples should always be as representative as possible of the population under study." "[A] major concern of the behavioral scientist is to ensure that the sample itself is a good representative {sic} of the population." (The sources of these quotations do not matter; they come from an accidental sample of books on my shelf.)

The trouble with these remarks is not that they are false—sometimes they are true—but that they are unqualified. Representativeness of sample is of vital importance for certain purposes, such as survey research. For other purposes it is a trivial issue.[4] Therefore, one must evaluate the sampling procedure in light of the purpose—separately, case by case.

Taking the Package Apart

Everyone knows that we make experimental settings artificial for a reason. We do it to control for extraneous variables and to permit separation of factors that do not come separately in Nature-as-you-find-it. But that leaves us wondering how, having stepped out of Nature, we get back in again. How do our findings apply to the real-life setting in all its complexity?

I think there are times when the answer has to be, "They don't." But we then may add, "Something else does. It is called understanding."

As an example, consider dark adaptation. Psychophysical experiments, conducted in restricted, simplified, ecologically invalid settings, have taught us these things among others:

1. Dark adaption occurs in two phases. There is a rapid and rather small increase in sensitivity, followed by a delayed but greater increase.

2. The first of these phases reflects dark adaptation by the cones; the second, by the rods.

---

[4] There is another sense in which "generalizing to a population" attends most psychological research: One usually tests the significance of one's findings, and in doing so one speaks of sample values as estimates of population parameters. In this connection, though, the students are usually reassured that they can always define the population in terms of the sample and take it from there—which effectively leaves them wondering what all the flap was about in the first place.

Perhaps this is the place to note that some of the case studies I have presented may raise questions in the reader's mind that are not dealt with here. Some raise the problem of interpreting null conclusions; adequacy of controls for confounding variables may be worrisome; and the Brown and Hanlon (1970) study faced the problem of observer effects (adequately dealt with, I think; see Mook, 1982). Except perhaps for the last one, however, these issues are separate from the problem of external validity, which is the only concern here.

Hecht (1934) demonstrated the second of these conclusions by taking advantage of some facts about cones (themselves established in ecologically invalid photochemical and histological laboratories). Cones are densely packed near the fovea; and they are much less sensitive than the rods to the shorter visible wavelengths. Thus, Hecht was able to tease out the cone component of the dark-adaptation curve by making his stimuli small, restricting them to the center of the visual field, and turning them red.

Now let us contemplate the manifest ecological invalidity of this setting. We have a human subject in a dark room, staring at a place where a tiny red light may appear. Who on earth spends time doing that, in the world of affairs? And on each trial, the subject simply makes a "yes, I see it/ no, I don't" response. Surely we have subjects who "behave as little like human beings as possible" (Bannister, 1966)—We might be calibrating a photocell for all the difference it would make.

How then do the findings apply to the real world? They do not. The task, variables, and setting have no real-world counterparts. What does apply, and in spades, is the understanding of how the visual system works that such experiments have given us. That is what we apply to the real-world setting—to flying planes at night, to the problem of reading X-ray prints on the spot, to effective treatment of night blindness produced by vitamin deficiency, and much besides.

Such experiments, I say, give us understanding of real-world phenomena. Why? Because the *processes* we dissect in the laboratory also operate in the real world. The dark-adaptation data are of interest because they show us a process that does occur in many real-world situations. Thus we could, it is true, look at the laboratory as a member of a class of "target" settings to which the results apply. but it certainly is not a "representative" member of that set. We might think of it as a limiting, or even *defining*, member of that set. To what settings do the results apply? The shortest answer is: to any setting in which it is relevant that (for instance) as the illumination dims, sensitivity to longer visible wavelengths drops out before sensitivity to short ones does. The findings do not represent a class of real-world phenomena; they define one.

Alternatively, one might use the lab not to explore a known phenomenon, but to determine whether such and such a phenomenon exists or can be made to occur. (Here again the emphasis is on what can happen, not what usually does.) Henshel (1980) has noted that some intriguing and important phenomena, such as biofeedback, could never have been discovered by sampling or mimicking natural settings. He points out, too, that if a desirable phenomenon occurs under laboratory conditions, one may seek to make natural settings mimic the laboratory rather than the other way around. Engineers are familiar with this approach. So, for instance, are many behavior therapists.

(I part company with Henshel's excellent discussion only when he writes, "The requirement of 'realism,' or a faithful mimicking of the outside world in the laboratory experiment, applies only to . . . hypothesis testing within the logico-deductive model of research" [p. 470]. For reasons given earlier, I do not think it need apply even there.)

THE DRAMA OF THE ARTIFICIAL

To this point, I have considered alternatives to the "analogue" model of research and have pointed out that we need not intend to generalize our results from sample to population, or from lab to life. There are cases in which we do want to do that, of course. Where we do, we meet another temptation: We may assume that in order to *generalize* to "real life," the laboratory setting should *resemble* the real-life one as much as possible. This assumption is the force behind the cry for "representative settings."

The assumption is false. There are cases in which the generalization from research setting to real-life settings is made all the stronger by the lack of resemblance between the two. Consider an example.

A research project that comes in for criticism along these lines is the well-known work on obedience by Milgram (1974). In his work, the difference between a laboratory and a real-life setting is brought sharply into focus. Soldiers in the jungles of Viet Nam, concentration camp guards on the fields of Eastern Europe—what resemblance do their environments bear to a sterile room with a shock generator and an intercom, presided over by a white-coated scientist? As a setting, Milgram's surely is a prototype of an "unnatural" one.

One possible reaction to that fact is to dismiss the work bag and baggage, as Argyle (1969) seems to do: "When a subject steps inside a psychological laboratory he steps out of culture, and all the normal rules and conventions are temporarily discarded and replaced by the single rule of laboratory culture—'do what the experimenter says, no matter how absurd or unethical it may be'" (p. 20). He goes on to cite Milgram's work as an example.

All of this—which is perfectly true—comes in a discussion of how "laboratory research can produce the wrong results" (Argyle, 1969, p. 19). The wrong results! But that is the whole point of the results. What Milgram has shown is how easily we can "step out of culture" in just the way Argyle describes—and how, once out of culture, we proceed to violate its "normal rules and conventions" in ways that are a revelation to us when they occur. Remember, by the way, that most of the people Milgram interviewed grossly underestimated the amount of compliance that would occur *in that laboratory setting.*

Another reaction, just as wrong but unfortunately even more tempting, is to start listing similarities and differences between the lab setting and the natural one. The temptation here is to get involved in count-'em mechanics: The more differences there are, the greater the external invalidity. Thus:

> One element lacking in Milgram's situation that typically obtains in similar naturalistic situations is that the experimenter had no real power to harm the subject if the subject failed to obey orders. The subject could always simply get up and walk out of the experiment, never to see the experimenter again. So when considering Milgram's results, it should be borne in mind that a powerful source of obedience in the real world was lacking in this situation. (Kantowitz & Roediger, 1978, pp. 387–388)

"Borne in mind" to what conclusion? Since the next sentence is "Nonetheless, Milgram's results are truly remarkable" (p. 388), we must suppose that the remarks were meant in criticism.

Now the lack of threat of punishment is, to be sure, a major difference between Milgram's lab and the jungle war or concentration camp setting. But what happened? An astonishing two thirds obeyed anyway. The force of the experimenter's authority was sufficient to induce normal decent adults to inflict pain on another human being, even though they could have refused without risk. Surely the absence of power to punish, though a distinct difference between Milgram's setting and the others, only adds to the drama of what he saw.

There are other threats to the external validity of Milgram's findings, and some of them must be taken more seriously. There is the possibility that the orders he gave were "legitimized by the laboratory setting" (Orne & Evans, 1969, p. 199). Perhaps his subjects said in effect, "This is a scientific experiment run by a responsible investigator, so maybe the whole business isn't as dangerous as it looks." This possibility (which is quite distinct from the last one, though the checklist approach often confuses the two) does leave us with nagging doubts about the generalizability of Milgram's findings. Camp guards and jungle fighters do not have this cognitive escape hatch available to them. If Milgram's subjects did say "It must not be dangerous," then his conclusion—people are surprisingly willing to inflict danger under orders—is in fact weakened.

The important thing to see is that the checklist approach will not serve us. Here we have two differences between lab and life—the absence of punishment and the possibility of discounting the danger of obedience. The latter difference weakens the impact of Milgram's findings; the former strengthens it. Obviously we must move beyond a simple count of differences and think through what the effect of each one is likely to be.

VALIDITY OF WHAT?

Ultimately, what makes research findings of interest is that they help us understand everyday life. That understanding, however, comes from theory or the analysis of mechanism; it is not a matter of "generalizing" the findings themselves. This kind of validity applies (if it does) to statements like "The hunger-reduction interpretation of infant attachment will not do," or "Theory-driven inferences may bias first impressions," or "The Purkinje shift occurs because rod vision has *these* characteristics and cone vision has *those*." The validity of these generalizations is tested by their success at prediction and has nothing to do with the naturalness, representativeness, or even nonreactivity of the investigations on which they rest.

Of course there are also those cases in which one does want to predict real-life behavior directly from research findings. Survey research, and most experiments in applied settings such as factory or classroom, have that end in view. Predicting real-life behavior is a perfectly legitimate and honorable way to use research. When we engage in it, we do confront the problem of EV, and Babbie's (1975) comment about the artificiality of experiments has force.

What I have argued here is that Babbie's comment has force *only* then. If this is so, then external validity, far from being "obviously our ideal" (Campbell & Stanley, 1967), is a concept that applies only to a rather limited subset of the research we do.

A CHECKLIST OF DECISIONS

I am afraid that there is no alternative to thinking through, case by case, (a) what conclusion we want to draw and (b) whether the specifics of our sample or setting will prevent us from drawing it. Of course there are seldom any fixed rules about how to "think through" anything interesting. But here is a sample of questions one might ask in deciding whether the usual criteria of external validity should even be considered:

As to the sample: Am I (or is he or she whose work I am evaluating) trying to estimate from sample characteristics the characteristics of some population? Or am I trying to draw conclusions not about a population, but about a theory that specifies what *these* subjects ought to do? Or (as in linguistic apes) would it be important if *any* subject does, or can be made to do, this or that?

As to the setting: Is it may intention to predict what would happen in a real-life setting or "target" class of such settings? Our "thinking through" divides depending on the answer.

The answer may be no. Once again, we may be testing a prediction rather than making one; our theory may specify what ought to happen in *this* setting. Then the question is whether the setting gives the theory a fair hearing, and the external-validity question vanishes altogether.

Or the answer may be yes. Then we must ask, Is it therefore necessary that the setting be "representative" of the class of target settings? Is it enough that it be *a* member of that class, if it captures processes that must operate in all such settings? If the latter, perhaps it should be a "limiting case" of the settings in which the processes operate—the simplest possible one, as a psychophysics lab is intended to be. In that case, the stripped-down setting may actually *define* the class of target settings to which the findings apply, as in the dark-adaptation story. The question is only whether the setting actually preserves the processes of interest,[5] and again the issue of external validity disappears.

We may push our thinking through a step further. Suppose there are distinct differences between the research setting and the real-life target ones. We should remember to ask: So what? Will they weaken or restrict our conclusions? Or might they actually strengthen and extend them (as does the absence of power to punish in Milgram's experiments)?

Thinking through is of course another warm, fuzzy phrase, I quite agree. But I mean it to contrast with the cold creepies with which my students assault research findings: knee-jerk reactions to "artificiality"; finger-jerk pointing to "biased samples" and "unnatural settings"; and now, tongue-jerk imprecations about "external invalidity." People are already far too eager to dismiss what we have learned (even that biased sample who come to college and elect our courses!). If they do so, let it be for the right reasons.

REFERENCES

Argyle, M. (1969). *Social interaction*. Chicago: Atherton Press.

---

[5] Of course, whether an artificial setting does preserve the process can be a very real question. Much controversy centers on such questions as whether the operant-conditioning chamber really captures the processes that operate in, say, the marketplace. If resolution of that issue comes, however, it will depend on whether the one setting permits successful predictions about the other. It will not come from pointing to the "unnaturalness" of the one and the "naturalness" of the other. There is no dispute about that.

Babbie, E. R. (1975). *The practice of social research.* Belmont, Calif.: Wadsworth.

Bannister, D. (1966). Psychology as an exercise in paradox. *Bulletin of the British Psychological Society, 19,* 21–26.

Bickman, L. (1974, July). Social roles and uniforms: Clothes make the person. *Psychology Today,* pp. 49–51.

Brown, R., & Hanlon, C. (1970). Derivational complexity and order of acquisition in child speech. In J. R. Hayes (Ed.), *Cognition and the development of language.* New York: Wiley.

Brunswik, E. (1955). Representative design and probabilistic theory in a functional psychology. *Psychological Review, 62,* 193–217.

Campbell, D. T., & Stanley, J. C. (1967). *Experimental and quasi-experimental designs for research.* Chicago: Rand McNally.

Cappell, H., & Herman, C. P. (1972). Alcohol and tension reduction: A review. *Quarterly Journal of Studies on Alcohol, 33,* 33–64.

Deese, J. (1972). *Psychology as science and art.* New York: Harcourt Brace Jovanovich.

Hecht, S. (1934). Vision II: The nature of the photoreceptor process. In C. Murchison (Ed.), *Handbook of general experimental psychology.* Worcester, MA: Clark University Press.

Henshel, R. L. (1980). The purposes of laboratory experimentation and the virtues of deliberate artificiality. *Journal of Experimental Social Psychology, 16,* 466–478.

Higgins, R. L., & Marlatt, G. A. (1973). Effects of anxiety arousal on the consumption of alcohol by alcoholics and social drinkers. *Journal of Consulting and Clinical Psychology, 41,* 426–433.

Kantowitz, B. H., & Roediger, H. L., III. (1978). *Experimental psychology.* Chicago: Rand McNally.

Mello, N. K., & Mendelson, J. H. (1978). Alcohol and human behavior. In L. L. Iverson, S. D. Iverson, & S. H. Snyder (Eds.), *Handbook of psychopharmacology: Vol. 12. Drugs of abuse.* New York: Plenum Press.

Milgram, S. (1974). *Obedience to authority.* New York: Harper & Row.

Mook, D. G. (1982). *Psychological research: Strategy and tactics.* New York: Harper & Row.

Nisbett, R. E., & Ross, L. (1980). *Human inference: Strategies and shortcomings in social judgment.* New York: Century.

Orne, M. T., & Evans, T. J. (1965). Social control in the psychological experiment: Anti-social behavior and hypnosis. *Journal of Personality and Social Psychology, 1,* 189–200.

8

CRITICAL DIMENSIONS IN THE CHOICE AND MAINTENANCE OF SUCCESSFUL TREATMENTS: STRENGTH, INTEGRITY, AND EFFECTIVENESS

WILLIAM H. YEATON AND LEE SECHREST

Many of the issues confronted by research scientists are also likely to be quite relevant to professionals who evaluate and treat personal problems. We have recently written several papers that deal with issues of special interest to evaluation researchers in the fields of health and psychology. The concepts in these papers are not field-specific and appear to us to be quite pertinent to practicing clinicians as well. Our major purpose in the present article, then, is to suggest alternative perspectives on and procedures for clinical research and practice that may be particularly useful to clinicians. Testing these procedures in the growing grounds of clinical practice may in turn generate other new concepts of interest to research scientists.

Reprinted from the *Journal of Consulting and Clinical Psychology, 49*, 156–167. Copyright 1981 by the American Psychological Association.

ISSUES REGARDING THE CHOICE AND MAINTENANCE OF SUCCESSFUL TREATMENTS

There is a seemingly infinite number of aspects of the patient-problem nexus that will potentially influence the choice of treatments for clinical problems. However, our emphasis will instead be directed to important dimensions of the treatment itself. We maintain that these dimensions should be carefully considered in decisions regarding treatment choice. The strength, integrity, and effectiveness of treatment are central characteristics of any intervention strategy. They fully deserve a position more in line with their potential impact on clinical problems.

Strength of Treatment

By strength of treatment, we refer to the a priori likelihood that the treatment could have its intended outcome. Strong treatments contain large amounts in pure form of those ingredients leading to change. Assessments of strength are made independently of knowledge of outcome of treatment in any given case. Thus, certain chemotherapies may be regarded as strong treatments for cancer, even though not all, maybe not even most, cases recover. A clinician ought to specify both a treatment and the parameters of strength likely to change the problem behaviors. To illustrate, electric shock might be judged a strong treatment for deviant child behavior, and a verbal punishment approach would probably be judged as weak. But both treatments can vary along a continuum of strength so that it may be possible to implement electric shock therapy in a form that is relatively weaker than a strong form of verbal punishment therapy. A strong form of both treatments might require that they be administered at high intensity levels during frequent and lengthy treatment sessions.

Let us confess at the outset that we really do not know exactly how applicable the concept of strength of treatment may be in relation to interventions by psychologists. We believe that the concept is quite applicable, but we know that its application will not be easy. It is relatively easy to think, if not always to assess, in terms of strength of treatment in medicine. A strong chemotherapy is likely to be near the maximum that a patient can stand. However, a treatment may not be regarded as truly strong unless it is given in doses that would by other standards be regarded as massive. Aspirin has a long and generally successful history as an antifebrile agent, but it would not usually be regarded as a strong treatment. When one gets into interventions such as psychotherapy, thoughts about strength of treatment tend to get quite fuzzy. What would we ever mean by a "strong" psychotherapy? (On the other hand, we probably do have a reasonably good intuitive notion of what is meant by a weak treatment, e.g., a weak token economy, a weak relaxation treatment, a weak psychotherapy.) We confess that we do not know just how to answer many questions concerning strength of treatment, but we do not think that the issue will go away because we cannot. We will continue to be plagued with uncertainties about what it is that we are doing, what we are testing, and what we ought to do next until we can think our way through all of the problems surrounding the issue of strength of treatment.

For the moment, we think that strength has to do with the amount of treatment, so that longer treatment is stronger than shorter. It may have something to do with intensity in that 16 sessions over a period of 4 weeks may be stronger than 16 sessions over 16 weeks. Strength probably has to do with the adequacy of the theoretical rationale for a treatment, with the clarity of the links that tie the intervention to the outcome. To the extent that a treatment maximizes usage of these intervention-outcome linkages, it would tend to be judged as strong. We think that strength is also enhanced if there is a clear, detailed treatment protocol stipulating the precise conditions under which very specific interventions are intended to be delivered. We also think that, other things being equal, strength of treatment is positively related to the adequacy of training of those doing the treatment; an experienced professional is better than a novice. And, not to be exhaustive, we think that treatments may be regarded as stronger if sessions are planned ahead of time and involve considerable activity by therapist and patient, since both efficiency and expenditure of effort indicate attention to the task at hand.

The Problem of Specificity of Strength

Treatments are not universally strong. Treatments are strong for some problems but not for others. Morphine is a strong treatment for pain. Aspirin is a weak treatment for pain. Larger dosages might, however, enhance the strength of aspirin therapy for pain, at least up to a point. If a treatment is inappropriate for the presented problem, strength is simply an irrelevant dimension of treatment. Aspirin in any dose is not an effective treatment for a staphylococcus infection. Without knowledge of the kinds of problems likely to be modified by a given treatment, clinicians are doomed to intermittent failure.

So, a primary task is to learn which treatments are appropriate to which problems, an idea that we have termed the conceptual relevance of treatment (Yeaton & Sechrest, 1981). What we need is good theory, in the sense of an understanding of the mechanisms relating the causes and the problem as well as the presumed manner by which the treatment alleviates the problem. Only when we have such an understanding does strength become a relevant dimension of treatment. Should we suppose the cause of our client's depression to be a lack of personal reinforcers, we could easily recommend treatments of varying strengths. But, when conceptual relevance is unclear, as when relaxation training is suggested for everything from weight reduction to insomnia (Barlow, 1980), we have no basis to infer the value of stronger forms of treatment or even whether we know the parameters of strength.

Some readers may regard us as naive and wonder whether we really believe that psychological clinicians choose or decide on a treatment of a desired strength. No, we are not that naive. For one thing, many psychologists have only a narrow range of treatment options available to them and cannot choose in any real sense. Some treatments are relatively fixed with respect to parameters of strength. A case in point is the sex therapy program of Masters and Johnson (1970), which is designed to be a standard 2 weeks in duration, with daily sessions conducted by them and, presumably, with standard procedures. (However, see Zilbergeld & Evans, 1980, for critiques of the presumed standardization of techniques and the general accuracy of reporting results in the Masters and Johnson research.) Second, for some treatments, virtually the only dimension of strength that can be varied is duration. Traditional psychotherapy, as an instance, can often be obviously strengthened only by doing more of the same. In group settings, difficult cases may be assigned to more experienced therapists, and intensity may be varied within narrow limits, say between one and two sessions per week, but there may be limits of an economic or logistic nature even for intensity. Our experience and reading leads us to believe that considerably more conceptual development is going to be required before we will be able even to approach the quantification of the strength of a psychotherapeutic intervention. Some therapists may know how to vary emotional intensity within sessions, but it is doubtful if that could be regarded as stronger treatment. Is uncovering psychotherapy stronger than supportive psychotherapy? We are dubious of that proposition, especially since more serious problems like psychotic behavior are more likely to be treated with a supportive rather than an insight-oriented therapy. It is probable that in a large proportion of cases seen by psychologists, decisions about strength of treatment are guided by the patient's response to treatment rather than being planned on the basis of assessment and problem formulation. A clinician probably does not decide to carry out relaxation training for 20 minutes per session for 12 sessions. An experienced clinician may have some implicit norms for how long relaxation training will take, but if the patient responds more slowly or rapidly than usual, treatment will be adjusted accordingly.

Discriminating Strong and Weak Treatments

It requires good judgment and good theory to choose conceptually relevant treatments, but how good is our ability to recognize strong and weak treatment? We have sent descriptions of smoking treatments to judges who had considerable experience with smoking modification research and therapy. These experts were asked to estimate the extent of change they would expect from these treatments. These estimates were then compared with compared with the actual outcomes of the published studies. Assuming that strong treatments resulted in large changes in smoking behavior and that weak treatments resulted in small changes in behavior, we were able to assess the ability of experts to estimate strength of treatment. The average correlation between perceived strength and actual outcome was .47, though some judges attained correlations in the .70s. No doubt the relationship between judgment and outcome is attenuated somewhat by the unreliability of the outcome measure. This evidence suggests that experts at least can make reasonable estimates of strength of treatment even when hindered by lack of knowledge of the extent to which treatment was implemented as planned (i.e., treatment integrity). We also have some evidence that expert social psychological researchers can accurately assess the strength of experimental manipulations carried out in laboratories. However, a more satisfactory determination of psychologists to distinguish between treatments on the basis of strength awaits considerably more research scrutiny.

Problems With Too Weak or Too Strong Treatments

Realistically, we will often err in our choice of treatment strength. For example, we may choose a treatment that is too weak to modify the problem at hand. The problem may be more serious than simply managing the disappointment of patient and clinician at finding themselves where they were to begin with. The implications of using a weak antibacterial drug (too small a dose) can be quite severe. While relatively harmless strains of bacteria die, more potent strains are left alive to multiply and cause still more serious illness. Is the analogy applicable? A weak therapy approach may leave the problem more resistant to change than before the unsuccessful attempt, perhaps in part because of discouragement. (Note the paradox: The less buildup a treatment receives, the less likely it is to be effective, and the stronger the buildup it receives, the greater the disappointment when it fails.) Rather than bringing the solution closer to fruition, an initially weak treatment may actually increase the amount of time, energy, and money that must be spent.

The effect of unsuccessful, weak treatments is clearly illustrated in the case of punishment procedures. Ineffectual punishment procedures require rapidly escalating doses of punishment to suppress the target behavior (Azrin & Holz, 1966). Verbal nagging is often followed by physical threats and finally a "laying on of hands," as many an angry parent can attest. The flip side of this case may be an unsuccessful token program with inexpensive backup reinforcers that must be replaced with reinforcers considerably more costly than those that would have been required without the initial failure to achieve treatment goals.

Unsuccessful, weak treatments may also produce detrimental effects on the motivational level of the client. Unrewarded efforts are extinguished, and subsequent efforts may decrease in probability. Especially when considerable effort has been expended to no avail, we can expect remarkable decrement in the client's tendency to try to solve the problem or to seek assistance in its solution.

Not only can weak treatments have unintended effects, but strong treatments, though superficially successful, may produce undesirable effects. An obvious disadvantage of unduly strong treatments is the possibility of accruing unnecessary expense. Longer and more frequent sessions by trained staff translate into stronger but more expensive treatments. And a client with an accumulated history of strong treatment interventions may be immune to weak treatment strategies. Also, treatments judged to be strong (e.g., electric shock, drug therapy) may also tend to be less acceptable to consumers, thereby limiting the potential population who might benefit from treatment.

There may even be in psychological treatments some analogue to drug dependence. May it not be possible, for example, for some persons to get "hooked" on psychotherapy, and is that not more likely with intensive treatment? Caplan (1968) reported on an intervention program aimed at delinquents in which there was evidence of a treatment that was too strong. Caplan described a "blood, sweat, and tears index," which was a measure reflecting the intensity of involvement of a youth counselor with each case, which, incidentally, is one of the first and still rare instances of an attempt to assess strength of treatment. Analyses showed that there was a curvilinear relationship between the index and progress for the case. Beyond a point representing what one might think of as a turning point in the case, that is, where success seemed in sight, the relationship of further progress and the involvement index became negative. Thus, to the extent that intensity of involvement is a factor in strength of treatment, and to us that seems reasonable, for some cases the treatment was too strong.

Problems With Package Programs and Strength

We have been describing treatments as if they typically exist in pure form. The opposite is more likely to be the case. Treatments are very often packaged together in a kind of "something for everyone" manner (Baer, 1977), thereby minimizing the issue of individual differences. However, such a strategy has multiple shortcomings that are particularly obvious when viewed in the context of treatment strength. Any effort to bolster together individual treatments of unknown utility is potentially wasteful, at least to some clients. If a package program is successful, we are unable to say which elements are critical to its success. Confronted with treatment failure, we may then opt to increase treatment strength. But which ingredients should be increased in strength and how much? We can only guess, and often our guesses will be incorrect.

A Strategy For Choosing Treatment Strength

A clinician is confronted with the task of choosing a conceptually relevant treatment that is likely to solve a client's problem. A useful strategy to assist in the setting of the strength of this treatment choice would follow from a "weakest that works" rule of thumb. The rule is difficult to invoke in actual practice, but it does represent the concept of a treatment of ideal strength. It is very similar to the mathematical notion of a least upper bound. Physicians do not prescribe morphine for tension headaches. Neither do they persist in prescribing escalating doses of penicillin for gonorrhea when faced with an intractable case. Essentially, we want to use Solomon's wisdom to pick the minimum value of treatment strength from among all of the values that would prove to be successful. The risks and costs of being a bit too weak must be weighed carefully against the risks of choosing a stronger treatment than necessary. Obviously, the decision will depend on a multitude of factors, including the importance of the solution to the client, the necessity of finding an immediate solution, and the motivational level of the client. In general, however, we think that the strengths of treatments tend to be over- rather than underestimated. We are guessing that most clinicians have an intuitive understanding of the issues that are involved here; one begins with fairly modest efforts to produce weight gain with someone 15% underweight and with initially stronger efforts with a full-blown case of anorexia.

Integrity of Treatment

Strong, conceptually relevant treatments may prove ineffective if allowed to depart from the treatment protocol. Integrity of treatment refers to the degree to which treatment is delivered as intended (Sechrest & Redner, 1979; Sechrest, West, Phillips, Redner, & Yeaton, 1979). Boruch and Gomez (1977) have attributed the frequent lack of effectiveness of interventions evaluated in the field to the decreased integrity in field facsimiles of laboratory-proven, effective treatments. It is a relevant issue for all treatments and a dimension of treatment that clinicians should go to considerable efforts to guarantee. So too should researchers, though current standards do not require such practice. For example, in Volume 10 (1977) of the *Journal of Applied Behavior Analysis*, only 27% of the research articles presented data monitoring the independent variable (Yeaton, in press). It is obviously impossible to estimate the extent to which treatment is implemented as planned without a provision for monitoring. In this section of the article, we will explore some of the issues and implications for clinical practice of the relative presence and absence of treatment integrity.

Ease of Implementation of Treatments

There are undoubtedly inherent differences between treatments in the case with which they can be administered. Consequently, deficiencies in implementation of treatments cannot always be attributed simply to the carelessness of researchers or clinicians. Just as it is easier to administer 5 mg of Ritalin to the hyperactive child than it would be to administer x units of differential attention, it may be easier to deliver this behavioral regimen as intended than it would be to deliver a prescribed dosage of psychotherapeutic counseling. For highly skilled professionals, integrity may vary little across treatments, but at a paraprofessional level of training, differences in the integrity of treatments may be owing to the complexity of the treatment itself. Reports that show little difference between experts and paraprofessionals in the delivery of services may hold only for treatments that are easily implemented.

There are numerous instances that document the difficulties in implementing and maintaining treatments as planned. Wolf (1978) has noted that the lack of success in the initial replications of the Achievement Place model may have been due to the failure to stress the importance of warmth in the teacher-parents. Tharp and Gallimore (1979) have emphasized treatment integrity in their climax stage model for evaluating educational interventions with Hawaiian children. Also, Sechrest and Redner (1979), in the area of criminal rehabilitation, as well as Carnine and Fink (Note 1), with the DISTAR educational materials, have addressed the difficulties of implementing and maintaining complex treatments.

In general, we may expect that when an intervention is complex, demanding, tedious, extended in time, involves multiple participants, and so on, there are going to be serious problems in maintaining treatment integrity. It is precisely for such interventions that it is most important to have a specific plan for quality assurance, including both monitoring to detect lapses and mechanisms to repair them. Such systems of quality assurance are, in our experience, found less rather than more frequently with increasing levels of treatment complexity.

Problems Related to Levels of Treatment Integrity

When treatment integrity is low and is known to be low, possible conclusions about treatment ineffectiveness can be tempered by the expectation that higher levels of treatment integrity would bolster effectiveness. Since low treatment integrity attenuates treatment strength, we could easily attribute unexpected diminished effectiveness to this fact alone. Although the authors themselves do not make the interpretation, a good instance is provided by the study by Kassebaum, Ward, and Wilner (1971) of the effects of group counseling on prisoners. Once one understands that the documentation provided shows that the counseling was abysmally inadequate (Quay 1977), its failure to have any effects becomes totally uninteresting.

Much worse is the situation in which treatment integrity is low, but the problem is not detected. For example, the evaluation by Weissert, Wan, and Liveratos (Note 2) of the effects of day care and homemaker services to the chronically ill did not include documentation of the extent of service delivery. Given the almost minimal beneficial changes produced by the program, we are left with two equally possible conclusions: Treatment was ineffective, or treatment was not given in a form likely to have the potential to be effective. But if the second possibility is not considered, what follows is predictable and potentially wrong. An analysis like the one by Smith and Glass (1977) that pays no attention to either strength or integrity of treatment is in the long run virtually worthless. We suspect that few of the treatments that they included in their study were often delivered in anywhere near optimal form. Most were probably far from optimal. Maybe much larger effects would have been obtained with stronger treatments, but then again, maybe not. To make one obvious point, there is a great deal of difference between concluding that Therapy A produces better results than Therapy B and that Therapy A produces better results than Therapy B as usually done. We think it important to make clear that no amount of care in research design and statistical analysis can compensate for carelessness in planning and implementing treatments.

High integrity of treatment poses no direct problems, but the necessity to maintain high integrity in order to achieve desirable effects certainly has implications. It may mean that the treatment can be made available only in special circumstances, at high cost, and to a limited range of persons able to afford them. On the other hand, the need for high integrity may only imply the need for better training or for increased quality assurance.

Insulin-dependent diabetics need to be fairly rigorous in following the prescribed techniques and program for self-injection, but by learning and following the procedures, they save time and money and enhance their level of personal independence.

The requirement of high treatment integrity may also restrict the choice of procedures available for problem solution. For example, a clinician may find it impossible to recommend a relatively weak extinction procedure to parents as a treatment strategy for particular problem behaviors of their children that may be extremely difficult to ignore (e.g., loud swearing). Since any failure to follow the extinction regimen effectively places the child on an intermittent schedule of reinforcement, treatment options are limited to those clients who are able to ignore all instances of misbehavior by the child. But, had an alternative procedure been chosen that differentially reinforced any behavior other than swearing, one mistake of paying attention to an instance of swearing would not be critical to success. Efforts by clinicians to force compliance to an overly strict treatment regimen are probably wasted. Worse yet, this wasted effort may translate into poor rapport between clinicians and patients, an unintended effect that clinicians can ill afford to be burdened with.

Degradability of Treatments

Quite naturally, researchers and clinicians prefer that treatments be utilized as planned, a preference undoubtedly based on the possibly faulty assumption that any degradation of any treatment would necessarily lead to decreased effectiveness. Instead, it is probably more realistic to assume that some treatments are more immune to degradation than others and that degradation is less critical at some levels of treatment integrity than others. It would be invaluable to know which assumption is closer to the truth, but truth requires a commitment to monitor treatment delivery. In the absence of this commitment, we must weigh the plausible benefits of ensuring compliance against the possible costs of diminished treatment integrity.

A Strategy To Ensure Treatment Integrity

At the very least, a clinician should ask what level of integrity this treatment must be given. Then, a mechanism has to be created to ensure this level of integrity. Some researchers have made the mechanism physical, as when an automated device signals the designated time to smoke a cigarette (Azrin & Powell, 1968). On other occasions, the mechanism is financial, as illustrated by many smoking modification studies in which participants are required to give the researchers a refundable deposit that tends to guarantee attendance at regular treatment sessions (e.g., Best, 1975). Even in these instances, we cannot safely assume that integrity of treatment will occur. But high levels of treatment integrity are not likely to be maintained without appropriate contingencies for their occurrence. One is not surprised to discover that graduate students work diligently on their dissertation research when a nearly omnipotent major professor carefully supervises the quality and quantity of their efforts. Treatments are given (fairly) precisely as planned and with considerable enthusiasm. Unless a similar contingency is arranged by a clinician, it is a poor bet to assume that parents, spouses, or even major professors would implement a treatment as planned (cf. Yeaton, Greene, & Bailey, in press).

Effectiveness of Treatment

The fact that treatments can be implemented with varying degrees of strength and integrity gives clinicians considerable power to generate effective solutions to problems. This fact also contributes to the finding that some treatments will, therefore, produce larger effects than others. By an effect we mean the difference between measures obtained from experimental and control groups or the difference between two conditions of an experiment. The concept can easily be expanded to quasi-experiments as well as to subject and categorical differences. By way of example, Gilbert, McPeek, and Mosteller (1977) defined an effect as the difference between results obtained with innovative treatments and results obtained with standard treatments. If treatment in the experimental group was associated with a 60% success rate, and if a standard treatment had a 10% success rate, then the effect would be 50%, the difference between the respective group means.

The "quantification of effect" problem that we refer to in the preceding paragraph has concerned us for some time. We were disappointed to find purely statistical approaches, such as percentage of variance accounted for, to be of little value, since they rely so heavily on the specific features of a given experiment (Sechrest & Yeaton, Note 3). Consequently, we have begun to develop several empirical approaches to estimate the magnitude of experimental effects (Sechrest & Yeaton, in press-b) that are extremely pertinent to practicing clinicians. These approaches are relevant at two critical decision points: when a treatment must be chosen and when a decision must be made about whether to continue or alter the treatment regimen. In this section, we will review briefly several of the approaches that we have suggested and elaborate on their relevance to the practicing clinician.

Treatment Effect Norms

Clinicians wish to choose the most effective treatment among those currently available. However, such a strategy presupposes knowledge of the effects of other treatments for the same problem. To accomplish this task, results of previous studies can be aggregated to establish treatment effect norms. As an illustration of this approach (but one that we only partially approve), Smith and Glass (1977) constructed treatment effect norms based on the outcomes of several hundred therapy studies. Using the difference between the mean scores achieved by experimental and control groups divided by the control group standard deviation as their basic effect size measure, these researchers found the mean effect size to be .68 standard deviation units, whereas the standard deviation was .67 units. Treatment outcomes one standard deviation above the average effect size would exceed approximately 84% of the reported results and should therefore be regarded with relative optimism. Jeffrey, Wing, and Stunkard (1978) reported that an average of 11.5 pounds of weight loss could be expected based on their review of 21 recent weight control studies. Any treatment with the potential of much exceeding this average could be justified as a reasonable choice in a weight reduction program.

Normalization

A decision must be made by clinicians with regard to the extent of change necessary to solve a problem. A common goal is to restore the client to a level of functioning attained before the program developed. A physical therapist would logically terminate treatment when the size, strength, and flexibility of a broken left leg were comparable to these qualities in the right leg. Similarly, the modification of functioning to a level present in a peer-relative population is a generally admirable therapeutic goal. Minken et al. (1976) produced favorable changes in the conversational skills of predelinquents to a level attained by a relevant peer group of junior high students. The fact that conversational skills did not reach those of college students does not diminish the importance of their treatment.

These two illustrations suggest that a normal, but not super, state of functioning is likely to be the goal in most clinical interventions. Furthermore, when the definition of certain behavioral states (e.g., retardation, hyperactivity) relies on a normative classification scheme, a standard for treatment success is suggested. "Cure" can be argued when deviation from the norm has been eliminated. Indeed, O'Leary (1980) has implied that a treatment program for hyperactivity could legitimately be termed successful when the effects on the behavioral repertoires of individual subjects moves them within the level of functioning of children considered normal. Similarly, Ciarlo (1977) obtained community-wide norms against which to

justified. Though it is possible to take exception to the apparently faultless logic of this approach (Yeaton & Sechrest, 1981), both researchers and clinicians should be alert to those cases where there is general consensus for an existing standard to evaluate treatment success.

Social Validation

All of the previously described methods of demonstrating effectiveness (effect size norms, normalization, and standards) are mechanisms for validating the effectiveness of the treatments chosen, and each can be classified under the general rubric of social validation (Kazdin, 1977; Wolf, 1978). However, rating scale assessments by relevant judges are also an important validational tool for determining the effectiveness of treatment effects. Prototypically, to establish social validation, pre- and posttreatment videotapes are viewed by relevant judges, and subjective evaluations are made on Likert-type rating scales (e.g., Willner et al., 1977). Substantial change in pre–post ratings argues for an effective treatment, though the extent of change necessary for success is seldom specified, and there is evidence to suggest that the absolute extent of the change may often be small (Yeaton, in press).

Ironically, there are cases in which the change may be too extreme rather than too small (Van Houten, 1979). People may, as an instance, smile too much or offer too many compliments or be too assertive after training. In contrast, situations may arise when apparently small, quantitative change may be substantially important (Sechrest & Yeaton, in press-a), for example, when small initial changes disrupt vicious cycles. A medical intervention may be associated with minimal increases in life expectancy but substantially improve the quality of life in the interim. Caution must be taken to evaluate effectiveness of treatment in terms of all possible gains reaped by clients and not in sometimes simplistic, arbitrary measures.

Clinicians who might wish to use social validation techniques to argue that the goals of treatment have been reached must also be cautious in their choice of a relevant and discriminating set of judges to make the assessment. Greenwood, Walker, Todd, and Hops (1979) obtained both teacher and peer judgments of students' verbal interaction frequencies but found teacher judgments to correlate more highly with observational measures of actual interactions and to be more predictive of the most socially withdrawn children. Obviously, the assessments of some judges are likely to be superior to those of others, though it is not a simple matter to discriminate reliable from unreliable judges, since even expert judgment is open to criticism ("An Interview with Arthur Kantrowitz," 1980).

Cost, Benefit, and Risk Aspects of Treatment

In those rare instances when there are two or more equally effective treatments, clinicians need to take into account the probable costs and risks of implementing treatment. More likely are the cases in which more effective treatments are also more risky and costly. Then, choice of treatment is complicated by the subjective weighting of these positive and negative features. These issues have been elaborated upon elsewhere (Levin, 1975; Rothenberg, 1975; Sechrest & Yeaton, in press-b), but for purposes of the present discussion, we will only mention these facets as relevant to assessing the effectiveness of treatments and to choosing a given treatment over its competitors.

Across Time Assessment of the Strength, Integrity, and Effectiveness of Treatments

Clearly, there is a critical temporal dimension in the assessment of the problem behaviors of clients. Our discussion of the strength, integrity, and effectiveness of treatment is incomplete if we have failed to emphasize that these three dimensions undergo perpetual change during the course of treatment. Effectiveness changes are evident in the myriad patterns displayed in the within-subject designs of behavioral psychologists. But strong treatments become weak, and integrity may vacillate during the course of treatment. We know much less about the expected course of strength and integrity levels during the history of treatment and still less about how effectiveness is thereby altered.

Three-Dimensional Interactions

At best, we can offer some educated speculation about the kinds of probable interactions between strength, integrity, and effectiveness and the factors that may potentially influence the occurrence of these interactions. When a problem is severe, it may be extremely critical to maintain high levels of strength and integrity to preserve effectiveness. Weak treatments or strong treatments with low levels of integrity may be sufficient to sustain the gains produced by these initially strong treatments. It may be, too, that with increasing experience, clinicians may safely depart from treatment protocols without actually reducing treatment effectiveness; probably inexperienced clinicians should not be encouraged to innovate. Possibly, clinicians may be quite compulsive about assuring that treatments are delivered as planned during the first few sessions of treatment. With improvement, treatment specifications may be followed less explicitly. What will happen to effectiveness? The answer may depend on the particular problem being treated. There is considerable evidence that smoking cessation programs produce short-lived benefits, and in cases such as these, a decrease in treatment strength is an ominous sign of failure. If anything, one might argue for increasingly strong treatment during the duration of treatment. On the other hand, Stokes and Baer (1977) have used the expression "train loosely" to describe a planned treatment strategy not unlike a treatment administered at low integrity that enhances generalization in some instances. Without repeated measurements across time of the strength and integrity of treatment for different problems, it is impossible for clinicians to judge the importance of maintaining, increasing, or systematically diminishing treatment strength and integrity.

Effects on Treatment Decisions

It is extremely likely that clinicians will soon be required by third-party payment organizations to provide documentation of the effectiveness of treatments given to each client (Barlow, 1980). In earlier sections of the article, we offered suggestions to aid in choice of treatments. By monitoring the strength, integrity, and effectiveness of treatment across time, the clinician is also in a superior position to make midstream corrections in the treatment plan or to keep on a precharted course. To illustrate, we have reviewed approximately 50 smoking modification studies and have aggregated their success at monthly intervals in causing subjects to stop or decrease smoking. The curve that results when mean percentage decrease in smoking is graphed across time is remarkably similar to an extinction curve that plateaus around 20%. With these effectiveness data, the expected course of progress can be followed. Certainly, some treatment groups will follow the expected course more closely than others. Likewise, some treatments will induce change more or less quickly. However, extreme departures from this effectiveness curve may signal decreased strength or integrity of treatment, or the parameters of strength or integrity may be altered to diminish deviations from the curve. If these parameters are more expensive to implement, at least the clinician could justify the changes to the client or a third party who is paying for the treatment. When progress is sure but slow and follows the effectiveness curve, it should not be difficult to persuade a third party to continue payment for the treatment. When change is likely to be minimal from the continuation of treatment or when strong treatment and high levels of integrity do not diminish smoking levels still further, a decision to terminate treatment or to change treatments can be justified.

A CONCLUDING NOTE

As a field of study matures, it is inevitable that researchers and clinicians will begin to compare the efficacy of different treatments for the same problem. One naturally wonders which versions of various treatments would constitute a fair comparison. One obvious possibility is to compare treatments administered at the same level of strength and integrity, but which level? Should equally competent clinicians (we must now ignore the fact that we do not know how to measure competence either) be given randomly assigned halves of a subject pool and be asked to optimize their efforts at modifying the problem presented? Or should those versions of treatments more likely to be administered in everyday practice be compared even though treatments are not equated for strength and integrity? Whichever course is chosen, any valid comparison of effectivess of treatments simply cannot be made without considerable attention to their strength and integrity. Given our previous lack of attention and our current lack of understanding of the relationships among strength, integrity, and effectiveness, we question the validity of prior comparisons of treatment efficacy. This, we maintain, is a question in dire need of an answer.

REFERENCE NOTES

1. Carnine, D. W., & Fink, W. T. (1976, April). *Increasing rate of presentation and use of signals in direct instruction trainees* (Tech. Rep. 76-1, Appendix B). Eugene: University of Oregon.

2. Weissert, W. G., Wan, T. T. H., & Liveratos, B. B. (1980, February). *Effects and costs of day care and homemaker services for the chronically ill: A randomized experiment.* (NCHSR Research Services Report, DHEW Publication No. PHS 79-3258). Springfield, VA: National Technical Information Service.

3. Sechrest, L., & Yeaton, W. H. (1979). *Estimating magnitudes of experimental effects.* Unpublished manuscript. University of Michigan.

REFERENCES

Alexander, A. B., Cropp, G. J. A., & Chai, H. (1979). Effects of relaxation training on pulmonary mechanics in children with asthma. *Journal of Applied Behavior Analysis, 12,* 27–35.

Azrin, N. H., & Holz, W. C. (1966). Punishment. In W. K. Honig (Ed.), *Operant behavior: Areas of research and application.* New York: Appleton-Century-Crofts.

Azrin, N. H., & Powell, J. (1968). Behavioral engineering: The reduction of smoking behavior by a conditioning apparatus and procedure. *Journal of Applied Behavior Analysis, 1,* 193–200.

Baer, D. M. (1977). "Perhaps it would be better not to know everything." *Journal of Applied Behavior Analysis, 10,* 167–172.

Barlow, D. H. (1980). Behavior therapy: The next decade. *Behavior Therapy, 11,* 315–328.

Best, J. A. (1975). Tailoring smoking withdrawal procedures to personality and motivational differences. *Journal of Consulting and Clinical Psychology, 43,* 1–8.

Boruch, R. F., & Gomez, H. (1977). Sensitivity, bias, and theory in impact evaluations. *Professional Psychology, 8,* 411–434.

Caplan, N. (1968). Treatment intervention and reciprocal interaction effects. *Journal of Social Issues, 24,* 63–88.

Ciarlo, J. A. (1977). Monitoring and analysis of mental health program outcome data. *Evaluation, 4,* 109–114.

Foster, S. L., & Ritchey, W. L. (1979). Issues in the assessment of social competence in children. *Journal of Applied Behavior Analysis, 12,* 625-638.

Gilbert, J. P., McPeek, B., & Mosteller, F. (1977). Statistics and ethics in surgery and anesthesia. *Science, 198,* 684–689.

Greenwood, C. R., Walker, H. M., Todd, N. M., & Hops, H. (1979). Selecting a cost-effective screening measure for the assessment of preschool social withdrawal. *Journal of Applied Behavior Analysis, 12,* 639–652.

An interview with Arthur Kantrowitz. (1980, July). *Omni,* pp. 85–87; 112–113.

Jeffrey, R. W., Wing, R. R., & Stunkard, A. J. (1978). Behavioral treatment of obesity: The state of the art, 1976. *Behavior Therapy, 9,* 189–199.

Kassebaum, G., Ward, D., & Wilner, D. (1971). *Prison treatment and parole survival: An empirical assessment.* New York: Wiley.

Kazdin, A. E. (1977). Assessing the clinical or applied importance of behavior change through social validation. *Behavior Modification, 1,* 427–452.

Knatterud, G. L., Klimpt, C. R., Levin, M. E., Jacobson, M. E., & Goldner, M. G. (1978). Effects of hypoglycemic agents on vascular complications in patients with adult-onset diabetes: VII. Mortality and selected nonfatal events with insulin treatments. *Journal of the American Medical Association, 240,* 37–42.

Levin, H. M. (1975). Cost-effectiveness analysis in evaluation research. In M. Guttentag & E. L. Struening (Eds.), *Handbook of evaluations research* (Vol. 2). Beverly Hills, CA: Sage.

Masters, W. H., & Johnson, V. E. (1970). *Human sexual inadequacy.* Boston: Little, Brown.

Minkin, N., et al. (1976). The social validation and training of conversational skills. *Journal of Applied Behavior Analysis, 9,* 127–140.

O'Leary, K. D. (1980). Pills or skills for hyperactive children. *Journal of Applied Behavior Analysis, 13,* 191–204.

Pelham, W. E., Schnedler, R. W., Bologna, N. C., & Contreras, J. A. (1980). Behavioral and stimulant treatment of hyperactive children: A therapy study with methylphenidate probes in a within-subject design. *Journal of Applied Behavior Analysis, 13*, 221–236.

Quay, H. C. (1977). The three faces of evaluation: What can be expected to work. *Criminal Justice and Behavior, 4*, 341–354.

Rothenberg, J. (1975). Cost-benefit analysis: A methodological exposition. In M. Guttentag & E. L. Struening (Eds.), *Handbook of evaluation research* (Vol. 2). Beverly Hills, CA: Sage.

Sechrest, L., & Redner, R. (1979). Strength and integrity of treatments in evaluation studies. In *Evaluation reports*. Washington, DC: National Criminal Justice Reference Services.

Sechrest, L., West, S. G., Phillips, M., Redner, R., & Yeaton, W. (1979). Some neglected problems in evaluation research: Strength and integrity of treatments. In L. Sechrest et al. (Eds.), *Evaluation studies review annual* (Vol. 4). Beverly Hills, CA: Sage.

Sechrest, L., & Yeaton, W. H. (in press-b). Assessing the effectiveness of research: Methodological and conceptual issues. In S. Ball (Ed.), *New directions in evaluation research*. San Francisco: Jossey-Bass.

Sechrest, L. & Yeaton, W. H. (in press-b). Executive summary of "Empirical approaches to effect size estimation." In R. F. Boruch, P. M. Wortman, & D. S. Cordray (Eds.), *Secondary analysis in applied social research*. San Francisco: Jossey-Bass.

Smith, M. L., & Glass, G. V. (1977). Meta-analysis of psychotherapy outcome studies. *American Psychologist, 32*, 752-760.

Stokes, T. F., & Baer, D. M. (1977). An implicit technology of generalization. *Journal of Applied Behavior Analysis, 10*, 349–367.

Tharp, R. G., & Gallimore, R. (1975). The ecology of program research and evaluation: A model of successive evaluation. In L. Sechrest, S. G. West, M. A. Phillips, R. Redner, & W. Yeaton (Eds.), *Evaluation studies review annual* (Vol. 4). Beverly Hills, CA: Sage.

Van Houten, R. (1979). Social validation: The evolution of standards of competency for target behaviors. *Journal of Applied Behavior Analysis, 12*, 581–591.

Willner, A. G., et al. (1977). The training and validation of youth-preferred social behaviors of child-care personnel. *Journal of Applied Behavior Analysis, 10*, 219-230.

Wolf, M. M. (1978). Social validity: The case for subjective measurement or how applied behavior analysis is finding its heart. *Journal of Applied Behavior Analysis, 11*, 203-214.

Yeaton, W. H. (1979). *An analysis of a school crossing guard training program: Teaching pedestrian safety to young children.* Unpublished doctoral dissertation, Florida State University.

Yeaton, W. H. (in press). A critique of the effectiveness dimension in applied behavior analysis. In S. Rachman & H. Eysenck (Eds.), *Advances in behavior research and therapy*. Elmsford, NY: Pergamon Press.

Yeaton, W. H., Greene, B. F., & Bailey, J. S. (in press). Behavioral community psychology: Strategies and tactics for teaching community skills in children and adolescents. In A. E. Kazdin & B. B. Lahey (Eds.), *Advances in clinical child psychology.*

Yeaton, W. H., & Sechrest, L. (1981). Empirical approaches to effect size estimation in health research. In P. M. Wortman (Ed.), *Estimating effect size.* Beverly Hills, CA: Sage.

Zilbergeld, B., & Evans, M. (1980, August). The inadequacy of Masters and Johnson. *Psychology Today*, pp. 29–30; 33–34; 37–38; 40; 42–43.

9

WITHIN-SUBJECTS DESIGNS: TO USE OR NOT TO USE?

ANTHONY G. GREENWALD

Frequently an investigator faces the choice of whether to examine the effects of two or more experimental treatments by exposing each subject to (a) only a single treatment (between-subjects design) or (b) several or all of the treatments (within-subjects or repeated-measures design). Grice (1966) has pointed out that the pattern of treatment effects obtained may vary considerably between the two types of designs. However, only rarely does an investigator make a choice of type of design after consideration of the appropriateness of each type to the problem being investigated. I attempt to assemble here several considerations that may often be appropriate to the decision between a within-or between-subjects design.

Although they are mentioned briefly, statistical considerations relating to choice of design are not of primary interest here. These statistical matters are well handled in standard statistical texts, as referenced below.

Reprinted from the *Psychological Bulletin*, 83, 314–320. Copyright 1976 by the American Psychological Association.

Preparation of this report was facilitated by support to the author from National Science Foundation Grant GS-42981 and National Institute of Mental Health Grant MH-20527.

My aim, rather, is to detail the *psychological* considerations that are critical to the choice of design. Some of these points are also covered in statistical texts, particularly insofar as they may affect the choice of statistical procedures. I have added only a few novel points to these earlier treatments and have aimed more at (a) putting the several points together in a single place and (b) observing that the prevailing cautions against the use of within-subjects designs need to be moderated without, however, being abandoned.

Poulton (1973, 1974; see also Rothstein, 1974) has recently issued a general warning against within-subjects designs, pointing out that the context provided by exposure to other treatments ("range effect") may often alter the effect of a given treatment. This point is certainly valid and is acknowledged here by considering (a) how procedures may serve to minimize or maximize such context effects and (b) when it may or may not be appropriate to allow the occurrence of context effects. The context effects that may be generated by a within-subjects design are discussed under three headings: Practice, Sensitization, and Carry-Over.

Context Effects in the Between-Subjects Design

Poulton (1973) concluded that since context or range effects are to be expected in within-subjects designs, these designs should ordinarily be avoided or, if used, bolstered by between-subjects design results. Implicit in this conclusion is the principle that the between-subjects design provides a standard of validity against which results of a within-subject design must be evaluated. This may be questioned on three grounds. First, as Poulton (1973) noted, "The influence of range of stimuli cannot always be prevented by restricting each man to a single stimulus" (p. 115). This may be because extralaboratory experience leaves some residue of context. Second, even if the extralaboratory can be safely ignored, the presentation of a single treatment to each subject does not really achieve the *absence* of context, but rather the presence of the context provided by the single treatment. An example makes this clearer.

> Example 1: Researcher 1 uses two designs to study the effect of foreperiod duration on simple reaction time. In a between-subjects design, each subject is assigned to a single foreperiod treatment: 0, 200, 500, or 1,000 msec. In a parallel within-subjects design, each subject receives a series of trials in which the four treatments are randomly sequenced.

It is known that Researcher 1's results will be different for the two types of design. The within-subjects design may produce either an increasing or a decreasing function relating reaction time to foreperiod duration (see Poulton, 1973, Table 1). Which function will be obtained depends on whether the procedures are arranged to produce increasing or decreasing expectation of the response signal as the foreperiod grows. Thus, it may be said that the within-subjects design introduces an expectancy or readiness process that is affected by the context of other treatments (foreperiods).

Is this expectancy process absent from the between-subjects design? No—rather, readiness occurs and is focused at the end of the (single) expected foreperiod. Thus, the single treatment in the between-subjects design provides a very real context that influences performance. This context effect could be avoided by presenting each subject with only a single trial at the selected foreperiod duration, but this would be an impractical way of collecting data on the problem. Further, the researcher may well wish to *ignore* the first (or first several) trials, since these involve warm-up processes (effects due to lack of context!) that are not of interest.

These considerations raise the third basis for questioning the notion that between-subjects designs provide a standard of validity against which to evaluate within-subjects designs. In fact, the ecological or external validity (Campbell & Stanley, 1966) of a piece of research depends on the extent to which the research context approximates the context existing in the domain to which the researcher wishes to generalize the results. This point is considered further in the concluding section of this article.

Statistical Considerations

No attempt is made here to detail the technical problems involved in statistics used to analyze the within- or between-subjects designs. However, a few general principles of a statistical nature must be considered as background. A more complete discussion of these points may be found in standard sources such as Myers (1972, especially chapter 7) and Winer (1971, especially chapter 4).

Power

When each subject provides data for two or more treatments, the subject may be said to serve "as his own control" in comparisons among treatment effects (i.e., treatment differences are not confounded with subject differences). To the extent that the *subjects* classification in the ensuing analysis of variance constitutes a substantial source of variance, this feature of the within-subjects design results in substantially more sensitivity to treatment effects (power) than would characterize a between-subjects design employing the same number of observations. Since a k-treatment between-subjects design would employ k times the number of subjects used in a within-subjects design with the same number of observations, it is apparent that a within-subjects design might often reach a desired level of power while using fewer than $1/k$ times the number of subjects in an equally powerful between-subjects design. The within-subjects design can therefore represent an immense experimental economy, particularly when per-subject costs are considerable in relation to per-treatment costs.

Violation of Assumptions

The standard analyses of within-subjects designs depend on an assumption of equality of the variances of differences between pairs of treatments (Winer, 1971, p. 282). It has been noted by statisticians that real data often violate this assumption and that the standard F ratio tests may be biased considerably by such violations. For this reason, within-subjects designs must be treated with a certain amount of special statistical care. Nonetheless, the techniques for dealing with violations of assumptions seem well enough established so that such violations can be tolerated but not ignored. The appropriate procedures include tests for extent of departure from assumptions, adjustments in degrees of freedom to correct for such departures, and the use of alternative statistical tests such as the multivariate analysis of variance (see Poor, 1973), which make less restrictive assumptions.

CONTEXT EFFECTS IN WITHIN-SUBJECTS DESIGNS

Practice

Example 2: Researcher 2 is interested in assessing the effects of performance at a rotary pursuit task under three levels of distracting white noise: 75 db (A), 90 db (B), and 105 db (C). Should the effects of the three treatments be compared in a within- or between-subjects design?

A within-subjects design in which subjects were given Treatments A, B, C on Days 1, 2, 3 would suffer the obvious problem that the effects of treatments would be confounded with days. To the extent that performance on the motor skill task improves with practice, as is quite likely, this particular within-subjects procedure would yield seriously misleading results. There is a sometimes satisfactory remedy of *counterbalancing* the assignment of treatments to days in either (a) all possible combinations (six in this example) or (b) a balanced subset of combinations, as in a 3 × 3 Latin square design with *days* as the column factor, *groups of subjects* as the row factor, and *noise treatments* as the cell entries. This solution may not be satisfactory because the several treatments may be differently effective at different levels of practice. As a result, the observed treatment effects may be mixed inseparably with treatment-practice interactions.

At this point Researcher 2 should consider the relative interest of (a) treatment effects under minimum practice, (b) treatment effects under extensive practice, or (c) treatment effects across a range of practice levels (i.e., treatment–practice interaction). If the researcher is interested in treatment effects under minimum practice, the within-subjects design is inappropriate because subjects are providing data for two of the three treatments (more generally, $k - 1$ of k treatments) under more than minimum practice. A between-subjects design would be obligatory. If interest is in the treatment effect on the highly practiced skill, then a completely within-subjects design is possible, employing extensive practice to achieve a performance asymptote prior to administration of treatments in counterbalanced order. Finally, if interest is in the treatment effects across levels of practice, it may be best to use a combined between- and within-subjects design in which each subject provides data for performance at several levels of practice under only a single treatment condition.

The last design described above should be recognized as one of the most common instances of within-subjects designs—the learning experiment. Many psychologists would not think of studying practice effects with anything but a repeated-measurement assessment. Nonetheless, the decision to use a within-subjects design in a learning experiment should be made only after some thought. For a design with k different treatments and m levels of practice, it is possible to use km groups, each group being given a test for learning only once, after completion of the appropriate amount of practice. This might be advisable if the test for learning involves experiences that when applied repeatedly, might themselves affect performance. For example, paired-associate learning by passive exposure to word pairs could be tested after each passive exposure by presenting the first word of each pair and asking the subject to produce the second word that had been paired with each. For a variety of reasons, this type of test might affect later performance independently of what was learned during the exposure period. On the other hand, if an anticipation method is being used (learning trials consist of first-word presentation, after which the subject tries to produce the second before being shown it), then the researcher is able to obtain information on performance at various stages of practice without interfering in any way with the practice procedure. Here it would be folly to employ anything but a repeated-measurement procedure for the study of acquisition.

Summary

A within-subjects design should be avoided in studying effects of several treatments when the researcher is interested in the effects of the treatments in the absence of practice and practice is likely to affect performance (either a main effect of successive tests or an interaction of successive tests with treatments). For the purpose of using a within-subjects design, undesired practice effects may sometimes be controlled by counterbalancing the sequence of treatments, or may be avoided by providing extensive practice prior to administering any treatments. Choice among within- or between-subject procedures here should depend on the level(s) of practice at which it is appropriate to examine the treatment effects. Finally, the practice effect is often intended to be the direct object of study itself—in learning experiments. Here, within-subjects designs will often be appropriate, but only when performance information can be obtained (as it frequently can) without having an impact on the acquisition process.

Sensitization

> Example 3: Researcher 3 wishes to determine the effect of room illumination on worker productivity. Each subject is put to work on a well-learned task in a room in which the illumination is altered at periodic intervals in counterbalanced order across subjects, and the investigator determines the work rate under each illumination condition.

Researcher 3 should be concerned here with the possibility that the subject can readily discriminate the illumination differences and may thus be more sensitive and responsive to illumination than if there were exposure to only one of the several illumination level treatments. This sensitization to treatment variations may result in the subject's forming hypotheses about the treatment effects and responding to those perceived hypotheses rather than or in addition to the treatments themselves.

A variety of camouflaging strategies may be used to minimize the sensitization problem. The researcher in Example 3 may alter illumination from one treatment level to another so gradually that the subject will not notice it. In other circumstances, the experimenter may systematically alter several variables extraneous to the research design in order to draw attention away from a critical treatment variable (while, of course, not confounding the treatment with the extraneous variables).

The fact that perceptions of differences among treatments may be enhanced by their juxtaposition in a within-subjects design may be used to advantage in research when the experimenter is interested in observing the subject's capacity to discriminate such differences. Psychophysical studies constitute a large category of experiments in which the sensitization effect may be put to work for the researcher. In a brightness-judging experiment, for example, the experimenter is interested in the perceiver's sensitivity to brightness differences and wishes to optimize the conditions for observing such discrimination ability. By juxtaposing different treatments (brightnesses) in a within-subjects design, the limits of discrimination capacity can be assessed much more readily than in a between-subjects design.

Summary

A within-subjects design should be avoided when juxtaposition of treatments enhances perception of treatment variations *if* such perceptions can interfere with the processes the researcher desires to study. With ingenuity, it may often be possible to camouflage treatments so that this problem can be avoided. In quite a few experimental situations, particularly studies of perceptual discrimination, sensitization as a consequence of juxtaposing treatments (stimuli) in a within-subjects design will greatly facilitate the research.

Carry-Over

Example 4: Researcher 4 is interested in the effects of Drugs A, B, and C on performance on a simple reaction time task. In order to employ a within-subjects design, Researcher 4 gives each subject four performance tests separated by 20 minutes, each test being preceded by the administration of a standard dosage injection of one of the three drugs or a placebo control and with the sequence of treatments being counterbalanced across subjects.

In general, a carry-over effect occurs when the effect of one treatment persists in some fashion at the time of measurement of the effect of another. In Example 4, there are two types of potential carry-over. One is due to practice at the performance task and has been discussed separately above. The second is that traces of prior drug treatments may be present at the time of testing the effects of a later treatment. Counterbalancing provides an only partially adequate solution to this problem, since the interference effects may not be bidirectional and, further, they may obscure the treatment effects of the drugs taken individually.[1]

The chief means of reducing carry-over effects is to separate the treatments in time. This would likely be an effective means of applying a within-subjects design to the problem given in Example 4, assuming that practice effects are not also involved. In general, the strategy of separating treatments in time will be effective in reducing intertreatment carry-over only to the extent that the effects of any treatment are not permanent.

In addition to the study of learning, there are several other major areas of study in which the target of study is some process that can be

---

[1] This inadequacy of counterbalancing involves the same considerations mentioned in discussing the possible inadequacy of counterbalancing in removing practice effects. Practice is certainly an instance of the general class of carry-over effects, but has been discussed separately because of the special status of learning effects in psychological research.

interpreted as an intertreatment carry-over in the framework of a within-subjects design. Perceptual assimilation and contrast, incentive contrast, violation of expectation, transfer of training, primacy–recency in persuasion, resistance to extinction, and various types of adaptation are some of these. The fact that intertreatment carry-overs are likely to be a major source of serendipitous findings should not be overlooked as one of the virtues of employing within-subjects designs in which treatments that would otherwise not be examined in near temporal proximity are juxtaposed.

Procedures that permit the occurrence of carry-over effects present special problems for statistical analysis. Cochran and Cox (1957, pp. 133–142) discussed a variety of means of estimating separately the direct and carry-over effects of experimental treatments.

Summary

When treatments have persistent effects, a within-subjects design may be unsatisfactory because the effect of one treatment may still be in force at the time of measuring another's effect. However, the within-subjects design may be salvaged in this case by increasing the separation of the treatments in time. Effects dependent on carry-over or, more generally, upon the sequence in which treatments are administered and their temporal proximity are frequently of psychological interest in and of themselves.

EXTERNAL VALIDITY

Several of the concerns already treated are appropriate to evaluating the internal validity of an experiment—that is, Does the within-subjects design permit the experimenter to test the hypothesis of interest, or will consequences of using the design in some way contaminate (by practice, sensitization, or carry-over) the hypothesis test? Now we take up a matter that may be at odds with some of these considerations and ask how the choice of design affects the external (or ecological) validity of the experiment (i.e., the ability of the researcher to account for the effects of treatment variations as they may occur in interesting nonresearch settings). (See Campbell & Stanley, 1966, for an exposition of internal and external validity.)

Example 5: Researcher 5 is interested in the effects of source credibility on persuasion, and is considering two possible designs. In one, a between-subjects design, communications on two topics are attributed, for some subjects, to a trustworthy and expert source whereas, for other subjects, the same communications are attributed to an untrustworthy and inexpert source. In an alternate within-subjects design, each subject is exposed to the same two communications, but one is attributed to the high-credible source, the other to the low-credible source, with source-communication assignments being counterbalanced across subjects. Which design is preferable?[2]

Persons familiar with persuasion research will be aware that the between-subjects design is most often chosen for the examination of source credibility effects (but not always—see Osgood & Tannenbaum, 1955). But this is perhaps the less justifiable choice if the researcher's primary interest is in predicting or characterizing source effects in the non-laboratory environment. Consider that people tend to be exposed to persuasive communications in clusters in many mass communication settings, these communications frequently being identified with different sources (e.g., columns in a newspaper editorial section, political or product advertisements in magazines, or on radio or television). Therefore, the within-subjects design for studying the consequences of communicator credibility may have greater external validity than does the between-subjects design.[2]

Similar considerations would lead to a preference for the between-subjects design for other problems. For example, a researcher may be interested in studying the effect of reinforcement-based versus psychoanalytically based therapies for phobia symptoms. In such a situation exposure of the same subjects to several different treatments would create a situation rather lacking in external validity.

Considerations of external validity should not necessarily be uppermost in the researcher's mind. The between-subjects design may be preferred even in some situations for which the within-subjects design would have greater external validity, because the between-subjects design may allow cleaner tests of theoretical hypotheses. Example 6 presents such a case, in which internal validity is of more concern to the investigator than is external validity.

Example 6: Researcher 6 is interested in the effects of witnessing televised violence on subsequent aggressive behavior of children. A within-subjects design would involve exposure of each subject to several different program sequences of varying degrees of violence, each followed by the provision of some opportunity to act aggressively in a play situation with other children. Should this design be employed?

---

[2]Both of the designs mentioned in this example are within-subjects or repeated-measurement designs in that the effects of two communications are studied on each subject. However, the treatment variation of credibility is a between-subjects variation in the first design and a within-subjects variation in the second.

[3]Poulton's (1973) concerns about range effects are quite relevant here. The investigator who is interested in generalizing to nonlaboratory settings should be concerned to see that the range and distribution of treatment variations in the experiment correspond to their range and distribution in the appropriate nonlaboratory setting. Otherwise, the experimental treatment effects may misrepresent the effects of their nonlaboratory analogs.

In this case, the within-subjects design might not be preferable because the carry-overs among treatments (subjects still being under the influence of Program A at the time of Test B) might weaken the researcher's hypothesis test. Accordingly, the between-subjects design might be chosen even though the within-subjects design clearly has greater external validity in its correspondence to the mixture of types of programs the child would normally see on television.

In many cases, a greater stress on internal validity than on external validity would lead to a choice of the within-subjects design. This might be particularly true in cases of basic research for which there is no readily apparent nonlaboratory setting for which the research is an analog. For example, a neuropsychologist studying functions of single cells in the central nervous system should almost certainly examine the consequences of the range of treatments in which he or she is interested on each of the research subjects.

Summary

Considerations of external or ecological validity may sometimes be at odds with considerations related to practice, sensitization, and carry-over effects. Thus, the within-subjects design may often have greater external validity because it contains these confounds, but these may also interfere with the researcher's ability to isolate the treatment effects.

CONCLUSIONS

A general force operating in the direction of selecting a within-subjects design is the statistical efficiency afforded by the removal of subject variance from error terms used to test treatment effects. However, context effects may often interfere with hypothesis tests and, therefore, should take precedence over considerations of statistical efficiency when choosing a design. Context effects may occur in either a between- or a within-subjects design, but the range of possible effects is much greater in the latter type of design and, correspondingly, the experimenter has greater potential control over them by selecting ranges of treatments to administer. In many situations a within-subjects design can be made more acceptable by appropriate counter-balancing of treatment sequences (to control practice effects), by camouflaging treatments (to reduce sensitization to the treatment dimensions), or by separating treatments in time (to reduce carry-over effects). In still other circumstances, the deliberate introduction of these context effects in a within-subjects design may have the desirable consequences of permitting the study of some interesting aspect of the context effect itself or of increasing the external (ecological) validity of the research.

REFERENCES

Campbell, D. T., & Stanley, J. C. (1966). *Experimental and quasi-experimental designs for research.* Chicago: Rand McNally.

Cochran, W. G., & Cox, G. (1957). *Experimental designs.* New York: Wiley.

Grice, G. R. (1966). Dependence of empirical laws upon the source of experimental variation. *Psychological Bulletin, 66,* 488-498.

Myers, J. L. (1972). *Fundamentals of experimental design* (2nd ed.). Boston: Allyn & Bacon.

Osgood, C. E., & Tannenbaum, P. H. (1955). The principle of congruity in the prediction of attitude change. *Psychological Review, 62,* 42-55.

Poor, D. D. S. (1973). Analysis of variance for repeated measures designs: Two approaches. *Psychological Bulletin, 80,* 204-209.

Poulton, E. C. (1973). Unwanted range effects from using within-subjects experimental designs. *Psychological Bulletin, 80,* 113-121.

Poulton, E. C. (1974). Range effects are characteristic of a person serving in a within-subjects experimental design—A reply to Rothstein. *Psychological Bulletin, 81,* 201-203.

Rothstein, L. D. (1974). Reply to Poulton. *Psychological Bulletin, 81,* 199-201.

Winer, B. J. (1971). *Statistical principles in experimental design* (2nd ed.). New York: McGraw-Hill.

assess the effectiveness of mental health interventions. Treatment was considered successful when functional impairment was restored to a level of most other persons in the community.

There are many instances when a normalization approach to establishing appropriate effect size magnitudes can be inherently deficient. Often it is precisely the behavior of the normative group that is deficient. For example, unobtrusive videotapes of the pedestrian behavior of young children indicate severe deficiencies in their tendency to utilize safe street-crossing skills (Yeaton, 1979). Similarly, Foster and Ritchey (1979) have criticized efforts to teach social competence in children where peer norms are used as a basis for establishing success even when the norm may be unacceptable to society. Together, these examples support our contention that caution should always be exercised in the choice of an appropriate normative comparison group. With care and caution, however, the normative approach offers a strong rationale for a clinician's decision to terminate treatment.

Standards To Be Attained

For some treatments, it may be possible to utilize a well-defined standard whose attainment indicates that treatment can be considered to have been successful. As with the normalization approach, magnitude of effect per se is not determined, but a firm answer can be given to the question whether the change is big enough to reach an agreed-upon standard of adequacy. Actually the use of standards is a relatively common practice among researchers. For example, in their study of asthma in children, Alexander, Cropp, and Chai (1979) used nebulized isoproterenol hydrochloride as the standard for judging other treatments, since this pharmacological intervention is so widely used for symptomatic relief. Knatterud, Klimpt, Levin, Jacobson, and Goldner (1978) compared the effects of a variable insulin treatment regimen for diabetes with the commonly used standard involving fixed dosages (unless the patient's medical condition definitely warrants a nonstandard dosage). And Pelham, Schnedler, Bologna, and Conteras (1980) found that the combination of medication and behavior therapy maximally modified the behaviors of hyperactive children and argued that this combination should be considered a standard to judge the success of interventions with hyperactive children.

In some instances, there may exist absolute standards to judge the effectiveness of clinical interventions. Any treatment that could be credited with saving a life, avoiding a disabling injury, or alleviation serious disfigurement could be justified on the grounds that society values these benefits to the extent that any intervention producing them need not be

III

ASSESSMENT

Assessment is central to all research and evaluation. Demonstrating effects and interpreting outcomes depend on the quality of the assessment procedures. In this section, assessment topics are covered that are designed to facilitate development and interpretation of measures in clinical research.

BASIC CONCEPTS AND DESIGN OF MEASURES

In the first article, Bert Green (1981) concisely describes measurement concepts including reliability and validity, test development, administration, and scoring. The concepts are familiar, but not invariably considered in measurement selection. The initial article provides a basis for further concepts of assessment in clinical research.

René Dawis (1987) discusses the design, development, and evaluation of measures that are generated for research. The article focuses on devising the content and format of the scales in concrete terms. Different models of scale development are highlighted along with considerations that influence their selection. A number of specific issues are considered such as the development of unidimensional versus multidimensional scales, the role of factor analysis in scale evaluation, the relation of reliability and validity, and response bias. Each of these is important for scale development and for evaluation of scales that have been developed in prior research.

MEASUREMENT EVALUATION

The evaluation of a given scale is complex and never ending because each use of the scale has potential implications for the interpretation of the measure (construct validity). The quality of a measure, as defined by alternative types of reliability and validity, is critically important to inferences that can be drawn. Three of the most commonly used measures in clinical assessment are the Minnesota Multiphasic Personality Inventory, Rorschach Inkblot Test, and Wechsler Adult Intelligence Scale. The article by Kevin Parker, Karl Hanson, and John Hunsley (1988) evaluates psychometric properties of these three measures. The article is included to convey concretely some of the considerations that enter into scale evaluation. Not all forms of reliability and validity relevant to measurement evaluation are included nor are all scoring methods for these measures addressed. Nevertheless, the information conveys critical psychometric features.

Traditional concepts of reliability and validity play central roles in scale development and evaluation. Among the many advances in understanding assessment is *generalizability theory*. Generalizability theory extends assessment validation to consider multiple influences on measurement and the extent to which performance of an individual can be generalized to the universe of situations and circumstances other than those encompassed by the specific testing occasion and measure. Richard Shavelson, Noreen Webb, and Glen Rowley (1989) discuss generalizability theory in a clear and nontechnical fashion and convey what the approach adds conceptually to measurement evaluation.

BASIC CONCEPTS AND
DESIGN OF MEASURES

10

A PRIMER OF TESTING

BERT F. GREEN

Measurement in the physical sciences is now a fairly straightforward matter. With few exceptions, if a unit of measurement can be agreed upon, actual physical measurements are precise and uncontroversial. No one argues over the physical concepts of length, volume, mass, and momentum, nor is there serious disagreement over how these concepts should be measured.

In the social and behavioral sciences, however, the situation is fundamentally different. There is controversy not only about how concepts should be measured and the precision of those measurements, but there is also considerable controversy over the meaning of the constructs themselves. *Intelligence*, for example, as a concept or psychological construct, has no universally agreed upon definition among psychologists and educators. The measurement of intelligence is correspondingly problematic.

If we were to measure a person's height in the way that we must now

Reprinted from the *American Psychologist, 36*, 1001–1011. Copyright 1981 by the American Psychological Association.

measure psychological constructs, we would have to ask if the person was taller than a doorway, a car, a table lamp, a filing cabinet, and so on. Relative height could actually be measured by a series of such questions, and to do so would raise all of the questions to be discussed in the following articles.

A standardized test is a task or a set of tasks given under standard conditions and designed to assess some aspect of a person's knowledge, skill, or personality. A test provides a scale of measurement for consistent individual differences regarding some psychological concept and serves to line up people according to that concept. Tests can be thought of as yardsticks, but they are less efficient and reliable than yardsticks, just as the concept of verbal reasoning ability is more complex and less well understood than the concept of length. A test yields one or more objectively obtained quantitative scores, so that as nearly as possible, each person is assessed in the same way. The intent is to provide a fair and equitable comparison among test takers. In college admission or employee selection, for example, tests provide a common measure for all applicants. Techniques of constructing, evaluating, and using tests are well developed, and will be presented here in brief. More of the widely used standardized tests are made by professional testing agencies who all use essentially the procedures described here for constructing tests. These procedures have been developed and proven over many years, and they are generally applicable to a wide variety of tests, but the focus here will be on standardized, cognitive, multiple-choice tests.

This primer is intended for the reader who may not be familiar with basic concepts in tests and measurement. The majority of psychologists and educational researchers will be quite familiar with its contents. For readers desiring additional information, many good books provide more extensive treatment. Cronbach (1970) and Anastasi (1968) give good general discussions. For encyclopedic treatment, see *Educational Measurement*, edited by Thorndike (1971). Allen and Yen (1979) provide a good introduction to technical issues, and thorough advanced treatment of technical matters can be found in Lord and Novick (1968).

STATISTICS

A test is an actuarial instrument; it must be interpreted in terms of averages and probabilities. Saying that a student with a Scholastic Aptitude Test (SAT) score of 300 will fail at Harvard is like saying that a person who smokes four packs of cigarettes per day will die by the age of 60. Each is a good bet, but each is a statistical statement about averages and must be interpreted in the light of other information and with an appreciation of the uniqueness of each individual. Since the tests are actuarial, statistical methods must be used to assess their performance. A brief guide to statistical terminology will help.

When a test has been given to a group of persons and scored, the scores can be sorted and tallied in a *distribution* that shows how many people earned each possible score. The average score, or *mean*, of the score distribution is an index of the central tendency of the scores in the distribution. Individual scores deviate either upwards or downwards from the mean. The *standard deviation* is an index of the average amount of deviation, or spread, of the scores away from the mean. To compute this index, the individual deviations are squared and averaged, yielding the *variance*. The square root of the variance is the *standard deviation*. In the *normal* distribution, which is a particular mathematical form that often closely approximates actual score distributions, about two thirds of the scores deviate less than one standard deviation from the mean, and about 95% of the scores are within two standard deviations. Thus a normally distributed test with a mean score of 50 and a standard deviation of 10 will have about two thirds of its scores between 40 and 60, and about 95% of its scores between 30 and 70.

Scores on most ordinary tests, like the College Board's SAT, tend to have distributions that are slightly flatter than the normal form (with not quite as many scores near the mean), slightly more scores from one to two standard deviations from the mean, and fewer very extreme values, since, of course, the scores are limited by the number of items on the test. This shape results partly from the use of items that vary in difficulty; if all the items had about the same degree of difficulty, the distribution would be more nearly normal. Further, if most of the test items are too easy for the population of persons taking the test, the score distribution will be *negatively skewed*, with a concentration of high scores and a smattering of low scores. By contrast, a *positively skewed* score distribution results when the test is too difficult, so that most of the scores are low, with a smattering of high ones. In ordinary circumstances, the test will be appropriate to the population, so its score distribution will not be skewed, and it will not be much flatter than a normal distribution. The normal shape may be usually assumed, at least as a first approximation. In that case, the mean and standard deviation will serve to characterize the distribution.

A statistic is needed to characterize the relationship between two tests, or between a test and some other measure of performance, such as school grades, supervisor's ratings, and the like. The correlation coefficient, r, is the index commonly used. It is a ratio-like quantity, without units, with a maximum of 1 and a minimum of -1; r indicates the extent to which two measures tend to vary together. The index is positive when high scores on one measure tend to be accompanied by high scores on the other: $r = 1$ when the two tests give exactly comparable scores for each person in a population; $r = -1$ when there is a perfect negative relationship, with the highest score on one test corresponding to the lowest score on the other. When there is no degree of relationship between the tests, $r = 0$. Further properties of r will be discussed in considering reliability and validity, but suffice it to say that when comparing scores on two tests that supposedly measure the same thing, we would expect r to be at least .8 and would much prefer an r above .9. When comparing test scores with performance measures, like average college grades, we would expect rs in the range of .2 to .7. When $r = .2$, the relation is weak, when $r = .7$, the relation is moderately strong.

Although correlation is widely used, it has one unfortunate property—its size depends to some extent on the variability of the two measures being correlated. Two tests that correlate very well in a population with heterogeneous scores will not correlate as well in a population for which the test scores are more homogeneous. The effect is more pronounced when the correlation is high. Suppose the correlation between a math test and a verbal ability test is .5 in a heterogeneous population. If we remove everyone who scores below the mean on either test, the correlation of the tests determined from the remaining, severely restricted group is likely to fall to .1 or .2; thus, correlation must always be interpreted with respect to group variability.

KINDS OF TESTS

The multiple-choice pencil-and-paper test is the most common type of test, but other types are also used. Some free-answer tests are designed to elicit a list of words or phrases from the test taker. For example, one test of creativity asks for a list of different uses for a brick. Other tests have questions requiring a sentence or two as an answer. Essay questions require longer compositions. Performance tests are also common. For example, manual dexterity is usually tested by requiring manipulation of small objects, and a typing test may require that a document be typed.

Multiple-choice tests are preferred, where possible, because of the speed and objectivity with which they can be scored. A machine or a clerk with a list of the correct choices (a *key*) can score the test answers with little effort. The main disadvantage is the difficulty of preparing good items (the syntactically neutral term *item* is preferred to *question*, since most multiple-choice "questions" are actually declarative sentences). Many items are needed, since one item can usually cover only a small part of a given topic.

Shakespeare's test for determining the worth of Portia's suitors in *The Merchant of Venice* (a single three-option item: gold, silver, lead) would be considered too short by modern standards. Three options are also too few; professionals prefer four or five options, to reduce the value of guessing.

Critics of multiple-choice items claim that only surface facts can be tested in this way, not deep understanding. Professional testers disagree; items probing understanding are possible, but they are certainly difficult to devise. Many of the items that authors supply to accompany their textbooks are shallow, often concerning definitions, for example:

> The mean of a set of values is
> (a) the lowest value
> (b) the average value
> (c) the middle value
> (d) the most frequent value.

By contrast, consider:

> The correlation of SAT-verbal or SAT-math among all test-takers is about .5. For the group of applicants admitted to Harvard, the correlation is probably
> (a) greater than .5
> (b) about .5
> (c) less than .5
> (d) anything—there is no basis for a guess.

The students will have to reason that, since Harvard is a very selective school, the admitted group will have relatively homogeneous test scores, so the correlation will be less than in the national group. Probing items can be written about almost any subject, given enough time and thought.

A related criticism is that the very best students can often find some truth in an incorrect option or can find some fault with a supposedly correct option. Such items exist, although they are sufficiently rare that when they do occur they are news (Fiske, 1981). Number-series items are disconcerting to mathematicians. They claim that the next number in the series 1, 3, 5, 7, 9 could be 11, 63, 101, or any other number whatever. Testers argue that a good student would consider the general context and easily recognize that the "best" answer is 11. It is of course necessary that no other "obvious" rule will work, but arguments will seldom resolve such issues. Empirical data are needed. That is why items should be pretested by giving them to a group similar to the target population to see if most of the better students choose the keyed option and to see that none of the *distractors* (as incorrect options are called) are in fact selected by otherwise top scorers. If a distractor is popular with better students, the item must be revised or discarded.

Essay items are easy to prepare, but they are devilishly difficult to score objectively, as anyone who has ever tried knows. Even when strict criteria are established for what the essay must contain, many borderline answers will arise. Essay items are not immune from other flaws. They are sometimes misinterpreted, even by top students. Nor do essay items necessarily probe more deeply; presumably they offer the student the opportunity to display deep understanding, but some students will decline the offer and stay on the surface.

Nevertheless, the main problem with essay tests is consistent scoring. A famous example is the English Essay examination in the College Board's series of college entrance tests. Most people believe that the only way to test writing ability is to have students write. Further, college officials reason that if they require such a test, the secondary schools will have to teach composition. But scoring the English Essay Test has been a technical challenge. Hundreds of English teachers must be hired and brought together to evaluate the essays, following very detailed, strict criteria. Various quality controls are instituted and work is carefully supervised and checked. Yet, despite these considerable efforts, the essay scores are considerably less reliable than multiple-choice test scores. In fact, grades in college composition courses can be predicted at least as well by the SAT-V, a multiple-choice test of general verbal skill, and by objective tests of rhetoric. Consequently, the essay test has had a yo-yo existence over the years— used for a while, then abandoned, then reintroduced. Its main value has been its effect on curricula; its immediate practical value has been far less evident.

The English Essay Test exemplifies a general problem with any educational test that is singled out for special attention. The danger is that the test, or its absence, will influence the curriculum. Teachers may teach to the tests rather than teaching the subject matter. This problem is especially acute with minimum-competency tests for high school graduation. Excessive emphasis on these tests will help the poor student, but will not challenge the good student. Tests lose their value as measuring instruments under these circumstances. As a rule, a test measures best when it is used incidentally, in a nonreactive way.

Some tests are not professionally made and do not enjoy the advantages of the many careful procedures to be discussed below. Classroom tests may be adequate, but they are seldom up to professional standards. When I make a test for my statistics class, I cannot pretest all of the items, although I use some good items from earlier years. I don't have time to write dozens of deeply probing items or to develop elaborate standards for the consistent scoring of the essay questions. Magazines take even less care in their "tests" of marital compatibility, happiness, and the like, which may be tests by definition, but which have none of the properties of good tests. They generally have no theoretical basis and no empirical utility.

The testing profession has set up its own standards for good testing practice. The American Psychological Association, the American Educational Research Association, and the National Council on Measurement in Education have jointly established and published these standards (1974). A revision of these standards is currently in progress (see Novick, this issue). The most important standard states that "for each test there should be a test manual, perhaps with supplements, to provide enough information for a qualified user to make sound judgments regarding the usefulness and interpretation of test scores. Research is required prior to the release of the test or test scores for operational use" (APA, 1974, p. 5).

ATTRIBUTES OF TEST SCORES

For scores on a test to be useful, they must be both reliable and valid. Reliability refers to repeatability and stability of scores. Any measurement has some error. A student will not get exactly the same score on supposedly equivalent tests of verbal ability, just as his or her weight will not be exactly the same from day to day or from scale to scale. Reliability is assessed by correlating students' test scores with their scores on a replica or repetition of the test.

Validity assesses the extent to which the scores are related to other behaviors of interest. We measure the student's verbal ability or the applicant's typing speed because we suppose the measures will be related to future performance as a student or as a secretary, respectively. Validity is the ultimate index of utility, but validity is impossible without reliability. The extent to which test scores correlate with another measure depends on the extent to which the test and the other measure share common elements or require common skills. The measure that shares most with the test score is a replica of itself. Hence the validity of a test is limited by its reliability.

Reliability

One logical way to establish the reliability of a test score is to construct an equivalent (or "parallel") test, to give both tests to the same set of people, and to correlate the scores. A correlation of 1.0 would mean that the relative standing of the persons was exactly the same on the two tests. We cannot expect 1.0 on cognitive tests, but reliabilities above .90 are frequent.

In practice, a duplicate test is seldom administered, because of the possible fatigue of the test takers and because of the need to prepare two complete tests. Various alternatives are used, each appropriate for some kinds of tests. In the *test–retest* procedure, the same test is administered twice at different times to the same people, with the hope that at the second testing they will not remember either the items or their earlier responses. A test of physical endurance can be assessed in this way, if the two testing occasions are far enough apart for physical recovery, and not so far apart that the test takers can practice the task much or develop their endurance. In the *split-halves* procedure, the test is divided into two halves that are matched as well as possible and timed separately. This differs from the ideal case only in the lengths of the halves. Classical test theory provides the Spearman–Brown formula $R = 2r/(1 + r)$, by which the reliability of the total test, R, can be inferred from the correlation of the two halves, r.

The Spearman–Brown formula is one of many formulas that can be derived from the classical theory of mental tests first developed near the beginning of this century. This theory holds that a test score, x, has two additive components, an error component, e, representing variable error in a person's test responses, and a true component, t, representing the person's true score, devoid of random error. The true score is a hypothetical construct; it cannot be observed. It is defined to be independent of the errors, from which it follows that the variance of x is the sum of the variances of t and e. Two parallel tests have the same t but different es. When the test length is doubled by adding two parallel tests, the true score will simply be doubled; since the errors will tend to cancel each other out to some extent, the longer test will be more reliable, as the Spearman–Brown formula dictates.

Sometimes the two halves are not separately timed or separated in any other way; the items are simply divided into two sets after the test has been given. An automatic procedure is to split the odd-numbered items from the even-numbered items to get two half-test scores. The lack of separate timing is not critical unless there is substantial time pressure in the testing situation. For example, if college students were given a test consisting of two-digit addition problems $(12 + 25 = \_\_)$ with a short time limit, there would not be many errors, but some people would be able to work much faster than others. An odd-even split would give an over-estimate of the reliability. To see this, note that if there are *no* errors, the odd–even reliability would be 1.0, whereas parallel-form reliability would probably be smaller.

Another popular method of assessing reliability is based on the intercorrelation of the individual items on a test. Classical test theory can be applied at the item level. Each item can be viewed as a miniature test, with true and error components. The errors are not supposed to be correlated, so the item intercorrelations depend only on the true component. It follows that the reliability can be deduced from the intercorrelations among the items. The resulting reliability coefficient is called *alpha*.

The logic of alpha implies that if a test is long enough, its items do not have to intercorrelate very highly. In fact, on a 50-item test with a reliability of .90, the average item intercorrelation is only .15. That is, each individual item is mostly error. A test gains its reliability and its power by adding up a large number of homogeneous items. Flaws in individual items take on less importance in this context. Of course each item should be carefully designed and as good as possible, but no single item can ever do very much good or very much harm. Tests work by the weight of numbers. Multiple-choice tests can generally take more advantage of the weight of numbers that can essay tests, because multiple-choice tests usually have many more items.

Critics who are concerned about one or two particular items on a test miss the point. A poor item is likely to be completely uncorrelated with the other items, in which case it adds only error. Thus, a poor item reduces reliability, but otherwise does not distort test scores. Even good items can be criticized. Each item is of necessity particular. Journalists sometimes argue that a student's prospects are not much related to whether he or she knows the meaning of *archaic*, or some other particular word. This is true, but one item does not make a test. A student who does not know several particular words may well be a student with a limited vocabulary, and one who may be at a disadvantage in college or work when compared to the student who knows many more words. The fact that one item does little by itself is the main reason why professional testers eschew fixed cutting scores. Sometimes, as in competency tests, the situation forces establishment of a cutoff score, but since one item may well make the difference between passing or failing the cutoff, fixed cutting scores are to be avoided whenever possible.

Reliability is a correlation that, as noted above, is affected by group heterogeneity. A more nearly invariant index is the *standard error of measurement*, which indicates the extent to which test scores would vary if the test were repeated. In principle, if a person were to take many equivalent forms of a test, these scores would have a distribution around the person's "true" or average score. The standard deviation of the distribution of scores for that person is the standard error of measurement. Given an observed score on a test, the person's true score will be within one standard error of that observed score about two times out of three. For example, the SAT has a standard error of measurement of 30, so a score of 650 could just as easily have been 620 or 680, and it might even have been as low as 600 or as high as 700.

The standard error of measurement must be modified to answer a slightly different question: If a person takes the test twice, how big a difference in test scores can be expected? The standard deviation of a difference between two scores is 1.4 times the standard error of measurement. If the standard error of measurement is 30, and a person's test score is 600, the chances are 2 to 1 that the true score is between 570 and 630. But the chances are also 2 to 1 that if the person takes the test again, the second test score will be between 558 and 642. The larger interval occurs because there is error in both test scores, whereas in comparing a test score with a true score, the test score has error, but the true score has no error.

Validity

The validity of a test refers to many aspects of its use and definition, but the central feature is the correlation of the test with some other behavior of interest, such as performance in college or on the job. If a test is not reliable, it cannot be valid, because a test that does not correlate with itself cannot correlate with anything else. But a reliable test need not be valid. Validity also differs from reliability in that it is specific to some purpose. A test can be reliable in general—relative to the intended population of test takers. But a test cannot be valid in general; it is valid for a purpose. Indeed, a test may be both valid and not valid. For example, skill at algebra may be a valid predictor of science and math grades, but may not be valid for history or English.

Correlational validity is generally determined as follows. First, a group of applicants is tested. Second, some are then admitted or hired. Third, a measurement of performance, such as first-year grades or supervisory rating, is obtained. Fourth, the correlation between test scores and performance is found. There are several problems with this obvious procedure. First, the numbers of cases may be small. A solid base for a correlation is a group of 100 or more cases. Some credence can be given to correlations based on about 50 cases, but little weight can be given to a correlation based on less than 20 cases. The problem is simple: The sort of potential that is measured by tests is only one of many influences on performance. Many of these influences are idiosyncratic and will tend to balance out in a large group of cases, but when n is small, not all the individual effects are offset.

A second problem is the performance measure, often called the criterion. Like the test, it should be reliable and relevant. Most performance measures are much less reliable than the tests they are validating. An unreliable criterion is just as limiting as an unreliable test. The difference is that you know where you stand with an unreliable test (in need of a better test), but when the criterion is unreliable, the test may or may not be valid—there is no way to tell until a better criterion is found.

Perhaps the biggest problem with correlational validity is that the selection of acceptable applicants is likely to be made on the basis of the test scores, so the range of scores is limited as well as the range of performance. As noted above, the size of the correlation shrinks when the group variability is restricted. If poor scorers had also been selected and poor performance tolerated, a wide range of test scores and criterion measures would have been obtained, and the correlational validity would have been much higher. The problem is even more severe if there is competition for the most well-qualified applicants so that the best applicants are enticed elsewhere, thus selecting themselves out of the pool.

Validity can be assessed in other ways. *Face validity* means simply that the test appears, on the face of it, to be relevant to the performance (cf. Cole, this issue). A typing test has face validity for secretaries, but not for firefighters. *Content validity* involves a more detailed analysis of the skills measured by the test and the skills required for good performance in a particular job. For example, a test of quantitative ability might have predictive validity for selecting police officers, but unless it can be demonstrated that an important part of a police officer's job involves the use of the particular skills included in the test, the test would not be content valid. A test of quantitative ability might include arithmetic operations, simple algebra, and an understanding of graphs, with each of these categories possibly divided more finely. The nature of the police officer's job can also be analyzed into particulars. Assessing content validity involves matching the two sets of particulars.

Finally, a test has *construct validity* if the concept it is said to measure (verbal reasoning, for example) can be shown to make scientific and conceptual sense. This is usually done by examining the pattern of relationships of the test in question with tests measuring other constructs. Thus, if verbal reasoning is a meaningful concept, it should be strongly related to tests of reading comprehension, moderately related to vocabulary tests, mildly related to quantitative skills, and not at all related to physical strength.

It is sometimes argued (see Schmidt & Hunter, this issue) that tests of certain constructs are valid for certain species of jobs or schools because the construct is demonstrably or logically inherent in the expected performance. Verbal reasoning, for example, is logically inherent in almost all forms of academic endeavor and could be considered inherently valid for such activities. This is not what is meant by construct validity; rather, it is a species of content validity that presupposes valid constructs. In fact, verbal reasoning is demonstrably (as well as logically) valid for many academic pursuits, but it has less relevance in some branches of science and engineering. In fact, verbal reasoning is usually found to have at least moderate correlational validity for almost every kind of activity. Psychologists who believe that intelligence is unitary explain that verbal reasoning is the central core of intelligence. Psychologists who believe that intelligence has many facets are more suspicious. One reason for the ubiquity of verbal reasoning is that academic performance and job performance are often assessed by pencil-and-paper tests so that verbal reasoning is indeed a part of the performance measure, because of the way it is evaluated. Job performance is sometimes measured by success in on-the-job training programs that involve the usual verbally oriented academic training procedures. That is, the verbal reasoning construct can easily be an incidental component of the performance criterion. In general, it is wise to look behind the correlations.

BUILDING A TEST

Test construction involves first specifying the content of the test and then preparing a large number of items covering the specified content. A short test is not likely to be very reliable, since, as noted above, no one item does very much work. Furthermore, many more items must be written than will finally be used. Each item must be checked, edited, screened, and pretested, and some of them will not pass muster.

The items must first be checked by specialists in that subject matter, and the answers verified. Then the items should be edited for clarity, style, and brevity. Finally, they should be screened for bias and offensiveness, as well as for overspecialized content. Bias is a very complex issue (see Cole, this issue); here it simply refers to items involving incidental information that is much less familiar to one segment of the population than to another. An arithmetic item about golf scores assuming the knowledge that the lowest score wins might be biased against inner-city students; an item requiring the knowledge that a manhole cover is extremely heavy might be biased against rural children. Of course, an item has to have some content, and variety will tend to balance such factors, but narrowly based content should be avoided. Screening is necessary not only for political and cosmetic reasons, but mainly to avoid disturbing some test takers as they are taking the test, which would put them at a disadvantage and distort the test scores. Screening is best done by specialists who are especially sensitive to the issues. Few whites will notice all the aspects of items that bother blacks, just as few men will notice sexist terms.

Screened and edited items must then be pretested. Good judgment is dandy, but the proof is in the pudding. Pretesting means giving the items to test takers under conditions as nearly like the real test as possible. Ongoing testing programs simply put the new items into an actual test, either intermingled with the regular items or in a separate section. The items being pretested do not, of course, contribute to the test score, but merely provide data for item evaluation. Further, in large testing programs, not all candidates need to respond to each pretest item; a sample of 1,000 is considered adequate, so a large testing program can prepare many different versions of a test booklet, each with a different set of pretest items. When candidates discover, in their postmortem discussions, that they have seen different items, pretesting or equating (discussed below) is the reason.

Pretesting permits the assessment of the difficulty level and the discriminating power of each item. If a test is to be used as an aid in college admissions and employment selection, an item that is too easy or too hard is wasted, as is an item that does not discriminate between good and poor candidates. The index of difficulty is based on the proportion, p, of persons who answer the item correctly. (A transform of p is sometimes used.) Item discrimination is often expressed as the correlation between success on the item and score on the test as a whole; this index essentially checks whether this item is measuring the same thing that the other test items are measuring.

A third aspect of the item is the relative attractiveness of the distractors. One way to check this is to count the number of persons who chose a particular option and obtain the mean test score of those persons. An option that is never chosen should probably be replaced, and an incorrect option that is preferred by otherwise top-scoring students must be replaced.

Items that have passed the above hurdles can be included in the test. When the test is assembled, balanced coverage of topics must be checked. If item analysis has discarded all the items on an important topic, more items will have to be devised. Also, the easier items should come first and the positions of the correct option must be balanced. It will not do to have the correct choice always be c. The assembler must also check that the answer to one item is not disclosed in the stem of another item.

TEST ADMINISTRATION

When a test is to be given in more than a single location at more than one time, similarity of testing conditions is essential. Everyone must have an equal chance. Everyone should have a quiet environment, adequate light, a comfortable work space, and equivalent resources. Above all, everyone must have exactly the same amount of time to work on the test. When there are several parts of a test, proctors must ensure that students work only on the designated part in the given time.

A major problem arises for some handicapped students. Test booklets can be prepared in braille, in large type, or on audiocassettes for visually impaired students. There is no good way to equate testing conditions for these persons—generally, time constraints are relaxed considerably, but there is no assurance that the resulting test scores are comparable to scores of students tested under standard conditions.

Some tests, like the Stanford-Binet and the Wechsler intelligence tests, are administered individually; the tester must follow a carefully prescribed regimen in a reasonable environment. Some of the items may be of the free-answer type, in which case the tester must judge the response according to specified criteria. Sometimes this is easy, sometimes not. The Rorschach inkblot test of personality, for example, is relative easy to administer, but quite difficult to score reliably.

TEST SCORING

Free-answer items must be scored manually, whereas multiple-choice tests can be scored by machine. The machines rarely make errors, although quality control is necessary. Machines can, for example, score batches of answer sheets twice, using different settings for the required blackness of the marks. Studies show that machines, like human scorers, are mainly troubled by messy answer sheets on which the marks are actually ambiguous.

Guessing on multiple-choice tests is a quite different problem. If the test score is simply the number of items answered correctly, then candidates should mark an answer for every item; that is, they should guess. Random guessing increases the amount of error in a test score, and thus decreases reliability. One way to discourage random guessing is to tell the candidates that the number of right answers will be adjusted by the number of wrong answers. The correction is based on the assumption that a person either knows the right answer or guesses blindly. Since a blind guess on a five-option item will be right one time in five, there will be four wrong guesses to every right guess, on the average. Thus the expected number of right guesses is $\frac{1}{4}$ of the wrong guesses. Since by assumption all the wrong responses are guesses, the expected number of right guesses is $\frac{1}{4}$ of the number of wrong responses, so the score "corrected for guessing" is Rights minus $\frac{1}{4}$ Wrongs, $(R - W/4)$. In general, for k options the formula score is $R - W/(k-1)$.

The test takers must be told how their scores will be determined, and they should be given instructions about guessing that are consistent with the procedure that will be used. Since a test taker could be intimidated by the threat to penalize wrong responses, an exactly equivalent procedure that discourages guessing in a less punitive way has been devised. The candidates are told that they need not guess, since the official scorer will "guess" for them, crediting them with ⅕ (1/k in general) point for each item omitted. Since Rights plus Wrongs plus Omits equals N, the fixed number of items, it is easy to show that the formula R + O/k is equivalent to R − W/(k − 1), in the sense of giving scores that are perfectly correlated. Further, a more reasonable assumption can be made about guessing. The candidate is assumed to answer the test by using whatever misinformation or partial information he or she has, but omits certain items under formula-scoring directions, and answers them at random under "number right" directions.

Expert opinion differs from about procedure is fairer to all the candidates. Certainly a test taker's strategy should differ depending on whether the final score will be number right or one of the adjusted scores. Will all test takers be equally able to adapt their strategies? It is reasonable to assume that the low-scoring candidates are of most concern. The high scorers will know most of the answers, and so will have little need to guess. Further, the high scorers are more likely to be able to adjust their behavior to the instructions. By contrast, the low scorers are in trouble—they have plenty of opportunity to guess because they are sure of few of the answers, but they may be too unsure of themselves to guess. Many of their wrong responses will not be guesses; they will be the result of confusion or misinformation. Perhaps it is unfair to assume that they are guessing, even if it is to their advantage to do so. The dilemma of which instructions to give has no good, logical solution. Research results are also equivocal. The question deserves further study.

Scaled Scores

The number of items answered correctly is called the *rights score*; the guessing adjustment yields a *formula score*. Both are called *raw scores*. Neither provides a useful scale of measurement for a test. The percent correct is not much better; despite pretesting, a test may be too hard or too easy, so 80% could be a good, bad, or indifferent score. The test score acquires meaning from some external referent, which may be an absolute standard, as in competency tests, or only relative standing, as in most academic admissions and employment tests.

An absolute standard is difficult to specify because expert judgments are required. Experts must consider not only desired level of competence, but also the distribution of actual performance on the test in some relevant group and the nature of measurement error. Probably each item on the test should be readily answered by any competent person, yet competent people will misread questions and make other mistakes, so perfect test performance is not to be expected. (For a discussion of standard-setting issues in competency-based measurement, see Shepard, 1980.)

The two major ways to indicate relative standing are *percentiles* and *standard scores*. The percentile equivalent of a raw score is the percentage of persons who scored at or below that value. Percentiles have descriptive merit, but they have the difficulty that a difference between the 50th and 55th percentiles is a much smaller difference, in terms of raw score units, than is the difference between the 90th and 95th percentiles. This occurs because there are many more persons with scores in the vicinity of the 50th percentile than in the vicinity of the 90th. The raw score scale is humped in the middle and spread out near the extremes.

A standard score scale uses the standard deviation of the score distribution to set the unit. Raw scores are multiplied by the ratio of the specified standard deviation of the raw score distribution and then a constant is added to all scores so that the mean score has some convenient value. On a standard score scale, each additional item correctly answered provides the same increment in scaled score. The unit of measurement is related to the standard deviation of the scores. Statisticians would be happy with a scale that had a mean of 0 and a standard deviation of 1, but trying to explain a score of -1.20 to a candidate would be awkward. A scale with a mean of 50 and a standard deviation of 10 is a happier choice. The IQ scale has a mean of 100 and a standard deviation of 15. This scale can be misleading. (I once overheard a mother boasting of her son's IQ score of 88, "because 100 is as high as you can get.") Many tests, such as the SAT, use a scale with a mean of 500 and a standard deviation of 100. The scores on this scale cannot be mistaken for a percent-correct score, but they give the illusion of far greater precision than they enjoy; the illusion is not completely destroyed by setting the last digit always to zero. The standard error of measurement of the SAT is about 30, which means, for example, that if a person's "true" score is 600, his or her actual score can easily be anywhere from 570 to 630, and one third of the time it will be even more deviant.

Sometimes scores can best be interpreted not with reference to the groups who took the test, but with reference to a random or representative sample of some known group. Where an applicant stands with respect to all high school seniors will be quite different from where he or she stands with respect to all college applicants, or all applicants to four-year colleges. Score distributions for specified groups are called *norms*, and they are extremely useful in interpreting test scores.

Some procedures stretch and shrink the raw score scale here and there to force the score distribution to match a normal distribution exactly, on the ground that ability is normally distributed in nature. That ground is slippery—for what group would the normal distribution be natural?

Grade equivalents, or the similar concept of age equivalents, are attempts to indicate how advanced or retarded a student is with respect to schoolmates or to national samples of school children. By this scale distortion, the average raw score obtained by eighth-graders becomes an 8, the average raw score obtained by ninth-graders becomes a 9, and so on. Grade-equivalence scales depend on the particular curriculum in different grades and on promotion practices; the units depend strongly on the correlation of age or grade level with performance. When this correlation is low, small differences in raw test scores become amplified into large differences in grade equivalents. Some experts find grade-equivalent scales useful; others argue that a more appropriate comparison is the students' relative standing in their own grade, or in some other specified narrative group.

Equating

A severe scale problem arises when equivalent tests are to be given year after year, as in the common academic admissions tests. In this case, it is not appropriate to restandardize each time the test is given. Rather, the problem is to ensure that the same score, say 500, indicates the same ability that it did last year and the year before. The referent group is a set of test takers many years ago, when the test was first standardized. Each year, scores must be adjusted so that scores are equated for ability. Of course, scores are not directly equated with scores of 35 years ago. Rather, scores on this year's forms are equated to scores on last year's forms, which in turn had been equated to the previous years, etc. To forestall the scale from gently drifting year by year, equating can be done to two forms from different earlier years. This process becomes an elaborate statistical maze, but it can be done quite successfully.

Several procedures are currently used. The simplest way to equate a new form is to alternate the new form with one or more old forms at a single test administration, thus obtaining equivalent samples of candidates taking each of the forms. If a large number of students takes each form, then the scale (i.e., the mean and standard deviation) of the scaled scores on the new form can be set equal to the means and standard deviations of the scaled scores obtained at this time on the old forms. Note that a test given at one time cannot be equated in this simple way with a test given at a different time because the persons choosing to take the test at one time might (and generally do) differ from those taking the test at another time.

A more complicated procedure can be used without the need for several samples. Some items from earlier forms are included in each new test form. In essence, each person takes two tests—a short replica of the earlier form, and the new form, thus providing the needed comparison for the adjustment.

Both equating procedures require secure, undisclosed old forms or old items. If tests must be disclosed shortly after their use, much more costly, elaborate, and possibly less reliable equating methods are needed.

Equating works. A thorough statistical study of SAT scores over the past 20 years permits the conclusion that the observed decline in mean test scores is not due to any drift in equating, but is a real decline. The decline is partly due to a change in the college-bound population, the original standardization group having been rather elite. But changes in that population have been minimal in recent years, and the SAT scores have still continued to decline. Presumably a variety of societal factors are implicated in the more recent decline. Speculation is fruitless; we only know that the decline is not an artifact.

In considering mean declines, it is important to distinguish between the reliability of a single score and the reliability of an average. The standard error of measurement for a single score is about 30. Smaller score changes are not to be trusted. But the standard error of measurement of a mean of 100 scores is only 3, since the reduction is proportional to the square root of the number of scores being averaged. A mean of 10,000 cases is accurate to within .3 score points. Thus a mean drop of 5 points is a definite, statistically significant drop, whereas a change of 5 points in a single score would be of no consequence. (In fact, between 1967 and 1977, the mean score on the SAT declined by about 35 points, which is not only statistically significant, but large enough to be severely disturbing.)

SOME FUTURE PROSPECTS

Computers are beginning to play a larger role in testing. A computer can store a large collection of items and present them, one at a time, on a viewing screen. Efficiencies can come from *tailoring* the test to the candidate and not wasting time on items that are either too easy or too hard for a particular test taker. Tailored testing would represent a large change. With different candidates confronting different items, the test score cannot be the number of items correct—each item must be calibrated for difficulty. In essence, candidates would score more points for answering harder questions. The scores must also be adjusted for the fact that some items are more discriminating than others. The details of such procedures are available, but not much experience has accrued yet.

Equating tailored tests requires a new approach to the definition of the scale of the ability being tested. Classical test theory is not adequate to this task, and a new theory called Item Response Theory (IRT) is replacing it. Central to IRT is the notion that persons at any fixed level of "ability" have a certain probability, p, of responding correctly to a given item. As ability rises, so does p, the probability of being correct. The curve relating the probability of correct response to the ability level is called the item response curve, or item characteristic curve. Choosing a particular form for this curve fixes the scale. The form usually chosen is the cumulative logistic curve, which is nearly identical to the cumulative normal distribution and is mathematically more tractable. Each curve, and therefore each item, has two parameters: its difficulty, which can be specified as the ability level where $p, = .5$, and its discrimination (i.e., how fast the probability p changes with ability). Persons of very high ability are assumed to be virtually certain of answering correctly ($p = 1$), but at the low end of the scale, guessing must be considered. For items with five response options, the lowest possible p could be set at .2, on the grounds that in the absence of information, people guess. But the lowest possible probability can be left as a third parameter to be determined by the test data. A seductively simple version of IRT, called the Rasch model, ignores guessing and also assumes that all item curves have the same discrimination, thus differing only in difficulty. This simple model is adequate in some cases, but the more elaborate models will probably be preferred in general.

Some experimental psychologists have reasoned that answering a test item is a cognitive task and should be amenable to laboratory analysis. A clearer understanding of the item solving process should provide new insights into the nature of ability and its assessment (see Sternberg, this issue).

Testing has been one of the most successful applied enterprises in psychology. Perhaps its weakest aspect is the relative lack of progress over the past decades. With few exceptions, we are testing the same old things in the same old ways with the same moderate success. But today, testing is facing many difficult challenges. Large differences in test performance by different ethnic groups, especially blacks, have sparked claims of test bias. Consumer groups advocate disclosure of tests shortly after they have been used, thereby making the test process more "open," but also making tests more expensive to design and difficult to equate. Some tests are criticized for being susceptible to coaching. Competency testing has raised the problem of standard-setting. Tailored testing requires new scoring methods and new test theory. The guidance function of tests is not as well developed as the selection function. Such challenges are healthy. New problems have a way of invigorating a field, and testing is likely to prosper.

REFERENCES

Allen, M. J., & Yen, M. (1979). *Introduction to measurement theory*. Belmont, CA: Wadsworth.

American Psychological Association, American Educational Research Association, & National Council on Measurement in Education. (1974). *Standards for educational and psychological tests*. Washington, DC: American Psychological Association.

Anastasi, A. (1968). *Psychological testing* (3rd ed.). New York: Macmillan.

Cole, N. S. (1981). Bias in testing. *American Psychologist, 36,* 1067–1077.

Cronbach, L. J. (1970). *Essentials of psychological testing* (3rd ed.). New York: Harper & Row.

Fiske, E. B. (1981, March 17). Youth outwits merit exam, raising 240,000 scores. *New York Times*, pp. A1; C4.

Lord, F. M., & Novick, M. (1968). *The statistical theory of mental test scores*. Reading, MA: Addison-Wesley.

Novick, M. R. (1981). Federal guidelines and professional standards. *American Psychologist, 36,* 1035–1046.

Schmidt, F. L., & Hunter, J. E. (1981). Employment testing: Old theories and new research findings. *American Psychologist, 36,* 1128–1137.

Shepard, L. (1980). Standard setting issues and methods. *Applied Psychological Measurement, 4,* 447–467.

Sternberg, R. J. (1981). Testing and cognitive psychology. *American Psychologist, 36,* 1181–1189.

Thorndike, R. L. (Ed.). (1971). *Educational measurement* (2nd ed.). Washington, DC: American Council on Education.

11

SCALE CONSTRUCTION

RENÉ V. DAWIS

Scales are ubiquitous features of counseling psychology research. For instance, examination of a randomly chosen issue of the *Journal of Counseling Psychology* (1984, Vol. 31, No. 3) showed that all 12 major articles in the issue reported on studies that involved the use of scales.

As the term is used in counseling psychology research, a *scale* is a collection of items, the responses to which are scored and combined to yield a scale score. Scale scores can be categorized according to level of measurement. At the lowest, nominal level of measurement, scale scores are used to name or designate (identify) the classification categories to which the objects of measurement are grouped. At the ordinal level, scale scores rank order the measured objects along the classificatory dimension. At the interval level, scale scores reflect the relative distances between and among measured objects. At the ratio level, scale scores indicate the absolute

Reprinted from the *Journal of Counseling Psychology, 34,* 481–489. Copyright 1987 by the American Psychological Association.

distance of any measured object from a true-zero point on the scale. Few, if any, psychological scales are even-interval scales (Thomas, 1982).

Scales can also be classified according to the source of scale score variation, following Torgerson (1958), as stimulus-centered, subject-centered, or response scales. Scale scores in stimulus-centered scales (also called judgment scales) reflect stimulus (item) differences along the measurement dimension. An example would be a life events scale, in which a respondent rates or ranks particular life events in terms of respondent rates or ranks particular life events in terms of how stressful they are to the respondent. In contrast, for subject-centered scales (also called individual differences scales), scale scores reflect differences among the subjects (respondents) in terms of their standing along the scale's dimension. Personality trait scales of the inventory or questionnaire variety are common examples of subject-centered scales. Lastly, response scales are those for which scale score variation is attributed to both stimuli (items) and subjects (respondents). Scales constructed according to the Rasch scaling methodology (Wright & Masters, 1982) are examples of response scales.

For the purposes of this article, the term *scale* will be limited to those instruments that are constructed by researchers in order to obtain quantitative data on variables for which appropriate standardized instruments are not available. Examples of such variables are counselee and counselor perceptions (cognitions), evaluations, feelings, attitudes, plans, and actions (behaviors) as these occur before, during, and after the counseling process. To instrument such variables, researchers have often had to construct their own scales. Typically, such scales rely on the research participant's verbal report, and response by the participant is structured, that is, limited to given choices. This article focuses, therefore, on the construction of verbal, structured scales of the rating, questionnaire, or inventory type. I do not discuss the construction of tests or what Cronbach (1984) calls measures of maximum performance (i.e., ability, aptitude, achievement, knowledge, or skill tests), for which a large literature is available.

The scale construction process may be divided into three stages: design, development, and evaluation. Each stage is discussed in turn.

SCALE DESIGN

Designing a scale requires, first of all, some theory of the scale that includes a well-articulated definition of the psychological variable to be measured and indications of how it is to be measured. Definition of the variable depends on the larger theory that impels the research. Definition includes distinctions (what the variable is and what it is not), dependencies (how the variable is a function of more basic or previously defined terms), and relations (how the variable is related to other variables). How the variable is to be measured depends on a number of considerations, such as how best to represent the variable, who the respondents will be, the context and conditions under which the measure is to be administered, and the research design of the study, especially the analyses planned. In short, the theory of the scale should give the scale constructor directions as to scale content (the writing of items) as well as scale format (the type of scale to construct).

Scale Content

A useful preliminary to item writing is to conduct open-ended interviews with representative subjects from the target respondent population. Skillful interviewing can elicit a wide range of statements about the variable in question. The interviewee's own words can then be used in writing the items. Such use can provide a degree of authenticity that in turn can contribute to the scale's validity. For example, a scale to be filled out by clients to describe the counselor's behavior would be much more acceptable and credible to the clients if it were expressed in their (lay) language rather than in the more technical (if more precise) language of theory. Use of respondents' own words will also mean that readability of the scale will be less of a problem. Whether respondents' own words are used or not, it is good practice to check on the readability level of the scale to make sure that it is appropriate to the level of the respondent population. Useful hints on writing readable items are given by Payne (1951) and Fiske (1981).

The initial pool of items can be written to be homogeneous or heterogeneous in content. The scale design should indicate what degree of content heterogeneity is desired, based on the theory of the scale. A useful aid in this regard is to look at the scale data matrix as a two-factor, completely crossed with no replication analysis of variance design, in which the two factors are items and respondents. One can then see that, depending on the researcher's purposes, the scale can be so constructed as to maximize item effect only, respondent effect only, or item-by-respondent interaction. Maximizing item effect will require heterogeneous items; minimizing it will require homogeneous item content.

If items are explicitly derived from hypotheses from the larger theory, it might be useful to do a "back translation" (Smith & Kendall, 1963). That is, competent judges who were not involved in the writing of the items could be asked to assign the items back to the hypotheses or hypothesized categories. Back translation can be a useful check on the coverage of the content domain as outlined by the design of the scale.

Scale Format

Items in structured verbal scales typically consist of a stimulus part (the item stem) and a response part (the response choices). Item stems may consist of full sentences, phrases, or even single words. They may describe some attribute of an object (e.g., "The counselor appears trustworthy"), or the state of the object ("The counselor is passive"), or some event involving the object ("The counselor is reflecting the client's feelings"), to varying degrees of specificity or generality. Item stems ordinarily consist of single components but may have two or more components (as in paired comparison or multiple rank-order scales).

Response choices in structured verbal scales vary in their underlying measurement dimension (e.g., agree–disagree, like–dislike, important–unimportant). They also vary in response format. Rating response formats differ in the number of scale points (choices) given the respondents (2-, 3-, or 5-point scales are the most common), and in the way scale points are anchored. Anchors can be words (*yes–no, true–false*), phrases (*strongly agree–strongly disagree*), or more extended prose as in behaviorally anchored scales (e.g., Campbell, Dunnette, Arvey, & Hellervik, 1973). Rating scales may be anchored at each scale point or only at selected scale points (e.g., at the ends and the middle of the scale). Response choices may be unweighted (scored with 0, 1 weights), or weighted using multiple weights. Rating response formats may be one-sided (zero to positive or to negative values) or two-sided (with both positive and negative sides of the continuum).

Ranking response formats are fewer in number, differing only in the number of elements ranked within an item (e.g., paired comparison, multiple rank orders such as triads and tetrads, or, at the extreme, a single ranking of all elements). Ranking response formats use ranks rather than weights as scores and by convention, ranks are ordered in a manner opposite that of weights in the rating response format, that is, the lower the number, the higher the rank.

In choosing a scale format, the general rule might be to choose the simpler format. However, there are other considerations: More complex formats might make the task of filling out the scale more interesting for the more experienced or knowledgeable respondent. When rating response formats are used, more scale points are better than fewer, because once the data are in, one can always combine scale points to reduce their number, but one cannot increase that number after the fact. Also, more scale points can generate more variability in response, a desirable scale characteristic if the response is reliable. Inordinate use of the middlemost scale point can be avoided by eliminating that scale point, that is, by using an even number of scale points. This has the further advantage of ensuring that the underlying dimension will be linear or can be made linear. At times rank ordering may be easier to do than rating, but use of ranking response formats may place limits on the statistical analysis of the data. Finally, the amount of space available for the scale (e.g., in an extended questionnaire) might preclude the use of certain formats.

SCALE DEVELOPMENT

Scale development consists of collecting data with the use of a preliminary form and analyzing the data in order to select items for a more final form. ("More final" is intended to indicate that the process might have to undergo one or more iterations depending on the results of the evaluation stage.) It is always useful to conduct a small N pilot study before the main data collection effort. The pilot study can be used to check out such nuts-and-bolts points as how easily the scale instructions are followed, how well the scale format functions, how long the scale takes to complete, and especially, how appropriate the scale items are for the target respondent population.

As a rule, the development sample should be representative of the target respondent population. There can be exceptions, however; for example, in developing stimulus-centered scales, one could use a sample that is more homogeneous than samples from the target population.

At the heart of scale construction is the scaling method used to select items. Several methods are described, grouped according to the type of scale (stimulus-centered, subject-centered, or response) with which they are typically associated. A fourth group of methods, the external criterion methods, which select items on a different basis, are also described.

Stimulus-Centered Scale Methods

Because counseling psychology is concerned with the individual client, one might expect more frequent use of stimulus-centered scales than apparently is the case. How a particular client scales stimuli (e.g., stressfulness of life events, preference for occupations) regardless of how others do it should be just as significant for couseling as how the individual compares with others, if not more so. Stimulus-centered scales would appear to be particularly appropriate to use in monitoring the progress of the client during counseling.

The prototypic method for developing stimulus-centered scales was the Thurstone method (Thurstone & Chave, 1929). From this method developed the popular Q sort. Rank-order methods are also frequently used to construct stimulus-centered scales. Brief descriptions of these methods follow:

The Thurstone Method

Thurstone's groundbreaking insight was that questionnaires could be constructed as scales by the application of the methods of psychophysics. The Thurstone method proceeds as follows:

1. A large number of statements (say, 200 to 300) are written about the construct, to represent the range of the construct.

2. A number of judges (say, 20 to 30) are asked to sort the items with respect to the underlying measurement dimension and to assign an appropriate scale value (scale point on the numerical scale) to each item. An 11-point scale is typically used.

3. The central tendency and variability of scale values assigned to it are computed for each item.

4. On the basis of their average scale values, two or three items with the lowest variabilities are selected to represent each scale point. Thurstone scales typically have 22 items.

After the items have been selected, they are arranged in random fashion in a questionnaire. Respondents are instructed, for instance, in the case of an attitude scale, to identify those items that they endorse. (Similar instructions can be given for other types of scales, for example, identifying the items descriptive of self, or of another person being rated, or of the events being observed.) The scale score is calculated as the average of the scale values of the endorsed items.

The Thurstone method, although a historic methodological breakthrough, has not found much favor with scale constructors, and is practically unheard of in counseling psychology. Much better known is its derivative, the Q sort.

The Q-sort Method

The Q-sort method (Stephenson, 1953) has been used extensively in personality research, especially in research on the self-concept. The Q-sort method starts with a fixed set of stimuli (e.g., self-descriptive statements). The respondent is asked to sort the stimuli along a scale according to scale value (e.g., least to most descriptive). To ensure variability in the scores and to forestall response biases such as central tendency or leniency, the respondent might be asked to force the stimuli into a distribution, for example, for a 5-point scale, a 7%-24%-38%-24%-7% distribution.

The Q sort is useful in situations in which multiple response roles (positions) are taken with respect to the same set of stimuli (e.g., in self-concept research, "How I actually am," "How I would like to be," "How others see me," etc., are response roles that can be used with the same set of self-descriptors). Q-sort data are typically used in Q correlation (correlation between persons across variables) or in O correlation (correlation between occasions across variables). They may also be used in ordinary R correlation, unless the forced distribution method is used. In the latter case, the Q-sort scores will be ipsative. Ipsative scores (Clemans, 1966) are those in which the scores for an individual are distributed around that individual's mean and not around the population mean. Ipsative scores are not on a common scale for all individuals and therefore cannot be used in analyses that assume a common scale, for example, correlating variables across individuals, factor analysis, or analysis of variance. However, they would be appropriate in correlating individuals across variables (i.e., in Q correlation).

Rank-Order Methods

The two frequently used rank-order methods are the paired comparison method and the ranking method.

In the paired comparison method (Guilford, 1954), each stimulus (e.g., person, object, event, state, or condition) is paired with every other stimulus. The respondent's task is to select one stimulus from each pair on the basis of the scaling dimension, that is, the basis of comparison. From the number of times each stimulus is chosen, the stimuli can be rank ordered with more precise information than if all of the stimuli were just rank ordered in the usual way. (The additional information comes from circular triads, i.e., where A is chosen over B, B over C, and C over A. Such information is not obtained in ordinary ranking.)

Each stimulus' "score" (number of times chosen) can also be converted to a z score, using the normal curve table. Such z scores would be ipsative. The ipsative character of these z scores can be minimized by calibrating each individual's scores to that individual's zero point. This zero point can be ascertained (for each individual) by adding an absolute judgment scale (a two-categoried scale; see Guilford, 1954, pp. 171–173).

Because the number of pairs increases rapidly with increase in number of stimuli (for n stimuli, the total number of pairs equals $n\{n-1\}/2$), the paired comparison method becomes impractical when more than 20 stimuli are involved. For such situations, the method of multiple rank orders (Gulliksen & Tucker, 1961) can be used, in which, instead of presenting stimuli in pairs, they are presented in blocks of threes (triads) or more, but in such a manner that each stimulus is paired only once with every other stimulus. (Special designs are necessary to accomplish this. See

Guilliksen & Tucker, 1961.) If collected in this way, the data from the multiple rank orders can be reduced to paired comparisons, and then scaled as paired comparisons.

At the other extreme to paired comparisons is the ranking method. Ranking can be used with any number of stimuli. For small numbers, the instructions are straightforward. For large numbers of stimuli (i.e., more than 20), the reliability of the ranking can be improved by using the alternation ranking procedure, in which the respondent alternates between picking the highest and lowest ranks (i.e., first, the first ranked; next, the last ranked; then, the second ranked; then, the next to the last ranked; the third ranked, etc.). As with paired comparison data, ranking data can also be converted to z scores (Guilford, 1954).

Ranking data, that is, rank scores, whether obtained by the paired comparison, multiple rank orders, or ranking method, should be analyzed by using nonparametric statistics (Siegel, 1956), especially rank-order statistics. When converted to z scores with a zero point, however, the data can be analyzed with the use of ordinary parametric statistics.

Subject-Centered Scale Methods

Subject-centered scales are probably the kind of scale in most frequent use in counseling psychology research. Individual differences in both the clients and the counselors are thought to account for significant portions of counseling outcome variance. Also, possibly because individual differences variables are among the most easily accessible to researchers, much effort has been put into constructing and developing subject-centered scales.

The classic method for developing subject-centered scales is the Likert method. Refinements in the method have been introduced via factor analysis. A variant of the method, the semantic differential, has proven quite useful. These methods are described below.

The Likert Method
Just as Thurstone saw the application of psychophysical methods to scaling nonsensory stimuli, so did Likert (1932) see the application of psychometric methods to scaling nonability-test items. The Likert procedure can be described as follows:

1. A number of items are written to represent the content domain. Five-point anchored rating scales are typically used as response choices for each item (hence, the mistaken use of *Likert* to refer to the 5-point-rating item format). Scoring weights from 1 to 5 assigned to the five rating-scale points.

Direction of scoring (whether 1 or 5 is high) is immaterial provided it is consistent for all items.

2. The items are administered to a large group of respondents (N of at least 100). Each respondent's item rating choices are scored and the item scores summed to constitute the respondent's total score.

3. Items are selected according to their ability to discriminate between high and low scorers on total score. Likert used a group-difference procedure (difference in item means between high-scoring and low-scoring groups, e.g., uppermost 25% and lowermost 25%). One could also use an item-total-score correlation procedure, as is currently done in ability test construction. Maximizing item-total-score correlation will also maximize the scale's internal consistency reliability coefficient (coefficient alpha). Computer programs (e.g., the Statistical Package for the Social Sciences Reliability program) are available for use in this connection.

4. The best discriminating items are then selected to constitute the scale, and the scale score is obtained by summing the item scores for the selected items. At this point, scale scores can be treated as normative scores (i.e., transformed to standardized scores, used to determine percentile equivalents for specific populations, etc.).

Of all the scale construction methods, the most convenient for researchers is the Likert method because it can be employed with the use of ordinary SPSS programs. To implement the Likert method requires only (a) computing total score, (b) computing item-total-score correlations, and (c) computing alpha reliability for the final set of items. Incidentally, reliability should be computed for every research use of Likert scales, not just at scale development, because reliability is a function not only of the scale but also of the respondent sample.

Unfortunately, not all scales that are purported to be Likert-type scales are constructed according to the Likert procedure. They only look like Likert scales because of the use of the 5-point rating response format (Triandis, 1971). If, in such scales, the correlation of the items with total scale is not high, then the interpretation of the scale score is problematic.

Use of Factor Analysis

Factor analysis is a data reduction technique in which a large set of variables is reduced to a smaller set without much loss of information. The technique can be used to select items for Likert-type scales in the following way:

1. The items in the item pool are intercorrelated.

2. The item intercorrelation matrix is subjected to a principal components analysis. (This requires the use of the principal axis solution, with unities in the diagonal, and extracting only the first factor.)

3. The items with the highest loadings are selected for the scale. *Highest loading* can be defined in an absolute sense (e.g., at least .707 or .50, which would represent 50% and 25%, respectively, of the item variance) or in a relative sense (the loading squared, as a proportion of the communality, e.g., no less than 50%).

4. There may be instances in which certain items are essential to the definition of the scale but are not found among the highest loading ones, that is, are not selected by this procedure. In this case, the scale constructor can go back to the original item intercorrelation matrix and eliminate all items that correlate below a given level (e.g., .30) with the essential defining items. The reduced matrix can then be factor analyzed.

5. When a content domain represented in an item pool is thought or assumed to be multidimensional, factor analysis can be used to construct several scales at the same time. The procedure is the same as above, except that more than one factor (component) is extracted. An additional step, factor rotation, is usually required to find a best (simple structure) solution, the procedure most frequently preferred being orthogonal rotation to a varimax criterion. A scale is then constructed for each factor, with items selected as described above. If an item is selected for more than one scale, the researcher can choose (a) to assign it to the scale with the highest loading, (b) to assign it to all the scales for which it was selected, or (c) to leave it out altogether. Choices (a) and (c) waste some information, but choice (b) will contribute to an artifactual interscale correlation that is undesirable.

As with Likert scales, all scales developed via factor analysis should be evaluated for reliability each time they are used.

The Semantic Differential

The semantic differential (Osgood, Suci, & Tannenbaum, 1957), like the Likert, makes use of the rating response format. Unlike the Likert, which uses only one rating dimension for all items in a scale, the semantic differential uses several rating dimensions for rating the same item or stimulus object. Semantic differential rating dimensions are typically bipolar, anchored at both ends with contrasting adjectives, with a 7-point rating continuum. Provided that response distributions are not forced, semantic differential data can be treated like any other rating data.

If stimuli can be assigned scale scores and subjects can be assigned scale scores, the next logical development should be to develop scale construction methods that assign scale scores to both subjects and stimuli. Such development has been going on (e.g., Coombs, 1964) but has been the province mainly of psychologists interested in scaling models and psychological modeling. Only relatively recently has response scale development had an impact on instrument construction in applied psychology (e.g., Lord & Novick, 1968). It has had practically no impact on counseling psychology research.

For the sake of completeness, however, and to illustrate the response scale approach, one of the earliest and more influential scaling methods—Guttman's scalogram technique—will be described. A more recently developed technique, the Rasch (1960) method, will also be briefly discussed.

The Guttman Method

Guttman's (1944) concern was the property of unidimensionality in a scale. With a unidimensional scale, according to Guttman, knowledge of the respondent's scale score should permit the reproduction of the respondent's item score pattern. In a unidimensional scale, the items can be arranged in order (of endorsement or descriptiveness or whatever the underlying dimension is) in such a way that positive response to an item (e.g., *agree*, in an attitude scale) should imply positive response to all other items lower down the scale, and conversely, negative response to an item should imply negative response to all other items higher up the scale. To ascertain unidimensionality, Guttman developed the scalogram technique.

Suppose we had a unidimensional attitude scale that was administered to a group of individuals. The scalogram technique would call for the data to be displayed as follows: Items are displayed as columns and ordered (from left to right) according to endorsement level from the most to the least endorsed item. Individuals are displayed as rows and ordered (from top to bottom) according to total score, from highest to lowest score. If the test were perfectly unidimensional, then the scalogram would show an orderly stepwise progression of endorsement for both the individuals and the items. Any exceptions to this expectation can be easily seen in a scalogram display, and the number of exceptions can be expressed as a proportion of the total matrix (N individuals $\times$ m items). Guttman (1944) defines a *coefficient of reproducibility* as 1 minus the proportion of exceptions, where 1.00 means that the response pattern for any given scale score can be reproduced perfectly.

When the coefficient of reproducibility is not high (e.g., below .9 or

.8), the scalogram display will reveal the items that do not conform to expectation. After removing these items, the coefficient of reproducibility is recalculated, and the process repeated until the desired level of the coefficient is attained. Sometimes it may also be necessary to eliminate some aberrant individuals whose responses do not conform to the expected pattern. (This underscores the fact that response is a function not just of the scale or instrument but also of the respondent population. Aberrant individuals might be hypothesized to belong to a different population insofar as the scale is concerned.)

The classic Bogardus (1928) social distance scale illustrates what Guttman had in mind. Respondents were asked whether they would be willing to admit members of a race or nationality group (a) to close kinship by marriage, (b) to membership in their club, (c) to their streets as neighbors, (d) to employment in their occupation, (e) to citizenship in their country, (f) only as visitors to their country, or (g) whether they would exclude them completely from their country. Admitting individuals at one level implies admitting them at lower levels but does not imply admitting them at higher levels.

The Rasch Method

The Rasch model, one of a group of models originating from item response theory, was initially developed in connection with the construction of ability tests. The model expresses Guttman's basic ideas in a probabilistic manner, as follows: (a) Given any item, a person of higher ability should have a higher probability of getting the item right than would a person of lower ability, and (b) given any person, an item of lower difficulty should be solved (gotten right) with a higher probability than would an item of higher difficulty. The model has since been extended to the construction of nonability measures (e.g., attitude scales) by, among others, Wright and Masters (1982).

The Rasch model postulates that item response is a function of two parameters, an item parameter and a person parameter. As examples: For ability tests, the parameters would reflect item difficulty and person ability; for attitude scales, item endorsement, and person attitude; for interest measures, item liking (liking for an item) and person interest. The parameters are estimated from the item-by-score matrix (persons with the same scores are grouped together). Parameters are estimated from the data, given that the model is true (i.e., with the model as the premise). The data's fit to the model can be assessed, and if the fit is poor, one infers that the model's assumptions have not been met.

If the fit is acceptable, the data can be improved by eliminating the items that show a poor fit (and in theory, the persons that have a poor fit, as well). Thus, by eliminating poorly fitting items, the refined scale is assumed to be unidimensional. (The reader will note the similarity to the Guttman technique.)

Calculation of parameter estimates for the Rasch model is typically done via computer, although hand calculation methods are also available (Wright & Masters, 1982).

All of the scale development methods described thus far make use of the item-by-person data matrix in determining which items to retain in, or eliminate from, the scale. A final group of methods makes use of external criteria and the relation of items to external criteria in determining which items to select. These methods were developed in the context of the practitioner's problem of predicting outcomes (e.g., in vocational choice and personnel selection). For these methods, the choice of criterion (or criteria) is all-important because it preordains the items that are selected.

External Criterion Methods

Item selection, again, is the key question in scale construction by external criterion methods. The three most-used methods of item selection are (a) the group difference method, (b) the item validity method, and (c) the multiple regression method. It is assumed that the criterion variable has been selected and that an adequate measure of it is available. Criterion variables typically reflect whatever it is that psychologist-practitioners are trying to effect, for example, client satisfaction, client choice, client behavior. (To simplify discussion, a single criterion variable is assumed, although a scale can be constructed to predict to multiple criteria.)

In the group-difference method, items for the scale are selected according to the difference in mean item scores between two groups, a high criterion group and a low criterion group, or, alternatively, a criterion group (whose members meet one or more criteria) and a reference group (a baseline, or unselected, or typical-population group). The larger the mean difference, the more definitely the item should be selected for the scale. The size of the difference can be used to give differential weights to items and response choices (Strong, 1943), but when the number of items in the scale is large (20 or so), unit weights (0, 1) do just as well as differential weights (Clark, 1961).

Note that the group difference method is similar to Likert's original method. What differs is that Likert used an internal criterion (total score on the undeveloped scale), whereas the present method uses an external criterion. Otherwise, the statistical procedures are very much the same.

The item validity method is also similar to the Likert method except that instead of the Likert's item–total-score correlation, the external criterion method uses the correlation between item score and criterion score as the basis for item selection.

A more sophisticated external criterion method of item selection involves the use of multiple regression. The criterion variable is regressed on the items, with items being added to the regression equation one at a time, depending on the amount of explained variance the item contributes. This method tends to select items that correlate highly with the criterion and lowly or not at all with one another.

Scales developed by external criterion methods tend to be heterogeneous in content, because most criteria tend to be heterogeneous or multidimensional. If this is so, determining internal consistency reliability may not be appropriate for scales constructed by these methods. Rather, immediate test–retest or alternate-forms methods should be used to ascertain reliability.

Because external criterion methods tend to capitalize on chance (i.e., sample idiosyncracies), three preventive steps should be taken: (a) The contrast groups (high vs. low, criterion vs. reference) should be large (Strong, 1943, used groups of at least 400); (b) the mean item score differences or item–total-score correlations should be practical, not just statistical, significance; and (c) the developed scale, after item selection, should be cross-validated, that is, tried out on new samples from the same population as the development sample. Cross-validation, to see if the group differences or correlations hold up, is of the utmost importance in scale construction by external criterion methods.

The fact that external criterion methods are designed to maximize the prediction of criteria is both their strength and their weakness. When the purpose of constructing a scale is to predict to a given criterion, an external criterion method is still unsurpassed as the method of choice. However, a scale that is developed to predict to an external criterion is only as good as the criterion at the time of scale development. If the criterion changes with time (e.g., a shift in emphasis in the criterion from quantity to quality), then the scale can become obsolete. If the criterion happens to be biased against one sex or one ethnic group, then the scale will also be biased. With new criteria, new scales may have to be constructed, although not before the old scales have been tried and found wanting. Otherwise, a seemingly never-ending series of new scale construction may result. For this reason, use of external criterion methods may require prior resolution of the criterion problem on theoretical as well as on practical grounds.

SCALE EVALUATION

Scales, as measuring instruments, are evaluated primarily on the basis of two criteria: reliability, or the proportion of scale score variance that is not error variance, and validity, or the proportion of scale score variance that accurately represents the construct or the proportion of criterion variance that is predicted by the scale. These two criteria are complex concepts, and a full discussion of them will not be attempted. However, certain points need to be made in connection with the evaluation of newly constructed scales. (A necessary reference for all scale constructors is the American Psychological Association's *Standards for Educational and Psychological Testing*, 1985.)

That different kinds of reliability estimates may be required for different kinds of scales has already been mentioned. For stimulus-centered scales, the reliability concern is whether on immediate retest the stimuli (items) will be rank ordered in the same way by the same person. The variance of the difference scores between test and retest would be indicative of error variance. For subject-centered scales, the concern is whether individuals are rank ordered in the same way on immediate retest. Variability in individuals' standing would be error variance. For trait scales, reliability refers to the stability of scores (or rank-order standing) over considerable lengths of time. This assumes that individuals are mature on the trait (i.e., developmentally in the stage when the trait is presumed to be stable). For state scales, reliability is the ability of the scale accurately to reflect changes in direction or intensity, or both, in the state being measured. For homogeneous scales, internal consistency reliability is appropriate; for heterogeneous scales, it is immediate test–retest or alternate-forms reliability.

Also, because reliability is a function of sample as well as of instrument, it should be evaluated on a sample from the intended target population—an obvious but sometimes overlooked point.

With respect to validity, although the concept continues to evolve (Messick, 1981; Embretson, 1983), certain practices have come to be accepted as mandatory. One of these is the use of the multitrait–multimethod design (Campbell & Fiske, 1959) to evaluate a scale. At the very least, the scale constructor should compare the new scale with the best competing scale and with a measure of a construct that clearly contrasts with the new scale (e.g., a positive affect scale against a negative affect scale).

It is also common—and—good practice to ascertain the correlates of the scale (e.g., age, sex, experience). It is even better if the expectations about correlates are given by theory. In ascertaining such theory-derived correlates, the *nomological net* (Cronbach & Meehl, 1955) that characterizes the construct is given concrete definition. However, such a network of correlations and other relations only delimits the scale's *nomothetic span* (Embretson, 1983). If the scale purported to be a measure of a construct, validation studies would have to identify the mechanisms that produce the scale scores and relate these mechanisms to the construct (i.e., do what Embretson calls *construct representation*).

The practical validity or utility (usefulness in professional practice) of a scale is still mainly a matter of predicting to criteria, either concurrently or subsequently measured. The number and range of criteria to which a scale can predict delineate its utility. The most useful scales in professional psychological practice (e.g., Minnesota Multiphasic Personality Inventory {MMPI}, Strong–Campbell Interest Inventory {SCII}) are characterized by the large number and wide range of criteria for which the scales are valid predictors.

Prediction to a criterion can be evaluated in two ways: by correlation (proportion of criterion variance accounted for) or by hit-rate (proportion of predicted positives who are true positives). The two are related in the Taylor-Russell tables (Taylor & Russell, 1939), which show what the hit rate would be as a function of the validity coefficient, the base rate, and the selection ratio. Hit rate data are much more concrete and much more useful to the counseling psychology practitioner than are correlation data.

Although reliability and validity concerns are of the essence, there are other less important (but nonetheless, important) considerations. Some of these have been mentioned, for example, administrative concerns. Another concern is the character of the score distribution generated by the scale—in part, a function of the respondent sample. Most users would prefer a scale that ordinarily produces a reasonably normally distributed set of scores. However, if the scale were to be used for diagnostic purposes, a user might prefer one that generates a skewed distribution, the direction of skew depending on whether low scores or high scores are diagnostic. Scales, like ability tests, can be so constructed as to produce the shape of score distribution that is desired, by selecting the appropriate items. Another concern is that the scale produce sufficient score variation to be useful, that is, produce unattenuated correlations. An old rule of thumb is that the coefficient of variation (standard deviation divided by the mean) should be between 5% and 15% (Snedecor, 1946, p. 47).

A final concern is a practical one: Is the scale necessary? That is, are there other, less expensive ways of getting the same information or the same measurements? This concern could also be a matter of social sensitivity: Are there other, less intrusive ways of getting the same information or measurements?

Other Issues

A number of other issues continue to be controversial or, at least, matters of concern for scale constructors.

1. *Measurement versus statistics.* This is an old and continuing debate that has recently been renewed (Gaito, 1980; Townsend & Ashby, 1984). In brief, the proponents of measurement hold that level of measurement (nominal, ordinal, interval, ratio) constrains the kinds of statistical procedures that can be applied to the numerical data. The proponents of statistics maintain that, "(t)he numbers do not know where they come from" (Lord, 1953, p. 751), that the level of measurement is not a constraining factor. Those who accept the latter view tolerate the use of parametric statistics with scores from quasi-interval scales that actually are at the ordinal level of measurement, a common practice that is criticized by proponents of the former view.

2. *Bandwidth versus fidelity (Cronbach & Gleser, 1965).* This is the scale constructor's dilemma that can be illustrated as follows: Suppose, for whatever reason, you are limited to 30 items. Do you construct a scale that yields a single, highly reliable score from 30 items or a scale that can yield three independent scores from three 10-item subscales, even if these subscale scores are of marginal reliability? The trade-off is reminiscent of an older one called the *attenuation paradox* (Loevinger, 1954), which identified a trade-off between reliability and validity. That is, high reliability is achieved at the expense of validity and high validity is achieved at the expense of reliability. Ways out of the paradox have been suggested (Humphreys, 1956).

3. *Empirical versus rational scales.* Conventional wisdom in applied psychology used to hold that empirical (external criterion) scales were the more valid, whereas rational (internal criterion, intuitive) scales were the more reliable. The opinion—or at least the part about the superiority of empirical scales with respect to validity—has now been challenged (Ashton & Goldberg, 1973; Goldberg, 1972; Hase & Goldberg, 1967; Hornick, James, & Jones, 1977; Jackson, 1975).

4. *The reference group problem.* In the use of the external criterion method of scale construction, what should constitute a reference group? The answer to this question may seem obvious (i.e., a proportionately representative sample of the population), but more careful examination will show that the answer is not so obvious. What is the referent population? The general adult population? A particular age group or sex

group? On what variables should there be proportionate representation? Is equal representation better? The constitution of the reference group is important because the scoring key (items selected, weights for response choices) can change with the change of the reference group (as Kuder, 1977, did) and use the criterion group's responses to develop the scoring key.

5. *Response bias.* Ratings—whether self- or other-descriptive, general (abstract) or specific (behavioral), or other kinds— are susceptible to certain response biases on the part of respondents. A response bias is a response tendency that operates in all rating situations, regardless of the context. At least three types of bias can be identified: (a) level bias, or the tendency to locate the mean of the ratings high on the scale (leniency or generosity), low on the scale (strictness or severity), or in the middle (central tendency); (b) dispersion bias, or the tendency to constrain or to expand the distribution of ratings (use of a small segment of the scale vs. use of the full range); and (c) correlation bias, which applies when several rating scales, dimensions, or items, i.e., variables, are involved. In such a situation, a common tendency called the *halo effect* results in the high correlation of variables. The opposite tendency, resulting in low or zero correlations, is rarely, if ever, observed. Most of the controversy concerns correlation bias, with some (e.g., Jackson & Messick, 1961) arguing for its removal in every case, and others (e.g., Block, 1965) arguing that such correlations are not necessarily bias and could be veridical. In any event, a large first principal component in rating data is a common finding, sometimes contrary to the expectations of the scale constructor.

6. *Multimethod measurement.* It is conventional wisdom nowadays to advocate the use of more than one method of measuring any construct. Such a recommendation may overlook the possibility that a change of method can change what it is that is being measured. In other words, method of measurement should be an integral part of the definition and explication of a construct.

7. *Direction of measurement.* Seemingly bipolar variables sometimes pose problems for scale constructors in that scaling in one direction can result in a measure that does not correlate highly with another that is scaled in the opposite direction. Some constructs, such as masculinity–femininity and positive versus negative affectivity, initially construed as bipolar but unidimensional, have now been redefined as bidimensional. Others such as flexibility–rigidity, while still construed as unidimensional, nevertheless require two different scales for measurement at each pole. These phenomena underscore the

need for an adequate theory of the construct to start with, but also for theory to be open to modification in the light of data.

8. *A final issue.* The demand for some quantitative measure of the multitude of process or outcome variables in counseling psychology research, coupled with the convenience of putting together a structured verbal scale, especially one of the Likert type, has led to the almost exclusive or even automatic use of such measures in our field. That researchers are quantifying their variables through the construction and use of such scales is laudable. That such scales have become the instrument of choice in our field is somehow worrisome. Just as we have been criticized for having developed a psychology of the college sophomore, may we not now be accused of having developed a psychology of the Likert scale response?

A Concluding Note

In scale construction, as in much of human endeavor, there can be no single "best" method. One method may be best for one research problem but not for another. Purpose, context, and limitations on the researcher have to be taken into account. Trade-offs in advantages and disadvantages seem to be the rule. A hybrid approach, tailored to the situation, might be better than any of the standard approaches discussed here. Researchers should not be reluctant to experiment with different scale construction approaches—and should report their results, so that the rest of us can find out what method is best.

REFERENCES

Ashton, S. G., & Goldberg, L. R. (1973). In response to Jackson's challenge: The comparative validity of personality scales constructed by the external (empirical) strategy and scales developed intuitively by experts, novices, and laymen. *Journal of Research in Personality, 7,* 1–20.

Block, J. (1965). *The challenge of response sets: Unconfounding meaning, acquiescence, and social desirability in the MMPI.* New York: Appleton-Century-Crofts.

Bogardus, E. S. (1928). *Immigration and race attitudes.* Lexington, MA: Heath.

Campbell, D. T., & Fiske, D. W. (1959). Convergent and discriminant validation by the multitrait-multimethod matrix. *Psychological Bulletin, 56,* 81–105.

Campbell, J. P., Dunnette, M. D., Arvey, R. D., & Hellervik, L. V. (1973). The development and evaluation of behaviorally based rating scales. *Journal of Applied Psychology, 57,* 15–22.

Clark, K. E. (1961). *The vocational interests of non-professional men.* Minneapolis: University of Minnesota Press.

Clemans, W. V. (1966). An analytical and empirical examination of some properties of ipsative measures. *Psychometric Monographs (14)*.

Coombs, C. H. (1964). *A theory of data*. New York: Wiley.

Cronbach, L. J. (1984). *Essentials of psychological testing* (4th ed.). New York: Harper & Row.

Cronbach, L. J., & Gleser, G. C. (1965). *Psychological tests and personnel decisions*. Urbana: University of Illinois Press.

Cronbach, L. J., & Meehl, P. E. (1955). Construct validity in psychological tests. *Psychological Bulletin, 52*, 281–302.

Embretson (Whitely), S. (1983). Construct validity: Construct representation versus nomothetic span. *Psychological Bulletin, 93*, 179–197.

Fiske, D. W. (Ed.). (1981). *Problems with language imprecision*. San Francisco: Jossey-Bass.

Gaito, J. (1980). Measurement scales and statistics: Resurgence of an old misconception. *Psychological Bulletin, 87*, 564–567.

Goldberg, L. R. (1972). Parameters of personality inventory construction and utilization: A comparison of prediction strategies and tactics. *Multivariate Behavioral Research Monographs, 72(2)*.

Guilford, J. P. (1954). *Psychometric methods* (2nd ed.). New York: McGraw-Hill.

Gulliksen, H., & Tucker, L. R. (1961). A general procedure for obtaining paired comparisons from multiple rank orders. *Psychometrika, 26*, 173–183.

Guttman, L. (1944). A basis for scaling qualitative data. *American Sociological Review, 9*, 139–150.

Hase, H. D., & Goldberg, L. R. (1967). Comparative validity of different strategies of constructing personality inventory scales. *Psychological Bulletin, 67*, 231–248.

Hornick, C. W., James, L. R., & Jones, A. P. (1977). Empirical item keying versus a rational approach to analyzing a psychological climate questionnaire. *Applied Psychological Measurement, 1*, 489–500.

Humphreys, L. G. (1956). The normal curve and the attenuation paradox in test theory. *Psychological Bulletin, 53*, 472–476.

Jackson, D. N. (1975). The relative validity of scales prepared by naive item writers and those based on empirical methods of personality scale construction. *Educational and Psychological Measurement, 35*, 361–370.

Jackson, D. N., & Messick, S. (1961). Acquiescence and desirability as response determinants on the MMPI. *Educational and Psychological Measurement, 21*, 771–790.

Kuder, F. (1977). *Activity interests and occupational choice*. Chicago: Science Research Associates.

Likert, R. (1932). A technique for the measurement of attitudes. *Archives Of Psychology*, No. 140.

Loevinger, J. (1954). The attenuation paradox in test theory. *Psychological Bulletin, 51*, 493–504.

Lord, F. M. (1953). On the statistical treatment of football numbers. *American Psychologist, 8*, 750–751.

Lord, F. M. & Novick, M. (1968). *Statistical theories of mental test scores.* Reading, MA: Addison-Wesley.

Messick, S. (1981). Constructs and their vicissitudes in educational and psychological measurement. *Psychological Bulletin, 89*, 575–588.

Osgood, C. E., Suci, C. J., & Tannenbaum, P. H. (1957). *The measurement of meaning.* Urbana: University of Illinois Press.

Payne, S. L. (1951). *The art of asking questions.* Princeton, NJ: Princeton University Press.

Rasch, G. (1960). *Probabilistic models for some intelligence and attainment tests.* Copenhagen, Denmark: Danmarks Paedogogiske Institut. (Chicago: University of Chicago Press, 1980).

Siegel, S. (1956). *Nonparametric statistics for the behavioral science.* New York: McGraw-Hill.

Smith, P. C., & Kendall, L. M. (1963). Retranslation of expectations: An approach to the construction of unambiguous anchors for rating scales. *Journal of Applied Psychology, 47*, 149–155.

Snedecor, G.W. (1946). *Statistical methods.* Ames: Iowa State College Press.

Standards for educational and psychological testing. (1985). Washington, DC: American Psychological Association.

Stephenson, W. (1953). *The study of behavior.* Chicago: University of Chicago Press.

Strong, E. K., Jr. (1943). *Vocational interests of men and women.* Stanford, CA: Stanford University Press.

Taylor. H. C., & Russell, J. T. (1939). The relationship of validity coefficients to the practical effectiveness of tests in selection: Discussion and tables. *Journal of Applied Psychology, 23*, 565–578.

Thomas, H. (1982). IQ, interval scales, and normal distributions. *Psychological Bulletin, 91*, 198–202.

Thurstone, L. L., & Chave, E. (1929). *The measurement of attitude.* Chicago: University of Chicago Press.

Torgerson, W. S. (1958). *Theory and methods of scaling.* New York: Wiley.

Townsend, J. T., & Ashby, F. G. (1984). Measurement scales and statistics: The misconception misconceived. *Psychological Bulletin, 96*, 394–401.

Triandis, H. C. (1971). *Attitude and attitude change.* New York: Wiley.

Wright, B. D., & Masters, G. N. (1982). *Rating scale analysis.* Chicago: Mesa Press.

MEASUREMENT
EVALUATION

12

MMPI, RORSCHACH, AND WAIS: A META-ANALYTIC COMPARISON OF RELIABILITY, STABILITY, AND VALIDITY

KEVIN C. H. PARKER, R. KARL HANSON, AND JOHN HUNSLEY

The Minnesota Multiphasic Personality Inventory (MMPI) and the Rorschach Inkblot Test are two of the most frequently used personality tests (Lubin, Larsen, & Matarazzo, 1984). Not only are they popular clinical instruments, but they are also among the most widely researched psychological tests. Buros (1978) reported that there were at least 5,043 studies published on the MMPI and 4,942 studies on the Rorschach. Summary evaluations of their empirical status (e.g., Anastasi, 1982; Kendall & Norton-Ford, 1982; Korchin, 1976) often portray the MMPI as "the standard of psychological assessment" (Kendall & Norton-Ford, 1982, p. 310). The Rorschach, on the other hand, is described as an intriguing but unscientific instrument. Despite recent efforts to systematize scoring criteria (e.g., Exner, 1986), the view of most academics and many clinicians can still be summed up in this statement: "The rate of scientific progress in clinical psychology might well be measured by the speed and thoroughness with which it gets over the Rorschach" (Jensen, 1965, p. 238).

Reprinted from the Psychological Bulletin, 103, 367–373. Copyright 1988 by the American Psychological Association.

Discussions at this basic level are often brief and oversimplified, claiming that too many studies exist for a thorough evaluation to be feasible. We paraphrase Phares (1984, p. 290) as follows: One can enter the forest of MMPI and Rorschach research and emerge with pretty much what one chooses. In the context of this vast, seemingly contradictory literature, meta-analytic studies can be useful in identifying factors that contribute to differences among primary research studies. In his meta-analysis of Rorschach research, Parker (1983) found that studies guided by theory, prior research, or both tend to support the Rorschach but found little support for the Rorschach among studies in which experimental hypotheses lacked a theoretical or empirical rationale. In other meta-analytic studies, researchers have similarly found that conceptual, theory-based studies show greater support for the Rorschach than do undirected studies (Atkinson, 1986; Atkinson, Quarrington, Alp, & Cyr, 1986). Furthermore, the power of the statistics used to analyze the research findings has also been shown to influence the magnitude of the observed effects. Parker's findings were generally consistent with Cohen's (1983) position that the most powerful statistics are those that represent relations between fully continuous measures.

Atkinson (1986) used meta-analytic procedures to compare the relative validities of the MMPI and Rorschach. On the basis of a random sample of articles listed in *Psychological Abstracts*, he found that the conceptual validation studies of the Rorschach were as successful as the conceptual validation studies of the MMPI. Atkinson went on to suggest that the questionable status of the Rorschach may be based on sociocultural factors, not scientific evidence.

The purpose of the present study was to extend previous meta-analytic studies of the psychometric properties of the Rorschach and MMPI. In contrast to previous researchers, we examined several indicators of the tests' merits. These indicators included the test's reliability, including internal consistency and rater agreement; stability, which is the correlation with itself over time; and convergent validity, which is the extent to which the test correlates with relevant criteria.

Rather than assess the Rorschach and MMPI in isolation, we included the Wechsler Adult Intelligence Scale (WAIS) as a control with which to compare the two tests of interest. We selected the WAIS as a comparison test because it is commonly considered to be one of the most reliable and valid tests used in clinical assessment. To address the broad question of the relative psychometric properties of these tests, we treated them as if they were unitary wholes, ignoring differences among scales and subscales of the tests for the present analysis.

In the present research, we also examined the possible effects of editorial biases on the research literature published on the Rorschach and the MMPI. Rather than attempt to randomize the effects of specific editorial biases, as in Atkinson's (1986) article, we attempted to examine these editorial effects by comparing the findings on the MMPI and the Rorschach from two journals—the *Journal of Personality Assessment* (JPA) and the *Journal of Clinical Psychology* (JCP). We selected these journals for two reasons: First, both journals publish extensively on all three tests. Second, one could argue that the traditional association between Rorschach research and the JPA may encourage an editorial bias toward publishing research that is favorable to the Rorschach. (The JPA, originally entitled the *Rorschach Research Exchange*, has several proponents of the Rorschach on its editorial board.) The JCP, in contrast, has no historical allegiance to the Rorschach and seems to publish proportionately more MMPI research than does the JPA. A significant bias in the JPA articles could qualify Parker's (1983) generally favorable evaluation of the Rorschach that was based on studies selected only from this journal.

The three major issues addressed by the present research were the relative reliability, trait stability, and convergent validity of the MMPI and Rorschach, in relation to the WAIS. Our prediction was that the WAIS would lead in all areas and that the MMPI and Rorschach would show lower but similar values. This expectation runs counter to many descriptions of the relative psychometric properties of the MMPI and Rorschach; it is consistent, however, with the earlier meta-analyses of the Rorschach (Atkinson, 1986; Atkinson et al., 1986; Parker, 1983), and it is consistent with the standard references on these tests (Dahlstrom, Welsh, & Dahlstrom, 1972; Exner, 1986; Matarazzo, 1972). The other hypotheses examined in the present research were as follows: On the basis of traditional psychometric theory, reliability values should be greater than stability values, which, in turn, should be greater than validity values. Validity values, which were justified in a study on the basis of theory, prior research, or both, should show greater effects than values that lacked an empirical or theoretical rationale. Studies that used powerful statistics should have found larger effects than studies that used less powerful statistics. Finally, larger effects for the Rorschach should be found in the JPA than in the JCP, because of possible editorial biases.

METHOD

Selection of Studies

We selected the studies included in the meta-analysis from studies published in the JCP and the JCP between 1970 and 1981. We included in the analysis all studies that mentioned the WAIS, Rorschach, or MMPI in the title, abstract, summary, or results section and included sufficient information about the results. We excluded studies that used the tests only to select extreme or matched groups of subjects. The limited reporting of statistics caused the following types of studies to be eliminated from the analysis: (a) studies reporting only multivariate statistics and not the corresponding univariate tests, (b) studies reporting only the significant results when other statistics were obviously examined but not reported, (c) studies using statistics for which estimates of predictable variance could not be calculated (e.g., kappa, Mann-Whitney U, and percentage agreement), and (d) studies reporting only the significance level (e.g., $p<.05$) and not the test statistic and degrees of freedom. We did not estimate effect size from significance levels because the standard procedures for making such estimations (see Smith, Glass, & Miller, 1980) introduce a bias that reduces the calculated effect sizes. This bias is negligible when the expected effect sizes are small, but when the expected correlations are large (as with reliability and stability findings), including estimates based on the minimum value necessary for statistical significance would introduce a substantial bias in the results. When authors reported enough information to reproduce the necessary values, we computed these and retained the studies.

We conducted the present analyses on only those findings that were related to the most commonly used, core scales from each test. For the MMPI, these scales were the three validity scales, the nine clinical scales, and the Don't Know and Social Introversion scales. The core scales for the WAIS were Performance IQ, Verbal IQ, full-scale IQ, and the 11 subtests. The scales considered to be core scales for the Rorschach were those scales that Exner (1983, Table 2.1) chose to examine in detail for temporal stability: Color, Weighted Sum of Color Responses, Achromatic Color, Lambda, Affective Ratio, Egocentricity Index, Experience Actual, Percentage Good Pure Form, and Percentage Good Form. A total of 295 relevant studies were selected from the JCP, and 116 were selected from the JPA. (The complete list of studies used in the meta-analysis is available from Kevin C. H. Parker.)

Coding Measurement Categories

We classified each finding as a reliability, stability, or validity finding. Included in the reliability category were several types of findings, including interrater and intrarater reliability, K-R 20, alpha, and part-whole correlations. Following Jensen (1981), we considered stability separately from the other reliability measures and included correlations between repeated administrations of the same test. We further subdivided the stability findings on the basis of whether the original authors provided theory, prior empirical evidence, or both to indicate that they expected the stability of the test to be high (trait stability) or expected it to be low (state stability) or provided no clear expectations (unknown stability). We similarly subdivided the validity findings into convergent validity (expected), discriminant validity (not expected), and unknown validity, on the basis of the information and hypotheses provided by the original authors. We assumed relations between measures whose names suggested that they should be related to be convergent-validity findings. The unknown-validity category in the present study roughly corresponds to what Atkinson (1986) classified as undirected validation studies.

We placed each finding into one of these seven categories exclusively on the basis of the information provided in the introduction and method sections of the articles. There is the possibility, however, that the introductions could actually be post hoc explanations for unexpected findings. Such a practice could inflate the trait-stability and convergent-validity values observed in the present research, but there is no reason to assume that this potential bias is more pronounced for any one of the three tests.

We coded the type of statistics used to report the results by using Parker's 1983 categories. We placed each statistic into one of three categories: (a) correlation statistics, including Pearson correlations, Spearman rhos, and Cronbach alphas; (b) analysis of variance (ANOVA) statistics for multigroup designs using one continuous dependent variable; and (c) T statistics for two-group designs with one continuous dependent variable, including two-group ANOVA, point-biserial correlations, and t tests. We did not include studies using the chi-square statistic in the present analyses because they were infrequently used.

Coding Procedure

Three judges were involved in coding the observations into measurement categories. The first judge selected the articles, highlighted material in the introduction and method sections that was relevant for coding the observations, and then rated the measurement category for each observation. The second judge read the highlighted section of each article, rated each observation, and only then compared his ratings to the ratings of the first judge. The first and second judges resolved disagreements through discussion. In most cases, they agreed once on judge identified information that the other judge had overlooked. They resolved other disagreements through discussion with the third judge. Each of the three authors served as first, second, and third judges in a structured pattern. We were careful to avoid observing the statistical results in any article during the process of coding observations into measurement categories.

To check the reliability of the coding, we used a variation on the standard coding procedure for three journal volumes (1977 JCP and 1971 and 1977 JPA): The first judge selected the articles, rated each observation, but did not highlight the information that he used to make his ratings. The second judge read the articles selected by the first judge, highlighted the relevant material in the introduction and method sections, and then independently rated each finding. The third judge read the highlighted articles provided by the second judge and then rated each finding. The reliability of these nine comparisons (three raters for each of three volumes) was clearly respectable (median kappa = .89). Furthermore, the reliability of the regular coding would have been even greater than these estimates because the actual procedure involved two raters in each case, with disagreements resolved by using a third rater.

Plan of Analyses

The analyses are organized according to the statistical measure used as the dependent variable. The reliability and stability were always reported in terms of correlations; consequently, correlations are a natural choice for the dependent variable for tests with these types of findings. The validity findings, however, were expressed not only in terms of correlations but also in terms of other statistics, such as t and F. In their meta-analytic work, Parker (1983) and Atkinson (1986) summarized across findings reported with diverse statistics by using the proportion of predictable variance (eta-squared) as the common dependent variable. The use of variance-accounted-for measures in meta-analysis has been criticized, however, because (a) they are insensitive to the direction of the observed effects (Hedges & Olkin, 1985; Hunter, Schmidt, & Jackson, 1982) and (b) they are sensitive to design characteristics, such as the variance in the independent variable (Glass & Hakstian, 1969; Hedges & Olkin, 1985). The initial problem can be corrected by considering values as negative when they are opposite to the predicted direction. The second criticism applies equally to the other statistics that have been proposed for summarizing research, such as d statistics (Hedges & Olkin, 1985) and correlation coefficients. The major disadvantage of variance-accounted-for measures is that inferential statistical tests for these measures are unavailable because the sampling distribution of these statistics has not been sufficiently explored.

In consideration of the above issues, we used a combination of approaches to the data analyses. In the initial set of analyses, we analyzed the correlational findings (reliability, stability, and validity) by using the procedures developed by Hedges and Olkin (1985). These procedures provide unbiased estimators of correlation coefficients and provide a method similar to ordinary regression procedures for testing the influence of specified independent variables. Hedges and Olkin's procedures improve on the ordinary least squares regression that has been used in meta-analyses (e.g., Smith & Glass, 1977) by correcting the observed values for differences in variances (due to differences in sample sizes between studies). The initial set of analyses examined the relative reliability, stability, and validity of the three tests; the relative magnitude of expected versus undirected validity studies; and the evidence of a possible editorial bias between the two journals.

The second set of analyses focused on only the validity findings but was able to include noncorrelational studies. We used the proportion of predictable variance (η^2) as the dependent variable. We used the following equations to estimate this quantity for the different statistics: For F statistics and independent-groups t tests, we used Hays's (1973) ω^2 statistic. For paired t tests, we used the equation

$$\omega^2 = t^2(1 - r)/\{2n + t^2(1 - r)\},$$

where r is the Pearson correlation between the matched observations and n is the total number of pairs. We derived this equation by substituting Smith et al.'s (1980, p. 215) estimation of S^2 for dependent t tests for $\sigma y/x^2$ in Hays's (1981, p. 291) Equations 8.12.2 and 8.12.3. All correlation statistics (e.g., Pearson correlations and Spearman rhos) were simply squared. Multiple-group designs that lacked specific hypotheses were collapsed into a one-way ANOVA.

We made no attempt to assess the statistical significance of the findings that used the proportion of predictable variance as the dependent variable because the sampling distribution of η^2 (with the appropriate signs) is unknown and is likely to violate the assumptions of traditional regression analysis (i.e., normal distribution and equality of variances across studies). Instead, we informally compared the magnitude and rank order of the average values with the theoretically predicted values.

In the initial stage of data gathering, we collected approximately 11,000 findings from 411 studies. To control for the nonindependence of findings from a single study, we allowed each study to contribute only one observation for each combination of test, measurement category, and statistic used. When more than one observation was available, we used the median value; in the case of an even number of observations, we randomly selected the higher or lower value at the median. Some authors reported multiple studies in one article, and we retained an average of 1.5 observations per article in the present analyses. All analyses were based on these median values.

RESULTS

We calculated estimates of the reliability, trait stability, convergent validity, and unknown validity of the three tests from the correlational data by using the methods suggested by Hedges and Olkin (1985). These results are displayed in Table 1. Few correlational findings related to state stability (7), unknown stability (6), or discriminant validity (5). Because these categories were not directly relevant to the main hypotheses of this study, we did not consider findings in these categories further. We transformed all correlations to unbiased estimators of the population correlation coefficient $G(r)$, using Equation 3 from Hedges and Olkin's (1985, p. 225) book. We further transformed these values into Fisher's z scores to normalize the distribution. We based estimates for each category on weighted means, using weights of $(n_i - 3)/\{\sum_{i=1}^{N} (n_i - 3)\}$, where n is the

TABLE 1
Estimates Based on Correlational Statistics of the Reliability, Stability,
Convergent Validity, and Unknown Validity for the WAIS, MMPI, and
Rorschach

Value	Estimated r	95% CI	No. findings	No. subjects	Homogeneity within each class (Q)[a]
Reliability					
WAIS	.87	.86–.88	12	1,759	136.0**
MMPI	.84	.83–.85	33	3,414	337.3*
Rorschach	.86	.82–.90	4	154	11.6*
Stability					
WAIS	.82	.73–.88	4	93	3.0
MMPI	.74	.65–.80	5	171	4.8
Rorschach	.85	.79–.89	2	125	0.1
Convergent validity					
WAIS	.62	.60–.64	26	3,441	306.7**
MMPI	.46	.44–.48	30	4,980	165.5**
Rorschach	.41	.31–.51	5	283	24.6**
Unknown validity[b]					
WAIS	.33	.29–.36	15	2,594	122.2**
MMPI	.24	.21–.26	51	7,949	290.4**
Rorschach	.07	.01–.12	12	1,158	15.9

Note: WAIS = Wechsler Adult Intelligence Scale; MMPI = Minnesota Multiphasic Personality Inventory; CI = confidence interval.
[a]Significance indicates rejection of the hypothesis of homogeneity. [b]Unknown-validity findings lacked a theoretical or empirical rationale.
*p < .01   **p < .001.

sample size for each finding and N is the number of findings. We calculated 95% confidence intervals for the average z scores and expressed these values as their correlation coefficient equivalents. For ease of interpretation, the correlation coefficient equivalents of the average z scores are also presented in Table 1 and Figure 1. We indexed the variability of these estimates by using Hedges and Olkin's Q statistic. The Q statistic estimates the probability that the observed correlations were drawn from a population with the same underlying correlation. (The Q statistic follows the chi-square distribution with $N - 1$ degrees of freedom, where N is the number of findings.) In a preliminary stage of analysis, we noted all Q values greater than 10 and checked the raw data in the original articles. We identified three values as sufficiently anomalous not to be included in the findings summarized in Table 1.

Inspection of Table 1 indicates that the cell Q values were above chance levels in every cell except the three stability cells and the unknown-validity cell for the Rorschach. These significant Q values indicate that there was more variability in the correlations for the cell than would be expected if the observed correlations were all estimates of the same population correlation. This lack of homogeneity in the reliability and validity findings is not surprising when one considers that the estimates combined

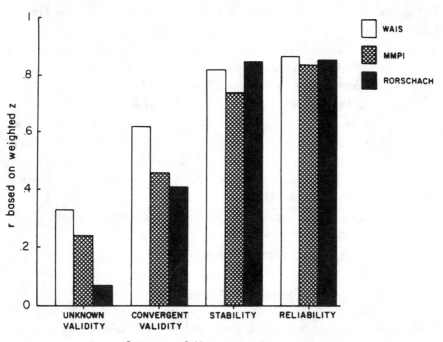

Figure 1: Estimated average correlations for reliability, stability, convergent-validity, and unknown-validity findings for the Wechsler Adult Intelligence Scale (WAIS), Minnesota Multiphasic Personality Inventory (MMPI), and Rorschach.

measures using different subscales, different subject populations, and, for the validity findings, different validity measures. Although the broad categories used in the present study appear to be heterogeneous, such a broad classification scheme is appropriate for addressing the equally broad question of the relative reliability, stability, and validity of the three tests.

We assessed differences among the three tests for each psychometric indicator by using the weighted regression procedures on the z values as suggested by Hedges and Olkin (1985). Weighted regression analyses indicated significant main effects for test ($Q_R = 20.9$, $df = 2$, $p < .011$) and measurement category ($Q_R = 1,306.5$, $df = 3$, $p < .001$), as well as a significant Test × Category interaction ($Q_R = 43.1$, $df = 6$, $p < .001$). The Q_R statistics are based on independent regression sum of squares. Even though the three effects above created a multiple correlation of .86, the regression model was far from correctly specified ($Q_E = 1,417.1$, $df = 194$, $p < .001$). Excess residual variance from the regression model is hardly surprising when one considers that most of the specific categories used in this analysis contained excessive variability themselves. Although poor model fit is not unexpected, the degree of specification error suggests that these regression analyses should be interpreted cautiously.

The average correlations (based on the weighted zs) for the different measurement categories clearly followed standard psychometric theory. Reliability values were greatest (average correlation of .85), followed by the values for stability (.80), convergent validity (.53), and finally, unknown validity (.24). The weighted regression contrasts were significant between all four categories: (a) reliability and stability ($Q_R = 9.0$, $df = 1$, $p < .005$), (b) stability and convergent validity ($Q_R = 87.6$, $df = 1$, $p < .001$), and (c) convergent and unknown validity ($Q_R = 560.7$, $df = 1$, $p < .001$).

Examination of the average correlations for the test main effect showed that the WAIS had the largest value (.63) when the data were collapsed over measurement categories, followed by the MMPI (.48) and the Rorschach (.31). On the basis of weighted regression, the contrast between the WAIS and MMPI was significant ($Q_R = 243.5$, $df = 1$, $p < .001$), as was the contrast between the MMPI and Rorschach ($Q_R = 64.5$, $df = 1$, $p < .001$).

The Test × Measurement Category interaction was significant, however, suggesting that the differences among the tests were not consistent across the measurement categories. Examination of the values in Table 1 indicates that the values within each test followed a consistent rank order from reliability, stability, convergent validity, to unknown validity. The range of values found within each measurement category did not overlap other measurement categories, with the one exception that the observed value for the stability of the Rorschach was marginally greater than the observed value for the reliability of the MMPI.

We used contrasts involving weighted regression to examine the differences among the tests within each measurement category. These contrasts involved 12 significance test (3 tests × 4 categories); consequently, we set the significance level for the contrast at $p < .001$, following the Bonferroni procedure. The average reliability of the WAIS (.87) was greater than the average reliability of the MMPI (.84; $Q_R = 16.1$, $df = 1$, $p < .001$). The average reliability of the Rorschach (.86) did not differ significantly from that of the WAIS ($Q_R = .10$, $df = 1$, $p > .50$) or the MMPI ($Q_R = 1.1$, $df = 1$, $p > .30$). Because the individual estimates of reliability for each test showed excessive variance, the test for model specification for the comparison among the reliabilities of each test showed a poor degree of fit ($Q_E = 484.6$, $df = 47$, $p < .001$).

The observed average stability value for the Rorschach (.85) was larger than the observed value for the WAIS (.82) and MMPI (.74), but these values were not significantly different ($Q_R = 6.9$, $df = 2$, $p < .05$). Because of the relatively small sample size and the low variance within each estimate, the weighted regression comparison among the stability of the three tests was the only model that was not significantly misspecified ($Q_E = 7.8$, $df = 8$, $p > .25$).

The average convergent-validity value for the WAIS (.63) was greater than the convergent-validity values for the MMPI (.46; $Q_R = 111.1$, $df = 1$, $p < .001$) and the Rorschach (.41; $Q_R = 21.9$, $df = 1$, $p < .001$). There was no significant difference between the average convergent-validity values for the MMPI and the Rorschach ($Q_R = .93$, $df = 1$, $p > .25$). The test for model specification for the comparison of the convergent-validity values showed a poor degree of fit ($Q_R = 496.3$, $df = 58$, $p < .001$).

The unknown validity value for the WAIS (.33) was greater than the value for the MMPI (.24; $Q_R = 18.6$, $df = 1$, $p < .001$). The value in the unknown-validity category for the MMPI was greater than that for the Rorschach ($Q_R = 30.0$, $df = 1$, $p < .001$), whose average value was only .07. The comparisons within the unknown-validity category again showed a poor degree of model specification fit ($Q_E = 428.4$, $df = 75$, $p < .001$).

The next set of analyses addressed possible editorial biases between the two journals. Unfortunately, only the MMPI had sufficient findings in both journals (23 in the JPA and 93 in the JCP) to justify statistical analysis. With weighted regression analyses, we found a significant effect for measurement category ($Q_R = 147.5$, $df = 3$, $p < .001$), but the effect for journal was insignificant ($Q_R = 2.1$, $df = 1$, $p > .10$). The Journal × Measurement Category interaction was marginally significant ($Q_R = 9.6$, $df = 3$, $p <$

.025), but it was unlikely to be meaningful when we considered the high degree of specification error in the regression model ($Q_E = 776.5$, $df = 109$, $p < .001$) and the lack of any a priori expectations for this interaction.

For the Rorschach, the average correlation (collapsed across measurement categories) found in the JPA was .33, compared with only .09 in the JCP, which seems to support an editorial bias. The value for the JCP, however, was based on only three validity articles, each of which lacked an empirical or theoretical rationale. We did not identify any articles on reliability, stability, or convergent validity of the Rorschach in the JCP. Similarly, we identified only two reliability, one convergent-validity, and two unknown-validity WAIS findings in the JPA. Consequently, we did not conduct statistical tests of editorial bias between journals for the Rorschach and the WAIS.

A final question that we addressed in the present study was the extent to which the statistics used to report the results influenced the magnitude of the findings. Table 2 contains the average predictable variance for the convergent-validity findings for each test for correlations, ANOVAS, and t tests. The present findings support the theoretical position that the statis-

TABLE 2
Convergent-Validity Scores for the WAIS, MMPI, and Rorschach

Tests	Mean predictable variance	Square root of predictable variance	SD of predictable variance	No. findings
Correlations				
WAIS	.41	.64	.24	26
MMPI	.24	.49	.16	31
Rorschach	.19	.44	.16	5
Pooled	.31			62
Analyses of variance				
WAIS	.29	.54	.05	6
MMPI	.14	.38	.15	15
Rorschach	.12	.35	.13	4
Pooled	.18			25
t tests				
WAIS	.11	.34	.08	7
MMPI	.15	.38	.19	20
Rorschach	.08	.28	.09	4
Pooled	.13			31

Note: WAIS = Wechsler Adult Intelligence Scale; MMPI = Minnesota Multiphasic Personality Inventory.

tics should be rank ordered from the most to the least powerful as follows: correlations, ANOVAs, and *t* tests.

DISCUSSION

The results support the traditional expectation that reliability findings should be greater than stability findings. The average reliability (.85) was similar to the average stability (.80) of the tests when we did not include in the stability estimates stability findings in which there was some reason to expect low stability (e.g., an experimental manipulation between administrations). Both the reliability and stability estimates were greater than the validity estimates.

As in previous meta-analytic reviews (Atkinson, 1986; Atkinson et al., 1986; Parker, 1983), the average correlation (averaged across studies and tests) for validity studies directed theoretically, empirically, or both (.53) was substantially greater than that for undirected, exploratory studies (.24). The average correlation found in the validation studies directed theoretically, empirically, or both for the MMPI and Rorschach was not significantly different. The MMPI and Rorschach both displayed adequate validity values (.46 and .41, respectively); the average convergent-validity value for the WAIS was .62. All three tests also showed stability and reliability values that were acceptable from traditional psychometric standards (generally greater than .80). These results indicate that researchers are likely to find support for each of the tests if they know what they are looking for and if they use the tests appropriately to test their hypothesis.

These results may surprise some readers, but it is worth noting that they are what would be expected if the standard references on these tests were taken at face value (i.e., Dahlstrom et al., 1972; Exner, 1986; Matarazzo, 1972). The present results were also similar to the previous meta-analyses of Parker (1983) on the Rorschach and Atkinson (1986) on the Rorschach and MMPI. Direct comparisons of the values in these meta-analyses and the present results were not possible because each study used somewhat different classification schemes. Nevertheless, these three studies suggest that the Rorschach and MMPI have acceptable and roughly equivalent psychometric properties when used in appropriate circumstances.

The moderate discrepancy between the WAIS validity value and the validity values of the other two tests is noteworthy, given that the reliability and stability values of the three tests were quite similar in magnitude. The criteria against which the WAIS was validated were typically measures such as other intelligence tests that are themselves considered to have higher validity and reliability than the measures against which the MMPI and the Rorschach were validated (e.g., clinical diagnoses). The differences between the personality tests and the intelligence test may be substantially smaller if corrected for attenuation because of the unreliability of the validation criteria.

The support found for the Rorschach should be interpreted cautiously, however, because we obtained all the data on reliability, stability, and convergent validity for the Rorschach from a single journal (the *JPA*). The historical association between the *JPA* and the Rorschach may create an editorial bias favorable to the Rorschach. Our attempt to empirically examine any possible bias proved unsuccessful because the other journal selected (the *JCP*) published only undirected validity studies on the Rorschach. It seems unlikely, however, that editorial bias provides a sufficient explanation for the current findings because Atkinson (1986) came to similar conclusions on the basis of a random selection of articles from a variety of journals.

A final variable examined in the present study was the type of statistic used to measure a relation. As Parker (1983) and Atkinson (1986) found, results reported with powerful statistics (e.g., r) accounted for greater amounts of predictable variance than did less powerful statistics (e.g., t and F). Cohen (1983) considered correlations to be more powerful statistics than F or t because whenever researchers artificially transform continuous data into discrete categories, they discard information. The fewer categories there are, the coarser the measurement and the more information that is lost. Our results provide support for Cohen's position.

Our questions and our conclusions have been rather general, but they are reasonably clear. The MMPI and Rorschach are both valid, stable, and reliable under certain circumstances. When either test is used in the manner for which it was designed and validated, its psychometric properties are likely to be adequate for either clinical or research purposes. More than anything else, the issue is to take the time and care to select a validated scale for the purpose at hand and to use that scale in a methodologically sound manner. Researchers using either test should reasonably expect to find significant results under appropriate circumstances. A corollary of this observation is that researchers have ample opportunity to find nonsignificant results if that is what they are looking for or if their selection of instruments or subjects is uninformed by sound theoretical or empirical rationales.

As one reviewer of a draft of this article put it, our article "paints with a very broad brush." This certainly is evidenced by the large Q_E values in almost every analysis, but this very general investigation is by no means the end of the matter. It merely sets the stage for more detailed analyses of these and other tests examining specific subscales, populations, and dependent variables. Smith and Glass's (1977) meta-analysis of therapy-outcome research also addressed a rather broad issue. That study has provided the impetus for more detailed meta-analyses of treatment efficacy (e.g., Dush, Hirt, & Schroeder, 1983; Miller & Berman, 1983). We hope that the findings of the present study will likewise encourage more detailed quantitative reviews of the psychological testing literature.

REFERENCES

Anastasi, A. (1982). *Psychological testing*. New York: Macmillan.

Atkinson, L. (1986). The comparative validities of the Rorschach and MMPI: A meta-analysis. *Canadian Psychology, 27*, 238–347.

Atkinson, L., Quarrington, B., Alp, I. E., & Cyr, J. J. (1986) Rorschach validity: An empirical approach to the literature. *Journal of Clinical Psychology, 42*, 360–362.

Buros, O. K. (1978). Introduction. In O. K. Buros (Ed.), *The eighth mental measurement yearbook* (Vol. 1, pp. xxxi-xliv). Highland Park, NJ: Gryphon.

Cohen, J. (1983). The cost of dichotomization. *Applied Psychological Measurement, 7*, 249–253.

Dahlstrom, W. G., Welsh, G. S., & Dahlstrom, L. E. (1972). *An MMPI handbook*. Minneapolis: University of Minnesota Press.

Dush, D. M., Hirt, M. L., & Schroeder, H. (1983). Self-statement modification with adults: A meta-analysis. *Psychological Bulletin, 94*, 408–422.

Exner, J. E., Jr. (1983). Rorschach assessment. In I. B. Weiner (Ed.), *Clinical methods in psychology* (2nd ed., pp. 58–99). New York: Wiley.

Exner, J. E., Jr. (1986). *The Rorschach: A comprehensive system* (2nd ed., Vol. 1). New York: Wiley.

Glass, G. V., & Hakstian, A. R. (1969). Measures of association in comparative experiments: Their development and interpretation. *American Educational Research Journal, 6*, 403–414.

Hays, W. L. (1973). *Statistics for the social sciences* (2nd ed.). New York: Holt, Rinehart & Winston.

Hays, W. L. (1981). *Statistics* (3rd ed.). New York: Holt, Rinehart & Winston.

Hedges, L. V., & Olkin, I. (1985). *Statistical methods for meta-analysis*. Orlando, FL: Academic Press.

Hunter, J. E., Schmidt, F. L., & Jackson, G. B. (1982). *Meta-analysis: Cumulating research findings across studies*. Berkeley, CA: Sage.

Jensen, A. R. (1965). A review of the Rorschach. In O. K. Buros (Ed.), *Sixth mental measurement yearbook* (pp. 501–509). Highland Park, NJ: Gryphon.

Jensen, A. R. (1981). *Bias in mental testing*. New York: Free Press.

Kendall, P. C., & Norton-Ford, J. D. (1982). *Clinical psychology.* New York: Wiley.

Korchin, S. J. (1976). *Modern clinical psychology.* New York: Basic Books.

Lubin, B., Larsen, R. M., & Matarazzo, J. D. (1984). Patterns of psychological test usage in the United States: 1935–1982. *American Psychologist, 39,* 451–454.

Matarazzo, J. D. (1972). *Wechsler's measurement and appraisal of adult intelligence.* Baltimore, MD: Williams & Wilkins.

Miller, R. C., & Berman, J. S. (1983). The efficacy of cognitive behavior therapies: A quantitative review of the research evidence. *Psychological Bulletin, 94,* 39–53.

Parker, K. C. H. (1983). A meta-analysis of the reliability and validity of the Rorschach. *Journal of Personality Assessment, 47,* 227–231.

Phares, E. J. (1984). *Clinical psychology: Concepts, methods and profession* (2nd ed.). Homewood, IL: Dorsey.

Smith, M. L., & Glass, G. V. (1977). Meta-analysis of psychotherapy outcome studies. *American Psychologist, 32,* 752–760.

Smith, M. L., Glass, G. V., & Miller, T. I. (1980). *The benefits of psychotherapy.* Baltimore, MD: Johns Hopkins University Press.

13

GENERALIZABILITY THEORY

RICHARD J. SHAVELSON, NOREEN M. WEBB AND
GLENN L. ROWLEY

Generalizability theory (Cronbach, Gleser, Nanda, & Rajaratnam, 1972) provides a framework for examining the dependability of behavioral measurements. Generalizability theory (GT) extends classical reliability theory most notably by recognizing and estimating the magnitude of the multiple sources of measurement error. In this article, we describe GT for an audience of psychologists, not psychometricians. To this end, we develop the theory's central concepts concretely and simply, linking the new theory to the classical theory (CT). We then describe some recent advances and conclude with a concrete application.

MOTIVATION FOR GENERALIZABILITY THEORY

CT partitions observed-score variance into two parts: that which is thought to be systematic (called true-score variance) and that which is

Reprinted from the *American Psychologist, 44,* 922–932. Copyright 1989 by the American Psychological Association.

thought to be random (called error variance). The results of this partition are elegant and satisfying.

CT's usefulness, however, depends on the researcher's ability to estimate true-score and error variances from data. With practical application of CT, we find that error variance is not a monolithic construct; error arises from multiple sources. Consequently, error estimates and estimates of reliability (the ratio of true- to observed-score variance) vary according to the data-collection design. Test–retest reliability counts day-to-day variation in performance as error, but not variation due to item sampling. An internal-consistency coefficient counts variation due to item sampling as error, but not day-to-day variation. Alternate-forms reliability counts both sources as error. CT, then, sits precariously on shifting definitions of true- and error-scores.

GT, in contrast, recognizes that there may be multiple definitions of true- and error-scores. Multiple sources of error define the universe of generalization, a fundamental notion in GT. A measurement taken on a person records a sample of behavior. A score

> is only one of many scores that might serve the same purpose. The decision maker is almost never interested in the response given to the particular stimulus objects or questions, to the particular tester, at the particular moment of testing. Some, at least, of these conditions of measurement could be altered without making the score any less acceptable to the decision maker. (Cronbach et al., 1972, p. 15)

A score's usefulness, then, largely depends on the extent to which it allows us to generalize accurately to behavior in some wider set of situations, a *universe of generalization.*

> That is to say, there is a universe of observations, any of which would have yielded a usable basis for the decision. The ideal datum on which to base the decision would be something like the person's mean score over all acceptable observations, which we shall call his "universe score." The investigator uses the observed score or some function of it as if it were the universe score. That is, he generalizes from sample to universe. (Cronbach et al., 1972, p. 15)

The concept of *reliability,* so fundamental to CT, is replaced by the broader and more flexible notion of *generalizability.* Instead of asking how accurately observed scores reflect their corresponding true scores, GT asks how accurately observed scores permit us to generalize about persons' behavior in a defined universe of situations. *"The question of 'reliability' thus resolves into a question of accuracy of generalization, or generalizability"* (Cronbach et al., 1972, p. 15).

A FRAMEWORK FOR ESTIMATING ERROR AND GENERALIZABILITY

GT can be described and illustrated within the analysis of variance (ANOVA) framework. GT is to measurement what the ANOVA is to substantive research. Just as the researcher attempts to identify and estimate the effects of potentially important independent variables, G theory attempts to identify and estimate the magnitude of the potentially important sources of error in a measurement. Just as the substantive researcher may manipulate some independent variables, control others, and ignore still others, so can the researcher concerned about measurement quality systematically manipulate certain facets of error, control others, and ignore still others.

The connection between GT and CT is paralleled by the connection between factorial and simple ANOVA. A researcher, using simple ANOVA, partitions variance into two parts, usually labeled "between" and "within." The former is thought of as systematic variance and is associated with the design factor that distinguishes groups from one another. The latter is thought of as random and treated as error because it is variance that obscures the researcher's focus on group differences. In the same way, CT partitions variance into true-score and error variance. The former is thought of as systematic variance, associated with differences between the objects of measurement (persons), whereas the latter is treated as random variance, unrelated to true-score variation.

By applying factorial instead of simple ANOVA, the researcher acknowledges multiple factors contributing to variance in data by partitioning data into segments corresponding to each factor, to the interactions among them, and to "random error." Simple ANOVA asks more limited questions, and addresses them with less efficiency, than does factorial ANOVA. Similarly, the extension of CT to GT acknowledges multiple influences on measurement variance. Whereas CT partitions variance into only two sources, GT partitions variance into many sources, corresponding to systematic variance among the objects of measurement, to multiple error sources, and to their interactions.

GT's multifaceted approach to error can be illustrated by a study of the dependability of measures of disaster survivors' psychological improvement (Gleser, Green, & Winget, 1978). Twenty adult survivors (S) were interviewed independently by two interviewers (I). Each interview was rated independently by two raters (R) as to the extent of each survivor's psychiatric impairment on a number of subscales (e.g., anxiety) of the Psychiatric Evaluation Form (Gleser et al., 1978). In differentiating survivors with respect to the extent of impairment, error in the measurement may arise from inconsistencies associated with interviewers, with raters, and with other unidentified sources. GT incorporates these potential sources of error into a measurement model and estimates the components of variance associated with each source of variation in the $20 \times 2 \times 2$ ($S \times I \times R$) design.

Table 1 presents the sources of variation and the estimated variance components for the anxiety subscale. Three components are large relative to the others. The first, for survivors, is analogous to true-score variance in CT and indicates that substantial differences among the survivors were detected, regardless of who interviewed them or who rated their interviews. The second, the survivor by interviewer interaction, represents one source of measurement error and is due to inconsistencies between the two interviewers in obtaining information from different survivors (e.g., the two interviewers may have provided protocols that led raters to rank order survivors differently). The third is the residual term representing the $S \times I \times R$ interaction and unidentified sources of measurement error. The lower variance components for R and I indicate that there were less systematic differences between raters in the overall level of the ratings that they gave and between interviewers in the data that they gathered. R did not interact substantially with S or with I, indicating that the differences among survivors and between interviewers were reported consistently by the two raters.

CONCEPTUAL UNDERPINNINGS OF GENERALIZABILITY THEORY

GT extends CT in several important ways. First, it recognizes multiple sources of measurement error, estimates each source separately, and provides a mechanism for optimizing the reliability. Second, although GT

TABLE 1
Generalizability of Measures of Disaster Survivors' Psychiatric Impairment

Source of variation	Estimated variance components
Survivors (S)	1.84
Raters (R)	0.21
Interviewers (I)	0.49
S × R	0.27
S × I	1.82
R × I	0.03
Residual (S × R × I, error)	1.58

provides a reliability coefficient, called a "generalizability coefficient," the theory self-consciously focuses on variance components that index the magnitude of each source of error. Third, GT distinguishes between *relative decisions*, where interest attaches to the dependability of the differences among individuals, and *absolute decisions*, where scores are themselves interpretable without reference to others' performance. Fourth, GT distinguishes between *generalizability* (G) and *decision* (D) studies. G studies estimate the magnitude of as many potential sources of measurement error as possible. D studies use information from a G study to design a measurement that minimizes error for a *particular* purpose.

Multiple Sources of Measurement Error

It was recognized early that the measurement error estimated in two applications of a test (retest method) was not necessarily the same as the error estimated with alternative forms of the same test (e.g., Goodenough, 1936; Thorndike, 1947). CT, however, cannot estimate the separate sources of error simultaneously. Hence, researchers who measure the achievement of five students on a four-item test on two test occasions have to decide whether to estimate the retest reliability of total scores or the internal consistency of the test on each of the two test occasions. Regardless, they cannot simultaneously estimate the impact of *test occasion* (o), *item homogeneity* (i), and their combination (o × i) on the reliability of the measurement. Without being able to estimate each potential source of error, how are they to decide, in order to achieve a desired level of reliability, whether to increase the number of occasions, the number of items, or some combination of the two?

GT addresses this problem by recognizing that behavioral measurements may contain multiple sources of error. The sources of error (e.g., occasions, raters, and items) are called facets, and the levels of the facets are called conditions. Hence, GT replaces CT's simple representation of a person's (p) observed score on a particular test (i), X_{pi}, as the sum of his or her true score (T_p) plus an undifferentiated error (E_{pi}) term—$X_{pi} = T_p + E_{pi}$—with a representation that includes multiple sources of error, such as occasions (o) and items (i) in our achievement example (Table 2).

Notice that in GT there is a variance associated with each component of an observed score—except for the constant μ. For example, the person effect, analogous to the true score in CT, has a variance over people: $E_p (\mu_p - \mu)^2 = \sigma^2_p$. GT, then, enables us to estimate the magnitude of the variance in observed scores due to universe-score variance and to multiple sources of error—*occasions* and *items* in our example.

TABLE 2
Decomposition of an Observed Score in Classical and Generalizability
Theory

Decomposition of observed score	Definition
Classical theory	
$X_{pi} = T_p$	True score for person p
$\quad + E_{pi}$	Error for person p on item i
Generalizability theory	
$X_{poi} = \mu$	Grand mean
$\quad + \mu_p - \mu$	Person effect
$\quad + \mu_o - \mu$	Occasion effect
$\quad + \mu_i + \mu$	Item effect
$\quad + \mu_{po} - \mu_p - \mu_o + \mu$	Person × occasion effect
$\quad + \mu_{pi} - \mu_p - \mu_i - \mu$	Person × item effect
$\quad + \mu_{oi} - \mu_o - \mu_i \mu$	Occasion × item effect
$\quad + $ residual	p × o × i, error

Note: p = person; i = item; o = occasion; μ = constant.

Estimated Variance Components

Variance component estimation is not unique to GT; it also underlies CT's approach to determining reliability. For example, a randomized blocks ANOVA can be used to estimate variance components and then calculate reliability. Only a single source of error (either occasions or items) can be considered at a time. If we consider occasions as introducing error, the score for each person on each occasion would be summed over items. The ANOVA provides mean squares (MS) for persons and the residual (person × occasion interaction confounded with random error). From the mean squares, variance components can be estimated. Table 3 provides the ANOVA summary information plus the expressions used to compute variance components for the persons-by-occasions (retest reliability) design. The reliability of the test is given by $(MS_p - MS_{res})/MS_p$ = true-score variance/observed-score variance. The procedures for determining internal consistency reliability (persons × items design) are analogous.

Suppose we expand the ANOVA approach of CT to include both error *facets* in the achievement example: occasions *and* items. We could then estimate variance components for seven sources of variation: persons (p), occasions (o), items (i), the two-way interactions po, pi and oi, and the three-way interaction confounded with error (poi, *e*). The magnitude of the variance components would tell us how much each facet contributes to measurement error (see Table 4).

TABLE 3
Expected Mean Squares for a Random-Effects Persons by Occasions Design

Source of variation	MS	Expected MS	Estimated variance component
Persons (p)	MS_p	$\sigma^2_{res} + n_o\sigma^2_p$	$\sigma^2_p = (MS_p - MS_{res})/n_o$
Occasion (o)	MS_o	$\sigma^2_{res} + n_p\sigma^2_o$	$\sigma^2_o = (MS_o - MS_{res})/n_p$
$p \times o, e$	MS_{res}	$\sigma^2_{po, e}$	$\sigma^2_{po, e} = MS_{res}$

Note: n_o = number of occasions; n_p = number of persons; e = error; res = residential.

TABLE 4
Generalizability Theory Applied to the Persons by Occasions by Items Design

Source of variation	Estimated variance component
Persons (p)	.06
Occasions (o)	.00
Items (i)	.03
$p \times o$	.01
$p \times i$	.00
$o \times i$	.00
Residual ($p \times o \times i$, error)	.24

Note: The Generalizability coefficient for two occasions, four items = .67, $\sigma^2_p/[\sigma^2_p + (\sigma^2_{po}/n_o) + (\sigma^2_{pi}/n_i) + (\sigma^2_{poi}/n_on_i)]$.

From these estimated variance components, a *generalizability coefficient*, analogous to a reliability coefficient, can be calculated by dividing the estimated person variance component by an estimated observed-score variance. A more formal development of the G coefficient, however, must await a treatment of relative and absolute decisions and their implication for the definition of what constitutes measurement error.

Relative and Absolute Decisions and the Generalizability Coefficient

CT is a theory of individual differences. In a p × o design, for example, there are three sources of variation (Table 3): p, o, and the p × o interaction confounded with error (we call the highest order interaction the residual). A reliability coefficient is calculated with two of the three sources of variation, persons and residual:

$$r_{xx'} = \frac{\hat{\sigma}^2_p}{\hat{\sigma}^2_p + \hat{\sigma}^2_{res}/n_o}.$$

The occasion effect should be zero because CT assumes strictly parallel measurements (but see Lord & Novick, 1968). Only the person and

GENERALIZABILITY THEORY   239

residual variation give rise to differences among individuals; the occasion effect is constant for all individuals in the p × o design.

Suppose, however, that to pass the written portion of a driving test one must answer at least 85% of the questions correctly. A passing score does not depend on the performance of others, and even if one ranks highly, a score of 84% will not be a passing grade. A large *occasion* effect suggests that one's score on the driving test depends on, for example, health or fatigue on the day one takes the test. When attention focuses on the actual value of the score and not one's standing among a group of individuals, as in driving tests, typing tests, or domain referenced tests, all three sources of variation in a p × o design (persons, occasions, and the residual) must be considered. Occasions can only be ignored if its variance component is very small.

GT distinguishes between decisions based on the relative standing of individuals (e.g., college admission) and decisions based on the absolute value of a score (e.g., driving license). Error in *relative decisions* arises from all nonzero variance components associated with rank ordering of individuals, other than the component for the object of measurement (persons). Specifically, variance components associated with the interaction of persons and each facet or combination of facets define error. In a p × o × i design, for example, the variance components that contribute to error for relative decisions (σ^2_{Rel}) are σ^2_{po}, σ^2_{pi}, and $\sigma^2_{\text{po,e}}$.

Decisions based on the level of the observed score, without regard to the performance of others, are called *absolute decisions*. All variance components associated with that score, except the component for the object of measurement, are defined as error. Error is associated not only with the ranking of individuals but also with constant effects associated with the facets. The difficulty of a particular test form or the stringency of a particular interviewer will influence an individual's observed score and, hence, absolute decisions about that individual. In a p × o × i design, then, the variance components that contribute to error variance for absolute decisions (σ^2_{Abs}) are σ^2_{o}, σ^2_{i}, σ^2_{po}, σ^2_{pi}, σ^2_{oi}, and $\sigma^2_{\text{poi,e}}$.

While stressing the importance of variance components and errors such as σ^2_{Rel}, GT also provides a coefficient analogous to the reliability coefficient in CT: true-score variance divided by observed score variance: $r_{xx'} = \sigma^2_t / \sigma^2_x$. GT's *generalizability coefficient*, E_ρ^2, is the ratio of the universe-score variance to the expected observed-score variance, that is, an intraclass correlation:

$$E_\rho^2\, \text{Rel} = \frac{\sigma^2_p}{E\sigma^2_x} = \frac{\sigma^2_p}{\sigma^2_p + \sigma^2\, \text{Rel}}.$$

(For absolute decisions, a generalizability coefficient can be defined in an analogous manner, using σ^2_{Abs}.) The expected observed-score variance is used because G theory assumes only random sampling of facet levels; observed-score variance may change from one application of the design to another. Sample estimates of the parameters in the G coefficient formula are used to estimate the G coefficient:

$$E_{\hat{\rho}}^2 \text{ Rel} = \frac{\hat{\sigma}^2_p}{\hat{\sigma}^2_p + \hat{\sigma}^2 \text{ Rel}}.$$

$E_{\hat{\rho}}^2$ is a biased but consistent estimator of E_{ρ}^2.

Generalizability (G) and Decision (D) Studies

A generalizability study is designed to estimate variance components underlying a measurement process by defining the universe of admissible observations as broadly as possible. Once data have been collected, a large set of variance components can be estimated. By optimizing the number of conditions of each facet, much in the way the Spearman-Brown prophecy formula does in CT, variance components can be reduced in magnitude and the measurement can be tailored to a particular purpose. Substantive studies that tailor the measurement to make decisions are known as D (for decision) studies. In distinguishing a G study from a D study, G theory recognizes that the former is associated with the development of a measurement procedure whereas the latter then applies the procedure.

By design, then, the G study systematically treats all the facets that are likely to enter into the generalizations of a diverse group of users. Hence, the G study will incorporate many more facets and variance component estimates than any one user would employ. To estimate all possible variance components, crossed designs are typically used.[1]

In planning a D study, the decision maker (a) defines the universe of generalization and (b) specifies the proposed interpretation of the measurement. These plans determine (c) the questions to be asked of the G study data in order to optimize the D study's measurement design.

Defining the Universe of Generalization

G theory recognizes that the decision maker will generalize to a universe made up of some subset of the facets in the G study. This universe of generalization may be defined by reducing the levels of a facet (e.g., creating a fixed facet; cf. fixed factor in ANOVA), by selecting and thereby controlling one level of a facet, or by ignoring a facet.

---

[1] The only exception would be D studies in which a particular nesting will definitely be used; in that case, the G study should incorporate the same nesting to provide the most precise estimates of the variance components corresponding to the nested facets; see Cronbach et al. (1972, p. 45).

Recognizing that there may be different universes of generalization allows us to resolve a paradox that is difficult to resolve with CT. Suppose that a performance is rated by several judges and that there are inconsistencies among them. The reliability of a composite score from all of the judges' ratings will be reduced by their disagreements and may even be increased by discarding all but one judge. However, even though the scores may be more reliable, who would prefer to use the score from a single judge rather than a composite score from many judges? Viewed from the framework of G theory, the choice is clear. The score from a single judge may be highly generalizable to a narrow universe: ratings given by that particular judge, with all of his or her idiosyncracies. A score obtained by combining ratings from several judges may be generalizable with less precision to a more interesting and important universe: ratings given by a population of judges.

Optimizing the Measurement Design

G studies provide information needed to optimize the measurement design for a D study. For example, in a study of hands-on performance of Navy machinist mates (Webb, Shavelson, Kim, & Chen, in press), variance components for a persons (machinist mates) × observers × tasks design were estimated. One question asked of the G study was whether the reliability of the measurement could be increased more efficiently by adding observers or tasks (Table 5). By adding tasks, we could reduce error variance much more than by adding observers, and the G coefficient would increase correspondingly. This is because the observer and persons × observer effects are remarkably small—a desirable measurement property if it arises from successful observer training and not from consultation among them.

TABLE 5
Estimated Variance Components for the Navy's Hands-on Performance
Tests of Machinist Mates: Engine Room

Source of variation	$N_{obs} = 1$ $N_{tasks} = 1$	$N_o = 2$ $N_t = 11$	$N_o = 1$ $N_t = 18$
Persons (p)	.00626	.00626	.00626
Observers (o)	.00000	.00000	.00000
Tasks (t)	.00979	.00088	.00054
po	.00000	.00000	.00000
pt	.02584	.00235	.00144
ot	.00003	.00000	.00000
po, e	.00146	.00007	.00008
Generalizability coefficients			
Relative	.19	.72	.80
Absolute	.14	.66	.75

D studies can be tailored not only by examining the trade-off between the number of conditions of different facets, but also by considering a wide variety of designs, including crossed, partially nested, and completely nested designs. All facets in the D design may be random (cf. random-model ANOVA), or only some may be random (cf. mixed-model ANOVA). Nested designs are often used for convenience, for increasing sample size, or for both. In general, the G study should be as fully crossed as possible, so that all sources of variation in the design can be estimated. From the results of a fully crossed G study, the generalizability for a wide variety of nested D study designs can be estimated.

Assumption of Steady State Behavior

Most measurement approaches, including CT and GT, assume that behavior remains constant over observations. Assessment of reliability is more complicated when behavior changes over time. Rogosa, Floden, and Willett (1984) showed that when behavior changes systematically over time (whether linearly or nonlinearly), the estimate of an individual's universe score will be time dependent. Inconsistent individual differences over time will arise whenever the trends for different individuals (whether they are due to unsystematic or systematic factors) vary.

A generalizability analysis with occasions as a facet can only identify some of these trends. Only when the variance components for occasions and the interaction between persons and occasions are both small can changes over time be ruled out. When one or the other component (or both) is relatively large, it is impossible to determine whether the changes over time are due to unsystematic variation in persons' behavior over time (the usual interpretation) or to different systematic trends over occasions for different people.

The best way to meet the steady state assumption is to restrict the time interval so that the observations of individuals' behavior represent the same phenomenon. If, even within a short time period, behavior cannot be assumed to be in a steady state, a generalizability analysis may not be appropriate. Rogosa et al. (1984) described ways to specify the process by which behavior changes over time and, consequently, to determine whether changes in behavior are systematic or unsystematic.

Rowley (in press) has pointed out that, even in the absence of any systematic time trend, there still may be dependencies among observations that may influence estimates of error variance and, hence, estimates of generalizability. When successive observations are correlated (e.g., there may be a nonzero correlation between the amount of time that an elementary school student spends reading from one occasion to the next; see

Leinhardt, Zigmond, & Cooley, 1981), the usual methods of estimating error variance will produce underestimates (Gottman, 1981), resulting in inflated estimated generalizability coefficients. This potential problem can be avoided by carrying out nonsuccessive observations (e.g., every third day rather than on consecutive days; see Rowley, in press).

NEW DEVELOPMENTS IN GENERALIZABILITY THEORY

A variety of new developments in GT have emerged since the publication of Cronbach et al.'s (1972) monograph. Here we touch on only a few: (a) a new procedure for estimating variance components, (b) treatment of fixed facets in D-study designs, (c) symmetry in G-study designs, and (d) generalizability of a multivariate profile.

Estimated Variance Components

Shavelson and Webb (1981) characterized problems in estimating variance components as the Achilles heel of GT *and* sampling theories in general. Especially with small sample sizes, ANOVA *estimates* of variance components are unstable and may even be negative (e.g., Cronbach et al., 1972; Lindquist, 1953; Shavelson & Webb, 1981; Smith, 1978).

Several methods have been proposed to treat negative estimates. Cronbach et al. (1972) recommended setting negative estimates to zero and carrying the zero through wherever that variance component enters the expected mean squares of another variance component. This produces biased estimates. Brennan (1983) recommended setting negative estimates to zero but using the negative estimate wherever that variance component enters the expected mean squares for another component. This procedure produces unbiased estimates. However, in neither case is it statistically comfortable to change estimates to zero.

Shavelson and Webb (1981) reviewed a Bayesian approach that sets a lower bound of zero on the estimated variance component and thereby produces nonnegative estimates. However, they concluded that this approach is not well enough developed to have widespread applicability.

Marcoulides (1987) examined another approach to estimating variance components that also restricts the estimate to zero or above: *restricted maximum likelihood estimation* (RMLE or REML now available in BMDP3V; see Genrich & Sampson, 1976). In all of his simulations, the RMLE variance component estimates were closer to the true parameters than those from ANOVA. In contrast to RMLE, the ANOVA was sensitive to distributional form, incorrectly estimated variance components for unbalanced designs, and produced negative estimates. Only with balanced data sets from normal distributions and balanced one-way dichotomous distributions did the two methods perform similarly. Compared to RMLE, ANOVA tended to underestimate universe score variance and overestimate error variances. So, on average, the RMLE method produced higher estimated G coefficients than ANOVA. With the real datasets, the two methods provided very similar estimates of variance components and G coefficients.

Fixed Facets in G Theory

A fixed facet in GT is analogous to a fixed factor in ANOVA—the conditions of the facet (levels of the factor) in the G study exhaust the possible conditions of interest. A fixed facet may arise because the entire universe of conditions is small and is included in the measurement design or because the decision maker is not interested in generalizing beyond the conditions observed in the G study.

Statistically, G theory treats a fixed facet by averaging over the conditions of the facet and examining the generalizability of these averages over the random facets (Cronbach et al., 1972, p. 60; see Erlich & Shavelson, 1976, for a proof). Averaging provides the best score for an individual because it represents the individual's universe score over all conditions of the fixed facet. The statistical analysis of data from G studies with a fixed facet leads to conclusions about scores averaged over the conditions of the fixed facet. The treatment of fixed facets shows that G theory is essentially a random facet measurement theory or, more specifically, a random-effects ANOVA theory (Rubin, 1974).

When Are Facets Fixed and When Are They Random?

A question immediately arises: Do we really randomly sample test items or test forms or judges (etc.)? In fact, we almost invariably take a convenient sample or include all possible levels of the facet (e.g., days of the week). Don't all psychometric procedures really produce fixed facets (Loevinger, 1965)?

There are several answers to this question. Cornfield and Tukey (1956) provided one answer: The inference is to the population from which the convenient sample was drawn. A second answer, perhaps somewhat less limiting, invokes the Bayesian notion of *exchangeability* (Novick, 1976): Even though conditions of a facet have not been sampled randomly, the facet may be considered to be random if conditions not observed in the G study are equally acceptable to, or exchangeable with, the observed conditions (see Shavelson & Webb, 1981, for details).

Procedures for Handling Fixed Facets

Sometimes it may not make sense to average over the conditions of a fixed facet. For example, Erlich and Shavelson (1978) calculated the generalizability of measures of teachers' behavior by averaging over measures taken during mathematics and reading instruction. This seemed to be averaging apples and oranges because of differences in the two types of instruction. If it does not make conceptual sense to average over the conditions of a fixed facet, or if conclusions about such averages are of little interest, a better strategy is to conduct a separate G study within each condition of the fixed facet. This permits, for example, different conclusions to be reached concerning the teaching of mathematics and reading.

An alternative strategy is to conduct a preliminary analysis, treating the fixed facet as random. If the variance components associated with that facet are small, we may (if it makes conceptual sense) average over the conditions of the fixed facet (see Shavelson & Webb, 1981, for details). If the component is large, we may conduct separate G studies for each condition of the fixed facet.

Subtests as Random Representatives of Their Domains

Cronbach (in press) has suggested a new treatment of reliability for test batteries in which several subtests measure a dimension. In the Stanford-Binet Intelligence Test, there are 15 subtests that index four dimensions: short-term memory, and verbal, quantitative, and abstract/visual reasoning. These dimensions are combined to create a composite or total standard age score. To determine the CT reliability of the composite, we would most likely calculate the reliability of each subtest and then use a version of the Jackson-Ferguson (1941) procedure to evaluate the reliability of the composite.

> But if subtests are indicators of a construct (e.g., verbal reasoning), the analysis might better view subtests as random and evaluate the adequacy of the test score as a representation of the domain of verbal reasoning subtests. It seems to me that an interpretation that a pupil is better in verbal than in Abstract Reasoning {sic} is a statement about the domain, not the fixed subtests. (Cronbach, personal communication, July 15, 1987)

Cronbach (in press) treated "subtests as random representatives of their domains, to evaluate how well each section {subtest} score measures its postulated latent trait" (p. 6). In estimating reliability, he considered each dimension separately (see the section on fixed facets presented earlier) and calculated an internal consistency coefficient treating variability among subtests within a dimension as measurement error.

In a G study of the Stanford-Binet, then, subjects would constitute the object of measurement (random). Dimensions would be considered a fixed facet covering the universe of dimensions of intelligence, or at least the universe to which the decision maker is interested in generalizing. Subtests would be considered a random facet, nested within their respective dimensions (cf. Cronbach et al., 1972, pp. 234–256).

Symmetry of Behavioral Measurements

The purpose of behavioral measurement has typically been to differentiate *individuals* and, more recently, to locate their scores within some subject matter or skill domain. In CT, we customarily think about persons as the objects of measurement and judge the suitability of a measure in terms of how well it enables us to distinguish between persons. All other facets (test items, occasions, raters, etc.) are treated as error. Cardinet and his colleagues (Cardinet & Tourneur, 1985; Cardinet, Tourneur, & Allal, 1976, 1981) recognized, however, that the *object of measurement* may change. Particularly in educational research, interest might attach to rates of success on a particular test item as an indicator of change, as has been the practice with the National Assessment of Educational Progress. Alternatively, classrooms, rather than individual students, might be the focus, even though we have a test score for each student in the class. In these cases, individual differences may give rise to measurement error (e.g., Gillmore, Kane, & Naccarato, 1978; Kane & Brennan, 1977).

Cardinet, Tourneur, and Allal (1976, 1981; Cardinet & Tourneur, 1985) proposed the *principle of symmetry* to enable G theory to address the situation in which the object of measurement might change. This principle asserts that any facet in a design may be regarded as the object of measurement. We may ask how well data enable us to distinguish among classes or schools or among instructional objectives. Such questions can be handled within GT: Differences among persons, instead of being the object of the measurements, obscure the distinctions being sought and are therefore "error." Variance components may be computed from a dataset regardless of the measurement design; the treatment of the variance components becomes necessarily asymmetrical only when a decision is made about the object of measurement. "Until the two kinds of problems (ANOVA estimates, measurement) were clearly disentangled, no multipurpose measurement was possible" (Cardinet, personal communication, May 9, 1980).

Generalizability of a Multivariate Profile

Behavioral measurements often involve multiple scores describing individuals' aptitudes or skills. As noted earlier, the Stanford-Binet intelligence test, for example, uses 15 subtests to measure four correlated dimensions. Although multiple scores may be conceived as vectors and thus should be treated simultaneously, the majority of G and D studies have not done so. Rather, each variable has been treated separately, perhaps because the multivariate literature is not easily comprehended (e.g., Bock, 1963, 1966; Cronbach et al., 1972). An attempt to elucidate multivariate G theory has been made elsewhere (e.g., Shavelson, 1985; Webb & Shavelson, 1981; Webb, Shavelson, & Maddahian, 1983), but several recent developments may be important to future work.

G Coefficient For a Multivariate Composite

In forming a composite for a multivariate measure such as the Stanford-Binet, a number of alternatives present themselves: Take the sum of the four dimensions, take a weighted sum based on expert judgment from theory, or take a weighted sum based on the variance of dimension scores. From a GT perspective, we might weight the dimension scores to maximize the G coefficient (Joe & Woodward, 1976; Woodward & Joe, 1973) and report a G coefficient for the multivariate composite. One problem with weightings based on variances or on maximizing a G coefficient is that the weights are "blind" to the theory that originally gave rise to the profile of measures. Statistical criteria for weighting measures do not necessarily make conceptual sense.

A second option, one based on the conceptual underpinnings of the profile, is to determine the weights by expert judgment. However, even expert judges may have differing views about the relative importance of elements in a composite. There may be no reason for preferring one judge's weights over another, and there is no guarantee that an average set of weights is in any sense the "correct" set. Another problem is that this choice of weights ignores the statistical properties of the data and therefore results in a composite whose psychometric properties may be poor.

A third alternative is to posit a conceptual model of the profile, fit this model statistically with confirmatory factor analysis, and then weight each variable in the composite according to its loading from the factor analysis. In this way, expert judgment in setting forth the conceptual model is combined with statistical accuracy for obtaining the appropriate weights to fit the model.

Short, Webb, and Shavelson (1986) compared these approaches in analyses of addition, subtraction, multiplication, and division subtests (Table 6). As expected, the multivariate G coefficient was highest with the weights derived for the coefficient itself. However, the weights derived from the confirmatory factor analysis produced nearly as high a multivariate G coefficient. Expert judgment resulted in a considerably lower G

TABLE 6
Generalizability (G) Coefficients Resulting From Four Weighting Schemes

Scheme	Weights			G coefficient	
	A/S[a]	M[b]	D[c]	$n_o = 1$[d]	$n_o = 2$[d]
Multivariate G	0.11	0.07	0.35	0.71	0.83
Decision maker	2.00	3.00	1.00	0.59	0.74
Unit weights	1.00	1.00	1.00	0.65	0.79
Factor loadings	2.05	2.09	4.87	0.70	0.82

[a]Addition/subtraction. [b]Multiplication. [c]Division. [d]Number of occasions.

coefficient. If this finding is replicated, confirmatory factor analysis and G theory might be merged to handle multivariate composites.

ILLUSTRATIVE APPLICATION

One of GT's greatest strengths lies in its ability to model a remarkably wide array of behavioral measurement applications. Here we present only one example, a study of the general educational development ratings contained in the *Dictionary of Occupational Titles* (U.S. Department of Labor, 1965). We hope it gives a flavor of the flexibility of the theory.

The U.S. Department of Labor (1972) developed the General Educational Development (GED) scale to characterize the amount of *reasoning, mathematics,* and *language* ability needed to perform various jobs. GED ratings are used in several employment and training situations, such as (a) estimating the time required to learn job skills; (b) deciding whether to refer persons to specific employers, job training programs, or remedial education programs; and (c) equating jobs with similar educational requirements.

In a G study of GED ratings (Webb & Shavelson, 1981; Webb, Shavelson, Shea, & Morello, 1981), job analysts were given written descriptions of jobs published in the *Dictionary of Occupational Titles* (DOT) and were asked to rate the jobs on three dimensions of the GED scale: reasoning development, mathematics development, and language development. Each of 71 raters from 11 field centers across the United States evaluated the three dimensions of a sample of jobs on two occasions. Different centers had from 2 to 12 analysts. Hence, the G-study design was a partially nested, unbalanced design with different numbers of raters nested within centers.

Because we were concerned with estimating the general educational development required to perform each job, *jobs* is the *object of measurement,* and the variance component for jobs, σ^2_j, is interpreted as the universe-score variance. All other variance components were considered measurement error because *absolute* decisions are made regarding GED requirements for each job. Measurement error, then, was defined as raters nested within center, centers, occasions, and all interactions.

Univariate G Study

Due to the unbalanced nature of the design, variance components were estimated in two ways (a) by dropping analysts randomly until we had two analysts per center, thus creating a balanced design; and (b) by Rao's MIVQUE procedure for estimating variance components in unbalanced designs (Hartley, Rao, & La Motte, 1978). We report the estimates in Table 7 for each dimension separately because we considered *dimension* to be a fixed facet, with the three ratings interpreted separately by decision makers.

The estimated variance components for jobs (universe-score variance) differ across GED ratings and are greatest for language. This indicates that jobs were seen to differ more in their demands for language than in their demands for mathematics and reasoning. The patterns of variance components contributing to error were consistent across dimensions: The interaction of raters with jobs accounted for most of the error variation, and occasions and centers accounted for little. This pattern suggested that, by taking the average ratings given by four raters, measurement error could be

TABLE 7
Univariate Generalizability Study of GED Ratings

Source of variation	Estimated variance component					
	Reasoning[a]	Math[a]	Language[a]	Reasoning[b]	Math[b]	Language[b]
Jobs (j)	.74	.63	1.01	.74	.63	1.01
Occasions (o)	.00	.00	.00	.00	.00	.00
Centers (c)	.00	.02	.05	.00	.02	.05
Raters (r:c)	.06	.02	.00	.02	.00	.00
jo	.00	.01	.01	.00	.01	.01
jc	.00	.00	.00	.00	.00	.00
jr:c	.13	.16	.14	.03	.04	.04
oc	.01	.00	.00	.01	.00	.00
or:c	.00	.09	.07	.00	.02	.02
joc	.00	.02	.01	.00	.02	.01
jor:c	.22	.25	.22	.06	.06	.05
Absolute error	.42	.57	.50	.11	.17	.18
$\hat{\rho}^2$ (Absolute G coefficient)	.64	.53	.67	.86	.79	.85

Note: Generalizability (G) study design is raters nested within centers crossed with jobs and occasions. GED = General Educational Development; n_r denotes number of raters; n_o is the number of occasions; n_c is the number of centers.
[a]$n_r = n_o = n_c = 1$. [b]$n_r = 4$, $n_o = 1$, $n_c = 1$.

reduced by about 75% and the G coefficient correspondingly increased to 0.86 for reasoning, 0.79 for mathematics, and 0.85 for language.

Multivariate G Study

For the multivariate G study, a random effects, multivariate ANOVA was used to estimate variance and *covariance* components with reasoning, mathematics, and language ratings as a vector of scores. Due to the limited capacity of computer programs available to perform the multivariate analysis and because geographic center contributed almost nothing to variability among job ratings, geographic center was disregarded in this analysis. (The reader may note that the case for dropping occasions was equally strong; this is reflected in the results that follow). The design, then, was raters crossed with jobs and occasions.

For each source of variation, variance and covariance component matrices were computed from the mean product matrices. One matrix, for example, contained estimated universe-score variances and covariances. All negative estimated variance components (diagonal values) were set equal to zero in further estimation. For this analysis, the variance component matrices, multivariate G coefficients, and canonical weights corresponding to each G coefficient were computed.

The estimated variance and covariance matrices are presented in Table 8.[2] Because centers were dropped, the variance components in Table 8 are similar to but do not equal those in the univariate analysis (Table 7). The components of covariance, however, provide new information. The large components for jobs reflect the underlying (disattenuated) covariances among the GED components. Jobs that require high reasoning ability are seen by raters to require high mathematics and language ability. The nonzero components of variance for raters indicate that some raters give generally higher ratings than others. The positive covariance components for raters indicate that the raters who give higher ratings on one GED component are likely to give higher ratings on the other GED components. The positive variance and covariance components for the job by rater interaction suggest that not only do raters disagree about which jobs require more ability but their disagreement is consistent across GED components. The nonzero components for error suggest that the unexplained factors that contribute to the variation of ratings also contribute to the covariation between ratings. As expected, the components of variance and covariance due to the occasion main effect and its interactions are negligible.

---

[2] Only the components for one rater and one occasion are included. To obtain results for four raters, the components corresponding to the rater effect and rater interactions only need to be divided by four.

TABLE 8
Estimated Variance-Covariance Components for the Multivariate Generalizability Study of GED Ratings

Source of variation	Reasoning	Math	Language
Jobs (j)			
Reasoning	.75		
Math	.64	.66	
Language	.88	.74	1.09
Occasions (o)			
Reasoning	.00		
Math	.00	.00	
Language	.00	.00	.00
Raters (r)			
Reasoning	.03		
Math	.03	.09	
Language	.03	.05	.05
jo			
Reasoning	.00		
Math	.00	.00	
Language	.00	.00	.00
jr			
Reasoning	.12		
Math	.11	.13	
Language	.09	.07	.11
or			
Reasoning	.00		
Math	.01	.01	
Language	.00	.00	.01
jro, e			
Reasoning	.21		
Math	.07	.29	
Language	.11	.10	.26

Note: The G study design is raters nested within centers and crossed with jobs and occasions with scores on reasoning, mathematics, and language.

The GED composites with maximum generalizability are presented in Table 9. When multivariate generalizability was estimated for one rater and one occasion, a single dimension emerged with a coefficient exceeding .50. This dimension is a verbal composite of reasoning and language. The analysis with four raters and one occasion produced two dimensions with coefficients over .50. One composite was defined by reasoning and language (G coefficients .74 and .92 for one and four raters, respectively); the other by a mathematics–language contrast with a G coefficient of .62 for four raters and one occasion.

SUMMARY

GT extends CT by recognizing and simultaneously estimating the magnitude of the multiple possible sources of error in a behavioral mea-

TABLE 9
Canonical Variates for Multivariate Generalizability Study of GED
Ratings

GED component	Canonical coefficients		
	Dimension I[a]	Dimension I[b]	Dimension II[b]
Reasoning	.34	.38	.05
Mathematics	.06	.06	−1.95
Language	.51	.57	1.33
Multivariate G coefficient	.74	.92	.62

[a]For Dimension I, $n_r = 1$ and $n_o = 1$ (n_r = number of raters and n_o = number of occasions). [b]For Dimensions I and II, $n_r = 4$ and $n_o = 1$.

surement, such as occasions, forms, raters, and items. The theory also goes beyond CT by distinguishing between the use of a measurement to make relative or "norm-referenced" decisions and absolute or "domain-referenced" decisions. Error is defined differently for decisions based on ordering of individuals (e.g., in selection situations) and on an individual's observed scores (e.g., typing speed test). Consequently, reliability (*generalizability*) is defined differently for the two types of decisions. GT also recognizes that there is a potentially large number of reliability (G) coefficients associated with a particular measurement. Different G coefficients can be defined according to how broadly or narrowly each decision maker proposes to generalize from a particular application of the measurement procedure. Finally, GT enables decision makers to pinpoint the major sources of error entering into the measurement and determine the most cost-effective ways to apply the measurement procedure for their purpose.

GT, then, provides perhaps the most flexible measurement theory available to psychologists, one that fits a wide variety of practical and theoretical applications. We surmise that the theory is not widely applied in psychological research because of its fairly formidable mathematical development (Cronbach et al., 1972; see also Brennan, 1983). The purpose of this article was to make GT accessible to the potential user. We hope that we succeeded by drawing an analogy between the use of ANOVA to address research questions and the use of GT to address measurement questions, by contrasting CT and GT, and by providing a practical application that illustrates GT's concepts and procedures.

REFERENCES

Bock, R. D. (1963). Multivariate analysis of variance of repeated measurements. In C. W. Harris (Ed.), *Problems of measuring change* (pp. 85–103). Madison, WI: University of Wisconsin Press.

Bock, R. D. (1966). Contributions of multivariate experimental designs to educational research. In R. B. Cattell (Ed.), *Handbook of multivariate experimental psychology* (pp. 820–840). Chicago: Rand McNally.

Brennan, R. L. (1983). *Elements of generalizability theory*. Iowa City, IA: American College Testing Program.

Cardinet, J., & Tourneur, Y. (1985). *Assurer la mesure* [Dependability of the measure]. Bern, Switzerland: Lang.

Cardinet, J., Tourneur, Y., & Allal, L. (1976). The symmetry of generalizability theory: Applications to educational measurement. *Journal of Educational Measurement, 13,* 119–135.

Cardinet, J., Tourneur, Y., & Allal, L. (1981). Extension of generalizability theory and its applications in educational measurement. *Journal of Educational Measurement, 18,* 183–204.

Cornfield, J., & Tukey, J. W. (1956). Average values of mean squares in factorials. *Annals of Mathematical Statistics, 27,* 907–949.

Cronbach, L. J. (in press). Stanford-Binet: Edition 4. In *Mental measurements yearbook.* Lincoln: University of Nebraska Press.

Cronbach, L. J., Gleser, G. C., Nanda, H., & Rajaratnam, N. (1972). *The dependability of behavioral measurements: Theory of generalizability of scores and profiles.* New York: Wiley.

Erlich, O., & Shavelson, R. J. (1976). *The application of generalizability theory to the study of teaching* (Technical Report No. 76-9-1, Beginning Teacher Evaluation Study). San Francisco: Far West Laboratory.

Erlich, O., & Shavelson, R. J. (1978). The search for correlations between measures of teacher behavior and student achievement: Measurement problem, conceptualization problem or both? *Journal of Educational Measurement, 15,* 77–89.

Genrich, R. I., & Sampson, P. F. (1976). Newton-Raphson and related algorithms for maximum likelihood variance component estimation. *Technometrics, 18,* 11–17.

Gillmore, G. M., Kane, M. T., & Naccarato, R. W. (1978). The generalizability of student ratings of instruction: Estimation of course and teacher effects. *Journal of Educational Measurement, 15,* 1–14.

Gleser, G. C., Green, B. L., & Winget, C. N. (1978). Quantifying interview data on psychic impairment of disaster survivors. *The Journal of Nervous and Mental Diseases, 166,* 209–216.

Goodenough, F. L. (1936). A critical note on the use of the term "reliability" in mental measurement. *Journal of Educational Psychology, 27,* 173–178.

Gottman, J. M. (1981). *Time-series analysis: A comprehensive introduction for social scientists.* Cambridge, England: Cambridge University Press.
Hartley, H. O., Rao, J. N. K., & La Motte, L. (1978). A simple synthesis-based method of variance component estimation. *Biometrics, 34,* 233–242.

Jackson, R. W. B., & Ferguson, G. A. (1941). *Studies on the reliability of tests.* Toronto: University of Toronto Press.

Joe, G. N., & Woodward, J. A. (1976). Some developments in multivariate generalizability. *Psychometrika, 41,* 205–217.

Kane, M. T., & Brennan, R. L. (1977). The generalizability of class means. *Review of Educational Research, 47,* 267–292.

Leinhardt, G., Zigmond, N., & Cooley, W. W. (1981). Reading instruction and its effects. *American Educational Research Journal, 18,* 343–361.

Lindquist, E. F. (1953). *Design and analysis of experiments in psychology and education.* Boston: Houghton-Mifflin.

Loevinger, J. (1965). Person and population as psychometric concepts. *Psychological Review, 72,* 143–155.

Lord, F. M., & Novick, M. R. (1968). *Statistical theories of mental test scores.* Reading, MA: Addison-Wesley.

Marcoulides, G. A. (1987). *An alternative method for variance component estimation: Applications to generalizability theory.* Unpublished doctoral dissertation, University of California, Los Angeles.

Novick, M. R. (1976). Bayesian methods in educational testing: A third survey. In D. M. N. de Gruijter & L. J. Th. van der Kamp (Eds.), *Advances in psychological and educational testing.* New York: Wiley.

Rogosa, D., Floden, R., & Willett, J. B. (1984). Assessing the stability of teacher behavior. *Journal of Educational Psychology, 76,* 1000–1027.

Rowley, G. (in press). Assessing error in behavioral data: Problems of sequencing. *Journal of Educational Measurement.*

Rubin, D. B. (Reviewer). (1974). The dependability of behavioral measurements: Theory of generalizability for scores and profiles [Review]. *Journal of the American Statistical Association, 69,* 1050.

Shavelson, R. J. (1985). *Generalizability of military performance measurements: I. Individual performance.* Washington, DC: National Research Council, Committee on the Performance of Military Personnel, Commission on Behavioral and Social Sciences and Education.

Shavelson, R. J., & Webb, N. M. (1981). Generalizability theory: 1973–1980. *British Journal of Mathematical and Statistical Psychology, 34,* 133–166.

Short, L., Webb, N. M., & Shavelson, R. J. (1986, April). *Issues in multivariate generalizability: Weighting schemes and dimensionality.* Paper presented at the meeting of the American Educational Research Association, San Francisco, CA.

Smith, P. (1978). Sampling errors of variance components in small sample multifacet generalizability studies. *Journal of Educational Measurement, 3,* 319–346.

Thorndike, R. L. (1947). *Research problems and techniques* (Report No. 3, AAF Aviation Psychology Program Research Reports). Washington, DC: U.S. Government Printing Office.

U.S. Department of Labor. (1965). *Dictionary of occupational titles* (3rd ed., vol. 2). Washington, DC: U.S. Government Printing Office.

U.S. Department of Labor. (1972). *Handbook for analyzing jobs*. Washington, DC: U.S. Government Printing Office.

Webb, N. M., & Shavelson, R. J. (1981). Multivariate generalizability of general educational development ratings. *Journal of Educational Measurement, 18,* 13–22.

Webb, N. M., Shavelson, R. J., Kim, K-S., & Chen, Z. (in press). Reliability (generalizability) of job performance measurements: Navy machinist mates. *Journal of Military Psychology.*

Webb, N. M., Shavelson, R. J., & Maddahian, E. (1983). Multivariate generalizability theory. In L. J. Fyans, Jr. (Ed.), *Generalizability theory: Inferences and practical applications* (pp. 67–81). San Francisco: Jossey-Bass.

Webb, N. M., Shavelson, R. J., Shea, J., & Morello, E. (1981). Generalizability of general educational development ratings of jobs in the U.S. *Journal of Applied Psychology, 66,* 186–191.

Woodward, J. A., & Joe, G. W. (1973). Maximizing the coefficient of generalizability in multi-facet decision studies. *Psychometrika, 38,* 173–181.

IV

DATA ANALYSIS, EVALUATION, AND INTERPRETATION

Research relies heavily on statistical evaluation to draw conclusions. The use of statistical analyses is not merely a matter of which tests to use. Rather, statistical analyses are fundamentally related to the conceptualization of the study, methods, and interpretation of the substantive findings. In the present section, several issues are related to alternative methods of evaluation and decision-making processes. Alternative tests and selection and use of novel methods of analysis presented in the articles are not only important in their own right, but also in conveying the integral role that data analyses play in all facets of research.

RESEARCH DESIGN AND STATISTICAL EVALUATION

The data analyses are always to be conducted in the service of the substantive ideas that underlie the investigation. As an abstract principle, this is well known. However, the connection between the design and statistical evaluation is often neglected at the design stage. In the planning of research, investigators often focus on the rationale for the study and several procedural decisions (introduction and method section material). Indeed, in graduate training, research proposals may include introduction and method sections without further material regarding the methods of statistical evaluation. However, the types of data analyses, characteristics of the data that are likely to emerge, and limitations of interpretation at the end of the study can be greatly aided by considering statistical evaluation before the design of the study is finalized. In short, statistical evaluation warrants treatment in planning the study. In the analysis of the results, the connection between the predictions and statistical analyses warrants clarification as well.

In the initial article, Bruce Wampold, Betsy Davis, and Roland Good (1990) introduce the notion of *hypothesis validity* to refer to the connections between the theory, hypotheses, and statistical evaluation. With examples from clinical research, they note the importance of specifying predictions and hypotheses and the relation of the specific analyses to these predictions. Several statistical evaluation issues are raised including the use of multiple statistical tests within a given study and the use and limits of omnibus tests.

The vast majority of psychological research focuses on null hypothesis testing and statistical significance. Statistical significance refers to conventions regarding when to consider a particular finding or difference as reliable or unlikely to be due to a "chance." The article by Michael Cowles and Caroline Davis (1982) discusses the origins of the use of $p < .05$ as a criterion for deciding statistical significance. The foundations of the criterion for statistical significance are important to understand because of the marked influence of this convention and how the criterion for significance relates to believability.

In the article by Ralph Rosnow and Robert Rosenthal (1989), several data analysis and statistical decision-making issues are highlighted. Rosnow and Rosenthal note the overreliance on dichotomous decisions based on statistical significance, the inadequacy of the statistical power of research studies, the importance of examining the magnitude of effects, and the need for replication studies. Several areas are introduced in this article that are pivotal to quantitative evaluation of the data.

Jacob Cohen has contributed significantly to research design and statistical evaluation. His most well-known contributions pertain to the importance of *power* in statistical evaluation. Power refers to the likelihood of detecting a difference in an investigation when in fact there is a genuine difference between conditions; alternatively, it is the likelihood of rejecting the null hypothesis (no difference) when that hypothesis is false. The article by Cohen (1990) discusses in an informal and highly engaging style critical issues related to power, data analyses, and design. Cohen discusses sample size, the number of variables included in the analysis, null hypothesis testing, p levels, and effect size, and their role in designing and interpreting research. The article ends with a discussion of how to use statistics in planning a study and interpreting the results.

SELECTED TESTS AND ANALYSES

Several articles address specific issues related to data analysis and its meaning. The article by Ralph Rosnow and Robert Rosenthal (1988) discusses significance tests (whether the difference between groups and conditions is statistically significant) and magnitude of effect (whether the difference is important, of practical significance, or large). Alternative measures for evaluating the magnitude of effects are presented. Concrete illustrations are provided to convey the implications of examining magnitude of the effects.

Invariably, investigators in clinical research examine multiple dependent variables. For example, in studies that evaluate treatment processes or outcomes, several different measures are used to provide multiple measures of a given construct and to assess related but somewhat different constructs. The analysis of multiple measures (multivariate data) raises critical questions. In the article by Carl Huberty and John Morris (1989), the relation of multivariate and univariate analyses of variance is discussed. Huberty and Morris convey that a common use of these analyses may be inappropriate and interfere with the investigator's purpose. The appropriateness of using one type of test (e.g., multivariate analyses of variance) versus another (e.g., univariate analyses) is often in question. In this article, considerations dictating the use of alternative methods of data analyses for a given data set are discussed.

In recent years, structural equation modeling has been accorded major attention as a method of analysis. The analysis, also known by other names including multivariate analyses with latent variables, causal modeling, and covariance structure analysis, tests hypotheses about constructs and their interrelations. There are special reasons for singling out structural equation modeling here. To begin with, the analysis raises the notion of *latent variables* or constructs. Latent variables require the use of multiple measures to assess a given construct and permit operationalization of the construct (e.g., depression and conflict) with different and multiple assessment methods. Second, the focus of structural equation modeling conveys the important relation between theoretical understanding, prediction, and data analyses. This method evaluates alternative models that stem from the investigator's conceptualization of how variables are represented and how variables relate to each other at a given point in time and over time. Finally, the method is used with increased frequency in the context of clinical assessment because of the ability to test alternative conceptual views and patterns of influence among multiple variables. The article by Richard Morris, John Bergan, and John Fulginiti (1991) provides an overview of structural equation modeling. Critical features of the analysis, meaning of the results, applications in clinical work, and limitations are presented.

INTERPRETATION OF RESEARCH OUTCOMES

Interpretation of the results of research raises important substantive issues related to the theory, hypotheses, and predictions. In addition, it is often at the interpretative stage that methodological issues and limitations of a study become most obvious. Methodological flaws, oversights, and limitations become apparent during interpretation of the findings because of what the investigator can and cannot say in light of the design. The present set of articles raises issues regarding interpretation of results of individual studies and bodies of research.

In the initial article, Peter Sedlmeier and Gerd Gigerenzer (1989) discuss statistical power. The article begins by examining a classic analysis of power completed by Jacob Cohen over 30 years ago. The original article by Cohen indicated that experiments are generally weak in their power and more often than not are unlikely to detect differences between groups (to reject the null hypothesis) even if differences truly exist. This article reviews many subsequent analyses of power and conveys that current research has not improved. The importance of power in research design and interpretation of results is discussed.

The weak statistical power in research is one reason why groups exposed to different experimental and control conditions may not differ from each other when the results are analyzed. The absence of differences between groups of conditions is referred to in many ways such as support for the null hypothesis or no-difference finding. More colloquially, the term *negative results* is often used to indicate that differences were not found. In any case, the absence of differences between groups has critically important methodological implications that affect all research independently of the nature of the findings. The article by Anthony Greenwald (1975) points out a bias against accepting the null hypothesis as a meaningful finding and discusses interpretive ambiguities such a finding can engender. More important for present purposes, the article presents ways of designing and executing experiments to enhance interpretation of the findings.

Evaluation of research extends beyond individual studies. Within the past 15 years, meta-analysis has emerged as a method to integrate and to evaluate large numbers of studies. Meta-analysis is a method of reviewing research but also, is itself a research method. Within clinical psychology, one of the more popular applications has been the use of meta-analysis to evaluate the effectiveness of alternative forms of psychotherapy. However, the method has broad applicability as a means of integrating research. In the article by Robert Bangert-Drowns (1986), the development and uses of meta-analysis are presented in a concise fashion. The article conveys what the analysis is, why and how it is conducted, alternative uses, and issues regarding interpretation of the conclusions. The article is included here because of the methodological issues raised in the context of examining the individual studies as well as for interpreting the outcomes of meta-analysis.

RESEARCH DESIGN AND
STATISTICAL EVALUATION

14

HYPOTHESIS VALIDITY OF CLINICAL RESEARCH

BRUCE E. WAMPOLD, BETSY DAVIS, AND ROLAND H. GOOD III

Clinical research spans a wide range of applied areas. To varying degrees, the basis of this research emanates from principles of behavior and behavior change. On the more technological side are treatment studies that answer the questions of whether a treatment works or which treatment is more effective (Kazdin, 1980; 1986), and status studies, which are designed to identify differences between populations. Yet certainly even these studies rely heavily on principles of behavior and behavior change to design the treatments, select measures, and interpret the results. For example, it is important to know whether maternal depression is associated with childhood problems; however, the curious investigator will soon seek to understand the nature of the relation between these two constructs (e.g., Dumas, Gibson, & Albin, 1989; Forehand, Lautenschlager, Faust, & Graziano, 1986; Hops et al., 1987). The link between theory and constructs in applied research is discussed by Cook and Campbell (1979):

Reprinted from the *Journal of Consulting and Clinical Psychology*, 58, 360–367. Copyright 1990 by the American Psychological Association.

Researchers would like to be able to give their presumed cause and effect operations names which refer to theoretical constructs. The need for this is most explicit in theory-testing research where the operations are explicitly derived to represent theoretical notions. But applied researchers also like to give generalized abstract names to their variables, for it is hardly useful to assume that the relationship between the two variables is causal if one cannot summarize these variables other than by describing them in exhaustive operational detail. (p. 38)

Although the importance of theory for the design of interpretation of clinical research is apparent, the mechanics of designing research in such a way that the results will be theoretically interesting are far from clear. The purpose of our article is to explore some of the aspects of clinical research that relate to theory. We have designated the term *hypothesis validity* to refer to the extent to which research results reflect theoretically derived predictions about the relations between or among constructs. If a study has adequate hypothesis validity, the results will be informative about the nature of the relation between constructs; that is, the study will inform theory. If a study has inadequate hypothesis validity, ambiguity about the relation between constructs will result, and indeed less certainty about the relation may exist than before the research was conducted. Hypothesis validity involves the development and statement of research hypotheses, the match of statistical hypotheses to research hypotheses, and the focus of statistical tests.

THE ROLE OF HYPOTHESES IN THEORY TESTING

Some important points from the philosophy of science as it relates to hypotheses supply the language to discuss and the base from which to develop hypothesis validity. Adopting the notation of Chow (1988), the crucial concepts needed for this discussion are illustrated in Table 1 and discussed below. Consider a theory T_1. Implication I_{11} of theory T_1 specifies an outcome that should occur given the mechanisms of the theory. $A.I_{11}$ represents the implication plus the auxiliary assumptions (e.g., normality of scores). X is an experimental expectation given $A.I_{11}$ (under the proper experimental conditions). Deductively, if the theory implies that X will occur (given the implication and the auxiliary assumptions, i.e., $A.I_{11}$) and if an experimental outcome D that is dissimilar to X is obtained, then the theory T_1 must be false. This approach to testing theory, which has been labeled *the falsificationist approach* (Popper, 1968), has bothered many philosophers of science, especially when used in conjunction with statistical tests (Folger, 1989; Mahoney, 1978; Meehl, 1978; Serlin, 1987; Serlin & Lapsley, 1985).

TABLE 1
Deductive Logic of Hypothesis Testing

Theory	T_1	T_1
Implication	I_{11}	I_{11}
	Falsification	Corroboration
Major premise	If $A.I_{11}$ then X under EFG	If $A.I_{11}$ then X under EFG
Minor premise	D is dissimilar to X.	D is similar to X.
Experimental conclusion	$A.I_{11}$ is false.	$A.I_{11}$ could be true.
Theoretical conclusion	T_1 is false.	T_1 could be true.

Note: T_1 = theory of interest; I_{11} = one implication of T_1; EFG = control and independent variables of the experiment; X = experimental expectation; A = set of auxiliary assumptions underlying the experiment; D = experimental outcomes (i.e., the pattern shown by the dependent variable in various conditions of the experiment). From "Significance Test or Effect Size?" by S. L. Chow, 1988, *Psychological Bulletin*, *103*, p. 107. Copyright 1988 by the American Psychological Association. Adapted by permission. See also Folger, 1989.

In the context of statistical hypothesis testing, falsification occurs when the null hypothesis is not rejected because the obtained result D is contrary to the expected result X. However, there are many ways that failure to reject the null hypothesis can result other than the fact that the theory is false, ruining the clean deductive nature of falsification (Folger, 1989). The obtained findings may be due to chance (Type II error), incorrect formulation of the implication of the theory, misspecification of the expected outcome X, low power, poor experimental methods, unreliable variables, or violated assumptions (Cook & Campbell, 1979; Folger, 1989).

Besides being epistemologically troublesome, falsification is not the modus operandi of research in the social sciences. If anything, there is a prejudice against research that fails to reject the null hypothesis, especially in clinically related areas (Atkinson, Furlong, & Wampold, 1982; Fagley, 1985; Greenwald, 1975; Mahoney, 1977). The alternative hypothesis holds the upper hand in psychological research; that is, researchers usually hope to reject the null hypothesis and lend support to a particular point of view. Furthermore, journal editors and reviewers look to significant results to inform the field (Atkinson et al., 1982). However, there are epistemological problems with this approach as well. The fact that the obtained pattern of results D is similar to the predicted pattern X does not imply that the theory T_1 is true, because other theories may also imply a predicted pattern X. Claiming the truth of a theory on the basis of the appearance of the expected pattern of results is a deductive error called *affirming the consequent*. The problems with affirming the consequent in psychological research have been acknowledged previously (e.g., Folger, 1989; Mahoney, 1978). Nevertheless, an experiment that produces the theoretically expected pattern of results has survived an attempt at falsification. In such a case, the theory is said to be *corroborated*; corroboration implies that the theory has been tested and has survived, which is quite different from implying that it has been confirmed (see Mahoney, 1978).

There is another problem with statistical testing and theory that is more subtle, and yet more troublesome, than the deductive problems we have discussed. In the hard sciences, as methods are refined (e.g., better measurement of phenomena), theories are winnowed, leaving fewer theories that are ascribed to with more confidence. Just the opposite is true in many areas of social science research. It is reasonable to believe that the null hypothesis is not literally true; that is, all constructs are related, even if to some small degree. As methods are refined, error variance will be reduced and statistical tests will be more powerful. As a consequence, it will be more likely that theories will be corroborated and less likely that they will be falsified and rejected. Instead of winnowing, theories will proliferate (Serlin, 1987; Serlin & Lapsley, 1985).

Several remedies to the philosophical problems of hypothesis testing have been suggested. An omnipresent suggestion involves the use of effect-size measures, confidence intervals, statements about power, measures of clinical significance, or other measures that reflect the degree to which the obtained results differ from that hypothesized under the null hypothesis (e.g., Cohen, 1988; Cook & Campbell, 1979; Fagley, 1985; Folger, 1989; Haase, Waechter, & Solomon, 1982; Jacobson, Follette, & Revenstorf, 1984; Rosnow & Rosenthal, 1988; Wampold, Furlong, & Atkinson, 1983). These measures are useful because they provide information in addition to the binary decision of whether the null hypothesis is rejected, although their use is controversial logically and statistically (Chow, 1988, 1989; Hollon & Flick, 1988; Mitchell & Hartmann, 1981; Murray & Dosser, 1987; O'Grady, 1982).

Another remedy to the traditional hypothesis-testing strategy is to use alternative statistical paradigms or to use no statistics at all. The Bayesian approach readjusts prior estimates of the probabilities of events with information provided by new samples (Schmitt, 1969). Serlin and Lapsley (1985) have promulgated the *good-enough principle*, which embodies a hypothesis-testing strategy in which, instead of hypothesizing a null effect, the researcher hypothesizes the magnitude of the effect that is sufficient to corroborate the theory or that is clinically significant. Of course, the researcher may eschew the use of statistical tests entirely; a significant body of knowledge has been accumulated in experimental and applied areas by the visual analysis of data generated by single-subject designs (Barlow & Hersen, 1984).

Hypothesis validity addresses the interrelations of theory, research hypotheses, and statistical hypotheses. Research hypotheses are derived from theory and can be characterized as statements about the presumed relations among constructs. In Chow's (1988) framework, the research hypotheses represent an implication of the theory. Research hypotheses should be stated in such a way that a theory is falsifiable and that competing theories can be winnowed. Clarity of a research hypothesis is vital to determine whether an obtained outcome is similar or dissimilar to the outcome predicted by theory.

Certain properties of statistical hypotheses are needed in order to assure adequate hypothesis validity. First, statistical hypotheses should be congruent with the research hypotheses. If the research hypotheses posit a relation between constructs on the basis of means, then the statistical hypotheses should be phrased in terms of μ, the population mean. However, a statistical hypothesis regarding μ would be inappropriate if the implication of the theory was phrased in terms of differences in variances. Second, statistical hypotheses must be sufficiently specific to determine whether the obtained result is similar or dissimilar to the predicted experimental outcome.

The relations among theory, research hypotheses, statistical hypotheses, and results are presented in Figure 1. The design of experiments involves deriving research hypotheses from theory, matching statistical hypotheses to research hypotheses, and creating the experiment in order to obtain the results. It is interesting to note that design texts and courses

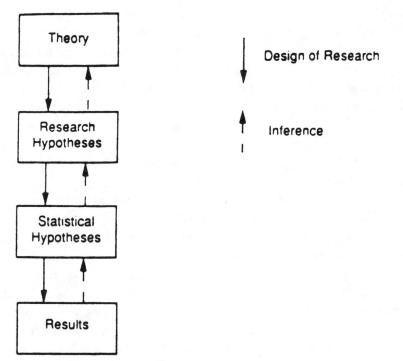

Figure 1: Design and inference in theory testing.

often focus on the last operation (i.e., design of the experiment rather than design of the research). Inference proceeds in the opposite direction. The results are used to make decisions about the statistical hypotheses (e.g., reject the null hypothesis), and these decisions indicate whether the predicted patterns stipulated in the research hypotheses have been verified, determining whether the theory is corroborated or falsified. Traditional statistics texts concentrate on making inferences from sample data (i.e., the results) to statements about population parameters (i.e., statistical hypotheses). Hypothesis validity involves both the design of research and the inferences made from the results of studies.

In the spirit of Campbell and Stanley (1966), Bracht and Glass (1968), and Cook and Campbell (1979), we discuss hypothesis validity in more detail by posing threats to hypothesis validity.

THREATS TO HYPOTHESIS VALIDITY

Inconsequential Research Hypotheses

In Chow's (1988) framework, I_{11} was an implication of theory T_1. There are many other implications from theory T_1 that could be made (i.e., I_{12}, I_{13}, etc.). An important question is whether I_{11} represents a crucial issue. That is, from the set of possible implications (some of which may not have been entertained by the researcher), is I_{11} central to determining the veridicality of the theory T_1 in comparison with T_2, T_3, and so forth? Implication I_{11} is suboptimal to the extent that competing theories would have implications similar to I_{11}. For example, if theory T_2 implied I_{21}, which was identical to I_{11}, then any experimental result corroborating T_1 would also corroborate T_2. The hypothesis validity of a study is strengthened when the number of tenable theories that have implications similar to I_{11} is small. Ideally, corroborating T_1 should simultaneously falsify a large number of competing theories.

In his discussion of strong inference, Platt (1964) discussed the importance of determining the crucial question and devising research so that various explanations for observed phenomena can be ruled out. Implication I_{11} is superior to other implications to the extent that research that is based on this implication will result in a clearer understanding of the relation between constructs than would research that is based on other implications, and to the extent that this understanding is important to understanding the psychological phenomena of interest. Thus, strong inference is based, in part, on inductive reasoning about the implications of the theory under scrutiny.

Framing the discussion of research questions notationally should not be construed to indicate that this process is necessarily formal or deductive. Essentially the researcher surveys existing knowledge relating to his or her problems and attempts to pose the important unanswered question. Examining crucial hypotheses leads to the extension of knowledge, the winnowing of theories, the clarification of discrepancies, the identification of active ingredients of treatments, and so on. Inconsequential research hypotheses, on the other hand, do not produce resolution because they do not lead to a convergence of knowledge.

Platt (1964) addressed the issue of inconsequential research hypotheses by advocating multiple hypotheses. He has claimed that sciences that progress rapidly are characterized by experimentation that tests one theory against another. In that way, the results simultaneously corroborate one theory while falsifying another. For example, in particle physics, two models might be postulated; one model cannot explain the appearance of a certain particle in an experiment, whereas the other can explain it. If the particle appears (reliably), the first model is abandoned, and the second is tentatively adopted until a competing model is developed and tested against the tentatively adopted model.

This multiple hypothesis idea has implications for the manner in which models are tested in psychological research, especially with the advent of modeling techniques such as LISREL (Jöreskog & Sörbom, 1988). Typically, a model is proposed (one that is based on theory, it is hoped), and its compatibility with sample data is assessed. If the sample data are not consistent with the model proposed, the model is rejected (e.g., a significant chi-square goodness-of-fit test is obtained). On the other hand, if the goodness of fit is not significant, the model is retained. However, it is not proved, because this conclusion would be affirming the consequent (Cliff, 1983); there may be other models that fit the data as well (or better) than the model proposed. According to the multiple-hypothesis concept, stronger inferences can be made by contrasting competing models. For example, using a LISREL analysis of attitudes, Kerlinger (1980) demonstrated that a model with separate conservative and liberal dimensions was superior to a model with conservatism and liberalism as poles on a single dimension.

Ambiguous Research Hypotheses

Ambiguous research hypotheses make it difficult to ascertain how the results of a study influence our theoretical understanding. If the experimental expectation (X in Chow's {1988} notation) is not specified sufficiently, it may well be impossible to determine whether the obtained results D are similar or dissimilar to what was expected. Ambiguity with regard to research hypotheses results in the inability to falsify a theory, a particularly troublesome state of affairs from a philosophy of science perspective (Mahoney, 1978; Platt, 1964; Popper, 1968).

Ambiguous research hypotheses are often stated in journal articles with phrases such as "the purpose of the present study is to explore the relation between . . ." or "the purpose is to determine the relation between. . . ." In one sense, such research cannot fail, because some relation between variables will be "discovered," even if the relation is null (i.e., no relation). In another sense, the research will always fail because the results do not falsify or corroborate any theory about the true state of affairs.

As an example of ambiguous research hypotheses, consider the following purpose of a study (Webster-Stratton, 1988) on parents' perceptions of child deviance:

> The present study attempted to determine (a) the relation of parental adjustment measures of such variables as depression, marital satisfaction, parenting stress, and other negative life stressors to mothers' and fathers' perceptions of their children's deviant behaviors; (b) the relation of teachers' independent perceptions of the children's behaviors to mothers' and fathers' perceptions; (c) the relation of mother, father, and teacher perceptions of child behaviors to observed mother, father, and child behaviors; and (d) the relation of parent measures to observed mother, father, and child behaviors. (pp. 909–910)

Interpretation of the results of this study was problematic because there was no predicted experimental outcome of results with which to compare the obtained pattern of results. It is not surprising that this research discovered some patterns that confirmed previous research (e.g., mothers' perceptions of their children's deviant behaviors were affected by mothers' personal adjustment) and some patterns that contradicted other previous research (e.g., that teacher reports were better than maternal depression for the prediction of mothers' reports of child deviance).

Although careful observation is an important step in the development of hypotheses in any science, reliance on exploratory research can result only in confusion, if for no other reason than that some of the observed patterns are due to chance. A preponderance of studies with ambiguous research hypotheses will tend not to converge on important principles of behavior but will result in post hoc attempts to reconcile discrepant findings. As a result, weak theories will proliferate.

An example of clear hypotheses is provided by Borkovec and Mathews (1988) in a study of nonphobic anxiety disorders: "Clients with predominantly cognitive symptoms might be expected to respond better to techniques addressing this symptom domain, whereas clients with predominantly somatic symptoms might improve more under coping desensitization" (p. 878). This hypothesis is specific enough that, if other aspects of the study are valid (including other aspects of hypothesis validity discussed later), the results can clearly corroborate or fail to support the Borkovec and Mathews prediction.

As a hypothetical example to illustrate research hypotheses (and later statistical tests), consider a treatment study contrasting a behavioral intervention and a cognitive intervention. To answer Paul's (1967) question about which treatments work with which type of clients, further suppose the differential effects of the treatment on two types of persons—cognitively oriented and noncognitively oriented. Suppose five dependent variables were used to operationally define the construct targeted for change (e.g., marital satisfaction). A reasonable and specific hypothesis would be that the behavior therapy would be effective with both types of subjects (i.e., cognitively oriented and noncognitively oriented), whereas the cognitive therapy would be effective only with the cognitively oriented subjects. The anticipated pattern of results is presented in Figure 2.

The argument for specificity in research hypotheses has been made in the context of traditional hypothesis testing. However, our points are as pertinent, if not more so, for many alternative strategies. For example, in the Bayesian approach, specificity is important because one has to stipulate prior probabilities. According to the good-enough principle, the minimal effect size that represents importance must be specified (Serlin & Lapsley, 1985).

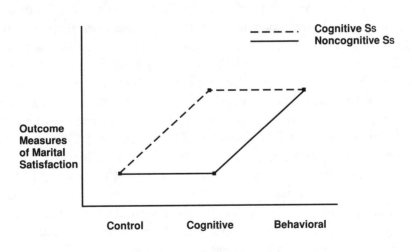

Figure 2: Predicted pattern for outcome variables for Type of Subject × Treatment. (Higher scores indicate more satisfaction.)

Noncongruence of Research Hypotheses and Statistical Hypotheses

To determine whether the obtained outcome D is similar or dissimilar to the experimental expectation X, the statistical hypothesis must correspond to the research hypothesis. When the research and statistical hypotheses are incongruent, even persuasive statistical evidence (small alpha levels, high power, large effect sizes) will not allow valid inferences to be made about the research hypotheses.

Although the problems of noncongruence seem obvious, consider the case in which the research hypothesis addresses differences in variances; that is, a treatment is expected to increase the variance (and quite possibly leave the mean unchanged). For example, a treatment for autoimmune deficiency syndrome could possibly prolong the lives of one half of the subjects and hasten the death of the other half. In such a case, it would be inappropriate to hypothesize mean differences à la an analysis of variance (ANOVA; viz., $\mu_1 = \mu_2 = \ldots = \mu_j$) when the question of interest is whether the variances are equal (viz., $\sigma_1^2 = \sigma_2^2 = \ldots = \sigma_j^2$). A perusal of the statistical tests used in clinical research convincingly demonstrates, we believe, that differences among groups are expressed as differences among means by default.

Diffuse Statistical Hypotheses and Tests

Statistical tests are used to evaluate the extent to which an observed experimental outcome D is similar or dissimilar to the experimental expectation X. If the research hypothesis is translated into one set of statistical hypotheses (a null and an alternative), then, if the statistical test is valid and is congruent to the research hypothesis, the results of the statistical test will provide information so that the researcher can decide whether D is similar to X. If the null hypothesis for this test is rejected in favor of an alternative hypothesis that is consistent with X, then the conclusion is made that D is similar to X. If the null hypothesis is not rejected, then the conclusion is made that D is dissimilar to X (Chow, 1988). Of course, the decisions made could be incorrect (viz., Type I and Type II error).

Diffusion of statistical tests is created in one of three ways: First, a specific research hypothesis can be (and often is) translated into many statistical hypotheses and tests. Second, the statistical test used may be an omnibus test that does not focus on a specific research question. Third, extraneous independent variables may be included.

Multiple Statistical Tests
When more than one set of statistical hypotheses is tested per re-

search hypothesis, theoretical ambiguity can result because it is not clear what pattern of results will corroborate or falsify the conjecture embodied in the research hypothesis. Specifically, many statistical tests per research hypothesis are problematic for two reasons. First, there is uncertainty with regard to the interpretation of many statistical tests because the results may not be consistent. Suppose that the researcher conducts two statistical tests. One yields a result consistent with the theory, and the other yields a result that is inconsistent with the theory, as might be the case when two dependent variables are used. Is this evidence for or against the theory?

The interpretation of multiple statistical tests is further compounded by the fact that some of the statistically significant results will have occurred by chance when there was no effect (Type I error), and some of the nonsignificant results will have occurred even though the expected effect was present (Type II error). Control of experimentwise Type I error will minimize the Type I errors but will lead to greater experimentwise Type II error. In any event, the question remains, "Which results were due to Type I and Type II errors?"

The problem with many statistical tests is illustrated by the Borkovec and Mathews (1988) study of nonphobic anxiety. For the specific hypothesis with regard to clients with cognitive and with somatic symptoms, several statistical tests were used. Predictably the outcome was ambiguous, giving rise to difficulties in interpretation: "Such an ambiguous outcome is open to a variety of interpretations" (Borkovec & Mathews, p. 882).

To further illustrate the ambiguity created by many statistical tests, consider the example presented earlier with regard to the behavioral and cognitive treatments for cognitively and noncognitively oriented subjects. To test the research hypothesis embodied in Figure 2, a series of t tests for each dependent variable could be conducted in which several tests would be expected to be significant and others nonsignificant. These t tests are presented in Table 2; 45 tests would be needed (9 for each dependent

TABLE 2
Pattern of Predicted Significant t Tests

Test	Significant
Control/cognitive Ss vs. control/noncognitive Ss	No
Cognitive Tx/cognitive Ss vs. cognitive Tx/noncognitive Ss	Yes
Behavioral Tx/cognitive Ss vs. behavioral Tx/noncognitive Ss	No
Control/cognitive Ss vs. cognitive Tx/cognitive Ss	Yes
Control/cognitive Ss vs. behavioral Tx/cognitive Ss	Yes
Control/noncognitive Ss vs. cognitive Tx/noncognitive Ss	No
Control/noncognitive Ss vs. behavioral Tx/noncognitive Ss	Yes
Cognitive Tx/cognitive Ss vs. behavioral Tx/cognitive Ss	No
Cognitive Tx/noncognitive Ss vs. behavioral Tx/noncognitive Ss	Yes

Note: S = subject. Tx = treatment.

variable). Clearly such an approach is questionable because it is unclear what degree of correspondence with the expected pattern of results in Table 2 would be required to corroborate the research hypothesis. Suppose that 1 of the t-test outcomes was not as expected; would that still be strong enough evidence to decide that the results were consistent with the prediction? What about 2 or 3, 35 or 40? As mentioned previously, this question is complicated by the fact that the probability of a Type I error has escalated dramatically. One could, of course, control the experimentwise Type I error rate with a Bonferroni type procedure, although this would be a very conservative approach, resulting in unacceptable experimentwise Type II error rates (Hays, 1988; Rosenthal & Rubin, 1984).

Omnibus Tests

Omnibus tests are problematic because they contain effects, contrasts, or combinations that do not reflect solely the research hypothesis. Hence, several different research hypotheses can lead to a significant omnibus test. For example, an omnibus F test in an ANOVA for a treatment study with several treatments may be due to the treatments' being superior to the control group, or may be due to one treatment's being superior to the other treatments and to the control group. Although differences may be explored post hoc, planned comparisons are advantageous for theory testing. The interpretation given to the results of a planned comparison (or any other focused test[1]) is a direct test of a specific hypothesis. On the other hand, if the omnibus F test is significant at a given level, then some possible post hoc comparison must be significant at that level (Hays, 1988; Wampold & Drew, 1990); however, there is no assurance that this comparison will be interpretable. Even if the comparison is interpretable, the interpretation is made post hoc, and correspondence to a predicted pattern is precluded.

There are problems with omnibus tests other than their questionable relation to theory. Omnibus tests (and post hoc follow-up tests) are statistically less powerful means to detect effects than are focused tests (Hays, 1988; Rosnow & Rosenthal, 1988). Furthermore, calculation and interpretation of effect sizes for omnibus tests are problematic (Rosnow & Rosenthal, 1988).

Returning to the marital satisfaction example, we could conduct a 3 (two treatments plus control group) × 2 (type of subject) ANOVA for each

---

[1]Focused tests have been defined by Rosnow and Rosenthal (1988) to be "significance tests that address precise questions, such as any t test, any F test with 1 df in the numerator, and any 1-df χ^2 test" (p. 204). However, there are tests with more than 1 df that answer specific questions. For example, a general linear model F test that all higher order interaction effects are zero could be used to show that a number of independent variables do not interact with a treatment variable.

dependent variable, a less diffuse choice than conducting the 45 t tests. However, this approach also suffers from multiple tests because it yields 15 F tests, 2 tests of main effects, and 1 test of the interaction effect for each of the five dependent variables. However, the omnibus F test for the ANOVA is particularly pernicious because it does not directly address the pattern of expected results. The research hypothesis embodied in Figure 1 combines a main effect and an interaction effect.

The expected pattern of results for this problem can be neatly expressed as a planned comparison (see display below). However, even though this comparison tests the research hypothesis directly, testing this comparison for each dependent variable maintains the multiple statistical test problem.

Tx:	Control	Control	Cognitive	Cognitive	Behavioral	Behavioral
Ss:	Cognitive	Noncognitive	Cognitive	Noncognitive	Cognitive	Noncognitive
Comparison:	-1	-1	$+1$	-1	$+1$	$+1$

The most focused test would be a multivariate planned comparison. This one test would answer the question of whether the expected pattern of means was reflected in the sample data and thus would avoid multiple statistical tests as well as omnibus tests. There would be no need to conduct follow-up tests because the research hypothesis did not specify differential effects for individual outcome variables; presumably the variables were measuring the same construct.

In this example, the focused test was one multivariate test. However, this example should not be taken to indicate that multivariate tests are necessarily less diffuse than univariate tests. A common practice is to conduct omnibus multivariate analyses of variance (MANOVAs) followed by omnibus univariate ANOVAs. This practice is diffuse because of the omnibus nature of the tests and because it is not clear which pattern of the univariate tests corroborates the research hypothesis. In fact, it is possible to reject the multivariate null hypothesis while not being able to reject any of the univariate null hypotheses (Huberty & Morris, 1989). It has been recommended that significant multivariate tests be followed by discriminant analyses so that the linear combination of variables that best differentiate the groups can be examined (e.g., Bray & Maxwell, 1982). Although this may be an improvement over univariate Fs, without hypothesizing linear combinations, it remains difficult to link the statistical results to the research hypotheses.

The choice of a multivariate test should depend on the research hypothesis. Multivariate tests often are advocated for the express purpose of controlling experimentwise Type I error (e.g., Leary & Altmaier, 1980). Although controlling Type I error is beneficial, consideration of hypothesis validity of the study should be the primary criterion in the choice of a statistical procedure. For example, when the dependent variables are conceptually independent and result in multiple research questions, multiple ANOVAs may be the appropriate procedures to answer specific research questions (Huberty & Morris, 1989).

Generally, the less diffuse the statistical tests (and hence statistical hypotheses), the greater the hypothesis validity of the study. To the extent possible, one statistical test should be focused on one research hypothesis. Accordingly, planned comparisons would be preferable to omnibus F tests in the ANOVA context, a test of a hypothesized curvilinear relation would treat other curvilinear relations as residual, higher order interactions with no theoretical relevance would not be tested, parameters would be contrasted rather than tested individually (e.g., tests of differences between correlations), and so forth.

The importance of focusing a few specific tests on research questions rather than using diffuse tests has long been emphasized. Serlin (1987) has succinctly summarized the theoretical problems associated with omnibus tests:

> But one still sees omnibus F tests performed in analysis of variance, even though almost all the contrasts subsumed by the omnibus null hypothesis have *no possibility of interpretation* {italics added}. In a similar fashion, the omnibus null hypothesis in multivariate analysis of variance subsumes an even larger set of mostly *uninterpretable* {italics added} contrasts performed on mostly *uninterpretable* {italics added} linear combinations of the dependent variables. Finally, the omnibus null hypothesis in regression analysis examines whether any of an infinite set of linear combinations of the predictor variables is related to the dependent variable. In each of these cases, *a consideration of the theoretically derived research questions under examination in the experiment would obviate the use of the omnibus hypothesis test* {italics added}. (p. 370)

Extraneous Independent Variables

Often independent variables are included in a study to increase the external validity of a study, that is, to increase the generalizability of the results across persons, settings, or time (Cook & Campbell, 1979). For example, to determine whether the results apply equally to men and women, gender may be added to a design as an independent variable. Of course, the set of possible independent variables related to persons, settings, or time is very large. With regard to persons, the most widely used variables include gender, ethnicity, socioeconomic status, and intelligence, although there are many other variables that could be included. Furthermore, each of these variables very likely glosses over other important distinctions. For example, gender ignores sex role orientation, and ethnicity ignores level of acculturation.

The choice of independent variables related to generalizability is difficult. We contend that this choice should be driven by theory to the extent possible. If there is good reason to believe that the results of a study will differ for men and women, then there is a good rationale to include gender in the study. However, if the theory implies that sex role orientation is the critical variable, then sex role orientation should be included.

Inclusion of extraneous variables inflates the number of hypotheses tested, increasing the diffusion of the statistical tests. In the typical factorial design, each independent variable added to the design introduces another main effect as well as interaction effects with the other independent variables. Additional independent variables also increase the likelihood that omnibus tests will be used because it becomes more difficult and less appropriate (without theory) to make specific predictions with regard to the main and, particularly, the interaction effects.

One could suggest another caution about additional independent variables. If an additional independent variable is important enough to be included in the study, it should be treated as a legitimate part of the design, and predictions should be made about the outcome for this variable. The irrelevance of independent variables is demonstrated when researchers conduct a preliminary test for differences on a variable such as gender and then collapse over this factor when no significant differences are found. This process rules out the possibility of detecting an interaction effect as well, which is often the most interesting of results from an external validity point of view.

CONCLUSIONS

The purpose of our article is to call attention to the connection between theory and results of individual studies. The concept of hypothesis validity has been introduced to emphasize the importance of drawing crucial implications from theory, stating clear research hypotheses, matching statistical hypotheses with research hypotheses, and focusing the statistical tests on the research hypotheses. We hope that the presentation of hypothesis validity provides a framework that is useful for the design and critique of clinical research.

Any conceptual framework is somewhat arbitrary; hypothesis validity is no exception. Hypothesis validity borders on both construct validity of putative causes and effects and statistical conclusion validity, as discussed by Cook and Campbell (1979). Construct validity of putative causes and effects involves determining the degree to which the variables included in a study reflect theoretical constructs. Clearly, construct validity plays an important role in the theoretical relevance of studies. However, hypothesis validity differs from construct validity by focusing on the relation between the constructs; construct validity focuses on the operationalization of the constructs.

Hypothesis validity is also related to statistical conclusion validity. Multiple statistical tests pose threats to statistical conclusion validity because of fishing and error rate problems (Cook & Campbell, 1979). However, even if these problems are attenuated by statistical means (e.g., using the Bonferroni inequality), ambiguity is present because of the difficulty in comparing the obtained pattern of results with the predicted pattern of results. Focused tests are advantageous primarily because they provide an explicit test of a specific hypothesis, although they are also desirable from a statistical point of view (e.g., increased power under certain circumstances).

Hypothesis validity applies most directly to theoretically driven clinical research. What about purely exploratory research or technological research? In any field of empirical inquiry, exploration is important. Most researchers enjoy searching through data to discover unanticipated relations among variables. Nevertheless, the search is guided by knowledge and understanding of theory, and interpretation of the discoveries is made within a theoretical context. Although the tenets of hypothesis validity do not apply as directly to purely exploratory research, they are critical to testing the conjectures that emanate from the exploratory phase.

Examples of purely technological research in clinical psychology are difficult to find. At first glance, comparative treatment studies may appear to answer the atheoretical question about the relative efficacy of two or more treatments (Kazdin, 1980, 1986). However, development of the treatment will most likely rely on principles of behavior change, selection of the dependent measures will be based on the intended outcome, and interpretation of the results will be explained within a theoretical context. Regardless of the degree to which such studies rely on theory, the principles of hypothesis validity are valuable. One still wants to conduct a study crucial to establishing the relative efficacy of a treatment, to state clearly the research hypotheses about relative efficacy, to match the statistical hypotheses to the research hypotheses, and so on.

We hope that describing the threats to hypothesis validity will result in more thought about the research hypotheses and how they can be tested elegantly. If a researcher uses a strong rope to lower himself or herself from theory to research hypotheses to statistical hypotheses and finally to the results of a study, then he or she will be able to climb back with the results so that a valid statement about theory can be made. If the rope is fatally frayed at some point, the results picked up at the bottom will be of little value (and may become burdensome weight) for the return journey.

REFERENCES

Atkinson, D R., Furlong, M. J., & Wampold, B. E. (1982). Statistical significance, reviewer evaluations, and the scientific process: Is there a (statistically) significant relationship? *Journal of Counseling Psychology, 29,* 189–194.

Barlow, D. H., & Hersen, M. (1984). *Single case experimental designs: Strategies for studying behavior change* (2nd ed.). New York: Pergamon Press.

Borkovec, T. D., & Mathews, A. M. (1988). Treatment of nonphobic anxiety disorders: A comparison of nondirective, cognitive, and coping desensitization. *Journal of Consulting and Clinical Psychology, 56,* 877–884.

Bracht, G. H., & Glass, G. V. (1968). The external validity of experiments. *American Educational Research Journal, 5,* 437–474.

Bray, J. H., & Maxwell, S. E. (1982). Analyzing and interpreting significant MANOVAs. *Review of Educational Research, 52,* 340–367.

Campbell, D. T., & Stanley, J. C. (1966). *Experimental and quasi-experimental designs for research.* Chicago: Rand McNally.

Chow, S. L. (1988). Significance test or effect size? *Psychological Bulletin, 103,* 105–110.

Chow, S. L. (1989). Significance tests and deduction: Reply to Folger. (1989). *Psychological Bulletin, 106,* 161–165, 778.

Cliff, N. (1983). Some cautions concerning the application of causal modeling methods. *Multivariate Behavioral Research, 18,* 115–126.

Cohen, J. (1988). *Statistical power analysis for the behavioral sciences* (2nd ed.). Hillsdale, NJ: Erlbaum.

Cook, T. D., & Campbell, D. T. (1979). *Quasi-experimentation: Design and analysis for field settings.* Chicago: Rand McNally.

Dumas, J. E., Gibson, J. A., & Albin, J. B. (1989). Behavioral correlates of maternal depressive symptomatology in conduct-disordered children. *Journal of Consulting and Clinical Psychology, 57,* 516–521.

Fagley, N. S. (1985). Applied statistical power analysis and the interpretation of nonsignificant results by research consumers. *Journal of Counseling Psychology, 32,* 391–396.

Folger, R. (1989). Significance tests and the duplicity of binary decisions. *Psychological Bulletin, 106,* 155–160.

Forehand, R., Lautenschlager, G. J., Faust, J., & Graziano, W. G. (1986). Parent perceptions and parent–child interaction in clinic-referred children: A preliminary investigation of the effects of maternal depressive moods. *Behaviour Research and Therapy, 24,* 73–75.

Greenwald, A. G. (1975). Consequences of prejudice against the null hypothesis. *Psychological Bulletin, 82,* 1–20.

Haase, R. F., Waechter, D. M., & Solomon, G. S. (1982). How significant is a significant difference? Average effect size of research in counseling psychology. *Journal of Counseling Psychology, 29,* 58–65.

Hays, W. L. (1988). *Statistics* (4th ed.). New York: Holt, Rinehart & Winston.

Hollon, S. D., & Flick, S. N. (1988). On the meaning and methods of clinical significance. *Behavioral Assessment, 10,* 197–206.

Hops, H., Biglan, A., Sherman, L., Arthur, J., Friedman, L., & Osteen, V. (1987). Home observations of family interactions of depressed women. *Journal of Consulting and Clinical Psychology, 55,* 341–346.

Huberty, C. J., & Morris, J. D. (1989). Multivariate analysis versus multiple univariate analyses. *Psychological Bulletin, 105,* 302–308.

Jacobson, N. S., Follette, W. C., & Revenstorf, D. (1984). Psychotherapy outcome research: Methods for reporting variability and evaluating clinical significance. *Behavior Therapy, 17,* 336–352.

Jöreskog, K. G., & Sörbom, D. (1988). LISREL VII: *A guide to the program and applications* [Computer program manual]. Chicago: SPSS.

Kazdin, A. E. (1980). *Research design in clinical psychology.* New York: Harper & Row.

Kazdin, A. E. (1986). The evaluation of psychotherapy: Research design and methodology. In S. L. Garfield & A. E. Bergin (Eds.), *Handbook of psychotherapy and behavior change* (3rd ed., pp. 23–68). New York: Wiley.

Kerlinger, F. N. (1980). Analysis of covariance structures test of a criterial referents theory of attitudes. *Multivariate Behavioral Research, 15,* 403–422.

Leary, M. R., & Altmaier, E. M. (1980). Type I error in counseling research: A plea for multivariate analyses. *Journal of Counseling Psychology, 27,* 611–615.

Mahoney, M. J. (1977). Publication prejudices: An experimental study of confirmatory bias in the peer review system. *Cognitive Therapy and Research, 1,* 161–175.

Mahoney, M. J. (1978). Experimental methods and outcome evaluation. *Journal of Consulting and Clinical Psychology, 46,* 660–672.

Meehl, P. (1978). Theoretical risks and tabular asterisks: Sir Karl, Sir Ronald, and the slow progress of soft psychology. *Journal of Consulting and Clinical Psychology, 46,* 806–834.

Mitchell, C., & Hartmann, D. P. (1981). A cautionary note on the use of omega squared to evaluate the effectiveness of behavioral treatments. *Behavioral Assessment, 3,* 93–100.

Murray, L. W., & Dosser, D. A., Jr. (1987). How significant is a significant difference? Problems with the measurement of magnitude of effect. *Journal of Counseling Psychology, 34,* 68–72.

O'Grady, K. E. (1982). Measures of explained variance: Caution and limitations. *Psychological Bulletin, 92,* 766–777.

Paul, G. L. (1967). Strategy of outcome research in psychotherapy. *Journal of Consulting Psychology, 31,* 104–118.

Platt, J. R. (1964). Strong inference. *Science, 146,* 347–353.

Popper, K. (1968). *Conjectures and refutations.* London: Routledge & Kegan Paul.

Rosenthal, R., & Rubin, D. B. (1984). Multiple contrasts and ordered Bonferroni procedures. *Journal of Educational Psychology, 76,* 1028–1034.

Rosnow, R. L., & Rosenthal, R. (1988). Focused tests of significance and effect size estimation in counseling psychology. *Journal of Counseling Psychology, 35,* 203–208.

Schmitt, S. A. (1969). *Measuring uncertainty: An elementary introduction to Bayesian statistics.* Reading, MA: Addison-Wesley.

Serlin, R. C. (1987). Hypothesis testing, theory building, and the philosophy of science. *Journal of Counseling Psychology, 34,* 365–371.

Serlin, R. C., & Lapsley, D. K. (1985). Rationality in psychological research: The good-enough principle. *American Psychologist, 40,* 73–83.

Wampold, B. E., Furlong, M. J., & Atkinson, D. R. (1983). Statistical significance, power, and effect size: A response to the reexamination of reviewer bias. *Journal of Counseling Psychology, 30,* 459–463.

Wampold, B. E., & Drew, C. J. (1990). *Theory and application of statistics.* New York: McGraw-Hill.

Webster-Stratton, C. (1988). Mothers' and fathers' perceptions of child deviance: Roles of parent and child behaviors and parent adjustment. *Journal of Consulting and Clinical Psychology, 56,* 909–915.

15

ON THE ORIGINS OF THE .05 LEVEL OF STATISTICAL SIGNIFICANCE

MICHAEL COWLES AND CAROLINE DAVIS

It is generally understood that the conventional use of the 5% level as the maximum acceptable probability for determining statistical significance was established, somewhat arbitrarily, by Sir Ronald Fisher when he developed his procedures for the analysis of variance.

Fisher's (1925) statement in his book, *Statistical Methods for Research Workers*, seems to be the first specific mention of the $p = .05$ level as determining statistical significance.

> It is convenient to take this point as a limit in judging whether a deviation is to be considered significant or not. Deviations exceeding twice the standard deviation are thus formally regarded as significant. (p. 47)

Cochran (1976), commenting on a slightly later, but essentially similar, statement by Fisher (1926), says that, "Students sometimes ask, 'how did the 5 per cent significance level or Type I error come to be used as a

---

Reprinted from the *American Psychologist*, *37*, 553–558. Copyright 1982 by the American Psychological Association.

standard?' . . . I am not sure but this is the first comment known to me on the choice of 5 per cent." (p. 15).

In the 1926 article Fisher acknowledges that other levels may be used:

> If one in twenty does not seem high enough odds, we may, if we prefer it, draw the line at one in fifty (the 2 per cent point), or one in a hundred (the one per cent point). Personally, the writer prefers to set a low standard of significance at the 5 per cent point, and ignore entirely all results which fail to reach this level. A significant fact should be regarded as experimentally established only if a properly designed experiment *rarely fails* to give this level of significance. (p. 504)

Cochran feels that Fisher was fairly casual about the choice, "as the words *convenient* and *prefers* have indicated" (p. 16). However, the statement quoted above leaves no doubt about Fisher's acceptance of the level as the critical cutoff point, once he had decided upon it.

Other writers, well-versed in the history and development of probability, have also fostered the attitude that the level is an arbitrary one. Yule and Kendall (1950), in the 14th edition of a book first published by Yule in 1911, state,

> In the examples we have given . . . our judgment whether P was small enough to justify us in suspecting a significant difference . . . has been more or less intuitive. Most people would agree . . . that a probability of .0001 is so small that the evidence is very much in favour . . . Suppose we had obtained $P = 0.1$. . . . Where, if anywhere, can we draw the line? The odds against the observed event which influence a decision one way or the other depend to some extent on the caution of the investigator. Some people (not necessarily statisticians) would regard odds of ten to one as sufficient. Others would be more conservative and reserve judgment until the odds were much greater. It is a matter of personal taste. (pp. 471–472)

Cramer (1955), in a completely rewritten version of a Swedish text first published in 1926, tells his readers,

> a value of t . . . will be denoted as *almost significant* if t exceeds the 5% value, but falls short of the 1% . . . called *significant* if t lies between the 1% and 0.1% values and *highly significant* if t exceeds the 0.1% value. This is, of course, a purely conventional terminology. (p. 202)

The issue to be considered is whether the choice of the 5% value was as arbitrary and casual as is so often implied. An examination of the history of probability and statistical theory, however, indicates that the choice was far from arbitrary and was influenced by previous scientific conventions that themselves were based on the notion of "chance" and the unlikelihood of an event occurring.

ORIGINS

As David (1962) has so articulately and elegantly described, the first glimmerings of an appreciation of long-run relative frequencies, randomness, and the unlikelihood of rare events being merely fortuitous go back at least to the Greek mathematicians and the Roman philosophers. Later, however, the spread of Christianity and the collapse of the Roman Empire made the Church the sole haven for scholars. This religious philosophy that accepted a universe in which every event, no matter how trivial, as being caused by an omnipotent God left no place for the investigation of random events. This is very likely the reason why the seeds of mathematical probability theory were not sown until late in 17th-century France. The opportunities had always been there: Because both the archaelogical and the written records show that gambling has been an ever-popular pastime, informal and relatively unsystematic "systems" for calculating "odds" were undoubtedly developed.

The questions posed by Antoine Gombauld, the Chevalier de Méré, related to certain gaming problems, sparked off the correspondence between Blaise Pascal and Pierre Fermat in 1654. Here are the beginnings of combinatorial algebra and mathematical probability theory (again see David, 1962).

In a slightly later (1662) development, John Graunt, a London haberdasher, constructed tables from the Bills of Mortality, parish accounts regularly recorded from early in the 17th century and, most importantly, used these tables for a series of statistical, actuarial inferences.

Graunt was, for example, able to reassure readers of his quite remarkable, unassuming, and refreshing work that,

> This *casualty* {Lunacy} being so uncertain, I shall not force myself to make any inference from the numbers, and proportions we finde in our Bills concerning it: onely I dare ensure any man at this present, well in his Wits, for one in the thousand, that he shall not die a *Lunatick* in *Bedlam*, within these seven years, because I finde not above one in about one thousand five hundred have do so. (Graunt, 1662/1956, p. 1430)

Here is a statement based on numerical data and couched in terms not so very far removed from those in reports in the modern literature.

In 1657, Huygens (1657/1970) published a tract, *On Reasoning in Games of Dice*, that was based upon the exchanges between Pascal and Fermat, and in 1713 Jacques Bernoulli's (1713/1970) book, *The Art of Conjecture*, developed a theory of games of chance. De Moivre's (1756/1967) *The Doctrine of Chances* was the most important of the gambling manuals; it appeared in three editions in 1718, 1738, and 1756. In the two later editions De Moivre presents a method, which he had first published in 1733, of approximating the sum of a very large number of binomial terms. It is safe to say that no other theoretical mathematical abstraction has had such an important influence on psychology and the social sciences as that method, for it generates the bell-shaped curve now commonly known by the name Karl Pearson gave it: the normal distribution.

The law of frequency of errors is often attributed to Laplace (1749–1827) and Gauss (1777–1855). Both men developed the use of the distribution ouside of gaming and in particular demonstrated its utility in evaluating the variable results of measurements and observations in astronomy and in geodetic surveying. With the introduction of this distribution into the field of the biological and social sciences, we may start to trace the path that leads to the $p = .05$ level.

THE NORMAL DISTRIBUTION

The credit for the extension of the use of calculations used to assess observational error or gaming expectancies into the organization of human characteristics goes to Lambert Adolphe Quetelet (1796–1874), a Belgian astronomer.

Quetelet (1849) found, for example, that the frequency distribution of the chest girths of 5,738 Scottish soldiers closely approximated the normal curve. Moreover, he used the curve to infer what he took to be a non-chance occurrence. In examining the distribution of the heights of 100,000 French army conscripts, he observed a discrepancy between the calculated and reported frequencies of men falling at the minimum height for military service. "Is it not a fair presumption that the . . . men who constitute the difference of these numbers have been fraudulently rejected?" (p. 97).

Sir Francis Galton (1822–1911) eagerly adopted the curve in the organization of the anthropometric data that he collected and introduced the concept of percentiles.

All persons conversant with statistics are aware that this supposition brings Variability within the grasp of the laws of Chance, with the result that the relative frequency of Deviations of different amounts admits of being calculated, when these amounts are measured in terms of any self-contained unit of variability, such as our Q. (Galton, 1889, pp. 54–55)

Q is the symbol for the semi-interquartile range, defined as one half of the difference between the score at the 75th percentile (the third quartile) and the 25th percentile (the first quartile). This means that in a distribution of scores, one half of the deviations fall within $\pm Q$ of the mean, which in the normal distribution falls at the 50th percentile (the second quartile). This measure of variability is equivalent to the *probable error*.

PROBABLE ERROR

The unit of measure of the abscissa of the normal distribution has had many forms. Today the *standard deviation* is the unit of choice, but for many years the probable error *(PE)* was in common use, and it is still used occasionally in the physical sciences. Fundamentally, probable error defines the deviation from a central measure between whose positive and negative values one half of the cases may be expected to fall by chance.

The term appeared in the early 19th century among German mathematical astronomers. Although De Moivre refers to the concept on which *PE* is based, Bessel used the term *(der wahrscheinliche Fehler)* for the first time in 1818. It was subsequently adopted by Gauss, who developed several methods of computing it (Walker, 1929). It was first used with the normal distribution in instances where it was necessary to determine the best possible value of the true position of a point from a series of measurements or observations all of which involved an element of error.

It remained for Karl Pearson (1894) to coin the term *standard deviation*, but the calculation of an equivalent value had existed since De Moivre. Simple calculation shows that the *PE* is equivalent to 0.674560, or roughly ⅔ of a standard deviation.

It was apparently normal practice for Quetelet and Galton to express values in a normal distribution as a function of *PE*, and it seems reasonable to assume that their preference was the overriding influence in its being used in subsequent statistical practice. It should be noted in passing that Galton (1889) objected to the name probable error, calling it a "cumbrous, slipshod, and misleading phrase."

The probable error is, quite clearly, not the most probable of all errors, and the use of the term *error* in describing the variation of human characteristics perhaps carries the analogy with measurement error distribution a shade too far.

STATISTICAL TESTS

In 1893 Pearson began his investigations into the general problem of fitting observed distributions to theoretical curves. The work led eventually to the formulation of the x^2 test of "goodness of fit" in 1900, one of the most important developments in the history of statistics.

Weldon, the co-founder with Pearson of the biometric school (both men, of course, being much influenced by Galton), approached the problem of discrepancies between theory and observation in a much more empirical way, tossing coins and dice and comparing the outcomes with the binomial model.

In a letter written to Galton in 1894, Weldon asks for a comment on the results of some 7,000 throws of 12 dice collected for him by a clerk at University College, London.

> A day or two ago Pearson wanted some records of the kind in a hurry, in order to illustrate a lecture, and I gave him the record of the clerk's 7,000 tosses . . . on examination he rejects them because he thinks the deviation from the theoretically most probable result is so great as to make the record intrinsically incredible. (E. S. Pearson, 1965/1970, p. 331)

This incident set off a good deal of correspondence and discussion among the biometricians. These interchanges contain various references to odds and probabilities beyond which one would be ready to assert that the outcome was unlikely to be chance. Certainly it seems to have been agreed that what we now call the alpha level should have a relatively low value.

But only with the publication of the X^2 test, the first test that enabled us to determine the probability of occurrence of discrepancies between expected and measured frequencies in a distribution, are indications of specific criteria to be found. Here we see the beginnings of standard rejection levels (i.e., points at which the probability of occurrence is so small as to make it difficult, perhaps impossible, for one to regard the observed distribution as a random variation on the theoretical distribution).

Pearson did not choose one particular value as the point of rejection. However, from an examination of the various examples of X^2 calculations presented, with their corresponding probability values, one can see the range within which what might be described as a mixture of intuitive and statistical rejection occurred. The following remarks are from Pearson's paper: $p = .5586$ ("thus we may consider the fit remarkably good" {p. 170}); $p = .28$ ("fairly represented" {p. 174}); $p = .1$ ("not very improbable that the observed frequencies are compatible with a random sampling" {p. 171}); $p = .01$ ("this very improbable result" {p. 172}).

From Pearson's comments, it appears that he began to have some doubts about the goodness of fit at the .1 level ("not very improbable" implies that the results were perhaps *a little* improbable); however, he was convinced of the unlikelihood of the fit at the .01 level. The midpoint between the two is, of course, the .05 level.

William Gosset (who wrote under the pen name of "Student") began his employment with the Guinness Brewery in Dublin in 1899. Scientific methods were just starting to be applied to the brewing industry. Among Gossett's tasks was the supervision of what were essentially quality control experiments. The necessity of using small samples meant that his results were, at best, only approximations to the probability values derived from the normal curve. Therefore the circumstances of his work led Gosset to formulate the small-sample distribution that is called the *t* distribution.

With respect to the determination of a level of significance, Student's (1908) article, in which he published his derivation of the *t* test, stated that "three times the probable error in the normal curve, for most purposes, would be considered significant" (p. 13).

A few years later, another important article was published under the joint authorship of an agronomist and an astronomer (Wood & Stratton, 1910). This paper was essentially to provide direction in the use of probability in interpreting experimental results. These authors endorse the use of *PE* as a measure: "The astronomer . . . has devised a method of estimating the accuracy of his averages . . . the agriculturist cannot do better than follow his example" (p. 425). They recommend "taking 30 to 1 as the lowest odds which can be accepted as giving practical certainty that a difference is significant" (p. 433). Such odds applied to the normal probability curve correspond to a difference from the mean of 3.2 *PE* (for practical purposes this was probably rounded to 3 *PE*).

What specifically determined the adoption of this convention is largely a matter of speculation. Perhaps it was a combination of the preferred use of the *PE* as a measure by early statisticians like Galton and the influence of Pearson and his statements about the unlikelihood of particular results. In any case, it is clear that as early as 1908 X $\pm$ 3 *PE* was accepted as a useful rule of thumb for rejecting differences occurring as the result of chance fluctuations.

Certainly by the time Fisher published his first book on statistical methods 17 years later, 3PE was a frequently used convention for determining statistical significance in a variety of sciences that employed statistical tests as experimental tools. For example, an article in the 1925 volume of the *British Journal of Psychology* reports that the chance occurrence of all calculated correlations is "greater than 3 times the *PE*" (Flugel, 1925).

McGaughy (1924) uses the term *critical ratio* for the expression X/3PE, where X represents a difference. This, he says, is "the accepted standard for the undoubted significance of an obtained difference between averages" and cites Jones (1921).

Having examined the events preceding Fisher's 1925 publication and remembering the context of his discussion, consideration of his first reference to $p = .05$ quite clearly indicates nothing startling or new, or for that matter arbitrary, about what he was suggesting.

A fact that would have been no surprise to most of those reading his book (and which, indeed, Fisher pointed out) is that "a deviation of three times the probable error is effectively equivalent to one of twice the standard error" (Fisher, 1925, pp. 47–48).

Fisher then cannot be credited with establishing the value of the significance level. What he can perhaps be credited with is the beginning of a trend to express a value in a distribution in terms of its own standard deviation instead of its probable error. Fisher was apparently convinced of the advantages of using standard deviation (SD), as evidenced by his remark that "The common use of the probable error is its only recommendation" (p. 48).

Fisher provided calculations for a "probability integral table," from which for any value (described as a function of its SD), one could find what proportion of the total population had a larger deviation. Therefore, when conducting any critical test, use of this table necessitated expressing the deviation of a value in terms of its SD.

Although, strictly speaking, the conventional rejection level of 3PE is equivalent to two times the SD (in modern terminology, a z score of 2), which expressed as a percentage is about 4.56%, one may hazard a guess that Fisher simply rounded off this value to 5% for ease of explanation. Furthermore, it seems reasonable to assume that as the use of statistical analysis was extended to the social sciences, the tendency to report experimental results in terms of their associated probability values rather than transforming them to z score values provided a broader base for general understanding by those not thoroughly grounded in statistical theory. In other words, the statement that the probablity of obtaining a particular result by chance was less than 5% could be more easily digested by the uninitiated than the report that the result represented a z score of approximately 2.

SUBJECTIVE PROBABILITY

How the 5% significance level came to be adopted as a standard has been considered. However, *why* this level seemed appropriate to early statisticians, or why it has continued to prevail in statistical analysis for so long, must be approached not so much from a historical point of view, but from a consideration of the concept of *probability*.

Definitions of the term are most frequently based on expositions of the formal mathematical theory of probability. This may reflect the need to bridge the reality of events in everyday life and the philosophy of logic. Probability in this sense is an objective exercise that uses numerical calculations based on the mathematical theories of arrangements and frequency for the purpose of estimation and prediction.

What often eludes precise definition is the idea that, fundamentally, probability refers to the personal cognition of individuals whereby their knowledge of past experience aids in the formation of a system of expectations with which they face future events. This has been called *subjective probability* to distiguish this notion from its more formal mathematical counterpart.

Alberoni (1962a, 1962b) has conceptualized the intellectual processes that underlie the operation of subjective probability. When individuals cannot find a cause or a regular pattern to explain some differences or variation in the real world, they arrive at the idea of *chance*. This, in turn, forms their expectations for future events. If, however, at some point the events begin to contradict the expectations they have formed, they introduce *cause* and abandon the idea of chance. The point at which this rejection occurs depends largely on the degree of discrepancy and how it is interpreted by each individual. Alberoni refers to this point as the "threshold of dismissal of the idea of chance."

The fundamental questions that remain are straightforward and simple: Do people, scientists and nonscientists, generally feel that an event which occurs 5% of the time or less is a rare event? Are they prepared to ascribe a cause other than mere chance to such infrequent events?

If the answer to both these questions is "Yes," or even "Generally speaking, yes," then the adoption of the level as a criterion for judging outcomes is justifiable.

There is no doubt that the "threshold of dismissal of the idea of chance" depends on a complex set of factors specific to each individual, and therefore varies among individuals.[1] As a formal statement, however, the level has a longer history than is generally appreciated.

REFERENCES

Alberoni, F. (1962). Contribution to the study of subjective probability. Part I. *Journal of General Psychology, 66,* 241–264. (a)

Alberoni, F. (1962). Contribution to the study of subjective probability: Prediction. Part II. *Journal of General Psychology, 66,* 265–285. (b)

Bernoulli, J. (1970) *The art of conjecture* (F. Maseres, Ed. & trans.). New York: Redex Microprint. (Originally published, 1795.)

---

[1]We have some evidence, based on both formal and informal data, that people, on average, do indeed approach this threshold when the odds reach about 1 in 10 and are pretty well convinced when the odds are 1 in 100. The midpoint of the two values is close to .05, or odds of 1 in 20. One is reminded that these subjective probability norms are congruent with the ideas expressed in Pearson's 1900 publication.

Bessel, F. W. (1818). *Ueber den Ort des Polarsterns*. Berlin: Berliner Astronomische Jahrbuch für 1818.

Cochran, W. G. (1976). Early development of techniques in comparative experimentation. In D. B. Owen (Ed.), *On the history of statistics and probability*. New York: Dekker.

Cramer, H. (1955). *The elements of probability theory*. New York: Wiley.

David, F. N. (1962). *Games, gods and gambling*. New York: Hafner.

De Moivre, A. (1967). *The doctrine of chances* (3rd ed.). New York: Chelsea. (Originally published, 1756.)

Fisher, R. A. (1925) *Statistical methods for research workers*. Edinburgh: Oliver & Boyd.

Fisher, R. A. (1926). The arrangement of field experiments, *Journal of the Ministry of Agriculture, 33*, 503–513.

Flugel, J.C. (1925). A quantitative study of feeling and emotion in everyday life. *British Journal of Psychology, 15*, 318–355.

Galton, F. (1889). *Natural inheritance*, London: Macmillan.

Graunt, J. (1956). Natural and political observations made upon the bills of mortality, 1662. In J. R. Newman (Ed.), *The world of mathematics*. New York: Simon & Schuster. (Originally published, 1662.)

Huygens, C. (1970). On reasoning in games. In J. Bernoulli (F. Maseres, Ed. & trans.), *The art of conjecture*. New York: Redex Microprint. (Originally published, 1657.)

Jones, D. C. (1921). *A first course in statistics*. London: Bell.

McGaughy, J. R. (1924). *The fiscal administration of city school systems*. New York: Macmillan.

Pearson, E. S. (1970). Some incidents in the early history of biometry and statistics, 1890–94. In E. S. Pearson & M. G. Kendall (Eds.), *Studies in the history of statistics and probability*. London: Griffin. (Originally published, 1965.)

Pearson, K. (1894). Contributions to the mathematical theory of evolution: I. On the dissection of asymmetrical frequency curves. *Philosophical Transactions*, Part I, pp. 71–110.

Pearson, K. (1990). On the criterion that a given system of deviations from the probable in the case of a correlated system of variables is such that it can be reasonably supposed to have arisen from random sampling. *Philosophical Magazine, 50*. 150–175.

Quetelet, L. A. (1849). *Letters on the theory of probabilities* (O. G. Downes, Trans). London: Layton.

Student {W. S. Gossett}. (1908). The probable error of a mean. *Biometrika, 6*, 1–25.

Walker, H. M. (1929). *Studies in the history of statistical method*. Baltimore, MD: Williams & Wilkins.

Wood, T. B., & Stratton, F. J. M. (1910). The interpretation of experimental results. *Journal of Agricultural Science, 3*, 417–440.

Yule, G. U., & Kendall, M. G. (1950). *An introduction to the theory of statistics* (14th ed.). London: Griffin.

16

STATISTICAL PROCEDURES AND THE JUSTIFICATION OF KNOWLEDGE IN PSYCHOLOGICAL SCIENCE

RALPH L. ROSNOW AND ROBERT ROSENTHAL

The exposure and castigation of error does not propel science forward, though it may clear a number of obstacles from its path.
—Medawar, 1969, p. 7

"Think Yiddish, write British" might be an apt slogan for the dominant discursive pattern of the intuitions and inductive inferences that characterize the scientific outlook in psychology during the entire 20th century. As is true in other fields, the inventive ways that psychological

Reprinted from the *American Psychologist, 44*, 1276–1284. Copyright 1989 by the American Psychological Association.

This article was completed while Ralph Rosnow was a Visiting Professor at Harvard University and Robert Rosenthal was a Fellow at the Center for Advanced Study in the Behavioral Sciences. We wish to thank these institutions for the generous support provided us. We also wish to acknowledge the funding received by Rosnow from Temple University through the Bolton Endowment and a National Institute of Health Biomedical Research Support Grant, and that received by Rosenthal from the National Science Foundation and the John D. and Catherine T. MacArthur Foundation. Portions of this article are based on presentations at the annual meeting of the American Psychological Association by Rosenthal in 1987 and by Rosnow in 1988.

researchers think frequently seem to resemble the hunches and intuitions, the illogical as well as logical inferences, of an astute Jewish grandmother. Indeed, it has been observed that the progress of science, as much as the saga of human discoveries in all fields, is not a history of stunning leaps of logic but is often the outcome of "happy guesses" and "felicitous strokes of talent" in ostensibly unrelated situations (Grinnel, 1987, p. 24). The creative process in psychological science, as in all scientific disciplines, might be compared to the energy that excites a neuron in the human nervous system. The energy used to excite the neuron is nonspecific. The same ion flow occurs whether one hits one's finger with a hammer, burns it on the stove, or has it bitten by a dog. As long as the excitation is there, the result will be the same—ignition. In science, it also seems to make little difference as to what circumstances provide the inspiration to light the fuse of creativity. As long as the situation is sufficiently stimulating to excite thought in the scientist, there will be "ignition."

In contrast, the rhetoric of psychological science, the tightly logical outcome of this "thinking Yiddish," tends to be consistent with the traditions of British empiricist philosophy. As much as in all fields of science, journal articles and research monographs that describe the way in which the scientific method was used to open up the psychological world fail to communicate the day-to-day drama of the interplay of discovery and justification, in which speculative ideas based on facts, theories, intuitions, and hunches exert a constant influence on each other (cf. Knorr-Cetina, 1981; Mahoney, 1976; Mitroff, 1974). One reason for this situation may be that language, insofar as it is limited (Polanyi, 1967), imposes limitations on the ability of scientists to justify what they feel that they know. Another plausible reason is that the world's richness of information often exceeds our capacity to process it directly. As a result, the knower's representation of what is "out there" is, like any model of reality, reduced and distorted to fit in with his or her own available schematisms (McGuire, 1986).

In this article, we are concerned with various specific aspects of the rhetoric of justification, which in part draws on the strict logical consequences of statistical data analysis to shore up facts and inductive inferences. Despite the great range of procedures employed, there are some common problems of methodological spirit and methodological substance that although they have been addressed before, nevertheless endure. By exposing these problems again, we hope it may be possible to weaken their influence. In modern philosophy, a nautical analogy may be used to compare the progress of science to a boat that must be reconstructed not in drydock but at sea, one plank at a time. The aspects of statistical data analysis that we discuss might be thought of as the connecting tools that help us hold fast our facts and inductive inferences. In our reliance on statistical data-analytic tools used to reinforce the empirical foundation of psychological science, we want to choose the right tools for the job and to use them properly.

We begin by discussing four matters pertaining to the methodological spirit, or essence, of statistical data analysis. They are (a) the overreliance on dichotomous significance-testing decisions, (b) the tendency to do many research studies in situations of low power, (c) the habit of defining the results of research in terms of significance levels alone, and (d) the overemphasis on original studies and single studies at the expense of replications. We then turn to a consideration of some matters of methodological substance, or form. These are primarily problems in the teaching and usage of data-analytic procedures. The issues to be considered here are the use of omnibus or multivariate tests, the need for contrasts or focused tests of hypotheses, and the nearly universal misinterpretation of interaction effects.

MATTERS OF METHODOLOGICAL SPIRIT

Dichotomous Significance-Testing Decisions

Far more than is good for us, psychological scientists have for too long operated as if the only proper significance-testing decision is a dichotomous one, in which the evidence is interpreted as "anti-null" if p is not greater than .05 and "pro-null" if p is greater than .05. It may not be an exaggeration to say that for many PhD students, for whom the .05 alpha has acquired almost an ontological mystique, it can mean joy, a doctoral degree, and a tenure-track position at a major university if their dissertation p is less than .05. However, if the p is greater than .05, it can mean ruin, despair, and their advisor's suddenly thinking of a new control condition that should be run.

The conventional wisdom behind the approach goes something like this: The logic begins, more or less, with the proposition that one does not want to accept a hypothesis that stands a fairly good chance of being false (i.e., one ought to avoid Type I errors). The logic goes on to state that one either accepts hypotheses as probably true (not false) or one rejects them, concluding that the null is too likely to regard it as rejectable. The .05 alpha is a good fail-safe standard because it is both convenient and stringent enough to safeguard against accepting an insignificant result as significant. The argument, although not beyond cavil (e.g., Bakan, 1967), affords a systematic approach that many researchers would insist has served scientists well. We are not interested in the logic itself, nor will we argue for replacing the .05 alpha with another level of alpha, but at this point in our discussion we only wish to emphasize that dichotomous significance testing has no ontological basis. That is, we want to underscore that, surely, God loves the .06 nearly as much as the .05. Can there be any doubt that God views the strength of evidence for or against the null as a fairly continuous function of the magnitude of p?

Gigerenzer (1987; Gigerenzer & Murray, 1987; Gigerenzer et al., 1989), in discussions that examined the emergence of statistical inference, reminded us that the notion of dichotomous significance testing was initially developed out of agricultural experimentalists' need to answer questions such as, "Is the manure effective?" It is perhaps harder to object to the necessity of an accept–reject approach when the experimental question is phrased in precisely this way. However, the composition of the data base of psychological science, certainly, is substantively different, as would seem to be the phraseology of the research questions that psychological experimentalists try to answer. Indeed, Fisher at one point (largely as a reaction against the criticisms of Neyman and E. S. Pearson) voiced his strong objections to the idea of a fixed, dichotomous decision-level approach and instead argued for a cumulative, more provisional conception of statistical data analysis in science (as discussed in Gigerenzer, 1987, p. 24)—an idea that we will discuss in more detail.

To be sure, determining the particular level of significance of the data at which a null hypothesis will be rejected is essentially a personal decision, and by extension a decision by the field at a given historical moment. It is well known that in other scientific fields there is a strong tradition of rejecting the null hypothesis at an alpha level other than 5%. In using the Bonferroni procedure, scientists further redefine the alpha level so as to protect against post hoc selection of the largest effects (e.g., Harris, 1975; Morrison, 1976; Myers, 1979; Rosenthal & Rubin, 1984). The essential idea at this point in our discussion is that, from an ontological viewpoint, there is no sharp line between a "significant" and a "nonsignificant" difference; significance in statistics, like the significance of a value in the universe of values, varies continuously between extremes (Boring, 1950; Gigerenzer & Murray, 1987).[1]

Working With Low Power

Too often, it seems that psychologists do significance testing with low

---

[1] Interestingly, Enrico Fermi, the great physicist, thought $p = .10$ to be the wise operational definition of a "miracle" (Polanyi, 1961), and recent findings would lead us to believe that a similar standard might seem reasonable as a kind of "last ditch threshold" (i.e., before accepting the null hypothesis as true) to many psychological researchers (Nelson, Rosenthal, & Rosnow, 1986).

power as a consequence of ignoring the extent to which, in employing a particular size of sample, they are stacking the odds against reaching a given p value for some particular size of effect. One reason for this situation may be that even though the importance of the implications of the mechanics of power analysis for practice were recognized long ago by psychological statisticians, these mechanics were dismissed in some leading textbooks for a time as too complicated to discuss (e.g., Guilford, 1956, p. 217). However, as a consequence of a series of seminal works by Cohen beginning in the 1960s (e.g., Cohen, 1962, 1965), the concept resurfaced with a vengeance in psychological science.

No matter the reasons why a sense of statistical power was never fully inculcated in the scientific soul of laboratory experimental psychology, it cannot be denied that this situation has led to some embarrassing conclusions. Consider the following example (the names have been changed to protect the guilty): Smith conducts an experiment (with $N = 80$) to show the effects of leadership style on productivity and finds that style A is better than B. Jones is skeptical (because he invented style B) and replicates (with $N = 20$). Jones reports a failure to replicate; his t was 1.06, $df = 18$, $p > .30$, whereas Smith's t had been 2.21, $df = 78$, $p < .05$. It is true that Jones did not replicate Smith's p value. However, the magnitude of the effect obtained by Jones ($r = .24$ or $d = .50$) was *identical* to the effect obtained by Smith. Jones had found exactly what Smith had found even though the p values of the two studies were not very close. Because of the smaller sample size of 20, Jones's power to reject at .05 was .18 whereas Smith's power (N of 80) was .60—more than three times greater.

Table 1 helps us to examine this problem more deeply. It shows ratios of Type II to Type I errors for sample sizes from 10 to 1,000. Type I errors may be thought of as inferential errors of gullibility or overeagerness, that is, an effect or a relationship is claimed where none exists. Type II errors may be thought of as inferential errors of conservatism or blindness, that is, the existence of an effect or a relationship that does exist is denied (cf. Axinn, 1966). This table shows what may be conceptualized as the perceived seriousness of Type II to Type I errors for the conventional .05 level of p, the "miraculous" .10 level of p, and levels of r that are frequently characterized as small ($r = .10$), medium ($r = .30$), and large ($r = .50$) in psychological science, following Cohen's (1977) suggestion. For example, if the likelihood of a Type II error = .90 and the likelihood of a Type I error = .10, then the ratio of $.90/.10 = 9$ would tell us that the error in rejecting the null hypothesis when it is true (Type I error) is taken nine times more seriously than the error in failing to reject the null hypothesis when it is false (Type II error).

Thus, the generally greater weight attached to the avoidance of Type

TABLE 1
Ratios of Type II to Type I Error Rates for Various Sample Sizes, Effect Sizes, and Significance Levels (Two-Tailed)

| | Effect sizes and significance levels | | | | | |
| | $r = .10$ | | $r = .30$ | | $r = .50$ | |
N	.05	.10	.05	.10	.05	.10
10	19	9	17	8	13	5
20	19	9	15	6	7	2
30	18	8	13	5	3	1
40	18	8	10	4	2	—
50	18	8	9	3	—	—
100	17	7	3	—	—	—
200	14	6	—	—	—	—
300	12	5	—	—	—	—
400	10	4	—	—	—	—
500	8	3	—	—	—	—
600	6	2	—	—	—	—
700	5	2	—	—	—	—
800	4	1	—	—	—	—
900	3	—	—	—	—	—
1,000	2	—	—	—	—	—

Note: Entries are to nearest integer; missing values <1.

I errors relative to Type II errors increases the smaller the effect size (i.e., r value), the smaller the N, and of course, the more stringent the p value. Although it might be argued that psychologists working in laboratories usually have plenty of power to detect even small effects because in laboratory experimentation error terms are often very small, we see that working simultaneously with a small effect, a small sample, and a binary decisional $p = .05$ might be compared to trying to read small type in a dim light: It is harder to make out the material. How much power is needed? Cohen (1965) recommended .8 as a convention for the desirable level of power. With a "small" effect (i.e., $r = .10$, $d = .20$), a power of .8 would require us to employ a total N of approximately 1,000 in order to detect various effects at $p = .05$, two-tailed (Cohen, 1977). With a "medium" effect (i.e., $r = .30$, $d = .63$), it would mean a total N of approximately 115 sampling units, and with a "large" effect (i.e., $r = .50$, $d = 1.15$) a total N of approximately 40 sampling units, to detect various effects at $p = .05$, two-tailed.[2] Given a typical medium-sized effect (Brewer, 1972; Chase & Chase, 1976; Cohen, 1962, 1973; Haase, Waechter, & Solomon, 1982; Sedlmeier &

---

[2] Small, medium, and large effects of d are conventionally defined as .2, .5, and .8, respectively, but we see that in actuality a somewhat larger effect of d is required when claiming correspondence with a medium or large effect of r (cf. Rosenthal & Rosnow, 1984, p. 361).

Gigerenzer, 1989), it would appear that psychological experimenters seemingly choose to work, or are forced to work by logistic constraints, in "dimly lit" rather than in "brightly lit" situations. This is not universally true in all fields, as we will show.

DEFINING RESULTS OF RESEARCH

The example of Jones and Smith would lead us to believe (quite correctly) that defining the results of research in terms of significance levels alone fails to tell the whole story. In his classic *Design of Experiments,* Fisher (1960) stated further that

> convenient as it is to note that a hypothesis is contradicted at some familiar level of significance such as 5% or 2% or 1% we do not . . . ever need to lose sight of the exact strength which the evidence has in fact reached, or to ignore the fact that with further trial it might come to be stronger or weaker. (p. 25)

He did not give specific advice on how to appraise "the exact strength" of the evidence, but the use of statistical power analysis, effect-size estimation procedures, and quantitative meta-analytic procedures (to which we refer later) enables us to do this with relative ease.

We have looked into power, and we now take another look at significance testing and effect-size estimation in the framework of a study with plenty of power overall. Before turning to this illustration, it may be worth reviewing the logic that insists that effect sizes be computed not only when p values in experimental studies are viewed as significant but also when they are viewed as nonsignificant. There are two good arguments for this recommended practice.

First, computing population effect sizes guides our judgment about the sample size needed in the next study we might conduct. For any given statistical test of a null hypothesis (e.g., t, F, χ^2, Z), the power of the statistical test (i.e., the probability of not making a Type II error) is determined by (a) the level of risk of drawing a spuriously positive conclusion (i.e., the p level), (b) the size of the study (i.e., the sample size), and (c) the effect size. These three factors are so related that when any two of them are known, the third can be determined. Thus, if we know the values for factors (a) and (c), we can easily figure out how big a sample we need to achieve any desired level of statistical power (e.g., Cohen, 1977; Kraemer & Thiemann, 1987; Rosenthal & Rosnow, 1984).

Second, it is important to realize that the effect size tells us something very different from the p level. A result that is statistically significant is not necessarily practically significant as judged by the magnitude of the effect. Consequently, highly significant p values should not be interpreted as automatically reflecting large effects. In the case of F ratios, a numerator mean square (MS) may be large relative to a denominator MS because the effect size is large, the N per condition is large, or because both values are large. On the other hand, even if considered quantitatively unimpressive according to the standards defined earlier, it could nevertheless have profound implications in a practical context.

The following example serves to illustrate that a test of significance without an effect size estimate gives an incomplete picture: In 1988, a major biomedical research study reported that heart attack risk in the population is cut by aspirin (Steering Committee of the Physicians' Health Study Research Group, 1988). This conclusion was based on the results of a five-year study of a sample of 22,071 physicians, approximately half of whom (11,037) were given an ordinary aspirin tablet (325 mg.) every other day, while the remainder (11,034) were given a placebo. Presumably, the way that aspirin works to reduce mortality from myocardial infarction is to promote circulation even when fatty deposits have collected along the walls of the coronary arteries. That is, aspirin does not reduce the chances of getting clotting but makes it easier for the transport of blood as the arteries get narrower. Part of the results of this study are shown in Table 2.

The top part of Table 2 shows the number of participants in each condition who did or did not have a heart attack. We see that 1.3% suffered an attack, and this event occurred more frequently in the placebo condition (1.7%) than in the aspirin condition (0.9%). Testing the statistical significance of these results yields a p value that is considerably smaller than the usual .05 decision cliff relied on in dichotomous significance testing, χ^2 (1, $N = 22,071$) = 25.01, $p < .00001$. This tells us that the results were very unlikely to be a fluke or lucky coincidence. However, when

TABLE 2
Aspirin's Effect on Heart Attack

Condition	MI absent	MI present
Presence or absence of MI in aspirin and placebo conditions		
Aspirin	10,933	104
Placebo	10,845	189
Binomial effect-size display of $r = 0.34$		
Aspirin	51.7	48.3
Placebo	48.3	51.7
Total	100.0	100.0
Fatal and nonfatal MIs in aspirin and placebo conditions		
	Nonfatal MI	Fatal MI
Aspirin	99	5
Placebo	171	18

Note: MI = myocardial infarction.

we compute the effect size (as a standard Pearson correlation coefficient), the result ($r = .034$) is so small as to be considered quantitatively unimpressive by methodological convention in our field.

Nevertheless, the implications are far from unimpressive, and we see this more clearly when we recast this magnitude of effect into the language of a binomial effect-size display (Rosenthal & Rubin, 1979, 1982). In such a display, the results are translated for simplicity into dichotomous outcomes such as success versus failure, improved versus not improved, or in this case, myocardial infarction (MI) present versus MI absent. Because discussions of this technique are already available (e.g., Rosenthal & Rubin, 1979, 1982; Rosenthal & Rosnow, 1984; Rosnow & Rosenthal, 1988), it will suffice to note that its use to display the increase in success rate due to treatment more clearly communicates the real-world importance of treatment effects than do the commonly used effect-size estimators based on the proportion of variance accounted for. The middle part of Table 2 provides us with a binomial effect-size display that corresponds to the $r = .034$ effect size computed on the results in the top part. It suggests that approximately 3.4% fewer persons who would probably experience a myocardial infarction (i.e., given the particular conditions of this investigation) will not experience it if they follow the regimen as prescribed in the aspirin treatment condition.

The bottom part of Table 2 shows a small subset of the sample that participated in this investigation, consisting of those persons who actually suffered a heart attack during the five-year period of observation. In the aspirin condition 4.8% had a fatal heart attack, whereas in the placebo condition 9.5% had a fatal heart attack. It appears that mortality from myocardial infarction decreased by approximately one half as a result of aspirin taken every other day. When we compute the effect size, we find it to be more than twice the size ($r = .08$) of that computed for the overall results. However, even though the effect size for the smaller subset is more impressive than the effect size for the entire sample, were we to rely on dichotomous significance testing for a yes-or-no-decision we would be led to not reject the null hypothesis. That is because $\chi^2 (1, N = 293) = 2.06$, $p = .08$ for the results in the bottom part of Table 2. Inasmuch as the sample size is relatively small, as seen in the context of the "small" magnitude of effect, we are operating with much less power than we were in the top part of Table 2. What is the lesson? Given the low level of power ($<.4$), this aspect of the investigation should be continued with a larger sample size before deciding that nothing happened.

Before leaving this section, it will be instructive if we briefly discuss the limitations of the findings in this study to underscore the idea that strength of effect is very context dependent. First, the sample in this study consisted entirely of male physicians, and the statistical results may not generalize in exactly the same way to the population at large. Furthermore, in prescribing aspirin, the physician would want to know about the medical history of the patient because the effects of aspirin could be dangerous to persons with ulcers, high blood pressure, kidney problems, or allergies to aspirin or who are about to undergo surgery. Thus, a further lesson is that, like a word or phrase framed by the context in which it is situated, it is important not to strip away the context from the content of a research study as we attempt to frame particular implications of the results.

Second, there is a growing awareness in psychology that just about everything under the sun is context dependent in one way or another (e.g., Gergen, 1973; Hayes, 1987; Hoffman & Nead, 1983; Jaeger & Rosnow, 1988; Lerner, Hultsch, & Dixon, 1983; McGuire, 1983; Mishler, 1979; Rosnow, 1978, 1981; Rosnow & Georgoudi, 1986; Sarbin, 1977; Smith, 1988; Veroff, 1983). Strength of effect measures are no exception, and it is therefore important to recognize how the study characteristics might influence the size as well as one's interpretation of the magnitude-of-effect estimate (e.g., Murray & Dosser, 1987; Rosenthal & Rosnow, 1984; Rosenthal & Rubin, 1979, 1982; Strube, 1988).

Overemphasis on Single Studies

The final matter of methodological spirit to be discussed concerns the importance of replication, a concept to which psychological journal editors, textbook writers, and researchers pay considerable lip service. In practice, however, the majority of editors, as much as most researchers, seem to be biased in favor of single studies at the expense of replications. Sterling (1959) found not a single replication in his classic review of experimental articles in four psychological journals during one year, and this practice does not appear to have changed much in more recent years (Mahoney, 1976).

Is it possible there are sociological grounds for this monomaniacal preoccupation with the results of a single study? Might those grounds have to do with the reward system of science, in which, in our perceptions, as much as in the realities of many academic institutions, merit, promotion, and the like depend on the results of the single study, which is also known as the "smallest unit of academic currency"? The study is "good," "valuable," and above all, "publishable" when $p < .05$. Our discipline might be farther ahead if it adopted a more cumulative view of science. The operationalization of this view would involve evaluating the impact of a study not strictly on the basis of the particular p level, but more on the basis of multiple criteria, including its own effect size as well as the revised effect size and combined probability that resulted from the addition of the new study to any earlier studies investigating the same or a similar relationship. This, of course, amounts to a call for a more meta-analytic view of doing science.

The name, meta-analysis, was coined by Glass (1976) to refer to the summarizing enterprise, although the basic quantitative procedures for combining and comparing research results were known some years earlier (Mosteller & Bush, 1954; Snedecor, 1946). Because numerous texts and articles are available on this subject (e.g., Cooper, 1984; Glass, McGaw, & Smith, 1981; Hedges & Olkin, 1985; Hunter, Schmidt, & Jackson, 1982; Mullen & Rosenthal, 1985; Rosenthal, 1984), we will mention only two, more or less secret, benefits to the research process of conducting meta-analytic reviews of research domains: the "new intimacy" and the "decrease in the splendid detachment of the full professor."

First, this new intimacy is between the researcher and the data. We cannot do a meta-analysis by reading abstracts and discussion sections. We have to look at the numbers and, very often, compute the correct ones ourselves. Meta-analysis requires us to cumulate *data*, not *conclusions*. Reading an original-study article is quite a different matter when one needs to compute an effect size and a fairly precise significance level—often from a results section that provides no information on effect sizes or precise significance levels. The *Publication Manual of the American Psychological Association* (American Psychological Association [APA], 1983) insists that when reporting inferential statistics, authors give the symbol, degrees of freedom, value, and probability level. The APA manual does not require that an exact significance level or the estimated effect size be reported, but what a boon it would be for meta-analysts if all journal editors required that authors also report all of their analyses and findings to even this limited extent.

Second, closely related to the first benefit is a change in *who* does the reviewing of the literature. Meta-analytic work requires careful reading of research and moderate data-analytic skills. One cannot send an undergraduate research assistant to the library with a stack of 5×8 cards to bring back "the results." With narrative reviews that seems often to have been done. With meta-analysis the reviewer must get involved with the data, and that is all to the good because it results in a decrease in the splendid detachment of the full professor.

There are other benefits of replications that are well known to scientists. The fact that the results can be repeated ensures the robustness of the relationships reported. The results also can be repeated by uncorrelated replicators (i.e., truly independent experimenters) in different situations, which ensures the further generality of the relationships. In spite of the recognized methodological and epistemological limitations, the importance of replications is supported by quite different methodological theories as essential in a pragmatic sense (e.g., Bakan, 1967; Brewer & Collins, 1981; Houts, Cook, & Shadish, 1986; Rosenthal & Rosnow, 1984; Rosnow, 1981).

MATTERS OF METHODOLOGICAL SUBSTANCE

Omnibus Tests

The first problem of methodological substance concerns the overreliance on omnibus tests of diffuse hypotheses that although providing protection for some investigators from the dangers of "data mining" with multiple tests performed as if each were the only one considered, do not usually tell us anything we really want to know. As Abelson (1962) pointed out long ago in the case of analysis of variance (ANOVA), the problem is that when the null hypothesis is accepted, it is frequently because of the insensitive omnibus character of the standard F-test as much as by reason of sizable error variance. All the while that a particular predicted pattern among the means is evident to the naked eye, the standard F-test is often insufficiently illuminating to reject the null hypothesis that several means are statistically identical.

For example, suppose the specific question is whether increased incentive level improves the productivity of work groups. We employ four levels of incentive so that our omnibus F-test would have 3 dfs in the numerator or our omnibus chi square would be on at least 3 dfs. Common as these omnibus tests are, the diffuse hypothesis tested by them usually tells us nothing of importance about our research question. The rule of thumb is unambiguous: Whenever we have tested a fixed effect with $df > 1$ for chi square or for the numerator of F, we have tested a question in which we almost surely are not interested.

The situation is even worse when there are several dependent variables as well as multiple degrees of freedom for the independent variable. The paradigm case here is canonical correlation, and some special cases are multiple analysis of variance (MANOVA), multiple analysis of covariance (MANCOVA), multiple discriminant function, multiple path analysis, and complex multiple partial correlation. Although all of these procedures have useful exploratory data-analytic applications, they are commonly used to test null hypotheses that are scientifically almost always of doubtful value (cf. Huberty & Morris, 1989). Furthermore, the effect size estimates they yield (e.g., the canonical correlation) are also almost always of doubt-

1.7; no distraction, 1.8, 2.4, 2.2, and 2.7. In the original published report the developmental change in treatment effect was tested by an omnibus F for the interaction of age by treatment, which the investigator found to be nonsignificant, that is, $F(3, 152) = 1.9$, $p = .13$. Hale reanalyzed the results by carving a focused F or contrast analysis between treatment and age trend out of the interaction sum of squares, which he found statistically significant, that is, $F(1, 152) = 4.3$, $p = .04$.

Discussions of contrasts have been primarily within the context of ANOVA, but their use is not restricted to this situation (cf. Bishop, Fienberg, & Holland, 1975; Rosenthal, 1984; Rosenthal & Rosnow, 1984, 1985). For example, Donald Rubin (in Rosenthal & Rosnow, 1985, pp. 48–49) has shown how contrasts can also be used when the obtained values are cast as frequency counts in a $2 \times C$ contingency table, in which the classes in one classification are ordered and the classes in the other classification are expressed as a proportion (see also Snedecor & Cochran, 1967, p. 247). Although most current textbooks of statistics describe the logic and the machinery of contrast analysis, one still sees contrasts employed all too rarely. That is a real pity given the precision of thought and theory they encourage and (especially relevant to these times of publication pressure) given the boost in power conferred with the resulting increase in .05 asterisks.

Interaction Effects

The final matter to be discussed concerns what are probably the universally most misinterpreted empirical results in psychology, the results of interaction effects. A recent survey of 191 research articles employing ANOVA designs involving interaction found only 1% of the articles interpreting interactions in an unequivocally correct manner (Rosnow & Rosenthal, 1989). The mathematical meaning of interaction effects is unambiguous, and textbooks of mathematical and psychological statistics routinely include proper definitions of interaction effects. Despite this, most of the textbooks in current usage and most psychological researchers reporting results in our primary journals interpret interactions incorrectly. The nature of the error is quite consistent. Once investigators find significant interactions they attempt to interpret them by examining the differences among the original cell means, that is, the simple effects. However, it is no secret that these condition means are made up only partially of interaction effects; main effects may contribute to simple effects even more than interactions (e.g., Lindquist, 1953). The origin of the problem, as Dawes (1969) suggested, may in part be a consequence of "the lack of perfect correspondence between the meaning of 'interaction' in the analysis of variance model and its meaning in other discourse" (p. 57). Whatever its etiology, however, the error of looking only to the uncorrected cell means for the pattern of the statistical interaction is deeply rooted, indeed.

Because we have discussed the treatment of this problem in some detail recently (Rosenthal & Rosnow, 1984; Rosnow & Rosenthal, 1989), we merely note here that if investigators are claiming to speak of an interaction, the exercise of looking at the "corrected" cell means is absolutely essential. Of course, this should not be viewed as an argument against comparing cell means (i.e., simple effects tests), as it often makes sense to focus on a comparison of means using planned contrasts and to deemphasize the traditional main and interaction effects when they are based only on omnibus F-tests. Our point here is that the interaction effect is defined basically in terms of the residuals, or leftover effects, after the lower order effects have been removed from the original cell means. This is true even though the mean square for interaction in the ANOVA can be viewed as variability of the differences between the (uncorrected) cell means for the various rows of the table of overall effects. That is, the mean square for interaction will have a nonzero value if the difference between any two cell means in any row differs from the corresponding difference in any other row. Nonetheless, in focusing attention only on the original cell means, one is essentially ignoring the form and degree of relationship of the interaction itself. Like peeling away the skins of an onion, we need to peel away the lower order effects in order to separate the effects of the interaction from the main effects.

The problem is compounded because users of SPSS, SAS, BMDP, and virtually all data-analytic software are poorly served in the matter of interactions. Almost no programs provide tabular output giving the residuals defining interaction. The only exception to that, of which we are aware, is a little-known package called Data-Text, developed by Armor and Couch (1972) in consultation with leading statisticians including William Cochran and Donald Rubin. Researchers claiming to speak of an interaction must avoid the pitfall described in the anecdote of the drunkard's search. A drunk man lost his house key and began searching for it under a street lamp, even though he had dropped the key some distance away. When he was asked why he did not look where he had dropped it, he replied, "There's more light here!" This principle teaches that looking in a convenient place but not in the right place will never yield the key that will answer the question.

A FINAL NOTE

We have examined a number of aspects of the rhetoric of justification, which in part depends on statistical data analysis to shore up facts and inductive inferences. In particular, we have exposed several problems of methodological spirit and substance that have become deeply rooted in psychological science. Because of the unifying influence of the institutionalization of the classical procedure, we have sought in this discussion to review some ways of improving it rather than to argue for an alternative procedure for statistical inference (e.g., Goodman & Royall, 1988). Much of what we have said has been said before, but it is important that our graduate students hear it all again so that the next generation of psychological scientists is aware of the existence of these pitfalls and of the ways around them.

REFERENCES

Abelson, R. P. (1962). *Testing a priori hypotheses in the analysis of variance.* Unpublished manuscript, Yale University, New Haven, CT.

American Psychological Association. (1983). *Publication manual of the American Psychological Association* (3rd ed.). Washington, DC: Author.

Armor, D. J., & Couch, A. S. (1972). *Data-text primer: An introduction to computerized social data analysis.* New York: Free Press.

Axinn, S. (1966). Fallacy of the single risk. *Philosophy of Science, 33,* 154–162.

Bakan, D. (1967). *On method: Toward a reconstruction of psychological investigation.* San Francisco, CA: Jossey-Bass.

Bishop, Y. M. M., Fienberg, S. E., & Holland, P. W. (1975). *Discrete multivariate analysis: Theory and practice.* Cambridge, MA: MIT Press.

Boring, E. G. (1950). *A history of experimental psychology* (2nd ed.). New York: Appleton-Century-Crofts.

Brewer, J. K. (1972). On the power of statistical tests in the *American Educational Research Journal. American Educational Research Journal, 9,* 391–401.

Brewer, M. B., & Collins, B. E. (Eds.). (1981). *Scientific inquiry and the social sciences: A volume in honor of Donald T. Campbell.* San Francisco, CA: Jossey-Bass.

Chase, L. J., & Chase, R. B. (1976). A statistical power analysis of applied psychological research. *Journal of Applied Psychology, 61,* 234–237.

Cohen, J. (1962). The statistical power of abnormal-social psychological research: A review. *Journal of Abnormal and Social Psychology, 65,* 145–153.

Cohen, J. (1965). Some statistical issues in psychological research. In B. B. Wolman (Ed.), *Handbook of clinical psychology* (pp. 95–121). New York: McGraw-Hill.

Cohen, J. (1973). Statistical power analysis and research results. *American Educational Research Journal, 10,* 225–229.

Cohen, J. (1977). *Statistical power analysis for the behavioral sciences* (2nd ed.). New York: Academic Press.

Cooper, H. M. (1984). *The integrative research review: A systematic approach.* Beverly Hills, CA: Sage.

Dawes, R. M. (1969). "Interaction effects" in the presence of asymmetrical transfer. *Psychological Bulletin, 71,* 55–57.

Fisher, R. A. (1960). *Design of experiments* (7th ed.). Edinburgh, Scotland: Oliver & Boyd.

Gergen, K. J. (1973). Social psychology as history. *Journal of Personality and Social Psychology, 26,* 309–320.

Gigerenzer, G. (1987). Probabilistic thinking and the fight against subjectivity. In L. Kruger, G. Gigerenzer, & M. S. Morgan (Eds.), *The probabilistic revolution* (Vol. 2, pp. 11–33). Cambridge, MA: Bradford/MIT Press.

Gigerenzer, G., & Murray, D. J. (1987). *Cognition as intuitive statistics.* Hillsdale, NJ: Erlbaum.

Gigerenzer, G., Swijtink, Z., Porter, T., Daston, L., Beatty, J., & Krüger, L. (1989). *The empire of chance: How probability changed science and everyday life.* Cambridge, England: Cambridge University Press.

Glass, G. (1976). Primary, secondary, and meta-analysis of research. *Educational Researcher, 5,* 3–8.

Glass, G., McGaw, B., & Smith, M. L. (1981). *Meta-analysis in social research.* Beverly Hills, CA: Sage.

Goodman, S. N., & Royall, R. (1988). Evidence and scientific research. *American Journal of Public Health, 78,* 1568–1574.

Grinnell, F. (1987). *The scientific attitude.* Boulder, CO: Westview Press.

Guilford, J. P. (1956). *Fundamental statistics in psychology and education.* New York: McGraw-Hill.

Haase, R. F., Waechter, D. M., & Solomon, G. S. (1982). How significant is a significant difference? Average effect size of research in counseling psychology. *Journal of Counseling Psychology, 29,* 58–65.

Hale, G. A. (1977). On use of ANOVA in developmental research. *Child Development, 48,* 1101–1106.

Harris, R. J. (1975). *A primer of multivariate statistics.* New York: Academic Press.

Hayes, S. C. (1987). A contextual approach to therapeutic change. In N. Jacobson (Ed.), *Psychotherapists in clinical practice: Cognitive and behavioral perspectives* (pp. 327–387). New York: Guilford.

Hedges, L. V., & Olkin, I. (1985). *Statistical methods for meta-analysis.* Orlando, FL: Academic Press.

Hoffman, R. R., & Nead, J. M. (1983). General contextualism, ecological sciences and cognitive research. *Journal of Mind and Behavior, 4,* 507–560.

Houts, A. C., Cook, T. D., & Shadish, W., Jr. (1986). The person–situation debate: A critical multiplist perspective. *Journal of Personality, 54,* 52–105.

Huberty, C. J., & Morris, J. D. (1989). Multivariate analysis versus multiple univariate analyses. *Psychological Bulletin, 105,* 302–308.

Hunter, J. E., Schmidt, F. L., & Jackson, G. B. (1982). *Meta-analysis: Cumulating research findings across studies.* Beverly Hills, CA: Sage.

Jaeger, M. E., & Rosnow, R. L. (1988). Contextualism and its implications for psychological inquiry. *British Journal of Psychology, 79,* 63–75.

Knorr-Cetina, K. D. (1981). *The manufacture of knowledge: An essay on the constructivist and contextual nature of science.* Oxford, England: Pergamon.

Kraemer, H. C., & Thiemann, S. (1987). *How many subjects? Statistical power analysis in research.* Beverly Hills, CA: Sage.

Lerner, R. M., Hultsch, D. F., & Dixon, R. A. (1983). Contextualism and the character of developmental psychology in the 1970s. *Annals of the New York Academy of Sciences, 412,* 101–128.

Lindquist, E. F. (1953). *Design and analysis of experiments in psychology and education.* Boston, MA: Houghton Mifflin.

Mahoney, M. J. (1976). *Scientist as subject: The psychological imperative.* Cambridge, MA: Ballinger.

McGuire, W. J. (1983). A contextual theory of knowledge: Its implications for innovation and reform in psychological research. In L. Berkowitz (Ed.), *Advances in experimental social psychology* (Vol. 16, pp. 1–47). New York: Academic Press.

McGuire, W. J. (1986). A perspectivist looks at contextualism and the future of behavioral science. In R. L. Rosnow & M. Georgoudi (Eds.), *Contextualism and understanding in behavioral science: Implications for research and theory* (pp. 271–301). New York: Praeger.

Medawar, P. B. (1969). *Induction and intuition in scientific thought.* Philadelphia, PA: American Philosophical Society.

Mishler, E. G. (1979). Meaning in context: Is there any other kind? *Harvard Educational Review, 49,* 1–19.

Mitroff, I. (1974). *The subjective side of science: A philosophical inquiry into the psychology of the Apollo moon scientists.* New York: Elsevier.

Morrison, D. F. (1976). *Multivariate statistical methods* (2nd ed.). New York: McGraw-Hill.

Mosteller, F. M., & Bush, R. R. (1954). Selected quantitative techniques. In G. Lindzey (Ed.), *Handbook of social psychology: Vol. 1. Theory and method* (pp. 289–334). Cambridge, MA: Addison-Wesley.

Mullen, B., & Rosenthal, R. (1985). BASIC *meta-analysis: Procedures and programs.* Hillsdale, NJ: Erlbaum.

Murray, L. W., & Dosser, D. A., Jr. (1987). How significant is a significant difference? Problems with the measurement of magnitude of effect. *Journal of Counseling Psychology, 34,* 68–72.

Myers, J. L. (1979). *Fundamentals of experimental design* (3rd ed.). Boston, MA: Allyn & Bacon.

Nelson, N., Rosenthal, R., & Rosnow, R. L. (1986). Interpretation of significance levels and effect sizes by psychological researchers. *American Psychologist, 41,* 1299–1301.

Polanyi, M. (1961). The unaccountable element in science. *Transactions of the Bose Research Institute, 24,* 175–184.

Polanyi, M. (1967). *The tacit dimension.* London, England: Routledge & Kegan Paul.

Rosenthal, R. (1984). *Meta-analytic procedures for social research.* Beverly Hills, CA: Sage.

Rosenthal, R. (1987). *Judgment studies: Design, analysis, and meta-analysis.* New York: Cambridge University Press.

Rosenthal, R., & Rosnow, R. L. (1984). *Essentials of behavioral research: Methods and data analysis.* New York: McGraw-Hill.

Rosenthal, R., & Rosnow, R. L. (1985). *Contrast analysis: Focused comparisons in the analysis of variance.* Cambridge, England: Cambridge University Press.

Rosenthal, R., & Rubin, D. B. (1979). A note on percent variance explained as a measure of the importance of effects. *Journal of Applied Psychology, 9,* 395–396.

Rosenthal, R., & Rubin, D. B. (1982). A simple general purpose display of magnitude of experimental effect. *Journal of Educational Psychology, 74,* 166–169.

Rosenthal, R., & Rubin, D. B. (1984). Multiple contrasts and ordered Bonferroni procedures. *Journal of Educational Psychology, 76,* 1028–1034.

Rosnow, R. L. (1978). The prophetic vision of Giambattista Vico: Implications for the state of social psychological theory. *Journal of Personality and Social Psychology, 36,* 1322–1331.

Rosnow, R. L. (1981). *Paradigms in transition: The methodology of social inquiry.* New York: Oxford University Press.

Rosnow, R. L., & Georgoudi, M. (Eds.). (1986). *Contextualism and understanding in behavioral science: Implications for research and theory.* New York: Praeger.

Rosnow, R. L., & Rosenthal, R. (1988). Focused tests of significance and effect size estimation in counseling psychology. *Journal of Counseling Psychology, 35,* 203–208.

Rosnow, R. L., & Rosenthal, R. (1989). Definition and interpretation of interaction effects. *Psychological Bulletin, 105,* 143–146.

Sarbin, T. R. (1977). Contextualism: A world view for modern psychology. In J. K. Cole & A. W. Landfield (Eds.), *Nebraska symposium on motivation* (Vol. 24, pp. 1–41). Lincoln, NE: University of Nebraska Press.

Sedlmeier, P., & Gigerenzer, G. (1989). Do studies of statistical power have an impact on the power of studies? *Psychological Bulletin, 105,* 309–316.

Smith, M. B. (1988). Beyond Aristotle and Galileo: Toward a contextualized psychology of persons. *Theoretical and Philosophical Psychology, 8,* 2–15.

Snedecor, G. W. (1946). *Statistical methods.* Ames, IA: Iowa State College Press.

Snedecor, G. W., & Cochran, W. G. (1967). *Statistical methods* (6th ed.). Ames, IA: Iowa State University Press.

Steering Committee of the Physicians' Health Study Research Group. (1988). Preliminary report: Findings from the aspirin component of the ongoing physicians' health study. *New England Journal of Medicine, 318,* 262–264.

Sterling, T. D. (1959). Publication decisions and their possible effects on inferences drawn from tests of significance—or vice versa. *Journal of the American Statistical Association, 54,* 30–34.

Strube, M. J. (1988). Some comments on the use of magnitude-of-effect estimates. *Journal of Counseling Psychology, 35,* 342–345.

Veroff, J. (1983). Contextual determinants of personality. *Personality and Social Psychology Bulletin, 9,* 331–343.

17

THINGS I HAVE LEARNED (SO FAR)

JACOB COHEN

What I have learned (so far) has come from working with students and colleagues, from experience (sometimes bitter) with journal editors and review committees, and from the writings of, among others, Paul Meehl, David Bakan, William Rozeboom, Robyn Dawes, Howard Wainer, Robert Rosenthal, and more recently, Gerd Gigerenzer, Michael Oakes, and Leland Wilkinson. Although they are not always explicitly referenced, many of you will be able to detect their footprints in what follows.

SOME THINGS YOU LEARN AREN'T SO

One of the things I learned early on was that some things you learn aren't so. In graduate school, right after World War II, I learned that for doctoral dissertations and most other purposes, when comparing groups,

Reprinted from the American Psychologist, 45, 1304–1312. Copyright 1990 by the American Psychological Association.

the proper sample size is 30 cases per group. The number *30* seems to have arisen from the understanding that with fewer than 30 cases, you were dealing with "small" samples that required specialized handling with "small-sample statistics" instead of the critical-ratio approach we had been taught. Some of us knew about these exotic small-sample statistics—in fact, one of my fellow doctoral candidates undertook a dissertation, the distinguishing feature of which was a sample of only 20 cases per group, so that he could demonstrate his prowess with small-sample statistics. It wasn't until some years later that I discovered (mind you, not invented) power analysis, one of whose fruits was the revelation that for a two-independent-group-mean comparison with $n = 30$ per group at the sanctified two-tailed .05 level, the probability that a medium-sized effect would be labeled as significant by the most modern methods (a t test) was only .47. Thus, it was approximately a coin flip whether one would get a significant result, even though, in reality, the effect size was meaningful. My $n = 20$ friend's power was rather worse (.33), but of course he couldn't know that, and he ended up with nonsignificant results—with which he proceeded to demolish an important branch of psychoanalytic theory.

LESS IS MORE

One thing I learned over a long period of time that *is* so is the validity of the general principle that *less is more*, except of course for sample size (Cohen & Cohen, 1983, pp. 169–171). I have encountered too many studies with prodigious numbers of dependent variables, or with what seemed to me far too many independent variables, or (heaven help us) both.

In any given investigation that isn't explicitly exploratory, we should be studying few independent variables and even fewer dependent variables, for a variety of reasons.

If all of the dependent variables are to be related to all of the independent variables by simple bivariate analyses or multiple regression, the number of hypothesis tests that will be performed willy-nilly is at least the product of the sizes of the two sets. Using the .05 level for many tests escalates the experimentwise Type I error rate—or in plain English, greatly increases the chances of discovering things that aren't so. If, for example, you study 6 dependent and 10 independent variables and should find that your harvest yields 6 asterisks, you know full well that if there were no real associations in any of the 60 tests, the chance of getting one or more "significant" results is quite high (something like $1 - .95^{60}$, which equals, coincidentally, .95), and that you would expect three spuriously significant results on the average. You then must ask yourself some embarrassing questions, such as, Well, which three are real?, or even, Is six significant *significantly* more than the chance-expected three? (It so happens that it isn't.)

And of course, as you've probably discovered, you're not likely to solve your multiple tests problem with the Bonferroni maneuver. Dividing .05 by 60 sets a per-test significance criterion of .05/60 = 0.00083, and therefore a critical two-sided t value of about 3.5. The effects you're dealing with may not be large enough to produce any interesting ts that high, unless you're lucky.

Nor can you find salvation by doing six stepwise multiple regressions on the 10 independent variables. The amount of capitalization on chance that this entails is more than I know how to compute, but certainly more than would a simple harvest of asterisks for 60 regression coefficients (Wilkinson, 1990, p. 481).

In short, the results of this humongous study are a muddle. There is no solution to your problem. You wouldn't, of course, write up the study for publication as if the unproductive three quarters of your variables never existed. . . .

The irony is that people who do studies like this often start off with some useful central idea that, if pursued modestly by means of a few highly targeted variables and hypotheses, would likely produce significant results. These could, if propriety or the consequences of early toilet training deemed it necessary, successfully withstand the challenge of a Bonferroni or other experimentwise-adjusted alpha procedure.

A special case of the too-many-variables problem arises in multiple regression–correlation analysis with large numbers of independent variables. As the number of independent variables increases, the chances are that their redundancy in regard to criterion relevance also increases. Because redundancy increases the standard errors of partial regression and correlation coefficients and thus reduces their statistical significance, the results are likely to be zilch.

I have so heavily emphasized the desirability of working with few variables and large sample sizes that some of my students have spread the rumor that my idea of the perfect study is one with 10,000 cases and no variables. They go too far.

A less profound application of the less-is-more principle is to our habits of reporting numerical results. There are computer programs that report by default four, five, or even more decimal places for all numerical results. Their authors might well be excused because, for all the programmer knows, they may be used by atomic scientists. But we social scientists should know better than to report our results to so many places. What, pray, does an $r = .12345$ mean? or, for an IQ distribution, a mean of 105.6345? For $N = 100$, the standard error of the r is about .1 and the standard error of the IQ mean about 1.5. Thus, the *345* part of $r = .12345$ is only 3% of its standard error, and the *345* part of the IQ mean of 105.6345 is only 2% of its standard error. These superfluous decimal places are no better than random numbers. They are actually worse than useless because the clutter they create, particularly in tables, serves to distract the eye and mind from the necessary comparisons among the meaningful leading digits. Less is indeed more here.

SIMPLE IS BETTER

I've also learned that simple is better, which is a kind of loose generalization of less is more. The simple-is-better idea is widely applicable to the representation, analysis, and reporting of data.

If, as the old cliché has it, a picture is worth a thousand words, in describing a distribution, a frequency polygon or, better still, a Tukey (1977, pp. 1–26) stem and leaf diagram is usually worth more than the first four moments, that is, the mean, standard deviation, skewness, and kurtosis. I do not question that the moments efficiently summarize the distribution or that they are useful in some analytic contexts. Statistics packages eagerly give them to us and we dutifully publish them, but they do not usually make it possible for most of us or most of the consumers of our products to see the distribution. They don't tell us, for example, that there are no cases between scores of 72 and 90, or that this score of 24 is somewhere in left field, or that there is a pile-up of scores of 9. These are the kinds of features of our data that we surely need to know about, and they become immediately evident with simple graphic representation.

Graphic display is even more important in the case of bivariate data. Underlying each product–moment correlation coefficient in an acre of such coefficients there lies a simple scatter diagram that the r presumes to summarize, and well it might. That is, it does so if the joint distribution is more-or-less bivariate normal—which means, among other things, that the relationship must be linear and that there are no wild outlying points. We know that least squares measures, like means and standard deviations, are sensitive to outliers. Well, Pearson correlations are even more so. About 15 years ago, Wainer and Thissen (1976) published a data set made up of the heights in inches and weights in pounds of 25 subjects, for which the r was a perfectly reasonable .83. But if an error in transcription were made so that the height and weight values for one of the 25 subjects were switched, the r would become $-.26$, a rather large and costly error!

There is hardly any excuse for gaps, outliers, curvilinearity, or other pathology to exist in our data unbeknownst to us. The same computer statistics package with which we can do very complicated analyses like quasi-Newtonian nonlinear estimation and multidimensional scaling with Guttman's coefficient of alienation also can give us simple scatter plots and stem and leaf diagrams with which we can see our data. A proper multiple regression/correlation analysis does not begin with a matrix of correlation coefficients, means, and standard deviations, but rather with a set of stem and leaf diagrams and scatter plots. We sometimes learn more from what we see than from what we compute; sometimes what we learn from what we see is that we shouldn't compute, at least not on those data as they stand.

Computers are a blessing, but another of the things I have learned is that they are not an unmixed blessing. Forty years ago, before computers (B.C., that is), for my doctoral dissertation, I did three factor analyses on the 11 subtests of the Wechsler-Bellevue, with samples of 100 cases each of psychoneurotic, schizophrenic, and brain-damaged patients. Working with a pad and pencil, 10-to-the-inch graph paper, a table of products of two-digit numbers, and a Friden electromechanical desk calculator that did square roots "automatically," the whole process took the better part of a year. Nowadays, on a desktop computer, the job is done virtually in microseconds (or at least lickety-split). But another important difference between then and now is that the sheer laboriousness of the task assured that throughout the entire process I was in intimate contact with the data and their analysis. There was no chance that there were funny things about my data or intermediate results that I didn't know about, things that could vitiate my conclusions.

I know that I sound my age, but don't get me wrong—I love computers and revel in the ease with which data analysis is accomplished with a good interactive statistics package like SYSTAT and SYGRAPH (Wilkinson, 1990). I am, however, appalled by the fact that some publishers of statistics packages successfully hawk their wares with the pitch that it isn't necessary to understand statistics to use them. But the same package that makes it possible for an ignoramus to do a factor analysis with a pull-down menu and the click of a mouse also can greatly facilitate with awesome speed and efficiency the performance of simple and informative analyses.

A prime example of the simple-is-better principle is found in the compositing of values. We are taught and teach our students that for purposes of predicting a criterion from a set of predictor variables, assuming for simplicity (and as the mathematicians say, "with no loss of generality"), that all variables are standardized, we achieve maximum linear prediction by doing a multiple regression analysis and forming a composite by weighting the predictor z scores by their betas. It can be shown as a mathematical necessity that with these betas as weights, the resulting composite generates a higher correlation with the criterion in the sample at hand than does a linear composite formed using any other weights.

Yet as a practical matter, most of the time, we are better off using unit weights: +1 for positively related predictors, −1 for negatively related predictors, and 0, that is, throw away poorly related predictors (Dawes, 1979; Wainer, 1976). The catch is that the betas come with guarantees to be better than the unit weights only for the sample on which they were determined. (It's almost like a TV set being guaranteed to work only in the store.) But the investigator is not interested in making predictions for that sample—he or she *knows* the criterion values for those cases. The idea is to combine the predictors for maximal prediction for *future* samples. The reason the betas are not likely to be optimal for future samples is that they are likely to have large standard errors. For the typical 100 or 200 cases and 5 or 10 correlated predictors, the unit weights will work as well or better.

Let me offer a concrete illustration to help make the point clear. A running example in our regression text (Cohen & Cohen, 1983) has for a sample of college faculty their salary estimated from four independent variables: years since PhD, sex (coded in the modern manner—1 for female and 0 for male), number of publications, and number of citations. The sample multiple correlation computes to .70. What we want to estimate is the correlation we would get if we used the sample beta weights in the population, the cross-validated multiple correlation, which unfortunately shrinks to a value smaller than the shrunken multiple correlation. For $N = 100$ cases, using Rozeboom's (1978) formula, that comes to .67. Not bad. But using unit weights, we do better: .69. With 300 or 400 cases, the increased sampling stability pushes up the cross-validated correlation, but it remains slightly smaller than the .69 value for unit weights. Increasing sample size to 500 or 600 will increase the cross-validated correlation in this example to the point at which it is larger than the unit-weighted .69, but only trivially, by a couple of points in the *third* decimal! When sample size is only 50, the cross-validated multiple correlation is only .63, whereas the unit weighted correlation remains at .69. The sample size doesn't affect the unit weighted correlation because we don't estimate unstable regression coefficients. It is, of course, subject to sampling error, but so is the cross-validated multiple correlation.

Now, unit weights will not always be as good or better than beta weights. For some relatively rare patterns of correlation (suppression is one), or when the betas vary greatly relative to their mean, or when the ratio of sample size to the number of predictors is as much as 30 to 1 and the multiple correlation is as large as .75, the beta weights may be better, but even in these rare circumstances, probably not much better.

Furthermore, the unit weights work well outside the context of multiple regression where we have criterion data—that is, in a situation in which we wish to measure some concept by combining indicators, or some abstract factor generated in a factor analysis. Unit weights on standardized scores are likely to be better for our purposes than the factor scores generated by the computer program, which are, after all, the fruits of a regression analysis for that sample of the variables on the factor as criterion.

Consider that when we go to predict freshman grade point average from a 30-item test, we don't do a regression analysis to get the "optimal" weights with which to combine the item scores—we just add them up, like Galton did. Simple *is* better.

We are, however, *not* applying the simple-is-better principle when we "simplify" a multivalued graduated variable (like IQ, or number of children, or symptom severity) by cutting it somewhere along its span and making it into a dichotomy. This is sometimes done with a profession of modesty about the quality or accuracy of the variable, or to "simplify" the analysis. This is not an application, but rather a perversion of simple is better, because this practice is one of willful discarding of information. It has been shown that when you so mutilate a variable, you typically reduce its squared correlation with other variables by about 36% (Cohen, 1983). Don't do it. This kind of simplification is of a piece with the practice of "simplifying" a factorial design ANOVA by reducing all cell sizes to the size of the smallest by dropping cases. They are both ways of throwing away the most precious commodity we deal with: information.

Rather more generally, I think I have begun to learn how to use statistics in the social sciences.

The atmosphere that characterizes statistics as applied in the social and biomedical sciences is that of a secular religion (Salsburg, 1985), apparently of Judeo–Christian derivation, as it employs as its most powerful icon a six-pointed cross, often presented multiply for enhanced authority. I confess that I am an agnostic.

THE FISHERIAN LEGACY

When I began studying statistical inference, I was met with a surprise shared by many neophytes. I found that if, for example, I wanted to see whether poor kids estimated the size of coins to be bigger than did rich kids, after I gathered the data, I couldn't test this research hypothesis, but rather the null hypothesis that poor kids perceived coins to be the same size as did rich kids. This seemed kind of strange and backward to me, but I was rather quickly acculturated (or, if you like, converted, or perhaps brainwashed) to the Fisherian faith that science proceeds only through inductive inference and that inductive inference is achieved chiefly by rejecting null hypotheses, usually at the .05 level. (It wasn't until much later that I learned that the philosopher of science, Karl Popper, 1959, advocated the formulation of falsifiable *research* hypotheses and designing research that could falsify *them*.)

The fact that Fisher's ideas quickly became *the* basis for statistical inference in the behavioral sciences is not surprising—they were very attractive. They offered a deterministic scheme, mechanical and objective, independent of content, and led to clear-cut yes–no decisions. For years, nurtured on the psychological statistics text books of the 1940s and 1950s, I never dreamed that they were the source of bitter controversies (Gigerenzer & Murray, 1987).

Take, for example, the yes–no decision feature. It was quite appropriate to agronomy, which was where Fisher came from. The outcome of an experiment can quite properly be the decision to use this rather than that amount of manure or to plant this or that variety of wheat. But we do not deal in manure, at least not knowingly. Similarly, in other technologies— for example, engineering quality control or education—research is frequently designed to produce decisions. However, things are not quite so clearly decision-oriented in the development of scientific theories.

Next, consider the sanctified (and sanctifying) magic .05 level. This basis for decision has played a remarkable role in the social sciences and in the lives of social scientists. In governing decisions about the status of null hypotheses, it came to determine decisions about the acceptance of doctoral dissertations and the granting of research funding, and about publication, promotion, and whether to have a baby just now. Its arbitrary unreasonable tyranny has led to data fudging of varying degrees of subtlety from grossly altering data to dropping cases where there "must have been" errors.

THE NULL HYPOTHESIS TESTS US

We cannot charge R. A. Fisher with all of the sins of the last half century that have been committed in his name (or more often anonymously but as part of his legacy), but they deserve cataloging (Gigerenzer & Murray, 1987; Oakes, 1986). Over the years, I have learned not to make errors of the following kinds:

When a Fisherian null hypothesis is rejected with an associated probability of, for example, .026, it is *not* the case that the probability that the null hypothesis is true is .026 (or less than .05, or any other value we can specify). Given our framework of probability as long-run relative frequency—as much as we might wish it to be otherwise—this result does not tell us about the truth of the null hypothesis, given the data. (For this we have to go to Bayesian or likelihood statistics, in which probability is not relative frequency but degree of belief.) What it tells us is the probability of the data, given the truth of the null hypothesis—which is not the same thing, as much as it may sound like it.

If the p value with which we reject the Fisherian null hypothesis does not tell us the probability that the null hypothesis is true, it certainly cannot tell us anything about the probability that the *research* or alternate hypothesis is true. In fact, there *is* no alternate hypothesis in Fisher's scheme: Indeed, he violently opposed its inclusion by Neyman and Pearson.

Despite widespread misconceptions to the contrary, the rejection of a given null hypothesis gives us no basis for estimating the probability that a replication of the research will again result in rejecting that null hypothesis.

Of course, everyone knows that failure to reject the Fisherian null hypothesis does not warrant the conclusion that it is true. Fisher certainly knew and emphasized it, and our textbooks duly so instruct us. Yet how often do we read in the discussion and conclusions of articles now appearing in our most prestigious journals that "there is no difference" or "no relationship"? (This is 40 years after my $N = 20$ friend used a nonsignificant result to demolish psychoanalytic theory.)

The other side of this coin is the interpretation that accompanies results that surmount the .05 barrier and achieve the state of grace of "statistical significance." "Everyone" knows that all this means is that the effect is not nil, and nothing more. Yet how often do we see such a result to be taken to mean, at least implicitly, that the effect is *significant*, that is, *important, large*. If a result is *highly* significant, say $p < .001$, the temptation to make this misinterpretation becomes all but irresistible.

Let's take a close look at this null hypothesis—the fulcrum of the Fisherian scheme—that we so earnestly seek to negate. A null hypothesis is any precise statement about a state of affairs in a population, usually the value of a parameter, frequently zero. It is called a "null" hypothesis because the strategy is to nullify it or because it means "nothing doing." Thus, "The difference in the mean scores of U.S. men and women on an Attitude Toward the U.N. scale is zero" is a null hypothesis. "The product–moment r between height and IQ in high school students is zero" is another. "The proportion of men in a population of adult dyslexics is .50" is yet another. Each is a precise statement—for example, if the population r between height and IQ is in fact .03, the null hypothesis that it is zero is false. It is also false if the r is .01, .001, or .000001!

A little thought reveals a fact widely understood among statisticians: The null hypothesis, taken literally (and that's the only way you can take it in formal hypothesis testing), is *always* false in the real world. It can only be true in the bowels of a computer processor running a Monte Carlo study (and even then a stray electron may make it false). If it is false, even to a tiny degree, it must be the case that a large enough sample will produce a significant result and lead to its rejection. So if the null hypothesis is always false, what's the big deal about rejecting it?

Another problem that bothered me was the asymmetry of the Fisherian scheme: If your test exceeded a critical value, you could conclude, subject to the alpha risk, that your null was false, but if you fell short of that critical value, you couldn't conclude that the null was true. In fact, all you could conclude is that you *couldn't* conclude that the null was false. In other words, you could hardly conclude anything.

And yet another problem I had was that if the null were false, it had to be false to some degree. It had to make a difference whether the population mean difference was 5 or 50, or whether the population correlation was .10 or .30, and this was not taken into account in the prevailing method. I had stumbled onto something that I learned after awhile was one of the bases of the Neyman–Pearson critique of Fisher's system of statistical induction.

In 1928 (when I was in kindergarten), Jerzy Neyman and Karl Pearson's boy Egon began publishing papers that offered a rather different perspective on statistical inference (Neyman & Pearson, 1928a, 1928b). Among other things, they argued that rather than having a single hypothesis that one either rejected or not, things could be so organized that one could choose between two hypotheses, one of which could be the null hypothesis and the other an alternate hypothesis. One could attach to the precisely defined null an alpha risk, and to the equally precisely defined alternate hypothesis a beta risk. The rejection of the null hypotheses when it was true was an error of the first kind, controlled by the alpha criterion, but the failure to reject it when the alternate hypothesis was true was also an error, an error of the second kind, which could be controlled to occur at a rate beta. Thus, given the magnitude of the difference between the null and the alternate (that is, given the hypothetical population effect size), and setting values for alpha and beta, one could determine the sample size necessary to meet these conditions. Or, with the effect size, alpha, and the sample size set, one could determine the beta, or its complement, the probability of rejecting the null hypothesis, the power of the test.

Now, R. A. Fisher was undoubtedly the greatest statistician of this century, rightly called "the father of modern statistics," but he had a blind spot. Moreover, he was a stubborn and frequently vicious intellectual opponent. A feud with Karl Pearson had kept Fisher's papers out of *Biometrika,* which Karl Pearson edited. After old-man Pearson retired, efforts by Egon Pearson and Neyman to avoid battling with Fisher were to no avail. Fisher wrote that they were like Russians who thought that "pure science" should be "geared to technological performance" as "in a five-year plan." He once led off the discussion on a paper by Neyman at the Royal Statistical Society by saying that Neyman should have chosen a topic "on which he could speak with authority" (Gigerenzer & Murray, 1987, p. 17). Fisher fiercely condemned the Neyman–Pearson heresy.

I was of course aware of none of this. The statistics texts on which I was raised and their later editions to which I repeatedly turned in the 1950s and 1960s presented null hypothesis testing à la Fisher as a done deal, as *the* way to do statistical inference. The ideas of Neyman and Pearson were barely or not at all mentioned, or dismissed as too complicated.

When I finally stumbled onto power analysis, and managed to over-come the handicap of a background with no working math beyond high school algebra (to say nothing of mathematical statistics), it was as if I had died and gone to heaven. After I learned what noncentral distributions were and figured out that it was important to decompose noncentrality parameters into their constituents of effect size and sample size, I realized that I had a framework for hypothesis testing that had four parameters: the alpha significance criterion, the sample size, the population effect size, and the power of the test. For any statistical test, any one of these was a function of the other three. This meant, for example, that for a significance test of a product–moment correlation, using a two-sided .05 alpha criterion and a sample size of 50 cases, if the population correlation is .30, my long-run probability of rejecting the null hypothesis and finding the sample correla-tion to be significant was .57, a coin flip. As another example, for the same $\alpha = .05$ and population $r = .30$, if I want to have .80 power, I could deter-mine that I needed a sample size of 85.

Playing with this new toy (and with a small grant from the National Institute of Mental Health) I did what came to be called a meta-analysis of the articles in the 1960 volume of the *Journal of Abnormal and Social Psychology* (Cohen, 1962). I found, among other things, that using the nondirectional .05 criterion, the median power to detect a medium effect was .46—a rather abysmal result. Of course, investigators could not have known how underpowered their research was, as their training had not prepared them to know anything about power, let alone how to use it in research planning. One might think that after 1969, when I published my power handbook that made power analysis as easy as falling off a log, the concepts and methods of power analysis would be taken to the hearts of null hypothesis testers. So one might think. (Stay tuned.)

Among the less obvious benefits of power analysis was that it made it possible to "prove" null hypotheses. Of course, as I've already noted, everyone knows that one can't actually prove null hypotheses. But when an investigator means to prove a null hypothesis, the point is not to demonstrate that the population effect size is, say, zero to a million or more decimal places, but rather to show that it is of no more than negligible or trivial size (Cohen, 1988, pp. 16–17). Then, from a power analysis at, say, $\alpha = .05$, with power set at, say, .95, so that $\beta = .05$, also, the sample size necessary to detect this negligible effect with .95 probability can be determined. Now if the research is carried out using that sample size, and the result is *not* significant, as there had been a .95 chance of detecting this negligible effect, and the effect was *not* detected, the conclusion is justified that no nontrivial effect exists, at the $\beta = .05$ level. This does, in fact, probabilistically prove the intended null hypothesis of no more than a trivially small effect. The reasoning is impeccable, but when you go to apply it, you discover that it takes enormous sample sizes to do so. For example, if we adopt the above parameters for a significance test of a correlation coefficient and $r = .10$ is taken as a negligible effect size, it requires a sample of almost 1,300 cases. More modest but still reasonable demands for power of course require smaller sample sizes, but not sufficiently smaller to matter for most investigators—even .80 power to detect a population correlation of .10 requires almost 800 cases. So it generally takes an impractically large sample size to prove the null hypothesis as I've redefined it; however, the procedure makes clear what it takes to say or imply from the failure to reject the null hypothesis that there is no nontrivial effect.

A salutary effect of power analysis is that it draws one forcibly to consider the magnitude of effects. In psychology, and especially in soft psychology, under the sway of the Fisherian scheme, there has been little consciousness of how big things are. The very popular ANOVA designs yield F ratios, and it is these whose size is of concern. First off is the question of whether they made the sanctifying .05 cut-off and are thus significant, and then how far they fell below this cut-off: Were they perhaps *highly significant* (*p* less than .01) or *very highly significant* (less than .001)? Because science is inevitably about magnitudes, it is not surprising how frequently *p* values are treated as surrogates for effect sizes.

One of the things that drew me early to correlation analysis was that it yielded an *r*, a measure of effect size, which was then translated into a *t* or *F* and assessed for significance, whereas the analysis of variance or covariance yielded only an *F* and told me nothing about effect size. As many of the variables with which we worked were expressed in arbitrary units (points on a scale, trials to learn a maze), and the Fisherian scheme seemed quite

ful value. Although we cannot go into detail here, one approach to analyzing canonical data structures is to reduce the set of dependent variables to some smaller number of composite variables and to analyze each composite serially (Rosenthal, 1987).

Contrast Analysis

Whenever we have $df > 1$ for chi square or for the numerator of an F-test, we would argue that contrasts become the appropriate data-analytic procedure given the usual situation of fixed effect analyses (Rosenthal & Rosnow, 1984, 1985; Rosnow & Rosenthal, 1988). Briefly, contrasts are 1 df tests of significance for comparing the pattern of obtained group means to predicted values, with predictions made on the basis of theory, hypothesis, or hunch. Among the practical advantages of contrasts are that they can be easily computed with a pocket calculator, can be computed on the data in published reports as well as with original data, and most important, usually result in increased power and greater clarity of substantive interpretation.

Writing over 25 years ago, Abelson (1962) made a strong case for the method of contrasts and its wide range of varied uses. Why this method, which goes back virtually to the invention of ANOVA, had not previously received a comprehensive, unified treatment was a mystery. He speculated that "one compelling line of explanation is that the statisticians do not regard the idea as mathematically very interesting (it is based on quite elementary statistical concepts) and that quantitative psychologists have never quite appreciated its generality of application" (p. 2). Later, a number of issues at the heart of Abelson's thesis were picked up by other authors working in quite different areas of psychology, but these efforts did not have any definite practical impact on the teaching and usage of data-analytic procedures.

For example, Hale (1977) demonstrated the utility of carrying out contrasts in the area of developmental research. He computed a contrast F-test to reanalyze a portion of another investigator's published data concerning the effects of a vigilance distractor on recall of relevant and irrelevant information. In the published study, 40 children per grade in the first, third, fifth, and seventh grades were instructed to attend to one element in each of several two-element pictures in order to perform what was represented as a memory game. Half of the participants were tested under distraction conditions in which a melody of high notes on a piano was interrupted periodically by single low-pitch notes. Incidental learning was assessed by asking the children which elements appeared together in each picture. The mean scores for the distraction and no distraction conditions at these four grade levels, respectively, were distraction, 2.6, 2.3, 2.5, and complete by itself and made no demands on us to think about effect sizes, we simply had no language with which to address them.

In retrospect, it seems to me simultaneously quite understandable yet also ridiculous to try to develop theories about human behavior with p values from Fisherian hypothesis testing and no more than a primitive sense of effect size. And I wish I were talking about the long, long ago. In 1986, there appeared in the *New York Times* a UPI dispatch under the headline "Children's Height Linked to Test Scores." The article described a study that involved nearly 14,000 children 6 to 17 years of age that reported a *definite* link between height (age- and sex-adjusted) and scores on tests of both intelligence and achievement. The relationship was described as significant, and persisting, even after controlling for other factors, including socioeconomic status, birth order, family size, and physical maturity. The authors noted that the effect was small, but *significant*, and that it didn't warrant giving children growth hormone to make them taller and thus brighter. They speculated that the effect might be due to treating shorter children as less mature, but that there were alternative biological explanations.

Now this was a newspaper story, the fruit of the ever-inquiring mind of a science reporter, not a journal article, so perhaps it is understandable that there was no effort to deal with the actual size of this small effect. But it got me to wondering about how small this significant relationship might be. Well, if we take significant to mean $p < .001$ (in the interest of scientific tough-mindedness), it turns out that a correlation of .0278 is significant for 14,000 cases. But I've found that when dealing with variables expressed in units whose magnitude we understand, the effect size in linear relationships is better comprehended with regression than with correlation coefficients. So, accepting the authors' implicit causal model, it works out that raising a child's IQ from 100 to 130 would require giving the child enough growth hormone to increase his or her height by 14 ft (more or less). If the causality goes the other way, and one wanted to create basketball players, a 4-in. increase in height would require raising the IQ about 900 points. Well, they said it was a small effect. (When I later checked the journal article that described this research, it turned out that the correlation was much larger than .0278. It was actually about .11, so that for a 30-point increase in IQ it would take only enough growth hormone to produce a 3.5-ft increase in height, or with the causality reversed, a 4-in. increase in height would require an increase of only 233 IQ points.)

I am happy to say that the long neglect of attention to effect size seems to be coming to a close. The clumsy and fundamentally invalid box-score method of literature review based on p values is being replaced by effect-size-based meta-analysis as formulated by Gene Glass (1977). The effect size measure most often used is the standardized mean difference d of power analysis. Several book-length treatments of meta-analysis have been published, and applications to various fields of psychology are appearing in substantial numbers in the *Psychological Bulletin* and other prestigious publications. In the typical meta-analysis, the research literature on some issue is surveyed and the effect sizes that were found in the relevant studies are gathered. Note that the observational unit is the study. These data do not only provide an estimate of the level and variability of the effect size in a domain based on multiple studies and therefore on many observations, but by relating effect size to various substantive and methodological characteristics over the studies, much can be learned about the issue under investigation and how best to investigate it. One hopes that this ferment may persuade researchers to explicitly report effect sizes and thus reduce the burden on meta-analysts and others of having to make assumptions to dig them out of their inadequately reported research results. In a field as scattered (not to say anarchic) as ours, meta-analysis constitutes a welcome force toward the cumulation of knowledge. Meta-analysis makes me very happy.

Despite my career-long identification with statistical inference, I believe, together with such luminaries as Meehl (1978) Tukey (1977), and Gigerenzer (Gigerenzer & Murray, 1987), that hypothesis testing has been greatly overemphasized in psychology and in the other disciplines that use it. It has diverted our attention from crucial issues. Mesmerized by a single all-purpose, mechanized, "objective" ritual in which we convert numbers into other numbers and get a yes–no answer, we have come to neglect close scrutiny of where the numbers came from. Recall that in his delightful parable about averaging the numbers on football jerseys, Lord (1953) pointed out that "the numbers don't know where they came from." But surely *we* must know where they came from and should be far more concerned with why and what and how well we are measuring, manipulating conditions, and selecting our samples.

We have also lost sight of the fact that the error variance in our observations should challenge us to efforts to reduce it and not simply to thoughtlessly tuck it into the denominator of an F or t test.

HOW TO USE STATISTICS

So, how would I use statistics in psychological research? First of all, descriptively. John Tukey's (1977) *Exploratory Data Analysis* is an inspiring account of how to effect graphic and numerical analyses of the data at hand so as to understand *them*. The techniques, although subtle in conception, are simple in application, requiring no more than pencil and paper (Tukey says if you have a hand-held calculator, fine). Although he recognizes the importance of what he calls confirmation (statistical inference), he manages to fill 700 pages with techniques of "mere" description, pointing out in the preface that the emphasis on inference in modern statistics has resulted in a loss of flexibility in data analysis.

Then, in planning research, I think it wise to *plan* the research. This means making tentative informed judgments about, among many other things, the size of the population effect or effects you're chasing, the level of alpha risk you want to take (conveniently, but not necessarily .05), and the power you want (usually some relatively large value like .80). These specified, it is a simple matter to determine the sample size you need. It is then a good idea to rethink your specifications. If, as is often the case, this sample size is beyond your resources, consider the possibility of reducing your power demand or, perhaps the effect size, or even (heaven help us) increasing your alpha level. Or, the required sample may be smaller than you can comfortably manage, which also should lead you to rethink and possibly revise your original specifications. This process ends when you have a credible and viable set of specifications, or when you discover that no practicable set is possible and the research as originally conceived must be abandoned. Although you would hardly expect it from reading the current literature, failure to subject your research plans to power analysis is simply irrational.

Next, I have learned and taught that the primary product of a research inquiry is one or more measures of effect size, not p values (Cohen, 1965). Effect-size measures include mean differences (raw or standardized), correlations and squared correlation of all kinds, odds ratios, kappas— whatever conveys the magnitude of the phenomenon of interest appropriate to the research context. If, for example, you are comparing groups on a variable measured in units that are well understood by your readers (IQ points, or dollars, or number of children, or months of survival), mean differences are excellent measures of effect size. When this isn't the case, and it isn't the case more often than it is, the results can be translated into standardized mean differences (d values) or some measure of correlation or association (Cohen, 1988). (Not that we understand as well as we should the meaning of a given level of correlation {Oakes, 1986, pp. 88–92}. It has been shown that psychologists typically overestimate how much relationship a given correlation represents, thinking of a correlation of .50 not as its square of .25 that its proportion of variance represents, but more like its cube root of about .80, which represents only wishful thinking! But that's another story.)

Then, having found the sample effect size, you can attach a p value to it, but it is far more informative to provide a confidence interval. As you know, a confidence interval gives the range of values of the effect-size index that includes the population value with a given probability. It tells you incidentally whether the effect is significant, but much more—it provides an estimate of the range of values it might have, surely a useful piece of knowledge in a science that presumes to be quantitative. (By the way, I don't think that we should routinely use 95% intervals: Our interests are often better served by more tolerant 80% intervals.)

Remember that throughout the process in which you conceive, plan, execute, and write up a research, it is on your informed judgment as a scientist that you must rely, and this holds as much for the statistical aspects of the work as it does for all the others. This means that your informed judgment governs the setting of the parameters involved in the planning (alpha, beta, population effect size, sample size, confidence interval), and that informed judgment also governs the conclusions you will draw.

In his brilliant analysis of what he called the "inference revolution" in psychology, Gerd Gigerenzer showed how and why no single royal road of drawing conclusions from data is possible, and particularly not one that does not strongly depend on the substantive issues concerned—that is, on everything that went into the research besides the number crunching. An essential ingredient in the research process is the judgment of the scientist. He or she must decide by how much a theoretical proposition has been advanced by the data, just as he or she decided what to study, what data to get, and how to get it. I believe that statistical inference applied with informed judgment is a useful tool in this process, but it isn't the most important tool: It is not as important as everything that came before it. Some scientists, physicists for example, manage without the statistics, although to be sure not without the informed judgment. Indeed, some pretty good psychologists have managed without statistical inference: There come to mind Wundt, Kohler, Piaget, Lewin, Bartlett, Stevens, and if you'll permit me, Freud, among others. Indeed, Skinner (1957) thought of dedicating his book *Verbal Behavior* (and I quote) "to the statisticians and scientific methodologists with whose help this book would never have been completed" (p. 111). I submit that the proper application of statistics by sensible statistical methodologists (Tukey, for example) would not have hurt Skinner's work. It might even have done it some good.

The implications of the things I have learned (so far) are not consonant with much of what I see about me as standard statistical practice. The prevailing yes–no decision at the magic .05 level from a single research is a far cry from the use of informed judgment. Science simply doesn't work that way. A successful piece of research doesn't conclusively settle an issue, it just makes some theoretical proposition to some degree more likely. Only successful future replication in the same and different settings (as might be found through meta-analysis) provides an approach to settling the issue. How much more likely this single research makes the proposition depends on many things, but not on whether p is equal to or greater than .05; .05 is not a cliff but a convenient reference point along the possibility-probability continuum. There is no ontological basis for dichotomous decision making in psychological inquiry. The point was neatly made by Rosnow and Rosenthal (1989) last year in the *American Psychologist*. They wrote "surely, God loves the .06 nearly as much as the .05" (p. 1277). To which I say amen!

Finally, I have learned, but not easily, that things take time. As I've already mentioned, almost three decades ago, I published a power survey of the articles in the 1960 volume of the *Journal of Abnormal and Social Psychology* (Cohen, 1962) in which I found that the median power to detect a medium effect size under representative conditions was only .46. The first edition of my power handbook came out in 1969. Since then, more than two dozen power and effect-size surveys have been published in psychology and related fields (Cohen, 1988, pp. xi–xii). There have also been a slew of articles on power-analytic methodology. Statistics textbooks, even some undergraduate ones, give some space to power analysis, and several computer programs for power analysis are available (e.g., Borenstein & Cohen, 1988). They tell me that some major funding entities require that their grant applications contain power analyses, and that in one of those agencies my power book can be found in every office.

The problem is that, as practiced, current research hardly reflects much attention to power. How often have you seen any mention of power in the journals you read, let alone an actual power analysis in the methods sections of the articles? Last year in *Psychological Bulletin*, Sedlmeier and Gigerenzer (1989) published an article entitled "Do Studies of Statistical Power Have an Effect on the Power of Studies?". The answer was no. Using the same methods I had used on the articles in the 1960 *Journal of Abnormal and Social Psychology* (Cohen, 1962), they performed a power analysis on the 1984 *Journal of Abnormal Psychology* and found that the median power under the same conditions was .44, a little worse than the .46 I had found 24 years earlier. It was worse still (.37) when they took into account the occasional use of an experimentwise alpha criterion. Even worse than that, in some 11% of the studies, research hypotheses were framed as null hypotheses and their nonsignificance interpreted as confirmation. The median power of these studies to detect a medium effect at the two-tailed .05 level was .25! These are not isolated results: Rossi, Rossi, and Cottrill (in press), using the same methods, did a power survey of the 142 articles in the

1982 volumes of the *Journal of Personality and Social Psychology* and the *Journal of Abnormal Psychology* and found essentially the same results.

A less egregious example of the inertia of methodological advance is set correlation, which is a highly flexible realization of the multivariate general linear model. I published it in an article in 1982, and we included it in an appendix in the 1983 edition of our regression text (Cohen, 1982; Cohen & Cohen, 1983). Set correlation can be viewed as a generalization of multiple correlation to the multivariate case, and with it you can study the relationship between anything and anything else, controlling for whatever you want in either the anything or the anything else, or both. I think it's a great method; at least, my usually critical colleagues haven't complained. Yet, as far as I'm aware, it has hardly been used outside the family. (The publication of a program as a SYSTAT supplementary module [Cohen, 1989] may make a difference.)

But I do not despair. I remember that W. S. Gosset, the fellow who worked in a brewery and appeared in print modestly as "Student," published the *t* test a decade before we entered World War I, and the test didn't get into the psychological statistics textbooks until after World War II.

These things take time. So, if you publish something that you think is really good, and a year or a decade or two go by and hardly anyone seems to have taken notice, remember the *t* test, and take heart.

REFERENCES

Borenstein, M., & Cohen, J. (1988). *Statistical power analysis: A computer program.* Hillsdale, NJ: Erlbaum.

Children's height linked to test scores. (1986, October 7). *New York Times*, p. C4.

Cohen, J. (1962). The statistical power of abnormal–social psychological research: A review. *Journal of Abnormal and Social Psychology, 65,* 145–153.

Cohen, J. (1965). Some statistical issues in psychological research. In B. B. Wolman (Ed.), *Handbook of clinical psychology* (pp. 95–121). New York: McGraw-Hill.

Cohen, J. (1982). Set correlation as a general multivariate data-analytic method. *Multivariate Behavioral Research, 17,* 301–341.

Cohen, J. (1983). The cost of dichotomization. *Applied Psychological Measurement, 7,* 249–253.

Cohen, J. (1988). *Statistical power analysis for the behavioral sciences* (2nd ed.). Hillsdale, NJ: Erlbaum.

Cohen, J. (1989). *SETCOR: Set correlation analysis, a supplementary module for SYSTAT and SYGRAPH.* Evanston, IL: SYSTAT.

Cohen, J., & Cohen, P. (1983). *Applied multiple regression/correlation analysis for the behavioral sciences* (2nd ed.). Hillsdale, NJ: Erlbaum.

Dawes, R. M. (1979). The robust beauty of improper linear models in decision making. *American Psychologist, 34,* 571–582.

Gigerenzer, G., & Murray, D. J. (1987). *Cognition as intuitive statistics.* Hillsdale, NJ: Erlbaum.

Glass, G. V. (1977). Integrating findings: The meta-analysis of research. In L. Shulman (Ed.), *Review of research in education* (Vol. 5, pp. 351–379). Itasca, IL: Peacock.

Lord, F. M. (1953). On the statistical treatment of football numbers. *American Psychologist, 8,* 750–751.

Meehl, P. E. (1978). Theoretical risks and tabular asterisks: Sir Karl, Sir Ronald, and the slow progress of soft psychology. *Journal of Consulting and Clinical Psychology, 46,* 806–834.

Neyman, J., & Pearson, E. (1928a). On the use and interpretation of certain test criteria for purposes of statistical inference: Part I. *Biometrika, 20A,* 175–240.

Neyman, J., & Pearson, E. (1928b). On the use and interpretation of certain test criteria for purposes of statistical inference: Part II. *Biometrika, 20A,* 263–294.

Oakes, M. (1986). *Statistical inference: A commentary for the social and behavioral sciences.* New York: Wiley.

Popper, K. (1959). *The logic of scientific discovery.* New York: Basic Books.

Rosnow, R. L., & Rosenthal, R. (1989). Statistical procedures and the justification of knowledge in psychological science. *American Psychologist, 44,* 1276–1284.

Rossi, J. S., Rossi, S. R., & Cottrill, S. D. (in press). Statistical power in research in social and abnormal psychology. *Journal of Consulting and Clinical Psychology.*

Rozeboom, W. W. (1978). Estimation of cross-validated multiple correlation: A clarification. *Psychological Bulletin, 85,* 1348–1351.

Salsburg, D. S. (1985). The religion of statistics as practiced in medical journals. *The American Statistician, 39,* 220–223.

Sedlmeier, P., & Gigerenzer, G. (1989). Do studies of statistical power have an effect on the power of studies? *Psychological Bulletin, 105,* 309–316.

Skinner, B. F. (1957). *Verbal behavior.* New York: Appleton-Century-Crofts.

Tukey, J. W. (1977). *Exploratory data analysis.* Reading, MA: Addison-Wesley.

Wainer, H. (1976). Estimating coefficients in linear models: It don't make no nevermind. *Psychological Bulletin, 83,* 213–217.

Wainer, H., & Thissen, D. (1976). When jackknifing fails (or does it?). *Psychometrika, 41,* 9–34.

Wilkinson, L. (1990). SYSTAT: The system for statistics. Evanston, IL: SYSTAT.

SELECTED TESTS AND ANALYSES

18

FOCUSED TESTS OF SIGNIFICANCE AND EFFECT SIZE ESTIMATION IN COUNSELING PSYCHOLOGY

RALPH L. ROSNOW AND ROBERT ROSENTHAL

Suppose you reached a fork in the road and were not sure which path, A or B, to take to reach your destination, Z. If you could ask one question of someone who knew the paths but who could respond only yes or no, which would it be: (1) Does A lead to Z? or (2) Does it make any difference which path I take? The answer, of course, is that you would ask Question 1 because it addresses the information you need in a focused or precise way, which Question 2 does not. No counseling researcher would make the mistake of asking an unfocused question in this situation, but many do follow the common practice of employing unfocused tests of hypotheses in their research when a focused test would be more appropriate. One purpose of this article is to illustrate the advantages of employing focused tests of significance in counseling research.

As implied by a number of writers (e.g., Haase, Waechter, & Solo-

Reprinted from the *Journal of Counseling Psychology*, 35, 203–208. Copyright 1988 by the American Psychological Association.

Preparation of this article was supported in part by the National Science Foundation and the Bolton Endowment of Temple University.

mon, 1982; Jacobson, Follette, & Revenstorf, 1984; Paquin, 1983; Serlin & Lapsley, 1985), a deepening chasm seems to exist between counseling researchers who examine the probability levels associated with statistical tests and practitioners who decry the irrelevance of most of this research for counseling or clinical practice. Various solutions to this problem have been suggested, including the adoption of new statistical conventions to reveal the practical as well as the statistical significance of research findings. One such convention that has been widely recommended is to report the magnitude of the effect in addition to reporting the statistical significance of the research results, because effect size (or the degree to which the relation studied differs from zero) tells us something very different from p level. A result may be statistically significant, but it is not necessarily practically significant as judged by the magnitude of the effect. Thus Haase et al. recommended estimating effect size by η^2, and Paquin reviewed ϵ, ω^2, and r^2 as procedures for estimating effect size.[1]

However there are some problems with the recommended direction. The most commonly used measure, r^2, although useful in some statistical applications (e.g., multiple regression and analysis of variance, ANOVA), only poorly reflects the practical value of any given correlation coefficient (Rosenthal & Rubin, 1982). Like η^2, r^2 suffers from the expository problem that psychologically important effects can appear to be far smaller than they are (cf. Abelson, 1985; Ozer, 1985). Similarly, whereas ϵ and ω^2 provide indexes of variability, they are not helpful in estimating effect sizes for 1-df contrasts (Rosenthal & Rosnow, 1985); in their effort to adjust for bias, these indexes remove part of the predicted effect. Thus, although it is recognized that a test of significance without an effect size estimate does not provide a full account of the relation studied, there may be some uncertainty as to which effect size estimate to use and how to interpret it.

We shall suggest a convenient measure of effect size, the product–moment r, which poses no particular problems of interpretation when used with focused tests of significance. The *Publication Manual of the American Psychological Association* (American Psychological Association, 1983) insists that when reporting inferential statistics, authors give the symbol, degrees of freedom, value, and probability level, which (as we shall show) is all the information that is needed for readers to make their own estimates of effect size. We shall also show how by recasting the effect size into a binomial display, it is possible to represent the practical importance in r in terms of some theoretically relevant dichotomous criterion (e.g.,

---

[1]Paquin's formula for estimating effect size by epsilon contains an error; it should read $\epsilon = \sqrt{[df_1(F - 1)]/[df_1(F) + df_2]}$, where df_1 is the number of degrees of freedom associated with the numerator of the F ratio and df_2 is the corresponding number of degrees of freedom for the denominator of F.

succeed–fail). By way of introduction, and to help readers sharpen their intuitive sense of the relation between r and p, we will discuss standards and limitations of interpretation imposed by normative and statistical conventions.

FOCUSED AND UNFOCUSED SIGNIFICANCE TESTS

By focused tests we mean significance tests that address precise questions, such as any t test, and F test with 1 df in the numerator, and any 1-df χ^2 test. By unfocused (or omnibus) tests we mean significance tests that address diffuse questions, such as any F test with > 1 df in the numerator and any >1 df χ^2 test. For example, a 1-df F is a focused significance test because it addresses the precise question of whether given the population from which two groups were drawn, there is (a) no difference between the groups or, equivalently, (b) no relation between membership in either group and scores on the dependent variable. An F with >1 df in the numerator is an omnibus significance test because it addresses the diffuse question of whether there are any differences among three or more groups, disregarding entirely the arrangement of the levels of the independent variable. We can illustrate this distinction and at the same time demonstrate some of the advantages of focused F tests over omnibus F tests when the implicit hypothesis calls for precise rather than diffuse significance testing.

Suppose counseling researchers interested in communication skill have children at five grade levels perform communication exercises before expert judges who rate the children on a 10-point scale. The researchers find that the mean scores of 10 children per grade in Grades 7, 8, 9, 10, and 11, respectively, are 2.5, 3.0, 4.0, 5.0, and 5.5. Whereas the scores suggest a developmental progression, the standard F that the researchers compute for grade levels is unimpressive. $F(4, 45) = 1.03$, $p = .40$. Should they conclude that grade level was not an effective predictor variable in this investigation? If they were to answer yes, they would be making a serious mistake, because they would be ignoring what we can see very plainly, namely, that performance increased in a monotonic fashion from the lowest to the highest grade. Indeed the product–moment correlation on the relation between grade level and mean performance level is $r = .992$, $p < .001$, two-tailed. (This "alerting" r is not the effect size r but is an aggregate correlation based on *average* performance. It is a poor estimate of the relation between *individual* children's grade and performance, because correlations based on aggregated data are often higher than those based on nonaggregated data.)

The problem is that the researchers' 4-df F test was diffuse and unfocused; it addressed the question of whether there were any differences among the five grade levels, disregarding entirely their temporal arrangement. The number of possible permutations, each containing five grade levels, that can be formed from a collection of five distinct grade levels is 120. Any of these 120 arrangements would have given the researchers the same f with the numerator $df = 4$. On the other hand, had they computed the f with weights of $-2, -1.0, +1, +2$ to test a linear contrast, their finding would have been that $F(1, 45) = 4.06, p = .05$. Because Fs employed to test contrasts have only 1 df in the numerator, they are all focused tests of significance. (Thus t tests are also focused tests, because taking the square root of the value of a focused F test is equivalent to computing a t test.)

The essential point of this illustration is to show that there is an increase in statistical power that derives from employing a focused rather than an omnibus test of significance. That is to say, there is an increase in the probability of not making a Type II error. Because counseling researchers want to use statistical tests that will lead to the rejection of the null hypothesis when it is false, our focused F test was more "useful" or more "successful" than was the researchers' omnibus F test. It is beyond the scope of this article to describe the calculations required to compute contrast Fs. However, suffice it to say that this kind of significance testing is easy to do with a pocket calculator, is not restricted to the ANOVA, and is useful for performing secondary analyses of other people's data (cf. Rosenthal, 1984; Rosenthal & Rosnow, 1985).

The reduction in statistical power is not the only disadvantage associated with omnibus F tests, however. Another drawback, as our example illustrates, is that the null hypothesis tested by an omnibus F is usually not of any great theoretical interest. Of what great interest is it to know that, ignignoring their temporal arrangement, the researchers' five means did not differ significantly? The question of theoretical interest to us as research consumers, and presumably to these researchers as well, concerns the nature of the relation among the five means that the omnibus F did not even address. A further disadvantage of omnibus F tests, very pertinent to this discussion, is that the use of r as an index of effect size in conjunction with these tests is problematic. Such effect size estimates with omnibus significance tests are difficult to interpret properly and are less useful than commonly realized (cf. Rosenthal & Rosnow, 1984), although (as we shall see) they usually pose no special problems of interpretation with focused significance tests.

NORMATIVE AND STATISTICAL CONVENTIONS

Before turning to procedures for the computation of r as an effect size index, we should review standards and limitations imposed by normative and statistical conventions. A very important general relation between rs of any form (or any other measure of the size of an effect or a relation) and a test of significance can be expressed by the following conceptual equation:

$$\text{Magnitude of Significance Test} = \text{Size of Effect} \times \text{Size of Study.} \quad (1)$$

This equation tells us that for any given (nonzero) effect size, the test of significance (e.g., t, F, χ^2, Z) will increase as the number of sampling units (size of study) increases. The particular index of the size of the study (e.g., N, df, $\sqrt{N}$, $\sqrt{df}$) varies with the index of effect size used, which in turn depends on the test of significance and the index of the size of the study (see, e.g., Rosenthal & Rosnow, 1984). The essential point is that highly significant p values should not be interpreted as necessarily reflecting large effects. In the case of F ratios, a numerator mean square (MS) may be large relative to a denominator MS because the effect size is large, the n per condition is large, or because both values are large. Any conclusions about the size of effect must be based on the direct calculation of an effect size index.

In a given situation it is certainly a personal decision to regard a particular n value as "low enough" to make us question the validity of the null hypothesis. Fisher (1960) put it this way:

> Convenient as it is to note that a hypothesis is contradicted at some familiar level of significance such as 5% or 2% or 1% we do not . . . ever need to lose sight of the exact strength which the evidence has in fact reached, or to ignore the fact that with further trial it might come to be stronger, or weaker. (p. 25)

Fisher did not give advice on how to appraise "the exact strength" of the evidence, but recent trends in statistical data analysis (e.g., power analysis and meta-analysis; cf. Rosenthal & Rosnow, 1984) pertain to making such an appraisal. Knowledge is a function of perceptions based in part on historically and socioculturally embedded conventions (cf. Rosnow, 1981; Rosnow & Georgoudi, 1986), and it is relevant to ask what current perceptions are essentially imposed on us by researchers and peer reviewers acting on convention.

This question was recently addressed by means of a survey study (Nelson, Rosenthal, & Rosnow, 1986). Psychological researchers and editors of leading psychological journals were sent questionnaires that asked them to report the degree of confidence they would have in research findings at 20 levels of p (.001 to .90) and 4 levels of r (.10, .30, .50, .70). As expected, an increase in confidence was found at more stringent levels of significance and with increasing magnitudes of effect size. Confidence ratings were also greater if the study size was represented as large rather than small—even though smaller samples speak for more dramatic results (at constant levels of p)—and greater when the study was a successful replication rather than an isolated study at the same p level. Another finding of considerable interest and relevance to this discussion was that there were abrupt drops in confidence in a p level just beyond the particular p for .05 and .10 significance levels. Convention dictates that the .05 significance level be regarded as the critical level to detect a "real" difference or a "real" effect in counseling psychology, but these findings raised the possibility that for many psychological researchers and peer reviewers $p = .10$ may be viewed as a kind of "last chance threshold" before making a Type II error.

Previously we alluded to statistical power analysis (cf. Cohen, 1977; see also discussion by Fagley, 1985), and it is of interest to ask how these two levels of p (.05, .10) and four levels of r (.10, .30, .50, .70) are related to one another in terms of considerations of power. Power $(1 - \beta)$ refers to the probability of not overlooking an effect or a relation that is really present. Power analysis tells us the extent to which in employing a particular size of sample, we are stacking the odds in favor of, or against, reaching a given p value for some particular size of effect. Table 1 addresses this question by showing ratios of Type II to Type I errors for sample sizes from 10 to 500. Type I errors represent inferential errors of gullibility or overeagerness (i.e., an effect or a relation is claimed where none exists), and Type II errors represent inferential errors of conservatism or blindness to a relation (i.e., the existence of an effect or a relation that does exist is denied). Thus Table 1 shows what may be conceptualized as the "perceived seriousness" of Type II to Type I errors for these two levels of p and four levels of r.

For example, if the likelihood of a Type II error = .20 and the likelihood of a Type I error = .10, then the ratio of $.20/.10 = 2$ would tell us that the error in rejecting the null hypothesis when it is true (Type I error) is taken twice as "seriously" as the error in failing to reject the null hypothesis when it is false (Type II error). We see that the generally greater weight attached to the avoidance of Type I errors relative to Type II errors increases the smaller the effect size (i.e., r value), the smaller the N, and, of course, the more stringent the p value. In other words, working with a small sample, a small effect, or a very stringent p value is a little like trying to read small type in a dim light: It is harder to make out the material. Table 1 implies that under most conditions of significance testing with which readers are familiar (cf. Haase et at., 1982), counseling researchers seemingly choose to work in "dimly lit" rather than in "brightly lit" situations.

TABLE 1
Ratios of Type II/Type I Error Rates for Various Sample Sizes, Effect Sizes, and Significance Levels (Two-Tailed)

	Effect sizes and significance levels							
	r = .10		*r* = .30		*r* = .50		*r* = .70	
N	.05	.10	.05	.10	.05	.10	.05	.10
10	19	9	17	8	13	5	6	2
20	19	9	15	6	7	2	—	—
30	18	8	13	5	3	1	—	—
40	18	8	10	4	2	—	—	—
50	18	8	9	3	—	—	—	—
60	18	8	7	2	—	—	—	—
70	17	8	6	2	—	—	—	—
80	17	8	4	1	—	—	—	—
90	17	8	4	1	—	—	—	—
100	17	7	3	—	—	—	—	—
120	16	7	2	—	—	—	—	—
140	16	7	1	—	—	—	—	—
160	15	6	—	—	—	—	—	—
180	15	6	—	—	—	—	—	—
200	14	6	—	—	—	—	—	—
300	12	5	—	—	—	—	—	—
400	10	4	—	—	—	—	—	—
500	8	3	—	—	—	—	—	—

Note: Entries are to nearest integer; missing values <1.

COMPUTING EFFECT SIZE

This brings us to the question of how best to compute, and then to interpret, effect size. The procedures we suggest in this section are simple enough that they can be performed with a pocket calculator, using the raw ingredients stipulated by the APA *Publications Manual*. In the following section we then discuss the interpretation of the results of such computations. To reiterate, we shall be emphasizing the product–moment r as a measure of effect size interpretable with focused tests of significance, where r can be defined as

$$r_{xy} = (\Sigma\, Z_x Z_y)/N; \qquad (2)$$

that is, the correlation between x and y is equal to the sum of the cross-products of the Z scores of x and y divided by the number (N) of pairs of x and y scores. (This is not an "alerting" r based on group means or aggregated data but one based on individual scores or nonaggregated data.) Cohen (1977) proposed as a convention that psychological researchers call rs of .1 "small," rs of .3 "medium," and rs of .5 "large." Interestingly, Haase et al. (1982) reported that the median effect size of research in the *Journal of Counseling Psychology* for the years 1970–1972 was of a magnitude corresponding to what Cohen defined as medium sized.

When the significance test is a t test, the corresponding effect size index can be calculated as follows:

$$r = \sqrt{t^2/(t^2 + df)}, \tag{3}$$

where t is the value of the test of significance employed to judge the tenability of the null hypothesis of no relation between two variables. Suppose a counseling researcher interested in assertiveness training reported the results of an evaluation study in which 20 subjects were randomly assigned either to the counseling treatment or to a zero control group. The reported finding is that subjects who received assertiveness training were evaluated as significantly more assertive afterward than were subjects in the control condition, with $t(18) = 1.735$, $p < .05$, one-tailed. Substituting in Equation 3, we find $r = \sqrt{(1.735^2)/(1.735^2 + 18)} = .38$, which in conventional terms would be called a medium effect size.

Suppose the research finding were reported instead as $F (1, 18) = 3.010$. Because $F = t^2$ for 1-df F tests, it is easy to take the square root of 3.010 and calculate r by using Equation 3. Alternatively, we can calculate r directly given the following identity:

$$r = \sqrt{F/(F + df\ \text{error})}, \tag{4}$$

where F is the value of the test of significance used to judge the tenability of the null hypothesis of no relation between two variables, and df error denotes the degrees of freedom for the denominator of the F ratio. Readers familiar with η will recognize that Equation 4 is derived from the more general equation:

$$\eta = \sqrt{[F(df\ \text{effect})]/\{F(df\ \text{effect}) + df\ \text{error}\}}, \tag{5}$$

where df effect always equals 1 in the case of focused F tests. An alternative equation for calculating η from the sums of squares (SS) directly is

$$\eta = \sqrt{SS\ \text{effect}/(SS\ \text{effect} + SS\ \text{error})}, \tag{6}$$

where η is equal to the square root of the SS for the effect of interest divided by the SS for that effect plus the SS for the error term. Returning to Equation 4 to compute the size of effect, $r = \sqrt{3.010/(3.010 + 18)} = .38$.

Another way to view correlation is in the context of 2×2 contingency tables, in which one test of statistical significance is χ^2 with 1 df and the corresponding effect size correlation coefficient is r_ϕ:

$$r_\phi = \sqrt{\chi^2(1)/N}, \tag{7}$$

where r_ϕ (the product–moment r in which the variables are dichotomous) is computed as the square root of the value of 1 df χ^2 divided by the number of independent scores in the study (N). Suppose a counseling psychologist wanted to know whether there were any association between clients' sex and their preferences in being treated by a male counselor or a female counselor. The responses of 50 male and 50 female clients suggest the answer is yes, with $\chi^2(1) = 3.84$, $p = .05$. By substitution in Equation 7, $r_\phi = \sqrt{3.84/100} = .20$, which might be tagged a small effect.

INTERPRETING EFFECT SIZE

Just as there are different indexes of effect size and different computational procedures for each index, there are alternative ways of viewing them. Previously we mentioned that r^2 has been the most commonly used measure of effect size. Referred to as the coefficient of determination, r^2 is viewed as the proportion of variation among the y scores that is attributable to variation in the x scores and vice versa. This is sometimes expressed by the following identity:

$$r^2 + k^2 = 1.00, \tag{8}$$

where $k = \sqrt{1 - r^2}$ is called the coefficient of alienation, r^2 is the amount of explained variance, and k^2 is the amount of unexplained variance.

As traditional as r^2 is as a gauge of the accuracy of prediction, it has been observed that even many experienced researchers do not have an intuitive sense of what "explained variance" means in either practical or theoretical terms (Rosenthal & Rubin, 1979). It was previously noted that r^2 is also a misleading index of the influence of systematic factors because it grossly underestimates the practical effects of individually tiny influences that cumulate to produce meaningful outcomes (Abelson, 1985). Thus, even though there is a direct relation between r^2 and r, the distinction between them is more than merely stylistic. That r is more informative than r^2 can be readily shown by recasting r into a binomial display, which at the same time serves to reveal the practical significance of any given magnitude of effect in terms of whatever equivalency measure is appropriate (e.g., improvement rate, success rate, survival rate).

The utility of this procedure, the binomial effect-size display (BESD), is illustrated in Table 2 (Rosenthal & Rubin, 1979, 1982). In this approach, effect size is viewed in the context of a symmetric 2 × 2 contingency table the purpose of which is to display the effect size index, r_ϕ, as a dichotomous (binomial) outcome. That is, the raw frequencies are recast into a two-way table in which the two rows correspond to the independent variable displayed as a dichotomous predictor (treatment vs. control) and the two columns correspond to the dependent variable displayed as a dichotomous outcome (e.g., improved vs. not improved). Table 2 provides an illustration

TABLE 2
Binomial Effect-Size Display for $r = .38$

| | Success rate | | |
| | Improved | Not improved | Total |
Condition			
Treatment	69	31	100
Control	31	69	100
Total	100	100	

based on the previously noted example, in which the reported finding was that subjects who received assertiveness training (treatment) were then evaluated as significantly more assertive than were subjects in the nontreatment group (control), with $t (18) = 1.735$, $r = .38$.

The traditional practice of relying on the squared correlation as a coefficient of determination might lead someone to state that the effect size was "only" .14. That is, it might be construed that $r = .38$ was a trivial effect, because it leaves 86% of the variance unaccounted for. However, relying on the value of r itself, we see that the distribution of cases reflects an "improvement rate" from 31 in the control group, calculated as $(.50 - r/2) \times 100 = 31$, to 69 in the treatment condition, calculated as $(.50 + r/2) \times 100 = 69$. The difference between these two values is equivalent to a 38% increase in success rate due to assertiveness training, which is not a trivial effect in a practical sense.

TABLE 3
Increases in Success Rates Corresponding to Different Values of r

| r | $r^2 \times 100$ | Increase in success rate | | Difference in success rate |
		From	To	
.01	<1%	.495	.505	.01
.02	<1%	.490	.510	.02
.03	<1%	.485	.515	.03
.04	<1%	.480	.520	.04
.05	<1%	.475	.525	.05
.06	<1%	.470	.530	.06
.07	<1%	.465	.535	.07
.08	<1%	.460	.540	.08
.09	<1%	.455	.545	.09
.10	1%	.450	.550	.10
.20	4%	.400	.600	.20
.30	9%	.350	.650	.30
.40	16%	.300	.700	.40
.50	25%	.250	.750	.50
.75	56%	.125	.875	.75
1.00	100%	.000	1.000	1.00

Note: Values in column 3 calculated as $.50 - r/2$; values in column 4 calculated as $.50 + r/2$.

Table 3 gives a general summary of the relation between increases in success rates and various values of r and $r^2 \times 100$. Column 5 shows the difference in success rates (column 4 minus column 3), which we note is identical to r itself (column 1). In other words, the absolute value of the correlation coefficient provides a generally interpretable gauge of effect size. Were we to multiply the values in column 5 by 100 and compare them with the corresponding values in column 2, we would see that r^2 is more likely to mislead than to aid researchers in evaluating the practical significance of their treatment effects. That is, except for extreme cases (rs of .01 and 1.00), r^2 consistently underestimates the practical significance of the effect. Thus the squared correlation is not a very useful index, whereas r itself is a very useful index of "practical significance." Further, although it may appear that BESD can be used only when the criterion measure provides for a dichotomous outcome, it can be shown that for many distributions there is quite good agreement between the r between the treatment variable and the continuously distributed outcome variable and the r_ϕ between the treatment variable and the dichotomous outcome variable (Rosenthal & Rubin, 1982). (For further discussion of the correlation coefficient as a directly interpretable gauge of effect size in the context of 2 $\times$ 2 contingency tables, see also Ozer, 1985.)

A FINAL NOTE

Previously we alluded to the work of Haase et al. (1982) in counseling psychology and Paquin (1983) in psychotherapy research. Haase et al. entitled their illuminating article "How Significant is a Significant Difference?"—thus seemingly ignoring the "significance" of statistically nonsignificant differences. This other side of the question of "How big is big?" is examined in Table 4, which summarizes population effect sizes and results of significance testing as joint determinants of inferential problems. Instead of specifying particular "critical" levels of r and p in this table, we use the terms *acceptable* and *unacceptable* as tag labels; the choice of a particular value of r or p as being large enough or sufficiently stringent to detect the presence of a "real" effect or a "real" difference is, as we have said, a personal decision. The idea of a "fixed critical level of significance" is also not one that is universally shared by data-analytic statisticians, who instead often recommend that researchers report the actual p level obtained along with a statement of the effect obtained (e.g., Snedecor & Cochran, 1980).

Suppose a nonsignificant p but a large r—what should this tell us as research consumers? Paquin (1983) admonished psychotherapy researchers about being naively overdependent on levels of significance to the exclu-

TABLE 4
Potential Problems of Inference as a Function of Obtained Effect Sizes and Significance Levels

| Level of significance | Effect size | |
	Acceptable	Unacceptable
Acceptable	No inferential problem	Inference of counseling importance from very significant results
Unacceptable	No inference of counseling importance from nonsignificant results	No inferential problem

sion of effect size indexes when evaluating clinical programs and research. To conclude that nothing happened would mean that in "being naively overdependent on levels of significance," we have possibly fallen victim to an inferential error. Low power may have led to failure to detect the true effect, and this line of investigation ought to be continued with a larger sample size before concluding that "nothing happened." On the other hand, suppose a significant p and a small r—what should this tell us as research consumers? The answer depends on the sample size and on what we consider the practical importance of the estimated effect size to be. With a large N we may mistake a result that is merely very significant for one that is of practical importance.

Table 4 thus underscores the importance of computing the effect size not only when p values are viewed as acceptable (i.e., statistically "significant") but also when they are viewed as unacceptable. Not only do counseling psychologists want to step beyond significant yet possibly meaningless research results (as Paquin put it), but they also want to give careful consideration to the plausible importance of even "small effects." A test of significance without an effect size estimate fails to tell the whole story.

REFERENCES

Abelson, R. P. (1985). A variance explanation paradox: When a little is a lot. *Psychological Bulletin, 97,* 129–133.

American Psychological Association. (1983). *Publication manual of the American Psychological Association* (3rd ed.). Washington, DC: Author.

Cohen, J. (1977). *Statistical power analysis for the behavioral sciences* (2nd ed.). New York: Academic Press.

Fagley, N. S. (1985). Applied statistical power analysis and the interpretation of nonsignificant results by research consumers. *Journal of Counseling Psychology, 32,* 391–396.

Fisher, R. A. (1960). *Design of experiments* (7th ed.). Edinburgh, United Kingdom: Oliver & Boyd.

Haase, R. F., Waechter, D. M., & Solomon, G. S. (1982). How significant is a significant difference? Average effect size of research in counseling psychology. *Journal of Counseling Psychology, 29,* 58–65.

Jacobson, N. S., Follette, W. C., & Revenstorf, D. (1984). Psychotherapy outcome research: Methods for reporting variability and evaluating clinical significance, *Behavior Therapy, 15,* 336–352.

Nelson, N., Rosenthal, R., & Rosnow, R. L. (1986). Interpretation of significance levels and effect sizes by psychological researchers. *American Psychologist, 41,* 1299–1301.

Ozer, D. J. (1985). Correlation and the coefficient of determination. *Psychological Bulletin, 97,* 307–315.

Paquin, M. J. R. (1983). Beyond significant yet meaningless results in psychotherapy research. *Psychotherapy: Theory, Research and Practice, 20,* 38–40.

Rosenthal, R. (1984). *Meta-analytic procedures for social research.* Beverly Hills, CA: Sage.

Rosenthal, R., & Rosnow, R. L. (1984). *Essentials of behavioral research: Methods and data analysis.* New York: McGraw-Hill.

Rosenthal, R., & Rosnow, R. L. (1985). *Contrast analysis: Focused comparisons in the analysis of variance.* Cambridge, United Kingdom: Cambridge University Press.

Rosenthal, R. & Rubin, D. B. (1979). A note on percent variance explained as a measure of the importance of effects. *Journal of Applied Social Psychology, 9,* 395–396.

Rosenthal, R., & Rubin, D. B. (1982). A simple general purpose display of magnitude of experimental effect. *Journal of Educational Psychology, 74,* 166–169.

Rosnow, R. L. (1981). *Paradigms in transition: The methodology of social inquiry.* New York: Oxford University Press.

Rosnow, R. L., & Georgoudi, M. (Eds.). (1986). *Contextualism and understanding in behavioral science: Implications for research and theory.* New York: Praeger.

Serlin, R. C., & Lapsley, D. K. (1985). Rationality in psychological research: The good-enough principle. *American Psychologist, 40,* 73–83.

Snedecor, G. W., & Cochran, W. G. (1980). *Statistical methods* (7th ed.). Ames: Iowa State University Press.

19

MULTIVARIATE ANALYSIS VERSUS MULTIPLE UNIVARIATE ANALYSES

CARL J. HUBERTY AND JOHN D. MORRIS

The analyses discussed in this article are those appropriate in research situations in which analysis of variance techniques are useful. These analyses are used to study the effects of treatment variables on outcome/response variables (in ex post facto as well as experimental studies). We speak of a *univariate analysis of variance* (ANOVA) when a single outcome variable is involved; when multiple outcome variables are involved, it is a *multivariate analysis of variance* (MANOVA). (Covariance analyses may also be included.)

With multiple outcome variables, the typical analysis approach used in the group-comparison context, at least in the behavioral sciences, is to either (a) conduct multiple ANOVAs or (b) conduct a MANOVA followed by multiple ANOVAs. That these are two popular choices may be concluded from a survey of some prominent behavioral science journals. The 1986 issues of five journals published by the American Psychological Association were surveyed: *Journal of Applied Psychology, Journal of Counseling*

Reprinted from the *Psychological Bulletin*, 105, 302–308. Copyright 1989 by the American Psychological Association.

Psychology, Journal of Consulting and Clinical Psychology, Developmental Psychology, and *Journal of Educational Psychology.* In addition, one journal published by the American Educational Research Association, *American Educational Research Journal,* was included in the survey. The results of the survey are given in Table 1.

A few comments about these results would be appropriate. First, only one count was made per article, even though some articles reported analyses for multiple experiments or studies. Only the main analysis for an experiment was considered; so-called preliminary analyses were not tallied. Sometimes there were only two groups involved; in this case, multiple *t* tests were considered multiple ANOVAs, and a Hotelling T^2 analysis was considered a MANOVA. For the second analysis approach (MANOVA plus ANOVAs), interpretations or explanations were invariably based on the multiple ANOVAs. In six articles in which multiple ANOVAs were used, three justifications for not doing a MANOVA were given: (a) low outcome variable intercorrelations; (b) small number of outcome variables; and (c) small design cell frequencies. After a MANOVA, multiple ANOVAs were often used implicitly or explicitly to assess relative variable importance. Reasons given for conducting multiple ANOVAs after a MANOVA were (a) to clarify the meaning of significant discriminators; (b) to explain the results of the MANOVA; and (c) to document effects reflected by the MANOVA. In one case, multiple ANOVAs were conducted even though results of the MANOVA were nonsignificant. In 2 of the 88 analyses that involved a MANOVA plus multiple ANOVAs, discriminant functions were briefly considered, but the main interpretation focus was still on the multiple ANOVAs. One of the three

TABLE 1
Frequencies of Alternative Analyses With Multiple Outcome Variables in
1986 Journal Issues

		Analysis Approach			
Journal	Volume	Multiple ANOVAS	MANOVA plus ANOVAS	MANOVA	Total
Journal of Applied Psychology	71	10	10	1	21
Journal of Counseling Psychology	33	18	15	1	34
Journal of Consulting and Clinical Psychology	54	24	41	0	65
Developmental Psychology	22	48	12	0	60
Journal of Educational Psychology	78	19	4	1	24
American Educational Research Journal	23	12	6	0	18
Total		131	88	3	222
Percentage		59.0	39.6	1.4	100

Note: ANOVA = analysis of variance; MANOVA = multivariate analysis of variance.

MANOVA-only applications resulted in nonsignificance. The other two applications incorporated descriptive discriminant analysis techniques. In none of the 222 multiple outcome variable studies was there much interest expressed in any structure associated with the MANOVA results.

Our thesis is that the MANOVA-ANOVAS approach is seldom, if ever, appropriate. Discussions of the appropriateness of the multiple-ANOVAS approach and the strict multivariate approach are given. The Type I error protection issue is briefly reviewed prior to some concluding comments.

ANALYSIS PURPOSES

The primary reason for conducting a MANOVA or an ANOVA is to determine if there are any treatment (used generically) variable effects; in a one-way layout, this amounts simply to determining (by a statistical test) if any group differences exist. These effects or differences may pertain to a collection of outcome variables or to a single outcome variable. In addition to using the statistical test, however, a researcher will want to understand (explain/describe/interpret) the resulting effects or differences. An understanding of resulting ANOVA effects may be gained through the study of explained variation and univariate group contrasts. An understanding of resulting MANOVA effects may be gained through the study of explained variation, multivariate group contrasts, linear discriminant functions (LDFs), and LDF-outcome variable correlations.

We contend that an understanding of resulting MANOVA effects may not be gained by studying the significance of multiple ANOVAS. (As can be seen from the summary reported in Table 1, the MANOVA-ANOVAS approach is fairly common, at least in some areas of study.) A significant MANOVA difference need not imply that any significant ANOVA effect or effects exist; see Tatsuoka (1971, p. 23) for a simple bivariate example.

A justification often given for conducting a MANOVA as a preliminary to multiple ANOVAS is to control for Type I error probability (see, e.g., Leary & Altmaier, 1980). The rationale typically used is that if the MANOVA yields significance, then one has a license to carry out the multiple ANOVAS (with the data interpretation being based on the results of the ANOVAS). This is the notion of a protected (multivariate) F test (Bock, 1975, p. 422). The idea that one completely controls for Type I error probability by first conducting an overall MANOVA is open to question (Bird & Hadzi-Pavlovic, 1983; Bray & Maxwell, 1982, p. 343), because the alpha value for each ANOVA would be less than or equal to the alpha employed for the MANOVA only when the MANOVA null hypothesis is true. This notion does not have convincing empirical support in a MANOVA-ANOVAS context (Wilkinson, 1975), the Hummel and Sligo (1971) and Hummel and Johnston (1986) studies notwithstanding.

From a statistical point of view, one purpose of conducting a MANOVA should not be to serve as a preliminary step to multiple ANOVAs. The multivariate method and the univariate method address different research questions. The choice to conduct a strictly multivariate analysis or multiple univariate analyses is based on the purpose or purposes of the research effort.

RESEARCH QUESTIONS

The guiding force of an empirical research effort should be the question or set of questions formulated by the researcher. Research questions suggest not only the appropriate design and data collection procedures but also the data analysis strategy or strategies. It is recognized that additional research questions may be formulated after data collection commences and that results from initial analyses may suggest research questions in addition to those originally posed.

Univariate Questions

Obviously, research questions that would call for multiple ANOVAs pertain to individual outcome variables. For example, with respect to which outcome variables do the groups differ? Or, the treatment variable has an effect on which outcome variables?

There are, perhaps, four situations in which multiple ANOVAs may be appropriate. One is when the outcome variables are "conceptually independent" (Biskin, 1980, p. 70). (This is the antithesis of a situation involving a variable system, a notion discussed in the next section.) In such a situation one would be interested in how a treatment variable affects each of the outcome variables. Here, there would be no interest in seeking any linear composite of the outcome variables; an underlying construct is of no concern. In particular, an underlying construct would perhaps be of little interest when each outcome variable is from an unrelated domain. Dossey (1976), for example, studied the effects of three treatment variables (Teaching Strategy, Exemplification, Student Ability) on four outcome variables: Algebra Disjunctive Concept Attainment, Geometric Disjunctive Concept Attainment, Exclusive Disjunctive Concept Attainment, and Inclusive Disjunctive Concept Attainment. Considering these outcome variables as conceptually independent, four three-way ANOVAs were conducted.

A second situation in which multiple univariate analyses might be appropriate is when the research being conducted is exploratory in nature. Such situations would exist when new treatment and outcome variables are being studied, and the effects of the former on the latter are being investigated so as to reach some tentative, nonconfirmatory conclusions. This might be of greater interest in status studies, as opposed to true experimental studies.

A third situation in which multiple ANOVAs may be appropriate is when some or all of the outcome variables under current study have been previously studied in univariate contexts. In this case, separate univariate analysis results can be obtained for comparison purposes, in addition to a multivariate analysis if the latter is appropriate and desirable.

Finally, there is an evaluation design situation in which multiple univariate analyses might be conducted. This is when some evidence is needed to show that two or more groups of units are equivalent with respect to a number of descriptors. These analyses might be considered in an in situ design for the purpose of a comparative evaluation of a project. In this situation, evidence of comparability may be obtained via multiple informal ("eyeball") tests or formal statistical tests.

Some four situations have been presented that would seem appropriate for multiple univariate analyses. Multiple ANOVAs might be conducted to (a) study the effects of some treatment variable or variables on conceptually independent outcome variables; (b) explore new treatment–outcome variable bivariate relationships; (c) reexamine bivariate relationships within a multivariate context; and (d) select a comparison group in designing a study.

Any empirical interrelationships among the outcome variables are completely ignored when conducting multiple ANOVAs; this is no problem if one can argue for conceptual independence. It should be recognized, however, that because of the nature of behavioral science variables, redundant information will usually be obtained with multiple ANOVAs. For example, suppose Variable 1 yields univariate significance and that Variable 2 is highly correlated with Variable 1. Significance yielded by Variable 2, then, would not be a new result. Van de Geer (1971) pointed out that "with separate analyses of variance for each variable, we never know how much the results are duplicating each other" (p. 271). Thus, asking questions about individual outcomes may very well imply asking redundant questions. Asking redundant questions may be acceptable in some research contexts; however, the researcher should be cognizant of the redundancy.

Multivariate Questions

The basic MANOVA question is, Are there any overall (interaction, main) effects present? In addition, questions pertaining to simple effects and to group contrast effects may be addressed. (See Huberty, 1986, for a discussion on these and subsequent questions in this section.) After addressing the effects questions, there are other research questions that may be addressed via a multivariate analysis. These questions pertain to (a) determining outcome variable subsets that account for group separation; (b) determining the relative contribution to group separation of the outcome variables in the final subset; and (c) identifying underlying constructs associated with the obtained MANOVA results. None of these questions may be adequately addressed by conducting multiple ANOVAs. To appropriately address them, one must consider outcome variable intercorrelations.

The three questions in the preceding paragraph, from a strict multivariate point of view, are now briefly reviewed. In some instances it may be desirable to determine if fewer outcome variables than the total number initially chosen should form a basis for interpretation. This is the so-called *variable selection problem,* and it is discussed in some detail by Huberty (in press). This question might be considered so as to seek a parsimonious interpretation of a system of outcome variables. It should be noted that this is not an imposed parsimony, as one might get with multiple univariate analyses, but is a parsimony that takes into consideration the correlations among the outcome variables.

A second potential reason for conducting a multivariate analysis is to make an assessment of the relative contribution of the outcome variables to the resultant group differences or to the resultant effects of the treatment variable or variables. This is the so-called *variable ordering problem.* Although the assessment of variable importance is problematic in all multivariable analyses (including multiple and canonical correlation, factor analysis, and cluster analysis), some potentially useful indexes have been proposed for the MANOVA context (see Huberty, 1984). Of course, a meaningful ordering of variables can only be legitimately accomplished by taking the variable intercorrelations into consideration.

(It should be pointed out that typically employed criteria for variable selection and variable ordering are sample and system specific. What a good variable subset or a relatively good individual variable is depends upon the collection of the variables in the system being studied. How well the proposed selection and ordering results hold up over repeated sampling needs to be addressed with further empirical study. Of course, replication is highly desirable. The rank-order position of a given variable in a system of variables may change when new variables are added to the system. The same may be said for the composition of a good subset of variables. Hence, a conclusion regarding the goodness of a variable subset and the relative goodness of individual variables must be made with some caution {see Huberty, in press, and Share, 1984, for elaboration}.)

The identification of a construct that underlies the collection of outcome variables to be studied is more a matter of art than statistics. This identification process is legitimate only if the collection of variables constitutes a system. A *system* of outcome variables may be loosely defined as a collection of conceptually interrelated variables that, at least potentially, determines one or more meaningful underlying variates or constructs. In a system, one has several outcome variables that represent a small number of constructs, typically one or two. For example, Watterson, Joe, Cole, and Sells (1980) studied a system of five outcome measures on attitudes (based on interview and questionnaire data) that led to two meaningful constructs, political attitude and freedom of expression; Hackman and Taber (1979) studied a system of 21 outcome measures on student performance (based on interview data) that yielded two meaningful constructs, academic performance and personal growth.

A goal of a multivariate analysis may be to identify and interpret the underlying construct or constructs. For such potential constructs to be meaningful, the judicious choice of outcome variables to study is necessary; the conceptual relationships among the variables must be considered in light of some overriding theory. A multivariate analysis should enable the researcher to "get a handle" on some characteristics of his or her theory: What are the emerging variables?

These emerging variables are identified by considering some linear composites of the outcome variables, called *canonical variates* or *linear discriminant functions* (LDFs). Correlations, sometimes called structure coefficients, between each outcome variable and each LDF are found. Just as in factor analysis, the absolute values of these correlations, or loadings, are used in the identification process: Those variables with high loadings are tied together to arrive at a label for each construct.[1] We subscribe to the use of structure coefficients to label or name the construct identified with each LDF. This is in opposition to the use of the so-called standardized LDF weights for this purpose, which is espoused by Harris (1985, p. 319).

Sometimes a researcher is interested in studying multiple systems, or

---

[1] It has been pointed out by Harris (1985, pp. 129, 257) and proven by Huberty (1972) that in the two-group case, the squared LDF–variable correlations are proportional to the univariate F values. Thus, it might seem that if a system structure is to be identified via loadings, then multiple univariate analyses would suffice. In the multiple-group case in whic at least two LDFs result, however, identification of the multiple constructs by multiple univariate analyses is generally problematic; an exception may be if only one interpretable construct results (Rencher, 1986).

subsystems, of variables. These subsystems may be studied for comparative purposes (see, e.g., Lunneborg & Lunneborg, 1977) or simply because different (conceptually independent?) constructs based on unrelated variable domains are present (see, e.g., Elkins & Sultmann, 1981). In this case, a separate multivariate analysis for each subsystem would be conducted.

The notion of a construct varies across different types of multivariate analyses. For the group-comparison or treatment-variable-effects situation on which we focus herein, the identified constructs are extrinsic to the set of outcome variables. That is, the optimization of the composites (i.e., LDFs) is based on a criterion that is external to the outcome variables, namely, the maximization of effects. Similar optimization of composites (linear classification functions) that is based on an external criterion occurs in the context of predictive discriminant analysis (see Huberty, 1984) in which classification accuracy is maximized. On the other hand, in component analysis, for example, the identified constructs are intrinsic to the set of outcome variables. That is, the optimization of the composites (i.e., components) is based on a criterion that is internal to the outcome variables, namely, the maximization of variance accounted for in the variable set. Furthermore, an extrinsic–intrinsic situation could result when one conducts a MANOVA or a classification analysis using component or factor scores as input (for an example, see Huberty & Wisenbaker, 1988; see Dempster, 1971, for more on data structure).

In a multiple-group situation, the study of system structure and of variable importance may lead to some interesting and informative conclusions. In the univariate case, group contrasts (pairwise or complex) are often of interest in addition to, or in lieu of, the omnibus intergroup comparison. Group contrasts may also be studied with multiple outcome variables, that is, multivariate group contrasts. The construct associated with one contrast may be characterized quite differently from that associated with another contrast. Also, the variable orderings for effects defined by two contrasts may be quite different. For a detailed discussion of this analysis strategy, see Huberty and Smith (1982).

None of the above three data analysis problems (selecting variables, ordering variables, identifying system structure) can be appropriately approached via multiple univariate analyses. As Gnanadesikan and Kettenring (1984) put it, an objective of a multivariate analysis is to increase the "sensitivity of the analysis through the exploitation of the intercorrelations among the response variables so that indications that may not be noticeable in separate univariate analyses stand out more clearly in the multivariate analysis" (p. 323). We interpret "indications" to imply relative importance of variables and structure underlying the data.

An Example

Consider a three-group, 13-variable data set, obtained from Bisbey (1988). Group 1 consists of college freshmen in a beginning-level course in French; Group 2 involves freshmen in intermediate French; and Group 3 involves freshmen in advanced French. The 13 outcome measures consisted of five (English, Mathematics, Social Science, Natural Science, French) high school cumulative grade point averages; number of semesters of high school French; four American College Testing Program standard scores (in the first four areas of study just mentioned); two (Aural Comprehension, Grammar) scores on the Educational Testing Service Cooperative French Placement Test; and number of semesters since last high school French course was taken.

A basic intent of the analysis was to explain or describe the resultant intergroup differences, Wilks lambda = .231, $F(26, 276) = 11.455, p < .001$, eta-squared = .769. For purposes of this discussion, we focus on three aspects of explanation/description: (a) relative contribution of the outcome variables to intergroup differences; (b) the construct or constructs underlying the differences; and (c) variable subset selection. Values of indices and procedures used for these purposes from a multivariate analysis[2] may be compared with the 13 univariate ANOVA F values (see Table 2).

Just as in multiple regression analysis, we think it is important to take into full consideration the intercorrelations of the outcome variables when ordering variables in (descriptive) discriminant analysis. It may be shown (Urbakh, 1971) in the two-group case that the quotient of the square of a standardized LDF weight and an index of collinearity of the outcome variables is an estimate of the decrease in group separation when the corresponding variable is deleted. That is, variable rankings based on these quotients are identical to those based on F-to-remove values that are output from many statistical package programs, for example, SAS STEPDISC, SPSS[x] DISCRIMINANT, and BMDP7M. F-to-remove values are appropriate for

---

[2]A popular index used in assessing relative variable contribution is the standardized LDF weight. As popular as this index might be, we prefer the F-to-remove index discussed in the latter part of the section. One reason for not preferring the standardized weight index is that its sampling variability is not considered. Furthermore, how to utilize standardized LDF weights for variable ordering when there are more than two groups is somewhat open to question. One possibility is to use only the weights for the first LDF. Another possibility is to determine, for each variable, a linear composite of the (absolute) LDF weights using, say, the eigenvalues as the composite weights (Eisenbeis & Avery, 1972, p. 70). A comparison between variable orderings based on standardized weights for the first LDF and those based on the preferred F-to-remove values may be made for the example considered here. The two sets of ranks are given in Table 2; the ranks are determined by clustering comparable values of each index. The correlation between the two sets of ranks is .878, which is fairly high, indeed. For two other data sets, taken from Huberty and Wisenbaker (1988), the correlations between the two sets of ranks are only .352 and .359.

TABLE 2
Univariate F, F-to-Remove, Standardized LDF Weight, and Structure
Correlation Values for the Example

Variable	Univariate F		F to remove		Standardized LDF1 weight		Structure correlation	
	Value	Rank	Value	Rank	Value	Rank	LDF1	LDF2
X1	8.496	7	0.173	12.5	.040	12.5	.182	.388
X2	2.396	12	1.167	8.5	−.232	5.5	.052	.439
X3	9.276	4	1.731	5.5	.191	8.5	.140	.736
X4	5.842	9	6.854	3	.582	2.5	.113	.577
X5	35.602	3	5.067	4	.322	4	.409	.043
X6	8.227	7	1.310	8.5	.028	12.5	.158	.554
X7	8.844	5	1.358	8.5	.205	8.5	.230	−.065
X8	0.584	13	0.197	12.5	.079	11	.028	.211
X9	3.722	10.5	1.841	5.5	−.247	5.5	.131	.080
X10	3.361	10.5	0.835	11	−.164	8.5	.124	−.082
X11	67.869	2	16.483	2	.606	2.5	.555	−.480
X12	105.862	1	23.455	1	.686	1	.703	−.243
X13	7.967	7	1.531	8.5	.176	8.5	−.187	.230

Note: Ranks are based on "clusters" of values.

ranking variables when more than two groups are involved; see Huberty (in press) and Huberty and Wisenbaker (1988) for more details. One might ask if the univariate F values may be used for variable ordering, realizing, of course, that variable intercorrelations would be ignored. The rank ordering of the F values is not at all similar to that of the F-to-remove values (our preferred ordering basis), $r = .651$.

Now for some comments pertaining to underlying constructs. Using structure correlations from Table 2 to identify the two constructs, it may be seen that some joining of variables X12, X11, and X5 yields the dominant construct. The second construct is basically defined by variables X3, X4, X6, X11, and X2. We claim that it is illogical to consider using univariate F values to identify some constructs, which inherently depend on intercorrelations of constituent variables.

The use of univariate F values to determine good subsets of outcome variables is also a questionable practice. For example, according to F values, the subset {X12, X11, X5, X3, X7, X1} might be considered; this subset is actually worse than the 10th best subset of size six, in the sense of the smallest Wilks lambda value (see Huberty & Wisenbaker, 1988).

Finally, when examining the univariate analyses, one might conclude that variable X1 is significant, $F(2, 150) = 8.496$, $p = .0003$, eta-squared = .102. But, in the company of the other 12 variables, X1 does not appear to be contributing much at all to overall group differences nor to structure identification.

TYPE I ERROR PROTECTION

Whenever multiple statistical tests are carried out in inferential data analysis, there is a potential problem of "probability pyramiding." Use of conventional levels of Type I error probabilities for each test in a series of statistical tests may yield an unacceptably high Type I error probability across all of the tests (the "experimentwise error rate"). In the current context, this may be a particular issue when multiple ANOVAs are conducted.

If a researcher has a legitimate reason for testing univariate hypotheses, then he or she might consider either of two testing procedures. One is a simultaneous test procedure (STP) originated by Gabriel (1969), advocated by Bird and Hadzi-Pavlovic (1983), and programmed by O'Grady (1986). For the STP, as it is applied to the current MANOVA-ANOVAs context, the referent distribution for the ANOVA F values would be based on the MANOVA test statistic used. Bird and Hadzi-Pavlovic (1983, p. 168), however, point out that for the current context, the overall MANOVA test is not really a necessary prerequisite to simultaneous ANOVAs. Ryan (1980) makes the same point for the ANOVA contrasts context. These two contexts may be combined to a MANOVA-ANOVA contrasts context in which it would be reasonable to go directly to the study of univariate group contrasts, if univariate hypotheses are the main concern. The STP approach has not been used to any great extent. One reason for this is the low statistical power, a characteristic shared with the Scheffé test in a univariate context.

The second procedure for testing univariate hypotheses is to employ the usual univariate test statistics with an adjustment to the overall Type I error probability. How *overall* is defined is somewhat arbitrary. It could mean the probability of committing a Type I error across all tests conducted on the given data set, or it could mean the Type I error probability associated with an individual outcome variable when univariate questions are being studied. Whatever the choice (which can be a personal one and one that is numerically nonconventional; see Hall & Selinger, 1986), some error splitting seems very reasonable. Assuming that Type I error probability for each in a set of m tests is constant, the alpha level for a given test may be determined by using either of two approaches. One approach is to use an additive (Bonferroni) inequality: For m tests, the alpha level for each test (α_1) is given by the overall alpha level (α_m) divided by m. A second approach is to use a multiplicative inequality (Šidák, 1967): For m tests, α_1 is found by taking 1 minus the mth root of the complement of α_m (see Games, 1977). The per-test alphas, constant across the m tests, that are found using the two approaches are, for most practical purposes, the same.

In nearly all instances, outcome variables are interrelated. Thus, multiple ANOVA F tests are not independent. This lack of independence does not, however, present difficulties in determining the per-test alpha level to use. That this is the case may be seen by the following double inequality:

$$\alpha_m \leq 1 - (1 - \alpha_1)^m < m\alpha_1.$$

That is, either function of α_1 may be considered as an upper bound for the overall alpha, α_m.

It turns out that when conducting m tests, each at a constant alpha level, a considerably larger overall alpha level results. For example, six tests, each conducted using an alpha level of .05, yield an upper bound for the overall alpha level of .30 using the additive inequality and yield about .26 using the multiplicative inequality (the middle of the double inequality in the preceding paragraph).

Just as the STP approach may be lacking for statistical power, so too may the procedure of adjusting the Type I error probability. One way of obtaining reasonable power values is to use an adequate sample size (in relation to the number of outcome variables). This, however, may provide little solace to the practicing researcher. Modifications of the adjustment procedure have been proposed by Larzelere and Mulaik (1977) and by Schweder and Spjøtvoll (1982). We recommend a modified adjustment procedure to control for experimentwise Type I error when conducting multiple statistical tests.

DISCUSSION

Even though it is a fairly popular analysis route to take in the behavioral sciences, conducting a MANOVA as a preliminary step to multiple ANOVAs is not only unnecessary but irrelevant as well. We consider to be a myth the idea that one is controlling Type I error probability by following a significant MANOVA test with multiple ANOVA tests, each conducted using conventional significance levels. Furthermore, the research questions addressed by a MANOVA and by multiple ANOVAs are different; the results of one analysis may have little or no direct substantive bearing on the results of the other. To require MANOVA as a prerequisite of multiple ANOVAs is illogical, and the comfort of statistical protection is an illusion. The view that it is inappropriate to follow a significant MANOVA overall test with univariate tests is shared by others (e.g., Share, 1984).

If the researcher is interested in outcome variable selection or ordering, or in variable system structure, then a multivariate analysis should be done. It has been argued (e.g., by Conger, 1984, p. 303) that a weighted composite of the outcome variables (i.e., an LDF) is not readily interpretable. That may be the case when a small number of diverse outcome variables is being studied. This should not, however, be considered a drawback to conducting a MANOVA. Obtaining an uninterpretable structure does not logically lead to the use of multiple ANOVAs. Is it reasonable to shift from a multivariate-type research question to an ANOVA-type research question just because the multivariate question is difficult to answer? The possibility of obtaining an interpretable composite when outcome variables are judiciously chosen for study may very well enhance analysis findings. This is a plus!

On the basis of the limited journal survey completed, one might conclude that the multiple-ANOVAs analysis strategy will be appropriate for many empirical studies. If this conclusion is in fact correct, then the assessment of relative outcome variable importance and the discovery and interpretation of data structure will apparently be of little interest. There will be little concern, too, for the potential of finding and reporting results that may be redundant across the set of outcome variables.

Whether a researcher conducts a multivariate analysis or multiple univariate analyses, it is strongly recommended that the outcome variable intercorrelations be reported, or at least be made available. Typically, these correlations would be reported in the form of a matrix. At the very least, a descriptive summary of the distribution of the correlations should be reported.

REFERENCES

Bird, K. D., & Hadzi-Pavlovic, D. (1983). Simultaneous test procedures and the choice of a test statistic in MANOVA. *Psychological Bulletin, 93*, 167–178.

Bisbey, G. D. (1988). [Characteristics of college freshmen in three levels of French instruction]. Unpublished raw data.

Biskin, B. H. (1980). Multivariate analysis in experimental counseling research. *The Counseling Psychologist, 8*, 69–72.

Bock, R. D. (1975). *Multivariate statistical methods in behavioral research.* New York: McGraw-Hill.

Bray, J. H., & Maxwell, S. E. (1982). Analyzing and interpreting significant MANOVAs. *Review of Educational Research, 52*, 340–367.

Conger, A. J. (1984). Statistical consideration. In M. Hersen, L. Michelson, & A. S. Bellack (Eds.), *Issues in psychotherapy research* (pp. 285–309). New York: Plenum.

Dempster, A. P. (1971). An overview of multivariate data analysis. *Journal of Multivariate Analysis, 12*, 316–346.

Dossey, J. A. (1976). The relative effectiveness of four strategies for teaching algebraic and geometric disjunctive concepts and for teaching inclusive and exclusive disjunctive concepts. *Journal for Research in Mathematics Education, 7,* 92–105.

Eisenbeis, R. A., & Avery, R. B. (1972). *Discriminant analysis and classification procedures.* Lexington, MA: Heath.

Elkins, J., & Sultmann, W. F. (1981). ITPA and learning disability: A discriminant analysis. *Journal of Learning Disabilities, 14,* 88–92.

Gabriel, K. R. (1969). Simultaneous test procedures: Some theory of multiple comparisons. *Annals of Mathematical Statistics, 40,* 224–250.

Games, P. A. (1977). An improved table for simultaneous control on g contrasts. *Journal of the American Statistical Association, 72,* 531–534.

Gnanadesikan, R., & Kettenring, J. R. (1984). A pragmatic review of multivariate methods in applications. In H. A. David & H. T. David (Eds.), *Statistics: An appraisal* (pp. 309–337). Ames: Iowa State University Press.

Hackman, J. D., & Taber, T. D. (1979). Patterns of undergraduate performance related to success in college. *American Educational Research Journal, 16,* 117–138.

Hall, P., & Selinger, B. (1986). Statistical significance: Balancing evidence against doubt. *Australian Journal of Statistics, 28,* 354–370.

Harris, R. J. (1985). *A primer of multivariate statistics.* New York: Academic Press.

Huberty, C. J. (1972). Regression analysis and 2-group discriminant analysis. *Journal of Experimental Education, 41,* 39–41.

Huberty, C. J. (1984). Issues in the use and interpretation of discriminant analysis. *Psychological Bulletin, 95,* 156–171.

Huberty, C. J. (1986). Questions addressed by multivariate analysis of variance and discriminant analysis. *Georgia Educational Researcher, 5,* 47–60.

Huberty, C. J. (in press). Problems with stepwise methods: Better alternatives. In B. Thompson (Ed.), *Advances in social science methodology* (Vol. 1). Greenwich, CT: JAI Press.

Huberty, C. J., & Smith, J. D. (1982). The study of effects in MANOVA. *Multivariate Behavioral Research, 17,* 417–432.

Huberty, C. J., & Wisenbaker, J. M. (1988, April). *Discriminant analysis: Potential improvements in typical practice.* Paper presented at the annual meeting of the American Educational Research Association, New Orleans.

Hummel, T. J., & Johnston, C. B. (1986, April). *An empirical comparison of size and power of seven methods for analyzing multivariate data in the two-sample case.* Paper presented at the annual meeting of the American Educational Research Association, San Francisco.

Hummel, T. J., & Sligo, J. R. (1971). Empirical comparison of univariate and multivariate analysis of variance procedures. *Psychological Bulletin, 76,* 49–57.

Larzelere, R. E., & Mulaik, S. A. (1977). Single-sample tests for many correlations. *Psychological Bulletin, 84,* 557–569.

Leary, M. R., & Altmaier, E. M. (1980). Type I error in counseling research: A plea for multivariate analyses. *Journal of Counseling Psychology, 27*, 611–615.

Lunneborg, C. E., & Lunneborg, P. W. (1977). Is there room for a third dimension in vocational interest differentiation? *Journal of Vocational Behavior, 11*, 120–127.

O'Grady, K. E. (1986). Simultaneous tests and confidence intervals. *Behavior Research Methods, Instruments, & Computers, 18*, 325–326.

Rencher, A. C. (1986, August). *Canonical discriminant function coefficients converted to correlations: A caveat*. Paper presented at the annual meeting of the American Statistical Association, Chicago.

Ryan, T. A. (1980). Comment on "Protecting the overall rate of Type I errors for pairwise comparisons with an omnibus test statistic." *Psychological Bulletin, 88*, 354–355.

Schweder, T., & Spjøtvoll, E. (1982). Plots of *p*-values to evaluate many tests simultaneously. *Biometrika, 69*, 493–502.

Share, D. L. (1984). Interpreting the output of multivariate analyses: A discussion of current approaches. *British Journal of Psychology, 75*, 349–362.

Šidák, Z. (1967). Rectangular confidence regions for the means of multivariate normal distributions. *Journal of the American Statistical Association, 62*, 626–633.

Tatsuoka, M. M. (1971). *Significance tests*. Champaign, IL: Institute for Personality and Ability Testing.

Urbakh, V. Y. (1971). Linear discriminant analysis: Loss of discriminating power when a variable is omitted. *Biometrics, 27*, 531–534.

Van de Geer, J. P. (1971). *Introduction to multivariate analysis for the social sciences*. San Francisco: Freeman.

Watterson, O. M., Joe, G. W., Cole, S. G., & Sells, S. B. (1980). Impression management and attitudes toward marihuana use. *Multivariate Behavioral Research, 15*, 139–156.

Wilkinson, L. (1975). Response variable hypotheses in the multivariate analysis of variance. *Psychological Bulletin, 82*, 408–412.

20

STRUCTURAL EQUATION MODELING IN CLINICAL ASSESSMENT RESEARCH WITH CHILDREN

RICHARD J. MORRIS, JOHN R. BERGAN, AND JOHN V. FULGINITI

There is growing interest in structural equation modeling in a variety of areas in the social and behavioral sciences (e.g. Breckler, 1990; Martin, 1987), with most of this interest focusing on the use of structural equation techniques in causal modeling (see, for example, Mulaik, 1987). This interest has paralleled the recent advances in computer technology that have permitted the testing of complex structural models derived from theorized cognitive, affective, and behavioral processes related to clinical phenomena (e.g., Bentler, 1987b; Crano & Mendoza, 1987). Structural equation techniques can also be used for the more fundamental purpose of validating measures used in research and practice. We will focus on the validation of clinical child assessment instruments and will show how structural equation procedures can be applied in clinical assessment research and used to overcome various validity problems that have become apparent in many currently available clinical assessment devices used with children.

Reprinted from the *Journal of Consulting and Clinical Psychology*, 59, 371–379. Copyright 1991 by the American Psychological Association.

OVERVIEW OF STRUCTURAL MODELING IN CLINICAL ASSESSMENT RESEARCH

The validation of clinical assessment instruments involves the investigation of two types of hypotheses. The first has to do with the extent to which the items selected to assess a given construct such as fear or anxiety actually do adequately measure that construct. The second has to do with relationships between the constructs being assessed and other variables. Both of these types of hypotheses are directly related to the notion of "construct validity" in the psychological assessment and measurement literature (e.g., Anastasi, 1988; Cronbach, 1984; Messick, 1988). In Figure 1, a path diagram illustrates the hypotheses associated with the validation of clinical assessment instruments. The squares in the diagram indicate observed variables (i.e., scores derived through clinical assessment). The circles in the diagram indicate hypothesized constructs to be measured by clinical assessment instruments. These constructs, school performance fears and social interaction fears, are not directly observed but rather are latent variables inferred from assessment data. Straight arrows in the diagram indicate the direct effects of the latent variables on other variables. The arrows from the latent variables to the physical complaint variable indicate hypothesized relationships between school fears and physical symptoms manifested by children. The arrows from the latent variables to the observed measures of school fears indicate that the latent variables are assumed to determine performance on the clinical assessment devices measuring children's fears. The curved arrow indicates covariation between the two fear variables with no assumption as to causation.

Measuring Hypothetical (Latent) Constructs

In clinical assessment as well as other types of assessment, hypothetical constructs are generally measured by scales that quantify variations in the level of the constructs being assessed. The construct is treated as a quantitative dimension. Location on the dimension is represented by a test score where, for example, as revealed in Figure 1, the practicing clinician may use an assessment scale to measure level of anxiety or fear in a child who has been referred to a clinic. In this case, the child's location on the measure is represented by his or her test score.

As indicated in Figure 1, the quantitative dimension being assessed is not directly observable. Rather, it is a latent (or hypothetical) variable whose presence must be inferred from observable responses to test items. These observable responses may be thought of as manifest indicators of the latent variable. The time-honored approach to validating the assumption

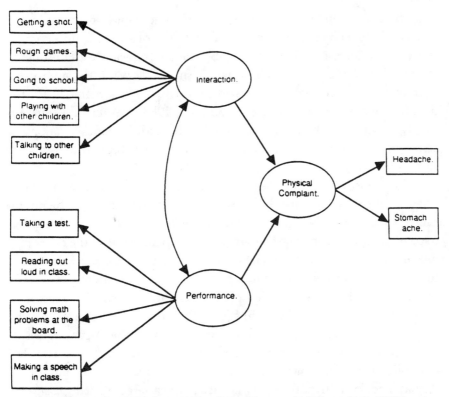

Figure 1: Preferred structural equation model for effects of fears on physical complaints. (Circles represent latent variables; boxes represent observed variables; straight arrows represent direct effects; curved arrow represents covariation without the assumption of causality.)

that a latent variable can be inferred from a set of observed variables is factor analysis. Factor analysis is the approach used within the structural equation paradigm for validating latent variables (McDonald, 1985). However, there are important differences between the approach to factor analysis used in structural equation modeling and traditional factor analytic procedures.

One major difference between the two approaches, which is well recognized in the literature (see, for example, McDonald, 1985), is that traditional factor analytic techniques do not afford a way to test hypotheses regarding the measurement of latent variables, whereas the factor analytic procedures used in structural equation modeling do allow for hypothesis testing. Traditional factor analysis is often described as "exploratory factor analysis" to distinguish it from the hypothesis testing approach used in structural equation modeling, which is called "confirmatory factor analysis" (e.g., McDonald, 1985).

Hypotheses in confirmatory factor analysis are generally tested in the following manner: First a hypothesized model is specified. A correlation matrix or covariance matrix is generated on the basis of the expectation that the model under examination is true. The values in the expected matrix are then compared with the values in the observed sample correlation or covariance matrix using a suitable statistic, typically the chi-squared statistic. When the value of chi-square is small relative to the number of degrees of freedom, the model is said to provide an acceptable fit for the data (see, for example, Jöreskog & Sörbom, 1988). Because chi-square is highly sensitive to variations in sample size under minor violations of assumptions, various additional indices have been advocated to assess the fit of a model to the data (e.g., Bentler, 1990).

The contribution of a specific parameter or set of parameters to the fit of a model to the data may be assessed by comparing the fit of hierarchically related models (see, for example, Hayduk, 1987). Two models are said to be hierarchical when one contains all of the parameters of the other plus one or more additional parameters. Under these conditions, the chi-square for the model with the larger number of degrees of freedom can be subtracted from the chi-square for the model with the smaller degrees of freedom. The result will be a chi-square that assesses whether or not the additional parameters contained in the model with the larger degrees of freedom contribute significantly to the fit of the model to the data. For example, the model shown in Figure 1 was compared with a hierarchically related model that hypothesized a single latent variable labeled *school fears*. The single-fear model did not provide an acceptable fit for the data. Moreover, the model assuming two fears improved significantly on the single-fear model. Thus, the two-fear model was preferred over the single-fear model.

When factor analysis is undertaken to validate a theory rather than to engage in exploratory data analysis, the confirmatory approach is more appropriate to the needs of the investigator than is traditional factor analysis. This is certainly the case in clinical assessment. For example, clinical researchers interested in measuring constructs such as fear and anxiety generally select items on the basis of the assumption that these items are indicators of an underlying latent trait or hypothetical construct. Confirmatory factor analysis allows the clinical researcher to validate constructs by testing hypotheses about the relationships between manifest variables and the latent traits they are assumed to measure (Jöreskog & Sörbom, 1988).

The importance for the practitioner of empirical validation of constructs such as fear or anxiety cannot be overestimated. When a test reflects a construct conveyed through a name such as the Children's Fear Assessment Inventory or Children's Anxiety Inventory (fabricated test names), the practitioner may assume that the test is measuring what the title says it measures. Without construct validation, that assumption is simply not justified. Unfortunately, the clinical assessment field is filled with instruments with similar interesting titles that reflect little or no construct validity (see, for example, Barrios & Hartmann, 1988; Frame & Matson, 1987; Holden & Edwards, 1989; King, Hamilton, & Ollendick, 1988; Knoff, 1986; Morris & Kratochwill, 1983).

Confirmatory factor analysis makes hypothesis testing possible by allowing the investigator to construct and statistically test models expressing hypotheses about the relationships between observed variables and latent variables assumed to underlie those indicators (Jöreskog & Sörbom, 1988). Factor analysis models are expressed through equations that specify relationships between model parameters and observed variables. For example, in the simplest case, a test item score may be described by the following simple regression equation, which specifies that the score (x) is a function of a factor loading (λ) times a factor score (f) plus a residual term (e):

$$x = \lambda f + e.$$

The factor loading, the factor, and the residual term are parameters in the model that must be estimated from the available data. The starting point for the estimation process is the correlation or covariance matrix specifying the relationships among the observed variables (test items) assumed to underlie the latent variable (Jöreskog & Sörbom, 1988). The tradition in factor analysis calls for a correlation matrix. However, the use of a correlation matrix assumes that it is appropriate to measure all of the variables under examination on the same scale. This is often not a reasonable assumption. Moreover, standardizing variables in a sample, which is what is done when a correlation is used, does not guarantee that the variables will be standardized in the population represented by the sample (McDonald, 1985). Thus, contemporary investigators generally prefer to analyze a covariance matrix rather than a correlation matrix (see, for example, Jöreskog & Sörbom, 1988).

In the case in which ordinal variables are to be analyzed, it is appropriate to carry out the analysis starting with a matrix of polychoric correlations (Jöreskog & Sörbom, 1988). This matrix is then weighted by the asymptotic covariance matrix to yield a distribution free matrix for analysis (Jöreskog & Sörbom, 1988). For example, the analysis of the data reflected in in Figure 1 used a polychoric correlation matrix and the associated asymptotic covariance matrix. The reason for using this approach with ordinal data involves the fact that no assumptions can be made regarding the distance between points on an ordinal scale. Thus, it does not make sense to assume that one ordinal variable is measured on a different scale from another.

After model parameters have been estimated, they can be used to produce an expected correlation or covariance matrix. This matrix gives the values of correlations or covariances among manifest variables that are expected under the assumption that the model being tested is true. The correspondence between the observed values in the matrix for manifest indicators and the expected values can be assessed using the chi-squared (X^2) statistic (see, for example, Jöreskog & Sörbom, 1988).

There are important differences between confirmatory factor analysis and traditional factor analysis. The confirmatory factor analysis approach allows the clinical investigator to impose restrictions on model parameters that make it possible to test a broad range of hypotheses that may be of interest. For instance, in the example used to illustrate confirmatory factor analysis in Figure 1, we assumed that a set of test items measured two different kinds of fears in children: (a) school performance fears related to classroom activities such as taking a test, reciting, and giving a speech and (b) social interaction fears related to such activities as playing rough games, playing with other children, and talking with other children. The confirmatory approach allowed us to restrict factor loadings of items related to social interaction to be zero on the factor assessing school performance fears. Likewise, we were able to restrict factor loadings assessing school performance to be zero on the social interaction factor. Restrictions of this kind are not possible using traditional factor analytic techniques (McDonald, 1985).

A second difference between contemporary confirmatory factor analysis procedures and traditional factor analytic procedures has to do with the analysis of ordinal data such as test items. Traditional factor analytic procedures assume that manifest indicators are normally distributed continuous variables (McDonald, 1985). Test items are generally dichotomous or polytomous variables that reflect no more than an ordinal scale. Thus, a normal distribution cannot be assumed. Traditional practice has been to ignore the requirement of continuous normally distributed variables and to factor analyze test items. The result of this approach is biased estimates of model parameters (Jöreskog & Sörbom, 1988).

A number of approaches are now available that provide ways to carry out confirmatory factor analyses with ordinal data and obtain unbiased estimates of model parameters (Mislevy, 1986). Applications of these techniques with clinical assessment instruments are largely lacking. Thus, the state of affairs that exists at present is that little attempt has been made to establish the construct validity of large numbers of clinical assessment instruments that are used with children. In those cases in which instruments have been validated through the use of traditional factor analysis, the procedures afford no way to test hypotheses necessary for construct validation. Moreover, because clinical instruments typically involve items reflecting an ordinal scale, traditional factor analysis can be expected to produce biased estimates of model parameters. There is no way to know what the implications of this problem are for the practitioner. Of particular concern is the issue of the validity of using existing assessment instruments for referral, diagnosis, treatment selection, forensic evaluations, and the evaluation of treatment outcome. Our own data do not provide an optimistic picture in that the results of traditional factor analyses were quite different from the results obtained with confirmatory factor analysis using procedures that produce unbiased parameter estimates with ordinal data. There is certainly a need, therefore, to apply confirmatory factor analysis technology to increase confidence in the validity of clinical child assessment instruments.

Construct Validity, Causal Modeling, and the Concept of Causality

The validation of clinical assessment instruments involves not only the problem of measuring latent variables by means of manifest indicators but also the problem of validating hypothesized relationships among the constructs being assessed. More often than not, these relationships are assumed to be causal in nature. For example, as shown in Figure 1, physical complaints are assumed to be caused by school-related fears. Structural equation techniques provide a way of investigating hypothesized causal relationships, between physical symptoms and hypothesized constructs such as school-related fears, that are of interest to clinicians.

Although cogent arguments for the use of structural equation models have been advanced (e.g., Bentler, 1987a; Muthen, 1987), there has been some objection in the literature to the use of structural equation techniques in the examination of causal hypotheses (see, for example, Freedman, 1987). Thus, some attention to the justification for the structural equation approach to causal modeling in clinical assessment is warranted.

Objections to the structural equation approach to causal modeling come mainly from those who are strict adherents to the traditional experimental paradigm. The view taken in this paper is that the theoretical assumptions underlying clinical research and practice are antithetical in fundamental ways to the traditional experimental paradigm used to validate causal inferences in research. Clinicians operating from a variety of theoretical perspectives assume that cognitions and related affective states are significant factors influencing human thought and action (Bandura, 1977; 1986; Dreikurs & Soltz, 1964; Ellis & Bernard, 1983; S. Freud, 1909/ 1963; Kanfer & Gaelick, 1986; Klein, 1932; Meichenbaum, 1986; Rogers, 1951; Rotter, 1954). The experimental tradition in psychology assumes that causal inferences should be confined to those cases in which independent variables are actively manipulated through random assignment. The assumption that causal inferences should be restricted to research involving random assignment imposes constraints on scientific investigation that effectively rule out the study of causal influences of cognitive and affective states on human functioning (Mulaik, 1987). Advocates of structural equation modeling conceptualize causality in ways that provide an alternative to the traditional randomization requirement, therefore allowing for the study of causal influences of cognitive and affective processes as well as effects of experimental variables. For this reason, structural equation modeling is well suited to the problems addressed in clinical research and in the validation of clinical assessment instruments.

It should be noted that neither the experimental paradigm nor the structural equation approach is totally congruent with the historical intuitive concept of causality (Marini & Singer, 1988). Philosophical assumptions about causality (Hume, 1739/1969; 1777/1975) assert that one phenomenon causes another when the first always occurs before the second, when there is a mechanism by which the first can affect the second, and when the action of the first determines some aspect of the second. For example, one might assume that fear of taking a test could cause physical symptoms such as epigastric discomfort, nausea, rapid heart rate, and palpitation, as well as palmar sweating, flushing of the face, and dilated pupils (see, for example, Morris & Kratochwill, 1983). In order for this assumption to be justified, the fear would have to occur before the physical symptoms. A mechanism (presumably physiological) linking the affective state to the physical symptom would have to be identified, and there would have to be a one-to-one correspondence between the occurrence of the fear and the physical symptom.

Both the experimental and structural equation paradigms differ from the philosopher's view with respect to the requirement of determinism. Within both of these paradigms, the relationship between a causal variable and the variable that it is assumed to affect is probabilistic rather than deterministic. For example, there is no expectation that every subject in an experimental treatment will outperform every subject in a control condition. Likewise, the relationship between a causal variable and the variable that it is presumed to influence is generally assumed to be less than perfect. One conclusion to be drawn here is that the experimental paradigm has no unique claim on the concept of causality (Mulaik, 1987; White, 1990).

The experimental paradigm in psychology has strong ties to logical positivism (e.g., Misiak & Sexton, 1966; Mulaik, 1987; Skinner, 1938, 1953; Watson, 1924). The assumption here is that those events that cannot be directly observed and manipulated should not be assigned a causal status. Cognitive processes are therefore ruled out of consideration by fiat.

The basis for this view is that investigations of unobserved variables such as cognitive processes have not proved fruitful (e.g., Skinner, 1974). This argument for ruling out unobserved variables is now widely questioned (Mulaik, 1987).

Arguments For and Against Causal Status for Nonexperimental Variables

The most common argument against the inclusion of nonexperimental (i.e., nonmanipulated) variables in causal studies lies in the familiar maxim that correlation does not imply causation. The basis for this maxim is that some unknown variable or variables may be correlated with both the causal variable and the dependent variable. The unknown variable(s), then, explain the covariation between the causal variable and the dependent variable. Superstitious behaviors provide a good example of what the experimentalist is concerned about. For example, athletes often go through ritualistic behaviors before action because these behaviors have been associated in the past with successful athletic performance. However, theoretically these behaviors ought to have no causal influence on performance.

When covariation between variables is explained by other variables that have not been explicitly recognized in a causal model or when the direction of causal effects is not correctly identified, the model is said to be "misspecified" (e.g., Hayduk, 1987). Model misspecification is the danger recognized in the old saw that correlation does not imply causation. The concern of researchers with model misspecification must be taken seriously because model misspecification can lead to seriously erroneous conclusions regarding causal effects. Moreover, as the experimentalists argue, random assignment to treatment conditions is a useful procedure for minimizing the possibility of model misspecification. When subjects are assigned at random to treatment conditions, the possibility that unknown variables may be responsible for covariation between causal and dependent variables is minimized.

The point at which we take issue with the experimentalist tradition lies in the assumption that the possibility of model misspecification justifies restricting the concept of causality only to those instances in which random assignment to treatment conditions and manipulation of independent variables are possible. This restriction rules out the study of hypotheses about causal relations among cognitive and behavioral processes that undergird the bulk of clinical theory and practice with children (e.g., Axline, 1947; Bandura, 1986; Dreikers & Solz, 1964; Ellis & Bernard, 1983; A. Freud, 1981; Kratochwill & Morris, 1991; Ollendick & Hersen, 1989).

The solution to the problem of model misspecification lies in the careful design of studies. What is required is attention to rival hypotheses and an effort to take them into account in the design of a study. The ruling out of rival hypothesis will invariably not be possible within a single study. Many investigations will be required, each taking account of alternative explanations for the observed covariation between a hypothesized causal variable and a dependent variable. It should be pointed out that the problem of ruling out rival hypotheses is inherent in the experimental paradigm as well as in nonexperimental approaches to causal questions. Moreover, the strategy of multiple investigations, each aimed at eliminating various alternative explanations for observed findings, is the strategy invariably followed in the experimental tradition.

In summary, structural equation modeling addresses two major problems in clinical assessment research with children. The first is that of validating hypothetical constructs or latent variables assumed in clinical theory and research to play a contributing role in the functioning of the individual. The second is to provide a mechanism for investigating causal relations involving cognitive, physiological, and motoric processes that are not amenable to experimental manipulation and that are assumed to have causal effects on client functioning. The benefit to the practicing clinician is that structural equation models afford a way to address questions involving the effects of the many variables that are assumed to influence the adjustment of the client and that cannot be investigated within the constraints imposed by the randomization requirement in experimental research. It should be noted that there is nothing in the statistical techniques typically used in experimental investigations that precludes the examination of causal questions with nonexperimental variables. The familiar practice of dividing continuous variables into categories in analysis of variance designs (e.g., Kirk, 1967) illustrates the inclusion of nonexperimental variables into experimental designs.

AN ILLUSTRATIVE EXAMPLE OF STRUCTURAL MODELING IN CLINICAL ASSESSMENT RESEARCH

To illustrate the use of structural equation techniques in clinical assessment research, we analyzed a selected data set on children's school-related fears and physical symptoms (specifically, headache and stomach-ache) collected in 15 elementary schools in Uppsala, Sweden (Morris, Melin, & Larsson, 1986). The schools comprised Grades 1-6 and included 3,438 children between the ages of 7 and 12 years. Ratings used in the present illustrative example were on 1,036 boys and girls from the fourth, fifth, and sixth grades. Teachers who agreed to participate in the study were asked to rate those children that they had known for at least 6 months. The Likert-type rating scale included nine items that were adapted from the Louisville Fear Survey Schedule (Miller, Barrett, Hampe, & Noble, 1972) and translated into Swedish, complemented with two additional items involving ratings of the frequency and intensity of children's headaches and stomachaches. The rating scale was administered through personal visits conducted at each school by a graduate student from Uppsala University. Teachers were assured of the anonymity of their ratings of individual children. The data were analyzed using traditional common factor analytic techniques and structural equation techniques.

Traditional Factor Analyses

Traditional factor analyses were carried out using the SPSS/PC+ computer program (Norusis, 1988). Principal axis analyses were carried out on the matrices of Pearson product-moment correlations computed from the data for fourth-, fifth-, and sixth-grade children. The results were rotated using the oblimin procedure (Harman, 1960). Scree plots were examined to determine the number of rotated factors to include. Examination of the scree plots (Gorsuch, 1983) for the rotated factors suggested that only one factor be retained for Grades 4 and 6. By contrast, two factors were retained for Grade 5. The factor structures giving the rotated factor loadings are shown in Table 1. The factor revealed in Grades 4 and 6 was labeled *school-related fears*. The two factors identified for Grade 5 were labeled *school performance fears* and *social interaction fears*.

The items with high loadings across on the performance factor included fear of reading out loud in class, fear of solving math problems at

TABLE 1
Factor Loadings: Exploratory Principal Axis With Oblique Rotation

Fear variables	4th grade (n = 327) School-related fears	5th grade (n = 239)		6th grade (n = 380) School-related fears
		Interaction	Performance	
Getting a shot	.40	.34	−.16	.49
Rough games	.51	.32	−.27	.46
Taking a test	.76	.40	−.34	.54
Going to school	.79	.74	−.31	.64
Reading out loud in class	.72	.26	−.55	.66
Blackboard excercises	.69	.25	−.47	.70
Playing with other children	.83	.68	−.17	.77
Talking with other children	.86	.64	−.39	.70
Making a speech in class	.71	.36	−.96	.64

Note: Range of ordinal scale values for fear variables: 0 to 5. Correlations between factors for 5th grade: $r = -.45$.

the board, and fear of making a speech in class. These fears are all related to classroom performance. The items with high loadings on the social interaction factor included fear of going to school, fear of talking with other children, and fear of playing with other children. These items all involve interactions with others. It was suspected that fear of interacting with peers was related to the phenomenon of bullying, which is a concern in many Swedish schools.

The major finding of concern related to the traditional factor analytic approach is the inconsistency in factor structure observed across grade levels. The question that immediately arises is whether or not the observed inconsistency is a function of true differences across grades or of the inadequacy of the traditional factor analytic approach with respect to the problem of testing the hypothesis of congruence in factor structure across grade levels.

Structural Analyses

Confirmatory factor analyses were implemented as part of the larger structural equation model shown in Figure 1 examining hypothesized relationships between fears and physical complaints (i.e., stomachaches and headaches) manifested by children. Because the data under examination were ordinal, the usual assumptions that the variables under examination were continuous and normally distributed could not be justified. When ordinal variables are used, the interpretation of measures of variability, such as the variance and standard deviation, is compromised. This is the case because there is no equal interval scale underlying an ordinal variable. Analyzing a covariance matrix composed of ordinal variables can lead to distorted parameter estimates and incorrect chi-square goodness-of-fit measures and standard errors (Jöreskog & Sörbom, 1988). A number of distribution free estimation procedures have been developed for dealing with the problem of biased parameter estimates associated with ordinal variables (Mislevy, 1986). We used a weighted least squares approach implemented by the PRELIS (Jöreskog & Sörbom, 1986) and LISREL (Jöreskog & Sörbom, 1988) computer programs to obtain unbiased estimates of model parameters. First, the matrices of polychoric correlations among the variables under study were computed using the PRELIS program. Second, the asymptotic covariance matrices associated with the polychoric correlation matrices were computed using PRELIS. The asymptotic covariance matrices were used to provide weights in the weighted least squares analyses, which were carried out using the LISREL program. Use of the weighted least squares approach gives asymptotically distribution free estimators for which correct asymptotic chi-squares and standard errors may be obtained (Jöreskog & Sörbom, 1986). It should be emphasized that the use of the polychoric matrix alone does not solve the problem of biased parameter estimates. Polychoric correlations assume an underlying normal distribution. The asymptotic covariance matrix must be used in conjunction with the polychoric matrix in order to obtain distribution free estimates.

Hypothesized factors for the structural models were based on the observations of school children in Sweden and on discussions with Swedish psychologists and school personnel by one of the authors (RJM). In Sweden, children may experience fear related to school for two reasons: First, they may fear social interactions with peers because of the occurrence of bullyism in some elementary schools. Second, they may experience anxiety and fear because of difficulty in performing certain academic tasks at an acceptable level. Accordingly, two factors were hypothesized, a classroom performance factor and a social interaction factor. The structural models examined in the study were constrained to reflect these two factors. The following items were restricted to have zero loadings on the performance factor: getting a shot, engaging in rough games, going to school, playing with other children, and talking to other children. These items were restricted to have zero loadings on the interaction factor: taking a test, reading out loud in class, solving math problems at the board, and making a speech in class. In addition, the model constrained the loadings across all three grade levels to be identical.

The fit of the model to the data was assessed by comparing the covariance matrices expected under the assumption that the model being examined was true to the observed covariance matrices using the chi-squared statistic. The model provided an excellent fit for the data, $\chi^2(129, N = 1,036) = 96.57$, $p = .99$. The total coefficient of determination for all structural equations jointly was .89. This coefficient may be thought of as the proportion of variance in the dependent measures determined by variables affecting the dependent measures.

It should be pointed out that the chi-squared statistic is extremely sensitive to variations in sample size when even minor violations in assumptions are present (see, for example, Bentler, 1990). Other indices of fit are available to deal with this problem (see, for example, Bentler, 1990; Jöreskog & Sörbom, 1988). It was not necessary to use any of these indices in the present example.

Factor loadings for the confirmatory factor analyses for Grades 4, 5, and 6 are shown in Table 2. There are a number of differences between these loadings and the loadings obtained in the traditional factor analysis. One difference is that the loadings from the confirmatory factor analyses cannot be compared directly with the loadings in the traditional analyses.

TABLE 2
Factor Loadings: Confirmatory Approach With Correlated Factors, Invariant Across Grades

	Factor	
Fear variables	Interaction	Performance
Getting a shot	.83	.00
Rough games	.83	.00
Taking a test	.00	.95
Going to school	1.00	.00
Reading out loud in class	.00	.97
Solving math problems on the blackboard	.00	1.00
Playing with other children	.99	.00
Making a speech in class	.00	.95

Note: Coviarance between fear factors = .80

The traditional factor loadings are the correlations of the items with the factors. This is not the case in the confirmatory analyses because the solution was not standardized. The confirmatory loadings reflect covariation between the items and the factors, but they are not correlation coefficients. In the confirmatory analyses, one variable was selected to establish a metric for each factor. That variable was assigned a loading of 1.00. Because the matrices subjected to analysis were polychoric correlation matrices and because 1 was selected as the metric for the factors, the loadings have similar values to correlations, but they are not correlations. One consequence of this fact is that the confirmatory loadings can exceed 1.

In the confirmatory factor analysis, certain items were constrained to have zero loadings on each factor. Moreover, the constraints were maintained across all three grade levels. In the traditional factor analyses, there was no way to impose constraints that limited the items allowed to have particular loadings on a factor. As a result, it was necessary to make subjective judgments as to whether or not a given loading was sufficiently high to warrant the assumption that the item was a suitable manifest indicator for the factor. The ambiguity in linking items to factors and in establishing the number of factors to be retained in the traditional approach made interpretation of the results difficult.

The confirmatory analysis constrained the loadings across grade levels to be identical, whereas this was not possible in the traditional analyses. The confirmatory approach revealed that a model assuming consistency across grades fit the data very well. The loadings in the traditional analyses varied substantially across grades leading to the erroneous conclusion of inconsistency with respect to the factor structure.

Another major difference between the traditional and confirmatory analyses involved the covariation between factors. The traditional approach revealed a negative correlation between the two factors that emerged in the fifth grade. By contrast, the confirmatory approach revealed a strong positive relationship between the factors. A model constraining the confirmatory factors to be orthogonal was tested and found to provide an unacceptable fit for the data. The chi-squared value was well over 1000. This was not surprising because the confirmatory model allowing covariance between the factors revealed covariation of substantial magnitude (.81).

Traditional factor analytic procedures do not provide a convenient way to examine causal relations between fears and physical complaints. The closest approximation is to look at the criterion-related validity (see, for example, Nunnally, 1978) of the fear factors by correlating them with physical complaints. The examination of the relationships between fears and physical complaints was accomplished in the traditional analyses by correlating the factor scores with the two physical complaint items, stomachaches and headaches. The results are shown in Table 3. This table indicates that school-related fears correlated with the physical complaint items at all three grade levels. However, in Grade 5 the performance factor correlated negatively with physical complaints, whereas the social interaction factor correlated positively with physical complaints.

In the structural analysis, the relationship between fears and physical complaints was addressed through the structural equation model depicted in the path diagram in Figure 1. Residual terms were omitted to avoid unnecessary complexity in the diagram.

The model was validated across three grade levels. This was accomplished by constraining parameter estimates to be equal across grade levels and testing the fit of the constrained model to the data. Validation of the model across three different grade levels provides evidence of the consis-

TABLE 3
Correlations Between Factor Scores and Physical Complaints

Physical complaint variables (by grade)	Correlations	
	Factor I	Factor II
Fourth grade		
Headache	.44	
Stomachache	.60	
Fifth grade		
Headache	.51	−.28
Stomachache	.48	−.20
Sixth grade		
Headache	.46	
Stomachache	.59	

tency and generality of the findings. As indicated earlier, the model provides an excellent fit for the data indicating that the assumption of consistency across grade levels is congruent with the data.

Commentary

Despite this good news, there are problems with this model. The model illustrates a very common problem in causal modeling research. The model assumes that fears affect physical complaints. This implies that the fears arose prior to the complaints. Unfortunately, there is no way to verify this. The ratings of fears and complaints were made at the same time. Moreover, even if they had not been, one could not necessarily conclude that fears arose before physical complaints. For example, suppose that fears were rated in the winter and complaints were rated in the spring. All that could be concluded is that fears and complaints were measured at different times. One could not conclude that they arose at different times. What is needed is some concrete evidence as to when fears and physical complaints developed. In the absence of this, it would have been useful to measure each of these variables at two points in time. This would have provided some evidence of temporal ordering for the variables.

The theory underlying the model provides some justification for assuming that fears precede physical complaints. It is reasonable that these fears could cause physical symptoms. Moreover, it is somewhat difficult to justify the alternative view that physical complaints would cause these two different kinds of fears. Nonetheless, it is possible that physical complaints generate fears. Accordingly, the model may be misspecified. Additional research that takes account of the ordering of the variables is required to validate the model.

Despite the possibility of model misspecification, the observed relationship between fear and physical complaints is of interest and does support the hypothesis that fears may produce physical symptoms. It is certainly important to know that children's fears may cause physical symptoms.

In summary, the traditional approach revealed inconsistent findings that were difficult to interpret. By contrast the structural equation approach revealed highly consistent results. Two factors emerged in the structural analyses, whereas this did not occur in the traditional analyses. The inconsistency in the traditional approach is not surprising given the fact that the estimates of model parameters could be expected to be biased. Also, a high degree of subjectivity is involved in the traditional approach in that there is no way to impose restrictions on model parameters and no way to test hypotheses about model parameters.

IMPLICATIONS OF STRUCTURAL MODELING FOR THE CLINICAL RESEARCHER AND PRACTITIONER

In considering the use of structural equation modeling versus traditional factor analysis and criterion-related validity studies, the question arises as to what are the benefits of one approach over the other from the point of view of both the practitioner and the clinical researcher. From the viewpoint of the practitioner, one benefit of using an assessment instrument whose construct validity is based on structural equation modeling is that the individual can have more confidence in the results obtained with the confirmatory approach used in structural equation modeling than with the approach associated with traditional factor analysis procedure. This is illustrated in the present example by the difference in the consistency of results between the traditional and confirmatory approaches. In short, the practitioner using the structural approach can be more assured that a particular test or assessment instrument is measuring what it purports to measure than is the case when traditional factor analysis is used.

Structural equation modeling also permits the researcher who is constructing a test to provide the practitioner with information regarding causal relationships between various constructs that are being assessed, something that is not accomplished with traditional test validation procedures. For instance, in the present example, the criterion-related validity coefficients presented in the traditional analysis do not lend themselves to causal interpretations. It is safe to assume that more often than not clinicians are interested in relationships among variables such as fears and physical complaints because they assume that causal relations are present. One of the main advantages of structural modeling for the clinical researcher is that it provides the researcher with the opportunity to validate constructs through the testing of causal hypotheses about relationships between latent variables.

As we pointed out earlier, practitioners operate from a variety of theoretical perspectives, each of which involves the specification of causal relationships between variables—many of which are assumed to be true without the provision of empirical support. Structural equation modeling provides a means by which the practitioner and clinical researcher can obtain this empirical support as well as test out a broad range of additional hypotheses that may be of interest to both. The power of the structural equation approach to deal with causal assumptions may encourage the researcher and clinician to work more closely than previously possible in developing models relevant to practitioner needs.

Despite the advantages of structural equation modeling, we do not assume that it should be the procedure of choice in every situation. The question of which approach to use depends on the purpose of the research being proposed. If the purpose is merely to demonstrate a relationship between variables or items on an assessment instrument like a children's fear inventory, then establishing criterion-related validity by correlating measures with suitable criterion variables is satisfactory in clinical assessment research. If, on the other hand, the purpose is to test the assumption that children's school-related fears influence the occurrence of physical complaints, then structural modeling is the procedure of choice.

REFERENCES

Anastasi, A. (1988). *Psychological testing* (6th ed). New York: Macmillan.

Axline, M. (1947). *Play therapy.* Boston: Houghton Mifflin.

Bandura, A. (1977). *Social learning theory.* Englewood Cliffs, NJ: Prentice-Hall.

Bandura, A. (1986). *Social foundations of thought and action: A social cognitive theory.* Englewood Cliffs, NJ: Prentice-Hall.

Barrios, B. B., & Hartmann, D. P. (1988). Fears and anxieties. In E. J. Mash & L. G. Terdall (Eds.), *Behavioral assessment of childhood disorders* (2nd ed., pp. 196-262). New York: Guilford Press.

Bentler, P. M. (1987a). Drug use and personality in adolescence and young adulthood: Structural models with nonnormal variables. *Child Development, 58,* 65-79.

Bentler, P. M. (1987b). Structural modeling and the scientific method: Comments on Freedman's critique. *Journal of Educational Statistics, 12,* 151-157.

Bentler, P. M. (1990). Comparative fit indexes in structural models. *Psychological Bulletin, 107,* 238-246.

Breckler, S. J. (1990). Applications of covariance structure modeling in psychology: Cause for concern? *Psychological Bulletin, 107,* 260-273.

Crano, W. D., & Mendoza, J. L. (1987). Maternal factors that influence children's positive behavior: Demonstration of a structural equation analysis of selected data from the Berkeley Growth Study. *Child Development, 58,* 38-48.

Cronbach, L. (1984). *Essentials of psychological testing* (4th ed.). New York: Harper & Row.

Dreikurs, R., & Solz, V. (1964). *Children: The challenge.* New York: Hawthorn Books.

Ellis, A., & Bernard, M. E. (Eds.). (1983). *Rational-emotive approaches to the problems of childhood.* New York: Plenum Press.

Frame, C., & Matson, J. L. (Eds.). (1987). *Handbook of assessment in childhood psychopathology.* New York: Plenum Press.

Freedman, D. A. (1987). As others see us: A case study in path analysis. *Journal of Educational Statistics, 12,* 101-128.

Freud, A. (1981). Foreword to "Analysis of a phobia in a five-year-old boy." *The writings of Anna Freud: Vol. 3. 1970–1980*. New York: International Universities Press.

Freud, S. (1963). The analysis of a phobia in a five-year-old boy. *The standard edition of the complete psychological works of Sigmund Freud* (Vol. 10, pp. 149–289). London: Hogarth Press. (Original work published 1909)

Gorsuch, R. L. (1983). *Factor analysis* (2nd ed.). Hillsdale, NJ: Erlbaum.

Harman, H. H. (1960). *Modern factor analysis*. Chicago, IL: University of Chicago Press.

Hayduk, L. A. (1987). *Structural equation modeling with LISREL*. Baltimore: Johns Hopkins University Press.

Holden, G. W., & Edwards, L. A. (1989). Parental attitudes toward child rearing: Instruments, issues, and implications. *Psychological Bulletin, 106*, 29–58.

Hume, D. (1969). *A treatise of human nature*. Baltimore, MD: Penguin. (Original work published 1739 and 1740)

Hume, D. (1975). *Enquiries concerning human understanding and concerning the principles of morals*. Oxford, England: Clarendon. (Original work published 1777)

Jöreskog, K. G., & Sörbom, D. (1986). *PRELIS: A preprocessor for LISREL*. Mooresville, IN: Scientific Software, Incorporated.

Jöreskog, K. G., & Sörbom, D. (1988). *LISREL 7: A Guide to the program and applications*. Chicago, IL: SPSS.

Kanfer, F. H., & Gaelick, L. (1986). Self-management methods. In F. H. Kanfer & A. P. Goldstein (Eds.), *Helping people change* (3rd ed., pp. 283–345). Elmsford, NY: Pergamon Press.

King, N. J., Hamilton, D. I., & Ollendick, T. H. (1988). *Children's phobias: A behavioral perspective*. New York: Wiley.

Kirk, R. E. (1967). *Experimental design: Procedures for the behavioral sciences*. Belmont, CA: Brooks/Cole.

Klein, M. (1932). *The psychoanalysis of children*. New York: Delacorte Press.

Knoff, H. (Ed.). (1986). *The assessment of child and adolescent personality*. New York: Guilford Press.

Kratochwill, T. R., & Morris, R. J. (Eds.). (1991). *The practice of child therapy* (2nd ed.). Elmsford, NY: Pergamon Press.

Marini, M. M., & Singer, B. (1988). Causality in the social sciences. In C. C. Clogg (Ed.), *Sociological Methodology* (pp. 347–409). Washington, DC: American Sociological Association.

Martin, J. A. (1987). Structural equation modeling: A guide for the perplexed. *Child Development, 58*, 33–37.

McDonald, R. P. (1985). *Factor analysis and related methods*. Hillsdale, NJ: Erlbaum.

Meichenbaum, D. (1986). Cognitive behavior modification. In F. H. Kanfer & A. P. Goldstein (Eds.), *Helping people change* (3rd ed., pp. 346–382). Elmsford, NY: Pergamon Press.

Messick, S. (1988). Validity. In R. L. Linn (Ed.), *Educational measurement* (3rd ed., pp. 13–103). New York: Ace Macmillan.

Miller, L. C., Barrett, C. L., Hampe, E., & Noble, H. (1972). Factor structure of childhood fears. *Journal of Consulting and Clinical Psychology, 39,* 264–268.

Misiak, H., & Sexton, V. S. (1966). *History of psychology: An overview.* New York: Grune & Stratton.

Mislevy, R. (1986). Recent developments in the factor analysis of categorical variables. *Journal of Educational Statistics, 11,* 3–31.

Morris, R. J., & Kratochwill, T. R. (1983). *Treating children's fears and phobias: A behavioral approach.* Elmsford, NY: Pergamon Press.

Morris, R. J., Melin, L., & Larsson, B. (1986). *School related fears in elementary school age children in Sweden.* Unpublished manuscript, Uppsala University, Uppsala, Sweden.

Mulaik, S. A. (1987). Toward a conception of causality applicable to experimentation and causal modeling. *Child Development, 58,* 18–32.

Muthen, B. O. (1987). Response to Freedman's critique of path analysis: Improve credibility by better methodological training. *Journal of Educational Statistics, 12,* 178–184.

Norusis, M. J. (1988). *SPSS/PC+ advanced statistics V3.0.* Chicago, IL: SPSS.

Nunnally, J. C. (1978). *Psychometric theory.* New York: McGraw-Hill.

Ollendick, T. H., & Hersen, M. (Eds.). (1989). *Handbook of child psychopathology* (2nd ed.). New York: Plenum Press.

Rogers, C. (1951). *Client-centered therapy: Its current practice, implications, and theory.* Boston: Houghton Mifflin.

Rotter, J. B. (1954). *Social learning and clinical psychology.* Englewood Cliffs, NJ: Prentice-Hall.

Skinner, B. F. (1938). *The behavior of organisms.* New York: Appleton-Century-Crofts.

Skinner, B. F. (1953). *Science and human behavior.* New York: Macmillan.

Skinner, B. F. (1974). *About behaviorism.* New York: Knopf.

Watson, J. B. (1924). *Behaviorism.* Chicago, IL: University of Chicago Press.

White, P. A. (1990). Ideas about causation in philosophy and psychology. *Psychological Bulletin, 108,* 3–18.

INTERPRETATION OF
RESEARCH OUTCOMES

21

DO STUDIES OF STATISTICAL POWER HAVE AN EFFECT ON THE POWER OF STUDIES?

PETER SEDLMEIER AND GERD GIGERENZER

Since J. Cohen's (1962) classical study on the statistical power of the studies published in the 1960 volume of the *Journal of Abnormal and Social Psychology*, a number of power analyses have been performed. These studies exhorted researchers to pay attention to the power of their tests rather than to focus exclusively on the level of significance. Historically, the concept of power was developed within the statistical theory of Jerzy Neyman and Egon S. Pearson but was vigorously rejected by R. A. Fisher. Fisher compared statisticians concerned with Type II errors (beta) or power (1-beta) to "Russians," who were trained in technological efficiency as in a 5-year plan, rather than in scientific inference (Fisher, 1955, p. 70). Neyman, also with reference to the issue of power, called some of Fisher's testing methods "worse than useless" in a mathematically specifiable sense (Stegmüller, 1973, p. 2). The unresolved controversies about statistical

Reprinted from the *Psychological Bulletin, 105*, 309–316. Copyright 1989 by the American Psychological Association.

This research was supported by an Akademie Stipendium from the Volkswagen Foundation and by Grant 17900585 from the University of Konstanz to the second author.

inference within statistics proper had their impact on psychological research, although here the controversial issues have been for the most part neglected (Gigerenzer, 1987). In psychological textbooks, an apparently uncontroversial hybrid theory is taught, which contains concepts from both camps (e.g., null hypothesis testing, following Fisher, and Type II error and specification of the Type I error before the data has been obtained, following Neyman and Pearson). This hybrid statistics is usually taught as statistics per se, without mention of the originators of the respective ideas, and this mixture of concepts certainly would not have been approved by either of the originators (Gigerenzer & Murray, 1987, chap. 1).

It is important to understand the unresolved issue of power in psychological studies against the background of this unresolved debate in statistics rather than as an isolated issue. We shall come back to this connection in the Discussion section.

POWER STUDIES

In the Neyman-Pearson theory, power (1-beta) is defined as the long-run frequency of acceptance of H_1 if H_1 is true. Recall that in their theory two point hypotheses, often called H_0 and H_1, are formulated, and this allows both alpha and beta to be determined. Beta cannot be calculated in Fisher's theory of null hypothesis testing, where only one point hypothesis, the null, is specified and tested (Fisher, 1935/1966). There are three major factors that influence the magnitude of the power: effect size in the population, level of significance, and number of observations. The effect size expresses the discrepancy between H_0 and H_1; for example, for a t test between sample means, it is the standardized difference between the two population means posited by H_0 and H_1 (J. Cohen, 1977). Everything else being constant, the greater the effect size, the greater the power. The level of significance, alpha, is the long-run frequency of rejecting H_0 if H_0 is true, which must be posited before the data are obtained, according to Neyman-Pearson theory. Note that in Fisher's theory of null hypothesis testing, the effect size is not a concept, and the level of significance can be determined after the data have been obtained (compare his later writings, e.g., Fisher, 1956). Everything else being constant, the smaller the level of significance, the smaller the power. Finally, when the number n of observations increases, the standard deviations of the sampling distributions for H_0 and H_1 become smaller. Thus the distributions will overlap less, and the power will increase. Besides these three major factors, the assumptions of the statistical model are important insofar as they affect the power if they do not hold. Examples are violation of independence (Edgell & Noon, 1984), false assumptions concerning the equality of variances (Petrinovich & Hardyck, 1969), and false assumptions about measurement scales and shapes of distributions (Trachtman, Giambalvo, & Dippner, 1978).

For the purpose of power analysis, it is assumed that the assumptions of the statistical model hold. In that case, any of the four variables—effect size, n, alpha, and power—can be determined as a function of the other three. The usual procedure for calculating the power of published studies is to determine the n of a test, to assume that alpha has been set as .05 in advance (which is not clearly stated in many studies), and to calculate the power depending on an assumed effect size. Generally, three levels of effect size, as suggested by J. Cohen (1962, 1969), are used. For the purpose of planning research, that is, for prospective rather than retrospective power analysis, the procedure is different. There are two major possibilities. The first is to calculate n, given a conventional alpha, a size of effect estimated from previous research, and a desired power. J. Cohen (1965), for instance, recommended .80 as a convention for a desirable power. The second possibility is to calculate alpha, given n, a size of effect, and a desired power. The second possibility has almost never been considered in actual research. The reason for this neglect can be seen in the widespread interpretation of alpha as a conventional yardstick for inductive influence. The calculations can be facilitated using the tables provided by J. Cohen (1969, 1977), in which (a) the power of commonly used (parametric) tests is listed as a function of effect size, n, and three levels of alpha (.01, .05, .10; one- and two-tailed tests) and (b) n is listed as a function of the other three variables. J. Cohen (1970) also offered rule-of-thumb procedures that allow a rough estimation of power for seven standard test statistics.

The first systematic power analysis was conducted by J. Cohen (1962), analyzing all studies published in the 1960 volume of the *Journal of Abnormal and Social Psychology*. He distinguished between major and minor research hypotheses and calculated the mean and median power of all significance tests performed in an article, for each kind of hypothesis. The calculations were based on alpha = .05 and on three effect sizes—small, medium, and large—corresponding to the dimensionless Pearson correlations .20, .40, and .60, respectively. His results, together with those of subsequent studies that appeared after a time lag of a decade, are depicted in Table 1. Cohen found a mean power of only .18 for detecting small effects, of .48 for medium effects, and of .83 for large effects. If one follows his judgment that medium effects are what one can expect in this area of research, then if follows that the experiments were designed so that the researcher had less than a 50% chance of obtaining a significant result if there was a true effect. Note that Cohen did not calculate the sample effect

TABLE 1
Results of Power Studies (Arithmetical Means)

Journal	Study	Effect size		
		Small	Medium	Large
Journal of Abnormal and Social Psychology	J. Cohen (1962)	.18	.48	.83
American Journal of Educational Research	Brewer (1972)	.14	.58	.78
Journal of Research in Teaching	Brewer (1972)	.22	.71	.87
The Research Quarterly	Brewer (1972)	.14	.52	.80
Journal of Communication	Katzer & Sodt (1973)	.23	.56	.79
Counselor Education and Supervision	Haase (1974)	.10	.37	.74
American Sociological Review	Spreitzer (1974; cited in Chase & Tucker, 1976)	.55	.84	.94
American Forensic Association Journal, Central States Speech Journal, Journal of Communication, The Quarterly Journal of Speech, Southern Speech Communication Journal, Speech Monographs, The Speech Teacher, Today's Speech, Western Speech	Chase & Tucker (1975)	.18	.52	.79
American Speech and Hearing Research, Journal of Communication Disorders	Kroll & Chase (1975)	.16	.44	.73
Journalism Quarterly, The Journal of Broadcasting	Chase & Baran (1976)	.34	.76	.91
Journal of Applied Psychology	Chase & Chase (1976)	.25	.67	.86
Journal of Marketing Research	Sawyer & Ball (1981)	.41	.89	.98

sizes in the 1960 volume. His definitions of small, medium, and large effect sizes were based on judgment but seem to be indirectly supported from calculations of sample effect sizes in related areas of research (Haase, Waechter, & Solomon, 1982), although these are not without problems (Murray & Dosser, 1987). Cooper and Findley (1982) concluded from their effect size study in social psychological research that it seems reasonable to assume a medium effect size (Cohen's definition) in power analysis. Most power studies have used Cohen's definitions; and the present study gives direct evidence for the validity of his definition with respect to his own study (J. Cohen, 1962).

The other studies shown in Table 1 are comparable to Cohen's study, because those authors followed Cohen's procedure, with the exception of Brewer (1972), who used single tests rather than articles as units.[1] Four

---

[1] The power values of Cohen's original study are not strictly comparable with those of the later studies summarized in Table 1. The reason is that Cohen has lowered over time the criteria of what constitutes a small, medium, or large effect for some statistics, and the later studies all used his criteria published in

other studies could not be included in Table 1 because they were not comparable; these studies did not use dimensionless measures of effect size (Freiman, Chalmers, Smith, & Kuebler, 1978), confused population effect size with obtained sample effect size (Ottenbacher, 1982), used only one "median total sample size" (Arvey, Cole, Hazucha, & Hartanto, 1985), or examined problems in a specific area of research (King, 1985). Most of these studies were conducted in the 1970s and show about the same low average power as that in Cohen's study, although there are a few journals with considerably more powerful tests, such as the *American Sociological Review* and the *Journal of Marketing Research*.

In general, these studies reveal an apparently paradoxical state in research. Given the high premium placed by both researchers and journal editors on significant results (see Atkinson, Furlang, & Wampold, 1982; Bredenkamp, 1972; L. H. Cohen, 1979; Coursol & Wagner, 1986; Greenwald, 1975; Melton, 1962), it seems strange that research was planned and conducted to give only a low chance of a significant result if there was a true effect. Researchers paradoxically seem to prefer probable waste of time, money, and energy to the explicit calculation of power.

24 YEARS LATER: A CASE STUDY

The question of interest is whether studies of power have an effect on the power of studies. Because methodological innovations, be they wrong or right, often have an incubation time on the order of decades rather than years, it is fair to use as a case study the influence of Cohen's analysis, which is both the oldest and the most prominent analysis. What impact did Cohen's analysis have on the power of studies published later in the same journal? That journal has meanwhile been divided into the *Journal of Abnormal Psychology* and the *Journal of Personality and Social Psychology*. We decided to analyze all studies published in the 1984 volume of the *Journal of Abnormal Psychology*. Twenty-four years should be sufficient time for a methodological innovation to be established. Of course, our comparison between the 1960 and the 1984 volumes cannot prove a causal connection; all that we can do is to establish whether there is a change or not.

1969 (or 1977). For instance, in 1962, a Pearson correlation of .2, .4, or .6 was defined as a small, medium, or large effect, respectively, whereas in 1969 (and 1977) the corresponding values were .1, .3, and .5. This systematic lowering of the effect size conventions has the effect of slightly lowering the calculated power, too. We have taken account of this problem in comparing the states of affairs of now and then (1984 and 1960) by using Cohen's original criteria whenever possible.

Method

J. Cohen (1962) calculated the power using articles as units, but 24 years later, articles often contain more than one experiment. We have treated different experiments within the same article as separate units if they used different samples of subjects. Power calculations were made using two different units: articles, as in J. Cohen (1962), and experiments. For each unit, all tests were classified into tests either of major or of minor hypotheses, following J. Cohen (1962). Then the power of each test was calculated for small, medium, and large effect sizes; for most tests, J. Cohen's (1977) tables could be used. For all calculations, alpha was assumed to be .05 (two-tailed for the unadjusted procedures; for the multiple comparison procedures the corresponding error rates [see, e.g., O'Neill & Wetherill, 1971] were used). Nonparametric tests that occasionally occurred were treated like their corresponding parametric tests (e.g., Mann-Whitney U tests, Kruskal-Wallis tests, and Spearman correlations were treated like t tests, F tests, and Pearson correlations, respectively); this usually results in a slight overestimation of power (J. Cohen, 1965).

The major difference between the tests published in 1960 and 1984 was the frequent use of alpha-adjusted procedures. These were practically nonexistent in 1960. In order to control for the effect of alpha adjustment, we calculated the power of each unit of analysis both including and excluding these procedures. In the latter case, alpha-adjusted tests like t tests, F tests, and chi-square were treated as if they were not adjusted, and multiple comparison procedures were excluded. For the Newman-Keuls, Duncan, and Tukey procedures the tables of Harter (1969) were used, and for the Scheffé test the tables of Hager and Möller (1985, 1986) were used.[2]

Results

The 1984 volume of the *Journal of Abnormal Psychology* contained 56 articles. One of them discussed previous research and contained no statistical tests; another used descriptive statistics concerning the major hypotheses and only one marginal test. These two articles were not evaluated. The remaining 54 articles employed statistical testing of hypotheses in 64 experiments. Alpha-adjusted procedures were used in 28 articles (31 experiments). In seven articles (seven experiments) at least some research hypotheses were stated as statistical null hypotheses. In these cases, any conclusion

---

[2] The number of tests, the test statistic used, the n used and whether a test concerned a major or minor hypothesis were evaluated by an independent rater. This rater analyzed 10 randomly chosen articles. The average amount of agreement between the authors and the independent rater was 98%.

that nonsignificance supports the research hypotheses is unwarranted without power considerations.

Remarks on power were found in only two cases, and nobody estimated the power of his or her tests. In four additional articles, alpha was mentioned, either by saying that it was set at a certain level (.05) before the experiment or by referring to the danger of alpha inflation. No author discussed why a certain alpha or n was chosen or what effect size was looked for. This first result shows that concern about power is almost nonexistent, at least in print.

Our calculations of power, based on either experiments or articles as units of analysis, resulted in practically identical values, the median and maximum absolute deviations being .01 and .04, respectively. Similarly, the tests of major and minor hypotheses were indistinguishable with respect to average power. For these reasons, we do not distinguish between these here, and we report the power of major tests using experiments as a unit. Table 2 reports the power of major tests using experiments as units, excluding alpha-adjusted procedures. This simulates the situation 24 years earlier, when those procedures were not common. A small number of experiments had very high power (see columns labeled *Small effects* and *Medium effects*); because of these outliers, we consider the medians rather than the means as

TABLE 2

Power of 64 Experiments Published in the 1984 Volume of the *Journal of Abnormal Psychology*, Excluding Alpha-Adjusted Procedures (Alpha = .05, Two-Tailed Tests)

Power	Small effects		Medium effects		Large effects	
	Frequency	Cumulative percentage	Frequency	Cumulative percentage	Frequency	Cumulative percentage
.99	1	100	5	100	21	100
.95–.98	—	98	—	92	4	67
.90–.94	—	98	2	92	8	61
.80–.89	—	98	6	89	12	48
.70–.79	3	98	4	80	7	30
.60–.69	1	94	6	73	6	19
.50–.59	—	94	4	64	2	9
.40–.49	1	92	7	58	2	6
.30–.39	5	91	10	47	1	3
.20–.29	8	83	15	31	1	2
.10–.19	34	70	4	8	—	—
.05–.09	11	17	1	2	—	—
N	64	—	64	—	64	—
M		.21		.50		.84
Mdn		.14		.44		.90
SD		.19		.27		.18
Q_1		.10		.28		.76
Q_3		.22		.70		.99

representing the average experiment's power. The median power for small, medium, and large effects was .14, .44, and .90, respectively. Twenty-four years earlier, the median power was .17, .46, and .89, respectively. As a general result, therefore, the power has not increased after 24 years. Although there are now a small percentage of experiments in which the chance of finding a significant result if there is an effect is high, even for small and medium effects, the respective median power for medium effects is slightly lower than that 24 years earlier.

For the purpose of comparison with the 1960 volume, where alpha adjustment was practically nonexistent, we have ignored these techniques in calculating the power in Table 2. However, as was mentioned previously, about 50% of all articles used at least one of the various alpha-adjusted procedures to test major research hypotheses. Because the power increases with alpha, the real power of the 64 experiments is smaller than that in Table 2. The effect of the alpha-adjusted procedures on the power of the tests is shown in Table 3, both for the entire set of experiments and for those using adjustment procedures. Results show that the use of alpha adjustment in 1984 decreased the real median power considerably. Because of the emphasis on alpha adjustment, the median power of detecting a medium-sized effect if there is one is only .37. Thus, we must conclude that 24 years later, the power of the tests has decreased instead of increased. The two bottom rows in Table 3 show an interesting state of affairs. Experiments using alpha-adjusted procedures have on the average smaller power than those that do not, even when these procedures are excluded from our calculations. This smaller power is then once more diminished by the adjustment, resulting in a median power of .28 for medium effects. Thus the researchers using alpha adjustment designed their experiments as if they believed that alpha adjustment compensated for the factors that increase power (such as large n), whereas in fact it decreases power.

TABLE 3
Impact of Alpha Adjustment on the Power of the 64 Experiments From the 1984 Volume of the *Journal of Abnormal Psychology* (Values Are Medians)

Condition	Effect size		
	Small	Medium	Large
All experiments ($N = 64$)			
Including alpha adjustment	.12	.37	.86
Excluding alpha adjustment	.14	.44	.90
Experiments using alpha adjustment ($N = 31$)			
Including alpha adjustment	.10	.28	.72
Excluding alpha adjustment	.14	.37	.85

The ratio of beta to alpha implies a conception of the relative seriousness of the two possible errors. This ratio varies between 14:1 and 11:1 for the conditions in Table 3, assuming a medium effect size. This means that researchers act as if they believe that mistakenly rejecting the null hypothesis is 11 to 14 times more serious than mistakenly accepting it.

We now shall address a specific issue: null hypotheses as research hypotheses. As was stated previously, in seven experiments (11%) at least some null hypotheses (no difference between treatments) were operationalizations of the research hypotheses. None of these tests became significant, and this result was unanimously interpreted by the authors as a confirmation of their research hypothesis. The power of these tests should have been particularly high in order to justify such conclusions (e.g., .95, which would correspond roughly to the case in which alpha = .05 and H_1 is the research hypothesis). Otherwise, in the case of unknown and probably low power, a nonsignificant result signifies that no conclusion should be drawn, that is, that one should not affirm the null hypothesis with an uncontrolled error rate (beta error) and that the experiment probably was a waste of time and money. The actual median power in these nonsignificant tests was .25, with a range between .13 and .67 for a medium-sized effect. This means that the experimental conditions, such as number of observations, were set up in such a way that given a true medium effect, the research (null) hypothesis would nevertheless be "confirmed" in 75% of the cases. There can be no doubt that such tests of research hypotheses are empirically worthless and the positive conclusions unwarranted, and the question arises, How can such tests and conclusions be accepted and published in a major journal?

DISCUSSION

We found almost no concern with power expressed in the 1984 volume, and no increase in the power of tests from 1960 to 1984, but rather a considerable decrease of power due to the frequent use of alpha-adjusted procedures. J. Cohen's (1962) seminal power analysis of the *Journal of Abnormal and Social Psychology* seems to have had no noticeable effect on actual practice as demonstrated in the *Journal of Abnormal Psychology* 24 years later.[3] Must we conclude that researchers stubbornly neglect a major

---

[3] Although the power did not increase over the years, at least in the present case study, references to power as measured by the citation frequency of J. Cohen's (1969, 1977) book multiply. The Science Citation Index (including additional citations in the Social Science Citation Index) reports 4, 13, 83, 193, and 214 citations for the years 1971, 1975, 1980, 1985, and 1987, respectively. This indicates growing attention to the issue and, possibly, differences between journals.

methodological issue over decades? Or should we assume that they are intuitively right and that we really do not need more power than .37?

Comparability

One way to defend research practice against our conclusion of "no change in low power" would be to assume that Cohen's criterion for a medium effect does not hold for both the 1960 and the 1984 volumes and that effects actually studied in 1984 were considerably larger, which implies larger power. For instance, if the 1960 studies were primarily of problems that yielded small effect sizes, but the 1984 studies were of problems that yielded medium-sized effects, this would suggest a change in power. Because none of the articles specified the sought-after effect size before the experiment (as Neyman-Pearson logic implies one should), we can check this conjecture only with respect to the actual sample effect sizes (determined after the experiment). As we mentioned earlier, sample effect sizes were not determined by Cohen for the 1960 volume; he instead used rule-of-thumb definitions for effect sizes. Thus we calculated effect sizes for both the 1960 and the 1984 volumes, in order to determine whether there was an increase in sample effect size.

To test the comparability of actual sample effect sizes between 1960 and 1984, we drew random samples of 20 (experimental) articles from each of the volumes. Sample effect sizes were again calculated separately for major and minor tests and for articles and experiments as units (the 1960 sample contained 20 experiments, the 1984 sample, 25 experiments). The median effect sizes were .31 in the 1960 sample and .27 in the 1984 sample (all effect sizes were expressed as Friedman's r_m).[4] These median effect sizes were identical under all the conditions mentioned here. The ranges were .12 to .69 and .08 to .64, respectively. This shows (a) that Cohen's definition, assuming a medium effect size (Pearson r) of .40 (J. Cohen, 1962) and

---

[4] Calculations of sample effect sizes were based on degrees of freedom, values of test statistics, p values, and n reported, following Friedman (1968). In cases of missing information, we proceeded in the following way. If only means and variances were specified in t tests, we calculated the point-biserial correlation coefficient, following J. Cohen (1977). If a test result was only described as not significant and the n for the test could be determined, we calculated the sample effect size for $p = .05$ and divided the value by a factor of 2. We consider this to be a $p = .05$ and divided the value by a factor of 2. We consider this to be a reasonable approximation, but it results in a tendency to obtain larger sample effect sizes for smaller ns. Therefore, we also made a second calculation in which sample effect sizes for nonsignificant results were assumed to be zero. This second calculation resulted in median sample effect sizes that were .02 and .05 smaller than those reported in the text, for the 1960 and 1984 volumes, respectively. It should be noted that values in the text that follows are calculated using the first method. If authors reported p values only, but not the value of the test statistic, the latter was inferred using the tables of Dunn and Clark (1974) and Hager and Möller (1985). Tests for multivariate procedures (e.g., multivariate analysis of variance), alpha-adjusted procedures, and coefficients of reliability (e.g., interrater reliability) were not included in the analyses. The procedure for estimating sample effect sizes was the same for the 1960 and the 1984 volumes.

.30 (J. Cohen, 1969), was quite close to the actual median sample effect size found in our analysis, and most important, (b) that sample effect sizes did not increase from 1960 to 1984. In fact, our results show the opposite tendency: Median sample effect sizes decreased slightly. These results speak for the comparability of actual sample effect sizes and contradict the assumption of an increase in power due to an increase in actual sample effect size.

Furthermore, our analysis provides a check of Cohen's judgment of a medium effect size in the 1960 volume. Recall that in his original study, he defined $r = .40$ as a medium effect size, and so did we in the present study. Using his own criteria for comparing various measures of effect size (J. Cohen, 1977, p. 82), we calculated that a point biserial $r_p = .32$ corresponds to $r = .40$. Because Friedman's r_m is roughly equivalent to r_p (for this, see Cohen, 1965, pp. 104–105), we may conclude that Cohen's judgment of a medium effect size of $r_p = .32$ corresponds closely to the actual sample median of .31 found in our analysis of the 1960 volume. Although a strict numerical comparison poses numerous difficulties, we now have evidence that his judgment was very close to the true median sample effect size.

Intuitions on Compensation

As was mentioned previously, power is a function of effect size, n, and alpha. Assuming that alpha is constant, concern with power should lead experimenters to compensate for a small expected population effect size by obtaining a large n, and vice versa. Although we have established that with the exception of two articles in the 1984 volume, nobody talks about power in print, researchers might follow this compensation principle intuitively. In particular, if there was a change in intuitions, then the correlation between effect size and n should be negative and larger than that in 1960.

Because single experiments often involved numerous tests with varying ns, we checked the intuitions with respect to both n and the number of subjects N (as given in the subjects sections). The latter is probably the more salient figure for the experimenter. For the actual sample effect sizes available, we calculated a Pearson correlation (major hypotheses only) between sample effect size and N of −.35 in 1960 and .01 in 1984. Inspection of the data revealed that the zero correlation was due to one experiment that investigated an unusually large number of subjects (725) and that found a rather large sample effect size (.34). Excluding this experiment, the correlation was −.37 in the 1984 sample, similar to that in 1960. The corresponding values for all tests (including minor hypotheses) were −.34 and −.33 in the 1960 and 1984 samples, respectively. However, the Ns reported in the subjects sections may not be the best guess for the actual ns, because there are procedures such as the analysis of variance (ANOVA) with repeated measures that use a much larger n for the single test. The correlations between average ns and sample effect sizes per experiment were $-.34$ in 1960 and $-.47$ in 1984.[5] The corresponding values for all tests (including minor hypotheses) were $.07$ in 1960 and $-.36$ in 1984. The latter, less negative values could be seen to indicate some sensitivity for the relationship between power and the relative importance of a test, especially in the 1960 sample. However, the small difference in the correlations for major tests does not seem to warrant any conclusions of a change in intuitive power considerations.

Tentative Explanation for the Zero Impact of Power Studies

The question of how psychologists came to neglect power in the first place is a historical one. The question of why they continue to neglect power seems to be an institutional one. For historical reasons, psychologists became familiar first with Fisher's theory of null hypothesis testing, from about 1935 on, and only later, during World War II, with Neyman and Pearson's statistical theory (Acree, 1979; Gigerenzer, 1987; Lovie, 1979; Rucci & Tweney, 1980). Textbooks of psychology and education first taught the Fisherian message, but after World War II, textbook writers realized the impact of Neyman-Pearsonian theory within statistics proper and began to supplement the null hypotheses testing theory with concepts of the latter theory, such as power. The incorporation of Type II error and power was done reluctantly. This is not surprising, because Fisher (1955) himself rejected Neyman and Pearson's emphasis on power and utility analyses, and power could not be calculated within null hypothesis testing theory. For instance, in the third edition of his influential *Fundamental Statistics in Psychology and Education*, Guilford (1956) still declared the concept of power as too complicated to discuss (p. 217). Finally, the concepts of Type II error and power were added by the majority of textbook writers to the framework of null hypothesis testing but could not be numerically determined, because most textbooks did not teach students to set up a second point hypothesis, as in Neyman-Pearson theory, which would have been necessary for the calculation. The resulting hybrid theory was usually anonymously presented as inferential statistics per se, and the

---

[5] For correlations and chi-square (in the sample almost exclusively with $df = 1$), we used the given n for the test. The n for t tests was $df + 1$ and the n for F tests was $df_{denominator} + df_{numerator} + 1$ for main effects and $df_{denominator}$ + number of relevant cells for interactions. Occasionally occurring nonparametric tests were treated like their parametric counterparts. The correlations were calculated, excluding the outlier in the 1984 sample (see text) and one 1960 experiment in which a self-constructed ANOVA technique was used. Inclusion of these two extreme outliers would lead again to zero correlations ($-.09$) and positive correlations ($.35$), respectively.

controversial issues and the existence of alternative theories about statistical inference were neglected (Gigerenzer & Murray, 1987). This was a strange and rare event in psychology, where the presentation of alternatives and controversies had always been the rule rather than the exception and where no one would dare to mix, say, the theories of Freud and Adler and to present the result as psychoanalysis per se. With hindsight, the great error during that time (when inferential statistics became institutionalized) was the attempt to present ideas from two fighting camps as a single monolithic body of statistical knowledge rather than to present one theory after the other and to make their different concepts and points of view explicit. This historical accident suggested a single, mechanical solution to the problem of scientific inference, and there seemed to be no need for methodological alternatives, because no controversial issues seemed to exist.

The institutionalization of this hybrid theory, patched together from the opposing theories of Fisher and Neyman and Pearson and sometimes supplemented by a Bayesian interpretation of what significance means, was documented recently (Gigerenzer et al., 1989, chaps. 3 and 6). This attempt to fuse opposing theories into a single truth generated, as a necessary consequence, confusion and illusions about the meaning of the basic concepts. For instance, Fisher and Neyman and Pearson never agreed whether the level of significance should be determined before or after the experiment, whether it applied to the single experiment or to the long-run frequency of errors, whether significance generated new knowledge about hypotheses or not, and so on. Therefore, it is not surprising that the hybrid theory became a steady source of contradiction and confusion (see, e.g., Bakan, 1966; Oakes, 1986). The ongoing neglect of power seems to be a direct consequence of this state of affairs. With respect to this, important confusions are the ideas that the level of significance determines (a) the probability that a significant result will be found in a replication and (b) the probability that H_1 (or H_0) is true. These and related confusions can be found in well-known American and German textbooks (e.g., Bortz, 1985, p. 149; Brown, 1973, pp. 522–523; Nunnally, 1975, p. 195) and in editorials of major journals (e.g., Melton 1962, pp. 553–554). Furthermore, as research on statistical intuitions of researchers in psychology indicates, these confusions seem to be shared by many of our colleagues. Tversky and Kahneman (1971) inferred from a questionnaire distributed at meetings of the Mathematical Psychology Group and of the American Psychological Association that most respondents have wrong intuitions about the relationship between number of observations and power, that is, that they systematically overestimate the power of experiments and believe in the "law of small numbers." Oakes (1986) tested 70 academic psychologists and reported that 96% held the erroneous opinion that the level of significance specified the probability that either H_0 or H_1 was true. Given such misconceptions, the calculation of power may appear obsolete, because intuitively, the level of significance already seems to determine all we want to know.

Moreover, the average researcher is not entirely to blame for conducting studies with a power of only .37. It is a historical accident that Fisher's theory of null hypothesis testing, which opposed power calculations in the Neyman-Pearson framework, became the starting point of the inference revolution in psychology. But the researcher's alertness to alternatives has been dulled by the presentation of a hybrid theory as a monolithic, apparently uncontroversial theory of statistical inference. This may be responsible for current conservative attitudes, which shy away from a practical innovation. Innovations that are accepted, such as alpha adjustment, are those that adjust the theory that was historically the first: null hypothesis testing and its emphasis on the level of significance. The cumulations of beta errors, in contrast, have been payed almost no attention (see, however, Westermann & Hager, 1986).

This historical development explains why psychologists were not familiar with calculating the power of a test in the first place; and the merging of null hypothesis testing with Neyman-Pearson theory and the presentation of the resulting hybrid theory as a monolithic statistical theory explains to some degree the ongoing neglect. Even studies of power seem to have no effect on the power of studies, at least in the case investigated in this article. What can be done about this situation? We believe there is only one force that can effect a change, and that is the same force that helped to institutionalize null hypothesis testing as the sine qua non for publication, namely, the editors of the major journals. This situation will not change until the first editor of a major journal writes into his or her editorial policy statement that authors should estimate the power of their tests if they perform significance testing, and in particular if H_0 is the research hypothesis.

Do We Really Need Power?

Of the three major approaches to inductive inference and hypothesis testing—Bayes, Fisher, and Neyman-Pearson—power is a concept of central importance only in the latter. Thus, a fundamental question emerges: Do we need power at all? The answer to this provocative question depends on whether researchers believe that they have to make a decision after an experiment or not. Neyman-Pearson theory aims at a decision between hypotheses, and Neyman and Pearson's examples focus on applications such as quality control, in which the statistical procedure serves to direct a final practical decision, such as stopping the production if the quality has decreased. In fact, Neyman and Pearson's joint papers contain no application in which a scientific hypothesis was the sole or primary object (Birnbaum, 1977, p. 30). Although Fisher ridiculed their reject–accept notion in the context of scientific inference, his earlier work, in particular *The Design of Experiments* (Fisher, 1935/1966), which was so influential on psychology, could be understood by many as implying a reject notion on a conventional 5% level of significance. In fact, in the hybrid theory that was institutionalized in psychology, his null hypothesis testing became linked with the reject–accept notion. The essential question is whether psychological research needs yes–no types of decisions, as in quality control and related areas. We believe that there is no unique answer and that an answer depends on the specific content and will more often be positive in applied research than elsewhere. However, given the general belief among psychologists in the decision type of statistical inference, knowledge about power remains indispensable. If, at a future point, the influence of both Fisherian and Neyman and Pearsonian theories on psychological methodology can be transcended,[6] then the perceived importance of decisions based on significance might decrease, and other methodological principles could gain or regain importance. An example would be the fundamental principle of controlling the error before the experiment rather than after, that is, of manipulating conditions, tasks, and measurement procedures before the experiment until one has a very small error in the dependent variable. Today, fast data collection methods are often preferred, and the error is dealt with by inserting it into the t or F value after the experiment has been performed. One tends to wait to see whether it will turn out to be significant or not. Gosset, who developed the t test in 1908, anticipated this overconcern with significance at the expense of other methodological concerns: "Obviously the important thing . . . is to have a low real error, not to have a 'significant' result at a particular station. The latter seems to me to be nearly valueless in itself" (quoted in Pearson, 1939, p. 247). As long as decisions based on conventional levels of significance are given top priority, however, theoretical conclusions based on significance or nonsignificance remain unsatisfactory without knowledge about power.

REFERENCES

Acree, M. C. (1979). Theories of statistical inference in psychological research: A historico-critical study. *Dissertation Abstracts International, 39*, 5073B. (University Microfilms No. 7907000)

---

[6] Here, we refer to those parts of Fisher's and of Neyman and Pearson's theories that have been institutionalized as an instrument of scientific inference in psychology; there is of course much more contained in their theories.

Arvey, R. D., Cole, D. S., Hazucha, J. F., & Hartanto, F. M. (1985). Statistical power of training evaluation designs. *Personnel Psychology, 38,* 493–507.

Atkinson, D. R., Furlang, M. J., & Wampold, B. E. (1982). Statistical significance, reviewer evaluations, and the scientific process: Is there a (statistically) significant relationship? *Journal of Counseling Psychology, 29,* 189–194.

Bakan, D. (1966). The test of significance in psychological research. *Psychological Bulletin, 66,* 423–437.

Birnbaum, A. (1977). The Neyman-Pearson theory as decision theory, and as inference theory; with a criticism of the Lindsley-Savage argument for Bayesian theory. *Synthese, 36,* 19–49.

Bortz, J. (1985). *Lehrbuch der Statistik: Für Sozialwissenschaftler* (2nd ed.). Berlin: Springer-Verlag.

Bredenkamp, J. (1972). *Der Signifikanztest in der psychologischen Forschung,* Frankfurt/Main, Federal Republic of Germany: Akademische Verlagsgesellschaft.

Brewer, J. K. (1972). On the power of statistical tests in the American Educational Research Journal. *American Educational Research Journal, 9,* 391–401.

Brown, F. L. (1973). Introduction to statistical methods in psychology. Appendix in G. A. Miller & R. Buckhout, *Psychology: The science of mental life.* New York: Harper & Row.

Chase, L. J., & Baran, S. J. (1976). An assessment of quantitative research in mass communication. *Journalism Quarterly, 53,* 308–311.

Chase, L. J., & Chase, R. B. (1976). A statistical power analysis of applied psychological research. *Journal of Applied Psychology, 61,* 234–237.

Chase, L. J., & Tucker, R. K. (1975). A power-analytic examination of contemporary communication research. *Speech Monographs, 42,* 29–41.

Chase, L. J., & Tucker, R. K. (1976). Statistical power: Derivation, development, and data-analytic implications. *The Psychological Record, 26,* 473–486.

Cohen, J. (1962). The statistical power of abnormal—social psychological research: A review. *Journal of Abnormal and Social Psychology, 65,* 145–153.

Cohen, J. (1965). Some statistical issues in psychological research. In B. B. Wolman (Ed.), *Handbook of clinical psychology* (pp. 95–121). New York: McGraw-Hill.

Cohen, J. (1969). *Statistical power analysis for the behavioral sciences.* New York: Academic Press.

Cohen, J. (1970). Approximate power and sample size determination for common one-sample and two-sample hypothesis tests. *Educational and Psychological Measurement, 30,* 811–831.

Cohen, J. (1977). *Statistical power analysis for the behavioral sciences* (2nd ed.). New York: Academic Press.

Cohen, L. H. (1979). Clinical psychologists' judgments of the scientific merit and clinical relevance of psychotherapy outcome research. *Journal of Consulting and Clinical Psychology, 47,* 421–423.

Cooper, H., & Findley, M. (1982). Expected effect sizes: Estimates for statistical power analysis in social psychology. *Personality and Social Psychology Bulletin, 8,* 168–173.

Coursol, A., & Wagner, E. E. (1986). Effect of positive findings on submission and acceptance rates. A note on meta analysis bias. *Professional Psychology: Research and Practice, 17*, 136–137.

Dunn, O. J., & Clark, V.A. (1974). *Applied statistics: Analysis of variance and regression*. New York: Wiley.

Edgell, S. E., & Noon, S. M. (1984). Effect of violation of normality on the *t* test of the correlation coefficient. *Psychological Bulletin, 95*, 576–583.

Fisher, R. A. (1966). *The design of experiments* (8th ed.). Edinburgh, Scotland: Oliver & Boyd. (Original work published 1935)

Fisher, R. A. (1955). Statistical methods and scientific induction. *Journal of the Royal Statistical Society, Ser. B, 17*, 69–78.

Fisher, R. A. (1956). *Statistical methods and scientific inference*. Edinburgh, Scotland: Oliver & Boyd.

Freiman, J. A., Chalmers, T. C., Smith, H., Jr., & Kuebler, R. R. (1978). The importance of beta, the type II error and sample size in the design and interpretation of the randomized control trial: Survey of 71 "negative trials." *The New England Journal of Medicine, 299*, 690–694.

Friedman, H. (1968). Magnitude of experimental effect and a table for its rapid estimation. *Psychological Bulletin, 70*, 245–251.

Gigerenzer, G. (1987). Probabilistic thinking and the fight against subjectivity. In L. Krüger, G. Gigerenzer, & M. Morgan (Eds.), *The probabilistic revolution: Vol. 2. Ideas in the sciences*. Cambridge, MA: MIT Press.

Gigerenzer, G., & Murray, D. J. (1987). *Cognition as intuitive statistics*. Hillsdale, NJ: Erlbaum.

Gigerenzer, G., Swijtink, Z., Porter, T., Daston, L. J., Beatty, J., & Krüger, L. (1980). *The empire of chance: How probability changed science and everyday life*. Cambridge, England: Cambridge University Press.

Greenwald, A. G. (1975). Consequences of prejudice against the null hypothesis. *Psychological Bulletin, 82*, 1–20.

Guilford, J. P. (1956). *Fundamental statistics in psychology and education* (3rd ed.). New York: McGraw-Hill.

Haase, R. F. (1974). Power analysis of research in counselor education. *Counselor Education and Supervision, 14*, 124–132.

Haase, R. F., Waechter, D. M., & Solomon, G. S. (1982). How signficant is a significant difference? Average effect size of research in Counseling Psychology. *Journal of Counseling Psychology, 29*, 58–65.

Hager, W., & Möller, H. (1985). *Zentrale F-Verteilungen für zufällige Effekte und Signifikanzbeurteilungen*. Unpublished manuscript, Institute for Psychology, University of Göttingen, Göttingen, Federal Republic of Germany.

Hager, W., & Möller, H. (1986). Tables and procedures for the determination of power and sample sizes in univariate and multivariate analyses of variance and regression. *Biometrical Journal, 28*, 647–663.

Harter, H. L., (1969). *Order statistics and their use in testing and estimation: Vol. 1. Tests based on range and studentized range of samples from a normal population*. Washington, DC: U.S. Government Printing Office.

Katzer, J., & Sodt, J. (1973). An analysis of the use of statistical testing in communication research. *The Journal of Communication, 23,* 251–265.

King, D. S. (1985). Statistical power of the controlled research on wheat gluten and schizophrenia. *Biological Psychiatry, 20,* 785–787.

Kroll, R. M., & Chase, L. J. (1975). Communication disorders: A power analytic assessment of recent research. *Journal of Communication Disorders, 8,* 237–247.

Lovie, A. D. (1979). The analysis of variance in experimental psychology: 1934-1945. *British Journal of Mathematical and Statistical Psychology, 32,* 151–178.

Melton, A. W. (1962). Editorial. *Journal of Experimental Psychology, 64,* 553–557.

Murray, L. W., & Dosser, D. A., Jr. (1987). How significant is a significant difference? Problems with the measurement of magnitude of effect. *Journal of Counseling Psychology, 34,* 68–72.

Nunally, J. C. (1975). *Introduction to statistics for psychology and education.* New York: McGraw-Hill.

Oakes, M. (1986). *Statistical inference: A commentary for the social and behavioral sciences.* New York: Wiley.

O'Neill, R., & Wetherill, G. B. (1971). The present state of multiple comparison methods (With discussions). *Journal of the Royal Statistical Society, Ser. B, 33,* 218–250.

Ottenbacher, K. (1982). Statistical power and research in occupational therapy. *Occupational Therapy Journal of Research, 2,* 13–25.

Pearson, E. S. (1939). "Student" as statistician. *Biometrika, 30,* 210–250.

Petrinovich, L. F., & Hardyck, C. D. (1969). Error rates for multiple comparison methods: Some evidence concerning the frequency of erroneous conclusions. *Psychological Bulletin, 71,* 43–54.

Rucci, A. J., & Tweney, R. D. (1980). Analysis of variance and the "second discipline" of scientific psychology: A historical account, *Psychological Bulletin, 87,* 166–184.

Sawyer, A. G., & Ball, A. D. (1981). Statistical power and effect size in marmarketing research. *Journal of Marketing Research, 18,* 275–290.

Stegmüller, W. (1973). *"Jenseits von Popper und Carnap": Die logischen Grundlagen des statistischen Schliessens.* Berlin: Springer-Verlag.

Trachtman, J. N., Giambalvo, V., & Dippner, R. S. (1978). On the assumptions concerning the assumptions of a t test. *The Journal of General Psychology, 99,* 107–116.

Tversky, A., & Kahneman, D. (1971). Belief in the law of small numbers. *Psychological Bulletin, 76,* 105–110.

Westermann, R., & Hager, W. (1986). Error probabilities in educational and psychological research. *Journal of Educational Statistics, 11,* 117–146.

22

CONSEQUENCES OF PREJUDICE AGAINST THE NULL HYPOTHESIS

ANTHONY G. GREENWALD

In a standard college dictionary (*Webster's New World*, College Edition, 1960), *null* is defined as "invalid; amounting to nought; of no value, effect, or consequence; insignificant." In statistical hypothesis testing, the *null hypothesis* most often refers to the hypothesis of no difference between treatment effects or of no association between variables. Interestingly, in the behavioral sciences, researchers' null hypotheses frequently satisfy the nonstatistical definition of *null*, being "of no value," "insignificant," and presumably "invalid." My aims here are to document this state of affairs, to examine its consequences for the archival accumulation of scientific knowledge, and lastly, to make a positive case for the formulation of more potent and acceptable null hypotheses as a part of an overall research strategy.

Because of my familiarity with its literature, most of the illustrative

Reprinted from the *Psychological Bulletin, 82,* 1–20. Copyright 1975 by the American Psychological Association.

Preparation of this report was facilitated by grants from National Science Foundation (GS–3050) and U.S. Public Health Service (MH–20527–02).

material I use is drawn from social psychology. This should not be read as an implication that the problems being discussed are confined to social psychology. I suspect they are equally characteristic of other behavioral science fields that are lacking in well-established organizing theoretical systems.

The Lowly Null Hypothesis

My paraphrasing of some widespread beliefs of behavioral scientists concerning the null hypothesis appears below. Some partial sources for the content of this listing are Festinger (1953, pp. 142–143), Wilson and Miller (1964), Aronson and Carlsmith (1969, p. 21), and Mills (1969, pp. 442–448).

1. Given the characteristics of statistical analysis procedures, a null result is only a basis for uncertainty. Conclusions about relationships among variables should be based only on rejections of null hypotheses.

2. Little knowledge is achieved by finding out that two variables are unrelated. Science advances, rather, by discovering relationships between variables.

3. If statistically significant effects are obtained in an experiment, it is fairly certain that the experiment was done properly.

4. On the other hand, it is inadvisable to place confidence in results that support a null hypothesis because there are too many ways (including incompetence of the researcher), other than the null hypothesis being true, for obtaining a null result.

Given the existence of such beliefs among behavioral science researchers, it is not surprising that some observers have arrived at conclusions such as:

Many null hypotheses tested by classical procedures are scientifically preposterous, not worthy of a moment's credence even as approximations. (Edwards, 1965, pp. 401–402)

It {the null hypothesis} is usually formulated for the express purpose of being rejected. (Siegel, 1956, p.7)

Refutations of Null Hypothesis "Cultural Truisms"

I am sure that many behavioral science researchers endorse the beliefs previously enumerated but would have difficulty in providing a rational defense for these beliefs should they be strongly attacked. That is, these attitudes toward the null hypothesis may have some of the characteristics of cultural truisms as described by McGuire (1964). Cultural truisms are beliefs that are so widely and unquestioningly held that their adherents (a) are unlikely ever to have heard them being attacked and may therefore (b) have difficulty defending them against an attack. If I am correct, the reader will have difficulty defending the preceding beliefs against the following attacks (the numbered paragraphs correspond to those in the preceding listing.) Briefly stated, these attacks are:

1. The notion that you cannot prove the null hypothesis is true in the same sense that it is also true that you cannot prove *any* exact (or point) hypothesis. However, there is no reason for believing that an estimate of some parameter that is near a zero point is less valid than an estimate that is significantly different from zero. Currently available Bayesian techniques (e.g., Phillips, 1973) allow methods of describing acceptability of null hypotheses.

2. The point is commonly made that theories predict relationships between variables; therefore, finding relationships between variables (i.e., non-null results) helps to confirm theories and thereby to advance science. This argument ignores the fact that scientific advance is often most powerfully achieved by *rejecting* theories (cf. Platt, 1964). A major strategy for doing this is to demonstrate that relationships predicted by a theory are not obtained, and this would often require acceptance of a null hypothesis.

3. I am aware of no reason for thinking that a statistically significant rejection of a null hypothesis is an appropriate basis for assuming that the conceptually intended variables were manipulated or measured validly. The significant result (barring Type I error) does indicate that some relationship or effect was observed, but that is all it indicates. The researcher who would claim that his data show a relationship between two variables should be as clearly obliged to show that those variables are the ones intended as should the researcher who would claim that his data show the absence of a relationship.

4. Perhaps the most damaging accusation against the null hypothesis is that incompetence is more likely to lead to erroneous nonsignificant, "negative," or null results than to erroneous significant or "positive" results. There is some substance to this accusation—when the incompetence has the effect of introducing noise or unsystematic error into data. Examples of this sort of incompetence are the use of unreliable paper-and-pencil measures, conducting research in a "noisy" setting (i.e., one with important extraneous variables uncontrolled), unreliable apparatus functioning, inaccurate placement of recording or stimulating electrodes, random errors in data recording or transcribing, and making too few observations.

These types of incompetence are often found in the work of the novice researcher and are proper cause for caution in accepting null findings as adequate evidence for the absence of effects or relationships. Some other very common types of incompetence are much more likely to produce false positive or significant results. These types of incompetence result in the introduction of *systematic* errors into data collection. Examples of such sources of artifact (cf. Rosenthal & Rosnow, 1969) are experimenter bias, inappropriate demand characteristics, nonrandom sampling, invalid or contaminated manipulations or measures, systematic apparatus malfunction (e.g., errors in calibration), or systematic error (either accidental or intentional) in data recording or transcribing. This latter category of incompetence is by no means confined to novices and may be quite difficult to detect, particularly since our existing customs encourage greater suspicion of null findings than of significant findings.

Behavioral Symptoms of Anti-Null-Hypothesis Prejudice

We should not perhaps be very disturbed about the existence of the beliefs previously listed if those beliefs would prove to be unrelated to behavior. The following is a list of some possible behavioral symptoms of prejudice against null hypotheses: (a) designing research so that the personal prediction of the researcher is identified with rejection rather than acceptance of the null hypothesis; (b) submitting results for publication more often when the null hypothesis has been rejected than when it has not been rejected; (c) continuing research on a problem when results have been close to rejection of the null hypothesis ("near significant"), while abandoning the problem if rejection of the null hypothesis is not close; (d) elevating ancillary hypothesis tests or fortuitous findings to prominence in reports of studies for which the major dependent variables did not provide a clear rejection of the null hypothesis; (e) revising otherwise adequate operationalizations of variables when unable to obtain rejection of the null hypothesis and continuing to revise until the null hypothesis is (at last!) rejected or until the problem is abandoned without publication; (f) failing to report initial data collections (renamed as "pilot data" or "false starts") in a series of studies that eventually leads to a prediction-confirming rejection of the null hypothesis; (g) failing to detect data analysis errors when an analysis has rejected the null hypothesis by miscomputation, while vigilantly checking and rechecking computations if the null hypothesis has not been rejected; and (h) using stricter editorial standards for evaluating manuscripts that conclude in favor of, rather than against, the null hypothesis.

Perhaps the enumeration of the items on this list will arouse sufficient recognition of symptoms in readers to convince them that the illness of anti-null-hypothesis prejudice indeed exists. However, just as a hypochondriac should have better evidence that he is ill than that the symptoms he has just heard about seem familiar, so should we have better evidence than symptom recognition for making conclusions about the existence of prejudice against the null hypothesis.

A Survey to Estimate Bias Against the Null Hypothesis

In order to obtain some more concrete evidence regarding the manifestations of anti-null-hypothesis prejudice, I conducted a survey of reviewers and authors of articles submitted to the *Journal of Personality and Social Psychology (JPSP)*. The sample included the primary (corresponding) authors and the reviewers for all manuscripts that I processed as an associate editor of *JPSP* during a 3-month period in 1973. The sample thus consisted of 48 authors and 47 reviewers to whom I sent a questionnaire. Returns were obtained from 36 authors (75%) and 39 reviewers (81%). The major items in the questionnaire assessed behavior in situations in which bias for or against the null hypothesis could occur. These situations were (a) initial formulation of a problems, (b) setting probabilities of Type I and Type II error, and (c) deciding what action to pursue once results were obtained. All questions were stated with reference to a test of the "focal hypothesis" for a new line of research. The focal hypothesis test was further defined as "the one hypothesis test that is of greatest importance" to the line of investigation. Responses were indicated on probability scales that could range from 0 to 1.00. The major results are given in Table 1.

With the exception of responses to two questions, the results for authors and reviewers were quite similar. This was not terribly surprising because there was substantial overlap between the populations from which these two subsamples were drawn. From Questions 4a and 4d it can be seen that authors reported they were more likely to report null hypothesis rejections and less likely to abandon the problem following a null hypothesis rejection than were reviewers. Given these rather limited differences, the following discussion of these data treats only the overall responses for the combined sample.

The questionnaire results gave several strong confirmations of existence of prejudice against the null hypothesis. In the stage of formulation of a problem, respondents indicated a strong preference for identifying their own predictions with an expected rejection, rather than an acceptance of the null hypothesis. The mean probability of the researcher's personal prediction being of the null hypothesis rejection (Question 1:

TABLE 1

Results of Survey of JPSP Authors and Reviewers to Determine
Prejudice Toward or Against the Null Hypothesis

Question	Mean responses for			
	Reviewers	Authors	All	$SD_{M_{all}}$
1. What is the probability that your typical prediction will be for a rejection (rather than an acceptance) of a null hypothesis?	.790 (39)	.829 (35)	.803 (74)	.021
2. Indicate the level of alpha you typically regard as a satisfactory basis for rejecting the null hypothesis.	.043 (39)	.049 (35)	.046 (74)	.002
3. Indicate the level of beta you would regard as a satisfactory basis for accepting the null hypothesis.	.292 (18)	.258 (19)	.274 (37)	.045
4. After an initial full-scale test of the focal hypothesis that allows rejection of the null hypothesis, what is the probability that you will				
(a) submit the results for publication before further data collection,	.408 (38)	.588 (35)	.494 (73)	.033
(b) conduct an exact replication before deciding whether to submit for publication,	.078 (38)	.069 (35)	.074 (73)	.009
(c) conduct a modified replication before deciding whether to submit,	.437 (38)	.289 (35)	.366 (73)	.027
(d) give up the problem.	.077 (38)	.053 (35)	.066 (73)	.012
Total	1.000	1.000	1.000	
5. After an initial full-scale test of the focal hypothesis that does not allow rejection of the null hypothesis, what is the probability that you will				
(a) submit the results for publication before further data collection,	.053 (37)	.064 (35)	.059 (73)	.014
(b) conduct an exact replication before deciding whether to submit for publication,	.107 (37)	.098 (36)	.102 (73)	.013
(c) conduct a modified replication before deciding whether to submit,	.592 (37)	.524 (36)	.558 (73)	.025
(d) give up the problem.	.248 (37)	.314 (36)	.280 (73)	.023
Total	1.000	1.000	1.000	

Note: Table entries are means of respondents' estimates of probabilities, based on the number of responses given in parentheses.

$\overline{X} = .81 \pm .04$) is substantially greater than .50.[1] This state of affairs is consistent with supposing that researchers set themselves the goal of confirming a theoretically predicted relation between variables more often than refuting one, despite good reason to believe that knowledge may advance more rapidly by the latter strategy (Platt, 1964).

In setting the probability of Type I error, respondents indicated relatively close adherence to the .05 alpha criterion (Question 2: $\overline{X} = .046 \pm .004$). Responses to Question 3 indicated a substantial lack of standard practice with regard to Type II errors (i.e., accepting the null hypothesis when in truth it should be rejected). About 50% of the respondents failed to answer the question requesting specification of a preferred Type II error (beta) criterion. Those who did indicate a Type II error criterion indicated much more tolerance for this type of error than for a Type I error, the resulting estimate of beta being approximately .30 (Question 3: $\overline{X} = .27 \pm .09$). This estimate, it should be noted, is in line with Cohen's (1962) conclusion that studies published in the *Journal of Abnormal and Social Psychology* were relatively low on power (probability of rejecting the null hypothesis when the alternative is true; power $= 1.00 - $ beta). In regard to tolerance for Type I and Type II errors then, the questionnaire respondents appeared biased *toward* null hypothesis acceptance in the sense that they reported more willingness to err by accepting, rather than rejecting, the null hypothesis. Such a conclusion would, I think, be quite misleading. Rather, responses to other questions not summarized in Table 1 and the frequency of nonresponse to Question 3 indicated that most resondents did not take seriously the idea of setting a Type II error criterion in advance. For example, the responses to questions asking for probability of setting alpha and beta criterions in advance of data collection indicated a .63 ($\pm.09$) probability that alpha would be set in advance of data collection, compared with only a .17 ($\pm.06$) probability that beta would be set in advance. Rather than indicating a prejudice toward acceptance of the null hypothesis then, I think the responses to the questions on alpha and beta indicate that acceptance of the null hypothesis is not usually treated as a viable research outcome.

In terms of what is done after completion of a full-scale data collection to test a focal hypothesis, a major bias is indicated in the .49 ($\pm.06$) probability of submitting a rejection of the null hypothesis for publication (Question 4a) compared to the low probability of .06 ($\pm.03$) for submitting a nonrejection of the null hypothesis for publication (Question 5a). A secondary bias is apparent in the probability of continuing with a problem and is computed conditionally upon the decision to write a report having

---

[1]The errors of estimates given are equal to the limits of 95% confidence intervals, approximately plus or minus twice the standard deviation of the estimated mean.

not been made following data collection. This derived index has a value of .86 (±.05) when the initial result is a rejection of the null hypothesis, compared to .70 (±.05) when the initial result is a nonrejection of the null hypothesis, indicating greater likelihood of proceeding in the former case.[2]

In sum, the questionnaire responses of a sample of contributors to the social psychological literature gave self-report evidence of substantial biases against the null hypothesis in formulating a research problem and in deciding what to do with the data once collected. In the following section, the impact of these biases on the content of the archival literature is considered.

A MODEL OF THE RESEARCH-PUBLICATION SYSTEM

The alpha criterion most commonly employed in the behavioral sciences is .05. Without giving the matter much thought, one may guess on this basis that approximately 1 in 20 publications may be an erroneous rejection of a true null hypothesis. However, some thought on the matter soon brings the discovery that the probability of a published article being a Type I error depends on much more than (a) the researcher's alpha criterion. The other determinants include (b) the probability of accepting the null hypothesis when it is false (Type II error or beta), (c) the a priori probability of an investigator selecting a problem for which the null hypothesis is true or false, (d) the probability of rejections versus nonrejections of the null hypothesis being submitted for publication, (e) the probability of the researcher's giving up in despair after achieving a rejection versus a nonrejection of the null hypothesis, and (f) the probability of an editor's accepting an article that reports a rejection versus a nonrejection of the null hypothesis. All of these probabilities represent opportunities for the occurrence of strategies that discriminate against the null hypothesis. The model I develop functions to derive consequences for the content of published literature from assumptions made about these strategies.

Model Description

In the model employed for the research–publication system (see Figure 1), a critical notion is that of a *focal hypothesis test*. It is assumed that in any line of investigation, there is one statistical test that is of major interest.

---

[2]In the case of a result rejecting the null hypothesis, this index is computed as {(4b + 4c) ÷ (4b + 4c + 4d)}, the numbers referring to the responses to the questions given in Table 1.

This may be a test for a main or interaction effect in an analysis of variance, a test of the difference between two groups or treatments, a test of correlation between two variables, and the like. This statistical test is assumed to be made in terms of a rejection or acceptance (nonrejection, if you prefer) of a null hypothesis of no main effect, no interaction, and so forth. In conducting this focal hypothesis test, the researcher is assumed to have formulated an extent of deviation from the null hypothesis of no main effect, no interaction, and so forth. In conducting this focal hypothesis test, the researcher is assumed to have formulated an extent of deviation from the null hypothesis (an alternative hypothesis, H_1) that he would like to be able to detect with probability (power) $1-\beta$. In practice, this formulation of H_1 may often be an implicit consequence of setting a critical region for rejection of the null hypothesis with a given risk, α, of Type I error. For example, assuming $\beta = \alpha$, the start of the critical region is effectively a midpoint between the null hypothesis and H_1.

In the model, the fate of a research problem is traced in terms of the probabilities of alternative outcomes at four types of choice points: (a) the researcher's formulation of a hypothesis, (b) his collection of data, (c) his evaluation of obtained results, and (d) an editor's judgment of a manuscript reporting the research results. At each of these points in the research–publication process, behavioral bias relating to the null hypothesis may enter. The model incorporates parameters that serve to quantify these biases, and these are listed here in their sequential order of occurrence in the research–publication process.

The Probability That the Null Hypothesis Is True For the Focal Hypothesis

Specification of this parameter requires a clear definition of the null hypothesis. If by the null hypothesis one refers to the hypothesis of *exactly* no difference or *exactly* no correlation, and so forth, then the initial probability of the null hypothesis being true must be regarded effectively as zero, as would be the probability of any other point hypothesis. In most cases, however, the investigator should not be concerned about the hypothesis that the true value of a statistic equals exactly zero, but rather about the hypothesis that the effect or relationship to be tested is so small as not to be usefully distinguished from zero. For the purposes of the model then, the probability of the null hypothesis being true becomes identified with the probability that the true state of affairs underlying the focal hypothesis is within a *null range* (cf. Hays, 1973, pp. 850–853). In the model, the probability that the investigator's focal hypothesis is one for which truth is within such a null range is represented as h_0. The probability that truth is outside this range is $h_1 = 1.00-h_0$. One would have to be omniscient to be assured of selecting accurate values for the h_0 and h_1 parameters. It seems, however, that the values of these parameters should be clearly weighted in the direction of starting with a false null hypothesis (i.e., $h_1 > h_0$). Some reasons for this are that (a) researchers identify their personal predictions predominantly with the falsity of the null hypothesis (see Table 1, Question 1), and there may often be good reason for them to make these predictions; and (b) as argued by McGuire (1973), there is usually at least a narrow sense in which most researchers' predictions are correct. For no outstandingly good reason, the values of .20 and .80 were selected for h_0 and h_1, respectively. To compensate for the difficulty of justifying this initial assumption, system results are given below for other values of these parameters.[3]

Outcome of Data Collection

As used here *data collection* refers to the researcher's activities subsequent to problem formulation, up to and including the statistical analysis of results. It is assumed that any such data collection can be characterized by probabilities of Type I and Type II errors that are either explicitly chosen by the investigator or else follow implicitly (cf. Cohen, 1962) from his choices of sample size, dependent measures, statistical tests, and the like. (Because investigators may often examine data midway in a planned piece of research and thereupon terminate or otherwise alter plans, the notion of data collection is somewhat vague in practice and must necessarily be so in the model). The outcome of a data collection will either be a rejection or a nonrejection of the null hypothesis. The probability of rejection if the null hypothesis is true is characterized in the model as r_0 and is approximately equivalent to the researcher's alpha criterion. Based on the questionnaire responses, r_0 is estimated at .05. If the null hypothesis is false, then the probability of its rejection is characterized as r_1 and this should be approximately 1.00 minus the researcher's beta criterion. This value is estimated at .70 based on the questionnaire responses. Probabilities of nonrejection of the null hypothesis are 1.00 minus r_0 (which equals .95) or 1.00 minus r_1 (which equals .30), respectively.[4]

---

[3]The equations for computing system output in indexes have been prepared as a computer program in the BASIC language. This program generates system output indexes in response to values of the system input parameters entered at a terminal by the user. The program therefore permits ready examination of consequences of assumptions other than those made presently about values of the system's input parameters. A listing of this program may be obtained from the author.

[4]The .05 level is probably a conservatively low estimate of alpha employed by the researchers to whom questionnaires were sent. In response to a question that asked for an estimate of a level of alpha which "although not satisfactory for rejecting the null hypothesis, would lead you to consider that the null hypothesis is sufficiently likely to be false so as to warrant additional

Probability of Writing a Report

The model assumes that upon completing a data collection, the researcher examines his results and decides whether or not to write a report. The probability of deciding to write if the null hypothesis has not been rejected is represented as w_0 and is estimated at .06, based on the questionnaire results (see Table 1, Question 5a). When the null hypothesis has been rejected the probability of deciding to write is represented as w_1 and is estimated at .49, based on the questionnaire responses (Question 4a).

Probability of Editorial Acceptance

In order for the result of a data collection to appear in print, it has to be accepted for publication by an editor. In the model, an editor accepts an article with probability e_0 if it reports a non-rejection of the null hypothesis and e_1 if it reports a rejection of the null hypothesis. The questionnaire data did not permit any estimates of these parameters and they have been estimated, somewhat arbitrarily, as both being equal to .25. Thus, although the model permits analysis of the consequences of editorial discrimination for or against the null hypothesis, no initial assumption has been made regarding the existence of such bias.

If at First You Don't Succeed

The researcher may be left holding a bagful of data if (a) he has decided not to report the results or (b) he has decided to report them but has been unable to obtain the cooperation of an editor. At this point, the model allows the researcher to decide whether to continue research or to abandon the problem. If the result of the preceding data collection was a nonrejection of the null hypothesis, the probability of continuing is represented as c_0; if the result was a rejection of the null hypothesis, the probability of continuing is represented as c_1. Estimates of these parameters have been derived from the questionnaire responses by computing the probability of continuations b and c in response to Questions 4 and 5, conditional on a decision to write *not* having been made. The resulting estimates are .70 for c_0 and .86 for c_1.

The model assumes that the researcher continues research by return-

---

data collection before drawing a conclusion," the mean response was .11 ($\pm$.02). This suggests that researchers may be willing to treat "marginally significant" results more like null hypothesis rejections than like nonrejections. Further, the .05 estimate of r_0 is based on the classical hypothesis-testing assumption of an exact null hypothesis, rather than a range null hypothesis, as is employed in the model. The adoption of the range hypothesis framework has the effect of increasing alpha over its nominal level, the extent of the increase being dependent on the width of the null range in relation to the power $(1-\beta)$ of the research. Since full development of this point is beyond the scope of the present exposition, it shall simply be noted that the presently employed estimates of r_0 and r_1 are at best approximate. The estimates actually employed, as derived from the questionnaire responses, are conservative in the sense that they probably err by leading to an overly favorable estimate of system output.

ing to the data collection stage, at which point the fate of his research is subject to the r, w, e, and c parameters as before. In carrying out computations based on the model, a three-strikes-and-out rule was assumed. That is, if the researcher has not achieved publication after three data collections, it is assumed that he will abandon the problem. With parameter values estimated for the present system, 62% of lines of investigation are published or abandoned after three attempts in any case. The limitation to three data collections is of little practical importance since the major output indices of the model (see below) change little with additional iterations.

The Figure 1 representation of the model portrays the researcher's choice points as spinners in a game of chance, the parameter values then being represented by the areas in which each spinner may stop. This illustration is intended to make it clear that the model parameters are conditional probabilities, each indicating the probability of a specific departure from a choice point once that choice point has been reached, rather than being an attempted judgment of the research process.

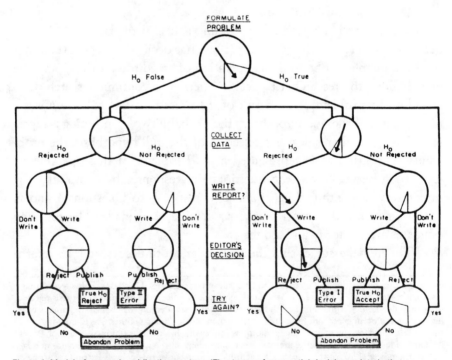

Figure 1: Model of research-publication system. (Five types of sequential decision points in the reaseach–publication process are represented by rows of circles that can be thought of as spinners in a board game, each spinner selecting one of two departures from the decision point. The spinners shown on four of the circles depict a published Type I error resulting from a researcher's first data collection on a problem.)

Limitations of the Model

No pretense is made for this model providing anything more than a potentially useful approximation to the research-publication system. Limitations in the accuracy with which some central model parameters can be estimated have already been mentioned. Perhaps the most glaring weakness in the model is its assumption that the probability of editorial acceptance of a report is independent of the sequence of events that precede submission to a journal. The model considers all manuscripts that reject the null hypothesis to be equivalent before the editorial process regardless of the number of data collections in which the null hypothesis was rejected. Similarly, all manuscripts that report acceptance of the null hypothesis are regarded as equivalent. Perhaps even more importantly, the model assumes the editorial process to be insensitive to the actual truth–falsity of the null hypothesis. The performance of the system would be at least a little better, on the various output criteria to be reported, if the model assumed some success of the editorial process in weeding out Type I and Type II errors rather than these having a likelihood of acceptance equal to true rejections and acceptances of the null hypothesis, respectively. These modifications have not been made partly because they would add complexity and also because the elaboration of additional parameters for the editorial process would not seriously affect the relations between the model's input parameters and its output indices. (They would affect absolute values of the output indices.)

Note a general caution: The model parameter estimates based on questionnaire responses are certainly more appropriate to some areas of behavioral science research than to others. Particularly, they are appropriate to areas of research in which null hypothesis decision procedures (Rozeboom, 1960) are dominant. Further, given the use of null hypothesis decision procedures, assumptions made about the present state of the system are most appropriate for those areas of research in which measurement error is substantial in relation to the magnitude of theoretically or practically meaningful effects. These are areas in which investigators are prone to work with relatively high risks of Type I error and to proceed otherwise in ways that tend to discriminate against acceptance of the null hypothesis. Within psychology, for example, much research in psychophysics, neuropsychology, and operant behavior would not properly be considered in terms of the present model. On the other hand, much research in social, developmental, experimental, clinical, industrial, and counseling psychology would, I expect, be reasonably well simulated by the model.

Model Output Indices

In order to illustrate how the model's output indices respond to change in model parameters, Figure 2 presents seven output measures as a function of the model parameter h_0 (probability that the null hypothesis is true for the focal hypothesis test). These results have been obtained with model parameters other than h_0 held constant at their previously described values (estimated from questionnaire responses).

If Type I and Type II errors are examined as a percentage of total journal content, it may be seen that these represent a gratifyingly small

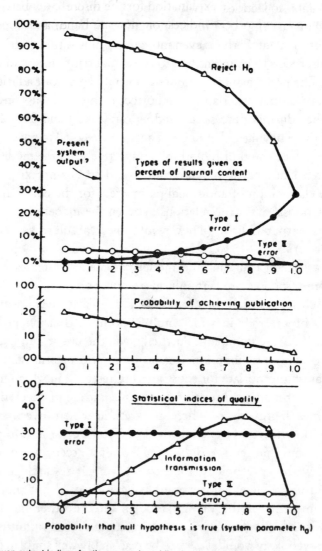

Figure 2: Seven output indices for the research–publication system model. (To illustrate responsiveness of output indices to an input parameter, the seven indices are plotted as a function of system parameter h_0 [which equals the probability that the researcher formulates a problem for which the null hyphothesis is, in fact, true].)

proportion of total published content (upper portion of Figure 2), given the estimated present-system value of $h_0 = .20$. It then becomes a bit disturbing to note that the Type I error rate of the system (system alpha) is rather high, .30. (System alpha is computed as the proportion of all publications on the right side of Figure 1 that are Type I errors.) System beta (the proportion of all publications on the left side of Figure 1 that are Type II errors) is quite low, .05.

It is somewhat coincidental, but nonetheless remarkable, that the system output levels of alpha (.30) and beta (.05) are exactly the reverse of the alpha ($r_0 = .05$) and beta ($1.00 - r_1 = .30$) levels used as estimates of model input parameters. The explanation for the discrepancy between the system alpha and system beta indices, on the one hand, and Type I and Type II errors considered as a percentage of all publications, on the other, can be found in an index giving the percentage of all publications in which the null hypothesis is reported as rejected for the focal hypothesis test (upper portion of Figure 2). This index has the quite high value of 91.5% when $h_0 = .20$. It is apparent then that the high value of system alpha, despite the low proportion of publications that are Type I errors, is a consequence of the fact that system output includes very few publications of true acceptances of the null hypothesis.

An Information Transmission Index

Because it is difficult to interpret the Type I and Type II percentage error indices or the system alpha and beta indices directly as measures of the quality of functioning of the research–publication system, it is desirable to have an index that better summarizes the system's accuracy in communicating information about the truth and falsity of researchers' null hypotheses to journal readers. An information transmission index, computed as shown in Table 2, can partially serve this purpose.

TABLE 2
Computation of Publication Information Transmission Index

Truth of H_0	Published result		Sum
	Not reject H_0	Reject H_0	
H_0 true	p_{00}	p_{01}	$p_{0.}$
H_0 false	p_{10}	p_{11}	$p_{1.}$
Sum	$p_{.0}$	$p_{.1}$	1.00

Note: Table entries are proportions of only those lines of investigation that have reached the stage of journal publication. The index is computed as (cf. Attneave, 1969, pp. 46 ff):

$$\left(- \sum_{i=0}^{1} p_{i.} \log_2 p_{i.}\right) + \left(- \sum_{j=0}^{1} p_{.j} \log_2 p_{.j}\right) - \left(- \sum_{i=0}^{1} \sum_{j=0}^{1} p_{ij} \log_2 p_{ij}\right).$$

To interpret the information transmission index, assume that a journal reader is presented with a list of the focal hypotheses tested in an upcoming journal issue. Maximally, reading the journal might reduce the reader's uncertainty about the truth–falsity of the several focal hypotheses by an average of 1.00 bit. The information transmission index will approach this maximum value to the extent that (a) there is a fifty–fifty likelihood that the null hypothesis is true or false for the published articles (i.e., the reader's uncertainty is maximal), (b) there is a fifty–fifty true–false reporting ratio for the null hypothesis in the published articles (i.e., the journal's content is maximally uncertain), and (c) the published conclusions are perfectly accurate (or perfectly inaccurate!) regarding the truth–falsity of the null hypothesis. It is important to note that this index bears little direct relation to the percentage of articles reporting a correct result. To appreciate this, consider that a journal may print nothing but correct rejections of the null hypothesis. By definition then, all of its content would be correct. However, the reader who had an advance list of the focal hypotheses of the to-be-published articles would gain *no* information regarding the truth–falsity of any focal null hypothesis from actually reading the journal, since he could know, by extrapolation from past experience, that the null hypothesis would invariably be rejected.

In Figure 2 (lower part), it is apparent that the information transmission index has a very low value (about .10 bits) given the present-system assumption that $h_0 = .20$. The fact that the information transmission index increases dramatically as h_0 increases reflects primarily some virtue in compensating, at the problem formulation stage, for biases against the null hypothesis residing elsewhere in the system.

Comment On the Information Transmission Index

A few of my colleagues have objected to the information transmission index as a summary of system functioning because it takes no account of their primary criterion for evaluating published research—the importance of the problem with which the research is concerned. These colleagues pointed out that archives full of confirmations and rejections of trivial null hypotheses would get high marks on the transmission index but would make for poor science. I am in full sympathy with this view and would not like readers to construe my preference for the information transmission index as a call for journals to catalog trivial results. Thus, it should be emphasized that the information transmission index is insensitive to several possible system virtues. Particularly, (a) it takes no account of the value to readers of the conceptual content of journal articles; (b) it ignores the information contained in tests of nonfocal hypotheses; and (c) by conceptualizing the test of the focal hypothesis as having just an accept–reject outcome, it ignores possible information in the direction or magnitude of effect shown by the focal hypothesis test. Further, the assumption implicit in the index—that readers can be aware in advance of articles' focal hypotheses—is obviously out of touch with reality. Despite these limitations, it is difficult to formulate an index that better summarizes functioning of the research–publication system.

There is an alternative form of the information transmission index that may seem preferable to the one shown in Table 2. This alternate index is based on *all* lines of investigation (not just those that reach the stage of publication) and classifies the outcomes of these lines as published rejection of the null hypothesis, published nonrejection, and also nonpublication. This index has the virtues of (a) summarizing activity in the whole system (rather than just the published portion) and (b) allowing nonpublication to provide information about the truth–falsity of the null hypothesis. Computations have been made for this index, the results indicating system functioning at about as poor a level as does the index described in Table 2. The alternate index has not been presented in Figure 2 chiefly because its implicit assumption—that system output watchers can keep track of lines of research that do not achieve publication—seems too unreasonable.

A final index shown in Figure 2, the probability of achieving a publication given embarcation on a research problem, is one that ought to be of practical concern to researchers. This index, plotted as a function of the h_0 parameter, indicates interestingly that the system "rewards" researchers with publications to the extent that they formulate a problem for which the null hypothesis is false.

A Check on the Model's Accuracy

One means of obtaining a rough check on the model's validity is to compare its predicted proportion of articles for which a focal null hypothesis is accepted against the actual content of the literature. With the assistance of John A Miller and Karl E. Rosenberg, such a check was made for the *Journal of Personality and Social Psychology* for the year 1972. Every article published that year was read to determine, first, what the focal null hypothesis was and, second, whether the article concluded in favor of acceptance or rejection of that null hypothesis. Out of 199 articles for which a focal null hypothesis was identified, 24 reported acceptance (or nonrejection) of that hypothesis. A 95% confidence interval for the proportion of articles reporting null hypothesis acceptance ($12.1\% \pm 4.5\%$) included the model's estimated value for the present system of 8.5%, providing some evidence supporting the model's validity. A similar check of four psychological journals in the mid 1950s by Sterling (1959) yielded a lower estimate of 8 out of 294 (which equals 2.7% ± 1.9%) articles that reported nonrejection of a focal hypothesis test. However, it is possible that Sterling may have used a more lenient criterion for declaring that an article rejected the null hypothesis for a focal hypothesis test (cf. Sterling, 1959, pp. 31–32).[5]

Toward a More Satisfactory System

The foregoing results strongly suggest that the research–publication system is functioning well below its potential in research areas characterized by prejudice against the null hypothesis. With the system model it is easy to demonstrate the improvement in system functioning that is potentially possible if biases against the null hypothesis are eliminated. Figure 3 shows

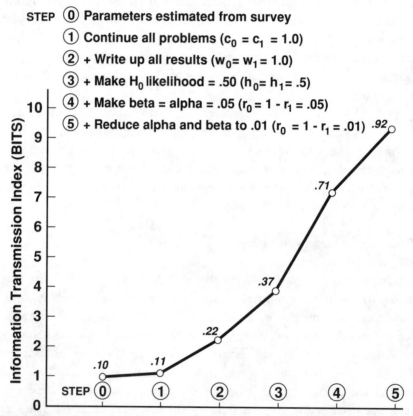

STEP ⓪ **Parameters estimated from survey**
① **Continue all problems ($c_0 = c_1 = 1.0$)**
② **+ Write up all results ($w_0 = w_1 = 1.0$)**
③ **+ Make H_0 likelihood = .50 ($h_0 = h_1 = .5$)**
④ **+ Make beta = alpha = .05 ($r_0 = 1 - r_1 = .05$)**
⑤ **+ Reduce alpha and beta to .01 ($r_0 = 1 - r_1 = .01$)**

Figure 3: Effects on information transmission index of step-by-step alterations in research–publication system parameters to reduce bias against the null hypothesis. (Present-system parameters estimated from survey results are given in the text. Hypothetical changed parameter values are indicated in parentheses in the legend, and characterize also all points to the right of the one in which the change is first indicated.)

---

[5] It gives me pause, in reading over this paragraph, to consider whether or not I would have reported the results of the content of *JPSP* if it had not been confirming of the model.

the consequences of step-by-step restoration of equal status to the null hypothesis, as reflected in values of the information transmission index. It is quite apparent from Figure 3 that unbiased behavior at the various stages of the research–publication process can have highly desirable effects on the informativeness of published research. The methods of achieving such unbiasedness are considered in more detail below.

System Effect on Generality of Research Findings

The information transmission and other system output indexes are insensitive to what may be the worst consequence of prejudice against the null hypothesis—the archival accumulation of valid results with extremely limited generality.

Consider the situation of the researcher who starts off with the hypothesis that an increase in variable x produces an increase in variable y. Since he is very convinced of the virtues of the theory that led to this prediction, he is willing to proceed through a number of false starts and pilot tests during which he uses a few different experimenters to collect data, a few different methods of minipulating variable x, a few different measures of variable y, and a few different settings to mask the true purpose of the experiment. At last, he obtains the result that confirms the expected impact of x on y but is properly concerned that the result may have been an unreplicable Type I error. To relieve this concern, he conducts an exact replication using the same combination of experimenter, operationalization of x, measure of y, and experimental setting that previously "worked," and is gratified to discover that his finding is replicated. Concerned about the validity of his procedures and measures, he also obtains evidence indicating that the manipulation of x was perceived as intended and that the measure of y had adequate reliability and validity. He then publishes his research concluding that increases in x cause increases in y and, therefore, that his theory, which predicted this relationship, is supported.

The potential fault in this conclusion should be obvious from the way I have presented the problem, but it is not likely to be obvious to the researcher conducting the investigation. Because of his investment in confirming his theory with a rejection of the null hypothesis, he has overlooked the possibility that the observed x–y relationship may be dependent on a specific manipulation, measure, experimenter, setting, or some combination of them. In his eagerness to proclaim a general x–y relationship, he has been willing to attribute his previous false starts to his (or, better, his research assistants') incompetence and, on this basis, does not feel it either necessary or desirable to inform the scientific community about them.

This style of researcher's approach has been well described by McGuire (1973):

> The more persistent of us typically manage at last to get control of the experimental situation so that we can reliably demonstrate the hypothesized relationship. But note that what the experiment tests is not whether the hypothesis is true but rather whether the experimenter is a sufficiently ingenious stage manager. (p. 449)

For further discussion of situations in which findings of limited generality appear to be much more general, I refer the reader to Campbell's (1969, pp. 358–363) typology of threats to valid inference.

SOME EPIDEMICS OF TYPE I ERROR

If the results generated by the model are to be believed, then the existing archival literature in the behavioral sciences should contain some blatant Type I errors. Although the absolute frequency of Type I error publications is not expected to be high, there should be some true null hypotheses for which only rejections of the null hypothesis have been published. About the only way to demonstrate the existence of Type I errors conclusively is to demonstrate that "established" findings cannot be replicated and that such failures to replicate cannot easily be regarded as Type II errors. As mentioned before, the fact that two of the three following cases are drawn from social psychology reflects only my familiarity with this field, not any belief that social psychology is more prone to such errors than are other areas of behavioral science research.

Attitude and Selective Learning

Between 1939 and 1958, approximately 10 studies (referenced in Greenwald & Sakumura, 1967) reported the consistent finding that subjects, when exposed to information on a controversial topic, more easily learned information that was agreeable rather than disagreeable to their existing attitude on the issue. This selective learning effect was regarded as sufficiently established to appear in many introductory psychology and social psychology textbooks, the study of Levine and Murphy (1943) particularly being regarded as somewhat of a classic.

Starting in 1963, however, almost all published studies that included a test of this hypothesis failed to confirm it (Brigham & Cook, 1969; Fitzgerald & Ausubel, 1963; Greenwald & Sakumura, 1967, Waly & Cook, 1966). In one study (Malpass, 1969) the hypothesis appeared to be confirmed in only one of three conditions in which it was tested. In general, the experiments reported since 1963 have been quite carefully done, each publication typically reporting the results of more than one replication of the hypothesis test and with careful attempts to control extraneous variables that might contaminate the tests. Therefore it does not seem reasonable to suggest that these recent findings should be regarded uniformly as Type II errors. Because the recent investigations have also made strenuous attempts, generally unsuccessful, to explain the earlier findings in terms of interactions with previously uncontrolled factors, the possibility that most of the earlier results were Type I errors is currently very plausible. This apparent epidemic of Type I error can be readily understood in terms of the hypothesized present research–publication system. Several of the earlier publications reported rejections of the null hypothesis with an alpha criterion greater than .05. After the selective learning effect had thus established some precedent in the literature, presumably researchers and editors were more disposed to regard a rejection of the null hypothesis as true than false. Possibly, also, investigators who could not obtain the established finding were content to regard their experiments as inadequate in some respect or other and did not even bother to seek publication for what they may have believed to be Type II errors, nor did they bother to conduct further research that might have explained their failure to replicate published findings.

The Sleeper Effect

The sleeper effect in persuasion is said to occur when a communication from an untrustworthy or inexpert source has a greater persuasive impact after some time delay than it does on original exposure. That is, the communication presumably achieves its effect while the audience "sleeps" on it. This result is established well enough so that it is described in most introductory social psychology texts. The research history of the sleeper effect demonstrates a variety of ways in which Type I publication errors may occur (if one assumes, that is, that the effect is not a genuine one).

The original report of a sleeper effect by Hovland, Lumsdaine, and Sheffield (1949) involved the use of an alpha criterion that was inflated by selective sampling from multiple post hoc tests of the hypothesis. That is, the effect was not predicted and was found on only a subset (not an a priori one) of the opinion items used by the investigators. In subsequent years, experimental investigators have chosen to look for the sleeper effect in terms of a comparison between the temporal course of opinion changes induced by the same communication from a trustworthy, versus an untrustworthy, source. That is, the increase in effect over time with the untrustworthy source should not be matched by a similar increase when the source is trustworthy. Significant interaction effects involving these two variables of source credibility and time since communication have been reported in a number of studies (e.g., Gillig & Greenwald, 1974; Hovland & Weiss, 1951; Kelman & Hovland, 1953; Shulman & Worall, 1970; Watts & McGuire, 1964). However, in *none* of these studies was there a significant increase in impact, with passage of time since the communication, for subjects receiving the communication from an untrustworthy source. That is, the interaction effects were due primarily or entirely to loss of effects, with passage of time, for subjects receiving the communication from a trustworthy source.

The sleeper effect, it is clear, was established in the literature by a series of studies, each of which employed an ostensible alpha criterion of .05 but for which the effective alpha criterion was substantially higher. In the original Hovland et al. (1949) study, alpha was inflated through the selective reporting of post hoc significance tests; in the later studies, it was inflated by use of an inappropriate overall interaction effect test instead of the simple effect of the time variable within the untrustworthy source conditions. Evidence that the original and subsequent sleeper effect reports are likely to have been Type I errors has come recently from a series of seven investigations by Gillig and Greenwald (1974) involving a total of 656 subjects. With their procedures, a true sleeper effect (increase over time) of .50 points on the 15-point opinion measure they used would have been detected with better than .95 probability. A 95% confidence interval (±.27 scale points) around the observed mean change of +.14 clearly included the hypothesis of zero change.

Quasi-Sensory Communication

A perennially interesting subject for the behavioral science research concerns the possibility of perception of events that provide no detectable inputs to known sensory receptors. Research on extrasensory perception or quasi-sensory communication (Clement, 1972; McBain, Fox, Kimura, Nakanishi & Tirada, 1970) is so plagued with research–publication system problems that no reasonable person can regard himself as having an adequate basis for a true–false conclusion. This state of affairs is not due to lack of research. It would be difficult to estimate, on the basis of the published literature, the amount of research energy that has been invested in para-psychological questions, and this is precisely the problem. It is a certainty that the published literature, both in favor of and against quasi-sensory communication, represents only a small fraction of the total research effort. Two anecdotes in my own experience are illustrative:

1. A physicist at Ohio State University once described to me an investigation, conducted with a colleague as a digression at their laboratory, into the detection of human-expressed af-

fect by plants.[6] They happened to have electronic apparatus of sufficient accuracy to detect electric potential charges of as small a magnitude as 10 nV between two points on the same or opposite surfaces of a leaf. This was approximately one part in 10^7 of the baseline voltage. They failed to detect responses of this magnitude reliably in a number of tests involving verbally and facially communicated threats to the plant. When I learned of this (at a cocktail party, of course) I asked if they had any intention either to publish their results or to repeat the experiment. The reply was negative, although I expect the scientific community would have been informed had their results been positive.

2. As an editorial consultant to a journal, I was asked to review an article that obtained an extrasensory perception effect that would reject the hypothesis of no effect if alpha were set at .10. I advised the editor that the result was one that had a higher probability of being Type I error than the ostensible .10, but the appropriate editorial response, since the study was competently done and the problem was interesting, was to guarantee to publish the results if the investigators would agree (a) to conduct a replication and (b) to publish the outcome of the replication (as well as the already submitted study). Two years later, the study was published (Layton & Turnbull, 1974; see also Greenwald, 1974) with the results of the replication *failing* to confirm the original findings.

Now we all know that anecdotes are unacceptable as scientific evidence because of the inflated probability that unusual events will be noticed and propagated as anecdotes. What is distressing is that the published literature on quasi-sensory communication (and other topics) also seems to be highly likely to detect and communicate relatively unlikely events. As it is functioning in at least some areas of behavioral science research, the research–publication system may be regarded as a device for systematically generating and propagating anecdotal information.

RATIONAL STRATEGIES REGARDING THE NULL HYPOTHESIS

My criticisms of researchers' null-hypothesis-related strategies are not new. They have been expressed, in part, by several previous writers, the article by Bakan (1966) being perhaps closest to the approach I have taken. The point that Type I publication errors are underestimated by reported

---

[6] I am grateful to James T. Tough and James C. Garland for permission to give this informal report of their investigation.

alpha criteria has been made also in critiques of the use of significance tests in sociology (Selvin, 1966) and psychology (Sterling, 1959) (see also the anthology edited by Morrison & Henkel, 1970). What I have attempted to add to the previous critiques is a quantitative assessment of the magnitude of the problem as it exists, by means of (a) a questionnaire survey and (b) a system simulation employing system parameters derived from the survey results. The obtained quantitative estimates must be regarded as frightening, even calling into question the scientific basis for much published literature.

Previous critics have not be negligent in suggesting remedies for what they too have regarded as an undesirable situation. Some suggestions have been intended for use in conjunction with the standard significance testing approach. For example, Cohen (1962) has pointed out that social psychological experiments often have power adequate to detect only relatively large effects. His suggestion for higher powered experiments, if adopted, should be expected to result in an increase in the frequency of null hypothesis rejections relative to nonrejections. However, it is also possible that increased awareness of experimental power may lead to taking null results more seriously. Hays (1963) has suggested using estimates of magnitude of association to accompany the standard reports of alpha levels. This would help to assure that trivial effects associated with a rejection of the null hypothesis would be recognized as such, but might have no systematic effect on the treatment of null results.

Other writers have recommended departures from the significance testing framework. Particularly, suggestions for the use of interval estimation (Grant, 1962) or Bayesian analytic techniques (Bakan, 1966; Edwards, Lindman, & Savage, 1963) would help to avoid prejudice against the null hypothesis, because with these procedures, results need not be stated in terms of acceptance or rejection of a null hypothesis. Despite the good reasons for using interval estimation and Bayesian techniques that have been advanced by several writers, inspection of current journals makes it apparent that tests of significance against point null hypotheses remain the predominant mode of analysis for behavioral data. (Further, there is little evidence that behavioral researchers have given increased attention to the power of their research designs or to magnitude of association, in pursuit of the suggestions by Cohen, Hays and others.)

It would be a mistake, I think, to expect that a recommendation to adopt some analysis strategy other than (or in addition to) significance testing might, by itself, eliminate bias against accepting the null hypothesis. This is because, as has been shown here, *the problem exists as much or more in the behavior of investigators before collecting and after analyzing their data as in the techniques they use for analysis.* Further, since a research enterprise may often be directed quite properly at the determination of whether a given relationship or effect does or does not approximate a zero value, it seems inappropriate to urge the dropping of methods of analysis in which null hypotheses are compared with alternatives. As noted earlier, a research question stated in null hypothesis versus alternative hypothesis form is especially appropriate for theory-testing research. In such research, a result that can be used to accept a null hypothesis may often serve to advance knowledge by disproving the theory.

For these reasons, *my basic recommendation is a suggested attitude change of researchers (and editors) toward the null hypothesis. Support for the null hypothesis must be regarded as a research outcome that is as acceptable as any other.* I cannot leave this recommendation just baldly stated because I suspect that most readers will not know how to go about analyzing and reporting data in a fashion that can lead to the acceptance of the null hypothesis. I conclude, therefore, by considering some technical points related to acceptance of the null hypothesis. I conclude, therefore, by considering some technical points related to acceptance of the null hypothesis. It should be clear to readers, as it is to me, that what follows is a rather low-level consideration of technical matters, directed at users around my own level of statistical naiveté but nonetheless accurate as far as I can determine through consultation with more expert colleagues.

How to Accept the Null Hypothesis Gracefully

Use a Range, Rather Than A Point, Null Hypothesis
The procedural recommendations to follow are much easier to apply if the researcher has decided, in advance of data collection, just what magnitude of effect on a dependent measure or measure of association is large enough not to be considered trivial. This decision may have to be made somewhat arbitrarily but seems better to be made somewhat arbitrarily before data collection than to be made after examination of the data. The minimum magnitude of effect that the researcher is willing to consider nontrivial is then a boundary of the null range. The illustrations that follow employ a "two-tailed" null range that is symmetric around the zero point of a test statistic.

Select N on the Basis of Desirable Error of Estimate of the Test Statistic
Assume, for example, that in an experiment with one treatment condition and a control condition, the researcher had decided that a treatment versus control difference of .50 units on his dependent measure is a minimum nontrivial effect. (Therefore, the null range is $(-.50, +.50)$

on this measure). It would seem inappropriate to collect data with N only large enough so that the estimate of the treatment effect would have a standard error of, say, .50. To appreciate this, consider that a 95% confidence interval based on this imprecise an estimate would encompass about twice the width of the null range. I can think of no hard and fast way of specifying a desirable degree of precision, but I would suggest that an error of estimate of effect on the order of 10%–20% of the width of the null range may often be appropriate. (A 95% confidence interval then would be 40%–80% of the null range's width.) More precision than this may often be desirable, but the researcher has to make such decisions based on the cost of obtaining such precision relative t the value of the knowledge obtained thereby.[7]

Have Convincing Evidence that Manipulations and Measures Are Valid

Whether the data are to be used to accept or reject a null hypothesis or to make some other conclusion, it seems essential that the researcher be able to document the validity of his procedures relative to the conceptual variables being studied. In the case of accepting the null hypothesis, the results are patently useless if the researcher has not defended himself against the argument that his operations lacked correspondence with the variables that were critical to his hypothesis test. However, the researcher drawing a conclusion that rejects a null hypothesis should feel equal compulsion to demonstrate that his procedures were valid.

Compute the Posterior Probability of the Null (Range) Hypothesis

I refer the reader to statistical texts (e.g., Hays, 1973, chap. 19; Mosteller & Tukey, 1969, pp. 160–183; Phillips, 1973) for an introduction to Bayesian methods (see also Edwards et al., 1963). Figure 4 offers a comparison of three modes of analysis—significance testing, interval estimation, and Bayesian posterior probability computation—for some hypothetical data. These hypothetical data are for the difference between two correlated means on a measure for which the researcher's null range is $(-.50, +.50)$. The standard error of the difference scores is assumed to be 1.00, and the obtained sample mean difference (M_D) is $+.25$, a point clearly within the null range. Each analysis method is presented for three sample sizes as an aid to comparing the different analysis procedures.

The first analysis employs a standard two-tailed significance test for a

---

[7] Setting N to achieve a given level of precision requires some advance estimate of variability of the data. If such information is unavailable at the outset of data collection, it may then be necessary to determine this variability on the basis of initial data collection.

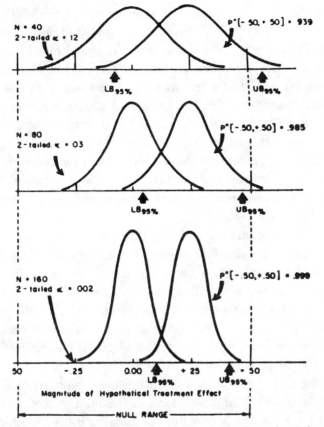

Figure 4: Comparison of significance testing, confidence interval estimation, and posterior probability estimation for three sample sizes. (The example assumes a null hypothesis range of (−.50, +.50), a variance of 1.00, and an obtained sample estimate of +.25 for a hypothetical treatment effect. The distribution centered over 0.00 is the expected distribution of sample mean estimates of the effect if the point null hypothesis of 0.00 is true. This is used to compute significance levels [αs]. The distribution centered over +.25 is the Bayesian posterior likelihood distribution, the posterior probability [P″] estimate being computed as the fraction of the area under this distribution falling in the interval (−.50, +.50). LB and UB are lower and upper confidence interval boundaries.)

point (not range) null hypothesis. This would seem to be the analysis currently preferred by most behavioral scientists. At $\alpha = .05$, this analysis does not reject the null (point) hypothesis for the smallest sample size shown but does do so for the two larger sample sizes, despite (a) the observed data point being well within the null range and (b) the fact that with the larger sample sizes we should have more confidence in the accuracy of this estimate. Clearly, computation of the significance level of an obtained result relative to an exact null hypothesis is not a useful way of going about accepting a range null hypothesis. With a relatively large N it is, rather, a good means of exercising prejudice against the null hypothesis.

The second analysis shown in Figure 4 presents 95% confidence intervals for the $M_D = +.25$ result for the three sample sizes. If we consider the containment of the 95% confidence interval within the null range as a criterion for accepting the null hypothesis, then we should accept the null hypothesis for the two larger sample sizes. This is definitely an improvement over the significance test analysis, but it still has some drawbacks. Particularly, (a) we are at a loss to make direct use of the data for the smallest sample size, for which the 95% confidence interval overspreads the null range; and (b) the conclusion does not reflect the increase in confidence that should be associated with the result for $N = 160$ relative to that for $N = 80$. It is apparent that these drawbacks of the confidence interval procedure stem from the awkwardness of relating the interval estimation procedure to a decision relative to the null hypothesis (cf. Mosteller & Tukey, 1969, pp. 180–183).

The final procedure illustrated in Figure 4 involves the computation of posterior likelihood distributions based on the obtained data. When in a Bayesian analysis one starts from ignorance (a "diffuse," "uniform," or "gentle" prior likelihood distribution), the posterior likelihood distribution is constructed directly from the mean and variability of the obtained data, much as is a confidence interval. A critical difference from the confidence interval analysis is that the assumptions underlying the Bayesian analysis facilitate drawing a conclusion about the acceptability of the null hypothesis. For the posterior distributions presented in Figure 4, a uniform prior distribution is assumed. The resulting posterior probability statements have the desirable feature of allowing us to conclude that the (range) null hypothesis is considerably more likely than its complement for all three sample sizes, while at the same time allowing expressions of the increased certainty afforded by the larger sample sizes for the $M_D = +.25$ result.

To provide a more concrete illustration of a posterior probability computation used as the basis for accepting a null hypothesis, consider the data from the Gillig and Greenwald (1974) sleeper effect study described in the earlier section on Type I errors. In this study, Gillig and Greenwald were employing a 15-point opinion scale as the dependent measure. They considered that a change from an immediate posttest to a delayed posttest of less than .50 on this scale was a trivial effect (.50 was less than 25% of the standard deviation of the obtained difference scores). They employed 273 subjects to estimate this change, so that the standard error of their estimate of the effect was .134 (which equals 13.4% of the $(-.50, +.50)$ null range). Computation of the posterior likelihood distribution of the hypothesis, assuming a uniform prior distribution, indicated that 99.6% of the area under the posterior distribution was within the null range. The .996 figure can therefore be taken as a posterior probability measure of acceptance of the null (range) hypothesis for these data. This figure can be expressed alternately as a posterior odds ratio of .996/(1 − .996) = 249:1 in favor of the null hypothesis. For comparison, an odds ratio of 19:1 (α = .05) is frequently considered "significant" in rejecting a point null hypothesis (as contrasted with all possible alternatives).

Report All Results of Research for Which Conditions Appropriate to Testing A Given Hypothesis Have Been Established

As has been demonstrated earlier, successful communication of information through archival publication is severely threatened by self-censorship on the part of investigators who obtain unpredicted (often meaning null) findings. The only justifiable basis for withholding a report of the results of a data collection should be that the hypothesis intended for testing was not actually tested. This could come about through failures of manipulation, measurement, randomization, and so forth. As previously noted, the investigator should be prepared for these possibilities, meaning that he should be able to support a decision to withhold data by demonstrating that such an invalidating condition obtained. Given a valid hypothesis test, the only justifiable procedure for reporting less than all of the data obtained is the decidedly dubious one of discarding portions of the data randomly; any nonrandom decision procedure with widespread application would result in publications being a biased sample of actual research results. Therefore, researchers should make a point of including at least brief mentions of findings of preliminary data collections, explaining why these results have been ignored (if they have), in reports of data on which more final conclusions have been based. It will be obvious that the admonition to publish all one's data fails to take into account the reality of editorial rejection. This point prompts a few final comments. First, it is a truly gross ethical violation for a researcher to suppress reporting of difficult-to-explain or embarrassing data in order to present a neat and attractive package to a journal editor. Second, it is to be hoped that journal editors will base publication decisions on criteria of importance and methodological soundness, uninfluenced by whether a result supports or rejects a null hypothesis.

CONCLUSIONS

As has, I hope, been clear there is a moral to all this. In the interest of making this moral fully explicit (and also for the benefit of the reader who has started at this point), I offer the following two boiled-down recommendations.

1. Do research in which any outcome (including a null one) can be an acceptable and informative outcome.

2. Judge your own (or others') research not on the basis of the results but only on the basis of adequacy of procedures and importance of findings.[8]

REFERENCES

Aronson, E., & Carlsmith, J. M. (1969). Experimentation in social psychology. In G. Lindzey & E. Aronson (Eds.), *Handbook of social psychology* (2nd ed., Vol. 2), Reading, MA: Addison-Wesley.

Attneave, F. (1959). *Applications of information theory to psychology.* New York: Holt.

Bakan, D. (1966). The test of significance in psychological research. *Psychological Bulletin, 66,* 432–437.

Binder, A. (1963). Further considerations of testing the null hypothesis and the strategy and tactics of investigating theoretical models. *Psychological Review, 70,* 107–115.

Brigham, J. C., & Cook, S. W. (1969). The influence of attitude on the recall of controversial material: A failure to conform. *Journal of Experimental Social Psychology, 5,* 240–243.

Campbell, D. T. (1969). Prospective: Artifact and control. In R. Rosenthal & R. L. Rosnow (Eds.), *Artifact in behavioral research.* New York: Academic Press.

Campbell, D. T., & Stanley, J. C. (1963). Experimental and quasi-experimental designs for research on teaching. In N. L. Gage (Ed.), *Handbook of research on teaching.* Chicago: Rand McNally.

Clement, D. E. (1972). Quasi-sensory communcation: Still not proved. *Journal of Personality and Social Psychology, 23,* 103–104.

Cohen, J. (1962). The statistical power of abnormal-social psychological research: A review. *Journal of Abnormal and Social Psychology, 65,* 145–153.

Edwards, W. (1965). Tactical note on the relation between scientific and statistical hypotheses. *Psychological Bulletin, 63,* 400–402.

Edwards, W., Lindman, H., & Savage, L. J. (1963). Bayesian statistical inference for psychological research. *Psychological Review, 70,* 193–242.

Festinger, L. (1953). Laboratory experiments. In L. Festinger & D. Katz (Eds.), *Research methods in the behavioral sciences.* New York: Holt.

Fitzgerald, D., & Ausubel, D. P. (1963). Cognitive versus effective factors in the learning and retention of controversial material. *Journal of Educational Psychology, 54,* 73–84.

---

[8] Concluding note: Although I have not had occasion to cite their work directly in this report, the articles of Binder (1963), Campbell and Stanley (1963), Lykken (1968), and Walster and Cleary (1970) have stimulated some of the ideas developed here.

Gillig, P. M., & Greenwald, A. G. (1974). Is it time to lay the sleeper effect to rest? *Journal of Personality and Social Psychology, 29,* 132–139.

Grant, D. A. (1962). Testing the null hypothesis and the strategy and tactics of investigating theoretical models. *Psychological Review, 69,* 54–61.

Greenwald, A. G. (1974). Significance, nonsignificance, and interpretation of an ESP experiment. *Journal of Experimental Social Psychology, 10.*

Greenwald, A. G., & Sakumura, J. S. (1967). Attitude and selective learning: Where are the phenomena of yesteryear? *Journal of Personality and Social Psychology, 7,* 387–397.

Hays, W. L. (1963). *Statistics for psychologists.* New York: Holt, Rinehart & Winston.

Hays, W. L. (1973). *Statistics for social scientists* (2nd ed.). New York: Holt, Rinehart & Winston.

Hovland, C. I., Lumsdaine, A. A., & Sheffield, F. D. (1949). *Experiments on mass communication.* Princeton: Princeton University Press.

Hovland, C. I., & Weiss, W. (1951). The influence of source credibility on communication effectiveness. *Public Opinion Quarterly, 15,* 635–650.

Kelman, H. C., & Hovland, C. I. (1953). "Reinstatement" of the communicator in delayed measurement of opinion change. *Journal of Abnormal and Social Psychology, 48,* 327–335.

Layton, B. D., & Turnbull, B. (1947). Belief, evaluation, and performance on an ESP task. *Journal of Experimental Social Psychology, 10,* in press.

Levine, J. M., & Murphy, C. (1943). The learning and forgetting of controversial material. *Journal of Abnormal and Social Psychology, 38,* 507–517.

Lykken, D. T. (1968). Statistical significance in psychological research. *Psychological Bulletin, 70,* 151–159.

Malpass, R. S. (1969). Effects of attitude on learning and memory: The influence of instruction induced sets. *Journal of Experimental Social Psychology, 5,* 441–453.

McBain, W. N., Fox, W., Kimura, S., Nakanishi, M., & Tirado, J. (1970). Quasi-sensory communication: An investigation using semantic matching and accentuated effect. *Journal of Personality and Social Psychology, 14,* 281–291.

McGuire, W. J. (1964). Inducing resistance to persuasion: Some contemporary approaches. In L. Berkowitz (Ed.), *Advances in experimental social psychology* (Vol. 1). New York: Academic Press.

McGuire, W. J. (1973). The yin and yang of progress in social psychology: Seven koan. *Journal of Personality and Social Psychology, 26,* 446–456.

Mills, J. (1969). The experimental method. In J. Mills (Ed.), *Experimental social psychology.* Toronto: Macmillan.

Morrison, E. E., & Henkel, R. E. (Eds.). (1970). *The significant test controversy.* Chicago: Aldine.

Mosteller, F., & Tukey, J. W. (1969). Data analysis, including statistics. In G. Lindzey & E. Aronson (Eds.), *Handbook of social psychology* (2nd ed., Vol. 2). Reading, Mass: Addison-Wesley.

Phillips, L. D. (1973). *Bayesian statistics for social scientists.* New York: Crowell.

Platt, J. R. (1964, October). Strong inference. *Science*, pp. 347–353.

Rosenthal, R., & Rosnow, R. L. (Eds.). (1969). *Artifact in behavioral research*. New York: Academic Press.

Rozeboom, W. R. (1960). The fallacy of the null-hypothesis significance test. *Psychological Bulletin, 57*, 416–428.

Selvin, H. C., & Stuart, A. (1966). Data-dredging procedures in survey analysis. *American Statistician, 20*, 20–23.

Shulman, G. I., & Worrall, C. (1970). Salience patterns, source credibility, and the sleeper effect. *Public Opinion Quarterly, 34*, 371–382.

Siegel, S. (1956). *Nonparametric statistics for the behavioral sciences*. New York: McGraw-Hill.

Sterling, T. D. (1959). Publication decisions and their possible effects on inferences drawn from tests of significance—or vice versa. *Journal of American Statistical Association, 54*, 30–34.

Walster, G. W., & Cleary, T. A. (1970). A proposal for a new editorial policy in the social sciences. *American Statistician, 24*, 16–19.

Waly, P., & Cook, S. W. (1966). Attitudes as a determinant of learning and memory: A failure to confirm. *Journal of Personality and Social Psychology, 4*, 280–288.

Watts, W. A., & McGuire, W. J. (1964). Persistency of induced opinion change and retention of the inducing message contests. *Journal of Abnormal and Social Psychology, 68*, 233–241.

Wilson, W. R. & Miller, H. (1964). A note on the inconclusiveness of accepting the null hypothesis. *Psychological Review, 71*, 238–242.

23

REVIEW OF DEVELOPMENTS IN META-ANALYTIC METHOD

ROBERT L. BANGERT-DROWNS

When Glass (1976) first coined the term *meta-analysis*, he meant it to refer to no new or specific technique. Instead, Glass advocated the application of familiar experimental methodologies to summarize research findings in the social sciences. As he put it later, "'Meta-analysis' is nothing more than the attitude of data analysis applied to quantitative summaries of individual experiments . . . it is not a technique; rather it is a perspective that uses many techniques of measurement and statistical analysis" (Glass, McGaw, & Smith, 1981, p. 21).

Recently, there has been disagreement over what exactly constitutes meta-analysis. For example, Hunter, Schmidt, and Jackson (1983) have referred to their meta-analytic work as "state-of-the-art meta-analysis . . . the most complete meta-analysis procedure now known" (p. 140). Hedges and Olkin (1982) regard Glass's original formulation as outdated and present what they believe to be a more technically adequate form.

Reprinted from the *Psychological Bulletin*, 99, 388–399. Copyright 1986 by the American Psychological Association.

Glass has recently restated his confidence in his original formulation of meta-analysis and called for greater specificity in the use of the term (Glass & Kleigl, 1983).

These disagreements only further obscure what was ironically intended to be a tool of clarification. Readers, researchers, editors, and research reviewers need to be better informed if they are to be intelligent consumers and critics of meta-analytic reviews. Meta-analysis is becoming an increasingly commonplace tool of social science. J. A. Kulik (1984) estimates that about 300 meta-analyses have already been conducted. Despite the increase in meta-analytic literature, S. E. Jackson (1984) found that only 33% of a sample of *Psychological Bulletin* authors described themselves as fairly familiar or very familiar with this type of review. The need for more information about this method is, therefore, also growing.

This article provides some of the needed information. A brief history of the development of meta-analysis is given, and then five alternative approaches to meta-analysis are distinguished and suggestions for their use made.

BRIEF HISTORY OF META-ANALYSIS

Research reviews can be arranged into four classes (Cooper, 1982; G. B. Jackson, 1980). The first type of review identifies and discusses new developments in a field. The second uses empirical evidence to highlight, illustrate, or assess a particular theory or to tentatively propose new theoretical frameworks. Third, a reviewer can organize knowledge from divergent lines of research.

Meta-analysis belongs to the fourth class of review, the integrative review. The integrative review is "primarily interested in inferring generalizations about substantive issues from a set of studies directly bearing on those issues." (G. B. Jackson, 1980, p. 438). The meta-analytic reviewer will typically collect a group of studies that investigate the same question through roughly similar procedures. Of course there would be little need for review if this convergence of hypothesis and research design produced identical results in all the studies. On the contrary, the social sciences are replete with research, especially applied research, that has attempted to verify or extend previous research in an unsystematic way (e.g., Shaver & Norton, 1980). Diversity in study outcomes may therefore be due to subtle differences in setting, subjects, and researcher. This is precisely what meta-analysis hopes to answer: Are some regular patterns discernable in a body of studies on a given topic that show divergent outcomes?

Meta-analysis applies statistics to the treatment of quantitative representations of study outcomes. This distinguishes meta-analysis from more informal narrative forms of review. Perhaps the most statistically sensitive type of narrative review is the "vote-counting" or "box-score" review (Light & Smith, 1971).

In a box-score review, the studies are grouped into three sets: those significantly favoring the control group, those significantly favoring the experimental group, and those with nonsignificant outcomes. The modal category is taken as the best representation of the outcomes of this research area. Outcomes of lesser frequency are attributed to chance or undetected experimental error. Counting statistically significant findings gives a crude idea of how large and consistent a particular finding is in a body of research.

Vote counting, however, will only reliably represent the size of a treatment's effect if the collected studies have the same sample sizes and a unimodal distribution reflecting one population. There are two reasons for this. First, statistical significance is a product of both the treatment's effect and the sample size. If the sample sizes of the studies differ, conclusions from studies with larger samples are more likely to be significant even when the underlying treatment effect is small or the same as in the other studies. Secondly, a multimodal distribution could suggest that factors other than the treatment alone are mediating study outcomes.

Meta-analysis is not hampered by these problems. It does not rely on frequency counts or statistical significance within studies. Instead it applies statistics to numerical representations of the studies' dependent measures. Further, it typically investigates the influence of mediating factors on the independent variable.

Early Meta-Analytic Studies

Glass cites two reviews that exemplify earlier applications of meta-analytic ingenuity (Glass et al., 1981, p. 24). Underwood (1957) graphed the apparently divergent outcomes of 16 studies on recall interference. He discovered a significant relation between the number of prior lists learned and recall ability. This relation was not detected in any individual study. Sudman and Bradburn (1974) gathered hundreds of studies investigating response effects in survey research. These reviewers applied statistical methods to assess the influence of survey design and use on survey results.

Other well-known examples are not hard to find. Ghiselli (1949, 1955, 1973) averaged correlation coefficients from numerous studies to estimate the validity of different tests in predicting proficiency in different occupations. Bloom (1964) aggregated correlation coefficients to summarize evidence of stability and change in behavior. Cartwright (1971) quantified and cumulated study outcomes to show that group influence is trivial in risky shift research. Erlenmeyer-Kimling and Jarvik (1963) aggregated more than 30,000 correlation pairings from 52 studies to discover orderly relations between intelligence and genetic history.

One can trace meta-analysis to earlier roots (Hedges & Olkin, 1982). In the first third of this century, agricultural experimenters assembled a large body of studies bearing on identical questions. Interpretation of these study findings was hampered as interpretation in the social sciences is today. As Yates and Cochran (1938) observed, "difference in soil, agronomic practices, climatic conditions and other variations in environment" (p. 556) introduced uncontrolled factors into experiments. Secondly, the amount of land needed for an adequate experiment was often not available at a single site. "The agricultural experimenter is thus frequently confronted with the results of a set of experiments on the same problem" (Yates & Cochran, 1938, p. 556).

Tippitt (1931) answered the difficulty by supplying methods to test the statistical significance of results combined from separate experiments. Other researchers, such as Fisher (1932), K. Pearson (1933), and E. S. Pearson (1938), followed in this tradition. They sought ways to combine probability values from tests of significance.

Cochran (1937) and Yates and Cochran (1938) set out to answer the difficulty in a different way. They developed methods to estimate the mean effect and variability of a particular treatment examined at different agricultural centers. Furthermore, Cochran (1943) discussed the importance of comparing different dependent measure criteria for compatibility and relative accuracy before combining study findings.

Wilkinson (1951) proposed a method to interpret multiple outcomes from single studies in the social sciences. He observed that, because study results are either significant or nonsignificant, the binomial distribution could be used to determine the expected number of significant results given a true null hypothesis. This estimate of expected studies could be tested against the actual number of significant findings as a check on the assumption about the null hypothesis.

Jones and Fiske (1953) went further to import the meta-analytic attitude of agricultural research to the social sciences. They extended Wilkinson's proposition and argues that Fisher's (1932) and K. and E. S. Pearson's methods of combining probabilities could be used to combine findings in education and psychology. Mosteller and Bush (1954) also established combined probabilities as a useful tool in social science integration.

As early as the 1950s, therefore, combining probabilities was advocated as a reasonable way of statistically integrating social science research.

However, no integrative technique similar to Cochran's was formally developed for the social sciences. That is, no one advocated a coherent method to estimate the mean and variation of a social or psychological treatment. Two remaining methodological problems blocked this development.

Two Obstacles to Meta-Analysis

Dissimilar dependent measures and variations in study features presented difficult obstacles to the translation of the meta-analytic attitude into a coherent meta-analytic method. Though a group of studies might investigate the same question with similar methods, the reviewer could not be sure to what degree the combined results were distorted due to differences in the criterion scale used and differences in study features. Three important articles offered solutions to these problems and in may ways anticipated what would become modern meta-analytic method.

In his well-known article "The statistical power of abnormal-social psychological research," Cohen (1962) indirectly spoke to some of the gaps in meta-analytic method. He set out to review the power of all the studies appearing in Volume 61 of the *Journal of Abnormal and Social Psychology*. He made three calculations of statistical power for each article, each calculation corresponding to hypothetical population effects of different degrees: low, medium, or large. Given such calculations, Cohen showed that 78 articles were poorly designed to detect false null hypotheses when effect sizes were medium or low.

To the historian of research integration, Cohen's review contributed to meta-analytic theory in three important ways. First, he showed a way of statistically summarizing a diverse literature without taking recourse to counting or combining significance levels. Each study was represented in the review by three power estimates. These estimates were summarized in terms of central tendency (mean and median) and variation.

Secondly, because effect size is a factor in determining a study's power, any call to power analysis must also be an encouragement for an analysis of effect size. Cohen did not calculate the effect size for each study, a procedure that is common in modern meta-analysis. He did, however, underscore the convenience of the use of effect size in statistical research integration. Faced with "diverse content areas, utilizing a large variety of dependent variables and many different types of statistical tests . . . size of effect was expressed quantitatively in terms not dependent on the specific metric of the variable(s) involved" (1962, p. 446).

Third, Cohen suggested a rudimentary form by which the relations between study features and study findings could be examined. He realized that the power of major statistical tests, tests on the central hypotheses of the article, may be greater than the power of more peripheral statistical tests. He classified these separately, performing his analysis on the major tests, then analyzing the power of the peripheral tests to see if there were differences between the classes. In this way, the influence of a study feature on findings was empirically assessed.

In their article "The teaching-learning paradox: A comparative analysis of college teaching methods," Dubin and Taveggia (1968) attempted an ambitious statistical integration of findings from 74 studies comparing forms of college teaching. Like many reviewers before them, they categorized findings into three groups (favored treatment A, favored treatment B, and no difference) and performed simple sign tests on the frequency distributions.

However, these researchers complained that "the sign test does not give us any indication of the magnitude or distribution of differences between any two methods of teaching" (Dubin & Taveggia, 1968, p. 59). Fifty-six of the 74 studies reported group means, standard deviations, and sample sizes. They calculated t values for the findings of these studies as a measure of the magnitude of the difference between means. These t values were averaged and the average was tested to see if it differed significantly from zero. They concluded that the various college teaching methods did not differ significantly.

From a meta-analytic perspective, this review suffered from at least two faults. (a) The t value is inferior to Cohen's effect size as a measure of treatment magnitude because it is dependent on sample size. Two applications of a treatment may produce effects of identical magnitude, yet if one application involved a larger sample, its corresponding t value would also be larger. (b) In addition, the authors did not attempt to examine any relations between treatment effects and features of the studies.

However, Dubin and Taveggia (1968) did anticipate meta-analysis in several ways. First, they recognized the value of using a standardized measure of magnitude that can be compared across studies and across criterion scales. Second, they insisted on the review of research from probabilistic standpoint. As Taveggia (1974) later put it, "Research results are *probabilistic*. . . . In and of themselves, the findings of any single research is meaningless—they may have occurred simply by chance" (p. 398). Third, the authors believed that measures of treatment effect representing each study could be treated as data points and summarized and tested statistically.

A third article speaks to the development of meta-analytic method. In "Accumulating evidence: Procedures for resolving contradictions among research studies." Light and Smith (1971) proposed an alternative to narrative methods of research integration. Their alternative, called "cluster analysis," involves five steps.

First, only studies that are methodological replications are admitted to cluster analysis. Second, the reviewer must gather the original data reflected in the studies' findings. Third, the reviewer must determine natural aggregations or clusters into which the data can be regrouped. Fourth, the reviewer must investigate differences among the clusters, comparing means, variances, relations between independent and dependent variables, subject/treatment interactions, and subject/cluster interactions, to see if differences among clusters explain study outcome variation.

Finally, in those cases in which no differences are found, clusters can be combined to increase sample sizes. At the end of a cluster analysis, a reviewer should be able to draw conclusions from larger samples or attribute differences in study findings to identifiable differences among the clusters. Of course, such an analysis may also fail and the variation in the original studies be found to be unexplainable.

In many ways, cluster analysis is distinguishable from the meta-analytic tradition. Cohen (1962) and Dubin and Taveggia (1968) were willing to quantitatively represent each study in their reviews and perform analyses on these statistical representations. This resembles modern meta-analytic procedure. Light and Smith, on the other hand, relied on original data. In this way, cluster analysis is more a form of secondary analysis, the reanalysis of original data, than a form of meta-analysis and is impossible to do in the numerous cases in which original data is unavailable (Cordray & Orwin, 1983; Glass, 1976).

Yet Light and Smith (1971) made an important theoretical contribution to the maturation of meta-analysis. Their interest was, after all, in the synthesis of diverse study outcomes. They reaffirmed the importance of finding a statistically sensible way to resolve apparent contradictions in research findings. More importantly, their work underscores the necessity of the search for subject/setting interactions as an essential focus of any research integration and an essential means for explaining variation in study findings.

FIVE FORMS OF META-ANALYTIC METHOD

In 1976, the same year that Glass first coined the term "meta-analysis," Rosenthal published his book *Experimenter effects in behavioral research* and Schmidt and Hunter were working on a validity generalization technique. These three concurrent efforts established three distinguishable meta-analytic approaches. Since the late 1970s, two other coherent methods have been formulated as elaborations of Glass's approach (Hedges, 1982a; Mansfield & Busse, 1977).

It would be incorrect to think that these five approaches are the last word in meta-analysis. They only indicate the present moment in the continuing evolution of review methodology. Users may in fact select and apply elements of these five without committing themselves to all the features of any one approach. I present these approaches as five separate and coherent methods because they have been most frequently used this way and because no one has yet documented the differences among all five methods. They are distinguishable on four factors: purpose, unit of analysis, treatment of study variation, and products of the meta-analysis (Table 1).

Glassian Meta-Analysis

Scientific literature does not just record the measured effects of controlled treatments. It is also an enduring record of the way scholars think about their field, the way they conduct research, the way they organize their data, and the assumptions implicit in their taxonomies and interpretations. An ambitious integrative project would evaluate such features of research as well as summarize study outcomes to assess the scientific enterprise in a given area.

Glass has endeavored to apply meta-analysis in this way. The meta-analyses of psychotherapy effectiveness and class size influence are classics of research integration (Glass, Cahen, Smith, & Filby, 1982; Smith, Glass, & Miller, 1980). Other reviewers have followed his lead (e.g., Hansford & Hattie, 1982; Hartley, 1978; Walberg & Haertel, 1980, pp. 103-133; White, 1982).

Glassian meta-analysis proceeds through three steps. First, all studies relevant to a defined question are collected. Glass uses liberal criteria for inclusion, accepting studies of widely varying methodological quality to his synthesis. Second, the outcomes of each study are transformed to a common metric to allow comparisons across the different scales of different dependent measures. Glass's effect size (*ES*), a modified form of Cohen's *d*, divides the difference between experimental and control means by the control group's standard deviation.

The study finding is the unit of analysis in Glass's method. That is, one study may produce several findings from several dependent measures. Each finding is transformed into a separate effect size. The more dependent measures a study has, the more frequently it is represented in the overall meta-analysis.

After the first two steps, a Glassian meta-analyst can describe an average outcome of a group of studies and the variance of those outcomes. Glass wants to additionally search for significant relations between inde-

TABLE 1
Five Methods of Meta-Analysis

Descriptive label	Purpose	Unit of analysis	Treatment of study variation	Outcomes of analysis
Glassian meta-analysis	To review what a literature says about the scientific process in a given area	Study finding	Examine relations between effect sizes and preestablished categories	Average effect size; comparisons of effect sizes in preestablished categories; regression models
Study effect meta-analysis	To review what a literature says about a treatment's effectiveness	Study	Examine relations between effect sizes and preestablished categories; apply strict study inclusion criteria	Average effect size; comparisons of effect sizes in preestablished categories; regression models
Combined probability method	To estimate a treatment effect and the reliability of this finding	Study, for effect size; subject, for combined probability	Crude division of studies into groups analyzed separately	Average effect size; combined probability; fail-safe N
Approximate data pooling with tests of homogeneity	To estimate population treatment effects	Subject	Apply tests of homogeneity	Average effect sizes for homogeneous groups
Approximate data pooling with sampling error corrrection	To estimate population treatment effects	Subject	Compare variation among studies to variation attributable to sampling error; test for moderating variables	Average effect size; study variation; variation attributable to sampling error; list of moderators accounting for remaining variation; regression models

pendent variables and dependent measures. Every study is coded on a number of quantitative dimensions (e.g., number of sessions of psychotherapy) and categorical variables (e.g., random assignment of subjects vs. nonrandom assignment). For example, Smith and Glass (1977) coded at least 16 independent variables for each study. Variables are preselected by the reviewer as potential determinants of variability in study findings. They represent differences in treatment application, methodological differences and controls for validity, differences in publication history, and differences in experimental setting. Parametric tests are applied to identify relations between study outcomes and the coded study features.

Critics of Glassian meta-analysis have found fault with four features that are peculiar to this approach. These features are the inclusion of methodologically poor studies in the review (the "garbage in-garbage out" complaint), the use of overly broad categories in averaging effects across independent and dependent variables (the "apples-and-oranges" problem), and the representation of individual studies by multiple effect sizes, resulting in nonindependent data points (the nonindependence problem) and misleadingly large samples (the problems of "inflated Ns"). These complaints can be recast in terms of threats to internal, construct, statistical conclusion, and external validities (Cook & Campbell, 1979; Wortman, 1983).

Glass's liberal inclusion of studies regardless of methodological quality flies in the face of integrative tradition. The traditional reviewer gives greater weight to findings of greater internal validity. Mansfield and Busse (1977) argued for the elimination of methodologically inferior studies from meta-analysis. Eysenck (1978) more disparagingly referred to meta-analysis as "mega-silliness" and complained that the inclusion of methodologically inadequate research only demonstrates the axiom "garbage in-garbage out."

Replying to this criticism, Glass takes an empirical stand (e.g., Glass et al., 1981, pp. 220–226). He agrees that internal validity can effect the outcome of research, but he argues that this is an empirical question, one that meta-analysis is equipped to handle. By coding studies for various threats to internal validity, relations between effect sizes and these threats can be determined, if they exist.

Some authors have found fault with this reply (Bryant & Wortman, 1984: Cook & Leviton, 1980). It makes sense to look for relations between effect size and methodological flaws only if the available research provides a wide range of experimental rigor. If studies with numerous threats to validity predominate a review's sample, there may not be a sufficient number of well-controlled studies to provide a comparison. "When all studies share a common bias, this all-inclusive approach can be misleading. . . . Without well-designed studies that can be used as a baseline for comparison, it is impossible to determine how methodological quality affects resresults" (Bryant & Wortman, 1984, p.12).

Critics also complain about the apples-and-oranges problem. At the level of the independent variable, Glass's form of meta-analysis can obscure critical differences among subgroups of studies. For example, Glass's investigation of psychotherapy effectiveness included psychodynamic, Adlerian, eclectic, transactional analysis, rational-emotive, Gestalt, client-centered, systematic desensitization, implosion, and behavior modification therapies (Smith & Glass, 1977). These were collapsed into two "superclasses," behavioral and nonbehavioral, and even averaged across all groups for a total "psychotherapy effect" measure. Presby (1978) complained that important differences "are cancelled in the very use of broad categories, which leads to the erroneous conclusion that research results indicate negligible differences among outcomes of different therapies" (p. 514).

In question then is the construct validity of Glassian meta-analyses. Do the categories established by the Glassian meta-analyst accurately reflect relevant underlying constructs? Glass has said that the construct validity can only be assessed against the purposes of the reviewer. Whether the reviewer has a specific hypothesis in mind or is simply trying to summarize a literature in broad strokes will determine to a great degree the validity of the categories used (Glass et al., 1981). Cooper (1982) has defined "integrative review" by the fact that it can encompass more operational definitions than primary research. As Wortman (1983) put it, "If a policy decision to reimburse clinical psychologists for psychotherapy is being considered, than a general question concerning the effectiveness of all therapies seems appropriate" (p. 240). Besides, an overall effect size can later be broken into effects related to specific treatments.

An apples-and-oranges treatment of dependent measures, however, seems less defensible (J. A. Kulik, 1984; Landman & Dawes, 1982). Glassian meta-analysis records and uses an effect size from every finding, even if a study produces more than one finding. In studies of computer-based instruction, for example, achievement test scores, ratings of attitudes toward computers, and ratings of attitudes toward course content cannot be said to measure the same construct. How would one interpret their combination? "Computer-based instruction produces increases of 0.30 standard deviations in . . . " what? Meta-analysis may quantify a combined effect, but readers of reviews are generally not interested in such abstractions; effects of a treatment however defined, must be effects on something specific.

Another difficulty arising from the calculation of effect sizes for every dependent measure is the nonindependence of the resulting data points. Even Glass et al. (1981) recognized this as a cogent criticism. Landman and Dawes (1982), in their reanalysis of a sample of Glass's psychotherapy data, found five different types of violation of the assumption of independence.

Inferential statistics are less reliable when applied to such data and this poses a significant threat to the statistical conclusion validity of the review.

A fourth criticism results from the calculation of effect sizes for every dependent measure. That is, studies are represented in the meta-analysis by the number of findings they report. Thus, any report, even if it is atypical or of marginal quality, can have greater influence on meta-analytic findings if it uses many dependent measures. The ratio of study findings to studies can be extreme at times. Burns (1981), for example, gathered 413 effect sizes from 33 reports. Some studies contributed as many as 120 effect sizes, others as few as 1.

"Inflated Ns" threaten the generalizability or external validity of meta-analyses. Because individual studies can be arbitrarily overrepresented in a review, the definitions of the sample and target population become unclear. The problem is compounded when effect sizes are divided into study feature categories. Categories that only represent data from one or two studies do not offer generalizable information, even if they have a large number of effect sizes.

An example of the potential confusion is offered by the Educational Research Service's (1980) critique of Glass's class size meta-analysis. Fourteen of the 76 studies were considered well-controlled. These 14 well-controlled studies produced 110 comparisons, but 73% of the 110 came from 4 of the 14 studies. Glassian meta-analysts must use some procedure to protect against biases that may result when a small group of studies contributes too much data.

Glass has been disappointed by the dearth of variables found to significantly explain diversity in study findings (Glass, 1979). However, Glass recently restated his confidence in the general robustness and usefulness of his method (Glass & Kleigl, 1983). He also made his view of the purposes of meta-analysis explicit. The goal of meta-analysis is larger than simply summarizing the outcomes of a sample of research, according to Glass. It endeavors "to determine how and in what ways the judgments, decisions, and inclinations of persons (scholars, citizens, officials, administrators, policy makers) ought to be influenced by the literature of empirical research" regarding a defined enterprise (Glass & Kleigl, 1983, p. 35). To accomplish this, the meta-analyst evaluates not only a treatment and its effect but the method of research and the taxonomical structure used by researchers in a field.

Study Effect Meta-Analysis

Mansfield and Busse (1977) were early critics of Glass's meta-analytic approach. They outlined an alternative specifically designed to summarize study findings on the effect of a particular treatment and to avoid the problems of study inclusion and apples-and-oranges combinations. Since 1979, J. A. Kulik and his colleagues have produced about 15 meta-analyses that are consistent with the suggestions of Mansfield and Busse (e.g., Bangert-Drowns, Kulik & Kulik, 1983; J. A. Kulik & Bangert-Drowns, 1983/1984; J. A. Kulik, C.-L. C. Kulik, & Cohen, 1979). Other examples of this type of meta-analysis are offered by Landman and Dawes (1982) and Wortman and Byrant (1985).

Perhaps the most significant feature of this form of meta-analysis is that it differs from Glassian meta-analysis regarding the appropriate unit of analysis. For Glass, the unit of analysis is the study finding; an effect size is calculated for every study outcome. In the alternative form of meta-analysis, the study itself is the unit of analysis. If a study uses more than one dependent measure, the corresponding effect sizes are either combined if they represent the same construct (e.g., academic achievement) or they are sent to separate analyses if they represent different constructs (e.g., one analysis for academic achievement data, another for attitude toward school data).

By using the study as the unit of analysis, this meta-analytic type avoids several pitfalls of Glass's approach, such as nonindependence of effect sizes, inflated Ns, and the apples-and-oranges problem. Dependent measures are analyzed separately if they are assumed to gauge different constructs, protecting construct validity. The number of studies reviewed is equal to the number of effect sizes, protecting the overall results from being biased by a small number of studies that may produce many outcomes. The independence of the effect sizes allows the reviewer to use statistics with more confidence.

Because using the study as the unit of analysis is a central feature of this approach, I refer to it as *study effect meta-analysis* (SEM) to distinguish it from Glassian meta-analysis. Study effect meta-analysis and Glassian meta-analysis are similar in some ways. Both use quantitative and categorical variables to code study features as independent variables. Glass's ES is used as an outcome measure and parametric statistical tests are used to identify relations between study features and study outcomes.

Study effect meta-analysis is usually more exclusive than the Glassian form in selecting studies for review. In Kulik's research, for example, if any study suffers from flaws that may obscure treatment effects or if the study's method deviates too greatly from standard experimental practice, the study is rejected. All studies must possess experimental and control groups. If subjects are not randomly assigned to these groups, there must at least be evidence that the two groups show pretreatment equivalence. Any study whose treatment specifically trains the experimental group on the dependent measure is excluded. The experimental treatment in each accepted study must roughly fit criteria established by experts in the area under review. Control groups must undergo treatment that is roughly equivalent across studies.

In addition to Kulik, other meta-analysts have applied the study effect approach. Wortman and Bryant (1985), for example, developed 33 criteria for study exclusion in their meta-analysis of desegregation research. Threats to construct and external validity were used to determine a study's relevance for the review. Threats to internal and statistical conclusion validity were used to decide whether a relevant study was of acceptable quality (Bryant & Wortman, 1984).

In addition, the dependent measures that were examined by Wortman and Bryant (1985) were fairly homogeneous; that is, mathematics and reading achievement test performances were used to calculate effect sizes. In some ways, their treatment of effect sizes resembled the Glassian approach. Effect sizes were calculated for grade level and for reading and mathematics achievement, resulting in 106 effect sizes for 31 studies. "The overall analyses, however, used the study as the unit of analysis by averaging the results within each study and combining these average effect sizes" (Wortman & Bryant, 1985, p. 302).

Landman and Dawes (1982) used SEM to reanalyze a sample of studies randomly selected from Smith and Glass's (1977) psychotherapy review. Their results suggest that the inclusion of methodologically poorer studies and the calculation of more than one effect size for each study may have served to lower the average effect sizes Smith and Glass computed. Landman and Dawes found that the apples-and-oranges problem at both the independent and the dependent variable level may have more seriously obscured some potentially important relations.

The differences between the study effect method and Glass's method are few, but they betray the different purposes in these meta-analytic approaches. Glass, with his liberal standards of inclusion and empirical attitude toward methodological flaws and differences in dependent criteria, seeks to use quantitative means to assess a scholarly subculture, to examine modes of inquiry and construct definition as well as to estimate treatment effects. Study effect meta-analysis, on the other hand, seeks to represent what the available research says about a treatment's effectiveness. In doing so, SEM seems especially sensitive to the limits that the quality, quantity, and historical context of published research impose on integrative interpretations.

This approach is not without its shortcomings. With stricter inclusion standards and only one effect size from each study, one should expect a smaller sample size than with Glass's approach. If less than 10 studies pass the screening stage, such small samples would be prohibitive. Study exclusion may also provide an undesirable opportunity for a reviewer's biases to creep into the review, and it deprives a meta-analyst of the chance to determine whether and how some methodological shortcomings affect study outcomes. However, if a reviewer has a group of 20 or more studies, if it is likely that differential representation of studies will effect the meta-analytic findings, if the reviewer has a focused concern in mind and is not as interested in a general evaluation of a scientific field, and if the reviewer is willing to explicitly define and adhere to standards for inclusion, SEM is an attractive alternative to Glass's approach.

Combined Probability Method

Since 1976, Rosenthal and his colleagues (Cooper, 1979; Rosenthal, 1976, 1978, 1983; Rosenthal & Rubin, 1982a, 1982b) have developed two distinguishable meta-analytic methods; the more recent form is discussed later in this article. The combined probability method, discussed here, has been used to survey a number of areas (e.g., Arkin, Cooper, & Kolditz, 1980; Cooper, 1979; Dusek & Joseph, 1983; Rosenthal, 1976; Rosenthal & Rubin, 1978; Wolf, Savickas, Saltzman, & Walker, 1983).

Meta-analysis based on these techniques have a typical format (e.g., Cooper, 1979). The reviewer specifies an area of interest and all relevant studies are collected. For each study, exact one-tailed p values are calculated and their corresponding standard normal deviate (Z) listed. Additionally, Cohen's d is calculated for each study as a measure of effect that is more independent of sample size than is a p value. (Cohen's d is sometimes also represented as Cohen's U_3, the percentage of control group subjects with dependent measures less than the mean of the experimental group.)

Finally, the average effect size and a combined probability measure are calculated. The ds (and U_3s) are averaged to provide an overall effect size measure. Stouffer's method (Rosenthal, 1978) is used to combine the Zs corresponding to each study. The resulting Stouffer's Z defines the probability that the pooled subjects would be distributed among treatments as they are in the collected studies. The "fail-safe N" is calculated using an extension of the Stouffer method and is a more intuitively understandable form of the combined Z. The fail-safe N indicates the number of additional studies of no effect needed to reduce a significant combined probability to nonsignificance. (Note that the fail-safe N represents the number of unlocated studies of *zero effect*. There may in fact be a smaller number of *negative* studies, studies favoring the control group, that would reduce the meta-analytic outcome to nonsignificance [Cooper, 1979; Rosenthal, 1979].)

The unit of analysis in the calculation of the average d is clearly the study. Each study contributes one effect size and these are simply averaged across studies. Stouffer's Z, however, is not a simple average across studies, but a Z score of a cumulation of Z scores. Because the probabilities corresponding to each Z are already sensitive to sample size, the unit of analysis in determining overall probability is the subject.

This meta-analytic approach is not as comprehensive as the others. What is most conspicuously absent from this form of meta-analysis is rigorous attention to differences in study features. This method is not as attentive to outcome variation as it is to the degree of outcome convergence. Decisions regarding the inclusion or exclusion of methodologically inferior studies are left to the reviewer's discretion. Only very few or very basic differentiations are made in a literature, for example, the differentiation between studies examining race and studies examining sex as bases of teacher expectation (Dusek & Joseph, 1983). A reviewer might use this approach to gain a rough impression of a group of studies but must borrow from other approaches for more subtle analysis.

Unlike Glassian and study effect meta-analysis, the implicit purpose of the combined probability approach is not to review a literature but to estimate a treatment effect and provide some measure of the estimate's reliability. These measures are intended to be broadly generalizable. Cooper (1979), for example, went so far as to use his meta-analytic findings to predict the results of future research. In keeping with this goal of deriving generalizable conclusions, Rosenthal's method has begun to focus on the subject as the unit of analysis, an effort to draw conclusions from large samples of subjects. Rosenthal's combined probability method can be seen as a transitional form of meta-analysis between, on the one hand, meta-analyses whose conclusions are interpreted as specific to the studies reviewed and, on the other hand, meta-analyses that attempt to determine population parameters and "true" treatment effects.

Approximate Data Pooling With Tests of Homogeneity

Rosenthal's combined probability method hints at an alternative use of meta-analysis. Instead of critically reviewing a body of studies, perhaps studies' summary statistics could be used to approximate the pooling of all the subjects from all the studies into one large comparison. That is, perhaps meta-analysis could be used to approximate data pooling.

Two methodological modifications are immediately implied. If we are concerned with pooling data across studies, we must attend not only to variability among studies as Glass prescribes, but also to the variance associated with each effect size as a summary statistic. Second, Glassian meta-analysis is meant to test differences between a priori categories. An alternative is to provide some overall test to determine whether such categorical tests are necessary at all. If a group of effect sizes is found to be homogeneous, the effect sizes can be averaged without further fuss. The crucial question is whether the variation among effect sizes is due to real mediators or simply to sampling error.

Hedges (1982a) and Rosenthal and Rubin (1982a) have devised tests for the homogeneity of effect sizes. Variability among study outcomes is represented as the sum of squared differences between each effect size and the weighted average effect size. The ratio of this sum of squared differences to the sum of sampling variances in all the effect sizes is distributed as a chi-square. If this ratio, designated H, is approximately 1, variation among studies is approximately the same as sampling error of the studies. If H is large or statistically significant, the variation among studies cannot be attributed to sampling error only.

Hedges (1982b) extends the use of this test of homogeneity. If the overall H is large, the effect sizes can be broken into smaller categories that may differ in average effect size. If H within a category is small, the effect sizes within the category are assumed to be homogeneous and to represent a single population treatment effect. A variant of the H statistic, H_B, describes the degree to which the categories vary among each other. As with the partitions of variation in an analysis of variance, the overall H is equal to the sum of the within-category H and between-categories H_B. By sensitizing regression to the sampling error of the effect sizes, the H statistic can be applied to continuous data as well (Hedges, 1982c).

Rosenthal and Rubin (1982a, 1982b) suggest a simple formula to test for significant differences among effect sizes in a heterogeneous group. The concept is analogous to contrasts in analysis of variance. The sum of appropriately weighted effect sizes is distributed as a standard normal deviate. This Z can be easily tested for statistical significance.

Hedges (1981) proposed several adjustments to increase the accuracy of the effect size as an estimator. Some of these are not practically important. For example, using Hedge's correction for estimator bias, Bangert-Drowns et al. (1983) found a correlation of .999 between corrected and uncorrected effect sizes in a meta-analysis of 27 studies. Corrected and uncorrected estimators are virtually equivalent for greater than 10 df (Hedges, 1982a, p. 492; Rosenthal & Rubin, 1982a, p. 504). Similarly Hedge's corrections for unreliability and invalidity of dependent measures are generally impractical because they require information that is rarely available, such as the reliabilities of the dependent measure and of a valid response measure, and the correlation between the two measures.

However, Rosenthal and Rubin (1982a) and Hedges (1981) also

sought a weighting procedure that would minimize the variance of the cumulated effect size. The frequency-weighted effect size, that is, the effect size multiplied by the ratio of its sample size to the sum of all sample sizes, appears to adequately approximate the optimally weighted effect size (Hunter et al., 1983).

The use of the test of homogeneity bears some resemblance to Light and Smith's (1971) cluster analysis. Cluster analysis attempted to group original data into natural clusters of homogeneity. Hedges and Rosenthal have weighted effect sizes to reflect differences in sample size and sampling error. These subject-sensitive statistics are clustered and reclustered as they form natural aggregations of greater homogeneity, tested by subject-sensitive significance criteria. The subject is the unit of analysis even though this unit is mediated by the summary statistic, effect size.

Hedges appears to be as willing as Glass to include studies of diverse quality and treatment features. The tests of homogeneity can be used to empirically determine whether this diversity produces heterogeneous outcomes (Hedges & Olkin, 1982). However, Hedges will not allow the averaging of effects from dependent measures representing different constructs. To estimate single population effects, effect size estimates must come from dependent measures that can be assumed to be linearly equitable.

The practical usefulness of tests of homogeneity is unclear. Rosenthal and Rubin (1982a) warn that the behavior of statistics used in this meta-analytic type is not fully understood for small or nonnormal samples. Hedges and Stock (1983) reexamined the continuous model offered by Glass relating class size to student achievement. Their conclusions largely duplicated Glass's findings.

In addition, some authors have spoken against the use of tests of homogeneity. Hunter et al. (1983), for example, developed a test of homogeneity for use with the correlation coefficient. This test is identical to Hedges's and Rosenthal and Rubin's. However, Hunter et al. (1983) "do not endorse this significance test because it asks the wrong question. Significant variation may be trivial in magnitude, and even nontrivial variation may still be due to research artifacts" (p. 46). Hedges (1982a) warns, "When the sample sizes [within studies] are *very* large, it is probably worthwhile to consider the actual variation in [the effect sizes] because rather small differences may lead to large values of the test statistic" (p. 493).

Approximate Data Pooling With Sampling Error Correction

Hunter and Schmidt became interested in quantitative research synthesis as a tool to investigate the differential validity of employment tests for blacks and whites (Hunter & Schmidt, 1978; Hunter, Schmidt, &

Hunter, 1979; Schmidt, Berner, & Hunter, 1973). They found in summarizing test validity research that "72% of the variation across studies is accounted for by four artifacts: sampling error, variation in criterion reliability, variation in test reliability, and variation in range restriction" (Hunter & Schmidt, 1981, p. 7). Their meta-analytic technique, therefore, is designed to check for such artifactual mediators.

In many ways this fifth and final form of meta-analysis is a variation of that advocated by Hedges and by Rosenthal and Rubin. The two methods agree in basic purpose and analytic strategy. Their greatest difference is that Hunter and Schmidt will not use tests of homogeneity.

Studies are collected; each study is represented in the analysis by one effect size. All studies that bear on the question of interest are included regardless of methodological adequacy. Effect sizes for each study are individually corrected for unreliability or other statistical artifacts when appropriate information is given. If such information is sporadically given, say in only 20 of 50 collected studies, Hunter and Schmidt recommend using the average of the measures found in the 20 studies to correct all the effect sizes.

To measure the overall variability of the effect sizes, the sum of squared differences between each effect size and the estimated population effect is calculated and weighted by proportional sample sizes. The amount of variation attributable to sampling error is calculated next. This calculation is identical to the sampling error approximations used by Hedges and by Rosenthal and Rubin. However, Hunter and Schmidt do not test for homogeneity. Instead, they subtract the variation due to sampling error from the total variation. If sampling error removes approximately 75% of the overall variation, the effect sizes are assumed to estimate one parameter (i.e., they are homogeneous) and the frequency-weighted effect is the best estimate of the parameter.

If the variation is still large after correcting for sampling error, the meta-analyst should investigate the influence of moderator variables. The meta-analyst develops and codes a set of independent variables representing study and treatment features suspected of producing outcome variation. Effect sizes can be divided into groups according to these categories. If a variable really acts as a moderator, the means of the categories should be different, and their variation should be less than variation for the mixed group. Alternatively, correlations can be taken between effect sizes and study features (and these correlations can be corrected for sampling error in the effect sizes) to assess the influence of moderators.

This type of meta-analysis has a number of products. There is an overall mean and standard deviation corrected for statistical artifacts. Once moderating variables have been identified, Hunter and Schmidt recommend the use of regression on the effect sizes as individual data points in much the way Glass recommends. Such a procedure allows the meta-analyst to estimate the distribution of the treatment effects when study characteristics are at their means and when they are varied.

The Hunter-Schmidt procedure is consistent with the goals of meta-analysis described by Hedges and by Rosenthal and Rubin. These researchers wish to base causal conclusions on larger groups of subjects. When primary data is not available, meta-analysis can approximate cluster analysis by grouping effect sizes into natural aggregations. However, instead of testing for statistical significance, Hunter and Schmidt resort to real measures of variance and approximate sampling error. Using these, the meta-analyst is more aware of the real magnitude of variation being examined, not just its statistical significance.

Use of the real measures allows for more creative manipulations of data variation. DerSimonian and Laird (1983), for example, used a meta-analytic procedure that approximates data pooling without recourse to homogeneity tests. They showed that in studies of Scholastic Aptitude Test coaching, sampling error could be estimated more exactly than the estimation routinely used in the test of homogeneity.

When tests of homogeneity calculate sampling error for a group of studies, they assume that each study is a "posttest only" design (C.-L. C. Kulik & J. A. Kulik, 1985). Sampling error estimates are not adjusted when additional information is available from pretests or covariates. DerSimonian and Laird estimated sampling error from gain scores, that is, with variation reduced by information about subjects' pretreatment aptitude. Thus, by *not* applying statistical tests, these reviewers more flexibly and accurately examined the magnitude of variation produced by different categories of effect sizes.

DISCUSSION

Research outcomes vary in ways that make generalizable interpretations difficult. Such variation comes from a number of sources. It may reflect real population variation, the effects of different treatment features or study settings, sampling error, selection biases of the reviewer, publication biases, the effects of erroneous or insufficient reporting (unreported spurious influences, computational errors, typographical errors), differing degrees of validity and reliability in the outcome measures, and differences in the range or intensity of the independent variable. The task is enormous, but the power of social scientific inquiry would greatly increase if patterns could be found amid this outcome variation.

A number of processes have been used to attempt this task. These processes can be arranged on a continuum according to the degree of quantification. At one extreme, there is the informal narrative review that, at its simplest, lists the outcomes of some sample of studies and presents the reviewer's reasoned speculations regarding their interpretation. At the other extreme, there are the forms of secondary analysis, such as cluster analysis (Light & Smith, 1971). Cluster analysis groups original data from varied research sources into smaller, natural aggregations. Where no differences are found among aggregations, original data is pooled into samples of larger sizes.

Meta-analysis lies between these two extremes. Its procedures are more approximate than those of cluster analysis. Yet meta-analysis is more statistically rigorous than is the typical narrative review. It attempts to identify some central tendency in the outcomes of a group of studies and additionally to analyze their variation without resorting to original data.

Because meta-analysis is not a single method, the user must make a number of decisions in conducting such a review. This article does not advocate any particular approach as entirely superior to the others. Instead, general guidelines and cautions are offered regarding the applications of elements of these approaches.

Purpose

The meta-analytic reviewer must first decide the intention of the review. Two alternatives are possible. A reviewer may primarily want to describe a body of literature. Such analyses seek to answer questions of the form "What does available research say about treatment X's effects?" (Glass et al., 1981; J. A. Kulik, C.-L. C. Kulik, & Cohen, 1979). On the other hand, some meta-analyses attempt to approximate an increased sample size in order to test a specific hypothesis and to determine a generalizable estimate of a treatment effect. In intent, these reviews are similar to cluster analyses or data pooling and seek to answer questions of the form "What is the real effect of treatment X?" (Hedges, 1980; Hunter et al., 1983; Rosenthal & Rubin, 1982a).

The difference between these alternatives is not a trivial one. A meta-analyst's choice will determine how outcome variation is treated and how the findings are interpreted and generalized. Indeed, it will determine how the meta-analyst conceives of the whole meta-analytic enterprise.

Meta-analysts who stand closer to the cluster analysis/data pooling/ secondary analysis traditions identify their work with the work of primary researchers. They attempt to answer the same questions as primary researchers, only these meta-analysts hope to use larger samples. "In meta-analysis, the parameter of interest is the population standardized mean difference" (Hedges, 1980, p. 25); "Only cumulation of results across studies can generate {adequate} sample sizes in most areas of contemporary research" (Hunter & Schmidt, 1981, p. 6); and, "We are able to extend traditional limits of meta-analysis to obtain results previously available only when the original data were analyzed" (DerSimonian & Laird, 1983, p. 6).

Other meta-analysts, whose concerns are more in the tradition of "literature review," have pointedly distinguished their work from the work of primary researchers. As Glass put it, "The literature on psychotherapy outcomes is distinct from psychotherapy outcomes themselves by a sequence of translations too obvious to enumerate" (Glass & Kleigl, 1983, p. 35). For Glass, the work of the primary researcher is to construct and test theory; for the meta-analyst, it is to accurately summarize research as it is reported.

Glass's comment is sobering. It reminds us that publicly available reports may not be simple indicants of all the research being done nor of the real effects of a specific treatment. It has been repeatedly observed, for example, that effect sizes taken from published articles are consistently higher than those found in dissertations (Bangert-Drowns, Kulik, & Kulik, 1984; Smith, 1980). There is the forbidding possibility that a meta-analyst's findings may say more about editorial preference, the politics of research finance, or the differential capabilities and biases of professionals and graduate students than about real treatment effects. This dilemma is more serious for meta-analyses that propose to estimate treatment parameters. Those reviews that more modestly claim to only characterize the available findings can fulfill their purposes whether or not publication histories differentiate those findings.

Treatment of Study Variation

Once a purpose is clarified, the meta-analyst must decide how variations among studies will be handled. The meta-analyst must consider three kinds of variation. First, differences in research quality must be considered. Most meta-analysts are fairly liberal in their inclusion of studies of differing quality. However, some (e.g., J. A. Kulik, C.-L. C. Kulik, & Cohen, 1979; Wortman & Bryant, 1985) may eliminate many studies on the grounds of methodological inferiority.

Glass has criticized the use of inclusion standards. Disregarding studies a priori from review because their quality introduces the reviewer's biases and removes a large sample of findings that may in fact differ little from more controlled research. It militates against the possibility of discovering some potentially important relations between methodological variety and outcome variance.

Even the most liberal reviewers will exclude some studies, such as those with insufficient or obviously incorrect reports. Because all meta-analysts deal with inclusion decisions to some degree, two rules should apply. First, criteria for inclusion must be so explicitly stated that others may replicate the results or evaluate the limitations of the review. Second, the meta-analyst must test to determine whether differences in quality are related to differences in outcome. The reviewer can then decide whether research features are confounding treatment effects.

The second issue regarding study variation is the apples-and-oranges problem. A reviewer's interest may be broader than the primary research-er's, for example, an interest in psychotherapy rather than just behavior modification (Cooper, 1982; Wortman, 1983). A reviewer may therefore mix independent variables that primary researchers had tested separately. Such "mixed" independent variables can at times be somewhat artificial or remote from real applications. However, reviewers should define a research area according to their purposes, remembering that a broadly defined independent variable can later be split into smaller components.

Mixing dependent measures that examine different constructs is less justifiable, however. Treatments may influence many phenomena but averaging measures of all these phenomena only confuses our picture of the treatment. A drug may cure cancer but make colds worse. Averaging these effects would obscure important information about the drug and produce a single effect size that is difficult to interpret. It seems better to let every averaged effect size represent one type of dependent measure.

The third issue regarding study variation is the management of out-come variance. Two approaches are available. The first is to treat each study or study finding as a single data point. Traditional statistical tests are applied to relate these collected data points to features of the studies from which they came. This approach is consistent with the use of meta-analysis for literature review (Glassian and study effect meta-analysis).

The alternative is to recognize that each effect size is a summary statistic describing the varied performance of a group of subjects. Each effect size, therefore, has its own sampling error. By accounting for this sampling error, perhaps more accurate estimates can be made of the treat-ment effects. This is consistent with the use of meta-analysis to approxi-mate data pooling either with or without tests of homogeneity.

Users should note some final cautions regarding the homogeneity tests. Rosenthal and Rubin (1982a) warn that the accuracy of the homoge-neity tests for small or nonnormal samples is not certain. Studies that have compared the homogeneity procedures with Glass's have largely replicated

Glass's findings. In addition, Hunter and Schmidt offer an alternative, a method that allows the reviewer to approximate data pooling without resorting to homogeneity tests. Their procedure attends to the real magnitude of variation instead of significance tests and thereby encourages more flexible treatment of sampling error, as in DerSimonian and Laird (1983).

Unit of Analysis

Meta-analysts must also decide which will be the review's unit of analysis, the study itself or the study finding. For cases in which a meta-analyst is approximately data pooling, procedures applied to effect sizes are subject-sensitive and the subject may be regarded as the unit of analysis. Even in these cases, however, one must still decide which will be the basis of the effect sizes, the study or the finding.

There are too many difficulties associated with the study finding as unit of analysis to warrant its continued use. Multiple effect sizes from any one study cannot be regarded as independent and should not be used with statistical tests that assume their independence. Differential contributions of effect sizes from the studies means that some studies will have greater influence on overall findings than others. If effect sizes are divided into smaller categories, whole categories can be dominated by one or two studies and therefore not provide reliably generalizable information. As a rule, each study should be represented only once to an analysis.

Outcomes of Analysis

Of course the outcomes of the analysis are highly dependent on the methods used. Of the five described here, Rosenthal's combined probability method is perhaps the most unique. Its products are an average effect size, a measure of the combined probability of the study outcomes, and the fail-safe N. Even more notable, however, is what is lacking. This approach to meta-analysis makes little or no attempt to examine the relation between study features and study outcomes.

Meta-analysis at its present level of development should be expected to provide more than just measures of central tendency. It should also systematically attempt to relate study features or treatment characteristics to the study outcomes. The combined probability method therefore must be used only in conjunction with elements of other approaches that will better address study outcome variation.

CONCLUSION

The systematic differences in meta-analysis have been largely overlooked. It is time they are clarified so the limitations of this approach to research integration can be more realistically assessed. These differences should not be taken as evidence of some inherent weakness of meta-analysis. It is merely a reflection of the natural evolution of a new social scientific tool. Perhaps meta-analytic methods appropriate to different purposes and different research areas will ultimately be distinguished.

Meta-analysis is not a fad. It is rooted in the fundamental values of the scientific enterprise: replicability, quantification, causal and correlational analysis. Valuable information is needlessly scattered in individual studies. The ability of social scientists to deliver generalizable answers to basic questions of policy is too serious a concern to allow us to treat research integration lightly. The potential benefits of meta-analysis method seem enormous.

REFERENCES

Arkin, R., Cooper, H., & Kolditz, T. (1980). A statistical review of the literature concerning the self-serving bias in interpersonal influence situations. *Journal of Personality, 48*, 435–448.

Bangert-Drowns, R. L. Kulik, J. A., & Kulik, C.-L., C. (1983). Effects of coaching programs on achievement test performance. *Review of Educational Research, 53*, 571–585.

Bangert-Drowns, R. L., Kulik, J. A., & Kulik, C.-L. C. (1984, August). *The influence of study features on outcomes of educational research*. Paper presented at the 92nd annual meeting of the American Psychological Association, Toronto.

Bloom, B. S. (1964). *Stability and change in human characteristics*. New York: Wiley.

Bryant, F. B., & Wortman, P. M. (1984). Methodological issues in the meta-analysis of quasi-experiments. In W. H. Yeaton & P. M. Wortman (Eds.), *Issues in data synthesis* (pp. 5–24). San Francisco: Jossey-Bass.

Burns, P. K. (1981). A quantitative synthesis of research findings relative to the pedagogical effectiveness of computer-assisted mathematics instruction in elementary and secondary schools. *Dissertation Abstracts International, 42*, 2946A. (University Microfilms No. 81-28, 378)

Cartwright, D. (1971). Risk taking by individuals and groups: An assessment of research employing choice dilemmas. *Journal of Personality and Social Psychology, 20*, 361–378.

Cochran, W. G. (1937). Problems arising in the analysis of a series of similar experiments. *Journal of the Royal Statistical Society, 4* (Suppl.), 102–118.

Cochran, W. G. (1943). The comparison of different scales of measurement for experimental results. *Annals of Mathematical Statistics, 14*, 205–216.

Cohen, J. (1962). The statistical power of abnormal–social psychological research: A review. *Journal of Abnormal and Social Psychology, 65*, 145–153.

Cook, T. D., & Campbell, D. T. (1979). *Quasi-experimentation: Design and analysis issues for field settings.* Boston, MA: Houghton Mifflin.

Cook, T. D., & Leviton, L. C. (1980). Reviewing the literature: A comparison of traditional methods with meta-analysis. *Journal of Personality, 48*, 449–472.

Cooper, H. M. (1979). Statistically combining independent studies: A meta-analysis of sex differences in conformity research. *Journal of Personality and Social Psychology, 37*, 131–146.

Cooper, H. M. (1982). Scientific guidelines for conducting integrative reviews. *Review of Educational Research, 52*, 291–302.

Cordray, D. S., & Orwin, R. C. (1983). Improving the quality of evidence: Interconnections among primary evaluation, secondary analysis, and quantitative synthesis. In R. J. Light (Ed.), *Evaluation Studies Review Annual: Vol. 8* (pp. 91–119). Beverly Hills, CA: Sage.

DerSimonian, R., & Laird, N. M. (1983). Evaluating the effect of coaching on SAT scores: A meta-analysis. *Harvard Educational Review, 53*, 1–15.

Dubin, R., & Taveggia, T. C. (1968). *The teaching-learning paradox: A comparative analysis of college teaching methods.* Eugene: University of Oregon Press.

Dusek, J. B., & Joseph, G. (1983). The bases of teacher expectancies: A meta-analysis. *Journal of Educational Psychology, 75*, 327–346.

Educational Research Service (1980). Class size research. A critique of recent meta-analysis. *Phi Delta Kappan, 62*, 239–241.

Erlenmeyer-Kimling, L., & Jarvik, L. F. (1963). Genetics and intelligence: A review. *Science, 142*, 1477–1479.

Eysenck, H. J. (1978). An exercise in mega-silliness. *American Psychologist, 33*, 517.

Fisher, R. A. (1932). *Statistical methods for research workers* (4th ed.). London: Oliver & Boyd.

Ghiselli, E. E. (1949). The validity of commonly employed occupational tests. *University of California Publications in Psychology, 5*, 253–288.

Ghiselli, E. E. (1955). The measurement of occupational aptitude. *University of California Publications in Psychology, 8*, 101–216.

Ghiselli, E. E. (1973). The validity of aptitude tests in personnel selection. *Personnel Psychology, 26*, 461–477.

Glass, G. V. (1976). Primary, secondary, and meta-analysis research. *Educational Researcher, 5*, 3–8.

Glass, G. V. (1979). Policy for the unpredictable. *Educational Researcher, 8*, 12–14.

Glass, G. V., Cahen, L. S., Smith, M. L., & Filby, N. N. (1982). *School class size: Research and policy.* Beverly Hills, CA: Sage.

Glass, G. V., & Kliegl, R. M. (1983). An apology for research integration in the study of psychotherapy. *Journal of Consulting and Clinical Psychology, 51*, 28–41.

Glass, G. V., McGaw, B., & Smith, M. L. (1981). *Meta-analysis in social research.* Beverly Hills, CA: Sage.

Hansford, B. C., & Hattie, J. A. (1982). The relationship between self and achievement/performance measures. *Review of Educational Research, 52,* 123–142.

Hartley, S. S. (1978). Meta-analysis of the effects of individually paced instruction in mathematics. *Dissertation Abstracts International, 38,* 4003A. (University Microfilms No. 77-29, 926)

Hedges, L. V. (1980). Unbiased estimation of effect size. *Evaluation in Education: An International Review Series, 4,* 25–27.

Hedges, L. V. (1981). Distribution theory for Glass's estimator of effect size and related estimators. *Journal of Educational Statistics, 6,* 107–128.

Hedges, L. V. (1982a). Estimation of effect size from a series of independent experiments. *Psychological Bulletin, 92,* 490–499.

Hedges, L. V. (1982b). Fitting categorical models to effect sizes from a series of experiments. *Journal of Educational Statistics, 7,* 119–137.

Hedges, L. V. (1982c). Fitting continuous models to effect size data. *Journal of Educational Statistics, 7,* 245–270.

Hedges, L. V., & Olkin, I. (1982). Analyses, reanalyses, and meta-analysis. *Contemporary Education Review, 1,* 157–165.

Hedges, L. V., & Stock, W. (1983). The effects of class size: An examination of rival hypotheses. *American Educational Research Journal, 20,* 63–85.

Hunter, J. E., & Schmidt, F. L. (1978). Differential and single-group validity of employment tests by race: A critical analysis of three recent studies. *Journal of Applied Psychology, 63,* 1–11.

Hunter, J. E., & Schmidt, F. L. (1981). *Cumulating results across studies: Correction for sampling error. A proposed moratorium on the significance test and a critique of current multivariate reporting practices.* Unpublished manuscript, Michigan State University, East Lansing.

Hunter, J. E., Schmidt, F. L., & Hunter, R. (1979). Differential validity of employment tests by race: A comprehensive review and analysis. *Psychological Bulletin, 86,* 721–735.

Hunter, J. E., Schmidt, F. L., & Jackson, G. B. (1983). *Meta-analysis: Cumulating research findings across studies.* Beverly Hills, CA: Sage.

Jackson, G. B. (1980). Methods for integrative reviews. *Review of Educational Research, 50,* 438–460.

Jackson, S. E. (1984, August). *Can meta-analysis be used for theory development in organizational psychology?* Paper presented at the 92nd annual meeting of the American Psychological Association, Toronto.

Jones, L. V., & Fiske, D. W. (1953). Models for testing the significance of combined results. *Psychological Bulletin, 59,* 375–382.

Kulik , C.-L. C., Kulik, J. A. (1986). *Estimating effect sizes in quantitative research integration.* Manuscript submitted for publication.

Kulik, J. A. (1984, April). *The uses and misuses of meta-analysis.* Paper presented at the meeting of the American Educational Research Association, New Orleans.

Kulik, J. A., & Bangert-Drowns, R. L. (1983/1984). Effectiveness of technology in precollege mathematics and science teaching. *Journal of Educational Technology Systems, 12*, 137-158.

Kulik, J. A., Kulik, C.-L. C., & Cohen, P. A. (1979). A meta-analysis of outcome studies of Keller's personalized system of instruction. *American Psychologist, 34*, 307-318.

Landman, J., & Dawes, R. M. (1982). Psychotherapy outcome. *American Psychologist, 37*, 504-416.

Light, R. J., & Smith, P. V. (1971). Accumulating evidence: procedure for resolving contradictions among different research studies. *Harvard Educational Review, 41*, 429-471.

Mansfield, R. S., & Busse, T. V. (1977). Meta-analysis of research: A rejoinder to Glass. *Educational Researcher, 6*, 3.

Mosteller, F. M., & Bush, R. R. (1954). Selected quantitative techniques. In G. Lindzey (Ed.), *Handbook of social psychology: Vol. 1. Theory and method.* Cambridge, MA: Addison-Wesley.

Pearson, E. S. (1938). The probability integral transformation for testing goodness of fit and combining tests of significance. *Biometrika, 30*, 134-148.

Pearson, K. (1933). On a method of determining whether a sample size n supposed to have been drawn from a parent population having a known probability integral has probably been drawn at random. *Biometrika, 25*, 379-410.

Presby, S. (1978). Overly broad categories obscure important differences between therapies. *American Psychologist, 33*, 514-515.

Rosenthal, R. (1976). Interpersonal expectancy effects; A follow-up. In R. Rosenthal, *Experimental effects in behavioral research* (pp. 440-471). New York: Irvington.

Rosenthal, R. (1978). Combining results of independent studies. *Psychological Bulletin, 85*, 185-193.

Rosenthal, R. (1979). The "file drawer problem" and tolerance for null results. *Psychological Bulletin, 86*, 638-641.

Rosenthal, R. (1983). Assessing the statistical and social importance of the effects of psychotherapy. *Journal of Consulting and Clinical Psychology, 51*, 4-13.

Rosenthal, R., & Rubin, D. B. (1978). Interpersonal expectancy effects; The first 345 studies. *Behavioral and Brain Sciences, 1*, 377-386.

Rosenthal, R., & Rubin, D. B. (1982a). Comparing effect sizes of independent studies. *Psychological Bulletin, 92*, 500-504.

Rosenthal, R., & Rubin, D. B. (1982b). Further meta-analytic procedures for assessing cognitive gender differences. *Journal of Educational Psychology, 74*, 708-712.

Schmidt, F. L., Berner, J. G., & Hunter, J. E. (1973). Racial differences in validity of employment tests: Reality or illusion? *Journal of Applied Psychology, 58*, 5-9.

Shaver, J. P., & Norton, R. S. (1980). Randomness and replication in ten years of the *American Educational Research Journal, Educational Researcher, 9*, 9-16.

Smith, M. L. (1980). Publication bias and meta-analysis. *Evaluation in Education, 4*, 22-24.

Smith, M. L., & Glass, G. V. (1977). Meta-analysis of psychotherapy outcome studies. *American Psychologist, 32,* 752–760.

Smith, M. L., Glass, G. V., & Miller, T. I. (1980). *The benefits of psychotherapy.* Baltimore, MD: Johns Hopkins University Press.

Sudman, S., & Bradburn, N. M. (1974). *Response effects in surveys: A review and synthesis.* Chicago: Aldine.

Taveggia, T. (1974). Resolving research controversy through empirical cumulation. *Sociological Methods and Research, 2,* 395–407.

Tippett, L. H. C. (1931). *The methods of statistics.* London: Williams & Norgate.

Underwood, B. J. (1957). Interference and forgetting. *Psychological Review, 64,* 49–60.

Walberg, H. J., & Haertel, E. H. (Eds.). (1980). *Evaluation in education: An international review series (Vol. 4).* Oxford, England: Pergamon Press.

White, K. R. (1982). The relation between socioeconomic status and academic achievement. *Psychological Bulletin, 91,* 461–481.

Wilkinson, B. (1951). A statistical consideration in psychological research. *Psychological Bulletin, 48,* 156–158.

Wolf, F. M., Savickas, M. L., Saltzman, G. A., & Walker, M. L. (1983). *A meta-analytic evaluation of an interpersonal skills curriculum for medical students: Synthesizing evidence over successive occasions.* Unpublished manuscript, University of Michigan, Ann Arbor. (Preliminary version presented at the meeting of the American Educational Research Association, Montreal, April 1983)

Wortman, P. M. (1983). Evaluation research: A methodological perspective. *Annotated Review of Psychology, 34,* 223–260.

Wortman, P. M., & Bryant, F. B. (1985). School desegregation and black achievement: An integrative review. *Sociological Methods and Research, 13,* 289–324.

Yates, F., & Cochran, W. G. (1938). The analysis of groups of experiments. *Journal of Agricultural Science, 28,* 556–580.

V

SPECIAL TOPICS IN CLINICAL RESEARCH

A variety of special circumstances, methods, and problems emerge in clinical research. Articles in this section illustrate special situations and methods for research and evaluation and, hence, supplement more traditional methods previously covered.

CASE STUDY AND SMALL SAMPLE RESEARCH

Much of clinical research and evaluation is conducted with one or only a few clients, as in psychotherapy. In such cases of course, the usual methods and designs are strained and cannot properly provide strong bases for drawing inferences. In clinical work, assessment and evaluation are no less important. However, alternative methods may be needed to provide such an evaluation. In the first article (Kazdin, 1981), I discuss the case study in the context of clinical work. The article suggests that cases can be evaluated in such a way as to permit causal inferences to be drawn about the impact of alternative interventions. Specific assessment practices and

469

special information about the case can enhance the understanding of influences well beyond the yield from traditional anecdotal case studies.

The previous article suggests methods that can be brought to bear to evaluate cases in practice but do not constitute true experiments. Steven Hayes (1981) extends the discussion to present single-case experimental designs. These designs are rarely taught in research training in clinical psychology despite their potential for widespread use. In this article, essential features of the designs, options for conducting careful evaluations, and integration of the designs with clinical exigencies are discussed.

Clinical research often focuses on complex interpersonal variables that require fine-grained analyses of small numbers of cases. William Henry, Thomas Schacht, and Hans Strupp (1986) focus on a small number of therapists and clients to examine therapeutic relationship and treatment-process issues. They illustrate a novel method of analysis (Structural Analysis of Social Behavior {SASB}) that permits evaluation of several interpersonal processes.

DESIGN, TREATMENT EVALUATION, AND CHANGE

Research with clinical populations in applied settings often places special constraints on the design related to the number of subjects available for participation in the study, random assignment of subjects to conditions, and retention of subjects within the study and within the conditions to which they were assigned. Helena Kraemer (1981) suggests strategies to cope methodologically with many of the constraints of clinical research. Issues related to sample size, criteria for case selection, random assignment, the importance of measurement selection, and alternative methods of data analyses are discussed. Alternative design options and strategies are presented to increase the strength of the design and sensitivity of experimental tests.

In psychotherapy outcome research, a central task is to understand the impact of alternative forms of treatment. The impact of treatment is likely to depend on a variety of factors and influences including the specific intervention, characteristics of clients and therapists, alternative processes that emerge within treatment, and other conditions of administration. To say that treatment depends on multiple factors means that treatment is moderated by or interacts with these other factors. Bradley Smith and Lee Sechrest (1991) discuss the study of Treatment–Aptitude interactions. In this context, aptitude is used as a term to reflect diverse variables (client, therapist, setting, and other) that may moderate the impact or outcome. The article is important in addressing substantive, methodological, and data analytic issues in examining interactions of treatment with other variables. Although the focus is on therapy research, the points and analytic issues apply more broadly in the search for interactions among variables.

An issue in psychotherapy research has been the role of nonspecific factors in therapeutic change. The underlying research question, stated generally, is whether treatment outcomes are attained because of factors included by the conceptual underpinnings of treatment or because of more general factors such as attending treatment, talking with a professional, and expecting improvement. Of course, treatment outcome does not have to result from either specific treatment influences (e.g., altered cognitions or resolution of psychodynamic conflict) or nonspecific effects. Yet, the control of nonspecific effects has raised important issues regarding the interface of conceptual and methodological features of therapy research. In the article by Morris Parloff (1986), placebo controls are discussed in the context of current psychotherapy research. The article raises issues about the nature of therapy, the meaningfulness of the concept of placebo, and the difficulty in developing appropriate control conditions. The article ends with recommendations regarding how to design therapy research.

Research in clinical psychology frequently focuses on changes over time. Among the examples are studies of therapy, recidivism, and changes over the course of development. In these and other areas, the researcher is concerned with such changes as improvement, the course of functioning, and the onset or termination of some target event. The article by David Francis, Jack Fletcher, Karla Stuebing, Kevin Davidson, and Nora Thompson (1991) discusses the analysis of change. The article is included here because central topics are covered such as alternative measures and models of change, issues raised by different methods of computing change (e.g., difference scores), and alternative statistical measures to focus on change of individuals as well as groups. An example of one method of evaluating change is also included.

Evaluation of the change is usually based on statistical criteria (statistical significance). In clinical psychology, treatment outcome serves as a frequent focus of research. The interventions are designed to have an impact that is clinically significant. Clinical significance is concerned with the findings of whether the impact makes a difference to the individual in everyday life. Clinical significance has been defined in many ways, such as whether the individual seen in treatment has returned to normative levels of functioning at the end of treatment, whether the problem that led to treatment has been eliminated, and whether others in contact with the client (e.g., spouses and peers) subjectively view the client as improved. In the article by Neil Jacobson and Paula Truax (1991), clinical significance is discussed in relation to the amount of change an individual makes over the course of treatment. A statistic referred to as the *reliability of change index* is proposed as a measure to evaluate whether the change is clinically important.

CASE STUDY AND SMALL
SAMPLE RESEARCH

24

DRAWING VALID INFERENCES FROM CASE STUDIES

ALAN E. KAZDIN

The case study has played a central role in clinical psychology. Indeed, understanding the individual person is occasionally considered to be a distinguishing characteristic of clinical psychology relative to other branches of the field (Korchin, 1976; Watson, 1951). The intensive study of the individual has contributed to clinical research and practice by providing a rich source of hypothesis about the bases of personality and behavior and by serving as a place to develop and apply intervention techniques (Bolgar, 1965; Garfield, 1974; Kazdin, 1980; Lazarus & Davison, 1971).

Despite its recognized heuristic value, the case study is usually considered to be inadequate as a basis for drawing valid scientific inferences. Relationships between independent and dependent variables are difficult to discern in a typical case study because of the ambiguity of the factor(s)

Reprinted from the *Journal of Consulting and Clinical Psychology, 49*, 183–192. Copyright 1981 by the American Psychological Association.

Preparation of this manuscript was facilitated by Grant MH31047 from the National Institute of Mental Health.

responsible for performance. For example, treatment for a particular clinical case may be associated with therapeutic change. However, the basis for the change cannot be determined from an uncontrolled case study. Even if treatment were responsible for change, several alternative interpretations of the case might be proposed. These alternative interpretations have been catalogued under the rubric of "threats to internal validity" (Campbell & Stanley, 1963).[1]

The case study has been discounted as a potential source of scientifically validated inferences, because threats to internal validity cannot be ruled out in the manner achieved in experimentation. Even though the case study is not experimental research, under several circumstances it can lead to knowledge about treatment effects for a given client that approximates the information achieved in experimentation. The present article examines the case study and its variations as a research tool. Alternative ways in which case studies are conducted and reported have important implications for drawing scientifically validated information. The present article discusses what can be done with the clinical case to improve the scientific inferences that can be drawn.

The case study as a potential source of scientifically valid information warrants careful scrutiny for several reasons. First, the case study has had tremendous impact on psychotherapy. Individual cases (e.g., Little Hans, Anna O., Little Albert) and series of cases (e.g., Masters & Johnson, 1970; Wolpe, 1958) have exerted remarkable influence on subsequent research and practice. Second, the case study draws attention to the frequently lamented hiatus between clinical practice and research. Clinicians have access to the individual case as their most convenient and feasible investigative tool, but inadequacies of the case study as a research strategy limit the inferences that can be drawn. Researchers often rigorously investigate psychotherapy but may sacrifice clinical relevance in the populations, therapeutic conditions, and standardization of treatment that research may require. Hence, investigation of psychotherapy often obscures aspects of the phenomenon of interest (Strupp & Hadley, 1979), and even under the best conditions, treatment may only be an "analogue" of the clinical situation (Kazdin, 1978).

One suggestion to help bring research and practice of psychotherapy

---

[1] The threats to internal validity refer to classes of variables that might produce effects mistaken for the effects of treatment. The major threats include the influence of (a) history (specific events occurring in time), (b) maturation (processes within the person), (c) testing (repeated exposure to the assessment procedures), (d) instrumentation (changes in the scoring procedures or criteria over time), (e) statistical regression (reversion of scores toward the mean or toward less extreme scores), (f) selection (differential composition of subjects among the groups), (g) mortality (differential attrition among groups), and (h) selection–maturation (and other) interactions (where differential changes occur as a function of other threats with selection). For additional threats, see Cook and Campbell (1979) and Kazdin (1980).

closer together is to encourage clinicians to utilize single case experimental designs (Hersen & Barlow, 1976). The designs permit experimental investigation of the single case. The designs have been applied successfully and often dramatically in case reports where the effects of treatment have been carefully documented with complex clinical problems seen in individual treatment. However, single-case experimental designs often impose special requirements (e.g., withdrawing or withholding treatment at different points in the designs) that are not always feasible in the clinical situation. Hence, some authors have suggested that the designs have not really been applied as widely as they should (Barlow, 1980) and perhaps often cannot be applied, because of the ethical, methodological, and practical obstacles inherent in clinical settings (Kazdin & Wilson, 1978).

Apart from the merits of single-case experimentation, nonexperimental alternatives need to be examined carefully. Indeed, in other areas of psychology, experimentation is not always possible. In such instances, important alternatives have been provided by elaborating the requirements for quasi-experiments (Campbell & Stanley, 1963), which can achieve some if not all of the goals of experimentation. Similarly, in the context of clinical practice, experiments are to be encouraged when opportunities exist. However, it is very important to elaborate the conditions that can be invoked to achieve several goals of experiments when rigorous investigations are not possible. The uncontrolled case study is a widely available investigative tool, and its methodological limitations, advantages, and alternatives need to be elaborated.

Characteristics of the Case Study

The case study has been defined in many different ways. Traditionally, the case study has referred to intensive investigation of the individual client. Case reports often include detailed descriptions of individual clients. The descriptions rely heavily on anecdotal accounts of the therapist to draw inferences about factors that contributed to the client's plight and changes over the course of treatment. Aside from the focus on the individual, the case study has come to refer to a methodological approach in which a person or group is studied in such a fashion that inferences cannot be drawn about the factors that contribute to performance (Campbell & Stanley, 1963; Paul, 1969). Thus, even if several persons are studied, the approach may still be that of a case study. Often cases are treated on an individual basis, but the information that is reported is aggregated across cases, for example, as in reports about the efficacy of various treatments (e.g., Lazarus, 1963; Wolpe, 1958). Hence, there is some justification for not delimiting the case study merely to the report of an individual client.

In general, the case study has been defined heterogeneously to denote several different things, including the focus on the individual, reliance on anecdotal information, and the absence of experimental controls. A central feature of the diverse definitions is that case studies differ from experimental demonstrations. Texts on methodology usually discount the case study as a preexperimental design and use it as a point of departure to show that experimentation is the alternative means for obtaining scientifically validated knowledge (Campbell & Stanley, 1963; Hersen & Barlow, 1976; Kazdin, 1980). However, the purpose of the present article is to suggest that case studies and experiments fall on a continuum that reflects the degree to which scientifically adequate inferences can be drawn. More importantly, several types of uncontrolled case studies can be identified that vary in the extent to which they permit valid conclusions.

The purpose of experimentation is to rule out threats to internal validity, which serve as alternative rival hypotheses of the results. For example, in clinical treatment research, single-case or between-groups experimental designs are required to rule out the impact of extraneous factors that might account for the findings. Case studies do not provide the arrangements that permit conclusions that are as clear as those available from experimentation. However, many of the threats to internal validity can be ruled out in case studies so that conclusions can be reached about the impact of treatment.

DIMENSIONS FOR EVALUATING CASE STUDIES

Case studies have been loosely and heterogeneously defined to include a variety of uncontrolled demonstrations aimed at showing that treatment produces therapeutic change. However, case studies may vary in how they are conducted and reported. The distinctions that can be made among case studies have important implications for drawing unambiguous conclusions. Major dimensions that can distinguish case studies insofar as they relate to internal validity, are presented below.

Type of Data

The main criterion that distinguishes case studies is the basis for claiming that a change has been achieved. At one extreme, anecdotal information may be relied on and include narrative accounts by the client and/or therapist regarding how client functioning has improved. Anecdotal reports are subject to a variety of limitations and sources of bias that need not be elaborated here. Suffice it to say that the anecdotal reports usually are not sufficient to conclude that changes really occurred in client behavior.

Case studies can include objective information, which refers to the large category of measurement strategies in which systematic and quantitative data are obtained. The specific measures encompass the gamut of assessment modalities and techniques (e.g., self-reports, ratings by others, overt behavior). Depending on other dimensions discussed below, objective information is a basic condition of a case study that has important implications for drawing inferences about the effects of treatment. The type of data obtained in a case study, that is, anecdotal or objective information, perhaps is the most important precondition for drawing inferences from a case study. Without some systematic data collection, other dimensions that might be applied to evaluate the case become almost irrelevant. Scientific inferences are difficult if not impossible to draw from anecdotal information. Indeed, it is the anecdotal information that is the problem rather than the fact that an individual case is studied. Even a rigorously designed experiment would be completely uninterpretable if anecdotal reports rather than objective assessment procedures served as the dependent measures.[2]

Assessment Occasions

Other dimensions that can distinguish case studies are the number and timing of assessment occasions. The occasions in which this objective information is collected have extremely important implications for drawing inferences from the case. Major options consist of collecting information on a one- or two-shot basis (e.g., posttreatment only, pre-and posttreatment, respectively) or continuously over time (e.g., every day or a few times per week) for an extended period.

When information is collected on one or two occasions, say before or after treatment, difficulties arise in inferring that change has occurred as a result of treatment. Other interpretations of the change might be proposed (e.g., testing, instrumentation, statistical regression). With continuous as-

---

[2] The absence of quantitative information may not necessarily rule out drawing causal inferences. Occasionally, intervention effects are so powerful that qualitative changes appear to be produced, and the certainty of change and the reason for this change are relatively unambiguous. These effects, occasionally referred to as "slam bang" effects (Gilbert, Light & Mosteller, 1975), are evident throughout the history of medicine and psychology. For example, Shapiro (1963) described a case of a patient with terminal cancer who showed a dramatic remission of symptoms on separate occasions as a function of receiving inert substances (an inactive drug and water). In this case, the changes were so strong and immediate ("slam bang" effects) that the absence of careful measurement did not pose as serious a problem for drawing inferences that the administration of treatment led to change. Apart from occasional examples, in most instances, quantitative information is required to attest to the fact that changes have in fact occurred and that these changes can be assessed with procedures that are replicable.

sessment over time conducted before or after treatment, artifacts associated with the assessment procedures become less plausible. That is, changes as a function of the measurement instrument, if evident, normally would be detected prior to treatment and would not necessarily obscure the pattern of data relied on to infer changes associated with treatment.

Continuous assessment provides an additional advantage that can strengthen the internal validity of the case study. Data from continuous assessment prior to treatment can serve as a basis for making predictions about likely performance in the future. Extrapolations about the likely direction of performance provide implicit predictions about what performance would be like. The effects of treatment can be judged by the extent to which departures in the data are evident from the previously projected performance.

Past and Future Projections

The extent to which valid inferences can be drawn about treatment effects is influenced by past and future projections of performance. The past and future projections may derive from continuous assessment which shows that the problem is stable and has not changed for an extended period. As noted above, continuous assessment can provide information extrapolated to the future that may serve as an implicit but testable prediction. If behavior appears stable for an extended period, changes that coincide with treatment suggest that the intervention may have led to change.

Past and future projections of performance also may be derived from understanding the course of a particular clinical problem. For some problems (e.g., obesity, social withdrawal), and extended history may be evident. The extended history is important from the standpoint of drawing inferences when change occurs. When change has occurred for a client whose problem has been evident for a long period, the plausibility that treatment caused the change is greatly increased. On the other hand, an acute clinical problem that has emerged relatively recently or is associated with a clear precipitating event may make evaluation of treatment slightly more difficult than it would be for a chronic problem. The acute or even episodic problem might be more amenable to the influence of extraneous (i.e., nontreatment) factors. Hence, it will be relatively difficult to rule out factors other than treatment that may account for the changes.

Projections of what the problems would be like in the future derived from understanding the particular clinical problem are also very relevant to drawing inferences about treatment. Research may suggest that a particular clinical problem is very likely to improve, worsen, or remain the same over a period of time. These alternative prognoses may be important when drawing inferences about treatment effects in a given case. For example, knowledge about the disorder may suggest that the problem will deteriorate over time (e.g., terminal cancer). The likely future for such a problem is highly relevant for evaluating whether treatment may be responsible for change. In the case of a patient with a terminal disease, improvements associated with a highly experimental treatment provide a strong inferential basis. Patient improvement strongly attests to the efficacy of treatment as the important intervention, because change in the disorder controverts the expected prediction.[3] Of course, with some clients and clinical problems, the future projections may indicate that improvements are likely even if no treatments are provided. For example, in treatment of children who have specific fears, conclusions about the short-term or long-term effects of treatment in a clinical case may be difficult to reach, because the projection for the future is for improvement (Agras, Chapin, & Oliveau, 1972). In general, inferences about the effects of treatment in a given case are more easily made to the extent that predictions can be made on the basis of extraneous information that the problem, if untreated, will follow a particular course. The plausibility that the changes are a result of treatment depend in part on the extent to which changes in client performance depart from the expected and predicted pattern of performance.

Type of Effect

The degree to which inferences can be drawn about the causal agent in the treatment of a clinical case also depends on the kinds of changes that occur. The immediacy and magnitude of changes contribute to judgments that treatment may have caused the change. Usually, the more immediate the therapeutic changes after the onset of treatment, the stronger a case can be made that treatment was responsible for the change. Of course, as any other of the dimensions discussed, showing that the conditions are met, in this case an immediate change, does not by itself mean that treatment was responsible for the change. But the more immediate the change, the less likely alternative sources of influence coincident with treatment account for the change. Alternatively, when change is gradual or delayed rather than immediate, the plausibility of associating the change with a particular

---

[3] This, of course, is not to say that the component the investigator believes to be important in the treatment was the one actually responsible for change, but only that the treatment and all that the treatment encompassed was the important event. The aspect(s) of treatment that caused change in experimentation is not a question of internal validity but rather one of construct validity (Cook & Campbell, 1976, 1979). In experimental research, the particular aspect of treatment may still be debated (construct validity), even though the experiment has ruled out the impact of extraneous influences (internal validity).

event in the past (i.e., treatment) decreases. As the latency between treatment administration and behavior change increases, the number of extraneous experiences that could account for the change increases as well.

Aside from the immediacy of change, the magnitude of change also contributes to the extent to which treatment can be accorded a causal role. More confidence might be placed in the causal role of treatment when relatively large changes are achieved. Of course, the magnitude and immediacy of change when combined increase the confidence that one can place in according treatment a causal role. Rapid and dramatic changes provide a strong basis for attributing the effects to treatment than more gradual and relatively small changes. A rapid and large change suggests that a particular intervention rather than randomly occurring extraneous influences accounts for the pattern of results.

Number and Heterogeneity of Subjects

Dimensions related to the subjects may influence the confidence that can be placed in conclusions about treatment effects. The number of cases included is important. Obviously, a stronger basis for inferring the effects of treatment stems from demonstrations with several cases rather than one case. The more cases that show changes associated with treatment, the more unlikely an extraneous event is responsible for change. An extraneous event that covaries with treatment and leads to therapeutic change is an unlikely rival hypothesis of the results, because the event must be common to all of the cases. The sheer number of cases obviously can contribute to the extent to which conclusions about treatment can be drawn by making implausible other explanations.

Aside from the number of cases, the heterogeneity of the cases may also contribute to drawing inferences about the cause of therapeutic change. If change is demonstrated across several clients who differ in various subject and demographic characteristics and the time that they are treated, the inferences that can be drawn are much stronger than if this diversity does not exist. Essentially, different persons have different histories and rates of maturation. As the diversity and heterogeneity of the clients and the conditions of treatment increase, it becomes increasingly implausible that the common experience shared by the clients (i.e., treatment) accounts for the changes.

APPLICATION OF THE DIMENSIONS

The above dimensions do not necessarily exhaust all of the factors that contribute to drawing firm conclusions from case studies. Also, each of the dimensions is discussed separately. Yet, any particular case can be examined in terms of where it lies on each of the dimensions. Precisely where a particular case falls on all of the dimensions determines the extent to which particular threats to internal validity or rival alternative hypotheses can be ruled out in interpreting the results.

All of the possible combinations of the dimensions would yield a large number of types of case studies that cannot be presented here. Many of the dimensions represent continua where an indefinite number of gradations are possible so a large set of types of cases could be enumerated. However, it is important to look at selected types of cases that vary on the dimensions mentioned earlier to show how internal validity can be addressed.

Table 1 illustrates a few types of cases that differ in their standing on the dimensions mentioned earlier. The extent to which each type of case rules out the specific threats to internal validity is also presented using a format that parallels similar analyses for true and quasi-experiments (Campbell & Stanley, 1963). For each case type, the collection of objective data was included. As noted earlier, the absence of objective or quantifiable data usually precludes drawing firm conclusions about whether change occurred. Drawing conclusions about the basis for change is premature, because the change itself has not been carefully documented. In the case types illustrated in Table 1, the assumption will be made that some

TABLE 1
Examples of Types of Cases and the Threats to
Internal Validity That They Address

Measure	Case example		
	1	2	3
Characteristic of case			
Objective data	+	+	+
Continuous assessment	–	+	+
Stability of problem	–	–	+
Immediate and marked effects	–	+	–
Multiple cases	–	–	+
Major threats to internal validity			
History	–	?	+
Maturation	–	?	+
Testing	–	+	+
Instrumentation	–	+	+
Statistical regression	–	+	+

Note: + indicates that the threat to internal validity is probably controlled, – indicates that the threat remains a problem, and ? indicates that the threat may remain uncontrolled. In preparation of the table, selected threats (mortality, selection, and others; see Footnote 1) were omitted because they arise primarily in the comparison of different groups in experiments and quasi-experiments. They are not usually a problem for a case study, which of course does not rely on group comparisons.

form of assessment was completed, even if only one or two occasions to measure performance before and after treatment.

Case Example Type 1: With Pre- and Postassessment

A case study where a client is treated may utilize pre- and posttreatment assessment. The inferences that can be drawn from a case with such assessment are not necessarily increased by the assessment alone. Whether specific threats to internal validity are ruled out depends on characteristics of the case with respect to the other dimensions. Table 1 illustrates a case with pre- and postassessment but without other optimal features that would address and rule out threats to internal validity.

If changes occur in the case from pre- to posttreatment assessment, one cannot draw valid inferences about whether the treatment led to change. It is quite possible that events occurring in time (history), processes of change within the individual (maturation), repeated exposure to assessment (testing), changes in the scoring criteria (instrumentation), or reversion of the score to the mean (regression) rather than treatment led to change. Hence, even though the case included objective assessment, the conclusion that can be drawn about the basis for change is not greatly improved over an anecdotal report.

Case Example Type 2: With Repeated Assessment and Marked Changes

If the case study includes assessment on several occasions before and after treatment, and the changes that occur at the time or over the course of treatment are relatively marked, then the inferences that can be drawn about treatment are vastly improved. Table 1 illustrates the characteristics of the case along with the extent to which specific threats to internal validity are addressed.

The fact that continuous assessment is included is important in ruling out the specific threats to internal validity that are related to assessment. First, the changes that coincide with treatment are not likely to result from exposure to repeated testing or changes in the instrument. When continuous assessment is utilized, changes due to testing or instrumentation could have been evident before treatment began. Similarly, regression to the mean from one data point to another, a special problem with assessment conducted only at two points in time, is eliminated. Repeated observation over time shows a pattern in the data. Extreme scores may be a problem for any particular assessment occasion in relation to the immediately prior occasion. However, these changes cannot account for the pattern of performance for an extended period.

Aside from continuous assessment, this case illustration was proposed to include relatively marked treatment effects, that is, changes that are relatively immediate and large. These types of changes produced in treatment help rule out the influence of history and maturation as plausible rival hypotheses. Maturation in particular may be relatively implausible, because maturational changes are not likely to be abrupt and large. However, a "?" was placed in the table, because maturation cannot be ruled out completely. In this case example, information on the stability of the problem in the past and future was not included. Hence, it is not known whether the clinical problem might ordinarily change on its own and whether maturational influences are plausible. Some problems that are episodic in nature conceivably could show marked changes that have little to do with treatment. With immediate and large changes in behavior, history is also not likely to account for the results. However, a "?" was placed in the table here too. Without a knowledge of the stability of the problem over time, one cannot be too confident about the impact of extraneous events.

For this case overall, much more can be said about the impact of treatment than in the previous case. Continuous assessment and marked changes help to rule out specific rival hypotheses. In a given instance, history and maturation may be ruled out too, although these are likely to depend on other dimensions in the table that specifically were not included in this case.

Case Example Type 3: With Multiple Cases, Continuous Assessment, and Stability Information

Several cases rather than only one may be studied where each includes continuous assessment. The cases may be treated one at a time and accumulated into a final summary statement of treatment effects or treated as a single group at the same time. In this illustration as characterized, assessment information is available on repeated occasions before and after treatment as in the last type of case. Also, the stability of the problem is known in this example. Stability refers to the dimension of past–future projections and denotes that information is available from other research that the problem does not usually change over time. When the problem is known to be highly stable or follows a particular course without treatment, the clinician has an implicit prediction of the effects of no treatment. The results can be compared to this predicted level of performance.

As evident in Table 1, the threats to internal validity are addressed by a case report meeting the specified characteristics. History and maturation are not likely to interfere with drawing conclusions about the causal role of treatment, because several different cases are included. All cases are not likely to have a single historical event or maturational process in common that could account for the results. Knowledge about the stability of the problem in the future also helps to rule out the influence of history and maturation. If the problem is known to be stable over time, this means that ordinary historical events and maturational processes do not provide a strong enough influence in their own right. Because of the use of multiple subjects and the knowledge about the stability of the problem, history and maturation are considered to be implausible explanations of therapeutic change.

The threats to internal validity related to testing are handled largely by the assessment over time. Repeated testing, changes in the instrument, and reversion of scores toward the mean may influence a comparison of performance from one occasion to another. Problems associated with testing are not likely to influence the pattern of data over a large number of occasions. Also, information about the stability of the problem helps to further make implausible changes due to testing. The fact that the problem is known to be stable means that it probably would not change merely as a function of assessment.

In general, the case study of the type illustrated in this example provides a strong basis for drawing valid inferences about the impact of treatment. The manner in which the multiple case report is designed does not constitute an experiment, as usually conceived, because each case represents an uncontrolled demonstration. However, characteristics of the type of case study can rule out specific threats to internal validity in a manner approaching that of true experiments.

General Comments

From the standpoint of experimentation, all of the above types of cases share a similar methodological status by being preexperimental and by not providing a sufficient basis for drawing scientifically valid inferences. The results that may emerge are usually rejected, because the data are from case studies. However, it is extremely important to shift the focus from the type of demonstration (i.e., case study versus experiment) to the specific threats to internal validity that interfere with drawing valid inferences. The focus on rival alternative hypotheses that may be proposed draws attention to characteristics of the case reports that can be altered to improve the scientific yield.

The purpose of experimentation is to make as implausible as possible alternative explanations of the results. At the end of an experimental investigation, the effects of the treatment should be the most plausible and parsimonious interpretation of the results. Case studies can also rule out alternative explanations that might compete with drawing inferences about the impact of treatment.

Specific procedures that can be controlled by the clinical investigator can influence the strength of the case demonstration. First, the investigator can collect objective data in place of anecdotal report information. Clear measures are needed to attest to the fact that change has actually occurred. Second, client performance can be assessed on several occasions, perhaps before, during, and after treatment. The continuous assessment helps rule out important rival hypotheses related to testing, which a simple pre- and posttreatment assessment strategy does not accomplish.

Third, the clinical investigator can accumulate cases that are treated and assessed in a similar fashion. Large groups are not necessarily needed but only the systematic accumulation of a number of clients. As the number and heterogeneity of clients increase and receive treatment at different points in time, history and maturation become less plausible as alternative rival hypotheses. If treatment is given to several clients on different occasions, one has to propose an intricate explanation showing how different historical events or maturational processes intervened to alter performance. As in ordinary experimentation, in such cases, treatment effects become the more likely interpretation.

Some features of the case study that can help rule out threats to internal validity are out of control of the clinical investigator. For example, knowledge about the stability of the problem over time comes from information extraneous to a particular client. Knowledge about the course of the disorder is required. However, even though this is not controllable by the clinical investigator, he or she can bring available information to bear when interpreting results. This is already implicit in some instances where, for example, the problem in treatment is known to have a high remission rate (e.g., childhood fears). Remission of the problem, which may normally occur over time, requires special care for interpreting the long-term effects of treatment with any particular case or intervention.

The clinical investigator cannot easily control whether the changes in treatment are immediate rather than marginal. However, the data pattern that does result should be examined specifically in light of other rival hypotheses that might explain the results. Could any historical events (e.g., family processes, job experiences) or maturational processes (e.g., decreased depression as a function of the passage of time since divorce or death of a relative) be brought to bear that might explain the pattern of results? Perhaps the pattern of the data can help rule out specific rival hypotheses.

It is not merely how we conduct case studies that might warrant reconsideration but how we conceptualize them as well. Much can be done in carrying out case studies to increase the strength of the inferences about causal events. The well-known criticism of case studies as research tools has fostered a methodological learned helplessness about what can be done. In fact, much can be done to rule out specific threats to internal validity within case studies, such as the use of assessment on multiple occasions and the accumulation of several cases.

Some of the dimensions that help rule out threats to internal validity are out of the control of the clinical investigator. For example, one cannot by fiat achieve immediate and marked therapeutic changes nor be sure of the stability of the problem over the past and future. However, the clinical investigator can bring to bear the available research on the nature of the problem and evaluate the likelihood that historical events and maturational processes could achieve the sorts of changes evident in treatment. It is not necessarily the lack of control over the clinical situation that is a problem. Within the limits of the situation, the clinical investigator might keep in mind some of the specific alternative rival hypotheses that need to be ruled out or made less plausible.

CONCLUSION

The case study occupies an extremely important place in clinical work both in inpatient and outpatient care. Case studies are widely recognized to serve as an important place to develop hypotheses about clinical problems and to explore innovative treatments. However, cases are usually considered to be completely inadequate as a basis for drawing scientifically validated inferences.

Case studies encompass several types of demonstrations that may differ in the extent to which inferences can be drawn. The issue is not whether a particular report is a case study. The focus on classifying reports on the basis of their lack of experimental design detracts from the more pertinent issue. Drawing inferences, whether in case studies, quasi-experiments, or experiments, is a matter of ruling out rival hypotheses that could account for the results. In case studies, by definition, the number of rival hypotheses and their plausibility are likely to present greater problems than they would in experiments. However, it is possible to include features in the case study that help decrease the plausibility of specific rival hypotheses.

The present article discusses several possibilities for assessing performance that rule out selected threats to internal validity. The purpose in adopting this approach is not to legitimize the case study as a replacement for experimental research. Experiments based on intra- and intersubject methodology can uniquely rule out threats to internal validity and can provide relatively clear information about the impact of treatment. Although the case study is not a substitute for experimentation, it has and probably will continue to contribute greatly to the information available in the field. Hence, it is important to consider the case study as a potential source of scientifically useful information and to adopt procedures, where they exist, to increase the strength of case demonstrations in clinical situations when true or quasi-experiments are not viable options.

REFERENCES

Agras, W. S., Chapin, H. H., & Oliveau, D. C. (1972). The natural history of phobia. *Archives of General Psychiatry, 26,* 315–317.

Barlow, D. H. (1980). Behavior therapy: The next decade. *Behavior Therapy, 11,* 315–328.

Bolgar, H. (1965). The case study method. In B. B. Wolman (Ed.), *Handbook of clinical psychology.* New York: McGraw-Hill.

Campbell, D. T., & Stanley, J. C. (1963). *Experimental and quasi-experimental designs for research.* Chicago: Rand McNally.

Cook, T. D., & Campbell, D. T. (1976). The design and conduct of quasi-experiments and true experiments in field settings. In M.D. Dunnette (Ed.), *Handbook of industrial and organizational psychology.* Chicago: Rand McNally.

Cook, T. D. & Campbell, D. T. (Eds.). (1979). *Quasi-experimentation: Design and analysis issues for field settings.* Chicago: Rand McNally.

Garfield, S. L. (1974). *Clinical psychology: The study of personality and behavior.* Chicago: Aldine.

Gilbert, J. P., Light, R. J., & Mosteller, F. (1975). Assessing social innovations: An empirical base for policy. In C.A. Bennett & A.A. Lumsdaine (Eds.), *Evaluation and experiment.* New York: Academic Press.

Hersen, M., & Barlow, D. H. (1976). *Single-case experimental designs: Strategies for studying behavior change.* New York: Pergamon Press.

Kazdin, A. E. (1978). Evaluating the generality of findings in analogue therapy research. *Journal of Consulting and Clinical Psychology, 46,* 673–686.

Kazdin, A. E. (1980). Research design in clinical psychology. New York: Harper & Row.

Kazdin, A. E., & Wilson, G. T. (1978). *Evaluation of behavior therapy: Issues, evidence, and research strategies.* Cambridge, Mass.: Ballinger.

Korchin, S. J. (1976). *Modern clinical psychology.* New York: Basic Books.

Lazarus, A. A. (1963). The results of behaviour therapy in 126 cases of severe neurosis. *Behaviour Research and Therapy, 1,* 69–79.

Lazarus, A. A., & Davison, G. C. (1971). Clinical innovation in research and practice. In A. E. Bergin & S. L. Garfield (Eds.), *Handbook of psychotherapy and behavior change: An empirical analysis.* New York: Wiley.

Masters, W. H., & Johnson, V. E. (1970). *Human sexual inadequacy.* Boston: Little, Brown.

Paul, G. (1969). Behavior modification research: Design and tactics. In C. M. Franks (Ed.), *Behavior therapy: Appraisal and status.* New York: McGraw-Hill.

Shapiro, A. K. (1963). Psychological aspects of medication. In H. I. Lief, V. F. Lief, & N. R. Lief (Eds.), *The psychological basis of medical practice.* New York: Harper & Row.

Strupp, H. H., & Hadley, S. W. (1979). Specific vs. nonspecific factors in psychotherapy. *Archives of General Psychiatry, 36,* 1125–1137.

Watson, R. I. (1951). *The clinical method in psychology.* New York: Harper & Row.

Wolpe, J. (1958). *Psychotherapy by reciprocal inhibition.* Stanford, CA: Stanford University Press.

25

SINGLE CASE EXPERIMENTAL DESIGN AND EMPIRICAL CLINICAL PRACTICE

STEVEN C. HAYES

The progress of research in clinical psychology presents something of a paradox. The social need for clinical research can hardly be overestimated; the field incorporates many of the most serious social and personal ills of the day. Further, tremendous resources are available to the field in the numbers of professionals , training programs, employment opportunities, and (compared with many disciplines) funding patterns. Yet data abound that these needs and resources have not yet been fully combined to produce maximum research progress (Garfield & Kurtz, 1976; Kelly, Goldberg, Fiske, & Kilkowski, 1978; Levy, 1962).

This paradox has often been noted, especially in the well-worn discussion of the research/practice split (e.g. Leitenberg, 1974; Meehl, 1971; Peterson, 1976; Raush, 1969, 1974; Rogers, 1973; Shakow, 1976). Some psychologists have rationalized the split, pointing to the irrelevance of the traditional research enterprise to clinical practice (Holt, 1971; Meehl, 1971;

Reprinted from the *Journal of Consulting and Clinical Psychology*, *49*, 193–211. Copyright 1981 by the American Psychological Association.

Peterson, 1976; Raush, 1974). Others have denied the split, defending the scientist-practitioner model (e.g., Shakow, 1976) and calling for better, more controlled, and even more intricate clinical research (e.g., Meltzoff & Kornreich, 1970; Paul, 1969, cf. Thelen & Ewing, 1970). A third reaction has begun to receive some attention (e.g., Barlow, 1980). It attempts to dissolve the split, claiming that practicing clinicians may not be lacking a dedication to research, just tools for the task. If single case (or time series) methodology[1] would be taught in a manner that fits demands of the clinical environment (the thinking goes), practicing clinicians could produce more research data and make consumption of clinical research more worthwhile for the practitioner.

This view has been advanced periodically over the years (e.g., Barlow & Hersen, 1973; Browning & Stover, 1971; Chassan, 1967, 1979; Hersen & Barlow, 1976; Kazdin, 1978, 1980; Leitenberg, 1973; Svenson & Chassan, 1967). Most of the conceptual work to date, however, has been oriented toward the full-time clinical researcher, not the practicing clinician. Clinical researchers and academic clinicians have not been unresponsive to single case methodology, but group comparison approaches are often equally attractive and valuable. It is in the on-line clinical environment that the unique value of time series experimentation truly becomes apparent, yet little has been done to advance its use there.

The goodness of fit between clinical decision making and time series methodology is remarkable. As will be shown, good clinical practice seems often to be a type of single subject experimentation in that the logic of the two enterprises is so similar. The present article will argue that good practicing clinicians are already doing evaluations of potential scientific value with most clients they see. They need only (a) take systematic repeated measurements, (b) specify their own treatments, (c) recognize the design strategies they are already using, and (d) at times use existing design elements deliberately to improve clinical decision making.

---

[1]The terminological diversity surrounding this research strategy is enormous. These designs have been termed single subject, N = 1, or single case (e.g., Hersen & Barlow, 1976); intrasubject replication (Kazdin, 1980); intensive (Chassan, 1967, 1979); own control (e.g., Millon & Diesenhaus, 1972); and time series (e.g., Campbell & Stanley, 1963; Glass, Wilson, & Gottman, 1975), among other names (Jayaratne & Levy, 1979). I have chosen to use two terms somewhat interchangeably. The first is *time series experimentation*. It emphasizes the critical component of these designs. Its drawback is possible confusion with time series analysis, a statistical technique used to analyze time series data (e.g., Box & Jenkins, 1976; Gottman, McFall, & Barnett, 1969), or confusion with specific designs, such as Campbell and Stanley's name for an A/B design. The other term, *single case designs*, emphasizes the number of subjects as the central issue. For clinical work, analyzing the individual is a desirable end in and of itself (Bernard, 1865), and this is the most popular name for these designs. Nevertheless, many of these designs (e.g., multiple baseline across subjects) require several subjects, and all can be done with entire groups as the unit of analysis. Other terms are more problematic. "Intensive" carries an evaluative connotation. "Intrasubject replication" and "own control" wrongly assert that all control strategies in these designs are within subject when many of them (e.g., baseline-only control, multiple baseline across subjects) are not.

If this argument can be shown to be correct, then it is worth considering why single case experimentation, hardly a newcomer on the methodological scene, is so underutilized in applied settings. Several reasons might be suggested:

1. It is undertaught. In most training programs, methodological courses are taught by nonclinicians (e.g., statisticians, general experimental psychologists). With some notable exceptions (e.g., the experimental analysis of behavior), most of these other subfields are heavily committed to group comparison research.

2. It has not been aimed at the practicing clinician. Perhaps in order to show that time series methodology can be just as scientific as group comparison approaches, methodological niceties have often been overemphasized. Individual clinicians cannot be expected to distinguish between the core essentials and simple issues of degree, and it may be rejected because it is seemingly impractical to do it right.

3. It is associated with behaviorism. Historically, single case methodology has been most heavily developed and used by behaviorists (e.g., Sidman, 1960) and may often be rejected because of it. This is unfortunate, however, because the methodology is theory free. One can use time series experimentation to answer questions about self-disclosure as readily as behavioral indicants of anxiety, and about insight-oriented procedures as successfully as assertiveness training.

4. Clinicians may fail to distinguish between research methodology and group comparison approaches. To most clinicians, group comparison research is research. Individual clinicians (and clinical training programs) are likely to throw the single case baby out with the group comparison bathwater.

5. There are few outlets for on-line clinical research. On-line single case evaluations, modified as they frequently are by realities of clinical practice, may meet a severe reception in most clinical journals. Reviewers of such articles are themselves unlikely to be practicing clinicians, and appropriate standards for evaluations of actual clinical practice are still unformed.

6. Clinical agencies often provide little support for scientific work. Everything from case loads to secretarial help to agency policies concerning research may hinder on-line use of single case methodology. Fortunately, third-party payments are beginning to create counter pressures for clinical evaluation.

In the past few years, a whole host of professional developments have indicated the possible beginning of an empirical clinical movement based on the combination of single case methodology with the resources of the practicing clinician. These include books (e.g., Jayaratne & Levy, 1979), articles (Barlow, 1980; Levy & Olson, 1979; in fact the present series of articles), conferences (e.g., the Association for Advancement of Behavior Therapy adopted this issue as the theme of its 1980 convention), special issues of journals (e.g., a 1979 issue of the *Journal of Social Service Research*; an upcoming issue of *Behavioral Assessment*), workshops, and the like.

The present article will outline the nature of times series experimentation and underline ways it can fit into routine clinical practice. I have assumed that the clinician is working with actual paying clients (individuals, groups, agencies, etc.) who have given consent to routine clinical evaluation and treatment. No willingness to endure a significant increase in risk, cost, or time to the client beyond that required by good clinical decision making is assumed. Finally, I have not attempted to analyze in detail the many fine points and issues raised by single case experimentation (for that, the interested reader is referred elsewhere, e.g., Hersen & Barlow, 1976; Jayaratne & Levy, 1979; Kratochwill, 1978; Sidman, 1960), and general, noncontroversial recommendations drawn from such sources have not been referenced separately.

THE ESSENTIALS OF SINGLE CASE METHODOLOGY

All time series work is based on combining essential core elements into logical designs. In this section, the general rules of approach will be described. In the following sections, specific design elements will be detailed.

Repeated Measurement

The absolute core of time series methodology, as denoted by the very name, is repeated measurement of the client's behavior, including thoughts, feelings, and so forth. Because estimates of the stability, level, and trend of the data (against which treatment effects might be seen) are drawn within subject, the clinician must have a record of client progress across time (see Nelson, 1981). Repeated measurement also parallels rules of clinical practice. Practical clinical guides often exhort clinicians to "examine regularly and consistently whether therapy is being helpful" (Zaro, Barach, Nedelmann, & Dreiblatt, 1977, p. 157).

In clinical practice, repeated measurement should start early, using several measures if possible. An experienced clinician often has a good idea of several of the client's problems even before the end of the first session. If measurement is begun immediately, then when normal assessments ends, the clinician will often have a systematically collected baseline. Early collection of systematic measures will also often contribute to clinical assessment itself. Some problems, when measured repeatedly, will turn out not to be real difficulties. Measures should also be practical. It is better to collect measures of medium quality than to collect none because excessively high standards of measurement are set. Finally, they should be taken under reasonably consistent conditions to avoid variability caused by inconsistent measurement procedures.

Establishment of the Degree of Intraclient Variability

An estimate of the degree of variability in the client's behavior (as repeatedly measured) is critical in single case methodology. In the context of this estimate, determinations are made about the level and trend in the behavior, and predictions are drawn about the future course of the behavior. Measures need only be stable enough to see effects, should they occur. The target problem and probable effects of intervention bear heavily on issues of stability, the quesiton is always, Stable in terms of what? For example, if a total reduction of a behavior is anticipated, extreme variability would present no problem. Conversely, if measurement variability could not allow any treatment effect to be seen, then it would be foolish to proceed. This methodological advice dovetails nicely with clinical realities, however. For example, a client showing infrequent nondestructive outbursts of anger would probably not be treated for anger control if their frequency would be indistinguishable from that expected after treatment.

When the client's behavior is excessively variable, several actions can be taken. First, the clinician can simply wait until patterns become clearer. Often variability is temporary (for example, it may be caused by the initial effect of entering treatment), and it is frequently better to wait than to plunge ahead unnecessarily.

Second, if at times the client is behaving well and at times badly, the practicing clinician will probably begin to search for factors that account for these differences. For example, if a client's self-esteem (as measured, say, by a brief paper-and-pencil instrument before each therapy session) is high some weeks and very low others, the clinician may search for reasons accounting for it. Finding that the client's self-esteem is low only on weeks following rejection by potential dates might lead to a treatment program of social skills training or therapy around the issue of rejection. Further, the previously unstable measures might now be quite stable when organized into times following or not following instances of rejection.

A third strategy is to examine the temporal unit of analysis. Often measures are collected in particular units for convenience (e.g., clients are often asked to self-record in daily blocks). If the actual phenomena may be better seen in larger units, then the data may be blocked (or intraclient averaged). For example, a clinician working with a marital couple might find that daily records of arguments reveal extremely variable behavior, some days there are no arguments, and on others there are several. This may be expected, since all couples have some good days and some bad. More clinically important may be, for example, the average number of arguments in a week. When the data are blocked by weeks, stability may emerge. Some of the detail is lost, but this is always true: Organizing events by day disguises hourly variability; organizing them by hour disguises minute-by-minute effects. Part of good clinical skill seems to involve knowing when to ignore individual trees in order to see the forest.

A final strategy is to proceed anyway. If the effects are very strong, they may be seen. If not, enough may be learned that the next client may benefit.

Specification of Conditions

All research requires clear specification of the independent variable. In the clinic, true "technological" (Baer, Wolf, & Risely, 1968) specificity is sometimes difficult. Even when the therapist cannot specify the intervention, however, it may be possible to measure therapist behavior using some of the same within-clinic procedures for measuring client behavior (Nelson, 1981; for example, see Becker & Rosenfeld, 1976).

Replication

The logic of all time series designs requires replication of effects. In the clinic, this requirement is increased because of the methodological compromises often forced there. In addition, the external validity of single case research depends on systematic replications of effects in many clients.

An Attitude of Investigative Play

Undoubtedly the biggest difference between group comparison research and time series methodology is the overall approach that they encourage. Single case research should be a dynamic, interactive enterprise in which the design is always tenative, always ready to change if significant questions arise in the process. The data should be graphed frequently and in various forms so that apparent patterns can emerge and leads can be followed. Group comparison research, however, is usually planned out in detail beforehand and then simply carried out.

One of the common mistakes made by researchers in time series research is their approaching these tools as they would approach group comparison research, (e.g., deciding beforehand on a sequence of phases or setting specific phase length). Unforunately, clients' data often do not conform to the preset mold; these data often do not confirm preset hypotheses. When unanticipated effects are seen, the clinician must be ready to abandon previous design decisions and to let the client's data be the guide. This is also good clinical practice. For example, clinical guides advise clinicians to "be prepared to alter your style of dealing with a client in response to new information" and "be prepared to have many of your hypotheses disproved" (Zaro et al., 1977, p. 28).

Other Suggested Requirements

Many other rules about single case methodology are not essential but are issues of degree. One rule is to keep phases about the same length (Hersen & Barlow, 1976). Widely different phase lengths can produce errors in interpretation, but changing phases based on time alone can also produce unclear comparisons. This is a matter of degree, and its importance can be minimized by clear effects and systematic replication. Another rule is, "Change one variable at a time" (Hersen & Barlow, 1976). This rule is often a good one, but it can be easily misinterpreted (e.g., Thomas, 1978). The meaning of "variable" here is better conveyed by the phrase "condition you wish to analyze." Thus, entire packages may be varied when it is the package that is being evaluated.

Creative Use of the Design Elements

The creative use of time series designs may have been inadvertently hindered by the literature's emphasis on complete designs rather than on design elements. For example, designs such as an A/B/A or B/C/B/C have often been described as separate designs even though their logical structures are identical (e.g., Hersen & Barlow, 1976; Mahoney, 1978; indeed, virtually the entire literature in the area has followed this course). All single case designs are built from a small set of building blocks. There are potentially as many specific single case designs as there are designs for brick buildings, and the core elements of each are comparably simple.

The present article distills all time series work into a few core elements, organized by the nature of their estimates of stability and the logic of their data comparisons. These core elements can then be creatively combined to contribute to good clinical decision making. There are three general types of strategies used: within, between, and combined series. All current single case design elements can be readily organized into these three types.

WITHIN-SERIES STRATEGIES

The best known types of time series elements rely on changes seen within a series of data points (in a single measure or homogeneous set of measures). There are two subtypes of within-series strategies: the simple phase change and the complex phase change. Each of these will be described, and their use in clincal practice will be detailed.

The Simple Phase Change

The cornerstone of many of the most popular single case designs is the simple phase change. This element consists of (a) the establishment of stability, level, and trend within a series of data points across time, taken under similar conditions; (b) a change in the conditions impinging on the client; and (c) examination of concomitant changes in the stability, level, or trend in a series of data points taken under the new conditions. It is a within-series strategy in the sense that it is systematic changes seen within a series of data points across time that are examined.

A common example of the simple phase change is the A/B design. If the stability, level, or trend shown in A suddenly changes when B is implemented, our confidence increases that B is responsible for that change. Often there are possible alternative explanations for the effect (e.g., maturation, the effect of measurement, coincidental external events; see Campbell & Stanley, 1963; Hersen & Barlow, 1976; Kratochwill, 1978), and usually the effect must be replicated before our confidence in the effect is sufficiently high. One way is to repeat the phase change in reverse order (the A/B/A design). If the behavior tracks the change once again, our confidence increases further. This simple phase change process can be repeated indefinitely, each sequence forming a new completed design (e.g., A/B/A/B; B/A/B). Two treatments can be compared in the same manner (e.g., B/C/B; C/B/C/B). All of these are merely specific applications of the logic of the simple phase change, allowing us to ask questions such as, Does treatment work? or Which treatment is better?

Complex Phase Changes

The simple phase change can be coordinated into a more complex series of phases. Each of the complex phase change strategies specifies an overall integrative logic.

Interaction Element

This is a series of phase changes in which a treatment or treatment component (B) is alternately added or subtracted from another treatment or treatment component (C). A number of specific sequences are possible (e.g., B/B+C/B; C/C+B/C; B+C/C/B+C). Its logic is essentially identical to the simple phase change. This can be easily seen if instead of writing A/B/A one were to write the equally correct A/A+B/A. The question, however, seems a bit more complex, namely, What is the combined effect of two treatment components compared to one alone? As an example, suppose a clinician wonders if the empty-chair technique is really helpful in the treatment of unresolved grief. In the first phase, a specified set of techniques (B+C) might be used, including empty-chair exercises involving the lost loved one. This technique (C) might then be withdrawn and reinstituted, forming a B+C/B/B+C design. If the client's functioning tracks these changes, the role of this procedure in the overall package could be determined.

Combining Does B Work? And Does C Work? Elements

A simple phase change comparing two treatments does not make sense unless it is known that either works relative to baseline. If this is not known, the design must compare them with baseline as well as with each other by combining simple phase change strategies for determining their effectiveness. For example, the sequence A/B/A/C/A combines an A/B/A with an A/C/A. This allows us to ask if B and if C are effective. It also allows a comparison of the two treatments, but it is weak, because order effects are possible and noncontiguous data are being compared (the data in the B phase with those in the C phase). To strengthen this comparison, other subjects might receive an A/C/A/B/A sequence. If the conclusions are the same, then the believability of the treatment comparison is strengthened.

Changing Criterion

This element (see Hartmann & Hall, 1976) is usually based on the following line of reasoning: If you arbitrarily specify the level that a given behavior must reach to achieve an outcome, and the behavior repeatedly and closely tracks these criteria, then the criteria are probably responsible. Typically, this element is used when the behavior can only change in one direction, either for ethical or practical reasons. The logic of the maneuver, however, allows for criterion reversals when the behavior is reversable.

The weakness of the procedure is that it is not always clear when observed behavior is tracking criterion shifts. This problem can be alleviated by altering the length and magnitude of criterion shifts (or, if possible, their direction), as shown in Figure 1.

Other Strategies

Several other complex phase change strategies exist, although they are used infrequently in the applied literature. For example, an ascending/descending design element (see Sidman, 1960) is a popular research tool in basic operant psychology.

Using Within-Series Strategies

When a clinician begins to work with a client, be it an individual, group, or agency, it is rare that an elaborate clinical question springs forth in whole cloth. Clinical work usually involves a gradual process of investigation. The use of within-series strategies provides a good example of how single case methodology suits itself to this clinical reality. In the sections that follow, the sequence of events faced by a clinician doing a within-series evaluation will be described. The choice points and design options in this process will be given particular emphasis.

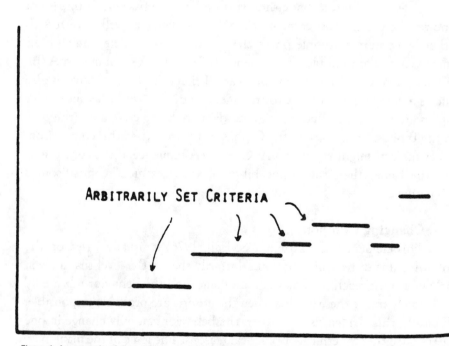

Figure 1: An example of the arbitrary manipulation of the length, depth, and direction of criterion shifts, making any behavioral correspondence with the criteria more obvious.

Establishing the First Phase

The clinician typically begins a therapeutic relationship with a period of assessment. If the advice offered earlier has been followed, when this period ends, a baseline is already in hand or nearly so. Several rules have been offered as to the adequacy of obtained baselines.

A first consideration is the length of the first phase. To establish estimates of stability, level, and trend, at least three measurement points seem to be needed (e.g., see Hersen & Barlow, 1976), though more are desirable. If fewer have been obtained, and the needs of the client are clear, then the practicing clinician must push ahead anyway. To do otherwise would be to delay treatment for research, not clinical, reasons. Short baselines are not necessarily lethal. There may be other information available about the problem being measured. For example, the disorder may have a known history and course (e.g., the social withdrawal of a chronic schizophrenic), or archival baselines may be available (e.g., records from previous therapists). Also, the clinician can often make up for short baselines by using other design elements later (e.g., withdrawals) or by replicating the effects with others (e.g., multiple baselines across subjects).

A second consideration is the stability of baseline. The earlier recommendations regarding stability all apply here, with one addition. If first-phase data are unavailable or excessively variable, and if treatment must begin, a design might be used that does not require a baseline (e.g., an alternating treatments design).

A final consideration is the trend in baseline. When the following phase is expected to produce increases in the data, a falling or flat baseline is desirable. When deceleration is expected, rising or flat trends are beneficial. These are not rigid rules, however. A slowly rising baseline may be adequate if treatment is expected to increase it substantially. Again, these methodological suggestions coincide closely with good clinical judgment. If the client is already improving maximally, then the therapist should wait before beginning treatment.

Once again, these considerations actually apply to any phase in a within-series strategy. The logic of simple and complex phase changes is the same whether one is going from A to B or from C to D.

Implementing the Second Phase

To begin with, is there a variable that needs to be controlled first? For example, could any effects be due simply to, say, encouragement to change and not to the specific treatment? If this is highly plausible, and especially if treatment is costly, difficult, aversive, or restrictive, the alternative treatment (e.g., encouragement) might be implemented first. This parallels good clinical decision making and may fit in with legal requirements, such as the initial use of the least restrictive alternative. If the less restrictive treatment does not work, there is still the option of implementing the full treatment (see below).

Another consideration in implementing treatment or any new phase is that it should begin in full force if possible. Gradual implementation might minimize apparent differences between phases. This is a difficult issue (Thomas, 1978), but violating this rule only makes positive findings less likely. Once found, clear results are not jeopardized.

When the second phase is implemented, only three outcomes are possible: no improvement, deterioration, or improvement. If there is no improvement, the clinician has three reasonable paths open, both clinically and methodologically. One is to wait to see if there is a delayed effect. A second option, also a common clinical step, is to try another treatment strategy. It is typically assumed that a phase producing no change can be with caution considered part of the previous phase (e.g., A=B/C). As phases are added, the plausibility of equivalence is jeopardized (e.g., an A=B=C=D=E/F/E/F design seems weak). The solution is to be had in systematic replication across clients (e.g., several A/F/A/F designs could be added to the one above). Finally, treatment can be altered by adding or subtracting components (e.g., A=B/B+C/B), also a common clinical step.

If treatment produces deterioration, the clear course is to withdraw treatment. If the behavior once again improves, the clinician will have documented an iatrogenic effect of treatment, often itself a significant contribution to the field.

The final possible effect of the second phase is improvement, which opens three possible paths. First, the clinician can continue treatment through to a successful conclusion and store the resulting A/B design. When a similar case presents itself, a multiple baseline across persons can be attempted. This is an extremely useful option and will be discussed at length later in the article. Second, if the client has other similar problems or problem situations, apply the same treatment to them (again, a multiple baseline). A final course of action is to withdraw the treatment or implement a treatment placebo. If improvement then slows, a treatment effect is more likely.

The use of withdrawal is so popular that many confuse this design option with all of single case methodology, so a more extended discussion is warranted. There are potential problems with the withdrawal of an apparently effective treatment. It raises ethical issues, client fee issues, potential client morale problems, and possible neutralization of subsequent treatment effects. Few data exist on the actual likelihood of these problems, however, and there are many important counterarguments to be made (e.g., Hersen & Barlow, 1976).

The issue of withdrawal relates in special ways to the practicing clinical environment. First, if the treatment is of unknown benefit, a withdrawal can avoid the unnecessary use of ineffective treatment. Physicians recognize this issue in the common practice of drug holidays (i.e., withdrawals) to assess the continued need for treatment. Second, withdrawals often present themselves naturally in treatment in the form of vacations, holidays, sickness, temporary treatment dropouts, and the like. These can then be incorporated into ongoing clinical evaluations by examining measurements taken during or after these periods but before reintervention. Unlike withdrawals determined by the clinician, however, natural withdrawals are more likely to reflect variables of importance to these measures. For example, deterioration following treatment dropout may be due to factors producing that very decision rather than to the withdrawal of treatment per se. Therefore, clinicians should specify reasons for natural withdrawals and stress greater caution and need for replication when presenting cases with natural withdrawals. Third, withdrawals need not be long and drawn out. The slight delay in treatment that they impose should be weighed against their clinical value. Fourth, a good rationale that will minimize client morale problems can usually be given. The rationale can be either absolutely honest (e.g., "You've been rather successful so far with this approach, but I'm not sure we still need to be following this course, so let's take a little breather and see where things go"), or they can be somewhat deceptive (e.g., giving the client the expectation that treatment is normally stopped now and that this often leads to even greater improvement). Such placebo rationales must be handled with care, of course, just as a placebo drug might be in medical practice. Fifth, withdrawals are often produced when turning to other issues. For example, the clinician may wish to spend a few weeks in reassessment of the client. While clinically valuable, this might constitute an attention placebo for a specific problem under treatment. This is a type of withdrawal, just as data taken during an initial assessment phase (which involves much more than mere baseline measurement) is thought of as baseline. Finally, withdrawals often have clear clinical benefit to the client. If behavior worsens, the client may become convinced that treatment is necessary and successful. If not, the client may see that the problem is now under control.

After Withdrawal

If the clinician returns to the first condition following improvement on the second, three possible outcomes once again occur: deterioration, no change, or continued improvement. If the behavior deteriorates, the clinical and methodological course is clear: Reimplement the effective treatment (e.g., an A/B/A/B). If the behavior shows continued and further improvement, several options are available. One option is simply to wait. As in any situation in which the behavior is already improving, there may be little reason to further intervene. Sometimes the behavior will soon stop improving or deteriorate, perhaps due to a short-lived carry-over effect from the second phase. If, however, the behavior keeps improving significantly, the clinician can allow the case to continue to a successful conclusion and store these data, waiting for a similar case. This sequence can then be repeated but with a longer or shorter initial phase as part of a multiple baseline across subjects. If the effect is subsequently replicated and order effects eliminated, nonreversible improvement due to treatment will have been documented. If improvement continues in the withdrawal phase, the same sequence can be followed with another of the client's problem behaviors or the problem behavior in another situation, again producing multiple baselines. If the continued improvement is not maximal, treatment can be reimplemented anyway. A subsequent increase in the rate of improvement would establish greater confidence in the treatment.

If no change is seen when the second phase is withdrawn (the behavior shows neither deterioration nor continued improvement), the options described above are open. The reimplementation option is particularly attractive. Some methodologists might be concerned over this advice, since the level of the behavior shown in baseline was not reattained in the return to baseline phase. This is a difficult argument for the clinician, since it implies that lack of maintenance of behavior change is a requirement in order to show treatment effects when using a withdrawal. Essentially, this would have clinicians document success by showing failure. Fortunately, it is the history of single case methodology, not its logic, that enables such a problematic argument to be made. For example, animal operant researchers (especially historically) have often seemed to assume that current behavior is primarily a function of immediately present environmental variables. Thus, behavior should be in one steady state when these variables are present and in another when they are not. This type of assumption pervades much of single case methodology, often to the detriment of its clinical uses.

The assumptions of the clinician are quite different. The clinician usually assumes that the current level of behavior is often a function of historical variables as much as current conditions. Greater improvement may be expected to be associated with treatment, but the actual level of behavior hopefully is maintained even when treatment is withdrawn (cf. Sidman, 1960, on transition states).

When these assumptions are applied to the logic of within-series strategies, it is apparent that deterioration (return to the previous level) is not required during withdrawal. If behavior improves faster during treatment than not, an effect is shown. It may be useful to regraph some data to underscore this. The top half of Figure 2, for example, shows an A/B/A/B sequence in which withdrawal produces less improvement but no clean reversals. The bottom half of the figure shows the same data calculated as difference scores from the trend in the previous phase (or same phase in the case of the first phase). When plotted in terms of improvement, a more classical pattern emerges.

There are many other ways in which the assumptions of the typical clinician overturn nonessentials of time series methodology as developed by operantly oriented psychologists and lead to new design options. For example, the notion of treatment phases as easily identifiable entities is jeopardized. A good deal of clinical work is done under 1 hour per week outpatient conditions. Sometimes, it is true, clinicians use this time to set up treatments that are obviously present throughout a specifiable time (e.g., a token economy for a noncompliant child). However, other clinicians (e.g., especially those working with adults) do not change obvious aspects of the client's environment outside of the clinical session itself. When, then, can treatment be said to be present? During that hour? That day? That week?

Ambiguity about the meaning of the word *phase* is not lethal to the clinical use of within-series strategies, but it does help open up new design options. It is not lethal, because (a) the effects of treatment often last well beyond the actual therapy hours (b) any ambiguity about the nature of phases (e.g., Thomas, 1978) makes only robust effects visible, and (c) phases usually incorporate considerable lengths of time. Thus, ambiguity about what is in one phase or in another is not a major threat to the internal validity of any clear effects actually obtained.

The design element opened up by this issue is the periodic treatments element (Hayes & Nelson, Note 1). The notion is that a consistent relationship between the periodicity of treatment and the periodicity of behavior change can demonstrate therapeutic effects. This relationship can only be shown when the frequency of behavioral measurement far exceeds the frequency of treatment sessions. An example may show the principle. The top half of Figure 3 shows the hypothetical record of positive social interactions self-recorded daily by a client. Arrows on the abscissa show days when the client saw a psychotherapist for 1-hour insight-oriented therapy sessions. Since the treatment sessions occur at varying intervals, and periods of improvement only follow them, these changes are likely due to treatment. The bottom half of the figure presents the data in difference score form,

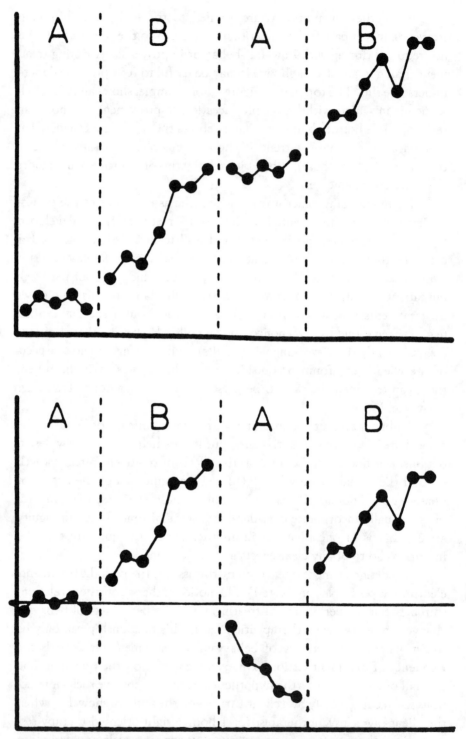

Figure 2: An example of the nondeterioration of behavior in the withdrawal phase of a within-series design, hypothetical data. (The lower graph is calculated in terms of improvement to highlight the control shown over the transitional state of behavior. The upper graph and lower graph both demonstrate experimental control despite nonreversibility; the lower is merely more obvious.)

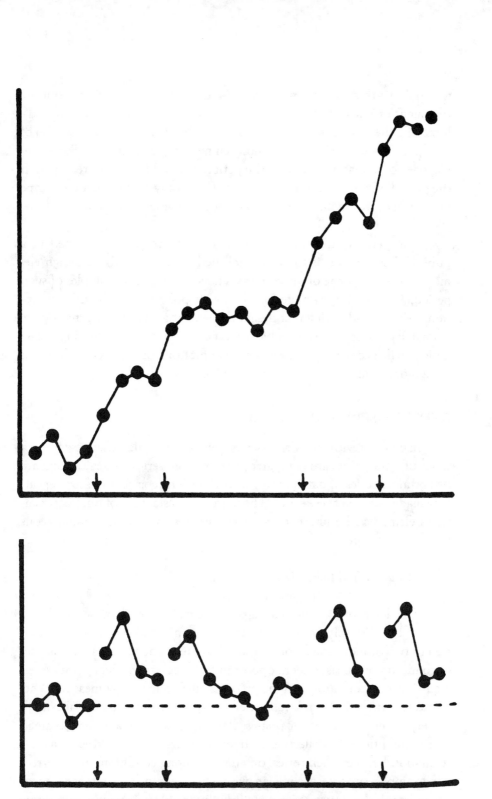

Figure 3: The periodic treatments effect is shown on hypothetical data. (Data are graphed in raw data form in the top graph. Arrows on the abscissa indicate treatment sessions. This apparent B-only graph does not reveal the periodicity of improvement and treatment as well as the bottom graph, where each two data points are plotted in terms of the difference from the mean of the two previous data points. Significant improvement occurs only after treatment. Both graphs show an experimental effect; the lower is merely more obvious.)

which draws this out even further. These data do not show what about the treatment produced the change (any more than an A/B/A design would). It may be therapist concern or the fact that the client attended a session of any kind. These possibilities would then need to be eliminated. For example, one could manipulate both the periodicity and nature of treatment. If the periodicity of behavior change was shown only when a particular type of treatment was in place, this would provide evidence for a more specific effect.

The periodic treatments element has apparently not be used in a published study (this is the first published description of the design element), although some of my own cases have shown clear examples of such periodicity (e.g., Hayes, Note 2). The major point is that clinical assumptions seem to lead to different design elements than those generated by the animal laboratory. It is possible that new developments in single case designs will occur as the needs and assumptions of practicing clinicians have more of an effect on the methodology itself.

BETWEEN-SERIES STRATEGIES

In contrast with the within-series elements, in which changes within a series of data points are compared, the between-series strategies compare two or more series of data points across time. The comparisons are repeatedly made between these series. There are two basic types of pure between-series elements: the alternating treatments design and the simultaneous treatments design.

The Alternating Treatments Design Element

The logic of the alternating treatments design (Barlow & Hayes, 1979) is based simply on the rapid and random (or semi-random) alternation of two or more conditions, in which there is one potential alternation of condition per measurement opportunity. Since a single data point associated with one condition may be preceded and followed by measurements associated with other conditions, there is no opportunity to estimate stability, level, and trend within phases. Rather, these estimates are obtained within conditions, by collecting each into a separate series. If there is a clear separation between such series, differences among conditions are inferred. For example, suppose a clinician wishes to examine the relationship of therapist self-disclosure to client self-disclosure. At the beginning of some sessions (randomly determined), the therapist self-discloses; in the other sessions, no self-disclosure is seen. Tape recordings of the sessions are rated (see Figure 4), with results demonstrating that therapist self-disclosure

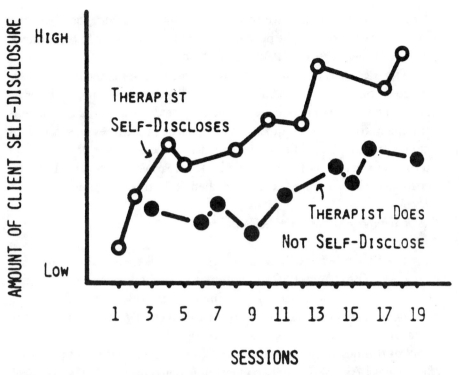

Figure 4: An example, using hypothetical data, of the alternating treatments design element. (The clear difference between the two conditions shows that more client self-disclosure is produced when the therapist self-discloses. The overall increase across time is not analyzed without the addition of other design elements; e.g., A phases before and after.)

increases client self-disclosure. Note that the comparison is made purely between series. The general upward trend in each condition is not analyzed and may be due to extraneous factors, but the major comparison is still sound. Thus, the alternating treatments strategy is viable even if within-series trends are extreme or are changing rapidly (e.g., in learning situations or with maturational phenomena).

One could think of this as an extremely rapid A/B/A (cf. Campbell & Stanley's, 1963, discussion of an "equivalent time samples" design), but they differ significantly. Not only are the estimates of variability and source of treatment comparisons different, but this design also minimizes order effects (by random sequencing) and can incorporate three or even more conditions into a single comparison sequence (see Barlow & Hayes, 1979).

This design strategy is often combined with other design elements (e.g., a baseline), though it is not required. It is particularly useful for the comparison of two or more treatments or when measurement is cumbersome or lengthy (e.g., an entire MMPI). Only four data points are absolutely needed (two in each condition). Each data point may incorporate many treatment sessions; the rapid alternation refers only to the rate of treatment alternation relative to the rate of measurement. On the other extreme, alternations might be made several times per session (e.g., Hayes, Hussian, Turner, Grubb, & Anderson, Note 3).

This design is also valuable when difficult assessment decisions are presented. Suppose, for example, that a client is presenting with social deficits. The clinician may have a difficult time determining if the client is more likely to respond to anxiety management procedures or social skills training procedures. Rather than guess, the clinician might do both in an alternating treatments fashion. The better treatment may quickly be revealed, and all treatment effort could then go in this direction.

The Simultaneous Treatment Design Element

The only other true between-series element is the simultaneous treatment design (Browning, 1967). It requires the simultaneous presence of two or more treatments. Since the treatments are truly available simultaneously, the client controls which treatment is actually applied (much as in a concurrent schedule design in animal operant work). Thus, a true instance of this design can only measure treatment preference, not treatment effectiveness. Apparently only one example (Browning, 1967) exists in the applied literature. (As for Kazdin & Hartmann, 1978, and McCollough, Cornell, McDaniel, & Meuller, 1974, see Barlow & Hayes, 1979.) However, many current applied questions (e.g., about the relative aversiveness or restrictiveness of treatments) are issues of preference, and the simultaneous treatments design might be of real use in these situations.

COMBINED-SERIES STRATEGIES

Several design elements in time series experimentation borrow from both of the previously described strategies. The combined-series elements utilize coordinated sets of comparisons made both between and within series of measurements.

The Multiple Baseline

Undoubtedly the most familiar combined-series element is the multiple baseline. Its logic is intended to correct for major deficiencies of a simple phase change (say, an A/B). In an A/B, any changes between the two phases could be due to coincidental extraneous events: maturation, cyclical behavior, baseline assessment, and so on. The multiple baseline solves these problems by replicating the A/B but with different lengths of baseline for each replication (a strategy that controls for the amount of baseline assessment or mere maturation) and with the actual time of the phase change arbitrarily altered (to reduce the possibility of correlated extraneous events).

As is show in Figure 5, a typical multiple baseline allows several comparisons. Some are identical to those made in a simple phase change, whereas others are between-series comparisons, examining patterns within an unchanged series compared to phase changes in other series.

A multiple baseline can be done with a similar behavior in two or more clients (across people), two or more behaviors in one client (across behaviors), or with a behavior in two or more settings in one person (across settings). The specific phase changes, however, must be the same—the same first condition must yield to the same second condition—since it is alternative explanations for a specific phase change effect that are being controlled.

The label *multiple baseline* is something of a misnomer. The logic of the comparison applies to any set of phase changes so arranged, whether or not there is a baseline present. For example, a series of B/C phase changes could easily be arranged into a multiple baseline (*multipe phase change* would actually be a clearer term). Sometimes it is used sequentially; for example, the sequence A/B/C (with A/C/B to control for order effects) can be put into a type of multiple baseline, as shown in the top half of Figure 6. This arrangement is problematic, since the third phase is introduced after equal second-phase lengths in each series (not controlling for sudden maturational or for phase length effects in the B/C comparison). A better sequential multiple baseline is shown in the bottom half of Figure 6.

No absolute rule can be given about the number of phase shift replications required between series in a multiple baseline element. The logic of the maneuver applies as well to a single replication as to several; it is simply that each additional series strengthens our confidence that much more. Thus, the clinician should not feel as though the element is useless when only two series are compared, though more are desirable. The same can be said about the differences in initial phase length. If one series has an initial phase only slightly longer or shorter than the other, this is less satisfactory than if there are large differences.

Much has been made of the need to avoid the multiple baseline when the specific series are interdependent (e.g., Kazdin & Kopel, 1975). If a phase shift in a multiple baseline is accompanied by behavior change not only within series but also between series, it is difficult to distinguish uncontrolled effects from true treatment effects. For example, in a multiple

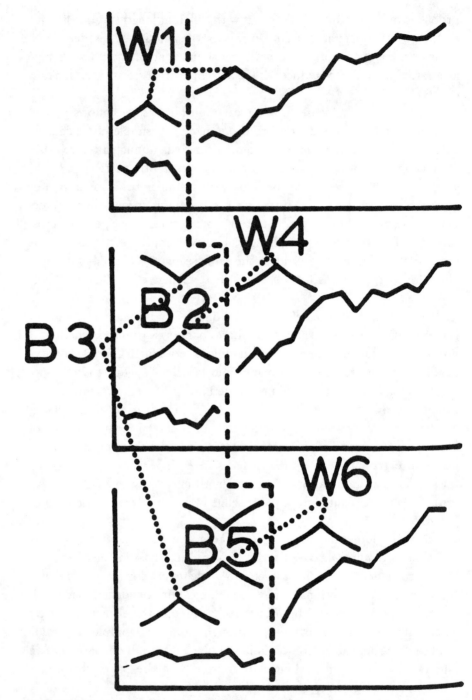

Figure 5: The types of comparisons made in a multiple baseline. (W = a within-series comparison, and B = a between-series comparison. The numbers show the usual sequence of comparisons).

baseline across behaviors, changes in one behavior may produce changes in another, because of actual processes of response generalization caused by treatment. Typically, this is not a problem in the use of multiple baseline elements so much as it is an opportunity to study generalization effects. Thus, the clinician in this situation could immediately embark on a new design (e.g., withdraw treatment and see if both behaviors stop improving), which would document that the multiple effects are actually being caused

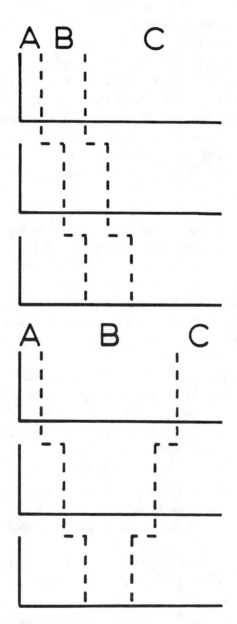

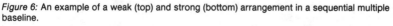

Figure 6: An example of a weak (top) and strong (bottom) arrangement in a sequential multiple baseline.

by treatment, an important contribution. Further, if several series are being compared, some interdependence can be tolerated (e.g., Hayes & Barlow, 1977; Hersen & Bellack, 1976) without undoing the design (Kazdin, 1980).

The opportunity to use the multiple baseline element in clinical practice is very large. Multiple baselines often form naturally across behaviors due to the tendency for practicing clinicians to tackle subsets of problems sequentially rather than all at once. Multiple baselines across settings are less common but also naturally occur when clinicians treat problem behavior shown in one specific condition first rather than treating the problem all at once (e.g., Hayes & Barlow, 1977).

The multiple baseline across people is probably one of the clearest examples of natural design elements that arise in clinical practice. Nothing could be more natural to clinical work than an A/B. To form a multiple baseline, all the clinician need do is save several of these with similar problems and the same treatment. Individual clients will inevitably have differing lengths of baseline, often widely so, due to case complexities or to matters of convenience. Thus, sequential cases usually lead to multiple baseline across people.

Some of the earliest applied literature on the multiple baseline (e.g., Baer, Wolf, & Risley, 1968) stated that multiple baselines across persons should always be done at the same time in the same setting with the same behavior. Saving cases, with perhaps periods of months or even years separating each, violates this rule, but fortunately the logic of the strategy does not really require it. If the time of the phase shift differs in real time from client to client, it is unlikely that important external events could repeatedly coincide with the phase changes. The control exerted by the different lengths of baseline remain.[2]

There is a potential difficulty, which was touched on in the earlier discussion of natural withdrawals. If the clinician is allowing the case itself to determine the exact length of baseline, there is the danger that the same factor which indicated that it is time to change phases is correlated with processes that produce behavior change. The main practical protections against this difficulty are replication (including several cases in natural multiple baselines) and information (reporting why the phase was changed for each client). If reasons for changing phases vary from client to client, it is unlikely that a third variable consistently produced changes in the second phase.

It is also essential that clinicians report all cases attempted, not just those showing the desired effect. If the effect is not seen in some of the

---

[2]A minor weakness is the fact that the events in real time that might have produced the phase change are not present in the other series. If effects are clear, this need not be a concern, since a series of such coincidences is still unlikely.

cases, the clinician should attempt to find out why; indeed this seems required by good clinical practice. A careful examination of possible differences between individuals accounting for variable results may lead to treatment solutions for nonresponsive clients. Data showing subsequent response would increase our knowledge about mechanisms producing change and about boundary conditions of a given treatment.

The multiple baseline across cases also provides a home for those cases in which just treatment is given (B only) and in which treatment is never given (baseline-only control; see below). As anchors in a series of cases arranged into a multiple baseline across subjects, such cases can provide evidence of the effectiveness of treatment even when no baseline is taken (B only), thus controlling for an unlikely order effect due to A or of the likelihood of change when no treatment is given (baseline-only control).

Crossovers

This maneuver (drawn from similar group-comparison approaches; see Kazdin, 1980) is based on two concurrent phase changes, one in reverse order of the other. For example, one subject may experience a B/C sequence; the other, a C/B. By changing phases at the same time, this strategy equalizes alternative sources of control that might have produced an apparent phase change effect (e.g., maturation, phase length). Since these sources are equalized, consistent within-series effects in the two series (e.g., if $B > C$ in both cases) provide evidence for the comparison. The controls are not strong, however (e.g., order effects are weakly dealt with), so the entire crossover should be replicated at least once with other clients. Some of these same issues apply to the true reversal, which also is a combined series element (see Leitenberg, 1973).

The Baseline-Only Control

Many times problems are repeatedly assessed but never treated. This may be done deliberately (e.g., assessing those on a waiting list) or serendipitously (e.g., assessing a problem behavior that is never treated, because the client moves away). Whatever else has been done, these data can be examined as a type of combined- or between-series comparison (e.g., Brownell, Hayes & Barlow, 1977; Hayes & Cone, 1977). The logic of this comparison is identical to the between-series comparisons made in a multiple baseline design (see Figure 5). Changes occurring elsewhere and not in the baseline-only control series are more likely to have been produced by treatment (cf. Campbell & Stanley's, 1963, equivalent time samples design).

ISSUES IN THE USE OF TIME SERIES DESIGN TOOLS

The purpose of the present article is to provide an overall framework for present single case design tools and to point out how they might fit into evaluations of actual clinical practice. If these tools are to be used by large numbers of practicing clinicians, many specific problems need to be solved (e.g., development of practical measurement tools, methods of specifying of treatment activities), but the most important problem is one of overall approach. By repeatedly emphasizing design elements rather than complete designs, the present organization is meant to encourage creative evaluations in actual clinical decision making. These are not static tools. It is quite possible to devise designs without names, designs in which many of the elements mentioned in the article are combined. As the clinician approaches each case, questions arise that require answers on clinical grounds. If the clinician is aware of available design options, some time series strategy is almost always available that fits closely with the logic of clinical decision making itself.

Table 1 presents some clinically important questions and examples of the various design elements useful in that situaiton. Within any row of this table, various elements can be combined to address a given clinical question. As different questions arise, different elements can be used (draw from different rows).

Another major stumbling block in the use of time series design tools in clinical practice is the historical status of the division between practice and research. At first glance, the distinction between research and treatment is clear cut and easily applied. Clinicians who have not used the type of approach advocated here often very easily define research and treatment in terms of their apparent structure (Hayes, Note 4), such as (a) Did the clinician collect systematic data? (b) Were the variables producing the impact systematically analyzed? (c) Were the results of this endeavor presented or published? The presence of any one of these is likely to lead to the endeavor's being termed "research." The consequences of this can be dramatic. We have generated a large number of protections in research with human subjects. It is possible, however, to use the structure of research to perform the function of treatment. This is treatment evaluation or empirical clinical practice (Jayaratne & Levy, 1979).

The ethical questions posed by treatment as opposed to treatment evaluation seem very similar. Indeed, the effects of evaluations of the sort

TABLE 1
Examples of the Use of Design Elements to Answer Specific Types of Clinical Questions

Clinical question	Design type		
	Within series	Between series	Combined series
Does a treatment work?	A/B/A/B/ ··· B/A/B/A/ ··· A/B (see combined designs) Periodic treatments design Changing criterion design	Alternating treatments (comparing A and B)	Multiple baseline across settings, behaviors, or persons comparing A and B Replicated crossovers (comparing A and B)
Does one treatment work better than another, given that we already know they work?	B/C/B/C/ ··· C/B/C/B/ ···	Alternating treatments (comparing B and C)	Replicated crossovers (comparing B and C) Multiple baselines (comparing B and C and controlling for order)
Does one treatment work, does another work, and which works better?	A/B/A/C/A combined with A/C/A/B/A	Alternating treatments (comparing A and B and C)	Multiple baseline (comparing A and B and C and controlling for order)
	Or combine any element from Row A with any element from Row B		
Are there elements within a successful treatment that make it work?	B/B+C/B B+C/B/B+C C/B+C/C B+C/C/B+C	Alternating treatments (comparing, for example, B and B+C)	Multiple baseline (comparing B and B+C, and C and B+C) Replicated crossovers (comparing B and B+C, and C and B+C)
Does the client prefer one treatment over another?		Simultaneous treatments (comparing B and C)	
Does a treatment work, and if it does, what part of it makes it work?	Combine any elements from Rows A or C with any element from Row D		
What level of treatment is optimal?	Ascending/descending design A/B'/B/B'	Alternating treatments (comparing B and B')	Multiple baseline (comparing B and B' and controlling for order) Replicated crossovers (comparing B and B')

described here seem beneficial on two grounds (Levy & Olson, 1979). First, the attempt to evaluate treatment is likely to contribute to clinical effectiveness by increasing feedback to the clinician and client alike, by increasing the clinician's involvement in the case, and by increasing information available about the client's response to treatment. Second, by increasing the knowledge base in the field more generally, such an approach would make successful treatment of others more likely.

Nevertheless, practicing clinicians (and society more generally) often make a distinction between treatment and evaluation based on mere appearance. In particular, evaluation is often grouped with research rather than with treatment per se. The effect of this is to discourage empirical clinical practice, since it leads to a number of additional protections beyond that required in the treatment environment itself. Unless this process is resisted (e.g., by not submitting routine clinical evaluation to human-subjects committees), strong negative pressure is put on the practicing clinician to avoid systematic evaluation.

Additional problems remain (Hayes, 1980; Levy & Olson, 1979; Thomas, 1978). For example, if the approach advocated here were adopted, a flood of information could emerge from the many thousands of practicing clinicians. Where would it be put? Who would publish it? Would it be simple-minded research anyway? Multiple case manuscripts might be a partial solution; a clearing-house-type arrangement might also be of aid, but it clearly would strain current information-handling systems.

Another problem is the importance of compromises forced by the clinical environment. There are a number of them (Thomas, 1978), although most seem soluble. The major solution is the same as that for most difficulties in time series designs more generally: replication. Only with the enormous resources provided by practicing clinicians does this advice seem practical. Without them, the external validity of single case work, which emerges only from replication (Hersen & Barlow, 1976), has little chance of full demonstration or analysis.

This, then, is the situation. Practicing clinicians are essential to the development of our knowledge base in clinical psychology, and time series experimentation seems fully applicable to the clinical environment. Indeed, the resources needed to repeatedly replicate single case experimentation are available only by including practicing clinicians. If combined, these needs, abilities, and resources could create a true revolution in clinical psychology. The question is, will they be?

REFERENCE NOTES

1. Hayes, S. C., & Nelson, R. O. *Realistic research strategies for practicing clinicians.* Workshop presented at the meeting of the Association for Advancement of Behavior Therapy, San Francisco, December 1979.
2. Hayes, S. C. *A component analysis of flooding relief.* Paper presented at the meeting of the American Psychological Association, Washington, D. C., September 1976.
3. Hayes, S. C. Hussian, R., Turner, A. E., Grubb T., & Anderson, N. *The nature, effect, and generalization of coping statements in the treatment of clinically significant anxiety.* Paper presented at the meeting of the Association for Advancement of Behavior Therapy, San Francisco, December 1979.
4. Hayes, S. C. *Ethical dilemmas of the empirical clinician.* Paper presented at the meeting of the Association for Behavior Analysis, Dearborn, Michigan, May 1979.

REFERENCES

Baer, D. M., Wolf, M. M., & Risley, T. R. (1968). Some current dimensions of applied behavior analysis. *Journal of Applied Behavior Analysis, 1,* 91–97.

Barlow, D. H. (1980). Behavioral therapy: The next decade: *Behavior Therapy, 11,* 315–328.

Barlow, D. H., & Hayes, S. C. (1979). Alternating treatments design: One strategy for comparing the effects of two treatments in a single subject. *Journal of Applied Behavior Analysis, 12,* 199–210.

Barlow, D. H., & Hersen, M. (1973). Single-case experimental designs: Uses in applied clinical research. *Archives of General Psychiatry, 29,* 319–325.

Becker, I. M., & Rosenfeld, J. G. (1976). Rational–emotive therapy—A study of initial therapy sessions of Albert Ellis. *Journal of Clincal Psychology, 76,* 12–26.

Bernard, C. (1865). *An introduction to the study of experimental medicine.* New York: Dover.

Box, G. E. P., & Jenkins, G. M. (1976). *Time series analysis: Forecasting and control.* San Francisco: Holden-Day.

Brownell, K. E., Hayes, S. C., & Barlow, D. H. (1977). Patterns of appropriate and deviant arousal: The behavioral treatment of multiple sexual deviations. *Journal of Consulting and Clincal Psychology, 45,* 1144–1155.

Browning, R. M. (1967). A same-subject design for simultaneous comparison of three reinforcement contingencies. *Behaviour Research and Therapy, 5,* 237–243.

Browing R. M., & Stover, D. O. (1971). *Behavior modification in child treatment: An experimental and clinical approach.* Chicago: Aldine-Atherton.

Campbell, D. T., & Stanley, J. C. (1963). *Experimental and quasi-experimental designs for research.* Chicago: Rand McNally.

Chassan, J. B. (1967). *Research design in clinical psychology and psychiatry.* New York: Appleton-Century-Crofts.

Chassan, J. B. (1979). *Research design in clinical psychology and psychiatry (2nd ed.).* New York: Irvington.

Garfield, S. L., & Kurtz, R. (1976). Clinical psychologists in the 1970s. *American Psychologist, 31,* 1–9.

Glass, G. V., Wilson, V. L., & Gottmann, J. M. (1975). *Design and analysis of time-series experiments.* Boulder: University of Colorado Press.

Gottmann, J. M., McFall, R. M., & Barnett, J. T. (1969). Design and analysis of research using time series. *Psychological Bulletin, 72,* 299–306.

Hartmann, D. P., & Hall, R. V. (1976). The changing criterion design. *Journal of Applied Behavior Analysis, 1976, 9,* 527–532.

Hayes, S. C. (1980). A review of Jayaratne & Levy's "Empirical clinical practice." *Behavioral Assessment, 2,* 306–308.

Hayes, S. C., & Barlow, D. H. (1977). Flooding relief in a case of public transportation phobia. *Behavior Therapy, 8,* 742–746.

Hayes, S. C., & Cone, J. D. (1977). Reducing residential electrical energy use: Payments, information, and feedback. *Journal of Applied Behavior Analysis, 10,* 425–535.

Hersen, M., & Barlow, D. H. (1976). *Single case experimental designs: Strategies for studying behavior change.* New York: Pergamon Press.

Hersen, M., & Bellack, A. S. (1976). A multiple baseline analysis of social skills training in chronic schizophrenics. *Journal of Applied Behavior Analysis; 9,* 527–532.

Holt, R. R. (Ed). (1971). *New horizons for psychotherapy: Autonomy as a profession.* New York: International Universities Press.

Jayaratne, S., & Levy, R. L. (1979). *Empirical clinical practice.* New York: Columbia University Press.

Kazdin, A. E. (1978). Methodological and interpretive problems of single-case experimental designs. *Journal of Consulting and Clinical Psychology, 46,* 629–642.

Kazdin, A. E. (1980). *Research design in clinical psychology.* New York: Harper & Row.

Kazdin, A. E., & Hartmann, D. P. (1978). The simultaneous-treatment design. *Behavior Therapy, 9,* 912–922.

Kazdin, A. E., & Kopel, S. A. (1975). On resolving ambiguities of the multiple-baseline design: Problems and recommendations. *Behavior Therapy, 6,* 601–608.

Kelly, E. L., Goldberg, L. R., Fiske, D. W., & Kilkowski, J. M. (1978). Twenty-five years later. *American Psychologist, 33,* 746–755.

Kratochwill, T. F. (1978). *Single subject research: Strategies for evaluating change.* New York: Academic Press.

Leitenberg, H. (1973). The use of single case methodology in psychotherapy research. *Journal of Abnormal Psychology, 82,* 87–101.

Leitenberg, H. (1974). Training clinical researchers in psychology. *Professional Psychology, 5,* 59–69.

Levy, L. H. (1962). The skew in clinical psychology. *American Psychologist, 17,* 244–249.

Levy, R. L., & Olson, D. G. (1979). The single subject methodology in clinical practice: An overview. *Journal of Social Service Research, 3,* 25–49.

Mahoney, M. J. (1978). Experimental methods and outcome evaluation. *Journal of Consulting and Clinical Psychology, 42,* 660–672.

McCollough, J. P., Cornell, J. E., McDaniel, M. H., & Meuller, R. K. (1974). Utilization of the simultaneous treatment design to improve student behavior in a first-grade classroom. *Journal of Consulting and Clinical Psychology, 42,* 288–292.

Meehl, P. E. (1971). A scientific, scholarly, non-research doctorate for clinical practitioners: Arguments pro and con. In R. R. Holt (Ed.), *New horizons for psychotherapy: Autonomy as a profession.* New York: International Universities Press.

Meltzoff, J., & Kornreich, M. (1970). *Research in psychotherapy.* New York: Atherton.

Millon, T., & Diesenhaus, H. I. (1972). *Research methods in psychopathology.* New York: Wiley.

Nelson, R. O. (1981). Realistic dependent measures for clinical use. *Journal of Consulting and Clinical Psychology, 49,* 168–182.

Paul, G. L. (1969). Behavior modification research: Design and tactics. In C. M. Franks (Ed.), *Behavior therapy: Appraisal and status.* New York: McGraw-Hill.

Peterson, D. R. (1976). Need for the doctor of psychology degree in professional psychology. *American Psychologist, 31,* 792–798.

Raush, H. L. (1969). Naturalistic method and the clinical approach. In E. P. Willems & H. L. Raush (Eds.), *Naturalistic viewpoints in psychological research.* New York: Holt, Rinehart & Winston.

Raush, H. L. (1974). Research, practice, and accountability. *American Psychologist, 29,* 678–681.

Rogers, C. R. (1973). Some new challenges. *American Psychologist, 28,* 379–387.

Shakow, D. (1976). What is clinical psychology? *American Psychologist, 31,* 553–560.

Sidman, M. (1960). *Tactics of scientific research.* New York: Basic Books.

Svenson, S. E., & Chassan, J. B. (1967). A note on ethics and patient consent in single-case design. *Journal of Nervous and Mental Disease, 145*(3), 206–207.

Thelen, M. H., & Ewing, D. R. (1970). Roles, functions, and training in clinical psychology: A survey of academic clinicians. *American Psychologist, 25,* 550–554.

Thomas, E. J. (1978). Research and service in single-case experimentation: Conflicts and choices. *Social Work Research and Abstracts, 14,* 20–31.

Zaro, J. S., Barach, R., Nedelmann, D. J., & Dreiblatt, I. S. (1977). *A guide for beginning psychotherapists.* Cambridge, England: Cambridge University Press.

26

STRUCTURAL ANALYSIS OF SOCIAL BEHAVIOR: APPLICATION TO A STUDY OF INTERPERSONAL PROCESS IN DIFFERENTIAL PSYCHOTHERAPEUTIC OUTCOME

WILLIAM P. HENRY, THOMAS E. SCHACHT, AND HANS H. STRUPP

Psychotherapy process and outcome factors are often split into three categories: (a) patient antecedents; (b) therapist techniques; and (c) relationship (so-called "nonspecific") variables. Research to date has emphasized antecedent patient and relationship variables, although generally failing to demonstrate unique effects of therapist technique, leading to unsettling speculations that perhaps therapist techniques are unimportant (e.g., Parloff Waskow, & Wolfe, 1978).

Traditional research methods foster this view of therapy as composed of discrete patient, therapist, and relationship variables. However, alternate approaches are possible. For example, Kiesler (1982) argued against considering patient and therapist variables isolated from their reciprocal dyadic context. Kiesler elaborated how problems in living appear as the sequelae of rigid, self-defeating communication patterns that collectively compose

Reprinted from the *Journal of Consulting and Clinical Psychology, 54,* 27–31. Copyright 1986 by the American Psychological Association.

This work supported in part by National Institute of Mental Health Grants MH-16247 and MH-20369, Hans H. Strupp, principal investigator.

an interpersonal evoking style. The central antecedent patient variable is the client's interpersonal evoking style, and the main therapist technique variable is the therapist's manner of responding to this style. Thus conceived, patient and therapist variables join in a final irreducible pathway: the therapeutic relationship.

In this view, interpersonal transactions in the therapy dyad should become the fundamental unit of psychotherapy process analysis. Accordingly, technique is not distinct from patient and relationship variables; instead, maintaining and exploring the relationship is therapy's central technical task (not simply an enabling background condition for application of techniques). Therapists do not simply supply a good or bad relationship; rather, they use it technically as both the context for and the substance of psychological change.

Unfortunately, most studies of patient–therapist interaction rely on crude measures of unilateral behaviors that neglect the exact nature of the dyadic transactions while also failing to articulate with any particular interpersonal theory. The present study reports a methodological demonstration designed to increase precision and/or ties to interpersonal theory in the study of psychotherapy transactions.

Circumplex models, from a psychometric standpoint, are the most sophisticated and theoretically coherent models of interpersonal behavior (cf. Wiggins, 1982, for review). Structural Analysis of Social Behavior (SASB; Benjamin, 1974, 1982) is the most detailed, conceptually rigorous, and empirically validated of current models. SASB was selected for the present study in accordance with Schaffer's (1982) guidelines for therapy process research. Specific advantages of SASB along these lines include the following: (a) It provides a research method congruent with theoretical premises about interpersonal process in psychotherapy; (b) it permits extremely fine-grained analysis of virtually any interpersonal event, and (c) it uses small rating units judged by methods requiring relatively low inference and permitting high specificity.

In the present demonstration, the SASB model was applied to 15-min segments of early therapy sessions drawn from four pairs of cases, each pair containing a high-change case and a low-change (i.e., good and poor outcome) case, treated by the same therapist under controlled conditions (described in Strupp, 1980a, 1980b, 1980c, 1980d). The following four hypotheses were designed to illustrate the kinds of clinically and theoretically meaningful questions addressable via the SASB model.

1. Communications should fall into different categories of interpersonal action (represented by SASB clusters) in high-change as compared to low-change cases.

2. Hostile and controlling therapist behavior (SASB Cluster 6, Surface 1) should predict poor outcome, consistent with Truax's (1970) observation that therapist's criticism was related to poor outcome and with Strupp's (1980a) finding that negative therapist reactions to patients' hostility were associated with low patient change.

3. Patients' evoking styles that fall into Cluster 6 of SASB Surfaces 1 or 2 (i.e., hostile controlling of others and hostile submission, respectively) should predict poor outcome. Previous studies (e.g., Crowder, 1972) using simpler methodology have correlated passive-resistant and passive-hostile patient behaviors with poor outcome.

4. As compared with high-change cases, low-change cases should be characterized by more negative (i.e., hostile and controlling) complementarity. Complementary interactions occur when a respondent acts in a manner that is prototypically pulled for by the other's evoking style.

METHOD

Subjects

Four psychotherapists (3 psychodynamic psychiatrists and 1 lay counselor) were each represented by both a high- and low-change case ($N = 8$). The actual interpersonal transactions, not the type of therapy, are of prime importance to the present research. Outcomes were measured by pre-post Minnesota Multiphasic Personality Inventory (MMPI) profiles and ratings of target complaints and global change by patients, therapists, and independent clinicians (Strupp, 1980a, 1980b, 1980c, 1980d). Patients were single men, aged 18-25 years old, with symptoms of anxiety, depression, and social withdrawal (elevated 2-7-0 MMPI profile). Each received individual psychotherapy twice weekly up to a 25-session limit (cf. Strupp & Hadley, 1979).

SASB Analysis

SASB is a system of three interrelated circumplex surfaces. Each surface presents, in a two-dimensional space, 36 interpersonal behaviors that represent unique combinations of the theoretically primitive interpersonal vectors of affiliation–disaffiliation and independence–interdependence. The 36 behaviors of each circumplex surface may be collapsed into eight psychometrically validated clusters or four quadrants (Benjamin,

1974, 1982; see Figure 1). Because of superior psychometric properties and ease of interpretation, the cluster level of the SASB model rather than the 36-point version was employed in the present study.

Each SASB surface defines a particular perspective, or focus, on interpersonal transactions. Surface 1 involves focus on another person (transitive action), and Surface 2 involves focus on the self (intransitive states).[1] SASB Surfaces 1 and 2 are structurally homologous (see Figure 1); furthermore, interpersonally complementary behaviors are represented at homologous points across the surfaces. *Complementarity* is defined as reciprocity on the interdependence (control) dimension and correspondence on the affiliative dimension. For example, "watching and managing" on Surface 1 is the interpersonal complement of "deferring and submitting" on Surface 2 (i.e., the former pulls for the latter).[2]

Procedure

Transcripts of third sessions were selected because prior research had indicated that the nature of the working alliance in time-limited therapy is well-established by this time and that this alliance predicts eventual therapeutic outcome (Suh, O'Malley, & Strupp, in press). Coding of the transcripts into the SASB model followed Benjamin, Giat, and Estroff's (1981) procedure manual. Initially, each transcription is broken into *thought units*, which are any portion of speech expressing one complete thought (independent judges usually have little disagreement when unitizing transcripts in this manner). Coding itself requires a series of three decisions. First, the focus (Surface 1 vs. Surface 2) of the thought unit is established. Normally the therapist focuses on *other* and the patient focuses on *self* (although this is not invariably the case). Second, the thought unit is rated on a 5-point scale representing the primitive affiliation–disaffiliation vector. Third, the

---

[1] Surface 3 represents intrapsychic actions resulting when focus on the other (Surface 1) is directed inward on the self (introjection). Surface 3 is normally used in content analysis rather than process analysis and, accordingly, is not incorporated into the present interpersonal process analysis.

[2] Because of the concept of focus, which gives rise to three separate circumplex surfaces, complementarity in the SASB system is more differentiated than in traditional one-surface circumplex models. In these traditional models (cf. Wiggins, 1982), the power dimension is represented by a single continuum ranging from dominance to submission. Thus a complementary interchange is one in which one party dominates and the other submits. In the SASB system, the meaning of the power dimension varies according to the interpersonal focus. On Surface 1 (focus on other), the continuum ranges from the traditional concept of dominance to autonomy-giving (freeing the other), whereas on Surface 2 (focus on self) the continuum moves from the traditional submission to autonomy-taking (asserting and separating from the other). In the SASB system then, the traditional dominance-submission definition of complementarity is supplemented by an additional complementary pattern in which one person is autonomy-giving (which differs from submission) and the other person is autonomy-taking (which differs from dominance). Further elaboration of this important advance in circumplex theory is given in studies by Benjamin (1974, 1982).

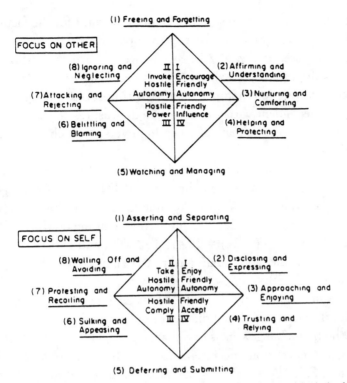

(1) Freeing and Forgetting

FOCUS ON OTHER

(8) Ignoring and Neglecting

(7) Attacking and Rejecting

(6) Belittling and Blaming

II I
Invoke | Encourage
Hostile | Friendly
Autonomy | Autonomy
Hostile | Friendly
Power | Influence
III | IV

(2) Affirming and Understanding

(3) Nurturing and Comforting

(4) Helping and Protecting

(5) Watching and Managing

(1) Asserting and Separating

FOCUS ON SELF

(8) Walling Off and Avoiding

(7) Protesting and Recoiling

(6) Sulking and Appeasing

II I
Take | Enjoy
Hostile | Friendly
Autonomy | Autonomy
Hostile | Friendly
Comply | Accept
III | IV

(2) Disclosing and Expressing

(3) Approaching and Enjoying

(4) Trusting and Relying

(5) Deferring and Submitting

Figure 1: Surface 1 (focus on other) and Surface 2 (focus on self) of the Structural Analysis of Social Behavior.

thought unit is rated on a 5-point scale representing the primitive independence–interdependence vector. Finally, the affiliation and autonomy ratings are used as Cartesian coordinate points to place the thought unit in its proper place. This position is subjected to a global judgment check (what Benjamin et al., 1981, called the "final clinical test"), which ratifies the interpersonal cluster into which the unit has been coded.

Raters who were blind to the outcome status of each case analyzed the first 150 thought units of each session (the first 15–20 min of the session). This segment was chosen arbitrarily, following the lead of Gomes-Schwartz (1978), who found no systematic difference in process scores attributable to the time sequence of rated segments. Transcripts and the original audio recordings were both used in the rating process. Independent interjudge agreement in SASB cluster assignment was high (Cohen's kappa = .91, based on 150 judgments). Instances of disagreement were resolved through discussion and mutual consent.

RESULTS

Prior to statistical analysis, observed frequencies in each SASB cluster for both patient and therapist were weighted to adjust for the fact that the proportion of thought units for the therapist versus the patient varied from case to case. Two $2 \times 2 \times 8$ (Change $\times$ Focus $\times$ SASB Cluster) analyses of variance (ANOVAs) were performed, one for data from patient utterances and one for therapist data. A within-subjects design was used, treating the dependent variables as repeated measures on the 4 therapists. This design removes the main effect of high versus low change due to the weighting procedure.

As expected, there was a main effect for focus for both the therapists, $F(1, 3) = 52.93$, $p < .004$; and the patients, $F(1, 3) = 94.88$, $p < .002$, indicating that therapists spent more time focusing on the other (i.e., the patient) and that patients devoted more time focusing on the self. Also as expected, therapists, $F(7, 21) = 20.41$, $p < .001$; and patients, $F(7, 21) = 10.36$, $p < .001$, did not equally utilize the eight available interpersonal clusters of the SASB.

The Outcome Status $\times$ Focus $\times$ Cluster interaction reveals that as predicted, therapists exhibited different interpersonal communication patterns in the high-change versus low-change cases, $F(7, 21) = 3.01$, $p < .02$. However, the corresponding interaction for the patients failed to reach significance, $F(7, 21) = 1.55$, $p < .20$ (see Discussion section).

Cluster Comparisons

Tukey's HSD statistic was used in a series of individual SASB cluster comparisons to establish the exact differences in evoking styles between patients and therapists in the high-change versus low-change conditions. As predicted (Hypotheses 2 and 3), differences between high and low cases ($p < .05$) appeared for both the patients and therapists on SASB Clusters 2 and 4, appeared for therapists on Cluster 6, and appeared for patients on Cluster 8 (see Table 1), indicating that in high-change cases the therapists were significantly more affirming and understanding (Cluster 2, Surface 1), more helping and protecting (Cluster 4, Surface 1), and less belittling and blaming (Cluster 6, Surface 1). Patients in the low-change cases were significantly less disclosing and expressing (Cluster 2, Surface 2), more trusting and relying (in a passive, deferent sense; Cluster 4, Surface 2), and more walling off and avoiding (Cluster 8, Surface 2).

Complementarity

Following Dietzel and Abeles (1975), the procedure for measuring interpersonal complementarity allowed assessment of degrees of complementarity. In addition, we separated positive complementarity (i.e.,

TABLE 1
Comparison of Structural Analysis of Social Behavior Cluster Means

Cluster	Therapist		Patient	
	High	Low	High	Low
Focus on other				
1. Freeing/forgetting	0.0	0.9	0.0	0.0
2. Affirming/understanding	14.2	7.8*	0.3	0.3
3. Nurturing/comforting	0.0	0.0	0.0	0.0
4. Helping/protecting	31.9	26.0*	1.0	0.0
5. Watching/monitoring	2.3	3.5	0.2	0.3
6. Belittling/blaming	0.3	5.2*	0.0	0.9
7. Attacking/rejecting	0.0	0.0	0.0	0.0
8. Ignoring/neglecting	0.0	1.7	0.0	0.0
Focus on self				
1. Asserting/separating	0.0	0.3	0.7	6.3
2. Disclosing/expressing	2.7	4.9	105.3	68.2*
3. Approaching/enjoying	0.0	0.0	0.0	0.0
4. Trusting/relying	0.5	0.2	6.5	17.8*
5. Deferring/submitting	0.0	0.5	0.0	6.2
6. Sulking/appeasing	0.0	0.4	0.0	4.5
7. Protesting/recoiling	0.0	0.0	0.0	0.0
8. Walling off/avoiding	0.0	0.8	0.0	9.6*

Notes: Scores represent weighted mean number of thought units per cluster.
*$p < .05$.

affiliative and autonomy-enhancing reciprocal interchanges) from negative complementarity (i.e., hostile or controlling reciprocal interchanges).

The eight cluster ratings were first collapsed into four quadrant ratings. Then a 4×4 matrix was established, with each row and column representing one of the four SASB quadrants. Each interchange between patient and therapist could be represented in 1 of the 16 matrix cells.

For each pair of turns at talk, the last thought unit of the speaker and the first thought unit of the respondent were selected for complementarity evaluation. The raw frequencies in each cell were weighted to remove the effect of differing numbers of turns at talk across cases. Because the circumplex surfaces have two dimensions, it is possible to have degrees of complementarity. The highest degree of complementarity occurs when an interaction is complementary on both the affiliation–disaffiliation and independence–interdependence dimensions. A smaller degree of complementarity is expressed when an interaction is complementary on only one of these dimensions (cf. Kiesler, 1983). Following this logic, each cell was assigned a complementarity weight (3, 2, or 1), and the weighted frequencies in each cell were then multiplied by the complementarity weights to produce the data for the complementarity analysis. Finally, each cell was assigned either a positive or negative valence. Cells in which both interactants were in an affiliative quadrant (i.e., Quadrants 1 or 4) were deemed to represent positive interpersonal events, whereas cells in which at least one of the participants was in a disaffiliative quadrant (Quadrants 2 or 3) were deemed negative.

For each case, weighted complementarity frequencies were summed separately across the positive and negative cells to produce positive and negative complementarity indexes and were summed together to produce a total complementarity index. Differences in complementarity for the high-change versus low-change conditions were evaluated via t tests ($n = 4$).

Results support Hypothesis 4. When analyzed from the perspective of the therapist speaking first (and the patient responding), all analyses were significant. High-change cases showed greater positive complementarity, $t(3) = 4.59$, $p < .01$; less negative complementarity, $t(3) = 2.66$, $p < .05$; and greater total complementarity, $t(3) = 7.30$, $p < .001$. Similar results obtained for the analysis in which the patient spoke first and the therapist responded. High-change cases showed greater positive complementarity, $t(3) = 3.0$, $p < .05$; and less negative complementarity, $t(3) = 3.0$, $p < .05$. There were no differences on total complementarity in this condition, $t(3) = 2.07$, ns.

Multiple Communications

A multiple communication is one in which a single thought unit communicates more than one interpersonal message (e.g., a message that simultaneously communicates acceptance and rejection). Although the pattern is overwhelmingly clear (multiple communications were far greater in the low-change cases), the intercase variability produced a variance that precluded significance testing because of the small sample size. It is worth noting, however, that in the low-change cases 22% of the therapists' and 17% of the patients' thought units conveyed a multiple interpersonal process, compared with 0% of the patients and 2% of the therapists in the high-change cases.

DISCUSSION

There are crucial differences between measuring categorical behaviors (such as specific types of interpretations) or global therapeutic climate (such as warmth) and studying small, specific units of interpersonal process. This study illustrates the potential value of fine-grained analysis of the interpersonal process between patient and therapist. High-change and low-change cases were differentiated via study of the interpersonal process early in treatment. Clear-cut patterns emerged, suggesting that a therapy might become infused with a pervasive interpersonal process rather early in treatment. The SASB-based research strategies permitted demonstration that as predicted, the same therapist, although using similar techniques with similar patients, nonetheless might exhibit markedly different interpersonal behaviors in low-change cases as compared to high-change cases. In the high-change cases none of the patients' communications and only 1% of the therapists' communications were judged to be hostile, whereas in the low-change cases the corresponding averages were 19% and 20%. However, because these conclusions are based on small segments from a limited number of cases, the generalizability of the current findings is unknown.

Interpersonal complementarity appears in the predictable patterns of dyadic elicitation-response sequences. Although the validity of complementarity as an organizing principle has been demonstrated repeatedly (cf. Dietzel & Abeles, 1975; Kiesler, 1982), the role of complementarity in psychotherapy remains controversial. One position proposed that treatment success requires therapists to respond in a noncomplementary or disconfirming manner to the patient's interpersonal evoking style (Kiesler, 1983). The patient's accustomed behavior is not reciprocally reinforced, creating opportunity for alternative patterns of interpersonal activity. Others (e.g., Swensen, 1967) hypothesized that noncomplementary interactions induce excess anxiety and argued that a highly complementary relationship should be the most harmonious and satisfying, leading to positive therapeutic outcomes. Dietzel and Abeles (1975) proposed a more complex alternative, in which the desirability of complementarity varies as a function of particular phases of therapy.[3]

Although seemingly contradictory, each theorist accepts the basic premise that complementary interactions tend to form stable patterns, whereas noncomplementary interactions are unstable and create conditions conducive to change. The apparent theoretical conflict results, we believe, from failure to distinguish positive from negative complementarity. Although affiliate (helping, trusting, etc.) sequences are the theoretical equivalent of hostile (blaming, appeasing, etc.) patterns in terms of complementarity, surely they are not therapeutically equal.

The present study separates positive from negative complementarity. Results indicate that compared with low-change cases, high-change cases were typified by higher levels of positive complementarity and lower levels of negative complementarity. In the condition in which the patient spoke first and the therapist responded (i.e., the procedure employed by Dietzel & Abeles, 1975, who found no effect), we also found no difference in

_____
[3] However, it must be noted that using a complementarity index similar to the procedure employed in the present study, Dietzel and Abeles (1975) found no difference in complementarity between successful and unsuccessful cases, either early in therapy or overall.

overall complementarity. When viewed from the foregoing perspective, however, the failure to find differences in overall complementarity appears to simply reflect the fact that positive and negative indexes, if lumped together, can cancel each other statistically and produce the erroneous impression that complementarity is unrelated to outcome.

Multiple communications were almost exclusively associated with therapies having a poor outcome. The following transcribed example offers a concrete illustration of the concept. Therapist and patient are discussing how the patient had been rudely rejected for a date, and the therapist has encouraged the patient to confront the girl about her behavior:

> Patient: (in a petulant tone of voice) "Well, what good is it going to do to say something to her?"
>
> Therapist: (in a critical manner) "It's not a question to me of whether it's going to do you any good or not, it's a question to me of whether you somehow have already told her it's all right to treat you that {rude} way."

In this exchange, the patient's communication takes the form of a query (SASB Cluster 4, trusting and relying). However, the context of the interchange and his tone of voice indicate that the patient is also protesting a previous therapist statement (SASB Cluster 6, sulking and appeasing). The therapist replies in a complementary manner to both parts of the patient's multiple communication. Although the form of the therapist's communication is of a helping analysis (SASB Cluster 4, helping and protecting), he simultaneously blames the patient for his predicament in a condescending manner (SASB Cluster 6, blaming and belittling). A more desirable therapist response to this patient's multiple communication might have been to respond in a complementary manner only to the positive portion of the patient's message.

The present study speaks to important methodological issues. For example, the problem of choosing units of analysis has long plagued psychotherapy research. Frequency counts of simple unidirectional units (e.g., counting the number of linking interpretations a therapist makes) have not demonstrated powerful relationships to outcome. Despite this, it is common procedure to construct therapy rating scales by combining items in a Likert-type format into a total score that purportedly reflects some facet of the therapeutic process. Findings are typically complex (e.g., 1 particular item scored low is more important than 10 items scored high, indicating that the absolute frequencies of therapeutic events need not be high to damage the therapeutic process). Researchers commonly deal with these complex relations by strategies such as item weighting, multivariate analysis, factor analysis, and so forth. However, although useful, statistical manipulations cannot substitute for weak theory. None of these approaches solves the basic problem of inadequate units of analysis or of research findings that lack a coherent relation to therapeutic action–plans.

An alternative represented here is to employ units of analysis sufficiently complex to capture equally complex interactive processes and yet also theoretically cogent and empirically reliable and validated. Interpersonal transaction patterns, expressed in terms of the SASB model, are one source of such complex units of analysis. In this view, the patterns of transaction between patient and therapist are studied per se, not each participant's unilateral contributions to the relationship. We concur with Kiesler's (1982) recommendation that these interpersonal transaction patterns should become a fundamental unit of empirical psychotherapy process research.

In summary, the methods illustrated by the present study permit fine-grained investigation of the therapeutic relationship as well as underlying theoretical issues such as the interpersonal theory of complementarity. Although technique varied substantially across the therapists studied (from traditional psychoanalytic technique to the directive folksy moralism practiced by the lay counselor), the actual interpersonal processes differentiating high-change and low-change outcomes were similar across cases.

This demonstration does not imply that technique factors are unimportant. To speak of the respective roles of technique (specific) versus relationship (nonspecific) variables is to participate in a misleading dichotomy (Henry, 1985). Techniques cannot be separated from the context of the interpersonal relationship, and indeed, future research is likely to reveal that management of the therapeutic relationship is itself a technical cornerstone (Strupp & Binder, 1984). Both research and clinical training would benefit, in our view, from efforts, such as the present study, to more directly integrate the study of interpersonal process and therapeutic technique.

REFERENCES

Benjamin, L. S. (1974). Structural analysis of social behavior. *Psychological Review, 81*, 392–425.

Benjamin, L. S. (1982). Use of structural analysis of social behavior (SASB) to guide intervention in psychotherapy. In J. C. Anchin & D. J. Kiesler (Eds.), *Handbook of interpersonal psychotherapy* (pp. 190–212). New York: Pergamon Press.

Benjamin, L. S., Giat, L., & Estroff, S. (1981). *Coding manual for structural analysis of social behavior (SASB)*. Unpublished manuscript, University of Wisconsin, Department of Psychiatry, Madison.

Crowder, J. E. (1972). Relationship between therapist and client interpersonal behaviors and psychotherapy outcome. *Journal of Counseling Psychology, 19,* 68–75.

Dietzel, C. S., & Abeles, N. (1975). Client–therapist complementarity and therapeutic outcome, *Journal of Counseling Psychology, 22,* 264–272.

Gomes-Schwartz, B. (1978). Effective ingredients in psychotherapy: Prediction of outcome from process variables. *Journal of Consulting and Clinical Psychology, 46,* 1023–1035.

Henry, W. P. (1985). The time-released placebo: A reply to Critelli and Neumann. *American Psychologist, 40,* 239.

Kiesler, D. J. (1982) Interpersonal theory for personality and psychotherapy. In J. C. Anchin & D. J. Kiesler (Eds.), *Handbook of interpersonal psychotherapy* (pp. 3–24). New York: Pergamon Press.

Kiesler, D. J. (1983). The 1982 interpersonal circle: A taxonomy for complementarity in human transactions. *Psychological Review, 90,* 185–214.

Parloff, M. B., Waskow, I. E., & Wolfe, B. E. (1978). Research on therapist variables in relation to process and outcome. In S. L. Garfield & A. E. Bergin (Eds.), *Handbook of psychotherapy and behavior change: An empirical analysis* (2nd ed., pp. 233–282). New York: Wiley.

Schaffer, N. D. (1982). Multidimensional measures of therapist behavior as predictors of outcome. *Psychological Bulletin, 92,* 670–681.

Strupp, H. H. (1980a). Success and failure in time-limited psychotherapy: A systematic comparison of two cases: Comparison 1. *Archives of General Psychiatry, 37,* 595–603.

Strupp, H. H. (1980b). Success and failure in time-limited psychotherapy: A systematic comparison of two cases: Comparison 2. *Archives of General Psychiatry, 37,* 708–716.

Strupp, H. H. (1980c). Success and failure in time-limited psychotherapy: With special reference to the performance of a lay counselor (Comparison 3). *Archives of General Psychiatry, 37,* 831–841.

Strupp, H. H. (1980d). Success and failure in time-limited psychotherapy: Further evidence (Comparison 4). *Archives of General Psychiatry, 37,* 947–954.

Strupp, H. H., & Binder, J. L. (1984). *Psychotherapy in a new key: A guide to time-limited dynamic psychotherapy.* New York: Basic Books.

Strupp, H. H., & Hadley, S. W. (1979). Specific versus nonspecific factors in psychotherapy: A controlled study of outcome. *Archives of General Psychiatry, 36,* 1125–1136.

Suh, C. S., O'Malley, S., & Strupp, H. H. (in press). The Vanderbilt psychotherapy process scale. In L. Greenberg & W. Pinsof (Eds.), *The psychotherapeutic process.* New York: Guilford Press.

Swensen, C. H. (1967). Psychotherapy as a special case of dyadic interaction: Some suggestions for theory and research. *Psychotherapy: Theory, Research and Practice, 4,* 7–13.

Truax, C. B. (1970). Therapist's evaluative statements and patient outcome in psychotherapy. *Journal of Clinical Psychology, 26,* 536–538.

Wiggins, J. S. (1982). Circumplex models of interpersonal behavior in clinical psychology. In P. C. Kendall & J. N. Butcher (Eds.), *Handbook of research methods in clinical psychology* (pp. 183–221). New York: Wiley.

DESIGN, TREATMENT EVALUATION, AND CHANGE

27

COPING STRATEGIES IN PSYCHIATRIC CLINICAL RESEARCH

HELENA CHMURA KRAEMER

With good reason, clinical researchers in psychiatry frequently lament that the classical methodological approaches to research learned in design/ analysis courses, in textbooks, and in seminars often seem irrelevant, inapplicable, unfeasible, and even when applicable, all too often unsuccessful. Such difficulties have their genesis in the fact that biostatisticians have been trained to function and, in turn, have trained researchers to function in a research world that essentially exists only in textbooks. In that idealized world, if one needs 100, 500, or 1,000 subjects to execute a research protocol, such subjects are not only accessible but are apparently ready and willing to participate in a research study. That there are legal and ethical strictures on the use of human subjects, particularly in psychiatric research,

Reprinted from the *Journal of Consulting and Clinical Psychology, 49,* 309–319. Copyright 1981 by the American Psychological Association.

This article is based on a speech delivered at the meeting of the Society for Psychotherapy Research at Asilomar, California, June 18, 1980. The research was supported by the National Institute of Mental Health Specialized Research Center Grant MH-30854 and was done in conjunction with consultation activities with regard to the NIMH Specialized Research Center Grant MH-30899 to Mardi Horowitz at the University of California, San Francisco.

and that informed consent is prerequisite to recruitment as well as to retention of subjects in any research project are factors that have no impact in that world.

Furthermore, in that world, subjects are random samples from a defined population of interest or, at least, representative samples. In reality, psychiatric clinical researchers may never in the course of a lifetime career have occasion to define a priori the population of interest, much less to select a random sample of that population or to guarantee a sample's representativeness.

In a clinical trial, in that ideal world, patients never refuse randomization. If assigned to a drug group in a drug–placebo trial, the patient does not dispose of the medication or share it or otherwise withhold compliance and, in effect, transfer himself to the placebo–control group. In a trial of relaxation training for control of hypertension, an attention–control patient does not read a book on the relaxation response and, in effect, transfer himself to the test group.

In that ideal world, patients do not drop out before the end of treatment. If they do, at least the reasons for dropping out are uncorrelated with response to treatment. All patients permit evaluation of their response: They do not refuse either to appear for final evaluation or to answer pertinent questions at that time.

Furthermore, it is not merely that there are unrealistic expectations of the behavior of sampling units. The common statistical analytic approaches are uniformly predicated on assumptions concerning the behavior of data that are also unrealistic. The analytic techniques used in the vast majority of psychiatric research reports (t-tests, analysis of variance, linear regression and correlation approaches, their multivariate extensions and their variations; Moore, 1975) are all based on assumptions that data are normally distributed, that variances in subgroups are equal, that associations between variables are linear, and that effects are additive. The fact is that data are almost never normally distributed, and other assumptions fail too often to be taken for granted. Despite comforting notions that seem inappropriately common, whether or not data behave in the manner they are assumed to behave may affect the validity of the results of the analysis based on those assumptions.

Historically, there is valid reason for such a disparity between the real world and the ideal. The common approaches to design and analysis evolved not in the context of clinical research but to a great extent in agricultural research, where the sample units were plots of land, and the responses measures of quantity and quality of crop yield. In fact, terminology in the design field (plot, blocks, crossover) reflects this history. The difficulty stems not from the formulation of statistical approaches but from the fact that we in psychiatric research continue to cling to approaches that are predicated on an expectation that patients behave like plots of land!

The research coping strategies that are described here are not the strategies that work optimally under optimal circumstances, as are the classical strategies, but ones that, in practice, tend to work well under the usual, far from optimal, circumstances of psychiatric research. Some may seem obvious. It is hoped that at least some will seem worth a try. Some may seem irrelevant or even wrong in the context of the reader's research. These strategies have evolved from the author's experience as consultant and collaborator on a wide range of psychological, psychiatric, and behavioral research projects and have been found successful in these contexts. The purpose of this presentation, however, is not to urge replacement of the classical approaches with these approaches but to encourage a critical, insightful, adaptive, and inventive philosophy about design and analysis issues, one in which methodological decisions are responsive to the exigencies of one's own research milieu and experience. Should this mean that in some cases thoughtful consideration would lead one to prefer the classical approaches to the author's or, better yet, some other approach to both as being better suited to the reader's research problems, that purpose will be well served.

SAMPLING

Sample Size

The single most frequently asked design question is, "How large a sample must I have?" The conventional approach requires (a) some knowledge of the characteristics of the population, (b) a specification of a clinically significant effect, and (c) a determination of the acceptable risk of failure (Cohen, 1969; Denenberg, 1976). Generally, at the time the question is asked (usually in formulating research proposals), (a) there is little or no knowledge of the population characteristics, (b) there is no peer-accepted definition of a clinically significant effect size, and (c) no researcher is willing to admit to accepting any risk of failure.

In the very rare circumstance that the conventional approach could be applied, conservative choices of clinically significant effect size and risk of failure tend to dictate the necessity of sample sizes of 100 or more. It is rare in clinical research that such sample size can be readily achieved outside of large-scale cooperative clinical trials or, in a single research center, by long-term research. Yet, funding agencies are loathe to approve studies involving the millions of dollars necessary for cooperative trials or 5–10 years in projected duration. Furthermore, individual researchers are reluctant to commit future efforts to very long-term research projects. As a result, the question phrased, "How large a sample must I have?" would more accurately be formulated as, "With how small a sample is it reasonable to proceed?" A simple coping strategy answer to that question is 20: no fewer than 10 per group in a treatment–control trial.

It should be clearly understood that this is not the sample size one would necessarily recommend if it were easy to obtain a larger sample size. What this number represents is a sample size that (a) seems acceptable in this field at this time, (b) generally seems feasible in those circumstances when recruitment of subjects is difficult or processing of each subject is expensive, (c) yields reasonable power for the magnitude of clinical effects that can be achieved in this area, and (d) provides a reasonable balance between the cost of the research project and its power. Acceptability, feasibility, power, and cost are the four factors with which one must come to terms. The larger the sample size, the greater the acceptability and power, but then the larger the sample size, the less feasible the completion of the project and the greater the cost. With these factors in mind, why 20 and not, for example, 10 or 30?

The results of public opinion or consumer surveys, a political poll, or an epidemiological study based on 100 or fewer subjects would be regarded as unacceptable and unconvincing by experts in these fields. At the other extreme, there was a time in the history of psychiatry when a single well-documented case history was accepted as convincing evidence for a theory. What is acceptable varies not only among research fields but even over time within a research field. As far as one can tell, what is or is not acceptable is not totally a function of the nature of the subjects, type of questions, quality of response measures, or statistical methods. In recent psychiatric clinical research, 20 seems a generally acceptable sample size (i.e., the basis of a peer-reviewed publishable research study; Agras & Berkowitz, Note 1), and this number also represents what seems acceptable in clinical research in general (Fletcher & Fletcher, 1979).

It is quite true that many studies with fewer than 20 subjects are published. Why not allow 10 subjects? The difficulty is that with fewer than 10 per group, one or two outliers can totally control the results, in which case the tail wags the statistical dog. With fewer than 10 per group, none of the statistical techniques for detecting outliers work, and it becomes impossible to distinguish a true value sampled from the tail of a distribution from a bad measurement. For these reasons, it is risky to allow group size to sink below about 10. In any case, with fewer than 10 subjects,

542   HELENA CHMURA KRAEMER

odds favor finding nonsignificant results (low power) even when the impact of the treatment is quite large.

On the other hand, it is also quite true that a minority of clinical research studies report 30–40 subjects. Why not recommend this sample size as a better minimal standard for the field? Table 1 presents the estimated power for 10, 20, 30, and 40 subjects. These figures are in fact based on the two-sample t-test, using a 5% one-tailed test, with an effect size of 1 (group means separated by one standard deviation). However, the type of pattern seen here is typical of a wide range of test procedures, and it is the pattern that is of interest.

One notes that each successive increase of 10 subjects "buys" less power. In raising sample size from 10 to 20, one gains a substantial 27% in power and changes the odds in this case from favoring a nonsignificant result to favoring a significant one. The next increase of 10 (20–30) gains a smaller 16%; the next (30–40), a very small 4%; and each succeeding increase of 10 (40–50, 50–60, etc.) will make little further practical difference.

What is the cost now of these buys of greater power? If each subject costs $100, say, to recruit and process, then the investment of $1,000 to raise the sample size from 10 to 20 is clearly a good investment. The next $1,000 to raise the sample size from 20 to 30 is more questionable, and the next does not seem worthwhile. In fact, however, in the circumstances under which clinical research is done, successive subjects accelerate in cost. A more realistic situation is that in which the first 10 may cost $1,000, but each successive 10 cost 50% more. The first $1,500 to raise the sample size from 10 to 20 still seems a worthwhile investment. Does an additional $2,000 to raise power from 68% to 84%? Our feeling is that it does not.

Clearly this is both a hypothetical and a restricted example. The general pattern, however, that of decelerating gains in power with increasing sample size and accelerating gains in cost, is quite general and realistic. A sample size of 20, which seems acceptable and feasible and which yields

TABLE 1
Power and Cost

n	% power	Cost[a]	
		Equal subject	Accelerating subject
10	41	1,000	1,000
20	68	2,000	2,500
30	84	3,000	4,500
40	92	4,000	6,000

[a]In dollars

reasonable power in well-designed research (based on our own experience as well as evidence in published research in this field), therefore seems a reasonable base level for sample size.

Inclusion/Exclusion Criteria

Subjects are, of course, not randomly selected, nor can they be unequivocally demonstrated to be representative of some predefined population. In general, they comprise whatever patients one is allowed to study and those who are able and willing to consent to be studied—in short, a sample of convenience. This sample represents some general population, but what population this is can only be suggested by a complete post hoc description of the entry characteristics of the sample. In fact, the only sampling option that can be exercised by the researcher is the definition of inclusion or exclusion criteria for entry into the study.

The conventional wisdom is that inclusion/exclusion criteria should be strictly set. It is argued that heterogeneity tends to attentuate the power of statistical tests and, therefore, to obscure all but the most blatant effects. However, it must be noted that the issue of power is related to heterogeneity of response, whereas the issue of entry criteria is related to heterogeneity of entry characteristics. Whether imposition of strict entry criteria leads to greater homogeneity of response is not at all assured. What is assured is a less attractive prospect.

First, clearly, since the results that one obtains from a research study generalize only to that population represented by the sample, the imposition of strict entry criteria restricts generalizability of results. Second, the imposition of strict entry criteria immensely increases the logistical problems of research. With fewer subjects eligible for entry, it may be near impossible to realize even the minimally acceptable sample size. Finally, there is a consequence that, while not assured, occurs too frequently to be dismissed. Patients who are relatively most healthy tend to be very unresponsive to treatment, as do patients who are relatively least healthy. If entry criteria favored either of these groups, there might be more homogeneous response, but it would be homogeneously a null response. In general, responsiveness to treatment may be related to the very criteria that one might restrict in defining entry criteria. There is no guarantee that eliminating heterogeneity of response is not concomitant with eliminating responsiveness to treatment.

The coping strategy that takes all these factors into consideration would be to set rather liberal entry criteria, eliminating only (a) those whom one would not consider for treatment either because of legal, ethical, or clinical reasons; (b) those who have a priori little capacity for change (e.g., the very healthy and the very sick); and (c) those who are unlikely to comply with the requirements of the protocol. If one wishes to isolate a particular subgroup for post hoc analysis, under these liberal criteria one may do so, whereas if only that particular subgroup were considered eligible for study, all post hoc options would be precluded.

Determination of eligibility and informed consent, of course, precede any research intervention with subjects, in particular that of assignment to treatment or control groups.

Randomization

Two considerations are relevant to assignment of patients to treatment or control groups: With sample sizes as small as these under consideration, there should be reasonable balance in group sizes, and, clearly, there should be no major difference between the groups in those patient characteristics that may influence response (i.e., no bias).

The conventional wisdom would have one randomize assignment using, for example, coin flips or random-number tables. If it were so done, in the long run, the sample sizes would be near equal (balance), and there would be but random differences in the entry characteristics of patients in the two groups (control of bias). Particularly unlikely would be major biases in those entry characteristics pertinent to response to treatment, whatever they may be.

The difficulty is, of course, that no researcher operates "in the long run." In small sample studies, a very common experience is that one ends with, for example, a 15-5 split. A sample size of 5 is, as noted earlier, unacceptable. With subjects entering the study sequentially, by the time it is clear that the imbalance is not just temporary, the study may be near completion. One strategy that should not be considered is that in which one alternates assignments to groups. Although this strategy produces balance, it has frequently been found that nurses, technicians, or researchers themselves consciously or unconsciously "gerrymander" order and, thereby, bias the samples. Even the risk of such bias is good reason to avoid this procedure.

We have found that an elegant and simple randomization procedure suggested by Efron (1971) copes well with this problem. In this procedure, the first subject who enters the study and any subject who is assigned when group sizes are equal is assigned randomly. Any subject who is assigned when group sizes are unequal has a 1-3 chance of entry into the majority group, 2-3 into the minority group. This is a randomization procedure that exerts a constant pressure to balance group sizes. Yet, at no point is there sure knowledge of assignment when crucial elegibility and consent decisions are being made.

The problem of bias is more difficult. Once again, in the long run, randomization produces unbiased samples, but randomization in small samples is no guarantee of control of bias. Conventional wisdom dictates that if bias is a vital issue, one should create subgroups matched in terms of the troublesome sources of bias and randomly assign subjects to treatment and control groups within each matched subgroup (preferably using the Efron procedure). In this case, there can be no bias in terms of the factors used for matching, and if properly analyzed (Kraemer, Jacob, Jeffrey, & Agras, 1979), this design may lead to an increase of power as well.

However, in a small sample design, it very often happens that one ends with only one subject per matched subgroup or two subjects both assigned to the same group. To retain control of bias, one is obliged to discard these subgroups. Thus, one loses a portion of what may already be minimal sample size. At the same time, the anticipated increase of power is realized only if the matching factors are well correlated with response. Once again, it is a common and dismaying occurrence to find after completion of a project that the factors one chose to match for are uncorrelated with response, whereas one that never entered a priori consideration is highly correlated and biases the groups. In this case, one must resort to post hoc analysis to assess the impact of bias on the results.

All things considered, as a coping strategy, the only factor that should ever be considered for matching procedures is one that unequivocally influences response (usually initial status of the response characteristic under study). All others may and should be evaluated in post hoc analysis.

DESIGN AND ANALYSIS

Decisions must be made as to when and how patient responses are to be evaluated. This is a huge and complex topic, but here only a few of the most common approaches and their relative advantages and disadvantages are mentioned as a paradigm of such evaluations.

One must consider four issues: the statistical validity (Cook & Campbell, 1976) of the design (Is it likely to lead to false conclusions?); its power (How likely is it to be successful?); its feasibility (Can one do it in the research context considered?); and finally, its clinical value (How clinically informative will its results be?).

The endpoint design, in which one evaluates response only at the end of treatment, is generally a valid design and one that is highly successful in many areas of medical research. In psychiatric research, however, data tend to be "soft." Such data have a high variability associated with individual differences, due not only to true physiological or psychological differences but also to differences in the ways subjects or observers evaluate and report, to variations in response styles, and to transient effects of the environment on behavior or perception. These accrue to reduce the power of this design. Furthermore, each patient who drops out is precluded from analysis. Clearly, this further reduces power. Even substantial and clinically significant responses are difficult to demonstrate as statistically significant.

Further, while the design tends to be easy to implement, it lacks important clinical information. Since initial status of patients is not measured, it is impossible to determine which individual patients respond and to what degree. To know approximately what percentage of patients respond and whether these patients share certain characteristics is vital in applying research results in a clinical setting.

A change design, in which one evaluates response both pre- and posttreatment in both treatment and control groups, is generally about as easy to implement as the endpoint design and is about as valid. However, for soft data, this design tends to yield more clinically useful information and more power. (However, see Cronbach & Furby, 1970.)

If the patient is informed that she/he has a 50–50 chance of being assigned to a placebo control group, this often exacerbates recruitment problems. The patient's awareness of this possibility also tends to encourage dropout from a study at whatever point the patient may assess her- or himself as feeling no benefit and, therefore, probably a placebo subject. When one adds to this list the fact that under the change design one can assess responsiveness to treatment on only half of what is already a small number of patients, considerable impetus is generated to consideration of a design in which, as the common phrase is, each subject "serves as his own control."

In the crossover design, each subject is exposed to a period of active treatment and a period of control treatment in random order. In theory, this design has even more power than the change design, yields even more clinically useful information, and facilitates recruitment and retention of subjects. The problem, however, is that the design is, in many cases, not a valid one. The crucial assumption is that following treatment a patient returns to baseline clinical state, an assumption very unlikely to be true, particularly when the anticipated clinical impact of treatment is on functioning or behavior (Brown, 1980). Despite its advantages, the risk of nonvalid results should produce a wariness in the clinical research use of this design.

However, extending the design principle of the change analysis in another direction, we have found, in company with Chassen (1967) and others, that the most successful approach is an intensive design, one in which response is monitored in both treatment and control groups, not only at baseline and endpoint but also at regular time points during treatment. The design itself creates few problems, but major problems arise in the statistical analysis procedures applied to it. It is unfortunately true that the most common analysis of this type of data is the repeated measures analysis of variance (ANOVA). It has long been known (e.g., McCall & Applebaum, 1973), and quite generally ignored, that this procedure is based on a set of assumptions that generally preclude its use in this time-series format. Results based on this analysis that are declared significant at the 5% level are achievable by chance as much as 20%–50% of the time. Use of this analytic strategy may lead to copious publications, but it is a disconcerting thought that many of these may report false positive results.

The reason these facts are so frequently ignored by researchers appears to be that the mechanism underlying the statistical problems with the approach seems to have been obscured rather than elucidated by the mathematical expositions of the facts. Yet, the only precise and accurate explanation of why and how repeated measures ANOVA fails in this context lies in the mathematics. Perhaps, however, the flavor of what happens can be conveyed as follows.

The ANOVA procedure attributes all that is common to the repeated measures on a subject to subject effect and all that is common to the multiple measures at a time point to the time effect. What remains when subject effects and the time effect are removed is attributed to error. When there are serial correlations between errors, as in a time series, there is a common thread linking the errors that will mistakenly be attributed to the subject effect and hence deducted from error. As a result, the error mean square (MS_e) tends to underestimate true error variance (σ_ϵ^2).

At the same time, and even more important, is the fact that only when errors are independent is the sum of squares for error distributed approximately as $\sigma_\epsilon^2{}^7 \chi^2$ with $(n-1)(t-1)$ degrees of freedom (n subjects, t time points). (The distribution is exact under normality assumptions.) With serial correlations, not only is the multiplier no longer ϵ_ϵ^2, but if χ^2 approximates the distribution at all, it is with fewer than $(n-1)(t-1)$ degrees of freedom. The cumulative effect of underestimation of error variance and overestimation of degrees of freedom associated with error is to exaggerate the significance of all the test results.

In the extreme case when there are near perfect serial correlations, error is almost totally confounded with subject effect and MS_e is near zero. Each of the F statistics in the ANOVA has the near zero MS_e as the divisor and is therefore extremely large. If one then proceeds mistakenly to refer these statistics to the critical values of F using $(n-1)(t-1)$ degrees of freedom for the MS_e, all effects are labeled extremely highly significant, even when there are no subject or treatment effects.

There are adjustments to the test procedure that produce conservative significance levels, primarily those of reducing the degrees of freedom associated with MS_e. These tend to sacrifice power to achieve validity. There are nonparametric approaches, in which no assumptions are made to quantitatively estimate separate subject effect and time effect. These procedures may have relatively more power, but they require complete data sets (i.e., no missing data or dropouts). Time-series analyses may be applied, although these frequently require strong data assumptions, such as multivariate normality, as well as complete data sets (Box & Jenkins, 1970). Yet, any one of these approaches is preferable to the common analysis of variance approach.

In fact, however, we have found remarkable success with another very simple coping strategy: We use a weighted average of observations to characterize each subject's response (usually the slope of response on time). Under this strategy, one loses very few subjects, since theoretically any subject with two or more visits can be included. The whole time course can be defined, not by the slopes but by true time-point averages. Factors correlated with responsiveness or with dropout can be identified. Finally, it is a valid design eliciting maximal power and maximal clinically useful information. Most often, because patients are monitored over the course of treatment in any case, the cost of implementing this design is only that of introducing systematic and regular recording of observed response.

In general, every design/analysis dyad is (a) optimal under certain circumstances, (b) acceptable under a somewhat broader range of circumstances, and (c) invalid under other circumstances. Depending on the research circumstances, that is, the nature of the population, what is feasible, and the nature of the measures of response, strategies are either preferred or excluded.

For example, unless there is absolutely no alternative, nonrandomized trials should be excluded. There is no mathematical procedure (e.g., analysis of covariance or path analysis; Overall & Woodward, 1977; Rogosa, 1980) that unequivocally corrects for nonrandom group composition. In such studies, a great deal of effort will have to be invested to exclude alternative explanations for apparently significant treatment effects, with little hope of excluding all such alternatives.

Trials with concurrent controls are always preferable, but convincing argument can sometimes be presented for historical controls (Gehan, 1974). A study with neither concurrent nor historical controls should be excluded from consideration.

Designs and analyses must surmount the problems associated with dropout and missing data. They must not have substantial risk of invalidity (as in the crossover or the repeated measures ANOVA); they must maximize power (as in preferring slopes to change scores) and must yield whatever information is necessary to interpret the results for clinical use.

MEASUREMENT

The only segment of the medical research community concerned with validity and reliability of data, it sometimes seems, is the psychiatry research group. It is argued that this differential focus is appropriate, since the parameters to be measured in psychiatry research are intangibles (depression, anxiety, stress, behavioral functioning), whereas parameters in other medical areas tend to define what may be seen, felt, weighted, counted, or dissected. This view has never been completely true and has become less true as behavioral or self-report measures such as pain assessment, patient satisfaction, and functional ability have become standard aspects of evaluation of medical and surgical treatments.

Reliability

One cannot overestimate the importance of reliable response measures. The power of a test, for example, depends not on the sample size per se but on the product of the sample size and coefficient of test–retest reliability (e.g., intraclass or product-moment correlation coefficient for near normally distributed data, Spearman rank correlation coefficient for ordinal data, kappa coefficient for nominal data; Bartko & Carpenter, 1976; Kraemer, 1979). Thus, one achieves the same power with 100 subjects and a coefficient of reliability of 20% (i.e., $r = .20$) as with 20 subjects and a coefficient of reliability equal to 100%. Since we are limited to small sample size, achieving high test–retest reliability is a necessity. One must, however, be realistic about what is achievable. I would suggest that a coefficient of 80% and above be regarded as almost perfect, 60%–80% as satisfactory, 40%–60% as acceptable but possibly improvable, 20%–40% as demanding improvement, and 20% or below as totally unacceptable and probably unimprovable (cf. Landis & Koch, 1977).

With these standards, it should be noted that the reliability of psychiatric diagnostic systems would have been considered acceptable 20 years ago before the massive investments of time and money to develop such systems in recent years. The facts that this investment has not demonstrably improved reliability (Spitzer & Fleiss, 1974) and, according to a recent study (Overall & Hollister, 1979), one may not even be able to claim face validity for these systems tend to support this view.

Nevertheless, this recommendation for realistic reliability goals stems not from these facts but from the following considerations. One can improve reliability of a clinical response measure by (a) standardizing conditions of testing, (b) training observers, and (c) clarifying definitions. However, the upper limit of test–retest reliability achievable by these strategies is not 100% but is determined by the moment-to-moment and day-to-day true lability of the subject's clinical condition. Thus, it may well be that the best of all possible measures may have a test–retest reliability of only 60%. In this case, futile efforts to increase reliability beyond this level may, in fact, be at the expense of validity.

In research, one can frequently tune out the effect of unreliability by use of multiple tests. Use of weighted averages of measures frequently steps up the reliability (Brown, 1910; Spearman, 1910), which is one of the reasons why the use of slopes in an intensive design often proves such a successful strategy. For these reasons, even if the best of all measures has a reliability of only 60%, testing in triplicate or combining three different measures of the same response may, in effect, amplify reliability to above 80%. In short, one may by brute force cope with low reliability. Validity is another matter.

Validity

Tukey (1979) comments on the "ivory-tower attitude" of placing the issue of reliability (the "good" measure) above that of validity (the "right" measure):

> Such a spirit can produce good measurement. But when the right thing can only be measured poorly, it tends to cause the wrong thing to be measured, only because it can be measured well. And it is often much worse to have good measurement of the wrong thing—especially when, as is so often the case, the wrong thing will IN FACT be used as an indicator of the right thing—than to have poor measurements of the right thing. (p. 486)

In a psychiatric clinical trial, one should use as primary measures of response those with face validity or those that have been validated. To set out on a trial without knowing that one has at least some right measures of response is both short-sighted and highly risky. Development of valid measures of clinical response is a highly complex and specialized task best left to psychometricians specializing in this area and not to be casually appended to clinical trials.

Sensitivity

One should seek measures that are as sensitive as possible. A frequent and costly error is to group valid and reliable quantitative responses, for example, comparing the response of those patients over 35 years of age with those under 35 rather than using age itself in analysis, or creating a 5-point scale out of an observed continuum of response. The effect of such grouping procedures is generally to decrease reliability, thereby obscuring the very effects one is seeking.

Redundancy

Finally, and very important, one should eliminate redundant response measures. It is a peculiar response to difficult problems of measurement that when one distrusts any one measure, one might believe that separate use of 5 to 10 such untrustworthy measures will clarify the situation. In general, the issues can only be further confused. From any such redundant set, one should discard any measures of questionable validity, any that are distinctly lower than others in reliability, and combine the remaining measures, if any, to step up reliability. The basic principle is that one has the best chance at solidly hitting a target by aiming carefully and taking one's best shot, not by spraying buckshot wildly in the general direction of the target.

DATA PROCESSING

The problem of redundant data is one that is rapidly escalating concurrently with the recent rapid increase in accessibility, capacity, and capability of computers. It would indeed be sad if what may be regarded as the most important technological advance of the 20th century, computers, might also be a facilitator of sloppy psychiatric research. More and more frequently, data are collected, stored, and analyzed, not because they are pertinent to the research questions and are valid and reliable but because they are available and computers are cheap. Statistical analysis techniques are applied to data not because they are the optimal approaches to clear answers to the research questions but because the data can be fit into the computer program's format, and why not?: Computers are cheap.

Computerized data and computer analysis are accorded an undeserved dignity. That data reside on computer discs rather than sheets of paper does not give the data greater value. That the analytic procedure is quickly done by a canned program rather than laboriously by hand does not mean that one is more meaningful or valid than the other. It is true that the computer is never wrong, but by the same token, the computer is never right. It is the researcher who decides what data to collect and how, what analytic techniques to use, how to enter the data into the analysis, how to interpret the results, who is right or wrong. It does not matter whether she/he utilizes a computer in the process. The infallibility of the computer confers no infallibility on the researcher. The computer simply performs the task more efficiently and more cheaply, even if the task performed is the wrong one.

Researchers should be urged to look, literally look, at their data to check its quality against their clinical knowledge and to gain a feel for its structure. They should be constrained to store no data that are not pertinent, valid, and reliable and to use no analytic program unless it is clearly understood what requirements are imposed by the design on the nature of data for validity of results and how to interpret results clearly and validly. If this means that one sacrifices complexity for clarity of results, so much the better.

Analysis Procedures

A few more comments are in order about the assumptions concerning the nature of the data that govern the validity of statistical tests. Most of the common procedures are specifically designed for normally distributed data—that most abnormal of all possible situations. However, there is (to this author's knowledge) no common procedure that depends for its validity on the normality of the data per se (t test, ANOVA, regression, correlation, etc.; Kraemer, 1980; Scheffé, 1959, chap. 10). Efforts, therefore, to normalize data are wasted.

However, these same procedures also assume equal variances, linearity, and additivity, and the evidence is very strong that these assumptions are essential to validity (Kraemer, 1980; Scheffé, 1959). A search for variance-stabilizing transformations or for nonparametric (Siegel, 1956) or robust alternatives (Mosteller & Tukey, 1977) to the common procedures is effort well placed. Robust procedures, that is, those that place minimal restrictions on the nature of the data for validity, have been in recent years a burgeoning area of statistical research in which there have been major advances. In consideration of the potential positive value and impact of such approaches in psychiatric research, these developments should be both monitored and rapidly incorporated into the methodological repertoires of psychiatric researchers.

Confirmatory and Exploratory Data Analysis

A scientific research project is designed to test certain hypotheses and is funded and executed for that purpose. If successful, it is confirmation of the theory via so-called confirmatory data analysis techniques that is publishable material. Without exception, however, the same research project should be a learning experience, a generator of new hypotheses. Methods that are directed not to confirmation of scientific hypotheses but simply to learning from data have been collectively called "exploratory data analysis" (Tukey, 1977). The philosophy underlying these approaches attempts to reverse that unfortunate recent trend in which both researchers and statisticians have distanced themselves from data, acting as if the rote computer procedures were able to perceive, evaluate, and project as well as the trained human mind. However, one must carefully avoid generating hypotheses and seeking to confirm them on the same data set—a procedure tantamount to offering to bet on a horse race after the finish of the race.

CONCLUSION

Courses, textbooks, and seminars in methodology equip a researcher with a basic kit of statistical all-purpose tools. However, in using these tools to the best purpose, it must be remembered that biostatistics is not a dead science in the sense that Latin is a dead language. Advances and developments are constantly taking place. Tools that were best 10 or 20 years ago may be either obsolete or superceded by newer, better, or more powerful tools. It may well be that the all-purpose tool should be supplanted by ones more specific to the job in hand. Totally new options may become available which could broaden one's conception of what jobs can be accomplished and how cost-effectively.

Whether one is planning one's own research, reviewing proposals for others' research, or reviewing papers for publication, it is vital to be open to new methodological as well as new therapeutic ideas. Psychiatric clinical research is not easy. Subjects are difficult to come by; they may tend to be particularly uncooperative and uncompliant. Response data tend to be soft. These facts, however, provide no excuse for soft scientific approaches, even if this means discarding the old traditions and placing oneself in the vulnerable position of launching new ones.

REFERENCE NOTE

1. Agras, W. S., & Berkowitz, R. *Clinical research in behavior therapy: Halfway there?* Manuscript in preparation, 1980.

REFERENCES

Bartko, J. J., & Carpenter, W. T. (1976). On the methods and theory of reliability. *Journal of Nervous and Mental Disease, 163,* 307–317.

Box, G. E. P., & Jenkins, G. M. (1970). *Time-series analysis: Forecasting and control.* San Francisco: Holden-Day.

Brown, W. (1910). Some experimental results in the correlation of mental abilities. *British Journal of Psychology, 3,* 296–322.

Brown, W., Jr. (1980). The cross-over experiment for clinical trials. *Biometrics, 36,* 69–79.

Chassen, J. B. (1967). *Research designs in clinical psychology and psychiatry.* New York: Appleton-Century-Crofts.

Cohen, J. (1969). *Statistical power analysis for the behavioral sciences.* New York: Academic Press.

Cook, T. D., & Campbell, D. T. (1976). The design and conduct of quasi-experiments and the experiments in field settings. In M. D. Dunette (Ed.), *Handbook of industrial and organizational psychology.* Chicago: Rand McNally.

Cronbach, L. E., & Furby, L. (1970). How we should measure change—Or should we? *Psychological Bulletin, 74,* 68–80.

Denenberg, V. H. (1976). *Statistics and experimental design for behavioral and biological researchers.* New York: Wiley.

Efron, B. (1971). Forcing a sequential experiment to be balanced. *Biometrika, 58,* 403–417.

Fletcher, R. H., & Fletcher, S. W. (1979). Clinical research in general medicine journals: A 30-year perspective. *New England Journal of Medicine, 301,* 180–183.

Gehan, E. R. (1974). Non-randomized controls in cancer clinical trials. *New England Journal of Medicine, 290,* 198–203.

Kraemer, H. C. (1979). Ramifications of a population model for k as a coefficient of reliability. *Psychometrika, 44,* 461–472.

Kraemer, H. C. (1980). Robustness of the distribution theory of the product-moment correlation coefficient. *Journal of Educational Statistics, 5,* 115–128.

Kraemer, H. C., Jacob, R. G., Jeffrey, R., & Agras, W. S. (1979). Empirical selection of matching factors in matched-pairs and matched-blocks small-sample research designs. *Behavior Therapy, 10,* 615–628.

Landis, J. R., & Koch, G. G. (1977). The measurement of observer agreement for categorical data. *Biometrics, 33,* 159–174.

McCall, R. B., & Applebaum, M. I. (1973). Bias in the analysis of repeated-measures designs: Some alternative approaches. *Child Development, 44,* 401–415.

Moore, M. (1975). The use of statistical techniques by psychological journal articles. *American Statistician, 29,* 68–69.

Mosteller, F., & Tukey, J. W. (1977). *Data analysis and regression.* Reading, MA: Addison-Wesley.

Overall, J. E., & Hollister, L. E. (1979). Comparative evaluation of research diagnostic criteria for schizophrenia. *Archives of General Psychiatry*, *36*, 1198–1205.

Overall, J. E., & Woodward, J. A. (1977). Nonrandom assignment and the analysis of covariance. *Psychological Bulletin*, *84*, 588–594.

Rogosa, D. (1980). A critique of cross-lagged correlation. *Psychological Bulletin*, *88*, 245–258.

Scheffé, H. (1959). *The analysis of variance*. New York: Wiley.

Siegel, S. (1956). *Non-parametric statistics for the behavioral sciences*. New York: McGraw-Hill.

Spearman, C. (1910). Correlations calculated from faulty data. *British Journal of Psychology*, *3*, 271–295.

Spitzer, R. L., & Fleiss, J. L. (1974). A re-analysis of the reliability of psychiatric diagnosis. *British Journal of Psychiatry*, *125*, 341–347.

Tukey, J. W. (1977). *Exploratory data analysis*. Reading, MA: Addison-Wesley.

Tukey, J. W. (1979). Methodology and the statistician's responsibility for *both* accuracy *and* relevance. *Journal of the American Statistical Association*, *74*, 786–793.

28

TREATMENT OF APTITUDE ×
TREATMENT INTERACTIONS

BRADLEY SMITH AND LEE SECHREST

Psychotherapy outcome research is a frustrating business. Experiments are not easy to arrange and control, outcomes are difficult to measure—often even to define—and results are often disappointing. Psychotherapy ought to work better than it appears to. One possible explanation for why it does not is that the effects of psychotherapy depend on specific characteristics of patients and the therapies to which they are exposed (i.e., effects of psychotherapy may depend on Aptitude × Treatment Interactions [ATIs; Cronbach & Snow, 1977]). More specifically, the ATI hypothesis states that appropriate matching of patients with treatment will result in better outcomes. This hypothesis has been optimistically interpreted by many clinical researchers to mean that ATI research can uncover psychotherapy effects that, compared with main effects, are stronger and more reliable. Unfortunately for the optimists, as we will assert and try to account for in this article, compared with main effects, ATIs in psychother-

Reprinted from the *Journal of Consulting and Clinical Psychology*, 59, 233-244. Copyright 1991 by the American Psychological Association.

apy research may be infrequent, undependable, and difficult to detect. The purpose of this article is to take a sober look at the realities and probable impact of ATI research in terms of psychotherapy theory and practice. The ATI approach is not a quick fix to the problem of disappointing results in psychotherapy research. This article outlines a variety of stringent conditions necessary for adequate ATI research. Ironically, if our recommendations are heeded, it is likely that subsequent research will uncover previously "hidden" main effects more frequently than interactions.

WHAT IS AN ATI?

To discuss Aptitude × Treatment interactions, it is necessary to agree on just what is meant by such an interaction. We do not have in mind the purely arithmetic fact that an interaction refers to a multiplicative rather than merely an additive effect of two or more variables, although people without much quantitative training often imagine that when two variables must be taken into account, that implies an interaction. Rather, we are concerned with the fact that an Aptitude × Treatment interaction may be manifest in different ways with entirely different implications. It needs to be noted, however, that demonstration of an interaction requires a minimum of four data points. It is not enough to show that Z therapy is superior to Y therapy with depressed clients in order to infer an interaction. One must show that for some other condition, say clients with anxiety, the difference between Z and Y therapy is either smaller or larger than for depressed patients. An interaction is always specific to particular contrasts. In our example, the contrast is with respect to the problem (psychopathology), but the contrast could be with respect to personal characteristics of patients (e.g., sex), characteristics of therapists (e.g., experience), circumstances of treatment (e.g., voluntary–involuntary), or site of treatment (e.g., inpatient–outpatient). Although Aptitude × Treatment interactions are typically defined as involving contrasts in patient characteristics, that limitation need not apply. The ideas and principles are the same. In essence, however, it is important to understand that the occurrence of an interaction implies a limitation on generalizability of effects of treatments. On the other hand, an interaction also implies a basis for optimism in that the treatment under study works *better* with some persons or under some conditions than under others.

The existence of an interaction does not necessarily mean that circumstances exist under which the two treatments are equal, or that if one is better for one thing, the other must be better for something else. Interactions can be *disordinal* or *ordinal* (Cronbach & Snow, 1977). In the case of disordinal interactions (panel 1 of Figure 1), the lines connecting the like treatment conditions cross. This, for some reason, is often taken as firmer evidence for an interaction than a "mere" ordinal interaction in which the lines do not cross (at least not within the range of variables studied; see panel 2 of Figure 1). If statistical significance means anything, it surely means that a significant ordinal interaction is just as dependable as a similarly significant distortional interaction. Some of the mythical superiority of disordinal interactions may be an artifact from the use of statistical models that give priority to main effects. Partialing out main effect variance has differential effects on disordinal and ordinal interactions, and, as a consequence, ordinal interactions may simply not be statistically significant after main effect variance is removed.

Moreover, under some circumstances, apparent ordinality may simply reflect limitations on the representations of independent or dependent variables (Cronbach & Snow, 1977). For example, consider the apparent ordinal interaction depicted in panel 3 of Figure 1. For therapists with 2 years of experience, therapy modalities Y and Z do not differ in effectiveness, but for therapists with 4 years, Z is superior. But consider the dotted lines extending to the level of 0 experience, a level not tested in the experiment.[1] The depiction suggests that the ordinal interaction actually observed would have been disordinal had different levels of the experience variable been included. For inexperienced therapists, Therapy Y would be a better choice. In fact, had only 0 and 2 years of experience been studied, one would have observed quite a different ordinal interaction with Y superior at the lowest level and Y and Z equal at the highest (2-year) level.

The interaction "results" displayed in Figure 1 also permit another observation: the pernicious potential of the inclination to connect two data points by a straight line. The line drawn in panel 4 almost cries out for the interpretation, "With increasing therapist experience, Z is increasingly the intervention to be recommended." That cry should be resisted for reasons portrayed in panel 4, where it is evident that lines of almost any sort may connect two data points. Nevertheless, a straight line is the best guess when only two data points are available. Therefore, anyone who intends to model growth and change should begin with a minimum of three data points. It may be that some ATIs can be measured only by nonlinear models.

---

[1] This hypothetical extrapolation is used here to make a point; we do not encourage such extrapolations from real data. We do, however, encourage studying broader ranges of variables.

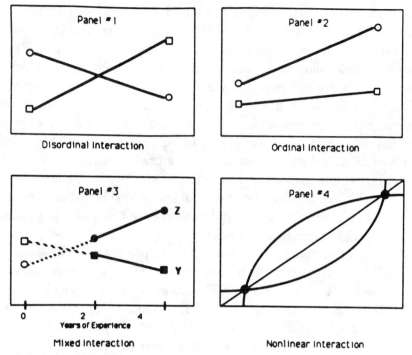

Figure 1: Illustrations of disordinal, ordinal, mixed, and nonlinear Aptitude × Treatment interactions.

VARIED INTERACTION EFFECTS

Interactions may be manifest in treatment effects in different ways with quite different implications. These are worth considering with some care.

First, and most commonly, an Aptitude × Treatment interaction is taken to refer to the greater effect of a treatment in the presence of some characteristics than others. For example, systematic desensitization is relatively more effective for patients with phobias than for patients with obsessive-compulsive disorders; certain forms of behavior modification are more helpful for obsessive-compulsive disorders than for phobias. Underlying such observations is the implicit idea of some absolute effect of therapies, a qualitative difference between them. A medical illustration of this type of interaction would be the use of quinine to treat malaria versus the use of penicillin to treat a bacterial infection.

A second way in which an Aptitude × Treatment interaction might be manifested, however, is in the relative *efficiencies* of two treatments. Whiskey is a "stronger" drink than beer, but that simply reflects the concentration of alcohol per fluid ounce. Beer is just as intoxicating as whiskey if one consumes enough of it. Similarly, two therapies could conceivably differ not in terms of the terminal effect but in the "dose" required to get there. One needs to be cautious in interpreting findings comparing 8 sessions of Therapy Y with 8 of Therapy Z. If Y takes 16 sessions to achieve the same effect of 8 Z sessions, that might make Z a preferable therapy (e.g., in terms of cost-effectiveness; Scott & Sechrest, in press), but that is not an absolute difference between the outcomes of the two therapies. Moreover, psychotherapeutic processes are not necessarily affected by the rate of change. Therefore, some ATIs may reflect differences in the rate of change rather than a qualitative difference in process and outcome.

A third possibility is that Aptitude × Treatment interactions may be specific to the outcome measure(s) chosen. Therapy Z may produce more improvement in self-esteem than Y for female than male patients, but no difference may be observable on any other outcome measure. An obvious implication is that researchers should use multiple outcome measures, and interpreters and users of research should be cautious in inferring the existence of generalized Aptitude × Treatment interactions without considering the possibility of an Aptitude × Treatment × Outcome interaction. It should be noted here, however, that a recent attempt to identify different outcomes for different treatments of depression failed to find any Treatment × Outcome interactions (Imber et al., 1990). This failure may have occurred because, although Imber et al. did enter client aptitudes into their analyses (level of depression), the interaction may not have been significant for a variety of other reasons, such as problems with statistical power, lack of measurement precision, or the simple possibility that there was no interaction effect.

WHO WILL BE AFFECTED BY ATI RESEARCH?

What are the boundaries of what constitutes "treatment" for the purposes of discussing Aptitude × Treatment interactions? If we consider the entire panoply of interventions relevant to the domain of "psychotherapy," then it is manifestly absurd to think that there are no ATIs (e.g., see Lazarus, 1990). It is now widely conceded that behavioral intervention involving exposure to the stimulus is the treatment of choice for phobias; however, such interventions would be irrelevant at best for a wide range of other conditions. For example, it is doubtful that simply exposing depressed patients to depressing stimuli will make them any better. Matching different problems with differentially effective treatments automatically makes for an interaction. Behavioral interventions tend by their very nature to be tailored somewhat to the requirements of different problems so that their use *assumes* an ATI. The recommendation of breathing retraining for hyperventilation is so obvious an instance of an assumed ATI that it is not even interesting; no one would suppose that breathing retraining would be useful in treating bruxism or brutomania.

On the other hand, if psychotherapy has no specific effects, if it is all just a matter of the quality of the relationship, then the search for ATIs is similarly diminished in interest. The search would be reduced to the search for therapist–patient matching variables that would foster the development of a high quality therapeutic relationship. Requirements for matching therapists and patients are not of great practical interest because they are difficult to meet under most conditions of practice. Therapists in agencies are usually under pressure to deliver services and do not often have the luxury of declining to treat a person because of less than optimal matching. Therapists in independent practice are under similar pressures, albeit for somewhat different reasons.

We assume that the interest in ATIs reflects assumptions about strategic and tactical options potentially open to therapists (i.e., that if a therapist knew of ATIs, the therapist could capitalize on them by optimal behavior). Interest in ATIs assumes that therapists are capable of planful flexibility in their decisions about how to approach cases. If the ATI reflects differences in the effectiveness of two or more *modalities* of therapy (e.g., as appears to be the case for treatment of phobias), the ethical therapist has either to master multiple modalities or decline to treat a patient nonoptimally and refer the patient to a therapist competent in the better modality. In actuality, most therapists probably consider themselves generalists and try to treat almost every patient who enters their office. Thus, ATIs may prove to be more interesting in theory development than in actual practice.

A medical analogy can further elucidate the complexity of treatment decisions in the context of ATIs. A cardiologist would not attempt to treat a patient presenting with a sore knee but would refer the patient to an orthopedist (another modality). The orthopedist might conclude that the first challenge would be to reduce swelling and inflammation and might prescribe an anti-inflammatory drug, rather than a painkiller. That tactical decision would involve an ATI. The physician's overall initial strategy might be to rely on natural healing processes on the assumption that the problem was caused by a severe sprain with no critical tissue damage. That strategic approach would involve an assumed ATI. If the problem were caused by tearing of the anterior cruciate ligament, then natural healing processes would produce an unsatisfactory outcome, and surgery would be recommended. The ATI would be a Diagnosis or Problem × Treatment interaction.

The same orthopedist might be faced with another patient who could be considered for a total knee replacement. The doctor might decide that the patient's age and lifestyle would not justify such a radical procedure. With a young but not highly active patient, watchful waiting could be a better treatment choice if a few years of moderate disability were rewarded by improvements in prosthetic technology during the waiting period. That would be a Patient Characteristic × Treatment interaction. If alternative treatments for a damaged knee involved a trade-off between discomfort and reduced mobility, that would be a Treatment × Outcome interaction.

In order to exploit ATIs when they are discovered, it is essential to know exactly how the treatment works and what the mechanisms are. Any ATI is observed in a particular context of therapists, patients, problems, circumstances, and so on. If we are to know how the observed ATI is to be applied to some new set of conditions, then we must know exactly the nature of the interaction in the first place. Our current understanding of most psychotherapies and behavioral interventions is scarcely more sophisticated than would be represented by a description of a medical "treatment" as "some red pills." A pharmacotherapy is not regarded as completely satisfactory until its specific mode of action is understood (i.e., which chemical operating on what structure to produce what response). Acetyl salicylate (aspirin), for example, was a useful therapeutic for centuries, but the medical community was never completely comfortable with it until they began, recently, to understand its various modes of action.

When one considers that a century after the invention of psychotherapy major disagreements still exist about such a fundamental issue as whether there are any specific treatment effects (e.g., Lazarus, 1990; Strupp, 1989), one can believe that we are still at the early aspirin stages in our understanding. Even if ATIs were found, we would not be in a position to interpret them correctly and exploit them in other than the most direct empirical way. In general, as we will elaborate on later, we expect psychotherapy theorists to benefit more from ATI findings than will practicing therapists.

COMPLEXITIES AND DIFFICULTIES IN ATI RESEARCH

Common sense suggests that there *should* be at least some Aptitude × Treatment interactions (ATI) in psychotherapy. The concept of the ATI has received serious attention in the educational psychology literature (see Cronbach & Snow, 1977) and has been proposed as an important, if not essential, strategy for research in all areas of psychology (e.g., Cronbach, 1975). Nonetheless, very little systematic work on ATIs in psychotherapy has been done, and very few replicable ATIs have been reported.

An important reason ATI research has not become a reality is the fact that measuring and interpreting interaction effects is much more difficult than dealing with main effects. ATI research requires greater precision than general effects research. Rather than comparing general packages of treatment delivered to a broad class of patients, in ATI studies one needs to know precisely what it is about the patient that interacts with a precisely defined component of treatment. Interaction effects need to be shown to occur above and beyond the additive influence of main effects, and this requires studies with large sample sizes and at least four treatment cells. Thus, compared with the search for main effects, research on interactions requires better measurement, more subjects, a wider variety of conditions, and specific a priori hypotheses.

To complicate further the problems of ATI research, traditional statistics are relatively insensitive to interaction effects (Wahlsten, 1990). Some of the statistical disadvantage in interaction research arises from the tendency of scientists to consider main effects before interaction effects. This preference is arbitrary, but it supposedly promotes parsimony and has become the accepted rule (actually it may be more parsimonious to propose one interaction instead of two main effects). Some consequences of the "parsimonious approach" are these: (a) Interactions have to be gleaned from the variance left over after main effects are removed, which reduces the likelihood that interactions will be significant; (b) the magnitudes of interaction effects may often be underestimated; and (c) the magnitudes of main effects are often overestimated. We are in general agreement with Dawes's (1988) point that interactions may not be very impressive after main effects are allowed for. But researchers who think interactions are important should understand the handicap they place themselves under in using analytical models that look for interaction effects only in the residuals from main effects predictions. Analyses of variance (ANOVAs) have that unhappy property, and the search for interaction effects might better be carried out by General Linear Models involving regression methods and individual growth curve analyses.

The search for ATIs is also impeded by the inclinations of many investigators to convert continuous measures to categorical measures, thereby sacrificing critical information. That inclination has probably been contributed to by a preference for ANOVA statistics and the custom of graphing interactions by the mean values of individual cells. What Cronbach and Snow (1977) refer to as "ATI regressions" are simply plots of regressions. These have the advantage of showing the shape of the entire function (e.g., revealing nonlinearity if it exists). Interactions will ordinarily be seen as differences in slopes of regression lines, although Cronbach and

Snow note that interactions may occasionally affect variances. Not only are regression analyses likely to have greater power for detection of interactions (Cohen & Cohen, 1983) but they are certain to be more sensitive to other features of the phenomena under study.

Few psychotherapy studies are planned to reveal interactions, and most of them have inadequate statistical power to detect interactions, especially given the preference researchers have shown for ANOVAs. Cronbach and Snow (1977) suggest, for example, that an ATI study with subjects assigned randomly to groups should have about 100 subjects *per treatment,* a sample size *much* larger than almost any psychotherapy studies. Blanchard, Appelbaum, Radnitz, Morrill, et al. (1990), in what is a fairly representative example of therapy research, had only 116 cases to allocate to four treatment conditions. It is not surprising that they found no differences among the three active treatments, although two actually had an odds ratio of better than 1.7 for producing improvement when compared with the third. Another study of treatment of a small sample of elderly patients found no differences between treatments (Thompson, Gallagher, & Breckenridge, 1987), although at the end of treatment "major depression still present" was twice as frequent in the cognitive as compared with the behavior therapy group. The possibility in such studies for detecting an interaction indicating that one of the treatments would be better than the others with a particular type of patient is virtually nil.

Unfortunately, power analyses are rarely reported for psychotherapy studies of any kind, an omission that is going to have to be corrected, but that is going to prove painful. Journal editors must begin to insist on properly done power analyses. Power analyses must be done before therapy studies are undertaken if they are to be useful. After the fact analyses permit capitalization on chance to a considerable, although unknown, degree because all the estimates must necessarily be considered biased.

With the exception of the above-mentioned statistical considerations and the minimum requirement that two treatments and two aptitudes must be compared, the difficulties of ATI research are basically similar to those faced in all types of psychotherapy research. Many of these issues are discussed elsewhere in great detail; however, it strengthens the purpose of this article to remind ATI researchers not to perpetuate problems that continue to plague psychotherapy research. As mentioned earlier, simply looking for ATIs will not automatically result in psychotherapy research successes. On the contrary, the ATI approach may exacerbate past problems that, if left uncorrected, could lead to dismal failure. Some of the more troublesome of these research liabilities are discussed later in this article.

DO ATIs REALLY EXIST?

Before discussing possible methodological problems that have made ATIs elusive, it is important to consider the possibility that ATIs do not exist, or at least that they are rare. Virtually every comprehensive analysis of psychotherapy outcomes (e.g., Smith, Glass, & Miller, 1980; Landman & Dawes, 1982; Luborsky, Singer, & Luborsky, 1975) ultimately concluded that type of therapy, experience of the therapist, credentials of the therapist, and so on are unrelated to outcome. If any client variables are consistently related to outcome of therapy, they generally support no more of a conclusion than that clients who are bright, verbal, motivated, and not so bad off in the first place tend to do better in therapy. Those are main effects, rather than interactions, and not very interesting ones. These conclusions have not, however, been much of a deterrent to speculation about ATIs. For example, an ATI reported by Jacobson, Follette, and Pagel (1986) for marital therapy was not only not particularly large in size but it was found only at immediate posttherapy measurement and not at follow-up. Talley, Strupp, and Morey (1990) found an interaction between therapists' tendencies toward affiliative or hostile response and patients' similar tendencies but only for therapist-rated improvement on a single item scale. Other interactions were reported, but they were similarly inconsistent across independent and dependent variables.

Despite the fairly consistently negative outcomes of the search for ATIs, the search is unabated. Why? One answer may lie in what Dawes (1979) calls "arguing from a vacuum." People have a strong tendency to believe and argue that if one desired solution does not work, it must be true that something else will. Psychotherapists would like to believe that therapist experience has a good bit to do with outcome, and when that cannot be shown, the response is to believe that the answer must lie in interactions. If type of therapy does not appear to be related to outcome of therapy, then the effect of type of therapy must lie in an interaction with other variables. All that remains is to ferret out and display the interaction.

In some important ways, the persistence of psychotherapy researchers in searching for ATIs resembles the error in thinking that Dawes (1988) identifies with the commitment to "sunk costs." So much effort has been expended in the attempt to find the "silver bullet" of psychotherapy that it is simply too painful to abandon all that investment, cut losses, and try something else. As the punch line of an old joke has it, "There must be a pony in there somewhere!"

To a metascientist the movement toward ATI research might be viewed as a symptom of a degenerating program of research. Programs can be said to be degenerating if they (a) fail to yield new predictions or empirical successes and/or (b) deal with empirical anomalies through ad hoc maneuvers that overcomplicate rather than clarify the problem of interest (Gholson & Barker, 1985). Perhaps psychotherapy researchers should be seriously and dispassionately reconsidering the core assumptions of their theories rather than building an elaborate ATI structure on a crumbling theoretical foundation.

The disappointment over empirical outcomes notwithstanding, the case for interactions is, unfortunately, a priori discouraging. Here is why, as Dawes (1991) makes clear. If there is an interaction but no main effect for the treatment variable, then either the interaction must be very small in magnitude in relation to unexplained (error) variance or the interaction must be disordinal (as in panel 1, Figure 1). Now if an interaction involving, for example, therapist experience were disordinal, that would mean that experienced therapists were less helpful, and perhaps harmful, to some clients. Not only would such a conclusion seem unlikely on the face of it, but it would immediately plunge the field into serious ethical difficulties. It would clearly be unethical to assign a client to any form of intervention *known* to be suboptimal. Thus, many ATIs, if they exist at all, may be more confusing and troublesome than past failures to find strong main effects.

TYPE III ERRORS IN PSYCHOTHERAPY RESEARCH

Failures of validity of experiments can lead to three types of errone-ous conclusions: (a) The treatment is judged to be effective when it is not (i.e., a Type I error); (b) the treatment is judged to be ineffective when it actually is effective (i.e., a Type II error); or (c) researchers conduct the wrong experiment (i.e., a Type III error). Type III errors occur when faulty measurements, experimental designs, or conceptualization of crucial vari-ables prohibit meaningful interpretation of experimental results. In the case of ATI studies, failures to understand aptitudes or treatments result in Type III errors.

Historically, the possibility of making Type I errors has been more carefully guarded against than the chance of making Type II errors. Mean-while, the possibility of making Type III errors has been virtually ignored. This oversight is serious because Type III errors override both Type I and Type II errors. Who cares if a hypothesis is erroneously accepted or rejected if the hypothesis is misspecified to begin with? Therefore, to minimize and control for Type I and Type II errors at the expense of Type III errors is a fallacy of misplaced precision (Mitroff & Featheringham, 1974). Most of the issues relevant to controlling and minimizing Type III errors fall under the province of what Mahoney (1978) calls "theoretical validity," which he defines as the extent to which an experiment has some logical bearing on a specific hypothesis or theory. Unfortunately, owing to the proliferation of diverse paradigms for explaining and studying human psychopathology, it is difficult to reach agreement on the minimum standards for theoretical validity. Nevertheless, some aspects of theoretical validity may be less debatable than others. For instance, determining whether a hypothesis is clearly stated a priori is much less problematic than trying to decide whether the hypothesis is theoretically relevant to a certain paradigm. Thus, even though many issues regarding theoretical validity are entrenched in specific schools of psychotherapy, it should be possible to list several methodological issues related to theoretical validity that are ubiquitous across paradigms of psychotherapy.

Concerns over Type III errors pertain to all four of the most widely recognized types of experimental validity: internal, external, construct, and statistical conclusion validity (Cook & Campbell, 1979). Of these four, statistical conclusion validity is probably the least affected by Type III errors. Nevertheless, calculations of statistical power may be dependent on theory-based estimates of treatment effect size (Scott & Sechrest, 1989). When this is the case and the wrong theory is applied or the right theory is misapplied, then a Type III error can result in a problem with estimating statistical power. Thus, statistical conclusion validity might be affected by Type III errors, although threats to statistical conclusion validity do not appear to contribute to Type III errors. Nonetheless, it should be emphasized that statistical conclusion validity issues are, on other grounds, critical to study and interpretation of ATIs.

Proper concern with Type III errors increases as attention shifts to internal validity. The confidence with which one can assert that the outcome of an experiment is attributable to the intervention and to no other variables (i.e., internal validity) is not a purely objective deduction. Formulations of experimental problems, and as a result internal validity, depend to a large extent on the researcher's ability to conceive of and control for rival explanations of treatment effects. Determining whether an effect occurred is a relatively simple endeavor compared with the process of attributing the effect to the independent variable. It is easier to show that a treatment works than to explain how it works, and misattributing a cause to an effect is a Type III error. For example, Jacobson, Follette, and Pagel (1986) may have shown that behavioral marital therapy is more beneficial for egalitarian couples than for others (although only immediately posttherapy), but that finding is not necessarily easily explained; and simply stating that the outcome was some ATI related to the "egalitarian" qualities of the couple would be a mistake. In order to reduce problems with Type III errors, we need to know more about specific and unique qualities of concepts such as "egalitarian" and "behavioral marital therapy."

Problems associated with misunderstanding how a treatment works are especially distressing when one attempts to disseminate findings from an effective study, a shortcoming recognized by Jacobson et al. (1986). The legitimacy of various generalizations of research findings across persons, places, and times (and other dimensions; see Cook, 1990) is the essence of external validity. Even though conclusive evaluation of external validity is based on empirical demonstrations of the replicability of treatment across different settings and subpopulations, most inferences about generalizability are based on theoretical interpretations of treatment. As a result, poor understanding of treatment variables can be expected to result in flawed generalization of treatment.

Out of Cook and Campbell's (1979) list of validities, construct validity is the most closely linked with Type III errors. Construct validity is completely subsumed by the concept of theoretical validity, although a few considerations pertinent to theoretical validity are not traditionally associated with construct validity (e.g., the issue of clinically vs. statistically significant change). We will not attempt to make sharp distinctions between theoretical and construct validity, and these terms may be used interchangeably, as they are in this article. However, we favor the expression "theoretical validity" because it emphasizes the importance of theory in psychotherapy research and promotes the notion that researchers should occasionally look beyond the four types of validity listed by Cook and Campbell (1979).

Theoretical validity refers to the adequacy of our understanding of the experimental variable(s) being studied. If the variables are not operationally defined in a manner that clearly and completely represents the theoretical construct of interest, then the experiment can result in a Type III error. Likewise, if the variables are not accurately described (i.e., poorly reported), there is a risk that subsequent readers and researchers will commit Type III errors. In summary, any severe threat to construct or theoretical validity will almost certainly result in a Type III error, and these errors imply that the worth of the entire experiment is diminished, at least in terms of theoretical or practical meaning. Unfortunately, the psychotherapy literature is replete with instances of poor, and probably inaccurate, description of interventions. Type III errors (i.e., failing to understand what treatment really is) could be the primary reason why main effects research has been disappointing. If these errors are left uncorrected, Type III errors could be an even more formidable barrier to ATI research.

A final note on the theoretical validity of treatment concerns the importance of the timing of formulations of theoretical explanations. Hypotheses that are formulated before the experiment (i.e., a priori hypotheses) are presumably tested by the experiment. Hypotheses generated after inspection of the data (i.e., a posteriori hypotheses) are actually untested and may represent little more than speculation. Thus, accepting a posteriori hypotheses as fact can result in Type III errors. An example is provided by the National Institute of Mental Health (NIMH) Depression Collaborative Research Program, for which a recent analysis (Elkin et al., 1989) appeared to show a reasonable, but unanticipated, ATI. More severely depressed patients got greater benefit from drug treatment than from other treatments, although no greater benefit from drugs existed for less severely depressed patients. This ordinal ATI would have been considerably more persuasive had it been predicted in advance, because compared with hindsight, a priori prediction suggests a greater understanding of the topic of interest.

SURMOUNTING THE BARRIERS TO ADEQUATE ATI RESEARCH

This article has described four major barriers to measuring ATI effects: (a) the need for relatively more complex designs and the ensuing practical and economic difficulties; (b) conditions that promote Type II errors, including small sample size and inappropriate statistical techniques for detecting interactions; (c) Type III errors, especially failing to understand the exact nature of treatments; and (d) the very real possibility that ATIs are infrequent and undependable. These barriers are formidable but not entirely insurmountable. The following section offers suggestions for overcoming adversity in ATI research.

Collaboration and More Appropriate Statistical Models

The requirement that experiments have sufficient designs and degrees of freedom to detect interactions is, obviously, not easy to meet, but ignoring that requirement has not gotten us, and will not get us, anywhere either. It will not do the field of psychotherapy any good simply to bemoan the fact that large sample sizes and elaborate designs are required for ATI research and then to ignore that fact in practice.

One possibility is that more studies can be carried out collaboratively. Successful completion of collaborative studies is not easy, but it is wasteful of money and effort to do studies that will not accomplish their aims. It should be recognized, however, that power to detect effects is not solely a matter of sample size (see also Higgenbotham, West, & Forsyth, 1988). It may be that for some effects the reduction of alpha from .05 to .10 would be justified; too much emphasis is placed on statistical significance in any case (Cohen, 1990). A second determinant of statistical power is the effect size anticipated, which may depend heavily on the strength of the intervention. Strength of intervention is often under the control of the investigative team, and treatment should be planned to be strong to begin with, and lapses in integrity of treatment should be protected against (Sechrest & Redner, 1979). Investigators should also, if they value and predict interactions, think of giving them priority over main effects in their statistical models. Finally, statistical power is a function in part of the size of the error term. The magnitude of experimental error is also very often under control of the investigative team. Experimental error can be reduced by decreasing heterogeneity in the sample, by better measurement procedures, by greater precision in conducting the experiment, and other maneuvers (Sechrest & Yeaton, 1981b).

Theory Driven Research

We believe strongly that if psychotherapeutic interventions are going to be improved substantially, and particularly if that improvement is to be derived from ATIs, better theory is going to be required, and that theory will have to have its basis in fundamental psychological research. Twenty-five years ago, Goldstein, Heller, and Sechrest (1966) proposed that psychotherapy should be, first and foremost, *psychological*, and that meant grounding theory and practice in the basic concepts and findings of the field. They did not believe that much progress could be made by trying to develop what would be a separate, isolated discipline of psychotherapy. Moreover, the three authors demonstrated by systematic reviews of research literature that hypotheses important to the psychotherapeutic enterprise could be derived from more basic research in the field. Despite a good bit of assent from others at the time, even some acclaim, the main thesis of Goldstein, Heller, and Sechrest has been, we think, largely ignored. Some of their ideas have been realized to some extent (e.g., the importance of generalization as an aspect of psychotherapy), but for the most part current literature on psychotherapy appears to pay scant attention to research on basic behavioral and conceptual processes. One cannot determine that, for example, cognitive therapy owes any more than the most general debts to cognitive psychology. If cognitive therapy is to develop and improve, one would think that it ought to take account of what cognitive psychologists are learning about cognition. A recent volume, *Psychotherapy and Behavior Change* (Higgenbotham et al., 1988), which is a descendent of Goldstein, Heller, and Sechrest, provides contemporary instances of the need to apply more basic research in developing thinking and research about psychotherapy. We would observe, however, that the material reviewed and the hypotheses developed tend strongly to suggest that any major improvements in psychotherapy are more likely to be in the form of main effects than ATIs.

Multitrait–Multimethod Experimental Designs

When testing psychological theories, researchers need to determine if their operationalization of the theory is accurate and representative of the problem of interest. Theoretical validity problems need to be subjected to the rigorous methodology of the multitrait–multimethod approach (Campbell & Fiske, 1959), which has been largely ignored in psychotherapy research. This approach attempts to get at the true meaning of a measure (the construct "true score") and, at the same time, to identify and attempt to neutralize the effect of any systematic bias introduced by measurement and analytic strategies. Thanks to modern statistical procedures such as structural modeling researchers are now in the position to undertake theory-driven determinations of convergent and divergent validity of experimental measures.

Manipulation Checks

Once the underlying traits of experimental measures are determined, dependent variables (DVs) can be chosen that should reveal the operation of the theorized mechanisms of change. For example, if a treatment for drug users focuses on self-concept because improved self-esteem is thought to result in better recovery, then treatment evaluation should use measures of self-esteem. Assuming that the DVs are perfectly psychometrically sound (which is rarely the case), if no reliable differences are recorded for these DVs, then the construct validity of the treatment should be questioned. In the drug abuser self-esteem example, failure to observe changes in self-esteem threatens the construct validity of treatment, at least to the extent that self-esteem is critical to the overall treatment theory. The methodology of recording changes in hypothesized mediating variables has been called "manipulation checks" (Aronson & Carlsmith, 1968). In our opinion, if the psychotherapy research paper does not report manipulation checks, then the reader should be skeptical about the construct validity of treatment.

Manipulation checks have also been shown to be useful in studying the believability of alternative treatments, especially those intended as placebos (Dush, 1987). If, as is usually assumed, placebos have their effect through arousal of expectancies for change, if they do not arouse those expectancies, they are not good placebos. Manipulation checks can be used to determine whether alternative treatments arouse similar expectancies, are equally believable, and so on. Alternatively, manipulation checks may reveal that alternative, nonspecific treatments were more "active" than they were intended to be. An example is provided by Blanchard, Appelbaum, Radnitz, Michultka, et al. (1990), who found that the placebo condition probably functioned much like a relaxation treatment. Elkin et al. (1989) also noted that the placebo condition in the National Depression Collaborative Research Program was not inactive.

We also think that manipulation checks should be more generally used to assess the nature of therapy *as perceived* by patients. For example, the National Depression Collaborative Research Program intended to compare the effects of interpersonal and cognitive behavioral therapies, for which extensive manuals were prepared in order to achieve uniformity in implementation of treatment. We are not, however, aware of any attempts to determine whether patients experienced the two therapies in any different ways (e.g., whether patients in cognitive behavior therapy viewed their therapists or therapy in any way different from the views of interpersonal therapy patients). This type of information is crucial to ATI research because patient aptitudes may have a major effect on perception of treatment and subsequent outcome. Unfortunately, with the exception of detailed process analyses on the role of patient expectancy in psychotherapy (e.g., Elliott, 1986), there appears to be very little information about the phenomenology of patienthood.

Dawes (1991) also makes the point that the fallback position of asserting that it is the importance of "the relationship" or the "therapeutic alliance" is weak unless we have measures of the relationship or alliance that predict outcome. Even then, the causal connection of the quality of the therapeutic alliance to outcome may be uncertain. The therapeutic alliance is likely to grow stronger when things are going well, and the perception of improvement (e.g., in symptoms) might well lag behind the perception of the quality of the alliance without any necessary inference of a causal relationship. In recovering from medical illnesses, people often report feeling much better or even "well" long before their relevant biomedical parameters have shown much change.

Strength of Treatment

A critical parameter in the understanding of any intervention, including psychotherapy, is the strength of the treatment. Strength is viewed here as a close analog to the strength of a drug treatment. A strong treatment of aspirin would be 10 mg; a weak treatment would be 2 mg. What would "strong" psychotherapy look like? We do not know. We can, however, conjecture as follows, allowing our description to reflect rather more common sense and consensus than actual empirical evidence. Strong psychotherapy might include

- Doctoral trained therapist;

- Therapist with at least 10 years experience;

- Therapist specialized in type of problem involved;

- Therapist well-versed in empirical and theoretical literature;

- Therapist highly regarded by peers for professional expertise;

- Well-developed therapy protocol (manual) for specific problem;

- Two sessions per week in the beginning, one per week thereafter;

- Intense sessions with minimum wasted time;

- Specific recommendations for intersession "practice" activities;

- Therapy of at least one year duration if required;

- Therapist is accountable for integrity of treatment and for its outcome.

Obviously, the characteristics listed are not likely to be orthogonal in real life (e.g., a therapist who is highly regarded is likely to have a doctorate and to have a good bit of experience). If all these characteristics were, however, descriptive of the therapy being provided to a client, we could probably all agree that the treatment should be regarded as strong. Conversely, a minimally trained, inexperienced therapist doing short-term, unfocused treatment not guided by protocol and at a low level of intensity for only a few weeks would be regarded as providing weak treatment or, at the very least, poorly understood treatment. The major problem is to understand just how strong and weak the two implementations would be and just where in between the two any other real-life instance of therapy might lie. For example, what about a new doctoral-level therapist a few months out of internship but very well-read, following a protocol, one session per week for 12 weeks? We are not even close to being able to estimate strengths of various psychotherapeutic interventions, but that is not because the task is impossibly difficult.

Treatment strength can be quantified. One could, for example, assemble panels of experts and ask them to assign weights to different aspects of therapeutic interventions. In a study of rehabilitative efforts directed at criminal offenders, for example, Sechrest and West (1983) found that professional training beyond the master's level was not accorded any additional weight. On the other hand, time in treatment was weighted in a virtually linear fashion. Alternatively, one could, perhaps by means of magnitude estimation techniques, ask experts to imagine "ideal" treatment and no treatment and then to assign a globally descriptive number to a description such as one of the above. We have regularly used a class exercise involving such judgments of smoking cessation interventions and have found graduate students quite sensitive to the methods and in generally good agreement in their judgments. Knowing the strength of treatments is crucial in ATI research because comparing weak with strong treatments is not likely to produce a very meaningful interaction effect (unless, of course, the "real-life" strengths of treatments are represented, and this also requires understanding the strength of treatment).

Manualized Treatment

A move toward "manualized" treatment appears to be developing, fostered by the examples used in the National Depression Collaborative Research Program (Elkin, Parloff, Hadley, & Autry, 1985). Brief focused treatment used for high utilizers of health services is another example (Cummings, Dorken, Pallak, & Henke, 1989). Manualized treatments (i.e., those with formal protocols) may well turn out to be stronger treatments. A study of chemotherapy for cancer patients done in Finland (Karjalainen & Palva, 1989), for example, showed that patients treated by a protocol had better outcomes than patients treated according to the clinical judgments of their physicians. Holding therapists accountable (e.g., by close supervision) may also strengthen treatment. Noting that their analyses suggested weaker treatment effects than in another similar study, Elkin et al. (1989) suggest that the results may be attributable to the fact that therapists in the other study (Rush, Beck, Kovacs, & Hollon, 1977) were more closely supervised.

Study a Broader Range of Variability

The size of any effect, whether measured in terms of mean differences produced or variance accounted for, depends in part on the strength of the intervention. In the case of psychotherapy, strength would be adjusted in terms of the "amount" or size of the "dose" of therapy. In the case of variables not directly manipulated, the strength of the intervention would be realized by the range of values over which the variables were studied. Thus, for example, if one wanted to determine the effect of therapist experience on outcome, one could include values of therapist experience ranging from no experience, to, say, 30 years. In fact, the first Vanderbilt Psychotherapy Research project (Strupp & Hadley, 1979) included untrained (no experience) therapists and others with an average of 23 years of experience. If one wanted to determine the relationship between initial level of depression and outcome of treatment, one could include clients ranging from those with very mild depression (or maybe no depression) to those with depression so severe that they require round-the-clock care. Amount of therapy could range from zero to at least hundreds of sessions. A type of therapy could be varied from just barely adherent to principles of a certain treatment approach to extraordinarily adherent to those principles.

Our impression is that, over the large body of studies that exist, many variables have been tested at fairly extreme values, but most individual studies have included only a fairly narrow range of values. Moreover, few studies have used extreme values of more than one variable, so that sensitivity to interactions has probably been limited. To wit, Wahlsten (1990) argues that reliable Heredity × Environment interactions have not been found in humans because only a narrow range of human environments have been studied. Although one may argue that studies should have representative designs, which might limit values of most variables to medium ranges, that argument may not be so strong if one believes that the main advantage of the search for interactions is the light it sheds on theoretical processes (see Shoham-Salomon & Hannah, 1991).

Using Strong Inference and Testing Alternative Models

For many years, research in psychotherapy was dominated by a strategy of opposing one therapy against one or more control groups chosen—or designed—to weaken or rule out some artifactual explanation for any therapeutic effect that might be found. Those artifacts to be ruled out often included, of course, nonspecific "ingredients" of treatment. If a therapeutic intervention proved no more effective than, for example, an intervention thought to do no more than arouse expectancies for improvement, then any appeal to a specific therapeutic effect was superfluous. That research strategy was quite consistent with the Popperian (Popper, 1959) epistemology emphasizing falsification of plausible rival hypotheses. However, more contemporary metascientists, especially Lakatos and Laudan, convincingly argue that different research traditions are not incommensurable and can be tested within the same experiment (Gholson & Barker, 1985).

At about the time psychotherapy had its beginnings, Chamberlin (1895/1965), a geologist, was urging the "method of multiple working hypotheses," insisting that progress in science would be faster if experimentation involved pitting alternative explanations against each other. Testing the effects of one variable against nothing is not at all efficient, nor is it very interesting. Many more ways exist for an idea to be wrong than right (Dawes, 1988), and showing that a hypothesis is not wrong (i.e., it is better than nothing) does not mean that the hypothesis is correct. Perhaps it is not even strengthened much by being found not wrong. On the other hand, if two rival explanations are pitted against each other, differing in some crucial respects, a result favoring one over the other is highly satisfying, even if not to be taken as proof. Cronbach and Snow (1977) point to the importance of selecting theoretically important variables from among the panoply imaginable and putting them to competitive tests, a process closely akin to what Platt (1964) called "strong inference."

Perhaps the time has come to abandon groups included in psychotherapy studies solely for the purpose of testing for nonspecific treatment effects. In fact, it has been suggested that strategies involving pitting of alternative therapies against each other should be adopted (Dance & Neufeld, 1988; Garfield, 1990). The need for "no treatment" controls may have diminished, or disappeared altogether, with the introduction of "norms" that can now be derived from the work of meta-analysts (Sechrest & Yeaton, 1981a). If, on the average, therapeutic interventions can be estimated to have an effect amounting to 0.6 standard deviations improvement on a relevant dependent measure, then one does not need a no-treatment group to determine whether that effect is achieved by a therapy being tested. If a standard therapy against which a new therapy is to be tested is known to have generally larger effects than those produced by nonspecific treatment groups, then one does not need to introduce such groups into every therapy study. Control groups do consume resources that might better be spent on improvements in comparisons between studies. A strong conceptual feature of the NIMH Treatment of Depression Collaborative Research Program (Elkin et al., 1985) was the use of imipramine plus clinical management as a "standard referent treatment."

The purposes of pitting therapies against each other would be broader than simply determining which might be most effective. Ideally, therapies should be pitted against each other because they involve different assumptions about mechanisms of action, likely outcomes, and so on.

Make Sure the ATI Is Meaningful

Last, but not least, if researchers are going to test ATI hypotheses, they need to justify the expense of the ATI research effort in terms of the meaningfulness of the interaction effect. If an interaction is ordinal (panel 2, Figure 1), the mean of clients in one condition would be higher overall than the mean of clients in the other condition. That is, there should be a main effect for that condition, although the main effect might be altogether spurious in the sense of being solely attributable to the interaction. If the interaction were strong, both the main effect and the interaction should be apparent. In any case, in a meta-analysis across a population of studies, one would think that an important interaction would be manifest in a consistent tendency for one condition, say experienced therapist, to have better outcomes than another (e.g., inexperienced therapist). Dawes (1988) also shows that ordinal interactions are usually very well estimated by separate linear effects so that even when they occur, they provide little improvement over estimates made by additive combinations of the variables involved (see Figure 2). This point is illustrated by the results of Kadden, Cooney, Getter, & Litt (1989) in which matching alcoholics with treatments improved R^2 from .10 to .16. Even though this ATI improved prediction *by* 60%, overall it resulted in an improvement *of* only 6% (see Pickering, 1983). A 6% gain is probably not enough to justify the considerable amount of effort required to effect differential assignment. Even from a purely theoretical perspective, it is questionable that such a small increase in explanatory power should be viewed as a particularly important finding.

Dawes's conclusions about the extent to which ordinal interactions may be approximated by additive linear effects are often obscured by the ways in which effects are graphed. Slopes can be made to appear flat or steep depending on the scales chosen for the ordinates and abscissae. One needs to determine the goodness of fit of the additive model by statistical, not visual, analyses.

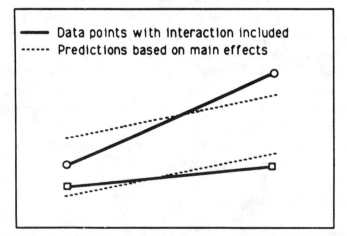

Figure 2: Illustration of the relative predictive value of main effects versus ordinal interactions.

An additional problem of interpretation is created by the fact that the metrics in which outcome measures are expressed often lack direct meaning (Cronbach & Snow, 1977; Sechrest & Yeaton, 1981c). What exactly does it mean when, according to their therapists, some clients are $-.5$ and others $.3$ on a standardized residual of global outcome rating (Talley, Strupp, & Morey, 1990)? (We do not mean to devalue this or any other studies cited but use them only as examples; the problem is ubiquitous.) The problem of difficult-to-interpret metrics is, of course, not peculiar to analyzing interactions, but it is more troublesome in ATI than in main effect research. A main effect of $.6$ merely suggests that all cases should be treated in a uniform way, which, unless the costs of doing so are large, poses no problem. An interaction requires, however, that treatment be differential, which means that differential classification must be carried out, that two or more forms of treatment be available, and so on. Consequently, the question of whether an effect size is large enough in some absolute and practically meaningful sense to justify accepting the implications of an interaction is potentially the most important question in ATI research.

CONCLUSIONS

We do not believe that it is fruitful to continue to try to "discover" ATIs in psychotherapy. In this discovery mode of research, therapeutic interventions are studied and, incidentally, a long list of other variables are measured. Then, especially in the context of failure to find anticipated main effects, a search for interactions is doomed to failure. Few ATIs are ever found, and those that are found prove to be trivial, ephemeral, or both.

We believe that if important ATIs are to be identified, it will be through deliberate tests of theoretically driven a priori hypotheses. First, ATI hypotheses must be justified in advance, just as main effects must be. No one would advocate trying interventions at random to see whether it might be possible to find one that works. Similarly, we do not think it worth looking randomly for ATIs. Second, we believe that a priori analysis of the practical or theoretical import of ATIs should be considered. If one has a notion that an ATI might have some practical value, then it ought to be possible to specify in advance just how and under what circumstances it might have value. One should also be able to say in advance just how the verification of an ATI intended to advance theory would actually advance it. Third, the treatment, or intervention, should be developed in such a way as to have a high likelihood of inducing the interaction and at sufficient strength to make it likely that the interaction could be detected if it is operative. Fourth, experiments must be of sufficient size to permit study of interactions. This means that power calculations need to be done for interactions rather than merely for main effects. Most therapy studies are not large enough to have reasonable power to detect interactions. But power calculations are not often done in any case. They must be done, and they must be done before the fact. Finally, statistical analyses should be appropriate to the problem posed and the data collected. The inclination to convert continuous variables into categorical variables must be abandoned (e.g., see Cronbach & Snow, 1977), and journal editors should begin enforcing that ban immediately. Much more attention needs to be paid to the possibility, indeed probability, that a large proportion of the relationships we are interested in are not linear, and some may not even be close to linear. We need not worry overly much about modest curvilinearity, but some variables are probably sharply curvilinear (e.g., asymptotic), and some may even be nonmonotonic. It is *possible*, as an instance, that the relationship between the amount of training for therapy and treatment outcome could be asymptotic or parabolic (i.e., an inverted U-shaped function). It is quite plausible that a moderate amount of training could produce maximum effects and, as a result, experience is not expected to be linearly related to therapeutic success.

The above discussion of therapist experience offers an example of how inaccuracy in measurement can lead to Type III errors. Therapist experience is a relatively easy-to-collect pseudomeasure of something researchers are truly interested in, that is, therapist competence. The lacunae in psychotherapy outcome research concerning the role of therapist competence is rather peculiar (see also Schaffer, 1982). To the best of our knowledge, therapist competence has never been directly assessed and studied in relation to therapy process or outcome. Inadequate proxies such as therapist training and years of experience have been used, and their observed effect seems to be nil. Competence needs to be assessed in some other, more meaningful way. Indeed, most constructs of interest to psychotherapists are measured very inaccurately. Until we set higher standards for the reliability and validity of our measures of aptitudes and treatments (As and Ts) it is very unlikely that we will find any ATIs.

We want to end by noting that, as in all scientific enterprises, knowledge about psychotherapy must advance by increments, usually small ones. Neither for main effects nor for ATIs are answers going to come from single studies. The task of generalizing from extant research is one whose difficulty has been greatly underestimated, as a reading of Cook (1990) will make clear. If we are to advance in our understanding, it will have to be on the basis of extensive research and broad wisdom and intelligence about it.

"Extrapolation and broad interpretation are guided by theoretical understanding, based on intelligent consideration of findings from the whole corpus of research" (Cronbach & Snow, 1977, p. 22). We agree.

REFERENCES

Aronson, E., & Carlsmith, J. M. (1968). Experimentation in social psychology. In G. Lindzey & E. Carlsmith (Eds.), *Handbook of social psychology* (Vol. 2, 2nd ed., pp. 1–79). Reading, MA: Addision-Wesley.

Blanchard, E. B., Appelbaum, K. A., Radnitz, C. L., Michultka, D., Morrill, B., Kirsch, C., Hillhouse, J., Evans, D. D., Guarnieri, P., Attanasio, V., Andrasik, F., Jaccard, J., & Dentinger, M. P. (1990). Placebo-controlled evaluation of abbreviated progressive muscle relaxation and relaxation combined with cognitive therapy in the treatment of tension headache. *Journal of Consulting and Clinical Psychology, 58,* 210–215.

Blanchard, E. B., Appelbaum, K. A., Radnitz, C. L., Morrill, B., Michultka, D., Kirsch, C., Guarnieri, P., Hillhouse, J., Evans, D. D., Jaccard, J., & Barron, K. D. (1990). A controlled evaluation of thermal biofeedback and thermal biofeedback combined with cognitive therapy in treatment of vascular headache. *Journal of Consulting and Clinical Psychology, 58,* 216–224.

Campbell, D. T., & Fiske, D. W. (1959) Convergent and discriminant validation by the multitrait–multimethod matrix. *Psychological Bulletin, 56,* 81–105.

Chamberlin, T. (1965). The method of multiple working hypotheses. *Science, 148,* 754–759. (Originally published 1895)

Cohen, J. (1990). Some things I have learned. *American Psychologist., 45,* 1304–1312.

Cohen, J., & Cohen, P. (1983). *Applied multiple regression-correlation: Analysis for the behavioral sciences.* Hillsdale, NJ: Erlbaum.

Cook, T. D. (1990). The generalization of causal connections: Multiple theories in search of clear practice. In L. Sechrest, E. Perrin, & J. Bunker (Eds.), *Research methodology: Strengthening causal interpretations of nonexperimental data* (pp. 9–31). Rockville, MD: Agency for Health Care Policy and Research.

Cook, T. D., & Campbell, D. T. (1979). *Quasi-experimentation: Design and analysis for field settings.* Boston: Houghton Mifflin.

Cronbach, L. J. (1975). Beyond the two disciplines of scientific psychology. *American Psychologist, 30,* 116–126.

Cronbach, L. J., & Snow, R. E. (1977). *Aptitudes and instructional methods: A handbook for research on interactions.* New York: Irvington.

Cummings, N. A., Dorken, H., Pallak, M. S., & Henke, C. (1989). *The impact of psychological intervention on health care utilization and costs: the Hawaii Medicaid Project.* Unpublished Final Project Report No. 11-C-98344/9.

Dance, K. A., & Neufeld, R. W. (1988). Aptitude-treatment interaction research in clinical settings: A review of attempts to dispell the "patient uniformity" myth. *Psychological Bulletin, 104,* 192–213.

Dawes, R. M. (1979). The robust beauty of improper linear models in decision making. *American Psychologist, 34,* 571–582.

Dawes, R. M. (1988). *Rational choice in an uncertain world.* New York: Harcourt Brace Jovanovich.

Dawes, R. M. (1991). *Professional practice versus knowledge in psychology.* Manuscript in preparation.

Dush, D. M. (1987). The placebo in psychosocial outcome evaluations. *Evaluation and the Health Professions, 9,* 421–438.

Elkin, I., Parloff, M., Hadley, S., & Autry, J. (1985). NIMH Treatment of Depression Collaborative Research Program: Background and research plan. *Archives of General Psychiatry, 42,* 305–316.

Elkin, I., Shea, M. T., Watkins, J. T., Imber, S. D., Sotsky, S. M., Collins, J. F., Glass, D. R., Pilkonis, P. A., Leber, W. R., Docherty, J. P., Fiester, S. J., & Parloff, M. B. (1989). National Institute of Mental Health Treatment of Depression Collaborative Research Program: General effectiveness of treatments. *Archives of General Psychiatry, 46,* 971–982.

Elliot, R. (1986). Interpersonal process recall as a psychotherapy process research method. In L. S. Greenberg & W. M. Pinsoff (Eds.), *The psychotherapeutic process: A research handbook.* New York: Guilford Press.

Garfield, S. L. (1990). Issues and methods in psychotherapy process research. *Journal of Consulting and Clinical Psychology, 58,* 273–280.

Gholson, B., & Barker, P. (1985). Kuhn, Lakatos, and Laudan: Applications in the history of physics and psychology. *American Psychologist, 40,* 755–769.

Goldstein, A. P., Heller, K. H., & Sechrest, L. B. (1966). *Psychotherapy and the psychology of behavior change.* New York: Wiley.

Higgenbotham, H. N., West, S. G., & Forsyth, D. R. (1988). *Psychotherapy and behavior change.* New York: Pergamon Press.

Imber, S. D., Pilkonis, P. A., Stotsky, S. M., Elkin, I., Watkins, J. T., Collins, J. F., Shea, M. T., Leber, W. R., & Glass, D. R. (1990). Mode-specific effects among three treatments for depression. *Journal of Consulting and Clinical Psychology, 58,* 352–359.

Jacobson, N. S., Follette, W. C., & Pagel, M. (1986). Predicting who will benefit from behavioral marital therapy. *Journal of Consulting and Clinical Psychology, 54,* 518–522.

Kadden, R. M., Cooney, N. L., Getter, H., & Litt, M. D. (1989). Matching alcoholics to coping skills or intractional therapies: Posttreatment results. *Journal of Consulting and Clinical Psychology, 57,* 698–704.

Karjalainen, S., & Palva, I. (1989). Do treatment protocols improve end results? A study of survival of patients with multiple myeloma in Finland. *British Medical Journal, 299,* 1069–1072.

Landman, T. J., & Dawes, R. M. (1982). Psychotherapy outcome: Smith and Glass's conclusions stand up. *American Psychologist, 37,* 504–516.

Lazarus, A. A. (1990). If this be research. . . . *American Psychologist, 44,* 670–671.

Luborsky, L., Singer, B., & Luborsky, L. (1975). Comparative studies of psychotherapy: Is it true that "everyone has won and all must have prizes"? *Archives of General Psychiatry, 32,* 995–1008.

Mahoney, M. J. (1978). Experimental methods and outcome evaluation. *Journal of Consulting and Clinical Psychology, 46,* 660–672.

Mitroff, I. A., & Featheringham, T. R. (1974). On systemic problem solving and the error of the third kind. *Behavioral Science, 19,* 383–393.

Pickering, T. G. (1983). Treatment of mild hypertension and the reduction of cardiovascular mortality: The "of or by" dilemma. *Journal of the American Medical Association, 249,* 399–400.

Platt, J. R. (1964). Strong inference. *Science, 146,* 347–353.

Popper, K. R. (1959). *The logic of scientific discovery.* New York: Basic Books.

Rush, A. J., Beck, A. T., Kovacs, M., & Hollon, S. (1977). Comparative efficacy of cognitive therapy and pharmacotherapy in the treatment of depressed patients. *Cognitive Therapy Research, 1,* 17–37.

Schaffer, N. D. (1982). Multidimensional measures of therapist behavior as predictors of outcome. *Psychological Bulletin, 92,* 670–681.

Scott, A. G., & Sechrest, L. (1989). Strength of theory and theory of strength. *Evaluation and Program Planning, 12,* 329–336.

Scott, A. G., & Sechrest, L. (in press). Theory driven approach to cost-benefit analysis: Implications of program theory. In H. Chen & P. Rossi (Eds.), *Policy studies organization.* Westport, CT: Greenwood Press.

Sechrest, L., & Redner, R. (1979). Strength and integrity of treatments in evaluation studies. In *How well does it work? Review of criminal justice evaluation, 1978: 2. Review of evaluation results, corrections* (p. 19–62). Washington, DC: National Criminal Justice Reference Service.

Sechrest, L., & West, S. G. (1983). Measuring the intervention in rehabilitation experiments. *International Annals of Criminology, 21*(1), 11–19.

Sechrest, L., & Yeaton, W. H. (1981a). Empirical bases for estimating effect size. In R. F. Boruch, P. M. Wortman, D. S. Cordray, & Associates (Eds.), *Reanalyzing program valuations: Policies and practices for secondary analysis of social and educational programs* (pp. 212–224). San Francisco: Jossey-Bass.

Sechrest, L., & Yeaton, W. H. (1981b). Estimating magnitudes of experimental effects. (*Journal Supplements Abstract Service: Catalog of Selected Documents in Psychology, 11,* Ms. No. 2355, 39 pp.)

Sechrest, L., & Yeaton, W. H. (1981c). Meaningful measures of effect. *Journal of Consulting and Clinical Psychology, 49,* 766–767.

Shoham-Salomon, V., & Hannah, M. T. (1991). Client–treatment interactions in the study of differential change processes. *Journal of Consulting and Clinical Psychology, 59,* 217–225.

Smith, M. L., Glass, G. V., & Miller, T. I. (1980). *The benefits of psychotherapy.* Baltimore: Johns Hopkins University Press.

Strupp, H. H. (1989). Psychotherapy: Can the practitioner learn from the researcher? *American Psychologist, 44,* 717–724.

Strupp, H. H., & Hadley, S. W. (1979). Specific vs. nonspecific factors in psychotherapy. *Archives of General Psychiatry, 36,* 1125–1136.

Talley, P. F., Strupp, H. H., & Morey, L. C. (1990). Matchmaking in psychotherapy: Patient–therapist dimensions and their impact on outcome. *Journal of Consulting and Clinical Psychology, 58,* 182–188.

Thompson, L. W., Gallagher, D., & Breckenridge, J. S. (1987). Comparative effectiveness of psychotherapies for depressed elders. *Journal of Consulting and Clinical Psychology, 55,* 385–390.

Wahlsten, D. (1990). Insensitivity of the analysis of variance to heredity-environment interaction. *Behavioral and Brain Sciences, 13,* 109–120.

29

PLACEBO CONTROLS IN PSYCHOTHERAPY RESEARCH: A SINE QUA NON OR A PLACEBO FOR RESEARCH PROBLEMS?

MORRIS B. PARLOFF

In an inconstant and uncertain world, it may be perversely comforting that over the past 80 years doubts, skepticism, and incredulity regarding the efficacy of psychological treatments have been dependably constant and certain. Neither variation in the nature of claimed effects not apparently authoritative evidence has diminished critics' regular and expectable expressions of mistrust.

Initially such doubts were stimulated by the lack of clear evidence that any form of psychotherapy was particularly effective (Eysenck, 1952, 1961, 1965; Levitt, 1957). More recently, skepticism was provoked by reports that a variety of different forms of psychosocial treatments are all effective and, furthermore, equally effective (Smith, Glass, & Miller, 1980; Shapiro & Shapiro, 1982). Neither of these sets of findings has been particularly reassuring.

Also provocative is the claim that psychosocial therapies are effective in their treatment of everything from chronic mental illness to the pan-

Reprinted from the *Journal of Consulting and Clinical Psychology, 54,* 79–87. Copyright 1986 by the American Psychological Association.

demic miseries of normalcy and the human condition. It is as if the field of psychotherapy has set about to rebut the thesis of Thomas Szasz's notorious volume, *The Myth of Mental Illness* (1961), by promoting the contrary view, the myth of mental health. The nonsomatic therapies have made rash claims of boundless dominion and continue to have difficulty defining not only what they are but, more important, what they are not.

The validity of the spate of nearly 600 controlled outcome studies (Smith et al., 1980; Shapiro & Shapiro, 1982) attesting to the efficacy of a wide range of psychosocial treatments is undergoing a renewed challenge. For example, Prioleau, Murdock, and Brody (1983) proposed, as have researchers before them (e.g., Meehl, 1955; Paul, 1966), that the scientific assessment of the efficacy of the psychosocial treatment approaches requires the determination of the relative contributions of the treatment and placebo control conditions to the measured treatment effects.

By reason of a semantic association between the terms *treatment* and *specific* and between *placebo* and *nonspecific*, such criticism holds that the observed treatment effects cannot be attributed to psychotherapy unless it is shown that they are due to specific rather than nonspecific therapeutic processes. Non-specific mechanisms are suspect because they cannot readily be differentiated from mechanisms that are disparagingly lumped under the ill-defined rubric of placebo. We are further warned that much of psychotherapy may represent the inadvertent application (even by the best-intentioned therapists) of what are merely plausible placebos (Critelli & Neumann, 1984; Shepherd, 1979; Wender & Klein, 1981). The placebo concept has become psychotherapy's most durable bogeyman.

PURPOSE

It is my general thesis that contrary to such assertions by methodologists, placebo controls do not serve as a primary test of the efficacy of psychosocial therapies. Moreover, the attempt to transpose the conceptually convoluted medical concept of placebo to the field of psychotherapy is potentially pernicious.

The placebo control study, if properly conducted, can more properly address questions about how a treatment works. It does not offer a unique or critical test of whether a treatment works. Placebo studies are particularly useful, for example, in testing theoretically based assumptions that unique and necessary relations exist between particular kinds of interventions, hypothetical modes of action, and actual therapeutic effects.[1,2]

---

[1]For heuristic purposes the generic term *psychotherapy* will be differentiated here from other psychological and psychosocial treatments and classes of procedures. This distinction is required particularly by advocates of the behavioral and cognitive schools of treatment, who believe that their theories and therapies are probably superior to the established psychodynamically oriented therapies and are certainly more empirically based.

Although I do not accept the view that placebo control groups provide a critical test of the efficacy of specified approaches to psychotherapy, I do believe that it remains an important and valid research task to clarify further the psychotherapeutic role of suggestion, faith, hope, therapist's attention, demand for improvement, and so forth. The primary research task is to identify and comprehend the strategies, agents, and mechanisms by which therapeutic elements—specific and nonspecific—produce their effects—beneficial or noxious.

Specifically, I shall first review some of the ambiguities and confusions associated with the concept of placebo; second, I shall identify some major problems that hamper the implementation of placebo controls in psychotherapy research; and finally, I shall propose an alternate research strategy.

The placebo issue has, of course, evoked some earlier thoughtful and measured discussions (e.g., Bok, 1974; Frank, 1973; Grünbaum, 1981; Jacobson & Baucom, 1977; Kazdin & Wilcoxon, 1976; O'Leary & Borkovec, 1978; Rosenthal & Frank, 1956; Shapiro, 1971; Shapiro & Morris, 1978). However, the strident and insistent nature of the current placebo attack requires its further examination and discussion.

There is a very ominous ring to the recent conclusion that "For real patients {neurotic individuals} there is no evidence that the benefits of psychotherapy are greater than those of placebo treatment" (Prioleau et al., 1983, p. 275). This option was echoed in the prestigious British medical journal *The Lancet*. An editorial, titled "Psychotherapy: Effective Treatment or Expensive Placebo?" (1984), asserted that the efficacy of psychotherapy, in contrast to behavior therapy and drug therapy, has never been established by scientific means.

I recognize that there are other reasons—more pragmatic and, therefore, perhaps more urgent—to account for the continued preoccupation with the comparison of the relative effects of psychotherapy and placebo treatments. For example, public and private third-party payers have increasingly shown a preference for those forms of health care services that are cost-effective as well as clinically safe and effective. (The concept of cost-effectiveness sometimes includes speed, scope, and durability of effects, as well as total costs of services to patients, family, and community; costs to therapists in terms of education and training required; availability

---

[2]The fact that a large body of outcome research evidence has failed to confirm the claimed preeminence of the newer forms of psychological treatments has not been gracefully and docilely accepted. Those engaged in this interschool rivalry would like to discount the apparent absence of differential effectiveness as specious—the unfortunate consequence of (a) flawed research design, particularly the lack of placebo control studies, and (b) the use of meta-analysis procedures to determine the effect sizes of independent outcome studies. (Because this article focuses primarily on the placebo control issue, I shall not comment here on meta-analysis critiques. My silence here does not imply a tacit acceptance of the criticisms.)

and acceptability of treatment to patients; and cost-offset, i.e., reduced medical treatment as a result of psychotherapy.)

A form of therapy unable to demonstrate that its therapeutic effects are superior to those of a less costly form of treatment—particularly if that less costly treatment were labeled *placebo*—might have difficulty in establishing its eligibility for support. Nevertheless, this supposition is not germane to the issue of establishing the clinical efficacy per se of a given treatment.

The current ipse dixit that placebo control studies are the sine qua non of scientific psychotherapy outcome research is accompanied by growlings and yowlings reminiscent of those evoked during the earlier spontaneous remission dispute (e.g., on one side, Eysenck, 1952, 1966; Levitt, 1957, 1963; Rachman, 1971; and on the other side, Bergin, 1971; Bergin & Lambert, 1978; Kiesler, 1966; Luborsky, 1954; Luborsky, Singer, & Luborsky, 1975; Rosenzweig, 1954; Slane, Staples, Cristol, Yorkston, & Whipple, 1975; Strupp, 1964; Subotnik, 1972).

Consider the hyperbolic and naively vulnerable position taken by one of psychotherapy's recent critics as he threw down the gauntlet: "I will publicly retract . . . any conclusions reached in our target article, if anyone can provide me with evidence of a study finding that psychotherapy leads to benefits that exceed those obtained for placebo treatments for neurotic outpatients" (Brody, 1983, p. 304).

This bravado probably does not bespeak a preference for life in the cool shade of the sword of Damocles, but rather a cool confidence that any study that purports to show that psychotherapy's benefits exceed those of placebo treatments is not likely to satisfy the selectively applied and often giddy standards of contrary-minded judges. As Smith et al. (1980) have noted, the experimenters' biases are highly correlated with the findings they report: "Where the allegiance was in favor of the therapy, the magnitude of effect was greatest. Where there was bias against the therapy, the effect was least" (p. 120). This inference is consistent, for example, with the tortuously shifting data base used in the research survey of Prioleau et al. (1983).

I am not sanguine that the doubts nurtured by psychotherapy's most intense and imaginative critics will soon by appeased by the tactic of casting before them yet another fresh supply of new and beautiful research findings. Experience now clearly indicates that such critics routinely tend to mistake such evidence for virginal sacrificial offerings.

I have chosen, therefore, not to enter the jousting lists of those who have picked up the now tattered gauntlet and earnestly but futilely presented what they correctly took to be responsive evidence (e.g., Andrews; Cordray & Bootzin; Eagle; Erwin; Frank; Garfield; Smith, Glass, & Miller;

Greenberg; Rosenthal; all included as commentary with Prioleau et a., 1983). Instead I shall attempt to show that the placebo challenge, as posed, is ill-conceived.

It is first helpful to recall that the scientific standard of efficacy, which the critics claim has not been, met, requires only that the effects of a specified treatment be better than no treatment or equal to or better than an effective alternate treatment (London & Klerman, 1982). I shall show that the inclusion of placebo controls in an efficacy research design does not afford a more compelling test of efficacy per se.

The criteria specified by London and Klerman are adequately met by the nonoverlapping body of 597 controlled comparative treatment studies (Smith et al., 1980; Shapiro & Shapiro, 1982). Of special relevance are three independent confirmations of the original Smith et al. (1980) findings based on reanalyses of subsets of their data: Andrews and Harvey (1981) identified 81 studies restricted to "real" patients, that is, neurotic individuals who had sought treatment; Landman and Dawes (1982) limited their sample to studies involving a strict random assignment of patients to either a treatment or control group, and Prioleau et al. (1983) initially confined their meta-analyses to 32 comparisons of psychotherapy versus placebo groups. (Their subsequent dismissal of these findings is based on a post hoc rejection of most of the 32 original studies for alleged limitations of design and internal validity.)

CONCEPT OF PLACEBO

Historically the term *placebo* ("I shall please") has referred to inactive medications prescribed primarily for purposes of placating or soothing the patient rather than directly treating any real disorder. Placebos were valued for their observed capacity to stimulate some patients to report varying degrees of improvement in mood, thought, and behavior. Also noted was the fact that occasionally patients reported noxious reactions. Thus placebos were always recognized as having the potential for producing active psychological effects—but merely psychological effects. Placebos influence the epiphenomena of illness but, by definition, do not treat the base of such ailments and, therefore, do not treat the real disorder. Pharmacologically inert placebos are not expected directly to benefit problems believed to be somatically based.

The application of the term placebo to the treatment of psychological disorders has been troublesome because the neat medical distinction between core somatic pathology and symptoms could not be maintained. Although psychodynamic and humanistic schools of psychotherapy have attempted to retain the conception that some form of psychopathology undergirds or directly produces psychological symptoms, nondynamic schools of psychotherapy reject the assumption of underlying pathology. As a consequence, the distinction between placebo and active treatment on the basis of differential effects is threatened. Psychotherapists no longer agree on the assumption that placebos produce only palliative symptomatic treatment (i.e., psychological changes tangential to the core problem), whereas true treatments effect cure or amelioration of the putative core problem.

If psychological problems require only the amelioration of symptoms, then the differentiation between the effects of placebos and psychotherapies may be merely one of degree of symptom amelioration, that is, incremental effectiveness, rather than differences in the nature or durability of changes.

Preliminary to examining the problems associated with the application of the medical concept of placebo to psychosocial treatment research, it is appropriate to review (a) the definitional consensus that guides and misguides the typical discussion of placebo and (b) the pejorative meaning that has come to be associated with the term placebo, especially in the field of psycho-social treatments.

Definition of Placebo

Almost all definitions of placebo, as evolved in the field of psychotherapy, include two basic elements: (a) The intervention or procedure must lack the specific ingredients believed to be prerequisite for the effective treatment of the specified condition, problem, disorder, and so forth and (b) individuals who are offered such hypothetically devitalized interventions must nonetheless be led to believe in their potency (Frank, 1973; Grünbaum, 1981; Shapiro, 1971; Shapiro & Morris, 1978).

The term placebo has often been used as a synonym for either the general rubric of nonspecific elements or any of its specified components such as suggestion, hope, persuasion, faith in the treatment, credibility of the treatment, confidence in the therapist, compliance with the demand characteristics of the situation, and so forth. Indeed, Critelli and Neumann (1984) have proposed that the definition of placebo could be made relatively objective by shifting from the current exclusionary requirement, that is, the identification and control by elimination of unique and active elements, to the seemingly simpler inclusionary requirement that the term placebo be applied to those treatment components that appear to be common to the psychotherapies.

In effect, they propose to finesse the onerous problems facing the researcher who attempts to apply the more usual definition of placebo. I am not persuaded that this semantic antic of arbitrarily equating the term placebo with whatever is to be labeled as a *common element* of psychotherapy adequately resolves the issue.

I recognize that the concept placebo has been applied with benign intent to such common and essential elements of treatment as establishing and maintaining a therapeutic relationship, enhancing patients' expectations of help, and developing confidence in the therapist. However, it is necessary to recognize its pejorative interpretation by critics.

Before exploring the implications for psychotherapy research of the conditions required by the usual definition of placebo, I wish to consider some of the common applications of the term placebo as an invective. I shall stress the inappropriateness of such usage and decry the unnecessary stigmatization of the term placebo. I see little advantage in counterphobically flaunting the term as if by so doing, the public will become desensitized to it.

PEJORATIVE MEANINGS ASSIGNED TO THE TERM PLACEBO

Placebo Effects Are Spurious

In surgery as in other fields of medicine, it is recognized that placebo effects are concomitants of any powerful treatment and may serve either to augment or inhibit the effects of treatment (Beecher, 1961; Wolf, 1950).

In the parent field of medicine, the theories of pathology and modes of action as well as the most credible index of change refer primarily to the biochemical or somatic. The most relevant empirical evidence, from this view, is physiological. If the disorder to be treated is viewed primarily as physiological, then any psychological effects (subjectively reported) not supported by independent evidence of objective physiological amelioration may be viewed as artifactual and classified as spurious, transitory, and tangential to the ultimate goals of treatment.

This classical emphasis on objective physiological evidence creates a special problem for the field of psychotherapy. In psychotherapy the action is intended to be primarily psychological, the problem treated is seen as psychological, and the changes are expected to be primarily psychological. In short, there is no expectation that the placebo control in psychotherapy research will control for the physiological, but only that it will control for the psychological elements deemed most relevant.

The central concepts and measures of change remain more psychological than somatic even in these days of saltatory advances in comprehension of brain functioning and despite the frenetic efforts at remedicalization of the practice of psychiatry.[3]

In the field of psychosocial treatments, unlike the field of pharmacotherapy, the fact of psychological change, independent of confirming evidence of physiological change, does not warrant the inference that the change is spurious. A clinically meaningful change is not to be dismissed peremptorily on the presumption that its parent techniques or mechanisms are illegitimate.

Real Problems Require Real Treatments

Should an individual's disorder appear to be effectively and enduringly benefited by a known placebo treatment, then doubts might be raised regarding the accuracy of the original diagnosis and whether the patient had, in fact, suffered from a real problem.

According to Prioleau et al. (1983) the class of real patients consists of those diagnosed as neurotic in contrast, presumably, to normal volunteers. Unfortunately the proposed patient restriction to this late-lamented diagnostic category does not clarify matters much. Research has thus far failed to show that a broad range of therapies differ in effectiveness in the treatment of the following: nonpsychotic depressions, mild-to-moderate anxieties, fears and simple phobias, compulsions, sexual dysfunctions; reactions to life crises of adolescence, midlife, and aging; and problems of everyday life such as vocational and marital adjustment.

Frank's (1975) characterization of patienthood has raised further doubts regarding the nature of the problems most effectively treated by all therapies. He believes that most patients come to therapy because they experience an overriding sense of helplessness, inability to cope, self-blame, feelings of worthlessness, hopelessness, and sense of alienation, that is, demoralization. He has proposed that "psychotherapy functions chiefly to restore morale, thereby increasing the patient's coping ability and reducing his symptoms" (Frank, 1975, p. 120). Thus, psychotherapy is thought to achieve its effects largely by directly treating demoralization and only indirectly treating overt symptoms or covert pathology.

If the problem requiring treatment is primarily a disorder of cognition, mood, behavior, or personality, then it is difficult to conceive of any nonspecific therapist–patient interaction as inert. If the disorder may be characterized as nonspecific in its nature and perhaps in its etiology—that

---

[3]It is recognized, of course, that placebos can and do produce objective physical change, and indeed, all human experience may be said to be biochemically mediated.

is, perception and interpretation of unfortunate and noxious social relationships—then perhaps effective treatment can also be nonspecific, involving amelioration by favorable relationships with the therapist. This
provides an opportunity for the patient to perceive and interpret events
and his or her own behavior more accurately.

The possibility remains that although all patients may share the
problem of demoralization, different classes of patients may respond better
to some interventions than to others. Where the problem may be biochemically triggered in response to constitutional factors or especially noxious
early life experiences, the treatment may require quite specialized interventions effective, for example, altered mood states, different states of consciousness, or the arousal and expression of strong emotions.

To the consternation of the clinician, the outcome evaluation literature has not yet convincingly identified the interactive roles among such
variables as classes of problems, characteristics of patients and therapists,
kinds of therapeutic interventions, and quality and quantity of change. In
the absence of such information, the myth has been allowed to grow that
each school of psychosocial treatment can provide effective and equally
effective, treatments for all kinds of problems and disorders and that all
treatment goals, no matter how lofty and expansive (e.g., psychodynamic
and humanistic) or prosaically symptomatic (e.g., behavioral), can also be
achieved. It has not served the credibility of the field to permit such myths
to go unchallenged. (In my view, these fantasies about the psychosocial
therapies are so far off target that they do not qualify even as near myths.)

Placebo's Mechanisms of Change Are Suspect

Some mechanisms of change are, ipso facto, less acceptable than
others. If the positive effects of psychotherapy are attributable primarily to
such mechanisms as suggestion, attention, or commonsense advice, then
the credibility of psychotherapy as a profession may be impugned.

Psychosocial therapies have long recognized the need to differentiate
themselves from suggestion or faith healing, which enjoy neither scientific
status nor dependable eligibility for coverage under health insurance plans.
Psychoanalysis has long viewed itself as the only form of psychosocial
treatment that is not dependent for its effects on the power of suggestions
(Gill, 1982).

It is likely that at the outset of treatment, the common aim of therapists of all schools is to establish the basis for a therapeutic alliance. In part
this involves the cultivation of the patient's hope and favorable expectations of receiving help. It is during this phase that psychotherapy is most
vulnerable to the criticism of emphasizing suggestion. Even the introduc-

tion of specific techniques may serve primarily to enhance, in the eyes of the patient, the credibility of the therapist and the particular form of therapy.

Although these elements are especially salient during the initial phases of therapy, they also serve as catalytic agents during the entire course of treatment. Indeed, some theorists have argued that the quality of the therapeutic relationship—a nonspecific element of all therapies—may provide not only the necessary but also the sufficient conditions for effective treatment (Rogers, 1957).

In later phases of therapy, psychotherapists may provide opportunities for patients to engage in activities consistent with the treatment theory represented. Such activities may include reality testing, discrimination learning, experiential as well as cognitive learning about self and others, social skills enhancement, and increasing one's sense of competence and self-esteem (Frank, 1975).

In essence, treatments may begin with efforts at instilling in the patient a sense of confidence in the therapist and therapy and then move toward the patient's developing a realistic sense of self-confidence, mastery, and self-efficacy.

PROBLEMS OF IMPLEMENTING PLACEBO CONTROLS IN PSYCHOTHERAPY RESEARCH

In view of these conceptual complexities and the negative and depreciatory aura that clings to the conception of placebo, formidable difficulties are associated with attempts to adapt the placebo definition to psychotherapy research. I shall consider, in turn, the problems of attempting to meet the two principal definitional requirements: (a) The placebo intervention must objectively lack the specific components hypothesized by the proponents of the experimental treatment to be prerequisite for its effective treatment of specified problems and (b) the patient must believe that the intervention is a potentially potent and effective treatment for his or her problems.

Placebo Must Lack Specific Prerequisite Treatment Components

To meet this requirement the research task requires the identification and elimination from the placebo control of those components of therapy thought to be specific—what Grünbaum (1981) has described as the characteristic components of the experimental therapy to be investigated.

The nonspecific or incidental or common elements of the experimental and placebo control treatments—components that are not believed to effect real or enduring change—are to be allowed to vary freely.

The research model assumes that only the experimental group includes the prerequisite specific therapeutic elements, whereas both the experimental and placebo groups share the nonspecific components. To implement this design requires a treatment dismantling strategy. This is a strategy that, as I shall indicate, cannot readily be applied to many of the established forms of psychotherapy.

The implementation of this design depends on the experimenter's ability to differentiate reliably specific from nonspecific treatment elements in order to omit the specific from the placebo control. Among the problems that face the researcher, six are particularly troublesome: (a) lack of standardization of placebos, (b) lack of standardization of psychotherapies, (c) problem of viewing psychotherapy as a technology (set of techniques), (d) difficulty of differentiating placebo controls from alternate forms of treatment, (e) insensitivity of measures, and (f) limits of generalization.

Lack of Standardization of Placebos

The discussion and integration of research reports involving placebo control groups give the unwarranted impression that a standard placebo group has been used, thereby permitting generalization to an entity known as *placebo controls*. However, there is no consistency from study to study regarding the standardized elements of placebo control groups, nor is this situation likely to change soon. The creation of such a standard control would require the prior establishment of a consensus among experts (theoreticians, researchers, and practitioners) about which elements of all psychotherapies are to be considered *nonplacebo* and which are to be labeled *placebo*. Such a consensus is conspicuously lacking in the field of psychotherapy.

In the field of pharmacological treatment and drug research, where the term placebo has gained great currency, emphasis is placed on maintaining a veridical and testable relation of what are considered the theoretically active, specific treatment elements to their empirically demonstrated therapeutic effects. Theory is guided by and amended to conform to objective evidence. In the field of psychotherapy, particularly in those instances where overt symptomatic change is less valued than basic change described in terms of hypothetical constructs, theory is given a more reverential role. Theory remains more insulated from the vagaries of empirical evidence, particularly evidence reported by researchers of alien theoretical orientation. Theory is rendered most credible to the psychosocial clinician through the testimony of authorized experts regarding potentially potent specific elements.

In the field of psychotherapy each school or form, based on its own vision of congenial and plausible theory, decides which elements of its treatment technology, procedures, or rituals are to be assigned the status of *specific*. The remaining elements, if acknowledged at all, are referred to as the *incidental*, or nonspecific, factors. These incidental and probably common factors are assumed, in this context, to be clinically inert, transitory, or tangential to the ultimate goals of treatment.

As a consequence, what is considered specific, active, and essential by advocates of one school of psychotherapy may be classed as nonspecific, inert, and incidental by another. The validity of labeling certain interventions as specific and others as nonspecific remains questionable because the practice appears to depend more on sheer conformity to theory than on inferences drawn from empirical evidence of differential therapeutic effects.

Because each placebo must be carefully designed and described to contrast with the particular experimental treatment for which it is to serve as a control, the hope of developing a standard placebo applicable to all treatments loosely identified as psychotherapy cannot be realized. If researchers attempted to device a standard placebo therapy that omitted all features hypothesized as the active ingredients of one or another of the ever-proliferating forms of psychotherapy, they would have to consider that there are now more than 250 brand names of psychotherapy (Herink, 1980). (The tribes of psychotherapy have faithfully followed the injunction to go forth and multiply and prosper, but it is not clear whether they have also been uniformly fruitful.) In this context, any placebo whose rationale was so ingenious as to elicit and sustain a high degree of credibility in patients would not long be considered theoretically inert.

Thus, the terms specific and nonspecific effects, as widely used, are actually tautological circumlocutions serving mainly to distinguish between different sources of treatment effects. Effects are labeled *specific* if they are attributed to what are believed to be theoretically essential (characteristic) factors of a given psychotherapy. Similar or identical effects may be termed *nonspecific* when they are assumed to derive from theoretically nonessential (incidental) treatment factors (Grünbaum, 1981). This practice represents an example of the theoretician's familiar acrobatic feat of executing backward leaps from foregone conclusions to unwarranted assumptions.

Lack of Standardization of Psychotherapies
In lieu of standard treatment forms in the field of psychotherapy, the

treatment approaches being compared must be well-specified and replicable. This is consistent with the growing recognition that it is necessary to identify, implement, and test the treatment factors hypothesized by given treatment approaches as therapeutic. To this end there has been a growing emphasis on the development of treatment manuals and programs for special training, supervision, and monitoring of therapist treatment behaviors. Also important is the effort of trainers to arrive at predetermined standards for judging therapists' levels of clinical mastery and implementation of training.

Until the recent development of treatment manuals in the field of psychotherapy (e.g., Beck, Rush, Shaw, & Emery, 1979; Klerman, Weissman, Rounsaville, & Chevron, 1984; Linehan, 1984; Luborsky, 1984; Strupp & Binder, 1982), the so-called specific and nonspecific elements were not operationally defined but tended to be attributed haphazardly to vague classes of therapist behaviors and attitudes.

A very vocal group of psychotherapists and researchers still remain unconvinced that any manual of treatment can be sufficiently sophisticated to represent the treatment adequately. At best, they hold, a manual can offer an approximation of treatment conducted by an experienced and flexible therapist who is sensitive to the unique needs of individual patients and the vicissitudes of the therapeutic alliance.

Clearly, in the absence of a distinctive, intelligible, and replicable description of the experimental treatment form, it is not possible to devise or select a useful placebo control.

Problem of Viewing Psychotherapy As a Set of Techniques

Implicit in the definition of placebo is the acceptance of the assumption that psychotherapy may be considered to be a technology whose components are amenable to detailed analysis. This inference is supported by the emphasis placed on specialized training by the proponents of the various schools of psychosocial therapies. The public has been led to believe that the techniques of therapy are the most conspicuous aspect of the different therapies.

At the same time, a serious complication has been introduced because many psychotherapists deemphasize the role of specific techniques and ascribe primary status to the nonspecific elements of therapy such as the quality and strength of the therapeutic relationship or working alliance (Bordin, 1974; Frank, 1974; Luborsky, 1984; Orlinsky & Howard, 1975; Rogers, 1957). No accurate census is available of the number of psychotherapists who accept the view that the effectiveness of psychotherapy depends on the therapeutic relationship as the necessary or necessary and sufficient condition. However, the advocates of these nonspecific factors—

whose orientation can be humanistic, experiential, or psychodynamic—represent an articulate and professionally much honored company.

With the possible exception of classical psychoanalysts, few dynamically oriented therapists continue to believe that effective treatment depends on the strict adherence to specific therapeutic techniques. It may ultimately be necessary to expand the concept of specificity to include the use of techniques intended to develop, modify, maintain, and resolve the therapeutic alliance. Techniques per se, of course, are not without their placebo concomitants. Patients tend to be impressed and reassured by the expertise and resourcefulness of therapists who offer a technique and procedure-oriented approach to treatment. As a consequence, some therapies that scrupulously emphasize their specificity may in the process be particularly effective in engendering significant placebo reactions.

Researchers who accept the clinicians' view of therapy as a nontechnical, nonspecific approach to treatment will find it idle to undertake to create or find placebos for such nonspecific therapies. Researchers cannot hope to omit from the placebo what the proponents of a nonspecific therapy believe are its relevant nonspecific elements.

Difficulty of Differentiating Placebo Controls From Alternate Forms of Treatment

The elements of the placebo, no less than the experimental treatment components that are to be controlled, must also be reliably identified. If the placebo includes ingredients hypothesized by any formal psychosocial treatment as specific for the treatment of specified problems, then the intended placebo, when applied to the same problems, must be considered an alternate treatment form rather than a placebo. In any event, whether placebo or an alternate treatment form, it must be described in sufficient detail to meet basic conditions of scientific research, that is, measurability and replicability.

An example of the difficulty in developing a psychotherapy–placebo condition is found in the National Institute of Mental Health's *Treatment of Depression Collaborative Research Program* (Elkin, Parloff, Hadley, & Autry, 1985). This multisite study involves two forms of psychotherapy (cognitive behavior therapy and interpersonal psychotherapy), a drug (imipramine plus clinical management), and a drug–placebo condition (pill–placebo plus clinical management). Despite serious efforts it was found that no placebo for psychotherapy per se could be devised that met the definitional requirements. Placebo conditions proposed were judged to be either too fanciful, implausible, unethical, or simply an attenuated version of an existing form of treatment.

Insensitivity of Measures

The clinical significance of a comparison of the placebo effects and psychotherapy effects depends on the adequacy and sensitivity of the measurements involved. Because such research is usually undertaken by critics and competitors of the practice of dynamic psychotherapy, the measurement of outcome is often limited to criteria and instruments of less interest to the dynamically oriented therapist.

Internal dynamic changes, so valued by the analytically oriented, are not usually represented (e.g., resolution of basic neurotic conflicts and reintegration of personality). Although psychotherapy and placebo effects may show no differences as measured on some scales, stable differences may yet be found on other measures of nature, quality, speed, durability, and scope of change, more valued by the psychodynamic therapist.

One of the obstacles to comparative research is the finding that the psychodynamic clinician is frequently more willing to enunciate the goals of treatment than to participate actively in developing reliable and valid measures for assessing the degree to which such goals have been attained. The actual or incidental self-protective nature of this stance has not escaped notice.

Limits of Generalization

I have earlier stressed that the difficulty of identifying the critical elements of a given form of psychotherapy as practiced creates problems in attempting to develop an appropriate placebo control group. The problems may be somewhat less acute in studies focusing on the newer forms of treatment.

The longer and the more widely a form of psychotherapy has been practiced, the less likely it is that the treatment conducted by a given therapist with a given patient will resemble the original theoretical version. Practitioners pride themselves on their ability to adapt, refine, and improve their ministrations on the basis of intuition, spontaneity, and sensitivity to the needs of the individual patient. This further limits the feasibility of developing a useful placebo control—one that faithfully represents the incidental elements of the treatment while faithfully omitting its characteristic elements.

As a consequence, generalizations based on the study of protean instances of a form of psychotherapy and an arbitrary placebo control condition (which may not, in fact, control for the essential elements of such treatments) cannot be firm. Such conditions to not permit generalization to a specified class of replicable therapies.

It is more likely that placebo controls can be usefully adapted for new forms of psychotherapy while such treatments are still relatively stable. Thus the preference in the research field is to conduct well-controlled investigations of new treatments in limited practice rather than inadequately controlled studies of old therapies in common practice.

As previously mentioned, in the absence of a standard placebo control that can be clearly described and readily replicated, the placebo control condition must be individually crafted to omit the specific procedures believed to characterize the therapy with which it is to be compared. However, generalizations from such comparisons have typically not been restricted to the particular forms of psychotherapy and the particular placebo used. Instead, generalizations have been made globally to entire classes of psychotherapy and indiscriminantly to all forms of placebo. Clearly this is unwarranted.

Patient Must Believe That the Intervention Is a Potentially Potent and Effective Treatment for His or Her Problems

Investigators in many fields of treatment have noted that the patient response to an intervention, be it surgical (Beecher, 1961), pharmacological (Lasagna, Mosteller, von Felsinger, & Beecher, 1954), or psychological (Kazdkin & Wilcoxon, 1976), is influenced by the practitioner's capacity to engender and maintain the patient's confidence in the clinician and the procedure.

In psychotherapy it is difficult to create the prerequisite conditions wherein therapists manage to develop as much enthusiasm for a treatment that they believe to be inert (at least for the condition being treated) as for the treatment in which the therapists may have a considerable ego investment. Unlike the therapist who participates in drug efficacy research, the psychotherapist cannot be kept blind with regard to the treatment he or she is offering. Under these conditions it may be difficult to recruit placebo therapists who can convey to their patients the hopefulness and enthusiasm necessary to enhance the credibility of the placebo condition. A study that could not establish the prerequisite research condition of providing equivalent therapist enthusiasm and patient confidence levels in both the placebo and experimental treatments would be seriously flawed.

Thus, in contrast to the critics who advocate the use of placebo control groups as the sine qua non for scientific research, I conclude that in the field of psychotherapy the term placebo is both conceptually grotesque and operationally infeasible—or nearly so.

RECOMMENDATIONS

I have attempted to identify some of the conceptual debris that clings to the construct placebo as it has been applied in this field of psychotherapy. I have also indicated research difficulties associated with the application of placebo control research to psychotherapy.

Not only is a placebo that approximates the classical definition difficult to achieve in the arena of psychotherapy research but also the information that may be gained from its use is not, I believe, commensurate with the effort required in the adaptation of the placebo model. Placebo control groups do not offer any more illuminating controls of the contribution of events assumed by theory to be specific, active, or characteristic of a given therapy than can be provided by its comparison with a well-specified alternate form of psychotherapy that does not share the same theoretical base. Similarly, the placebo control model does not offer any circumspect or appropriate control of the role of the so-called nonspecific, or incidental, elements common to the therapies being compared than can be provided by an active alternate treatment form.

A true placebo would be one that controlled for the actual active ingredients of a therapy, whether such ingredients were characteristic or incidental, unique or common. Such knowledge is not yet available. Investigators must content themselves with attempts to control for the hypothesized active ingredients.

Generalizations warranted from placebo control research are no less constrained by the need to identify the constituent elements of the particular experimental and control conditions than is the case in ordinary comparative studies.

I propose, therefore, that investigators adopt the less encumbered and potentially more informative research model of comparing known alternate treatment forms and modalities. The psychotherapies to be compared should preferably differ markedly—or appear to differ—in their theories, assumptions, and above all, their actual procedures. In effect, each would serve as a natural placebo control for the other in that each bases its treatment on hypothetical constructs not shared by the other. The use of active therapies to serve as placebos for each other was earlier described by Rosenthal and Frank (1956).

Because the major research question involves better understanding of how change is effected, I suggest that comparisons be limited to therapies that on the basis of previous small-scale (e.g., group or $N = 1$) studies have established records of efficacy with the particular disorder being studied. Under these conditions patients can in good conscience be assigned randomly to one or the other treatment condition. Another advantage of the alternate treatment design over the placebo control is that the treatments appear plausible to the therapists involved and therefore ultimately may be viewed as credible by the patients. A full range of effects should be assessed by use of the same instruments across the contrasted therapies.

The research design should permit the analysis and comparison of characteristic and incidental elements of the treatments. Because the aim of the proposed research is primarily to determine whether treatments involving quite different interventions produce different kinds of degrees of change with specified categories of problems, all other treatment elements should be kept as comparable as possible.

Therapists in each form of therapy should be encouraged to enhance the so-called nonspecific elements of their treatment, consistent with their optimal practice. Such elements may include trying to ensure a high quality of therapeutic relationship and encouraging confidence, hope, and favorable expectation of change. Ideally, the therapies being compared should be comparable on such variables as credibility of treatment to patients, duration of treatment, therapist attention, skills, and enthusiasm. These common nonspecific elements should, in effect, be comparable in the contrasted therapies. Empirically observed differences in outcome could then more readily be attributed to the differences among the specific procedures compared than to the elements common to these therapies.

If comparisons of the effects of therapies known to provide different interventions failed to reveal differences in nature, degree, speed, scope, or durability of change; patient attrition rates; or acceptability and feasibility of treatment, then it could be concluded that the differences in specific procedures and techniques were not critical. The focus of investigation could then more usefully be shifted to the study of the common elements and how they contribute to outcome effects.

Ideally the research design should permit the study of interaction effects. The typical treatment versus placebo control study is concerned primarily with determining whether the mean changes associated with the two treatments being compared are significantly different; that is, it is a study of the main effects. A potentially far more enlightening design is one that facilitates the analysis of interactions among treatment variables.

Multivariate or factorial designs involving comparisons of existing treatment approaches may contribute far more to the goal of understanding and enhancing treatment than designs asking simply whether Treatment A is better than Treatment B or Placebo X. The more appropriate designs permit the study of the effects on therapeutic outcome of various combinations of treatment components and attributes of patients and therapists.

Based in part on evidence of society's rising expectations from health care practitioners and in part on notable research advances, some practitioners now appear willing to extend to scientific research more than their usual minimal courtesy of sullen indifference. Now if our doctrinaire treatment-outcome assessors can be persuaded to make similar concessions of tolerance, then the research field can get on with its primary business of clarifying the mechanisms and processes of therapeutic change and thereby of ultimately enhancing the effectiveness of psychotherapy.

I believe that the placebo issue in psychotherapy should now be bronzed and put aside with other mementoes of psychotherapy's early developmental period. In short, the advocates of placebo control research are encouraged to go forth and sine qua non no more.

REFERENCES

Andrews, G., & Harvey, R. (1981). Does psychotherapy benefit neurotic patients? A reanalysis of the Smith, Glass and Miller data. *Archives of General Psychiatry, 38*, 1203–1208.

Beck, A. T., Rush, A. J., Shaw, B. F., & Emery, G. (1979). *Cognitive therapy of depression*. New York: Guilford Press.

Beecher, H. K. (1961). Surgery as placebo. *Clinical Science, 176*, 1102–1107.

Bergin, A. E. (1971). The evaluation of therapeutic outcomes. In A. E. Bergin & S. L. Garfield (Eds.), *Handbook of psychotherapy and behavior change* (pp. 217–270). New York: Wiley

Bergin, A. E., & Lambert, M. J. (1978). The evaluation of therapeutic outcomes. In S. L. Garfield & A. E. Bergin (Eds.), *Handbook of psychotherapy and behavior change: An empirical analysis* (2nd ed., pp. 139–189). New York: Wiley.

Bok, S. (1974, November). The ethics of giving placebos. *Scientific American, 231*, pp. 17–23.

Bordin, E. S. (1974). *Research strategies in psychotherapy*. New York: Wiley.

Brody, N. (1983). Author's response. In L. Prioleau, M. Murdock, & N. Brody: An analysis of psychotherapy versus placebo studies. *The Behavioral and Brain Sciences, 6*, 303–308.

Critelli, J., & Neumann, K. (1984). The placebo: Conceptual analysis of a construct in transition. *American Psychologist, 39*, 32–39.

Elkin, I., Parloff, M. B., Hadley, S. W., & Autry, J. H. (1985). NIMH treatment of depression collaborative research program. *Archives of General Psychiatry, 42*, 305–316.

Eysenck, H. J. (1952). The effects of psychotherapy: An evaluation. *Journal of Consulting Psychology, 16*, 319–324.

Eysenck H. J. (1961). The effects of psychotherapy. In J. J. Eysenck (Ed.), *Handbook of abnormal psychology: An experimental approach* (pp. 697–725). New York: Basic Books.

Eysenck, H. J. (1965). The effects of psychotherapy. *International Journal of Psychiatry, 1*, 97–178.

Eysenck, H. J. (1966). *The effects of psychotherapy.* New York: International Science Press.

Frank, J. D. (1973). *Persuasion and healing* (rev. ed.). Baltimore, MD: Johns Hopkins University Press.

Frank, J. D. (1974). Therapeutic components of psychotherapy. *Journal of Nervous and Mental Disease, 159*, 325–342.

Frank, J. D. (1975). General psychotherapy: The restoration of morale. In D. X. Freedman & J. E. Dyrud (Eds.), *American handbook of psychiatry* (2nd ed., Vol. 5, pp. 117–132). New York: Basic Books.

Gill, M. M. (1982). *Analysis of transference: Vol. 1. Theory and technique.* New York: International Universities Press.

Grünbaum, A. (1981). The placebo concept. *Behaviour Research and Therapy, 19*, 157–167.

Herink, R. (Ed.). (1980). *The psychotherapy handbook.* New York: New American Library.

Jacobson, N. S., & Baucom, D. H. (1977). Design and assessment of nonspecific control groups in behavior modification research. *Behavior Therapy, 8*, 709–719.

Kazdin, A., & Wilcoxon, L. (1976). Systematic desensitization and nonspecific treatment effects: A methodological evaluation. *Psychological Bulletin, 83*, 729–758.

Kiesler, D. J. (1966). Some myths of psychotherapy research and the search for a paradigm. *Psychological Bulletin, 65*, 110–136.

Klerman, G. L., Weissman, M. M., Rounsaville, B. J., & Chevron, E. S. (1984). *Interpersonal psychotherapy of depression.* New York: Basic Books.

Landman, J. T., & Dawes, R. M. (1982). Psychotherapy outcome: Smith and Glass' conclusions stand up under scrutiny. *American Psychologist, 37*, 504–516.

Lasagna, L., Mosteller, F., von Felsinger, J. M., & Beecher, H. K. (1954). A study of the placebo response. *American Journal of Medicine, 16*, 770–779.

Levitt, E. E. (1957). The results of psychotherapy with children: An evaluation. *Journal of Consulting Psychology, 21*, 189–196.

Levitt, E. E. (1963). Psychotherapy with children: A further evaluation. *Behaviour Research and Therapy, 1*, 45–51.

Linehan, M. M. (1984) *Dialectical behavior therapy for treatment of parasuicidal women: Treatment manual.* Seattle: University of Washington.

London, P., & Klerman, G. (1982). Evaluating psychotherapy. *American Journal of Psychiatry, 139*, 709–717.

Luborsky, L. (1954). A note on Eysenck's article, "The effects of psychotherapy: An evaluation." *British Journal of Psychology, 45*, 129–131.

Luborsky, L. (1984). *Principles of psychoanalytic psychotherapy: A manual for support-ive-expressive treatment.* New York: Basic Books.

Luborsky, L., Singer, B., & Luborsky, L. (1975). Comparative studies of psycho-therapies: Is it true that "everyone has won and all must have prizes"? *Archives of General Psychiatry, 32,* 995–1008.

Meehl, P. E. (1955). Psychotherapy. *Annual Review of Psychology, 6,* 357–378.

O'Leary, K. D., & Borkovec, T. D. (1978). Conceptual, methodological, and ethical problems of placebo groups in psychotherapy resarch. *American Psychologist, 33,* 821–830.

Orlinsky, D. E., & Howard, K. I. (1975). *Varieties of psychotherapeutic experience.* New York: Teachers College Press.

Paul, G. L. (1966). *Insight versus desensitization in psychotherapy: An experiment in anxiety reduction.* Stanford, CA: Stanford University Press.

Prioleau, L., Murdock, M., & Brody, N. (1983). An analysis of psychotherapy versus placebo studies. *The Behavioral and Brain Sciences, 6,* 275–310.

Psychotherapy: Effective treatment or expensive placebo? (1984, January 14). *The Lancet,* pp. 83–84.

Rachman, S. (1971). *The effects of psychotherapy.* Oxford: Pergamon Press.

Rogers, C. R. (1957). The necessary and sufficient conditions of therapeutic personality change. *Journal of Consulting Psychology, 21,* 95–103.

Rosenthal, D., & Frank, J. D. (1956). Psychotherapy and the placebo effect. *Psychological Bulletin, 53,* 294–302.

Rosenzweig, S. (1954). A transvaluation of psychotherapy—a reply to Hans Eysenck. *Journal of Abnormal and Social Psychology, 49,* 298–304.

Shapiro, A. K. (1971). Placebo effects in medicine, psychotherapy, and psycho-analysis. In A. E. Bergin & S. L. Garfield (Eds.), *Handbook of psychotherapy and behavior change* (pp. 439–473). New York: Wiley.

Shapiro, A. K., & Morris, L. A. (1978). The placebo effect in medical and psychological therapies. In S. L. Garfield & A. E. Bergin (Eds.), *Handbook of psychotherapy and behavior change: An empirical analysis* (2nd ed., pp. 369–410). New York: Wiley.

Shapiro, D. A., & Shapiro, D. (1982). Meta-analysis of comparative therapy outcome studies: A replication and refinement. *Psychological Bulletin, 92,* 581–604.

Shepherd, M. (1979). Psychoanalysis, psychotherapy, and health services. *British Medical Journal, 2,* 1557–1559.

Sloane, R. B., Staples, F. R., Cristol, A. H., Yorkston, N. J., & Whipple, K. (1975). *Psychotherapy versus behavior therapy.* Cambridge, MA: Harvard University Press.

Smith, M. L., Glass, G. V., & Miller, T. I. (1980). *The benefits of psychotherapy.* Baltimore, MD: Johns Hopkins University Press.

Strupp, H. H. (1964). The outcome problem in psychotherapy: A rejoinder. *Psychotherapy, 1,* 101.

Strupp, H. H., & Binder, J. L. (1982). *Time limited dynamic psychotherapy (TLDP):*

A treatment manual. Nashville, TN: Vanderbilt University, Center for Psychotherapy Research, Department of Psychology.

Subotnik, L. (1972). Spontaneous remission: Fact or artifact? *Psychological Bulletin, 77,* 32–48.

Szasz, T. S. (1961). *The myth of mental illness.* New York: Hoeber-Harper.

Wender, P. H., & Klein, D. F. (1981). *Mind, mood, and medicine: A guide to the new biopsychiatry.* New York: Farrar, Straus, Giroux.

Wolf, S. (1950). Effects of suggestion and conditioning action of chemical agents in human subjects pharmacology of placebos. *Journal of Clinical Investigations, 29,* 100–109.

30

ANALYSIS OF CHANGE: MODELING INDIVIDUAL GROWTH

DAVID J. FRANCIS, JACK M. FLETCHER, KARLA K. STUEBING, KEVIN C. DAVIDSON, AND NORA M. THOMPSON

The measurement and analysis of change plays a central role in many areas of clinical research. It would be difficult to provide an exhaustive list of clinical research endeavors in which this process is central. Many problems associated with the measurement and analysis of change are common to all such endeavors, including areas as diverse as examining the effectiveness of treatments for specific behavioral disorders, investigating developmental outcomes in impaired pediatric or adult populations, or identifying cognitive and emotional sequellae of acquired disorders. All these areas present researchers with difficult questions concerning the measurement and analysis of change. Ironically, some of these questions have been made

Reprinted from the *Journal of Consulting and Clinical Psychology*, 59, 27–37. Copyright 1991 by the American Psychological Association.

Preparation of this article was supported in part by National Institute of Neurological Disorders and Stroke Grant NS21889, "Neurobehavioral Outcome of Head Injury in Children," National Institutes of Health Grant CA33097-08, "The Neuropsychological Assessment of Children with Cancer," and National Institute of Child Health and Human Development Grants P01 HD21888, "Psycholinguistic and Biological Mechanisms in Dyslexia," and P50 HD25802, "Center for Learning and Attention Disorders."

more difficult by the volumes of well-intentioned, but often misleading, statistical and psychometric literature on change.

The present article attempts to clarify this literature in a manner accessible to the clinical researcher. We will show that some of the problems of measuring change are artifacts of an inappropriate conceptualization that has emphasized mean change over individual change (Rogosa, Brandt, & Zimowski, 1982; Willett, 1988). Secondly, we will attempt to demonstrate that it is both possible and desirable to model change at the individual level. To accomplish this objective, a conceptual formulation for modeling change and its correlates is presented (Willett, 1988) followed by an application from our research on recovery from closed head injury in children (Fletcher, Ewing-Cobbs, Miner, Levin, & Eisenberg, 1990).

TYPES OF CHANGE

The concerns addressed in this article do not encompass the whole of research on behavior change. Researchers in developmental psychology have distinguished between qualitative and quantitative behavior changes for many years (McCall, 1977; Wohlwill, 1973). Qualitative changes in behavior are typically evidenced through changes in the factor structure of instruments (Jöreskog, 1979). Constructs that change qualitatively with development have been labeled *dynamic constructs* (Collins, Cliff, & Dent, 1988). Labouvie (1981) has incorporated such structural changes into a general multivariate perspective on intraindividual change.

The methods discussed in our article are suitable whenever change occurs along strictly quantitative dimensions, and the instruments used provide equally precise scaling of individuals throughout the range of behavior to be measured over the entire span of the study. At the very least, this implies that the instruments represent interval scales that are safe from ceiling or floor effects.

TWO PERSPECTIVES ON QUANTITATIVE CHANGE

Change as Incremental

Research on traditional methods for the measurement and analysis of change has attempted to resolve several "problems." Foremost among them is how to measure change. A natural choice for measuring change from one occasion to the next would seem to be the difference score, quite simply $D_i = X_{2i} - X_{1i}$, where X_{2i} is the score on X (e.g., a measure of psychopathology) at Occasion 2 for person i, and X_{1i} the score on X for the same person at Occasion 1.

It is arguable whether any single issue has received more scrutiny in the statistical and psychometric literature than the use of the difference score in the study of change (Bereiter, 1963; Cronbach & Furby, 1970; Linn & Slinde, 1977; Lord, 1956, 1963; McNemar, 1958; Rogosa et al., 1982; Rogosa & Willett, 1985; Zimmerman & Williams, 1982a; 1982b). This attention has been mostly negative and has focused primarily on two issues: (a) the reliability (or unreliability) of the difference score and its inverse relationship to the correlation between X_2 and X_1 and (b) the correlation between the difference score and initial status (X_1) and its implications for using the difference score to study correlates of change. To resolve these problems a number of alternatives to the difference score have been recommended, including the base free measure of change (Tucker, Damarin, & Messick, 1966; Messick, 1981), the residualized change score (Webster & Bereiter, 1963), and Lord's (1956) regression-based estimate of true change. Zimmerman and Williams (1982b) have provided a recent comparison of several alternatives.

More relevant to the current discussion have been the efforts of Rogosa and his colleagues to present these alternatives from within a formal conceptual framework for modeling change (Rogosa et al., 1982; Rogosa & Willett, 1983, 1985; Rogosa, 1988; and Willett, 1988). Rogosa (1988) and Willett (1988) have provided the most generally accessible introductions to this framework. Willett (1988) argues that the problems that have been associated with the difference score stem more from the conceptualization of change that underlies their use than from any flaw in the difference score. To quote Willett (1988):

> Between the *idea* of measuring change and the *reality* of its empirical measurement has fallen the shadow of an unnatural, or at least unhelp-ful, conceptualization. .... It is a conceptualization that views individ-ual learning, not as a process of continuous development over time, but as the quantized acquisition of skills, attitudes, and beliefs. It is as though the individual is delivered of a quantum of learnings in the time period that intervenes between the premeasure and the postmeasure, and that our only concern should be with the size of the "chunk." (p. 347)

Change as a Process

When dealing with quantitative change, a compelling alternative to this traditional formulation is to consider change as reflecting a continuous process that underlies performance. The amount of true change that takes place for any given subject between any two time periods is a result of that subject's individual underlying growth trajectory. Viewing change in performance as a continuous process focuses the investigation of "change" on the description of the individual growth trajectories that reflect that process, not simply the amount of change taking place between arbitrary time points during the unfolding of that process. Of course, describing any trajectory that is not linear requires more than two observations on the same individual. Moreover, even if individual change is characterized by a straight line, errors of measurement necessitate that more than two observations be collected on an individual to precisely describe that line (Willett, 1988).

TWO APPROACHES TO MEASUREMENT AND DATA ANALYSIS

Incremental Approaches to Measurement

Warnings from the early statistical and psychometric literature have helped to promote and maintain several misunderstandings about the use of the difference score. It is not that these authors have misinformed researchers about the statistical and psychometric properties of the simple difference score and its alternatives. In many instances where difference scores are to be used as dependent or independent measures, these early warnings and recommendations are helpful. For example, these warnings are relevant when difference scores are used to compare competencies across domains, as in the comparison of achievement and intelligence test scores for the purposes of diagnosing learning disabilities (Fletcher et al., 1989) or the comparison of different subtests from an intelligence test. However, these same warnings have confused researchers interested in quantifying change over time. This confusion stems from the predominance of two-wave designs in longitudinal research, and the failure to recognize that quantification of change over time can be improved by collecting more than two waves of data (Rogosa, 1988; Willett, 1988). Nevertheless, it is instructive to consider the properties of the difference score for studying change in two-wave data because it is the most commonly used longitudinal design.

Measuring Change With Difference Scores: Reliability Versus Validity

The use of the difference score for measuring change has been criticized because of the inverse relationship between the reliability of the difference score and the correlation between X_1 and X_2 (e.g., pretest and posttest measures of anxiety). This inverse relationship concerns researchers because the correlation is interpreted as reflecting the extent to which the instrument measures the same construct at both times. This interpretation of the pretest–posttest correlation is reasonable, but only if the *individuals* are *not* changing at different rates between the two assessments. The reliability of a difference score taken between two time points is a function of several components: (a) precision in the individual measures (i.e., the reliability of the pretest and the posttest), (b) the length of time between the two measurements, and, most important, (c) the variability in true change (Rogosa et al., 1982). If subjects are changing at constant rates (not necessarily all equal), then as each of these individual components is increased, the reliability of the difference score likewise will increase. In fact, the reliability of the difference score can exceed that of the individual measurements (Zimmerman & Williams, 1982a). When the rate of change varies from subject to subject, it is simply not justifiable to interpret a low correlation between the pretest and posttest as a sign that the tests measure different constructs. On the other hand, when the amount of true change is nearly equal for all individuals, then the "low reliability of the difference score properly reveals that you can't detect individual differences {in growth} that ain't there" (Rogosa, 1988, p. 179).

Studying Correlates of Change With Difference Scores

A second criticism of the difference score, which has motivated several of its alternatives, is the often cited negative component to the correlation between the observed difference score and the pretest (Bereiter, 1963). As a result, it has been argued that use of the difference score as a measure of change gives an unfair advantage to persons with low initial values (Linn & Slinde, 1977). On the contrary, the difference score is an *unbiased*, albeit fallible, estimate of true individual change. The problem is that, although it is an unbiased measure of true individual change, fallibility makes the difference score inadequate for studying correlates of *true* change (Rogosa & Willett, 1983; 1985; Rogosa et al., 1982; and Willett, 1988). To understand this point fully, we need to distinguish the correlation between observed initial status and observed change from the correlation between true initial status and true change. Only this latter correlation is of any substantive interest, and it can, of course, be negative, zero, or positive (Rogosa & Willett, 1983). The actual value of this correlation is dependent only on the precise state of nature (e.g., change in aggression may correlate negatively with initial levels of aggressive behavior in children, whereas change in affectionate behavior may correlate positively with initial levels). Moreover, if subjects are changing at different rates, then the time chosen to represent initial status will affect the magnitude (and possibly the sign) of this correlation (Rogosa & Willett, 1983).

Unfortunately, the correlation between observed initial status and observed change is affected by several factors other than the population correlation of true initial status with true change. Principal among these factors is measurement error in the pretest and posttest (Rogosa & Willett, 1985). The net effect of these measurement errors is a negative bias in the observed correlation between status and change. In other words, although the observed correlation consistently estimates the population correlation between observed initial status and observed change, there is a tendency for the observed correlation to underestimate the real parameter of interest, namely, the population correlation between true initial status and true change (Willett, 1988).

It is one thing to say that the correlation between observed initial status and observed change is "negatively biased" and another thing to say that this correlation is negative. The effect of this negative bias is such that when the parameter of interest is small but positive, or zero (the condition studied most frequently in research on the statistical properties of the difference score), the correlation between observed status and observed change is expected to be negative (Rogosa et al., 1982; Rogosa & Willett, 1985). Although this is not strictly a problem of the difference score, it does indicate that interpretations of the observed correlation between the difference score and initial status may be invalid when the correlation between true initial status and true change is small or zero. Simply put, the raw difference score is not an optimal statistic for studying "correlates" of change (Willett, 1988), whether the correlate is initial status or some other variable.

Traditional Approaches to Data Analysis

This view of change as an increment in behavior that occurs between two occasions of measurement has fit easily into the traditional analytic framework of psychology. Coupling this view of change with the problems associated with the difference score in studying correlates of change, researchers in psychology have tended to analyze change over time as primarily a characteristic of groups at the expense of considering change as a characteristic of individuals.

There are numerous traditional methods that can be applied to longitudinal data for the purpose of studying mean group differences in change over time. These include the mixed model analysis of variance (ANOVA) and the multivariate approach to repeated measures analysis of variance

(MANOVA; O'Brien & Kaiser, 1985),[1] the analysis of covariance (ANCOVA) or residualized change analysis (Cronbach & Furby, 1970), and the analysis of covariance with reliability correction (ANCOVARC; Kenny, 1975). ANOVA and MANOVA are readily suited to the analysis of more than two waves of data, and it is also possible to extend the ANCOVA and ANCOVARC perspectives to more than two waves of data by path analysis and structural equation modeling (SEM; Jöreskog, 1979).

In discussing ANOVA and MANOVA, the method per se must be distinguished from the application of the method because it is possible to apply both ANOVA and MANOVA in a framework that is consistent with viewing change as a continuous process, namely, by polynomial trend analysis. Of course, not all applications of these methods to longitudinal data use trend analysis.

In two-wave data ($T = 2$), the analysis of variance (ANOVA and MANOVA) and analysis of covariance techniques (ANCOVA and ANCOVARC) address slightly different questions, but both perspectives are concerned with a type of mean change. The emphasis on mean change may be misleading, whether unadjusted, residualized on baseline scores, or residualized with reliability correction, because it incorrectly implies that two waves of data are adequate to study change (Rogosa, 1988) and that all individuals must be studied at the same fixed time points, which may not be optimal (Willett, 1988).

The most straightforward extension of ANOVA and MANOVA to data with $T > 2$ waves simply treats time as a qualitative factor with T levels. This approach is perfectly consistent with the incremental view of change in that the time-ordered nature of the observations is incorporated into the analysis as a series of successive differences between adjacent time waves, in essence quantifying change as the size of the increment between any two measurements. Group differences in change are evidenced as Group Factor × Time interactions, which are followed up by post hoc examination of simple effects of group at each time point, simple effects of time within group, and examination of group differences between adjacent time waves (e.g., do patients and controls show different amounts of change between the posttest and follow-up exams?).

However, in designs with $T > 2$, trend analysis provides an alternative approach to the application of ANOVA and MANOVA that constructs

---

[1]The reader should keep in mind that with only two waves of data, the ANOVA and MANOVA approaches to repeated measures analysis of variance yield identical results. Moreover, although either method can be used with more than two waves of data, these methods yield different results and differ in their assumptions. In general, the MANOVA assumptions are considered to be most plausible (O'Brien & Kaiser, 1985).

the time effect as a collection of $T - 1$ time-dependent trends in the means (McCall & Appelbaum, 1973). For example, it is possible to ask whether the means increase or decrease in a linear fashion. This analysis is consistent with the continuous process view of change because it treats the *pattern* of change as time dependent. In addition, it is possible to study the effects of subject variables on rates and patterns of change, provided that these variables can be included as grouping factors in the ANOVA or MANOVA design. The number of factors that can be incorporated into the design will be limited by sample size requirements, especially if some factors have more than two or three levels. One advantage of the MANOVA approach to repeated measures, including trend analysis, is the relatively nonrestrictive assumptions required for appropriate tests of significance. Provided that error variances and covariances are the same for all groups (an assumption made by all other methods discussed in this article, including the most common implementations of the growth curve methods to be described in the next section), the MANOVA approach will provide reasonable tests of hypotheses about group differences in trends. The same cannot be said for the ANOVA approach to repeated measures and trend analysis or the most common implementations of the growth curves approach to be described.

Although trend analysis offers a reasonable approach to the analysis of longitudinal data, there remain at least two significant shortcomings, the first of which is the restrictive design requirements. It is generally necessary that all subjects have data at all time points. Subjects with any missing data must typically be excluded from the analysis, or missing values must be estimated (Little & Rubin, 1983). Additionally, the spacing of the time points must be the same for all subjects. Hence, it is not possible to have some subjects seen at 6, 12, 24, and 36 months and others seen at 6, 10, 22, and 38 months. BMDP recently released MANOVA computer software capable of analyzing repeated measures data that are incomplete, namely, the BMDP 5V program (Schluchter, 1988). BMDP 5V accommodates the above design by treating the time sampling as fixed for all subjects (i.e., all subjects seen at 6, 10, 12, 22, 24, 36, and 38 months) with all subjects missing some observations. This approach may be problematic when the time sampling varies widely across subjects.

The second shortcoming of ANOVA and MANOVA is the ability to incorporate discrete, but not continuous, predictors of growth. These methods treat within-group individual differences in intraindividual change strictly as error. To the extent that these differences are predictable from continuously distributed characteristics of the individuals, these methods do not allow investigators to study important relations (e.g., one could not investigate the effect of resting heart rate on the rate of change in blood pressure in response to psychological vs. physiological stress in hypertensives, panickers, and normal control subjects).

Individual Growth Curves: Measurement and Analysis

It is possible and desirable to study change by first formulating a model for change at the individual level. Beginning with such an "individual growth model" focuses the study of change on interindividual differences in intraindividual change. This perspective to modeling longitudinal data has been discussed in the biological and statistical literature for some time. Recently there has been a developing interest in the application of individual growth models in psychology and education (Bryk & Raudenbush, 1987; Rogosa et al., 1982; Rogosa & Willett, 1985; Willett, 1988). Advocating the individual growth models perspective simply extends the search for aptitude–treatment interactions to the study of change.

Measuring Individual Change

In the incremental view of change, an individual's score at a given time, t, designated Y_{it}, is equal to her score at time $t - 1$ plus some increment. Given this view, behavior change is described by the difference in Y between times t and $t - 1$ (i.e., the difference score). In the process view of change, a person's score reflects an ongoing process that underlies continuous change in the expression of a characteristic (e.g., development or deterioration in cognitive skill). Given this view, behavior is best described by a continuous time-dependent curve that is characterized by a small set of parameters. As a result, change in behavior is measured by the parameters describing the relationship between behavior and time. For example, if performance for an individual increases (or decreases) linearly over time, then the rate of behavior change is the slope of the line relating behavior to time. Such a model is expressed as follows:

$$Y_{it} = \pi_{0i} + \pi_{1i}a_{it} + R_{it} \tag{1}$$

Equation 1 simply provides a description of a straight line, but it is a line with respect to time that is specific for subject i. Thus, the subscript i signifies a given individual subject, and the subscript t a given point in time from 1 to T_i (the total number of time points for that subject). The parameter π_{0i} is the intercept for the line, and thus describes the average level of Y for subject i when a is 0. Finally, and most important, the parameter π_{1i} describes the average rate of change in Y for subject i. We have kept this model simple, but it could be made more complex to allow for nonlinear change in Y.[2] At most, the model can be a polynomial of order $T_i - 1$ with T_i time points, although it will usually be a polynomial of order one or two. In developmental studies of change, a_{it} is usually taken to be the age of subject i at time t. However, it could be a different time-related marker, such as the number of months of follow-up, the number of completed therapy sessions, or the length of time postdiagnosis. The term R_{it} represents random error in Y for subject i at time t, that is, the R_{it} tell the extent to which the Y_{it} do not all fall on the curve given by Equation 1 for subject i. In its simplest form we assume only that R is normally distributed for all subjects and times, and that the Rs are uncorrelated across subjects at all time points. Depending on how we estimate the parameters of Equation 1, it may not be necessary to assume that the Rs are uncorrelated across time for a given subject (Bryk & Raudenbush, 1987; Willett, 1988).

It might seem that the above model is not different from trend analysis in ANOVA and MANOVA. In fact, the single most important feature of Equation 1 is the subscript i, which makes the model of Equation 1 different from the mean trend model. The subscript i associated with each of the growth parameters indicates that these values are subject specific (i.e., the growth parameters are allowed to vary across subjects). The extent to which the growth parameters vary across subjects indicates the possibilities for identifying correlates of change. In contrast, trend analysis allows growth parameters to vary, but only across groups of subjects. Within-group, individual variability in growth parameters is considered error.

Studying Correlates of Change

This alternative conceptualization of change permits a description of the change process for each individual separately and for groups of individuals collectively, leading to a different set of research questions. For example, what is the shape of the performance curve (e.g., is the memory decline in Alzheimer's disease accelerating {nonlinear} or constant)? Does the curve have the same shape for all individuals (e.g., is the memory decline accelerated for some patients and constant for others)? Are the parameter values constant across subjects, or do the magnitudes of certain parameters of the curve vary (e.g., although all patients show accelerated memory decline, is it more accelerated for some patients than for others)? Are such variations in the parameters of the curve systematically related to known characteristics of the individuals (e.g., is the rate of acceleration in memory decline related to a patient's age, diet, or level of family support)?

---

[2]In fact, in the example that follows we use a model $Y_{it} = \pi_{0i} + \pi_{1i}a_{it} + \pi_{2i}a^2_{it} + R_{it}$, which implies that there is some nonlinearity to the growth trajectories and that the extent of this nonlinearity varies over subjects.

Questions of this nature imply a second model in which the individual growth parameters (π_{0i} and π_{1i}) of Equation 1 are the dependent variables, and subject characteristics, such as initial status on Y or gender, are the independent variables. Specifically, correlates of change can be studied by developing a model that predicts π_{1i} from subject characteristics according to Equation 2:

$$\pi_{1i} = \beta_{10} + \beta_{11}X_{11i} + \cdots + \beta_{1p-1}X_{1p-1i} + U_{1i} \qquad (2)$$

where there are $p - 1$ measured characteristics (X_{1p}). The βs represent the effects of the pth characteristic on the rate of change in Y. U_{1i} is random error, or the extent to which variability in the rate of change is not fully explained by the set of subject characteristics. A similar model can be provided for the other parameters in Equation 1 (e.g., the intercepts, π_{0i}). Moreover, there is no need to use the same variables in Equation 2 to explain the different parameters from Equation 1.

Advantages to Modeling Individual Growth

This process view of change is very flexible, but most important, it emphasizes individual change and the correlates of change. The focus on the correlates of change comes from the fact that the parameters of the individual growth curves describe individual change. Consequently, subject characteristics that correlate with change will relate systematically to the parameters of the individual growth curves. Whereas Equation 1 measures individual change, Equation 2 allows the investigator to ask questions about individual and group change, thereby enhancing, rather than sacrificing, information about group mean change (Willett, 1988).

There are a number of additional advantages to the individual growth curves approach to the study of change. The first advantage is that this approach is well suited to designs with more than two waves of data. In fact, estimation of the parameters in Equations 1 and 2 will be improved as the number of time waves is increased. Moreover, the precise form of the growth curve in Equation 1 will become more apparent as the number of time waves is increased. A second advantage is that with more than two waves of data, it becomes possible to directly estimate the reliability of the growth parameters (i.e., how reliably *change* has been measured; Willett, 1988). Furthermore, these reliabilities can be used to disattenuate estimated correlations between subject characteristics and true change. Third, all of the available data for a given subject can be used, even if that subject was not measured on all occasions. This is a tremendous advantage over traditional methods of analysis, especially when working with field data. The individual change perspective uses whatever data is available for that person, provided that person has at least enough data to estimate the parameters of Equation 1. Even this condition is not necessary for some estimation procedures (Bryk & Raudenbush, 1987; Goldstein, 1987). Of course it is always important to examine the factors affecting missing data (e.g., attrition) so that differential influences on missing data can be controlled in the analysis. Finally, when one is studying the correlates of change in Equation 2, the individual growth curves perspective allows differential weighting of the data from individual subjects so that higher weight can be given to subjects whose change parameters have been estimated with greater precision (Bryk & Raudenbush, 1987; Goldstein, 1987; Willett, 1988). This differential weighting improves the study of correlates of change when not all of the subjects contribute equally precise estimates of individual change. This will happen when the time sampling is not the same for all subjects (Bryk & Raudenbush, 1987; Willett, 1988).

Combined models of the type displayed in Equations 1 and 2 are known by many names within the statistical literature, including random coefficient regression models, mixed general linear models, and multilevel or hierarchical linear models. No matter what the name, from a statistical standpoint the critical question is how to best estimate the parameters of the individual growth curves of Equation 1 and how to perform appropriate statistical analyses of the variability in these estimates in Equation 2. Willett (1988) describes some straightforward methods of estimation for Equations 1 and 2. Bryk and Raudenbush (1987) and Goldstein (1987) provide details on recent advances in statistics that can improve on traditional approaches to estimation. These alternatives are briefly discussed following an example from our research on recovery from closed head injury in children. However, before presenting these results, it is worthwhile to summarize the similarities and differences between trend analysis and individual growth curve analysis as it has been described here.

Summary: Comparison of Individual Growth Curves and Trend Analysis

Of the traditional analytic methods for longitudinal data, individual growth curves analysis is most directly related to trend analysis in ANOVA and MANOVA. Detailed comparison of these methods is beyond the scope of this article, but it is instructive to summarize their similarities, differences, advantages, and disadvantages.

Individual growth curves analysis is most closely related to trend analysis using ANOVA. If time sampling is the same for all subjects, no subjects have any missing data, and the predictors of individual growth are discrete, then the growth curves analysis of the preceding section and a trend analysis using ANOVA will yield identical results. Still, the growth curve approach has a certain conceptual appeal because it makes individual differences in growth the explicit focus of the study. Also, some effort is required to translate the results of the trend analysis into the language of growth curve analysis. For example, individual variability in growth rates is labeled Subject × Linear interaction in the ANOVA output and is not obtained by default using standard analytic packages. Although its design restrictions on time sampling are the same as ANOVA, MANOVA's assumptions about variances and covariances of observations are less restrictive. Consequently, MANOVA's tests of the trend hypotheses are valid under a wider variety of conditions (e.g., when errors of measurement are correlated across time waves). Although there is nothing about the growth curve analysis per se that requires the more stringent assumptions of univariate ANOVA, software for growth curve analysis that allows both flexible design and variance/covariance structures is not readily available.

The design requirements of ANOVA and MANOVA are highly restrictive and may be especially problematic in field studies, whereas the individual growth curves methodology is considerably more flexible. First, and foremost, predictors of growth can be either discrete or continuous. Consequently, in addition to the many other interesting relationships that can be studied (e.g., effects of depression on rate of memory decline in Alzheimer's disease), direct estimation of the correlation between growth and initial status becomes possible. Secondly, individual growth curves analysis allows the number and spacing of time points to vary across subjects. Thus, if subjects have missing data at certain occasions, or miss their appointment by 1 or 2 months, they may still be included in the analysis.

Other advantages exist for the growth curves analysis if certain approaches are used to estimate the parameters of Equations 1 and 2 (Bryk & Raudenbush, 1987; Goldstein, 1987). Specifically, these methods of estimation allow (a) the use of time varying covariates whose effects are fixed or random (e.g., using monthly assessments of treatment compliance in a longitudinal model of treatment for hypertension), (b) modeling correlates of change parameters in a fully multivariate context, and (c) inclusion of subjects with insufficient data to estimate the parameters of Equation 1.

Thus, it seems clear that individual growth curves analysis offers certain conceptual and statistical advantages over traditional methods for longitudinal data. Although some of these advantages are associated with specific approaches to the statistical estimation of Equations 1 and 2, the most important advantages result from adopting a conceptual framework that makes individual growth the explicit focus of the study and adopting a statistical model consistent with that focus.

APPLICATION OF INDIVIDUAL GROWTH MODELS

The example that follows is taken from our research on recovery from closed head injury in children. The example is limited to the presentation of a simple model for individual change that involves both linear and quadratic effects and a single model for predicting the within-subject growth parameters from a small set of subject and injury characteristics.

An Example from Clinical Neuropsychology

The children for this example were part of a cohort described by Fletcher et al. (1990). The subjects were 49 children, 6–15 years of age, who sustained mild to severe closed head injuries. Each child was initially studied on resolution of posttraumatic amnesia (baseline) and again at 6, 12, 24, and 36 months postinjury, although scheduling problems prevented all assessments from taking place at precisely these intervals. Children were excluded if they did not have at least four assessments, including a baseline measure of the dependent measure. A breakdown of the number of children seen at each time point is provided in Table 1. Children were classified into one of two injury severity groups based on the Glasgow Coma Scale (GCS; Teasdale & Jennett, 1974), an index of coma ranging from 3–15 and representing the best eye, motor, and vocal response of the subject. Severe closed head injury ($n = 14$) consisted of children with 24-hr GCS scores 8 and below. All other subjects were classified as mild–moderate ($n = 35$). Pupillary abnormalities, a sign of deep brain stem injury, were present in 33% of cases ($n = 16$), as determined by abnormalities in size or reactivity of the pupils at the time of admission. For the purposes of this study, we report on the effects of injury severity, coded as *mild–moderate* (0), *severe* (1), and the presence of pupillary abnormalities, coded as *absent* (0), *present* (1), and the joint effects of these two indicators. Sample sizes in the combined groups (severity, pupil) were $n = 28$ (0, 0), $n =$

TABLE 1
Sample Sizes and Descriptive Statistics for Age and Beery Visual
Motor Integration (VMI) at Each Time Point

| Variable | Occasion of measurement | | | | |
	1	2	3	4	5
Age at testing					
M	10.72	11.16	11.67	12.69	13.30
SD	2.89	2.94	2.91	2.92	2.87
Beery VMI					
M	13.92	15.96	17.37	18.06	18.85
SD	4.09	3.98	3.63	3.66	3.99
n	49	48	49	49	26

7 (0, 1), $n = 5$ (1, 0), and $n = 9$ (1, 1), respectively. Details of sample recruitment and demographics and additional injury characteristics are provided in Fletcher et al. (1990). The differences in sample sizes reported here reflect the inclusion of new subjects followed subsequent to the initial study and the use of different dependent measures and age ranges.

Analyses were performed using the Beery Test of Visual-Motor Integration (VMI; Beery & Buktenica, 1982) as an outcome measure. The test consists of 24 geometric line drawings of increasing complexity that the child must copy. The principal dependent measure is the number of correctly reproduced drawings. Descriptive statistics for continuously distributed variables used in the analysis are presented in Table 1.

Measuring Individual Rates of Change

There are numerous approaches to estimating the growth parameters of Equation 1 and the parameters of Equation 2. However, regardless of the approach taken to estimation, it is usually advisable to first graph the individual time series, fitting a straight line through the points. It is instructive to create such a graph for each individual as well as a composite graph that shows the collection of fitted curves. In fact, computer programs are available that will automatically fit linear, quadratic, and cubic curves to a set of data points, displaying both the fit and the residuals for all three curves on a single screen (e.g., Hintze, 1989). The practice of displaying the individual time series is very helpful in getting a rough idea of the order of the growth polynomial to be fitted in Equation 1, not to mention screening the data for extreme cases and helping to identify possible ceiling and floor effects in the instruments. The practice of graphing the time series is especially helpful if subjects were not all seen at the same fixed time intervals or ages, which is often the case in quasi-experimental research.

Figure 1 shows a graph including the 49 individual time series fitted with quadratic recovery curves. Each line in Figure 1 represents an estimated recovery curve for a specific subject. The recovery curves are presented in separate panels for subjects in each of the four combinations of severity and pupillary abnormality.

The fitted lines of Figure 1 were obtained using HLM (Bryk, Raudenbush, Seltzer, & Congdon, 1986). HLM was used in the present example because preliminary analyses indicated that a strictly linear growth model was probably not appropriate. HLM was chosen, in part, because it allowed fully multivariate, precision-weighted estimation of the parameters in Equations 1 and 2. Multivariate estimation at the second stage is desirable when the growth parameters (e.g., slopes and intercepts) are correlated, because it allows evaluation of the contribution of a predic-

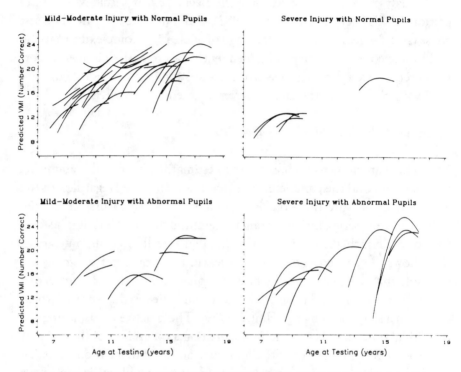

Figure 1: Quadratic recovery curves for visual-motor integration for individuals in four injury groups.

tor to a specific growth parameter, controlling for effects of that predictor on other growth parameters.

Estimates of the unconditional average intercept,[3] linear, and quadratic rates of recovery were 17.44, 2.12, and −.87, respectively. The mean constant rate of change (i.e., mean linear slope) of 2.12 indicates that subjects improved just over 2 designs per year, on average. At the same

[3] For ease of estimation, the age data for a subject were centered around that subject's mean age across all occasions of measurement. Thus the intercept value for a given subject reflects the expected level of performance on VMI when the subject is at his or her average age. This scaling complicates somewhat the interpretation of the average intercept, because this parameter reflects an average level of performance for children of different ages. However, the unconditional mean intercept (M = 17.44) can be thought of as the average expected performance at approximately 15.6 months postinjury (the average of 0, 6, 12, 24, and 36). The number of months postinjury is approximate because the time series is not the same for all subjects, a result of both missing data and scheduling problems.

time, the constant rates of recovery varied across subjects ($\hat{\sigma}_{\pi 1}{}^2 = 2.19$). This variance reflects both variance in the true slopes (variance that is systematic and could be related to subject characteristics) and sampling error. The variance in slope estimates adjusted for sampling error is 0.688. The reliability of the estimated growth rates is given by the ratio of the true variance:total variance ($.688/2.19 = 0.314$). It is important to keep in mind that the reliability of the growth rates indicates that 31.4% of the variance in the slope estimates is systematic and is potentially explainable on the basis of subject and injury characteristics. A similar analysis could be conducted for the quadratic rates of recovery and for the intercepts.

Correlates of Recovery Rate

Estimates of unconditional variance for all three sets of parameters are provided in the bottom half of Table 2, including the results of chi-square tests that these variances are 0. Because these tests indicate significant variance in slopes and intercepts, a second analysis was conducted to determine whether these parameters varied systematically on the basis of

TABLE 2
Effects of Injury and Subject Characteristics on Recovery Parameters
for Beery VMI

Variable	Intercept		Slope		Quadratic	
	Coefficient	SE	Coefficient	SE	Coefficient	SE
	Recovery parameter					
Fixed effect						
Constant	17.81****	0.36	2.25****	0.21	−.72****	0.16
Age at injury	0.62****	0.11	0.16**	0.06	−.20***	0.06
Initial status	0.30***	0.09	−0.26****	0.05	.20****	0.05
Pupils	−0.93	0.72	−0.82*	0.43	—	—
Severity	−2.01**	0.90	−1.33**	0.56	—	—
Severity × Pupils	2.36*	1.19	1.79**	0.72	—	—
	Variance estimates					
Random effect						
Total variance	12.71		2.19		2.94	
Unconditional parameter	10.54****		0.69***		0.25	
Conditional parameter[a]	2.17****		0.27**		—	
Variance explained						
R^2 (% total variance)	65.85		19.18		8.50	
R^2 (% parameter variance)[a]	79.41		60.87		—	

Note: VMI = Visual Motor Integration (Beery & Buktenica, 1982).
[a]Residual variance in the quadratic parameters was fixed at 0, indicating that all true parameter variance in this variance component was explained by the model.
*$p < .1$. **$p < .05$. ***$p < .005$. ****$p < .001$.

injury and subject characteristics. Quadratic growth rates were also modeled in spite of the nonsignificant chi-square test, because the set of predictors under consideration was relatively small and because the chi-square has low power for this effect as a result of the relatively short individual time series.

In this analysis, the within-subject growth parameters from the first analysis served as dependent variables and were predicted from injury characteristics of severity and abnormal pupils and from their interaction. In addition, the subject characteristics of age at injury and status on VMI at baseline were included. These later values were centered at their grand means to facilitate interpretation of the constants in the resulting model. Although we have described this analysis as taking place as a second step, in actuality, both the within-subject growth parameters and the effects of subject characteristics on those parameters are estimated at the same time under the method of estimation used in HLM (Bryk & Raudenbush, 1987).

The individual parameter estimates from the first analysis were not estimated with equal precision for all subjects. At least three elements contribute to the precision of a given estimate, including (a) the number of observations on a subject, (b) the spacing of those observations over time, and (c) the degree to which the model of Equation 1 provides an accurate description of that subject's trajectory. If we assume that the form of the model (e.g., linear, quadratic) has been correctly specified, then the estimates vary across subjects only as a result of (a) and (b). Incorporation of information about precision of the individual parameter estimates into the second stage analysis provides better estimation and more powerful tests of predictors of the individual growth parameters. This differential weighting of the individual parameter estimates is carried out automatically in HLM (Bryk & Raudenbush, 1987) but can also be accomplished in two-stage approaches to estimation of Equations 1 and 2, such as weighted least squares (Willett, 1988).

The results of this analysis are presented in the top half of Table 2 for the final model. This model was obtained by first specifying a full model consisting of the two injury characteristics and their interaction, the child's age at injury, and the baseline level of performance. Nonsignificant terms were then deleted from the model beginning with predictors for the higher order parameters (i.e., the quadratic change followed by the linear rate of change). These results indicated that the subject and injury characteristics included in the model relate to recovery in VMI in a complex way. The p values listed in Table 2 for individual predictors are best considered approximate because of the small sample sizes in some of the injury groups, the relatively short time series, and the backward stepwise deletion procedure used for trimming the model. The parameter estimates indicate a child with normal pupils and mild–moderate injury, who is of average age at the time of injury (approximately 10 years old) and who performs at the average level at the baseline assessment, is expected to improve on the VMI at approximately 2.25 designs per year. A similar child with a severe injury and normal pupils is expected to improve at a rate of approximately .92 designs per year, an estimated 1.33 designs per year slower. A similar statement can be made for a child of average age and initial VMI performance who has a mild–moderate injury but abnormal pupils. Such a child would improve at approximately 1.43 designs per year. The parameter estimate for age at injury indicates that, holding all other variables constant, for each year younger a child is at the time of injury, that child is expected to recover at a rate of approximately .16 designs per year slower. In other words, a child with a mild–moderate injury without pupillary abnormalities who is 7 years old at the time of injury but who is performing at the average level of approximately 13 designs correct at baseline, is expected to gain .48 designs less per year than a child of average age performing at the same level at baseline. In short, younger head-injured children have slower recovery rates on the VMI. Other studies have also suggested that recovery rates are poorer in younger head-injured children (see Fletcher & Levin, 1988), which contradicts commonly held assumptions concerning better recovery after brain injury in younger children due to greater brain plasticity. However, these hypotheses have not been adequately tested, and the null hypothesis of no age effects on recovery has often been accepted. These problems stem from the use of traditional ANOVA/MANOVA analyses, which must treat age at injury as a blocking variable with concomitant requirements for larger sample sizes to ensure adequate statistical power for testing hypothesized age effects on rates of change (Fletcher et al., 1990).

The interaction effect on the linear growth rates indicates that, surprisingly, children with severe injuries and pupillary abnormalities are, on average, recovering at about the same rate as children with mild–moderate injuries and normal pupils. A complete analysis of these data would investigate several possible explanations for this finding. First, examination of the individual parameter estimates and residuals may help explain this finding. An examination of the fitted lines in Figure 1 suggests that 3 subjects were contributing strongly to this effect. These subjects tended to be older and to have very poor performance early on in the recovery process. A factor not reflected in the modeling process that may account for this effect is that subjects with more severe injuries cannot be tested for longer periods postinjury, reflecting their greater posttraumatic amnesia. Further examination of Figure 1 indicates that this effect may stem in part from ceiling effects of the test. Because the mild–moderate injury subjects with normal pupils start out at higher levels than other groups, their growth rates will be more greatly constrained than those of other groups if the test lacks an adequate ceiling. Also, given the sample sizes in three of the four groups, the inclusion of additional subjects would be beneficial to evaluating the robustness of this finding. In addition, many important subject and injury characteristics have not been included in the analysis for the sake of parsimony in this demonstration. Given a sufficiently large sample of subjects and time points, the study of additional injury characteristics and investigation of more complex models may clarify these relationships further.

The availability of an estimate of the reliability in slope estimates allows a modified interpretation of R^2. The R^2 value for slopes in Table 2 indicates that the predictors accounted for 19% of the total variance in the estimates. However, the reliability of the slope estimates indicated that only 31.4% of the total parameter variance was systematic. Consequently, it is reasonable to consider that the model accounts for about 60% ($[.69 - .27]/ .69 = .61$) of the parameter variance in the linear growth rates that is potentially explainable (Bryk & Raudenbush, 1987). Moreover, the model accounts for close to 70% of the total variance in average VMI performance and almost 80% of the "true" parameter variance. These estimates of variance accounted for are much higher than commonly reported in traditional analyses of these data (Fletcher & Levin, 1988). Other injury and demographic variables are available that could be added to the model to further increase explanatory power.

CONCLUSIONS

The individual growth models perspective offers a particularly rich and flexible alternative to traditional methods for analyzing longitudinal data. A traditional analysis of the data presented in the previous section would have focused on incremental differences across fixed time points between injury severity groups. Group differences in the repeated measures effect would be further examined by contrasting groups at specific follow-up intervals. Typically, such an analysis would have been carried out on standard scores to control for age differences between injury groups. Trend analysis provides a somewhat more informative traditional analysis because it allows the investigation of smooth time-dependent change in the pattern of means. Admittedly, more than a few such analyses have been published by our research group (e.g., Fletcher et al., 1990).

Having appropriate statistical tools for data analysis is an important step in improving analyses of longitudinal data, but having appropriate instruments and sampling plans is even more fundamental. The use of age-standardized measures in psychological research virtually guarantees that information regarding heterogeneity in growth will be lost (Rogosa et al., 1982). Indeed, Fletcher et al. (1990) were not able to demonstrate relationships of alternative outcome measures with any injury or subject characteristics other than severity. The study of growth must incorporate measures capable of demonstrating change as well as individual differences in change when such differences exist. Such measures are not always available. One explanation for the reported findings concerning the interaction of pupillary abnormalities and injury severity is that the test lacks an adequate ceiling or does not afford equal scaling at all points on the score continuum. As researchers become more interested in the measurement and analysis of change from the individual growth models perspective, then greater emphasis on the development of instruments suitable for measuring change is likely to follow, as in the efforts of Collins et al. (1988).

Equally important is the time-dependent sampling of behavior. The data reported in the example were collected without regard for an explicit model for individual growth. If the study had been designed from an individual growth curves perspective, an explicit form for the individual trajectories would be required to guarantee that behavior was adequately sampled during the appropriate time frame. For example, the limited number of time points necessitated the use of polynomial models for the individual trajectories. It is quite possible that recovery follows a negative-exponential trajectory with performance reaching a plateau by 2 years postinjury. If so, then with limited time sampling early in recovery, it would not be possible to fit the most appropriate nonlinear model. The explicit model for the shape of the growth trajectories dictates the most appropriate design.

One difficulty in the practical application of individual growth models is the need for sufficiently long time series to precisely estimate the parameters of Equation 1. In the analysis of recovery from head injury, individual weights were employed in the estimation of Equation 2 in order to reflect the imprecision in estimates from Equation 1. The HLM analysis used here differentially weights subjects for their own data as compared with the data for the entire group. In essence, the estimates for a subject become weighted composites of two sets of estimates, (a) the individual estimates for that subject and (b) the estimates for that subject's group. Both the HLM program of Bryk et al. (1986) and the ML2 program of Rasbash, Prosser, and Goldstein (1989) use this type of precision-weighted approach to improve statistical estimation. Although there are technical differences between these specific programs, and others like them, at this time it is difficult to specify the practical implications of these differences. Kreft, de Leeuw, and Kim (1990) have compared these programs and others for estimating models other than growth models. A study is currently under way to evaluate several programs for the estimation of growth curves (Van der Leeden & de Leeuw, 1990).

The individual growth curves perspective has many applications in clinical research where change is quantitative. These methods could be applied in the study of any naturally changing phenomenon, such as the cognitive declines associated with normal aging as contrasted with dementia. These methods could also be applied in the evaluation of therapeutic outcomes, such as evaluating medication and psychotherapy in the treatment of depression. However, the real strength of this approach to the study of change is in the study of attribute–treatment interactions: For what types of subjects are treatments maximally (minimally) effective? What are the moderating effects of social support on cognitive declines in dementia? Researchers in clinical psychology are constantly confronted with questions that concern how individuals differ in their response to treatment and in their response to various environmental factors. To the extent that the response is measured quantitatively over time, the adoption of an individual growth models perspective will provide contextually richer answers to such questions.

REFERENCES

Beery, K. E., & Buktenica, N. (1982). *Developmental test of visual motor integration.* Chicago: Follett.

Bereiter, C. (1963). Some persisting dilemmas in the measurement of change. In C. W. Harris (Ed.), *Problems in measuring change* (pp. 3–20). Madison, WI: University of Wisconsin Press.

Bryk, A. S., & Raudenbush, S. W. (1987). Application of hierarchical linear models to assessing change. *Psychological Bulletin, 101,* 147–158.

Bryk, A. S., Raudenbush, S. W., Seltzer, M., & Congdon, R. J. (1986). *An introduction to HLM: Computer program and user's guide.* Chicago: University of Chicago.

Collins, L. M., Cliff, N., & Dent, C. W. (1988). The longitudinal Guttman simplex: A new methodology for measurement of dynamic constructs in longitudinal panel studies. *Applied Psychological Measurement, 12,* 217–230.

Cronbach, L. J., & Furby, L. (1970). How we should measure "change"—or should we? *Psychological Bulletin, 74,* 68–80.

Fletcher, J. M., Espy, K. A., Francis, D. J., Davidson, K. C., Rourke, B. P., & Shaywitz, S. (1989). Comparisons of cut-off score and regression based definitions of reading disabilities. *Journal of Learning Disabilities, 22,* 334–338.

Fletcher, J. M., Ewing-Cobbs, L. C., Miner, M. E., Levin, H. S., & Eisenberg, H. M. (1990). Behavioral changes after head injury in children. *Journal of Consulting and Clinical Psychology, 58,* 93–98.

Fletcher, J. M., & Levin, H. S. (1988). Neurobehavioral effects of brain injury in children. In D. Routh (Ed.), *Handbook of pediatric psychology* (pp. 258–296). New York: Guilford Press.

Goldstein, H. (1987). *Multilevel models in educational and social research.* London: Oxford University Press.

Hintze, J. L. (1989). *Number Cruncher Statistical System, Version 5.1-Graphics: Reference manual.* NCSS, Kaysville, UT.

Jöreskog, K. (1979). Statistical estimation of structural models in longitudinal–developmental investigations. In J. R. Nesselroade & P. B. Baltes (Eds.), *Longitudinal research in the study of behavior and development* (pp. 303–351). New York: Academic Press.

Kenny, D. A. (1975). A quasi-experimental approach to assessing treatment effects in the nonequivalent control group design. *Psychological Bulletin, 68,* 345–362.

Kreft, I. G. G., de Leeuw, J., & Kim, K. (1990). *Comparing four different statistical packages for hierarchical linear regression: GENMOD, HLM, ML2, and VARCL* (Technical Report No. 50). Los Angeles: UCLA, Statistics Series.

Labouvie, E. W. (1981). The study of multivariate change structures: A conceptual perspective. *Multivariate Behavioral Research, 16,* 23–35.

Linn, R. L., & Slinde, J. A. (1977). The determination of the significance of change between pre- and posttesting periods. *Review of Educational Research, 47,* 121–150.

Little, R. J. A., & Rubin, D. B. (1983). On jointly estimating parameters and missing data by maximizing the complete-data likelihood. *American Statistician, 37,* 218–220.

Lord, F. M. (1956). The measurement of growth. *Educational and Psychological Measurement, 16,* 421–437.

Lord, F. M. (1963). Elementary models for measuring change. In C. W. Harris (Ed.), *Problems in measuring change.* Madison, WI: University of Wisconsin Press.

McCall, R. B. (1977). Challenges to a science of developmental psychology. *Child Development, 48,* 333–344.

McCall, R. B., & Appelbaum, M. I. (1973). Bias in the repeated measures analysis of variance: Some alternative approaches. *Child Development, 44,* 333–344.

McNemar, Q. (1958). On growth measurement. *Educational and Psychological Measurement, 18,* 47–55.

Messick, S. (1981). Denoting the base-free measure of change. *Psychometrika, 46,* 215–217.

O'Brien, R. G., & Kaiser, M. K. (1985). MANOVA method for analyzing repeated measures designs: An extensive primer. *Psychological Bulletin, 97,* 316–333.

Rasbash, J., Prosser, R., & Goldstein, H. (1989). *ML2 software for two-level analysis: User's guide*. London: University of London, Institute of Education.

Rogosa, D. R. (1988). Myths about longitudinal research. In K. W. Schaie, R. T. Campbell, W. Meredith, & S. C. Rawlings (Eds.), *Methodological issues in aging research* (pp. 171–210). New York: Springer.

Rogosa, D. R., Brandt, D., & Zimowski, M. (1982). A growth curve approach to the measurement of change. *Psychological Bulletin, 90,* 726–748.

Rogosa, D. R., & Willett, J. B. (1983). Demonstrating the reliability of the difference score in the measurement of change. *Journal of Educational Measurement, 20,* 335–343.

Rogosa, D. R., & Willett, J. B. (1985). Understanding correlates of change by modeling individual differences in growth. *Psychometrika, 50,* 203–228.

Schluchter, M. D. (1988). *BMDP5V: Unbalanced repeated measures models with structured covariance matrices* (Technical Report No. 86). Los Angeles: BMDP Statistical Software.

Teasdale, G., & Jennett, B. (1974). Assessment of coma and impaired consciousness: A practical scale. *Lancet, 2,* 81–84.

Tucker, L. R., Damarin, F., & Messick, S. (1966). A base-free measure of change. *Psychometrika, 31,* 457–473.

Van der Leeden, R., & de Leeuw, J. (1990). *Comparison of four statistical packages for repeated measure and growth curve analysis*. Unpublished manuscript.

Webster, H., & Bereiter, C. (1963). The reliability of changes measured by mental test scores. In C. W. Harris (Ed.), *Problems in measuring change* (pp. 39–59). Madison, WI: University of Wisconsin Press.

Willett, J. B. (1988). Questions and answers in the measurement of change. In E. Z. Rothkopf (Ed.), *Review of Research in Education, 15,* 345–422.

Wohlwill, J. F. (1973). *The study of behavioral development*. New York: Academic Press.

Zimmerman, D. W., & Williams, R. H. (1982a). Gain scores in research can be highly reliable. *Journal of Educational Measurement, 19,* 149–154.
Zimmerman, D. W., & Williams, R. H. (1982b). The relative error magnitude in three measures of change. *Psychometrika, 47,* 141–147.

31

CLINICAL SIGNIFICANCE: A STATISTICAL APPROACH TO DEFINING MEANINGFUL CHANGE IN PSYCHOTHERAPY RESEARCH

NEIL S. JACOBSON AND PAULA TRUAX

There has been growing recognition that traditional methods used to evaluate treatment efficacy are problematic (Barlow, 1981; Garfield, 1981; Jacobson, Follette, & Revenstorf, 1984; Kazdin, 1977; Kendall & Norton-Ford, 1982; Smith, Glass, & Miller, 1980; Yeaton & Sechrest, 1981). Treatment effects are typically inferred on the basis of statistical comparisons between mean changes resulting from the treatments under study. This use of statistical significance tests to evaluate treatment efficacy is limited in at least two respects. First, the tests provide no information on the variability of response to treatment within the sample; yet information regarding within-treatment variability of outcome is of the utmost importance to clinicians.

Second, whether a treatment effect exists in the statistical sense has little to do with the clinical significance of the effect. Statistical effects refer

Reprinted from the *Journal of Consulting and Clinical Psychology*, 59, 12–19. Copyright 1991 by the American Psychological Association.

Preparation of this article was supported by Grants MH 33838-10 and MH-44063 from the National Institute of Mental Health, awarded to Neil S. Jacobson.

to real differences as opposed to ones that are illusory, questionable, or unreliable. To the extent that a treatment effect exists, we can be confident that the obtained differences in the performance of the treatments are not simply chance findings. However, the existence of a treatment effect has no bearing on its size, importance, or clinical significance. Questions regarding the *efficacy* of psychotherapy refer to the benefits derived from it, its potency, its impact on clients, or its ability to make a difference in peoples' lives. Conventional statistical comparisons between groups tell us very little about the efficacy of psychotherapy.

The effect size statistic used in meta-analysis seems at first glance to be an improvement over standard inferential statistics, inasmuch as, unlike standard significance tests, the effect size statistic does reflect the size of the effect. Unfortunately, the effect size statistic is subject to the same limitations as those outlined above and has been even more widely misinterpreted than standard statistical significance tests. The size of an effect is relatively independent of its clinical significance. For example, if a treatment for obesity results in a mean weight loss of 2 lb and if subjects in a control group average zero weight loss, the effect size could be quite large if variability within the groups were low. Yet the large effect size would not render the results any less trivial from a clinical standpoint. Although large effect sizes are more likely to be clinically significant than small ones, even large effect sizes are not necessarily clinically significant.

The confusion between statistical effect or effect size and efficacy is reflected in the conclusions drawn by Smith et al., (1980) on the basis of their meta-analysis of the psychotherapy outcome literature. In their meta-analysis, they found moderate effect sizes when comparing psychotherapy with no or minimal treatment; moreover, the direction of their effect sizes clearly indicated that psychotherapy outperformed minimal or no treatment. On the basis of the moderate effect sizes, the authors concluded that "Psychotherapy is *beneficial*, {italics added} consistently so and in many different ways. ... The evidence overwhelmingly supports the *efficacy* {italics added} of psychotherapy" (p. 184).

Such conclusions are simply not warranted on the basis of either the existence or the size of statistical effects. In contrast to criteria based on statistical significance, judgments regarding clinical significance are based on external standards provided by interested parties in the community. Consumers, clinicians, and researchers all expect psychotherapy to accomplish particular goals, and it is the extent to which psychotherapy succeeds in accomplishing these goals that determines whether or not it is effective or beneficial. The clinical significance of a treatment refers to its ability to meet standards of efficacy set by consumers, clinicians, and researchers. While there is little consensus in the field regarding what these standards should be, various criteria have been suggested: a high percentage of clients improving; a level of change that is recognizable by peers and significant others (Kazdin, 1977; Wolf, 1978); an elimination of the presenting problem (Kazdin & Wilson, 1978); normative levels of functioning by the end of therapy (Kendall & Norton-Ford, 1982; Nietzel & Trull, 1988); high end-state functioning by the end of therapy (Mavissakalian, 1986); or changes that significantly reduce one's risk for various health problems.

Elsewhere we have proposed some methods for defining clinically significant change in psychotherapy research (Jacobson, Follette, & Revenstorf, 1984, 1986; Jacobson & Revenstorf, 1988). These methods had three purposes: to establish a convention for defining clinically significant change that could be applied, at least in theory, to any clinical disorder; to define clinical significance in a way that was consistent with both lay and professional expectations regarding psychotherapy outcome; and to provide a precise method for classifying clients as "changed" or "unchanged" on the basis of clinical significance criteria. The remainder of this article describes the classification procedures, illustrates their use with a sample of data from a previous clinical trial (Jacobson et al., 1989), discusses and provides tentative resolutions to some dilemmas inherent in the use of these procedures, and concludes by placing our method within a broader context.

A STATISTICAL APPROACH TO CLINICAL SIGNIFICANCE

Explanation of the Approach

Jacobson, Follette, and Revenstorf (1984) began with the assumption that clinically significant change had something to do with the return to normal functioning. That is, consumers, clinicians, and researchers often expect psychotherapy to do away with the problem that clients bring into therapy. One way of conceptualizing this process is to view clients entering therapy as part of a dysfunctional population and those departing from therapy as no longer belonging to that population. There are three ways that this process might be operationalized:

(a) The level of functioning subsequent to therapy should fall outside the range of the dysfunctional population, where range is defined as extending to two standard deviations beyond (in the direction of functionality) the mean for that population.

(b) The level of functioning subsequent to therapy should fall within the range of the functional or normal population, where range is defined as within two standard deviations of the mean of that population.

(c) The level of functioning subsequent to therapy places that client closer to the mean of the functional population than it does to the mean of the dysfunctional population.

This third definition of clinically significant change is the least arbitrary. It is based on the relative likelihood of a particular score ending up in dysfunctional versus functional population distributions. Clinically significant change would be inferred in the event that a posttreatment score falls within (closer to the mean of) the functional population on the variable of interest. When the score satisfies this criterion, it is statistically more likely to be drawn from the functional than from the dysfunctional population.

Let us first consider some hypothetical data to illustrate the use of these definitions. Table 1 presents means and standard deviations for hypothetical functional and dysfunctional populations. The variances of the two populations are equal in this data set. Assuming normal distributions, the point that lies half-way between the two means would simply be

$$c = (60 + 40)/2 = 50$$

where c is the cutoff point for clinically significant change. The cutoff point is the point that the subject has to cross at the time of the posttreatment assessment in order to be classified as changed to a clinically significant degree. The relationship between cutoff point c and the two distributions is depicted in Figure 1. If the variances of the functional and dysfunctional populations are unequal, it is possible to solve for c, because

$$(c - M_1)/s_1 = (M_0 - c)/s_0;$$

or

$$c = \frac{s_0 M_1 + s_1 M_0}{s_0 + s_1}.$$

TABLE 1
Hypothetical Data From an Imaginary Measure Used To Assess
Change in a Psychotherapy Outcome Study

Symbol	Definition	Value
M_1	Mean of pretest experimental and pretest control groups	40
M_2	Mean of experimental treatment group at posttest	50
M_0	Mean of well functioning normal population	60
s_1, s_0	Standard deviation of control group, normal population, and pretreatment experimental group	7.5
s_2	Standard deviation of experimental group at posttest	10
r_{xx}	Test–retest reliability of this measure	.80
x_1	Pretest score of hypothetical subject	32.5
x_2	Posttest score of hypothetical subject	47.5

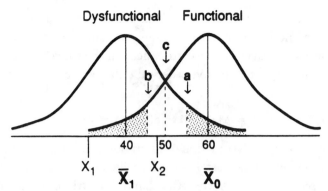

Figure 1: Pretest and posttest scores for a hypothetical subject (x) with reference to three suggested cutoff points for clinically significant change (a, b, c).

Because the cutoff point is based on information from both functional and dysfunctional populations and because it allows precise determination of which population a subject's score belongs in, it is often preferable to compute a cutoff point based only on one distribution or the other.

Unfortunately, in order to solve for c, data from a normative sample are required on the variable of interest, and such norms are lacking for many measures used in psychotherapy research. When normative data on the variable of interest are unavailable, the cutoff point can be estimated using the two standard deviation solution (a) suggested above as an alternative option. But because the two standard deviation solution does not take well-functioning people into account, it will not provide as accurate an estimate of how close subjects are to their well-functioning peers as would a cutoff point that takes into account both distributions. When the two distributions are overlapping as in the hypothetical data set, the two standard deviation solution will be quite conservative. As Figure 1 indicates, the cutoff point established by the two standard deviation solution is more stringent than c:

$$a = M_1 + 2s_1 = 40 + 15 = 55.$$

When functional and dysfunctional solutions are nonoverlapping, a will not be conservative enough. Not only are norms on functional populations desirable, but ideally norms would also be available for the dysfunctional population. As others have noted (Hollon & Flick, 1988; Wampold & Jensen, 1986), if each study uses its own dysfunctional sample to calculate a or c, then each study will have different cutoff points. The results would then not be comparable across studies. For example, the more severely dysfunctional the sample relative to the dysfunctional population as a whole, the easier it will be to "recover" when the cutoff point is study specific.

A third possible method for calculating the cutoff point is to adopt the second method mentioned above, and use cutoff point b, which indicates two standard deviations from the mean of the functional population. As Figure 1 shows, with our hypothetical data set the cutoff point would then be

$$b = M_0 - 2s_1 = 60 - 15 = 45.$$

When functional and dysfunctional distributions are highly overlapping, as in our hypothetical data set, b is a relatively lenient cutoff point relative to a and c (see Figure 1). On the other hand, if distributions are nonoverlapping, b could turn out to be quite stringent. Indeed, in the case of nonoverlapping distributions, only b would ensure that crossing the cutoff point could be translated as "entering the functional population." Another potential virtue of b is that the cutoff point would not vary depending on the nature of a particular dysfunctional sample: Once norms were available, they could be applied to any and all clinical trials, thus ensuring standard criteria for clinically significant change.

Which criteria are the best? That depends on one's standards. On the basis of our current experience using these methods, we have come to some tentative conclusions. First, when norms are available, either b or c is often preferable to a as a cutoff point: In choosing between b and c, when functional and dysfunctional populations overlap, c is preferable to b; but when the distributions are nonoverlapping, b is the cutoff point of choice. When norms are not available, a is the only cutoff point available: To avoid the problem of different cutoff points from study to study, a should be standardized by aggregating samples from study to study so that dysfunctional norms can be established. An example is provided by Jacobson, Wilson, and Tupper (1988), who reanalyzed outcome data from agoraphobia clinical trials and aggregated data across studies using the Fear Questionnaire to arrive at a common cutoff point that could be applied to any study using this questionnaire.

A Reliable Change Index

Thus far we have confined our discussion of clinically significant change to the question of where the subject ends up following a regimen of therapy. In addition to defining clinically significant change according to the status of the subject subsequent to therapy, it is important to know *how much* change has occurred during the course of therapy. When functional and dysfunctional distributions are nonoverlapping, this additional information is superfluous, because by definition anyone who has crossed the cutoff point would have changed a great deal during the course of therapy.

But when distributions do overlap, it is possible for posttest scores to cross the cutoff point yet not be statistically reliable. To guard against these possibilities, Jacobson et al. (1984) proposed a reliable change index (RC), which was later amended by Christensen and Mendoza (1986):

$$RC = \frac{x_2 - x_1}{S_{diff}}$$

where x_1 represents a subject's pretest score, x_2 represents that same subject's posttest score, and S_{diff} is the standard error of difference between the two test scores. S_{diff} can be computed directly from the standard error of measurement S_E according to this:

$$s_{diff} = \sqrt{2(S_E)^2}.$$

S_{diff} describes the spread of the distribution of change scores that would be expected if no actual change had occurred. An RC larger than 1.96 would be unlikely to occur ($p < .05$) without actual change. On the basis of data from Table 1,

$$S_E = s_1 \sqrt{1 - r_{xx}} = 7.5 \sqrt{1 - .80} = 3.35$$

$$s_{diff} = \sqrt{2(3.35)^2} = 4.74$$

$$RC = 47.5 - 32.5/4.74 = 3.16.$$

Thus, our hypothetical subject has changed. RC has a clearcut criterion for improvement that is psychometrically sound. When RC is greater than 1.96, it is unlikely that the posttest score is not reflecting real change. RC tells us whether change reflects more than the fluctuations of an imprecise measuring instrument.

AN EXAMPLE USING A REAL DATA SET

To illustrate the use of our methods with an actual data set, we have chosen a study in which two versions of behavioral marital therapy were compared: a research-based structured version and a clinically flexible version (Jacobson et al., 1989). The purpose of this study was to examine the generalizability of the marital therapy treatment used in our research to a situation that better approximated an actual clinical setting. However, for illustrative purposes, we have combined that data from the two treatment conditions into one data set. Table 2 shows the pretest and posttest scores of all couples on two primary outcome measures, the Dyadic Adjustment Scale (DAS; Spanier, 1976) and the global distress scale of the Marital Satisfaction Inventory (GDS; Snyder, 1979), and a composite measure,

TABLE 2
Individual Couple Scores and Change Status on Dyadic Adjustment
Scale, Global Distress Scale, and Composite Measures

Subject	Pretest	Posttest	Improved but not recovered	Recovered
Dyadic Adjustment Scale				
1	90.5	97.0	N	N
2	74.0	124.0	N	Y
3	97.0	97.5	N	N
4	73.5	88.0	Y	N
5	61.0	96.5	Y	N
6	66.5	62.5	N	N
7	68.5	112.5	N	Y
8	86.5	103.5	Y	N
9	88.5	90.0	N	N
10	68.5	82.5	Y	N
11	98.0	105.0	N	N
12	80.5	99.5	Y	N
13	89.5	112.5	N	Y
14	91.5	101.0	N	N
15	83.5	99.5	Y	N
16	60.5	79.5	Y	N
17	83.0	88.0	N	N
18	88.0	100.5	Y	N
19	98.5	119.0	N	Y
20	78.5	116.0	N	Y
21	99.5	116.0	N	Y
22	79.5	129.0	N	Y
23	84.5	113.0	N	Y
24	92.5	118.0	N	Y
25	93.0	92.0	N	N
26	85.0	114.0	N	Y
27	64.0	68.0	N	N
28	61.0	52.0	N	N
29	80.0	60.5	N	N
30	82.5	104.5	Y	N
Global Distress Scale				
1	68.0	62.5	N	N
2	74.5	56.0	N	Y
3	58.5	58.0	N	N
4	73.5	71.0	N	N
5	78.5	60.5	Y	N
6	76.0	77.0	N	N
7	76.5	58.5	N	Y
8	63.0	52.0	N	Y
9	70.0	65.5	N	N
10	75.0	73.0	N	N
11	63.5	64.0	N	N
12	73.5	55.5	N	Y
13	71.5	53.0	N	Y
14	63.5	55.0	N	Y
15	57.0	50.0	N	N
16	75.0	78.0	N	N
17	63.0	65.5	N	N

Table 2 (*continued*)

Subject	Pretest	Posttest	Improved but not recovered	Recovered
18	75.0	62.0	Y	N
19	71.5	60.5	Y	N
20	68.0	51.0	N	Y
21	75.5	50.0	N	Y
22	67.5	44.0	N	Y
23	62.5	55.5	N	N
24	69.5	56.0	N	Y
25	61.0	60.5	N	N
26	67.0	47.5	N	Y
27	75.5	—	—	—
28	75.5	—	—	—
29	69.5	—	—	—
30	66.5	—	—	—
		Composite		
1	64.8	57.9	N	N
2	75.9	43.0	N	Y
3	58.5	55.9	N	N
4	74.7	65.4	Y	N
5	82.4	57.3	N	Y
6	78.9	79.4	N	N
7	78.2	49.2	N	Y
8	64.6	50.7	Y	N
9	66.5	62.3	N	N
10	77.6	68.7	Y	N
11	59.6	54.8	N	N
12	71.6	53.9	N	Y
13	66.7	47.0	N	Y
14	62.6	53.0	Y	N
15	63.6	51.7	Y	N
16	81.3	72.0	Y	N
17	66.2	63.2	N	N
18	68.7	56.1	Y	N
19	62.6	47.1	N	Y
20	70.3	44.6	N	Y
21	63.7	44.2	N	Y
22	69.6	35.7	N	Y
23	65.3	47.8	N	Y
24	65.5	45.7	N	Y
25	60.9	59.4	N	N
26	66.9	43.9	N	Y
27	—	—	—	—
28	—	—	—	—
29	—	—	—	—
30	—	—	—	—

Note: Composite = Average of Dyadic Adjustment Scale and Global Distress Scale estimated true scores. Y = yes; N = no. Dash = information not available.

which will be explained below. Data from the DAS only are also depicted in Figure 2. Points falling above the diagonal represent improvement, points right on the diagonal indicate no change, and points below the line indicate deterioration. Points falling outside the shaded area around the diagonal represent changes that are statistically reliable on the basis of RC ($> 1.96 S_{diff}$); above the shaded area is "improvement" and below is "deterioration." One can see those subjects, falling within the shaded area, who showed improvement that was not reliable and could have constituted false positives or false negatives were it not for RC. Finally, the broken line shows the cutoff point separating distressed (D) from nondistressed (ND) couples. Points above the dotted line represent couples who were within the functional range of marital satisfaction subsequent to therapy. Subjects whose scores fall above the dotted line and outside the shaded area represent those who recovered during the course of therapy.

To understand how individual couples were classified, let us first consider Figure 3. Figure 3 depicts approximations of the distributions of dysfunctional (on the basis of this sample) and functional (on the basis of Spanier's norms) populations for the DAS. Using cutoff point criteria c, the point halfway between dysfunctional and functional means is 96.5. This is almost exactly the cutoff point that is found using Spanier's norms for functional (married) and dysfunctional (divorced) populations (cf. Jacobson, Follette, Revenstorf, Baucom, Hahlweg, & Margolin, 1984). If norms had not been available and we had to calculate a cutoff point based on the dysfunctional sample alone using the two standard deviation solution, the cutoff point would be 105.2. Finally, b, the cutoff point that signifies entry into the functional population, is equal to 79.4.

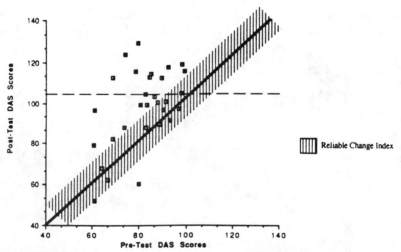

Figure 2: Scatter plot of pretest and posttest scores on the Dyadic Adjustment Scale with jagged band showing reliable change index.

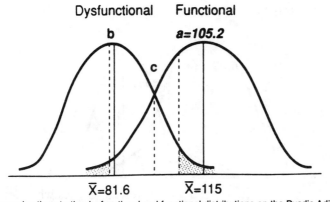

Figure 3: Approximations to the dysfunctional and functional distributions on the Dyadic Adjustment Scale with reference to three suggested cutoff points for clinically significant change (a, b, c).

Given that the dysfunctional and functional distributions overlap, we have already argued that c is the preferred criteria. Indeed, a convention has developed within the marital therapy field to use 97 as a cutoff point, which is virtually equivalent to c. However, there is a complication with this particular measure, which has led us to rethink our recommendations. The norms on the DAS consist of a representative sample of married people, without regard to level of marital satisfaction. This means that a certain percentage of the sample is clinically distressed. The inclusion of such subjects in the normative sample shifts the distribution in the direction of dysfunctionality and creates an insufficiently stringent c. If all dysfunctional people had been removed from this married sample, the distribution would have been harder to enter, and a smaller percentage of couples would be classified as recovered. An ideal normative sample would exclude members of a clinical population. Such subjects are more properly viewed as members of the dysfunctional population and therefore distort the nature of the normative sample. Given the problems with this normative sample, it seemed to us that a was the best cutoff point for clinically significant change. At least when a is crossed we can be confident that subjects are no longer part of the maritally distressed population, whereas the same cannot be said of c, given the failure to exclude dysfunctional couples in the normative sample.

Table 2 also shows how subjects were classified on the basis of RC. Some couples showed improvement but not enough to be classified as recovered, whereas others met criteria for both improvement and recovery. In point of contrast, Table 2 depicts pretest and posttest data for a second measure of marital satisfaction, the Global Distress Scale (GDS) of the Marital Satisfaction Inventory (Snyder, 1979). Subjects were also classified as improved (on the basis of RC) or recovered (on the basis of a cutoff point) on this measure. Figure 4 shows approximations of the dysfunctional

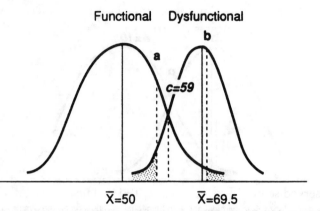

Functional   Dysfunctional

b

a

c=59

X̄=50   X̄=69.5

Figure 4: The same approximations of dysfunctional and functional distributions for Global Distress Scale of the Marital Satisfaction Inventory with reference to three suggested cutoff points for clinically significant change (a, b, c).

and functional populations. If we consider the three possible cutoff points for clinically significant change, criterion *c* seems preferable given the rationale stated earlier for choosing among the three. The distributions do overlap, and if *c* is crossed, a subject is more likely to be a member of the functional than the dysfunctional distribution of couples. The criteria for recovery on the GDS listed in Table 2 are based on the use of *c* as a cutoff point.

Table 3 summarizes the data from both the DAS and the GDS, indicating the percentage of couples who improved and recovered according to each measure. Not surprisingly, there was less than perfect correspondence between the two measures. It is unclear how to assimilate these discrepancies. Moreover, some subjects were recovered on one measure but not on the other, thus creating interpretive problems regarding the status of individual subjects.

Given that both the DAS and GDS measure the same construct, one solution to integrating the findings would be to derive a composite score. These two measures of global marital satisfaction can each be theoretically

TABLE 3
Percentages of Improved and Recovered Couples on DAS, GDS, and
Composite Scores

Measure	N	% improved	% recovered	% unimproved or deteriorated
DAS	30	30	33	37
GDS	26	12	42	46
Composite	26	27	46	27

Note: DAS = Dyadic Adjustment Scale, GDS = Global Distress Scale of the Marital Satisfaction Inventory, and composite-average of DAS and GDS estimate true scores.

divided into components of true score and error variance. However, it is unlikely that either duplicates the true score component of the construct "marital satisfaction." To preserve the true score component of each measure, a composite could be constructed that retained the true score component. Jacobson and Revenstorf (1988) have suggested estimating the true score for any given subject (j), using test theory, by adopting the formula

$$T_j = Rel(X_j) + (1 - Rel)M$$

where T represents true score, Rel equals reliability (e.g., test–retest), and X is the observed score (Lord & Novick, 1968). The standardized true score estimates can then be averaged to derive a multivariate composite. Cutoff points can then be established.

Tables 2 and 3 depict results derived from this composite. Because no norms are available on the composite, the cutoff point was established using the two standard deviation solution.[1]

Finally, let us use this data set to illustrate one additional problem with these statistical definitions of clinically significant change. We have been using a discrete cutoff point to separate dysfunctional from functional distributions, without taking into account the measurement error inherent in the use of such cutoff points. Depending on the reliability of the measure, all posttest scores will be somewhat imprecise due to the limitations of the measuring instrument. Thus, some subjects are going to be misclassified simply due to measurement error.

One solution to the problem involves forming confidence intervals around the cutoff point, using RC to derive the boundaries of the confidence intervals. RC defines the range in which an individual score is likely to fluctuate because of the imprecision of a measuring instrument. Figure 5 illustrates the use of RC to form confidence intervals. The confidence intervals form a band of uncertainty around the cutoff point depicted in Figure 5. On the basis of this data set, for the DAS a score can vary by as much as 9.83 points and still reasonably ($p > .05$) be considered within the bounds of measurement error. Variations of 10 points or more are unlikely to be explainable by measurement error alone. We then formed confidence intervals around the cutoff point, with the cutoff point serving as the midpoint of the interval. Approximately 10 points on either side of

---

[1]The proportion of recovered couples is greater in the composite than it is for the component measures for several reasons. First, there are four couples for whom GDS data are missing. In all four instances, the couples failed to recover. Composites could be computed only on the 26 cases for whom we had complete data. Second, in several instances couples were subthreshold on one or both component measures but reached criteria for recovery on the composite measure. It is of interest that in this important sense the composite measure was more sensitive to treatment effects than either component was.

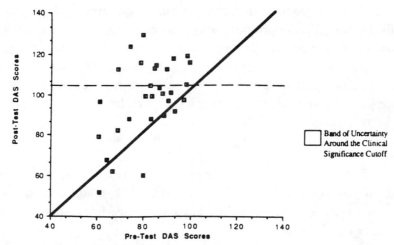

Figure 5: Scatter plot of pretest and posttest scores on the Dyadic Adjustment Scale including band of uncertainty around cutoff point for clinically significant change.

the interval are within the band of uncertainty, but beyond this band we felt confident that the cutoff point had truly been crossed.[2]

As Figure 5 shows, 14 subjects fell within the band of uncertainty created by these confidence intervals. Should these couples be classified as improved, recovered, deteriorated, or uncertain? One possibility would be to add a new category to the classification system: the proportion of subjects who fell within this band of uncertainty. These were couples about whose status we were unsure. If we added this category to our classification system, the revised percentages would be 20% recovered, 47% unclassifiable, and 33% unchanged or deteriorated. Having identified the proportion of subjects about whom we were uncertain, we could use the remainder of the sample and exclude the uncertain subjects in our calculations of proportions of recovered and unrecovered couples. This exclusion would lead to figures of 38% recovered, 19% improved but not recovered, and 44% unchanged or deteriorated. These proportions are probably a more accurate reflection of the true proportion of recovered subjects, inasmuch as subjects within the band of uncertainty are, on the average, going to be equally likely to fall into both categories. In fact, as Jacobson and Revenstorf (1988) noted, this latter suggestion is almost like splitting the difference (i.e., dividing the uncertain subjects equally between recovered and improved but not recovered groups). Although splitting the difference would not reduce ambiguity regarding the status of individual subjects who fall within the band of uncertainty, it would lead to a summary statistic that

---

[2]As Jacobson and Revenstorf (1988) noted, the use of confidence intervals in this manner is a convenience. The cutoff point is merely a theoretical point, and the actual measurement error logically pertains to individual subject's score.

would include the entire sample. Essentially, such a solution amounts to redistributing subjects within the band rather than ignoring it entirely. When equal numbers of subjects fall on either side of the cutoff point within the band, the proportion of recovered subjects will be identical to that calculated without consideration of measurement error at all. Splitting the difference with our sample data set would have resulted in 43% recovered, 23% improved but not recovered, and 34% unchanged or deteriorated.

CONCLUSION

In the past decade, the discussion of clinical significance has taken center stage in psychotherapy research. In a recent review appearing in the *Annual Review of Psychology*, Goldfried, Greenberg, and Marmar (1990) referred to it as one of the major methodological advances. There is no doubt that discussion has moved from occasional mention by a group of prescient observers (e.g., Barlow, 1981; Kazdin, 1977) to a lively topic for discussion and debate, as evidenced by the recent special issue of *Behavioral Assessment* devoted to the topic (Jacobson, 1988).

The editors of this special section have asked us to compare the results of using our system with what would have been obtained using standard inferential statistics or other criteria of improvement. When our statistics have been used, the impact has generally been to add additional information rather than to contradict the results of other data analytic strategies. However, the information from these additional analyses has generally led to more modest conclusions regarding the efficacy of the treatment in question. For example, Jacobson and colleagues (Jacobson, Follette, Revenstorf, Baucom, et al., 1984) reanalyzed data from previously published marital therapy outcome studies. Standard inferential statistical analyses yielded results that supported the effects of the marital therapies, in that treatments outperformed various control groups. The reanalyses reported by Jacobson and colleagues addressed the issue of clinical significance, and the results were somewhat disappointing: Fewer than half of the treated couples ended up in the happily married range after therapy on measures of marital satisfaction. Similar reanalyses based on studies looking at exposure treatments for agoraphobia led to similar results (i.e., treatments outperformed control groups but yielded a relatively small proportion of truly recovered clients; Jacobson, Wilson, & Tupper, 1988).

Experimenters who have used different statistical procedures based on similar principles have often found that clinical significance data make the treatments look less effective than standard statistical comparisons would imply. For example, Kazdin, Bass, Siegel, and Thomas (1989) recently reported on an apparently highly effective behavioral treatment for conduct-disordered children, but a clinical significance analysis suggested that celebration was perhaps premature. Whereas behavioral treatments outperformed a client-centered relationship therapy, comparisons with nonclinic samples revealed that the majority of subjects remained in the dysfunctional range on primary measures of conduct disorder. Similarly, Robinson, Berman, and Neimeyer (1990) recently reported a meta-analysis of studies investigating psychotherapy for depression. Whereas they reported substantial effect sizes for comparisons between psychotherapy and control groups, comparisons with normative samples suggested that subjects remained outside the normal range even after psychotherapeutic intervention.

The approach we have outlined is only one of many possible ways of reporting on clinical significance. On the one hand, our approach has a number of features that we believe should be part of any method for highlighting clinical significance: It operationalizes recovery in a relatively objective, unbiased way; its definition is not tied to a specific disorder, which means that it has potentially broad applicability; because of its general applicability, it could evolve into a convention within psychotherapy research, which in turn would facilitate comparison between studies; and it provides information on variability in outcome as well as clinical significance.

On the other hand, there are a number of unsolved problems that currently limit the generalizability of the method. First, it is unclear at present how robust the method will be to violations of the assumption that dysfunctional and functional distributions are normal. The concept that we have proposed for defining clinical significance does not depend on any formula. The formula is simply one way of determining the midpoint between functional and dysfunctional populations. Even when the formulas for RC and the cutoff points are not applicable, the concept can be applied by determining the cutoff point empirically. However, the formulas discussed in this and other articles assume normal distributions. Second, operationalizing clinical significance in terms of recovery or return to normal functioning may not be appropriate for all disorders treated by psychotherapy. For example, schizophrenia and autism are two disorders in which a standard of recovery would exceed the expectations of most who work in the field. Third, without psychometrically sound measures of psychotherapy outcomes, there are practical constraints that prevent optimal use of our methods, no matter how valuable they might be in theory. In particular, the absence of normative data for functional and dysfunctional populations on many commonly used outcome measures deters the development of standardized cutoff points.

In addition to these and other current problems, there are still a number of subjective decisions to be made regarding optimal use of these statistical methods. These were illustrated in our examples. Only by testing theoretical propositions with real data sets will these ambiguities be resolved. Thus, while it is not premature to expect psychotherapy investigators to report on the clinical significance of their treatment effects, it is far too early to advocate any particular method or set of conventions. Clinical significance has clearly arrived, but the optimal methods for deriving it remain to be determined.

REFERENCES

Barlow, D. H. (1981). On the relation of clinical research to clinical practice: Current issues, new directions. *Journal of Consulting and Clinical Psychology, 49*, 147–155.

Christensen, L., & Mendoza, J. L. (1986). A method of assessing change in a single subject: An alteration of the RC index. *Behavior Therapy, 17*, 305–308.

Garfield, S. L. (1981). Evaluating the psychotherapies. *Behavior Therapy, 12*, 295–307.

Goldfried, M. R., Greenberg, L. S., & Marmar, C. (1990). Individual psychotherapy: Process and outcome. *Annual Review of Psychology, 41*, 659–688.

Hollon, S. D., & Flick, S. N. (1988). On the meaning and methods of clinical significance. *Behavioral Assessment, 10*, 197–206.

Jacobson, N. S. (1988). Defining clinically significant change: An introduction. *Behavioral Assessment, 10*, 131–132.

Jacobson, N. S., Follette, W. C., Revenstorf, D., Baucom, D. H., Hahlweg, K., & Margolin, G. (1984). Variability in outcome and clinical significance of behavioral marital therapy: A reanalysis of outcome data. *Journal of Consulting and Clinical Psychology, 52*, 497–504.

Jacobson, N. S., Follette, W. C., & Revenstorf, D. (1984). Psychotherapy outcome research: Methods for reporting variability and evaluating clinical significance. *Behavior Therapy, 15*, 336–352.

Jacobson, N. S., Follette, W. C., & Revenstorf, D. (1986). Toward a standard definition of clinically significant change. *Behavior Therapy, 17*, 308–311.

Jacobson, N. S., & Revenstorf, D. (1988). Statistics for assessing the clinical significance of psychotherapy techniques: Issues, problems, and new developments. *Behavioral Assessment, 10*, 133–145.

Jacobson, N. S., Schmaling, K. B., Holtzworth-Munroe, A., Katt, J. L., Wood, L. F., & Follette, V. M. (1989). Research-structured versus clinically flexible versions of social learning-based marital therapy. *Behaviour Research and Therapy,* *27,* 173–180.

Jacobson, N. S., Wilson, L., & Tupper, C. (1988). The clinical significance of treatment gains resulting from exposure-based interventions for agoraphobia: A reanalysis of outcome data. *Behavior Therapy, 19,* 539–552.

Kazdin, A. E. (1977). Assessing the clinical or applied importance of behavior change through social validation. *Behavior Modification, 1,* 427–452.

Kazdin, A. E., Bass, D., Siegel, T., & Thomas, C. (1989). Cognitive–behavioral therapy and relationship therapy in the treatment of children referred for antisocial behavior. *Journal of Consulting and Clinical Psychology, 57,* 522–535.

Kazdin, A. E., & Wilson, G. T. (1978). *Evaluation of behavior therapy: Issues, evidence, and research strategies.* Cambridge, MA: Ballinger.

Kendall, P. C., & Norton-Ford, J. D. (1982). Therapy outcome research methods. In P. C. Kendall & J. N. Butcher (Eds.), *Handbook of research methods in clinical psychology* (pp. 429–460). New York: Wiley.

Lord, F. M., & Novick, M. R. (1968). *Statistical theories of mental test scores.* Reading, MA: Addison-Wesley.

Mavissakalian, M. (1986). Clinically significant improvement in agoraphobia research. *Behaviour Research and Therapy, 24,* 369–370.

Nietzel, M. T., & Trull, T. J. (1988). Meta-analytic approaches to social comparisons: A method for measuring clinical significance. *Behavioral Assessment, 10,* 146–159.

Robinson, L. A., Berman, J. S., & Neimeyer, R. A. (1990). Psychotherapy for the treatment of depression: A comprehensive review of controlled outcome research. *Psychological Bulletin, 108,* 30–49.

Smith, M. L., Glass, G. V., & Miller, T. I. (1980). *The benefits of psychotherapy.* Baltimore: Johns Hopkins University Press.

Snyder, D. K. (1979). Multidimensional assessment of marital satisfaction. *Journal of Marriage and the Family, 41,* 813–823.

Spanier, G. B. (1976). Measuring dyadic adjustment: New scales for assessing the quality of marriage and similar dyads. *Journal of Marriage and the Family, 38,* 15–28.

Wampold, B. E., & Jensen, W. R. (1986). Clinical significance revisited. *Behavior Therapy, 17,* 302–305.

Wolf, M. M. (1978). Social validity: The case for subjective measurement or how applied behavior analysis is finding its heart. *Journal of Applied Behavior Analysis, 11,* 203–214.

Yeaton, W. H., & Sechrest, L. (1981). Critical dimensions in the choice and maintenance of successful treatments: Strength, integrity, and effectiveness. *Journal of Consulting and Clinical Psychology, 49,* 156–167.

VI

ETHICS IN RESEARCH

Psychological research raises fundamental ethical issues that are intertwined with research design and methodology. Specific procedures and research practices, the extent to which information is disclosed, and the protection of privacy and anonymity raise explicit ethical concerns. Articles in this section discuss ethical issues and practices in research. The articles also highlight contemporary guidelines for ethical research practices and professional obligations in the conduct and reporting of research.

The American Psychological Association (APA) has provided a set of principles designed to guide psychological research with human subjects. The guidelines have been revised and updated repeatedly to handle the full range of circumstances in which psychologists in research and practice may function. In the 1989 article by APA in this section, a portion of the principles is presented from a larger statement. The principles give an overview of several areas of concern in addition to those issues raised by research. The principles are necessarily general because the full range of research practices cannot be enumerated to cover all experimental situations. Apart from the content of the individual statements, two overriding

649

tenets can be discerned. First, in considering research, the highest priority must be given to the protection of subjects. Second, the responsibilities for ethical conduct in research ultimately lie with the investigator.

Ethical issues generally arise during the conduct of research. Many practical issues emerge at the level of the investigation. In the article by Stanley Imber, Lawrence Glanz, Irene Elkin, Stuart Sotsky, Jenny Boyer, and William Leber (1986), ethical issues are raised in the context of psychotherapy research. Informed consent, random assignment of clinical cases to conditions, the use of placebo control conditions, confidentiality, and security of the data to protect individual rights are all salient issues. These are discussed in the context of the National Institute of Mental Health Collaborative Study on Depression, an investigation conducted on outpatient treatment at three different research sites. Issues and their practical resolution are discussed in the context of this study.

The evaluation of a specific research proposal entails examination of ethical issues and protection of the subjects. At universities where research is conducted, Institutional Review Boards (IRBs) are formed to review individual research proposals before the investigation can be conducted. The board comprises colleagues from diverse disciplines whose task is to review the ethical protections for the subject. The article by Stephen Ceci, Douglas Peters, and Jonathan Plotkin (1985) describes and evaluates the review process for deciding whether research is ethical. The focus of the article is on factors that contribute to approval or disapproval of research proposals. The article is included in this section because of the descriptions of the details, concerns, and operations of the IRB review process.

Ethical issues in research extend beyond the protection of subjects. There are several ethical issues related to the integrity of science and the obligations and responsibilities of the investigator in relation to one's colleagues, the profession, and scientific disciplines more generally. These issues include error, deception, fraud in science, allocation of credit for ideas and research efforts of one's colleagues and collaborators, and the sharing of materials to permit replication. Fraud in science, including the fabrication and misreporting of data, is the most significant violation of ethical responsibilities by the investigator. In the article by Mary Miers (1985), a brief perspective is provided from the National Institutes of Health (NIH), which funds a great deal of research in the sciences. The article discusses considerations of fraud and how NIH has dealt with allegations of fraud.

32

REPORT OF THE ASSOCIATION: ETHICAL PRINCIPLES OF PSYCHOLOGISTS

PREAMBLE

Psychologists respect the dignity and worth of the individual and strive for the preservation and protection of fundamental human rights. They are committed to increasing knowledge of human behavior and of people's understanding of themselves and others and to the utilization of such knowledge for the promotion of human welfare. While pursuing these objectives, they make every effort to protect the welfare of those who seek their services and of the research participants that may be the object

Reprinted from the *American Psychologist, 45*, 390–395. Copyright 1990 by the American Psychological Association.

This version of the *Ethical Principles of Psychologists* was adopted by the American Psychological Association's Board of Directors on June 2, 1989. On that date, the Board of Directors rescinded several sections of the Ethical Principles that had been adopted by the APA Council of Representatives on January 24, 1981.

These Ethical Principles apply to psychologists, to students of psychology, and to others who do work of a psychological nature under the supervision of a psychologist. They are intended for the guidance of nonmembers of the Association who are engaged in psychological research or practice.

of study. They use their skills only for purposes consistent with these values and do not knowingly permit their misuse by others. While demanding for themselves freedom of inquiry and communication, psychologists accept the responsibility this freedom requires: competence, objectivity in the application of skills, and concern for the best interests of clients, colleagues, students, research participants, and society. In the pursuit of these ideals, psychologists subscribe to principles in the following areas: 1. Responsibility, 2. Competence, 3. Moral and Legal Standards, 4. Public Statements, 5. Confidentiality, 6. Welfare of the Consumer, 7. Professional Relationships, 8. Assessment Techniques, 9. Research With Human Participants, and 10. Care and Use of Animals.

Acceptance of membership in the American Psychological Association commits the member to adherence to these principles.

Psychologists cooperate with duly constituted committees of the American Psychological Association, in particular, the Committee on Scientific and Professional Ethics and Conduct, by responding to inquiries promptly and completely. Members also respond promptly and completely to inquiries from duly constituted state association ethics committees and professional standards review committees.

PRINCIPLE 1: RESPONSIBILITY

In providing services, psychologists maintain the highest standards of their profession. They accept responsibility for the consequences of their acts and make every effort to ensure that their services are used appropriately.

   a. As scientists, psychologists accept responsibility for the selection of their research topics and the methods used in investigation, analysis, and reporting. They plan their research in ways to minimize the possibility that their findings will be misleading. They provide thorough discussion of the limitations of their data, especially where their work touches on social policy or might be construed to the detriment of persons in specific age, sex, ethnic, socioeconomic, or other social groups. In publishing reports of their work, they never suppress disconfirming data, and they acknowledge the existence of alternative hypotheses and explanations of their findings. Psychologists take credit only for work they have actually done.
   b. Psychologists clarify in advance with all appropriate persons and agencies the expectations for sharing and utilizing research data. They avoid relationships that may limit their objectivity or create a conflict of interest. Interference with the milieu in which data are collected is kept to a minimum.

c. Psychologists have the responsibility to attempt to prevent distortion, misuse, or suppression of psychological findings by the institution or agency of which they are employees.

d. As members of governmental or other organizational bodies, psychologists remain accountable as individuals to the highest standards of their profession.

e. As teachers, psychologists recognize their primary obligation to help others acquire knowledge and skill. They maintain high standards of scholarship by presenting psychological information objectively, fully, and accurately.

f. As practitioners, psychologists know that they bear a heavy social responsibility because their recommendations and professional actions may alter the lives of others. They are alert to personal, social, organizational, financial, or political situations and pressures that might lead to misuse of their influence.

PRINCIPLE 2: COMPETENCE

The maintenance of high standards of competence is a responsibility shared by all psychologists in the interest of the public and the profession as a whole. Psychologists recognize the boundaries of their competence and the limitations of their techniques. They only provide services and only use techniques for which they are qualified by training and experience. In those areas in which recognized standards do not yet exist, psychologists take whatever precautions are necessary to protect the welfare of their clients. They maintain knowledge of current scientific and professional information related to the services they render.

a. Psychologists accurately represent their competence, education, training, and experience. They claim as evidence of educational qualifications only those degrees obtained from institutions acceptable under the Bylaws and Rules of Council of the American Psychological Association.

b. As teachers, psychologists perform their duties on the basis of careful preparation so that their instruction is accurate, current, and scholarly.

c. Psychologists recognize the need for continuing education and are open to new procedures and changes in expectations and values over time.

d. Psychologists recognize differences among people, such as those that may be associated with age, sex, socioeconomic, and ethnic backgrounds. When necessary, they obtain training, experience, or counsel to assure competent service or research relating to such persons.

e. Psychologists responsible for decisions involving individuals or policies based on test results have an understanding of psychological or educational measurement, validation problems, and test research.

f. Psychologists recognize that personal problems and conflicts may interfere with professional effectiveness. Accordingly, they refrain from undertaking any activity in which their personal problems are likely to lead to inadequate performance or harm to a client, colleague, student, or research participant. If engaged in such activity when they become aware of their personal problems, they seek competent professional assistance to determine whether they should suspend, terminate, or limit the scope of their professional and/or scientific activities.

PRINCIPLE 3: MORAL AND LEGAL STANDARDS

Psychologists' moral and ethical standards of behavior are a personal matter to the same degree as they are for any other citizen, except as these may compromise the fulfillment of their professional responsibilities or reduce the public trust in psychology and psychologists. Regarding their own behavior, psychologists are sensitive to prevailing community standards and to the possible impact that conformity to or deviation from these standards may have upon the quality of their performance as psychologists. Psychologists are also aware of the possible impact of their public behavior upon the ability of colleagues to perform their professional duties.

a. As teachers, psychologists are aware of the fact that their personal values may affect the selection and presentation of instructional materials. When dealing with topics that may give offense, they recognize and respect the diverse attitudes that students may have toward such materials.

b. As employees or employers, psychologists do not engage in or condone practices that are inhumane or that result in illegal or unjustifiable actions. Such practices include, but are not limited to, those based on considerations of race, handicap, age, gender, sexual preference, religion, or national origin in hiring, promotion, or training.

c. In their professional roles, psychologists avoid any action that will violate or diminish the legal and civil rights of clients or of others who may be affected by their actions.

d. As practitioners and researchers, psychologists act in accord with Association standards and guidelines related to practice and to the conduct of research with human beings and animals. In the ordinary course of events, psychologists adhere to relevant governmental laws and institutional regulations. When federal, state, provincial, organizational, or institutional laws, regulations, or practices are in conflict with Association standards and guidelines, psychologists make known their commitment to Association standards and guidelines and, wherever possible, work toward a resolution of the conflict. Both practitioners and researchers are concerned with the development of such legal and quasi-legal regulations as best serve the public interest, and they work toward changing existing regulations that are not beneficial to the public interest.

PRINCIPLE 4: PUBLIC STATEMENTS

Public statements, announcements of services, advertising, and promotional activities of psychologists serve the purpose of helping the public make informed judgments and choices. Psychologists represent accurately and objectively their professional qualifications, affiliations, and functions, as well as those of the institutions or organizations with which they or the statements may be associated. In public statements providing psychological information or professional opinions or providing information about the availability of psychological products, publications, and services, psychologists base their statements on scientifically acceptable psychological findings and techniques with full recognition of the limits and uncertainties of such evidence.

a. When announcing or advertising professional services, psychologists may list the following information to describe the provider and services provided: name, highest relevant academic degree earned from a regionally accredited institution, date, type, and level of certification or licensure, diplomate status, APA membership status, address, telephone number, office hours, a brief listing of the type of psychological services offered, an appropriate presentation of fee information, foreign languages spoken, and policy with regard to third-party payments. Additional relevant or important consumer information may be included if not prohibited by other sections of these Ethical Principles.

b. In announcing or advertising the availability of psychological products, publications, or services, psychologists do not present their affiliation with any organization in a manner that falsely implies sponsorship or certification by that organization. In particular and for example, psychologists do not state APA membership or fellow status in a way to suggest that such status implies specialized professional competence or qualifications. Public statements include, but are not limited to, communication by means of periodical, book, list, directory, television, radio, or motion picture. They do not contain (i) a false, fraudulent, misleading, deceptive, or unfair statement; (ii) a misinterpretation of fact or a statement likely to mislead or deceive because in context it makes only a partial disclosure of relevant facts; (iii) a statement intended or likely to create false or unjustified expectations of favorable results.

c. Psychologists do not compensate or give anything of value to a representative of the press, radio, television, or other communication medium in anticipation of or in return for professional publicity in a news item. A paid advertisement must be identified as such, unless it is apparent from the context that it is a paid advertisement. If communicated to the public by use of radio or television, an advertisement is prerecorded and approved for broadcast by the psychologist, and a recording of the actual transmission is retained by the psychologist.

d. Announcements or advertisements of "personal growth groups," clinics, and agencies give a clear statement of purpose and a clear description of the experiences to be provided. The education, training, and experience of the staff members are appropriately specified.

e. Psychologists associated with the development or promotion of psychological devices, books, or other products offered for commercial sale make reasonable efforts to ensure that announcements and advertisements are presented in a professional, scientifically acceptable, and factually informative manner.

f. Psychologists do not participate for personal gain in commercial announcements or advertisements recommending to the public the purchase or use of proprietary or single-source products or services when that participation is based solely upon their identification as psychologists.

g. Psychologists present the science of psychology and offer their services, products, and publications fairly and accurately, avoiding misrepresentation through sensationalism, exaggeration, or superficiality. Psychologists are guided by the primary obligation to aid the public in developing informed judgments, opinions, and choices.

h. As teachers, psychologists ensure that statements in catalogs and course outlines are accurate and not misleading, particularly in terms of subject matter to be covered, bases for evaluating progress, and the nature of course experiences. Announcements, brochures, or advertisements describing workshops, seminars, or other educational programs accurately describe the audience for which the program is intended as well as eligibility requirements, educational objectives, and nature of the materials to be covered. These announcements also accurately represent the education, training, and experience of the psychologists presenting the programs and any fees involved.

i. Public announcements or advertisements soliciting research participants in which clinical services or other professional services are offered as an inducement make clear the nature of the services as well as the costs and other obligations to be accepted by participants in the research.

j. A psychologist accepts the obligation to correct others who represent the psychologist's professional qualifications, or associations with products or services, in a manner incompatible with these guidelines.

k. Individual diagnostic and therapeutic services are provided only in the context of a professional psychological relationship. When personal advice is given by means of public lectures or demonstrations, newspaper or magazine articles, radio or television programs, mail, or similar media, the psychologist utilizes the most current relevant data and exercises the highest level of professional judgment.

l. Products that are described or presented by means of public lectures or demonstrations, newspaper or magazine articles, radio or television programs, or similar media meet the same recognized standards as exist for products used in the context of a professional relationship.

PRINCIPLE 5: CONFIDENTIALITY

Psychologists have a primary obligation to respect the confidentiality of information obtained from persons in the course of their work as psychologists. They reveal such information to others only with the consent of the person or the person's legal representative, except in those unusual circumstances in which not to do so would result in clear danger to the person or to others. Where appropriate, psychologists inform their clients of the legal limits of confidentiality.

a. Information obtained in clinical or consulting relationships, or evaluative data concerning children, students, employees, and others, is discussed only for professional purposes and only with persons clearly concerned with the case. Written and oral reports present only data germane to the purposes of the evaluation, and every effort is made to avoid undue invasion of privacy.

b. Psychologists who present personal information obtained during the course of professional work in writings, lectures, or other public forums either obtain adequate prior consent to do so or adequately disguise all identifying information.

c. Psychologists make provisions for maintaining confidentiality in the storage and disposal of records.

d. When working with minors or other persons who are unable to give voluntary, informed consent, psychologists take special care to protect these persons' best interests.

PRINCIPLE 6: WELFARE OF THE CONSUMER

Psychologists respect the integrity and protect the welfare of the people and groups with whom they work. When conflicts of interest arise between clients and psychologists' employing institutions, psychologists clarify the nature and direction of their loyalties and responsibilities and keep all parties informed of their commitments. Psychologists fully inform consumers as to the purpose and nature of an evaluative, treatment, educational, or training procedure, and they freely acknowledge that clients, students, or participants in research have freedom of choice with regard to participation.

    a. Psychologists are continually cognizant of their own needs and of their potentially influential position vis-à-vis persons such as clients, students, and subordinates. They avoid exploiting the trust and dependency of such persons. Psychologists make every effort to avoid dual relationships that could impair their professional judgment or increase the risk of exploitation. Examples of such dual relationships include, but are not limited to, research with and treatment of employees, students, supervisees, close friends, or relatives. Sexual intimacies with clients are unethical.

    b. When a psychologist agrees to provide services to a client at the request of a third party, the psychologist assumes the responsibility of clarifying the nature of the relationships to all parties concerned.

    c. Where the demands of an organization require psychologists to violate these Ethical Principles, psychologists clarify the nature of the conflict between the demands and these principles. They inform all parties of psychologists' ethical responsibilities and take appropriate action.

    d. Psychologists make advance financial arrangements that safeguard the best interests of and are clearly understood by their clients. They contribute a portion of their services to work for which they receive little or no financial return.

    e. Psychologists terminate a clinical or consulting relationship when it is reasonably clear that the consumer is not benefiting from it. They offer to help the consumer locate alternative sources of assistance.

PRINCIPLE 7: PROFESSIONAL RELATIONSHIPS

Psychologists act with due regard for the needs, special competencies, and obligations of their colleagues in psychology and other professions. They respect the prerogatives and obligations of the institutions or organizations with which these other colleagues are associated.

a. Psychologists understand the areas of competence of related professions. They make full use of all the professional, technical, and administrative resources that serve the best interests of consumers. The absence of formal relationships with other professional workers does not relieve psychologists of the responsibility of securing for their clients the best possible professional service, nor does it relieve them of the obligation to exercise foresight, diligence, and tact in obtaining the complementary or alternative assistance needed by clients.

b. Psychologists know and take into account the traditions and practices of other professional groups with whom they work and cooperate fully with such groups. If a psychologist is contacted by a person who is already receiving similar services from another professional, the psychologist carefully considers that professional relationship and proceeds with caution and sensitivity to the therapeutic issues as well as the client's welfare. The psychologist discusses these issues with the client so as to minimize the risk of confusion and conflict.

c. Psychologists who employ or supervise other professionals or professionals in training accept the obligation to facilitate the further professional development of these individuals. They provide appropriate working conditions, timely evaluations, constructive consultation, and experience opportunities.

d. Psychologists do not exploit their professional relationships with clients, supervisees, students, employees, or research participants sexually or otherwise. Psychologists do not condone or engage in sexual harassment. Sexual harassment is defined as deliberate or repeated comments, gestures, or physical contacts of a sexual nature that are unwanted by the recipient.

e. In conducting research in institutions or organizations, psychologists secure appropriate authorization to conduct such research. They are aware of their obligations to future research workers and ensure that host institutions receive adequate information about the research and proper acknowledgment of their contributions.

f. Publication credit is assigned to those who have contributed to a publication in proportion to their professional contributions. Major contributions of a professional character made by several persons to a common project are recognized by joint authorship, with the individual who made the principal contribution listed first. Minor contributions of a professional character and extensive clerical or similar nonprofessional assistance may be acknowledged in footnotes or in an introductory statement. Acknowledgment through specific citations is made for unpublished as well as published material that has directly influenced the research or writing. Psychologists who compile and edit material of others for publication publish the material in the name of the originating group, if appropriate, with their own name appearing as chairperson or editor. All contributors are to be acknowledged and named.

g. When psychologists know of an ethical violation by another psychologist, and it seems appropriate, they informally attempt to resolve the issue by bringing the behavior to the attention of the psychologist. If the misconduct is of a minor nature and/or appears to be due to lack of sensitivity, knowledge, or experience, such an informal solution is usually appropriate. Such informal corrective efforts are made with sensitivity to any rights to confidentiality involved. If the violation does not seem amenable to an informal solution, or is of a more serious nature, psychologists bring it to the attention of the appropriate local, state, and/or national committee on professional ethics and conduct.

PRINCIPLE 8: ASSESSMENT TECHNIQUES

In the development, publication, and utilization of psychological assessment techniques, psychologists make every effort to promote the welfare and best interests of the client. They guard against the misuse of assessment results. They respect the client's right to know the results, the interpretations made, and the bases for their conclusions and recommendations. Psychologists make every effort to maintain the security of tests and other assessment techniques within limits of legal mandates. They strive to ensure the appropriate use of assessment techniques by others.

a. In using assessment techniques, psychologists respect the right of clients to have full explanations of the nature and purpose of the techniques in language the clients can understand, unless an explicit exception to this right has been agreed upon in advance. When the explanations are to be provided by others, psychologists establish procedures for ensuring the adequacy of these explanations.

b. Psychologists responsible for the development and standardization of psychological tests and other assessment techniques utilize established scientific procedures and observe the relevant APA standards.

c. In reporting assessment results, psychologists indicate any reservations that exist regarding validity or reliability because of the circumstances of the assessment or the inappropriateness of the norms for the person tested. Psychologists strive to ensure that the results of assessments and their interpretations are not misused by others.

d. Psychologists recognize that assessment results may become obsolete. They make every effort to avoid and prevent the misuse of obsolete measures.

e. Psychologists offering scoring and interpretation services are able to produce appropriate evidence for the validity of the programs and procedures used in arriving at interpretations. The public offering of an automated interpretation service is considered a professional-to-professional consultation. Psychologists make every effort to avoid misuse of assessment reports.

f. Psychologists do not encourage or promote the use of psychological assessment techniques by inappropriately trained or otherwise unqualified persons through teaching, sponsorship, or supervision.

PRINCIPLE 9: RESEARCH WITH HUMAN PARTICIPANTS

The decision to undertake research rests upon a considered judgment by the individual psychologist about how best to contribute to psychological science and human welfare. Having made the decision to conduct research, the psychologist considers alternative directions in which research energies and resources might be invested. On the basis of this consideration, the psychologist carries out the investigation with respect and concern for the dignity and welfare of the people who participate and with cognizance of federal and state regulations and professional standards governing the conduct of research with human participants.

a. In planning a study, the investigator has the responsibility to make a careful evaluation of its ethical acceptability. To the extent that the weighing of scientific and human values suggests a compromise of any principle, the investigator incurs a correspondingly serious obligation to seek ethical advice and to observe stringent safeguards to protect the rights of human participants.

b. Considering whether a participant in a planned study will be a "subject at risk" or a "subject at minimal risk," according to recognized standards, is of primary ethical concern to the investigator.

c. The investigator always retains the responsibility for ensuring ethical practice in research. The investigator is also responsible for the ethical treatment of research participants by collaborators, assistants, students, and employees, all of whom, however, incur similar obligations.

d. Except in minimal-risk research, the investigator establishes a clear and fair agreement with research participants, prior to their participation, that clarifies the obligations and responsibilities of each. The investigator has the obligation to honor all promises and commitments included in that agreement. The investigator informs the participants of all aspects of the research that might reasonably be expected to influence willingness to participate and explains all other aspects of the research about which the participants inquire. Failure to make full disclosure prior to obtaining informed consent requires additional safeguards to protect the welfare and dignity of the research participants. Research with children or with participants who have impairments that would limit understanding and/or communication requires special safeguarding procedures.

e. Methodological requirements of a study may make the use of concealment or deception necessary. Before conducting such a study, the investigator has a special responsibility to (i) determine whether the use of such techniques is justified by the study's prospective scientific, educational, or applied value; (ii) determine whether alternative procedures are available that do not use concealment or deception; and (iii) ensure that the participants are provided with sufficient explanation as soon as possible.

f. The investigator respects the individual's freedom to decline to participate in or to withdraw from the research at any time. The obligation to protect this freedom requires careful thought and consideration when the investigator is in a position of authority or influence over the participant. Such positions of authority include, but are not limited to, situations in which research participation is required as part of employment or in which the participant is a student, client, or employee of the investigator.

g. The investigator protects the participant from physical and mental discomfort, harm, and danger that may arise from research procedures. If risks of such consequences exist, the investigator informs the participant of that fact. Research procedures likely to cause serious or lasting harm to a participant are not used unless the failure to use these procedures might expose the participant to risk of greater harm, or unless the research has great potential benefit and fully informed and voluntary consent is obtained from each participant. The participant should be informed of procedures for contacting the investigator within a reasonable time period following participation should stress, potential harm, or related questions or concerns arise.

h. After the data are collected, the investigator provides the participant with information about the nature of the study and attempts to remove any misconceptions that may have arisen. Where scientific or humane values justify delaying or withholding this information, the investigator incurs a special responsibility to monitor the research and to ensure that there are no damaging consequences for the participant.

i. Where research procedures result in undesirable consequences for the individual participant, the investigator has the responsibility to detect and remove or correct these consequences, including long-term effects.

j. Information obtained about a research participant during the course of an investigation is confidential unless otherwise agreed upon in advance. When the possibility exists that others may obtain access to such information, this possibility, together with the plans for protecting confidentiality, is explained to the participant as part of the procedure for obtaining informed consent.

PRINCIPLE 10: CARE AND USE OF ANIMALS

An investigator of animal behavior strives to advance understanding of basic behavioral principles and/or to contribute to the improvement of human health and welfare. In seeking these ends, the investigator ensures the welfare of animals and treats them humanely. Laws and regulations notwithstanding, an animal's immediate protection depends upon the scientist's own conscience.

a. The acquisition, care, use, and disposal of all animals are in compliance with current federal, state or provincial, and local laws and regulations.

b. A psychologist trained in research methods and experienced in the care of laboratory animals closely supervises all procedures involving animals and is responsible for ensuring appropriate consideration of their comfort, health, and humane treatment.

c. Psychologists ensure that all individuals using animals under their supervision have received explicit instruction in experimental methods and in the care, maintenance, and handling of the species being used. Responsibilities and activities of individuals participating in a research project are consistent with their respective competencies.

d. Psychologists make every effort to minimize discomfort, illness, and pain of animals. A procedure subjecting animals to pain, stress, or privation is used only when an alternative procedure is unavailable and the goal is justified by its prospective scientific, educational, or applied value. Surgical procedures are performed under appropriate anesthesia; techniques to avoid infection and minimize pain are followed during and after surgery.

e. When it is appropriate that the animal's life be terminated, it is done rapidly and painlessly.

33

ETHICAL ISSUES IN PSYCHOTHERAPY RESEARCH: PROBLEMS IN A COLLABORATIVE CLINICAL TRIALS STUDY

STANLEY D. IMBER, LAWRENCE M. GLANZ, IRENE ELKIN, STUART M. SOTSKY, JENNY L. BOYER, AND WILLIAM R. LEBER

Curiously enough, there is little discussion in the literature regarding ethical problems that are present in the design and conduct of research in the psychotherapies. It seems unlikely that psychotherapy researchers are less sensitive to these matters than other researchers, but they may assume that the issues encountered in their investigations are not significantly different from those in the general or broader areas of psychological and behavioral research. In fact, however, there are more important ethical issues quite specific to psychotherapy work that deserve the careful attention of investigators (Imber, 1984).

In addition, there are two relatively recent developments in psychotherapy research—the increased use of controlled clinical trials and the advent of collaborative research arrangements—that make these issues

Reprinted from the *American Psychologist*, *41*, 137–146. Copyright 1986 by the American Psychological Association.

The NIMH Treatment of Depression Collaborative Research Program is a multisite program initiated and sponsored by the Psychosocial Treatments Research Branch, Division of Extramural Research Programs, NIMH, and is funded by Cooperative Agreements to seven participating sites.

more salient. The clinical trials paradigm is a relatively sophisticated design that focuses on experimental precision and controls, and collaborative work among investigators at different locations makes it possible to collect larger patient samples and data pools from more than a single site. All of these factors should allow for greater confidence in the validity and generalizability of findings. The methodological advantages of these procedures, however, are better understood than the ethical questions they raise.

This article describes a series of ethical issues that may be encountered in psychotherapy research and the ways they were addressed in the training/pilot phase of a large-scale collaborative study of two psychotherapies in which the research design was based on a clinical trials paradigm. Before we describe the research plan and ethical issues in executing the plan, it will be useful to review the literature on some of the ethical matters noted later in this presentation.

THE ISSUE OF INFORMED CONSENT

Current concepts of informed consent stem from relatively recent changes in cultural norms regarding the rights of the individual. It was only after the inhumane "medical" experiments conducted in Germany during the 1930s and 1940s that the Nuremberg Code (*Trials of War Criminals*, 1949) was developed, specifying that no category of persons is less worthy than any other. The Code stressed four major elements of informed consent: competence, voluntarism, full information, and comprehension. These elements are considered minimum requirements for assuring that self-determination of the individual is protected. Though greatly expanded, the same elements obtain in guidelines for the use of human subjects in research issued by the American Psychological Association (APA, 1981).

The concept of competence refers to the legal capacity of the subject to provide consent. Subjects must appreciate the nature and consequences of their participation in research studies. Competence requires that subjects be able to sort out relevant information in order to make a reasoned decision. Those who have difficulty reasoning, such as mentally retarded or psychotic subjects, must be protected, and court tests have generally placed stringent requirements on researchers to provide such protection. Controversial issues in the area of competence include guidelines for research with subjects who are not competent and clear criteria for the use of marginally competent subjects.

The issue of voluntarism also remains controversial. Patients have been asked to consent to experimental treatment when they were physically weak or overly motivated to be cooperative, or under a variety of other conditions that call into question the degree to which consent was fully voluntary and without distress (Schafer, 1982). Kelman (1972) noted that the experimental situation itself creates an inherent power advantage for the researcher over the subject, and he cautioned that subjects who occupy low-status or dependent positions in society are less likely to see themselves as having the option to refuse to participate. Reynolds (1979) suggested that research subjects should be selected only from higher socio-economic groups. The controversy highlights the continuing problems in defining what is meant by the term *voluntary*. Little research has been conducted in this area, perhaps because of the definitional difficulty. In a rare study, Fellner and Marshall (1970) suggested that family pressures may be especially influential in patients' "voluntary" decision making.

Provision of "full information" is an aspect of informed consent that has generated concern. Full information about research may be viewed as a contradiction in terms, because research ordinarily is conducted only where there is a lack of full information about the phenomenon under study. Also, some investigators apparently assume that certain informa-tion, if disclosed to patients, might be harmful or anxiety provoking, although empirical information on this point is sparse. One review of the medical literature (Lidz et al., 1984) cited equivocal evidence suggesting that although some patients suffer apprehensiveness or anxiety from dis-closure, other data indicate that informed patients are better prepared to face such serious procedures as major surgery. The practice recommended to the Department of Health, Education and Welfare was to advise poten-tial subjects fully of potential risks ("Protection of Human Subjects," 1975).

Comprehension is still another aspect of informed consent subject to varying interpretations. One study conducted for the National Commis-sion for the Protection of Human Subjects (1978) found that research consent forms contained language too complex for the average person. Grunder (1980) and Morrow (1980) have done work that support this finding, at least in medical research. Studies on the comprehensibility of psychiatric research (Carpenter, 1974; Siris, Docherty, & McGlashan, 1979) have suggested that psychiatric patients may have highly idiosyn-cratic ideas about research procedures. In a recent report on the results of the President's Commission for the Study of Ethical Problems in Medicine and Biomedical and Behavioral Research, Lasagna (1983) noted that lengthy and technical explanations of research procedures are not neces-sary, legally or ethically. Mutual respect of researcher and patient subjects was deemed to be at the heart of informed consent. Such matters are especially difficult for clinical investigators, who find themselves simulta-neously in the sometimes conflicting roles of helping agent and researcher.

THE ISSUE OF THE CONTROLLED CLINICAL TRIAL

The controlled clinical trial has become an increasingly popular experimental paradigm in medicine and pharmacology over the past three decades. The design refers to a controlled application of treatment procedures to patients with a specified disorder. As defined by Johnson (1983), the aim of the design is the efficient comparison of treatments. It may include, as a reference condition, a generally accepted treatment with known efficacy. It also includes standardized procedures for admitting subjects into the protocol and for evaluating the response to treatments. The design has only recently been put to use in psychotherapy studies, partly because of uncertainty that the conditions that make clinical trials appropriate for pharmacotherapy are relevant to psychotherapy.

The ethics of this research design have received little attention among psychotherapy investigators. Among the few commentators, DiMascio et al. (1979) and Richman, Weissman, Klerman, Neu, and Prusoff (1980), in discussing their work on the psychotherapy and pharmacotherapy of depression, have emphasized the need to achieve a balance between ensuring the safety of subjects and establishing the value of a therapeutic approach in adopting an appropriate control condition. Control techniques used in traditional research, such as waiting lists, nonspecific attention, and low or minimal contact, were considered too risky for depressed patients. They settled on a control condition comprising subject-initiated appointments. Patients in this condition received regular evaluations, could initiate appointments as needed, and were withdrawn from the protocol and referred for appropriate treatment when the frequency of their contacts exceeded once a month.

In pharmocology and medicine, Byar (1979) and Shaw and Chalmers (1970) are among a number of investigators who have described ethical problems in the use of the clinical trials design, such as the determination of an acceptable level of risk to subjects, and the proper circumstances for initiating a trial of a newly developed treatment. Lasagna (1979) pointed out the limited conclusions that can be drawn from clinical trials and suggested that they be supplemented by other methods, such as naturalistic studies.

Discussing randomized clinical trials of new cancer drugs, Marquis (1983) noted that the decision to undertake such a study often poses more difficult issues than the decision regarding when to terminate one. Where no scientific evidence exists that a new treatment may be of benefit, the decision to begin a series of clinical trials rests mainly on inferential, theoretical, and often very subjective grounds. Burkhardt and Kienle (1981, 1983) have asserted that pursuing a clinical trial beyond the establishment of a clear trend in the data subverts the doctor–patient relationship. The utilitarian standpoint on this issue is represented by Vere (1983), who argued for the ethical necessity of conducting rigorous trials that lead to optionally valid scientific conclusions. Vere's conclusions reflect the consensus on this issue at the Ditchley Park Conference ("The Scientific and Ethical Basis," 1980), which found that carefully constructed clinical trials are both ethically justified and necessary to the development of safe and effective medicine. The conference report stated that clinical investigators typically not only discharge their responsibilities to provide solicitous care to patients but are often supported by outstanding research and laboratory staffs and thus may provide better care than nonresearch physicians. The conferees stated that ethical researchers may discontinue trials that show an overwhelming trend, but more often it is ethically preferable to proceed with the entire sample. The conferees added that although risks to participants are an inevitable part of research, full informed consent results in a collaborative relationship between researcher and participant that adequately mitigates these risks.

One area of ethical concern that has received critical attention among psychotherapy investigators is that of placebos and placebo control groups (Paul, 1966; Shapiro, 1971). Despite the presumed inert nature of placebos, their utilization in research may do harm. O'Leary and Borkovec (1978) noted that sources of possible harm include "discomfort" due to deception, the deterring of patient-subjects from seeking active treatment, and frustration for subjects who fail to improve. The main argument for the use of a placebo is its value as the inefficacious control for comparison with the experimental treatment. O'Leary and Borkovec recommended that, when the risk to subjects is judged to be significant, alternatives to placebos should be used, such as the "best available" treatment or a standard reference condition against which to compare the untested treatments.

Although it has become accepted practice to fully inform potential subjects regarding their chances of being assigned to a placebo condition, Bok (1974) asserted that this is not sufficient to offset problems of implicit deception. In Bok's view, the setting of a hospital or doctor's office per se stimulates a sense of trust and faith conveying the impression that the prescribed remedy (even if a placebo) will lead to a beneficial outcome. She conceded that informed consent can help alleviate this problem but cautioned that reliance on placebo controls is excessive and warned that continuing use of this method affects the integrity of the investigator. Although Feinstein (1980) generally agreed that placebo controls are used more than necessary, he defended their value. He pointed out that in depressive disorders, for example, different patients may manifest a wide spectrum of symptoms and still be given the same diagnosis. This variability in clinical presentation may dilute the apparent effects of any one form of treatment. In such a case, the use of a placebo may be necessary to demonstrate that a medication is in fact superior to the placebo in relieving symptoms.

This brief review indicates the complexity of ethical issues in the conduct of experimental research. Unfortunately, there are few empirical investigations of ethics in psychotherapy research, as noted in a review by Haas, Fennimore, and Warburton (1983). Despite the increased use of clinical trials and of large-scale collaborative programs, the ethical questions raised by these advances are discussed only infrequently and subjected to empirical scrutiny even less often.

PROTOCOL OF THE NIMH TREATMENT OF DEPRESSION COLLABORATIVE RESEARCH PROGRAM

This report describes the principal ethical issues addressed in the design and implementation of the pilot phase of a multisite collaborative investigation utilizing a clinical trials design for evaluating the efficacy and safety of two forms of brief psychotherapy. Staff at seven sites participated in the program (see acknowledgment). Staff members at three research sites selected, evaluated, and treated patients suffering from nonbipolar major depressive disorder, in accordance with a common protocol. Staff members at three training sites were responsible for the training of therapists to certified standards, and those at one site were assigned the task of data analysis. An NIMH staff group (see acknowledgment) coordinated the overall activities and had developed the original research plan, taking into account ethical as well as methodological issues. A comprehensive description of the entire collaborative program may be found in Elkin, Parloff, Hadley, and Autry (1985).

The protocol involved the comparison of two forms of brief psychotherapy for the treatment of depression—cognitive–behavior therapy (Beck, Rush, Shaw, & Emery, 1979) and interpersonal psychotherapy (Klerman, Weissman, Rounsaville, & Chevron, 1984)—with a "standard reference" treatment (pharmacotherapy with the tricyclic antidepressant, imipramine). A double-blind placebo control condition was also included in the design to test the effectiveness of the medication as administered at the three research sites in this program, because only outpatients were treated in the protocol, and previous findings on imipramine had been derived principally from inpatient samples. The inclusion of a pill-placebo was deemed important also because of the variability of results reported both for imipramine and placebo response and for attrition rates in outpatient populations (Sotsky, Barnard, & Docherty, 1983).

All four treatments were designed to last 16 weeks, providing between 16 and 20 sessions, and were conducted in accord with the guidelines in treatment manuals provided by the training sites. Patients were assigned at random to one of four treatment conditions: cognitive–behavior therapy, interpersonal psychotherapy, imipramine, or a pill-placebo. The latter two treatments included a clinical management component. Patients did not pay fees for treatment. All treatment sessions and certain assessment interviews were video- and audiotaped.

Because several of the ethical issues to be discussed concern procedures in processing and evaluating patients, we will describe these procedures in some detail. Patients initially referred (from a variety of sources) as potentially eligible for the protocol were seen by trained clinical evaluators, who were psychologists and experienced clinicians. These evaluators conducted a standardized Schedule for Affective Disorders and Schizophrenia (SADS) interview (Endicott & Spitzer, 1978) and presented the case at a full research staff meeting during which decisions were made regarding patient qualifications and disposition. Patients were considered clinically eligible if they met Research Diagnostic Criteria (RDC) for a definite Major Depressive Disorder, namely, persistent depressed mood or pervasive loss of interest in normal activities, plus at least five of eight symptoms of depression, and impaired functioning or help seeking. Subjects were excluded if they were acutely suicidal or exhibited other severe psychopathology, such as psychotic features, bipolar affective disorder, or substance abuse.

Those patients who met inclusion criteria were given a thorough medical examination and were ruled out if a medical disorder was diagnosed that contraindicated the use of tricyclic antidepressant medication or that itself might be responsible for the depression. Following a rescreening one to two weeks after the first evaluation to assess the stability of the disorder, those subjects were admitted to the study who continued to meet RDC requirements and whose Hamilton scores (on a modified 17-item scale; Hamilton, 1967) persisted at 14 or more.

Patients were provided a detailed explanation of the research plan and the conditions of participation, including the four possible treatments and the fact of random assignment. This was done in the course of an unstructured interview that included an opportunity for responsive questions, conducted by the clinical evaluator or the project coordinator, who had the responsibility of ascertaining that patients comprehended the details of their participation and especially potential risks or costs. Patients who agreed to participate then signed consent forms that summarized information provided in the interview, for example, that treatment sessions would be videotaped and used for research purposes, that patients would be randomly assigned to one of the four treatments described, and that patients possessed the right to confidentiality and to withdraw from the study for any reason and at any point without penalty.

Patients received monthly assessment interviews conducted by the independent clinical evaluator during the course of treatment. In addition, an assessment was conducted at treatment termination and at a six-month follow-up point during the pilot phase (12- and 18-month follow-ups have since been added in the outcome study). Measures of patient status were made on a variety of instruments at the several evaluation points by patients, therapists, clinical evaluators, and significant other individuals. A list of these instruments may be found in Elkin et al. (1985).

THE ETHICAL ISSUES AND THEIR MANAGEMENT

The ethical issues denoted below and the account of how they were managed are organized in two categories: those related to the utilization of the clinical trials design and those that seem mainly a function of the collaborative nature of the research enterprise. With regard to clinical trials design, the following problems will be addressed: primacy of research staff in decision making on patient disposition; stipulation of specified treatment regimens rather than flexible clinical judgment; random treatment assignment without regard to patient preference; the appropriateness of placebo as a control condition; the waiting period for patients in acute crisis; debriefing and referral at termination; disposition of protocol "failures" and noncompliant patients.

Ethical issues to be discussed that may be particularly related to the collaborative format of the work are the following: ethical conduct as a collective or individual responsibility, site commitments to an adequate patient flow, the comprehensibility of informed consent forms; confidentiality in the use of audiovisual records, and security of data transmission.

Ethical Issues Related to the Clinical Trials Design

Primacy of Research Staff in Decision Making on Patient Disposition

In contrast to the usual treatment setting, in a clinical trials study the therapist is not consulted to determine acceptability of a particular patient for admission to the study. In addition, the therapist often has limited authority over whether a patient may be withdrawn from the protocol prior to completing treatment and whether referral for additional care is made when treatment is completed. In this clinical trials model, treatment qualification is determined by the independent clinical evaluator and research staff. Random assignment is made before the therapist sees the patient. The therapist may recommend withdrawal, but the principal investigator makes the ultimate recommendation, guided by the criteria previously drawn up. Similarly, referral for additional care at treatment termination is managed by the research staff and the principal investigator, with therapist recommendations considered but not necessarily decisive.

The ethical question here is the propriety of according ultimate authority to the research investigator in decisions that affect patient care and the apparent secondary consideration given the therapist. This is a common problem in applied research, and it reflects the difficulty in achieving a sensitive blending of the values of scientific research and practice. The tradition of science puts a special premium on rigorous methods, whereas clinical tradition places a primacy on patient care, even if that care at times must be based on tentative data or subjective judgment. These conflicting emphases of scientific and clinical method are at the center of several of the other ethical issues to be described.

In the present study, we dealt in several ways with the potential problem of research staff priority in decision making. The guidelines established for patient eligibility, withdrawal, and referral were based on clinical care considerations as well as on research purposes. Patients could drop out of the program unilaterally. The patients' preference and therapist's recommendations regarding withdrawal and referral tended to weigh heavily in the final decision. The independent clinical evaluations conducted monthly during treatment were also available on request by either patient or therapist. The evaluator had the prerogative to recommend withdrawal and/or referral. If differences in recommendations (for example, between therapist and clinical evaluator) could not be reconciled after staff conferencing, the matter would be reviewed by the independent senior clinician authorized to make the ultimate decision. The senior clinician at each site was a highly experienced psychiatrist with no clinical or administrative responsibilities in the study. The ethical relevance of the arbitration process was the provision of a means to offset the potential bias of the investigator to retain patients in the protocol as long as possible. The need for arbitration, however, was rare, occurring on a single occasion at one site.

Stipulation of Specified Treatment Regimens Rather Than Flexible Clinical Judgment

It has long been observed that the principled application of treatment depends at least as much on the ability to exercise the art of flexible clinical judgment as on the ability to use specific technical skills. A clinical trials study, however, ideally would ascertain that treatments are administered uniformly in accord with preestablished standards and that therapists meet particular performance criteria. Thus, the pilot phase of this program included the careful training, supervision, and continuous monitoring of therapist candidates, who were required to adhere closely to treatment manuals that provided guidelines for the treatment (Waskow, 1984).

The ethical question concerns the extent to which the research need to comply with a highly specific set of treatment "rules" may deprive therapists of flexibility in clinical judgment. It is clear that therapists have less opportunity to make free use of independent judgment in a clinical trials study than in usual clinical practice.

The manuals in the present study (Beck et al., 1979; Epstein & Fawcett, 1982; Fawcett & Epstein, 1980; Klerman et al., 1984) indeed specify procedures for therapists, but the instructions in each of them are more nearly broad guidelines and suggestions rather than rigid directives. Appropriate opportunities for individual clinical judgment are part of each of the three treatment methods. Nevertheless, therapists in this study occasionally expressed concern regarding what seemed to be restrictive conditions, such as the specified length of treatment, and pharmacotherapists sometimes viewed the proscription of psychotherapy interventions as constraining.

Random Treatment Assignment Despite Patient Preferences

Patients seeking treatment at any clinical setting often come with expectations or preferences regarding the treatments they will be offered. Even if these expectations or preferences are not met, patients probably anticipate that the treatment provided rests on a professional decision based on the evaluations they have undergone. As part of a clinical trials design, however, treatment assignment is made according to prespecified random order and is therefore unrelated to the evaluation findings, except for adherence to the inclusion and exclusion criteria. Unless patients insist on their treatment preferences, an action that automatically eliminates them from a study, they accept the condition of randomized assignment. Furthermore, each patient in this program has to accept the possibility that treatment assignment might be a pill-placebo, thus agreeing to an inactive medication as therapy for a four-month period.

The ethical issue is whether patients in a clinical trials study may be induced to accept the condition of random assignment, despite their prior treatment preference, by an enthusiastic research staff seeking to recruit as many candidates as possible. Do patients feel they really would have access to alternative treatments should they refuse the research protocol? In particular, we are concerned here with whether the nature of random assignment is understood and whether patient treatment preferences are observed, where appropriate.

In this program we attempted from the outset to cope with the question of randomization and patient preferences. During the recruitment or screening procedures, patients were given detailed information about the several treatments and told that they had no choice regarding which one they might ultimately be assigned. Every patient who insisted on a particular form of treatment or found one of the treatments unacceptable was provided with an alternative plan in the hospital setting or referral elsewhere.

Clinical evaluators and project coordinators were instructed not to exert pressure on potential patient candidates. There were no reported instances of patients later claiming they were misled or that their interests or needs were not respected. It is of interest to note that approximately 10% of patients at each site who did accept the condition of random assignment eventually dropped out, stating they preferred alternative treatment.

Appropriateness of Placebo as a Control Condition

The development of a satisfactory control for psychotherapy continues to defy the ingenuity of researchers. An adequate control would have to maintain the basic external structure of a particular psychotherapy without providing the specified active ingredients of that treatment. A pill-placebo may be viewed as a good approximation to a control condition, but it has serious deficiencies for that purpose. Typical activities engaged in by a pharmacotherapist are not used by the psychotherapist. These include the writing of prescriptions and dispensing of pills, questioning regarding somatic symptoms and side effects, and little effort to deal with interpersonal issues (specifically avoided in this protocol), except for the provision of support and encouragement. Thus, the pharmacotherapy session raises expectations of a process and mode of change and a patient role that are at variance with usual psychotherapeutic procedures.

The ethical question here relates to the assignment of patients to an inactive placebo treatment when "effective" treatments are available. Related to this question are the precautions taken to protect patients assigned to a double-blind, drug placebo condition.

The use of a pill-placebo in the present investigation is based upon design considerations quite different from those previously mentioned. The placebo was not posited as a control for the psychotherapy condition but rather as a control for the active medication, imipramine. As noted earlier, a clinical trials design permits the use of a standard reference treatment for comparison with the experimental treatment. In the present design, imipramine was the standard reference treatment selected. The use of the pill-placebo condition was deemed necessary, because the adequacy of the reference treatment could be challenged unless in efficacy was demonstrated for this sample.

The inclusion of the pill-placebo condition creates an even greater burden on investigators to protect subjects in the study. Safeguards included screening out individuals judged to be imminent suicidal risks, provision of regular contact with a pharmacotherapist, periodic independent evaluations, and the specification of a clear mechanism for patient withdrawal and referral to appropriate treatment.

The clinical management component of the pharmacotherapy condition was developed to ensure adequate clinical care throughout the treatment period, especially because of the inclusion of the placebo condition. This component comprised a weekly 20- to 30-minute session during which time the pharmacotherapist monitored symptoms and side effects, provided encouragement and support, and could provide direct advice when necessary.

The clinical management component essentially represented a balance between the integrity of the clinical trials design and adequate safeguards for patients assigned to the placebo condition. Of eight patients withdrawn for clinical deterioration and/or suicidal risk during the pilot study, only two had been receiving placebos. In addition, it should be noted that, at debriefing, placebo patients did not offer complaints when they learned their actual assignment.

The Waiting Period for Patients in Acute Crisis

In most clinical trials protocols, there may be fairly long delays before patients actually begin treatment. Usually such delays are due to extensive and multiple screening procedures and scheduling problems. In the present study, there was a delay of about three weeks (and occasionally longer) from the time of initial contact to treatment initiation.

The ethical problem relates to the fact that the clinical condition of patients in acute distress, including those with a high suicidal potential, might worsen considerably because treatment was not immediately provided. Are these patients put at unnecessary risk because of this situation? Can the long waiting period be justified?

In the present study, the principal reason for the wait had to do with the need to ascertain that a patient's clinical status did not fluctuate over time, thereby making the diagnosis uncertain. Thus, each patient was intensively interviewed by the clinical evaluator on two occasions during the intake period. In addition, patients who were taking certain drugs known to be contraindicated in combination with imipramine, or that would otherwise complicate outcome evaluations, entered a one- to two-week "wash-out" period, under the care and instructions of a physician. Also, patients underwent a comprehensive medical examination during this period to ensure that no medical condition existed that would disqualify them from participation in the program.

The protocol did provide for the timely management of patients in acute crisis prior to treatment assignment. When immediate treatment was deemed compelling, patients were removed from the screening process and promptly placed in appropriate treatment outside the program (e.g., hospitalized). We became aware during the pilot phase that patients who present a suicide risk often need special support during the screening–waiting period. Clinical evaluators took an active role in maintaining contact with these patients until they began treatment.

Referrals and Debriefing at Termination

Researchers interested in measuring possible persisting effects after therapy must confront the need of some patients for additional or supplementary treatments following the research treatment. On the one hand, if patients are provided with referrals, efforts to trace the long-term effects of the experimental treatment may be compromised, because follow-up evaluations are confounded by the introduction of a second treatment. On the other hand, adequate clinical care often may require that referrals be made. In addition, in a study such as the present one, in which active and placebo medication are administered double blind, breaking the blind at termination of treatment may influence evaluation and referral for further treatment during follow-up. When patients in the double blind medication condition have improved, there may appear no reason to break the blind immediately after treatment.

The ethical dilemma is how adequate clinical care can be assured during a naturalistic follow-up in the form of supplemental or additional treatments, when long-term results may thereby be confounded. Ethically, what procedures should the researcher follow to maintain good patient care as treatment ends? When is the proper time to debrief the pharmacotherapy patient?

In striking a balance between research values and good patient care, the investigators in this study made referral for further treatment at termination in accordance with the patient's improvement status at that time. All patients evaluated as unimproved were offered referrals. Patients evaluated as improved but who requested more treatment were encouraged to give their just concluded treatment a chance for further effect, but they were also provided with a follow-up appointment sooner than the routine six-month point, usually within one to two months. Furthermore, these patients were told to call for an even earlier appointment should they decide not to wait. In addition, marginally improved patients who did *not* request a referral at termination were nonetheless informed that they could receive a referral at any time should they request it. The treatment disposition of all patients was reviewed by the principal investigator and the research staff.

One group of patients in this program was unaware of the actual treatment they were receiving during the active treatment period. The pharmacotherapy patients were informed only at treatment termination of the nature of the pill that had been administered, that is, active medication or inert placebo. The determining factor for the investigators in arriving at the decision to disclose assignment at this point rather after follow-up, was the obvious lack of control over what might take place during the long follow-up interval. It seemed likely that some patients would seek additional forms of treatment, and these patients had an absolute need to know immediately what their experimental treatment was so that the information would be available in future treatment planning. Beyond this, however, it would seem ethically necessary that patients who had taken the risk of a placebo treatment be promptly and correctly informed at the conclusion of treatment. Once this information was divulged, considerations of alternative or further treatments were handled in the same way as already described for patients who were in one of the psychotherapy or active drug formats.

Disposition of Protocol "Failures" and Noncompliant Patients

Surely one of the more frustrating experiences for a research investigator is the loss, through dropout or withdrawal, of patients on whom there has been a considerable expenditure of time and energy in the form of assessment and treatment. For the researcher, these patients represent protocol "failures." They fail to complete the prescribed course of treatment, whether they are unilateral dropouts or patients withdrawn because of clinical deterioration or noncompliance with treatment requirements. In the present study there were, of course, dropouts and patients withdrawn because of noncompliance with their treatment formats, in the psychotherapies as well as in pharmacotherapy.

The ethical problem in this circumstance is how to ascertain that patients who provide so little in research returns and yet are so "costly" in time and effort receive full professional attention and appropriate services. The fact that they did not complete treatment suggests that they remained at risk and that efforts should be made to continue contact with them.

In this project, efforts were assiduously made to maintain contact and to provide consultation and referral for these patients. Such protocol "failure" patients continued to be scheduled for full-scale evaluations at the treatment termination point and at the follow-up period as well. Appropriate consultation and referrals were provided at these times.

Ethical Issues Related to the Collaborative Nature of the Research

Ethical Conduct as a Collective or an Individual Responsibility

In the planning and execution of a research endeavor, the burden of ethical responsibility ordinarily is placed directly on the individual investigator. In a collaborative arrangement, however, the design and its implementation involve a joint set of activities among various collaborating groups, and responsibility tends to be diffused. The present study is a case in point. There were agreed-upon procedures for almost every research and clinical activity, from the techniques for recruiting patients to the security of data, and from the precise criteria for excluding patient candidates to the methods for withdrawing patients from treatment. There was regular communication among the collaborating sites and NIMH. Particularly difficult issues, especially those that touched on ethical concerns, tended to receive close attention.

The ethical issue concerns whether the intimacy of a collaborative arrangement, which can foster a comfortable sense of shared, collective responsibility, diminishes the sense of individual accountability, which is the essence of ethical conduct. Can individual investigators retain a sense of responsible control over their work?

In this program we attempted to deal with the issue in a number of ways. For example, it was decided that when questions of individual patient care arose, decisions could not be made at a distance or collectively. Consultation and advice might be sought from other staff and from collaborating investigators, but the final decision was unambiguously that of the individual investigator at each site.

A quite different matter affecting individual ethical responsibility in collaborative projects has to do with publications issuing from the research. Typically, these involve listings of lengthy, multiple authorship because so many individuals at the several sites are directly involved in the work. Ethically, every coauthor is accountable for the basic integrity of a published report, but this obligation becomes inordinately difficult for the sixth and seventh author in a listing. To assist with this kind of problem and other issues, a publication board was established, comprising the principal investigator at each of the participating sites and representatives from NIMH. Prior to submission for publication, every manuscript is reviewed and approved for scientific integrity, as well as for authorship credit and citation.

Site Commitments to an Adequate Patient Flow

One important reason for bringing together several research institutions to work cooperatively on a common plan of research is the need to accumulate a sizable sample of subjects, ordinarily a most difficult task at any one site. Research sites in a collaborative enterprise make a kind of "commitment" to produce and maintain a good patient "flow." Although there was variability among the sites in this study with respect to the ease with which they were able to meet patient flow expectations, each site did experience continuing pressure to recruit patients and maintain them in the program.

The possible ethical question here is whether an effort to recruit patients may generate a large pool of patient candidates many of whom do not meet the criteria for acceptance in the program. Did the researchers spread their net too wide and stimulate expectations among patient candidates that would not be met? Were adequate efforts made to screen out promptly those who were unqualified?

In the present program, the process for screening patients produced a large number (more than 50%) who were excluded after presenting themselves for the initial screening. Clearly, there were many patients who experienced an imposition on their time and keen disappointment, although, where appropriate, alternate referrals were made.

Depending on local circumstances, the sites adopted different methods of patient recruitment, including the use of media sources, for example, press and television interviews in which the program might be mentioned (but not described in detail). If there was an ethical infringement in these actions, it took the form of investigator failure to anticipate the large number of patients who might possibly be dissatisfied and frustrated because they did not qualify after responding to what may have been too wide an "invitation" to participate. It should be noted, however, that the exclusion criteria were necessary to protect patients from being inappropriately included in the study, for example, where patients had medical contraindications, were imminently suicidal, or had another form of mental illness for which the experimental treatments were not appropriate. The balance between disappointing patients and protecting them is not easy to achieve.

Comprehensibility of Informed Consent Forms

It is a paradoxical consequence of the increased scrutiny of human use committees and institutional review boards that informed consent procedures have become so lengthy, detailed, and cumbersome that they may defeat the central purpose of informed disclosure. In addition, collaborative studies require explanation of the details of the relationship among the multiple sites and thus add further complexities to an already tedious procedure. In the present study, the contingencies of the research plan were numerous, including the screening and evaluation procedures, the several treatment methods, the video- and audiotaping provisions, the benefits and risks for participants, and so on. In the end, the patients had to deal with consent forms comprising a total of 2,000 words.

The ethical question is whether there can be sufficient comprehension of the procedures to permit a conclusion of fully informed consent, when the process is highly complex, detailed, and lengthy. Do some patients consent when in fact they may be intimidated by the intricacies of the procedures described? Do others become confused and refuse to participate, despite initial expressions of interest?

We attempted to cope with this problem in the study by carefully instructing the staff responsible for obtaining patient consent to interview each patient with considerable care regarding their understanding of the program. Patients were given time to consider privately the written materials presented them (e.g., to discuss them with family members or friends), and staff members were careful to avoid pressure on seemingly reluctant patients. Approximately 6% of all patient candidates who had met the screening criteria found the conditions of the study unacceptable for one reason or another and refused to sign the forms. Some, we suspect, were confused or put off by the complexity and lengthy details of the consent process.

An additional problem pertains to this project because of the nature of the disorder under study and the associated symptoms: Depressed patients frequently evidence memory and concentration deficits, and their information-processing system may become easily overloaded. It is possible that some patients were overwhelmed by the procedures and consented without adequate comprehension despite the best efforts of the research staff. There is, however, no certain way of knowing to what extent this occurred. We do know that among those patients who unilaterally dropped out of the program and who therefore might be expected to be especially critical of their experience in the study, none indicated there was misinformation or lack of information about any procedures or activities.

Confidentiality in the Use of Audiovisual Records

Large collaborative research programs, because of their size and complexity, often include procedures, data collection, and information not routinely found in less ambitious investigations. In this study, the collection of audiovisual tapes of treatment that were made during the course of the program represents just such a source of valued but relatively rare materials. In the interest of collegial cooperation and scientific advancement, the special materials derived from these large programs may be made available to other researchers. However, videotapes represent an uncommon form of patient records, because they provide both visual and auditory clues to patient identification and there is no easy means of removing clues without damaging the unique aspects of the materials that made them of special value in the first instance.

The ethical issue hinges on the adequacy of the precautions taken by the investigators to protect the privacy and confidentiality of patients when highly sensitive materials may be released and patients' anonymity cannot be fully guaranteed. Are investigators sufficiently alert to circumstances that increase the probability of patient identification?

In this study, explicit consent was obtained at intake for use of tapes for research purposes by authorized professional personnel, but patients were not required to consent to the possible dissemination of the tapes for training or teaching purposes as a condition for participation in the program. In fact, that consent was not requested until treatment had been completed, an important consideration because only then could patients know what they had disclosed in their sessions. Patients were informed that all tapes would be coded, with no names attached, and that names or identifying information would not be included in reports of the research.

However, the program participants became increasingly uncertain about releasing the tapes for training purposes outside the research program itself. Although professionals who make use of such materials are generally known to be sensitive to the issue of confidentiality, the recent proliferation of large workshops in therapy training could make the strict observance of privacy rules difficult to control. An increasing awareness of these difficulties during the pilot study has prompted a decision to restrict the use of these materials for training purposes to the collaborative personnel.

Security of Data Transmission

A typical feature of most multisite research programs, including this one, is that data storage and major analyses are done at a single, central facility. This fact means that staff at each site must transmit data to that facility, usually through the mails, and that there will be occasions when information exchange is necessary via telephone. In addition, periodic report summaries are likely to be transmitted back to the several sites from the data analysis facility.

The ethical problem concerns the procedures set up to assure the security of data transmission of confidential information via the public mails. Are these procedures adequate to protect privacy should the materials become lost?

In this program, the key procedure to the maintenance of security is the use of coding schemes for every datum transmitted. A research assistant at each site has the principal responsibility for the reduction to preset codes of information on all scales and questionnaires. This system has come into general use in multisite investigations and has been found to be efficient, with a high level of security. The central data facility in this collaborative program, moreover, has served that function in other large multisite investigations.

Even should the coded data be lost or misdirected in transmission, the materials are sufficiently disguised to prevent identification, and thus the system gives high assurance of protection of the confidentiality of the information provided. The collaborative program experienced no problems in this regard over the period of the pilot study.

DISCUSSION

This article focused on certain ethical issues in psychotherapy research and discussed how they were addressed in the conduct of a pilot study that preceded a major experimental investigation of psychotherapy outcomes. The specific problems described were presented as derivative of a clinical trials design and multisite collaborative arrangements. Although we focused on a variety of problems, it is important to recognize that significant positive ethical values also derive from these experimental procedures. The scientific rigor of a clinical trials design and the large sample sizes available in a multisite efforts seem more likely to yield valid and broadly generalizable findings than other alternative experimental procedures. The production of such findings surely could reduce the potential harm to human subjects in the use of unproven, uncontrolled, or innovative treatments where efficacy and safety tend to be poorly evaluated, if at all. Furthermore, collaborative arrangements have the virtue of permitting collective scrutiny and open collegial discussion of the many ethical issues that come up, especially in a large and long-term research program. These advantages must be weighed against the potential ethical difficulties cited in the body of this article.

The fact that this report is based on experience in a pilot study is also worthy of note. A carefully planned and systematically executed pilot study makes it possible to identify and to resolve outstanding ethical issues in advance of a main study. The opportunity, prior to the major study, to modify some of the conditions that helped create the issues has obvious advantages. Nevertheless, many of the most troubling issues indeed are not easily resolvable and present continuing dilemmas to the investigator. This is true for most of the problems described in the body of this article. For example, in our discussion of informed consent procedures, we made reference to the importance of the voluntary aspects of consent given by a participating human subject. Patients should understand that they may refuse an invitation to participate in a study and that they will be eligible for all the alternative services in the institution, and, should they consent to participate, they will be free to withdraw or drop out without penalty and with the provision of appropriate referrals. Yet voluntary consent is not easily defined, and the very nature of many psychiatric disorders complicates the problem further. In the case of depression, the volitional quality of an agreement is not easy to determine in the face of certain common features of the disorder, such as dependency, anxiety, apathy, and overcompliance.

Many of the ethical issues described in this article will be recognized as present and equally problematic in clinical research other than psychotherapy, such as drug studies. The increasing similarity of designs and procedures in the general field of efficacy studies partly accounts for this fact of shared issues and indicates that outcome investigations of structurally quite different treatment techniques are likely nonetheless to encounter similar problems that may have common resolutions.

Finally, the investigators in this study learned much about the necessity of making practical decisions about complex ethical issues. Given the sparsity of published reports on ethical considerations in the execution of psychotherapy research studies, the importance of other investigators presenting the ethical problems encountered in their work and the decisions made about them cannot be too strongly emphasized.

REFERENCES

American Psychological Association. (1981). Ethical principles of psychologists. *American Psychologist, 36*, 633–638.

Beck, A. T., Rush, A. J., Shaw, B. F., & Emery, G. (1979). *Cognitive therapy of depression*. New York: Guilford Press.

Bok, S. (1974). The ethics of giving placebos. *Scientific American, 231*, 17–23.

Burkhardt, R., & Kienle, G. (1981). Controlled trials—A social challenge. *European Journal of Clinical Pharmacology, 20*, 311–319.

Burkhardt, R., & Kienle, G. (1983). Basic problems in controlled trials. *Journal of Medical Ethics, 9*, 80–84.

Byar, D. P. (1979). The practical and ethical defects of surgical randomized prospective trials. In H. J. Tagnon & M. J. Stagnet (Eds.), *Controversies in cancer: Design of trials and treatment* (pp. 75–82). New York: Masson.

Carpenter, W. (1974). A new setting for informed consent. *Lancet, 1,* 500–501.

DiMascio, A., Klernman, G. L., Weissman, M. M., Prusoff, B. A., Neu, C., & Moore, P. (1979). A control group for psychotherapy research in acute depression: One solution to ethical and methodologic issues. *Journal of Psychiatric Research, 15,* 189–197.

Elkin, I., Parloff, M. B., Hadley, S. W., & Autry, J. H. (1985). The NIMH Treatment of Depression Collaborative Research Program: Background and research plan. *Archives of General Psychiatry, 42,* 305–316.

Endicott, J., & Spitzer, R. L. (1978). A diagnostic interview: The schedule for affective disorders and schizophrenia. *Archives of General Psychiatry, 35,* 837–844.

Epstein, P. S., & Fawcett, J. (1982). *Addendum to clinical-management-imipramine-placebo administration manual: NIMH Treatment of Depression Collaborative Research Program.* Chicago: Rush Presbyterian–St. Luke's Medical Center.

Fawcett, J., & Epstein, P. (1980). *Clinical-management-imipramine-placebo administration manual: NIMH Psychotherapy of Depression Collaborative Research Program.* Chicago: Rush Presbyterian–St. Luke's Medical Center.

Feinstein, A. R. (1980). Should placebo-controlled trials be abolished? *European Journal of Pharmacology, 17,* 1–4.

Fellner, C. H., & Marshall, J. R. (1970). Kidney donors—The myth of informed consent. *American Journal of Psychiatry, 126,* 1245–1251.

Grunder, T. M. (1980). On the readability of surgical consent forms. *New England Journal of Medicine, 302,* 900–902.

Haas, L. J., Fennimore, D., & Warburton, J. R. (1983). A bibliography on ethical and legal issues in psychotherapy, 1970–1982. *Professional Psychology Research and Practice, 14,* 771–779.

Hamilton, M. (1967). Development of a rating scale for primary depressive illness. *British Journal of Social and Clinical Psychology, 6,* 278–296.

Imber, S. D. (1984, May). *The ethics of psychotherapy research.* Address given at symposium in honor of Jerome D. Frank, Johns Hopkins University, Baltimore, MD.

Johnson, A. L. (1983). Clinical trials in psychiatry. *Psychological Medicine, 13,* 1–8.

Jonas, H. (1969). Philosophical reflections on experimenting with human subjects. *Daedalus, 98,* 219–247.

Kelman, H. C. (1972). The rights of the subject in social research: An analysis in terms of relative power and legitimacy. *American Psychologist, 27,* 989–1016.

Klerman, G. L., Weissman, M. M., Rounsaville, B. J., & Chevron, E. S. (1984). *Interpersonal psychotherapy of depression.* New York: Basic Books.

Lasagna, L. (1979). Placebos and controlled clinical trials under attack. *European Journal of Clinical Pharmacology, 15,* 373–374.

Lasagna, L. (1983). The professional-patient dialogue. *The Hastings Center Report, 13,* 9–11.

Lidz, C. W., Meisel, A., Zerubavel, E., Carter, M., Sestak, R. M., & Roth, L. H.

(1984). *Informed consent: A study of decisionmaking in psychiatry.* New York: Guilford Press.

Marquis, D. (1983). Leaving therapy to chance. *The Hastings Center Report, 13,* 40–47.

Morrow, G. R. (1980). How readable are subject consent forms? *Journal of the American Medical Association, 244,* 56–58.

National Commission for the Protection of Human Subjects of Biomedical and Behavioral Research (1978). Institutional review boards: Report and recommendation. *Federal Register, 43,* 56/74–56/98.

O'Leary, K. D., & Borkovec, T. D. (1978). Conceptual, methodological, and ethical problems of placebo groups in psychotherapy research. *American Psychologist, 33,* 821–830.

Paul, G. L. (1966). *Insight versus desensitization in psychotherapy.* Stanford, CA: Stanford University Press.

Protection of human subjects, 40 *Fed. Reg.* 11, 854(1975).

Reynolds, P. D. (1979). *Ethical dilemmas and social science research.* San Francisco: Jossey-Bass.

Richman, J., Weissman, M. M., Klerman, G. L., Neu, C., & Prusoff, B. A. (1980, February). Ethical issues in clinical trials: Psychotherapy research in acute depression. *IRB: A Review of Human Subjects Research, 2,* (2), 1–4.

Schafer, A. (1982). The ethics of the randomized clinical trials. *New England Journal of Medicine, 307,* 719–724.

The scientific and ethical basis of the clinical evaluation of medicines: Report of an international conference, held as a guest conference at the Ditchley Foundations, Ditchley Park, England, September 13–16, 1979. (1980). *European Journal of Clinical Pharmacology, 18,* 129–134.

Shapiro, A. K. (1971). Placebo effects in medicine, psychotherapy and psychoanalysis. In A. E. Bergin & S. L. Garfield (Eds.), *Handbook of psychotherapy and behavior change* (pp. 439–473). New York: Wiley.

Shaw, L. W., & Chalmers, T. (1970). Ethics in cooperative clinical trials. *Annals of the New York Academy of Sciences, 169,* 487–495.

Siris, S., Docherty, J., & McGlashan, T. (1979). Intrapsychic structural effects of psychiatric research. *American Journal of Pyschiatry, 136,* 1567–1571.

Sotsky, S. M., Barnard, N., & Docherty, J. (1983, July). *The anti-depressant efficacy of imipramine in outpatient studies.* Paper presented at the World Congress of Psychiatry, Vienna, Austria.

Trials of war criminals before the Nuremberg military tribunals under control council law no. 10. (1949). Washington, DC: U.S. Government Printing Office.

Vere, D. W. (1983). Problems in controlled clinical trials—A critical response. *Journal of Medical Ethics, 9,* 85–89.

Waskow, I. E. (1984). Specification of the technique variable in the NIMH Treatment of Depression Collaborative Research Program. In J. B. W. Williams & R. L. Spitzer (Eds.), *Psychotherapy research: Where are we and where should we go?* (pp. 150–159). New York: Guilford Press.

34

HUMAN SUBJECTS REVIEW, PERSONAL VALUES, AND THE REGULATION OF SOCIAL SCIENCE RESEARCH

STEHPEN J. CECI, DOUGLAS PETERS, AND JONATHAN PLOTKIN

Currently there is some dissatisfaction among social scientists with the concept of peer review, if not in principle at least as it is practiced (e.g., Bradley, 1981, 1982; Peters & Ceci, 1982). Crane (1967) alleged that journal editors, in their role as the "gate-keepers of science" (p. 195), employ extrascientific criteria to filter acceptable from unacceptable manuscripts. Since Crane made her claim, social scientists have focused attention on several extrascientific aspects of the peer review process for journals, including allegations of bias against authors affiliated with low-prestige institutions (Ceci & Peters, 1982; Peters & Ceci, 1982), bias against the publication of controversial findings (Goodstein & Brazis, 1970; Mahoney, 1977, 1979), poor reliability among reviewers' recommendations (Cicchetti, 1980, 1982; Cicchetti & Eron, 1979; Inglefinger, 1974; Watkins, 1979; also see Scarr & Weber, 1978; Whitehurst, 1984), and the effective-

Reprinted from the *American Psychologist*, 40, 994–1002. Copyright 1985 by the American Psychological Association.

This research was supported, in part, by grants from the College of Human Ecology, Cornell University, to S. J. Ceci, and from Division 9 of APA to D. Peters.

ness and public perception of practices such as blind reviewing (Bradley, 1981; Ceci & Peters, 1984).

The attention given to journal reviewing has led to the acknowledgment that, in many instances, the true gatekeepers of science may not be journal editors and reviewers but rather funding agencies' review panels and study groups. Decisions of funding agencies frequently dictate the form of research that later will be submitted for journal review. So, in a very real sense, it is the funding review process that occupies the gatekeeping function of filtering acceptable from unacceptable ideas. Consequently, researchers have started to turn their attention to factors suspected of influencing the reliability and fairness of funding decisions, including characteristics of the principal investigator (Chubin & Gillespie, 1984; Stark-Adamec & Adamec, 1981), characteristics of the reviewers (Cole, Cole, & Simon, 1981; Mitroff & Chubin, 1979), and characteristics of the research itself (Chubin & Gillespie, 1984; Mahoney, 1979; National Commission on Research, 1980). As a result of the attention given to the peer review process practiced by both journals and funding agencies, important knowledge about the early filtration of research has been gained, including factors that diminish the reliability and validity of the review process.

A case can be made, however, that there exists an even earlier filtration process that has yet to be examined for its gatekeeping function: the role played by human subjects committees (or institutional review boards—IRBs for short) in the regulation of research. Often, the first step (a required one in most cases) in undertaking research is to obtain the approval of one's IRB for the proposed treatment of human subjects. Yet, far more is known about far less important matters than about the functioning of IRBs. What knowledge does exist is an amalgam of facts, inferences, and suspicions. If IRB decisions were confined to the mandated considerations of the physical and mental risks to prospective research participants, further scrutiny along the lines we shall describe might not be warranted. However, there is mounting suspicion that in addition to their consideration of physical and mental risks, IRBs employ sociopolitical considerations in their judgments in ways that are explicitly prohibited by their federal mandate. Moreover, there is a growing awareness that social scientists' perceptions of their IRBs' political and social values influence their selection of research topics in ways that may be counterproductive to the development of the science (de Sola Pool, 1979; Glynn, 1978; Seiler & Murtha, 1980). Because no empirical, let alone experimental, study of these issues yet exists, we will describe some provocative findings from a recent study we conducted. But first it is useful to review some background information about IRBs that serves to underscore the importance of gaining direct knowledge of IRB decision making.

CHARACTERISTICS OF IRBs

How Extensive Is the IRB Process?

The Department of Health and Human Services (DHHS) requires IRB approval of a research proposal as a precondition for the release of its funds, as do most federal agencies, institutes, and foundations. Increasingly, private tax-exempt foundations have also begun to require IRB approval as a condition of funding, as a quick perusal of their literature will confirm. Perhaps more important, all institutions that receive DHHS funds are required to include an institutional assurance agreement in the materials they provide to DHHS, describing their policy governing the review of all research proposals, regardless of their funding (Chalkey, 1975). This agreement must describe how institutions intend to comply with federal standards. IRB review of nonfunded research proposals (i.e., cases in which investigators do not intend to pursue outside funding) has not been mandated since the 1981 revisions to the DHHS regulations ("Protection of Human Subjects," 1981) were adopted; however, review of nonfunded research is considered evidence of an "institutional willingness to afford human subjects protection" ("Human Research Subjects," 1981, p. 8366) and, by implication, "an institutional worthiness that justifies the receipt of federal funds" (Reynolds, 1982).[1] Consequently, in 1976 it was reported that 92% of all IRBs mandated the routine review of all proposals, not just those that are, or hope to be, funded (see Reynolds, 1982). An updated statistic in 1981 is remarkably close to this 1976 figure, with 91% of the 437 multiple-project assurances promising to use the same procedures to review funded as well as nonfunded research (Office of Protection from Research Risk, personal communication, June 1984).

How Expensive Is the IRB Process?

On the basis of two surveys, Cohen (1982, 1983) determined that the average IRB review of a proposal costs $160, taking into account the modal

---

[1] Prior to the adoption of the 1981 revisions, some researchers, angered over a broad interpretation of DHHS's standards, charged that requiring nonfunded research to be reviewed by an IRB whenever the researcher's institution received DHHS funds for other projects amounted to a First Amendment violation entailing prior review and restraint (Reynolds, 1982).

size of committees, the size of stipends paid to noninstitutional members, clerical support, and the assumption that institutional members of the IRB would be able to invest their time in other supported activities (e.g., teaching, research, advising, or other committee work) in lieu of attending IRB meetings and reviewing proposals. Cohen estimated that this potential redeployment of faculty members' time and the concomitant savings in clerical costs and external stipends would save U.S. institutions tens of millions of dollars annually. (However, in considering the financial aspects of IRBs, we need to bear in mind that IRBs have probably obviated a number of ethically questionable and dangerous practices that could have resulted in injury and death to subjects and costly liability suits against universities. Against the backdrop of litigation, the financial costs of IRBs might be regarded as a sound insurance policy in the event that they prevent even a single case of malfeasance.)

How Reliable Is the IRB Process?

Eaton (1983) reported an analysis of 111 research proposals of psychologists that were reviewed over a 10-month period by experienced reviewers (other members of the psychology department) for their treatment of human subjects. He found that reviewers were in agreement only 8% of the time (after correction for chance) regarding the appropriateness of the proposals for use with human subjects. These findings led him to remark that "reliability in ethics reviews cannot, it seems, be assumed or taken for granted" (Eaton, 1983, p. 17). Some have questioned whether reliability among IRB members is, in fact, something inherently desirable and worth striving for. Doob (1983) has argued that the role played by IRB members should not be likened to the "fact finder" role played by members of a jury. Rather, IRB members are selected to be representatives of different community values. Hence, diversity of opinions about the acceptability of research for use with human subjects is not only inevitable but also valuable. "Very high levels of agreement in ethical judgments may not be desirable; indeed, I would suggest that we even consider the view that high levels of agreement . . . reflect an inadequate sampling of views" (Doob, 1983, p. 269). However, to a researcher whose proposal is rejected or modified because of concerns expressed by only some members of an IRB, such an argument is likely to lack persuasiveness, especially if an IRB at a nearby institution has already approved a similar protocol, a real possibility facing collaborators employed at different institutions located in the same or neighboring communities. (Existing guidelines require the signed agreement of one IRB that it accepts the judgment of the other; hence it is necessary for each collaborator's IRB to be at least somewhat involved.)

Finally, there is some suggestion that members of IRBs tend to be more cautious in their risk assessments than either investigators or prospective subjects (Smith, 1981; Smith & Berard, 1982). For example, Smith and Berard (1982) asked students to evaluate the appropriateness of Solomon Asch's (1955) classic study of conformity for use with human subjects. They found that asking students to assume the role of IRB members who were called upon to decide the appropriateness of Asch's study resulted in their making significantly more restrictive judgments than when they were to participate in the study.

THE ROLE OF PERSONAL VALUES IN IRB REVIEW

In the most recent study of attitudes toward IRBs, Gray and Cook (1980) surveyed over 2,000 researchers at 61 institutions, including 800 IRB members. They found evidence of a growing dissatisfaction with some aspects of the IRB process: "Approximately one half of researchers said that their research had been impeded in a way that was not balanced by benefits of the review process" (p. 40). Because of the seriousness of allegations made against the IRB process—for example, that oblique sociopolitical values influence their decisions, and that there is a lack of scientfically adequate data for a critical evaluation—the following experimental study was carried out between August 1981 and February 1984.

Nine sample research proposals were developed, one of which was sent at random to each of the 375 university IRBs in the United States. The chairpersons of the IRBs were asked to participate in a study of factors presumed to influence IRB members' judgments by having their committees review the sample proposals sent to them. It was stressed that committees' reviews should be as naturalistic as possible and that the chairpersons should treat the sample proposals as if they were actually submitted by their own faculty members for consideration. No other details of the study or its hypotheses were divulged in order to avoid compromising the design.

All nine sample proposals dealt with an investigation of hiring discrimination, in particular, discrimination in the hiring of managerial positions by Fortune 500 corporations. The design was a 3×3 factorial representing three types of proposals, characterized by varying degrees of ethical problems or areas of special IRB consideration, within each of three levels of social sensitivity. The three levels of ethical problems were: (a) those involving only the use of deception (which is technically permissible in certain circumstances); (b) those involving the use of deception as well as a failure to debrief subjects at the conclusion of the study (which is impermissible under the DHHS general requirements for informed consent

["Protection of Human Subjects," 1981, pt. 46.116] except in the event that debriefing would endanger the subject); and (c) those involving no technical violations, according to the DHHS guidelines ("Protection of Human Subjects," 1981, pts 46.111–46.115). The three levels of social sensitivity were: (a) discrimination proposals that proposed to examine discrimination against minorities and women in corporate hiring practices (i.e., to document that minorities and women who possessed superior credentials and work histories were being bypassed in favor of white males possessing fewer qualifications); (b) reverse discrimination proposals that proposed to document discrimination against white males in corporate hiring (i.e., to examine the possibility that minorities and women who possessed inferior credentials and work histories were being given preferential treatment over white males possessing superior qualifications); and (c) nonsensitive proposals that proposed to examine discrimination against obese and short individuals (with no mention of race or sex) in the hiring practices of Fortune 500 corporations.

The nine sample proposals were similar in their wording and identical in their treatment of the prospective human subjects, who in all cases were to be personnel officers of Fortune 500 corporations. The only changes in wording were those made to emphasize the socially sensitive nature of some of the proposals. The following quotations are taken from the three types of proposals that were sent to IRBs for review and are illustrative of the differential social sensitivities that were examined. (Within each of these three types of proposals we varied the level of technical violations.) First, consider some key sections from the politically sensitive discrimination proposal, "A Proposed Study of Possible Discrimination in the Affirmative Action Hiring Practices of Fortunate 500 Corporations":

> This proposal is to examine factors associated with an applicant's success in obtaining managerial-level positions in business. We are particularly interested in applicants' physical characteristics (specifically their race and sex) and whether this might influence their being invited to interview for a position with a Fortune 500 corporation. The proposed study attempts to examine this issue of documented bias in naturalistic settings where variables can be controlled in order to rule out alternative explanations. It is hoped that the power of the proposed design will enable researchers to establish the magnitude of bias against minorities and women. . . . By conducting multiple comparisons of the interview rates in response to superior vitae, with those associated with inferior applicants, it will be possible to document the extent of bias against well-qualified minority and female applicants and to further strengthen the mounting the evidence of prejudice in corporate hiring. . . . At present, popularly held beliefs regarding "reverse discrimination" are little more than slogans, lacking sound empirical support, as the present study will attempt to demonstrate.

As can be seen from the above quotation, the proposals were not worded in the oblique language of some social science research but clearly displayed the hypothetical investigator's sociopolitical beliefs and expectations. Many such cases can be found in psychology, especially in the field of evaluation research, and the present proposal was modeled after an actual proposal we came across in the course of doing this study. In contrast to the discrimination proposal above, the reverse discrimination proposal, entitled "A Proposed Study of Possible Reverse Discrimination in the Affirmative Action Hiring Practices of Fortune 500 Corporations," conveyed an opposite sociopolitical orientation:

> This proposal is to examine factors associated with an applicant's success in obtaining managerial-level positions in business. We are particularly interested in applicants' physical characteristics (specifically their race and sex) and whether this might influence their being invited to interview for a position. . . . The proposed study attempts to examine the issue of alleged bias in naturalistic settings where all groups of applicants' credentials have been carefully controlled. It may be that minority and female applicants are not actually subjected to prejudicial treatment (as has been alleged) when their job-related credentials are equal to those of white males. . . . By conducting multiple comparisons of the interview rates in response to superior vitae with those associated with inferior vitae, it will be possible to determine whether racial or sexual discrimination exists, or whether reverse discrimination is a more adequate description of the modus operandi when comparisons are made between equally qualified applicants. . . . At present, popularly held beliefs regarding prejudicial employment {of minorities and women} are little more than slogans, lacking a sound empirical basis.

The nonsensitive proposal, which was entitled, "Proposed Study of the Relationship Between Perceived Weight of Applicants and the Hiring Practices of Fortune 500 Corporations," dealt with discrimination against obese and short individuals and was worded identically to the reverse discrimination proposal, except that the words *height* and *weight* were substituted for *race* and *sex* each time the latter appeared, as follows:

> This proposal is to examine factors associated with an applicant's success in obtaining managerial-level positions in business. We are particularly interested in applicants' physical characteristics (specifically their height and weight) and whether this might influence their chances of being invited to interview for a position with a Fortune 500 corporation. . . . It may be that very short and obese applicants are not actually subjected to prejudicial treatment when their job-related credentials are equal to those of normal weight and height individuals. . . . By conducting multiple comparisons of interview rates associated with superior individuals with those asociated with inferior applicants, it will be possible to determine whether weight discrimination is an adequate description of the modus operandi when comparisons are

made between equally qualified applicants. . . . At present, popularly held beliefs regarding prejudicial employment opportunities [of obese and short persons], are little more than slogans, lacking a sound empirical basis.

Within each of these three levels of political sensitivity, three types of proposals reflected varying degrees of ethically problematic, or at least ambiguous, procedures. Deception proposals involved the deception of Fortune 500 personnel officers. In these, it was proposed that hiring practices would be examined by sending strong and weak vitae in response to published announcements of managerial positions (a strong vita included a master's degree in business administration and relevant work history; a weak vita included a bachelor's degree and irrelevant work history). In these deception proposals, IRB members were told that personnel officers would not be informed that the vitae and letters sent to them in response to a position announcement were fictional and were being submitted as part of a study. The data of interest were the frequencies that applicants with each type of vita were selected for interviews. For example, in the reverse discrimination proposals, the data of interest were the frequencies of offers for interviews made by personnel officers to less qualified fictitious minority and female applicants, and in the height/weight proposals, the data of interest were the frequencies of offers for interviews based on the fictitious applicants' height and weight.

Proposals that contained deception *and* a planned omission of debriefing procedures were identical to the deception proposals except that a debriefing procedure described in the deception proposal was omitted, in contradiction of DHHS regulations ("Protection of Human Subjects," 1981, pt. 46.116), which specifies that in cases of deception, subjects should be debriefed upon conclusion of the study, except in the event that debriefing could lead to risk. The absence of a debriefing procedure was explicitly mentioned in the body of the proposal, and a rationale was provided for this decision. In particular, it was reasoned that debriefing could not be expected to add anything of a constructive nature to the personnel officers' unwitting participation and that the debriefing might actually produce in them a tendency to discount authentic applicants in the future in the mistaken belief that they were part of another study.[2]

Proposals that contained no ethically problematic procedures or conditions that required special IRB consideration differed from the other two types in that they proposed to describe the purpose of the study to the personnel officers at the study's outset and request their permission to

---

[2] The lack of debriefing was made explicit, along with a rationale, because research has demonstrated that disclosures of ethically questionable practices tend to be viewed more favorably by IRBs than failing to mention them in the proposal (Smith & Berard, 1982).

submit fictional vitae during the course of a 12-month period, without informing them of the nature of the vitae or when they would be submitted. These proposals also contained a debriefing provision.

Sample copies of each of these nine types of proposals (three levels of political orientation times three levels of ethical problems) were sent at random to U.S. universities, one per university, along with a cover letter requesting their participation. IRBs that agreed to participate were aware only of the single proposal they were sent. They were asked to provide a normal review and decision along with any narrative account of their deliberations that was routinely kept. Of the 375 IRBs that were sent a sample proposal, 171 responded. Of these, 14 declined to participate either because of scheduling problems ($N = 6$) or for unspecified reasons. Thus, we were left with a sample of 157 participating IRBs. It should be mentioned that many proposals did not reach the institutional office responsible for scheduling human subjects reviews because the names used to designate this office are quite varied—for example, IRBs, Ethics Committees, Institutional Research Committees, Research Committees, Human Subjects Committees, or Vice President's Office for Research. Often our correspondence was returned marked "address unknown." Thus, the actual participation rate is probably far higher than the 45% reported above—157 out of 375.

Table 1 shows the breakdown of IRBs for each type of proposal along with the IRBs' decisions. As can be seen, there were large differences in the outcomes for the nine types of proposals. Overall, the reverse discrimination proposals were the most difficult to get approved.[3] Collapsing over the three levels of ethical problems, 63% of these were considered problematic enough to warrant withholding approval until substantial changes were made.

The discrimination proposal nonapproval rate (51%) was slightly lower than the nonapproval rate for the reverse discrimination proposals (63%). However, in contrast to these socially sensitive proposals, the height/weight proposals fared much better, receiving nonapproval on only 26% of occasions. The differences among the approval rates of all nine types were significant, x^2 (8, $N = 157$) = 21.22, $p < .005$ (contingency coefficient = .361). A breakdown of the overall contingency revealed that

---

[3] Two raters coded each IRB decision as either approved or nonapproved. Included in the latter category were cases in which the approval was contingent upon the incorporation of strategic changes, for example, avoiding the use of deception or an insistence on debriefing. Included in the former category were cases in which approval was contingent upon the incorporation of nonstrategic changes, for example, enlarging the sample size or employing a different statistical model. (Because the variables like deception and nondebriefing were actually manipulated in the present study, an IRB approval that was contingent upon the removal of deception or nondebriefing was included in the nonapproved category to provide a comparison with its counterparts in the no-violation condition.) The two raters agreed on 146 out of 157 cases (95%).

TABLE 1
Frequencies of Approval as a Function of the Nature of the Proposal

Decision	Discrimination			Reverse discrimination			Height/weight		
	Deception	Deception & debriefing	No. violations	Deception	Deception & debriefing	No. violations	Deception	Deception & debriefing	No. violations
Approved	8	10	9	6	5	6	12	10	19
Nonapproved	8	10	10	9	10	10	7	7	1
Total	16	20	19	15	15	16	19	17	20

Note: The total number of proposals was 157.

the approval rates for the height/weight proposals were significantly higher than those associated with socially sensitive proposals (all $ps < .05$).

Of interest was the finding that the socially sensitive proposals' outcomes were not reliably influenced by the presence or absence of ethical problems or areas of special IRB consideration (all $ps > .10$). That is, sensitive proposals containing neither deception nor a failure to debrief were rejected as often as proposals that did contain such violations. The presence of ethical problems, however, was a potent predictor of the height/weight approval rate. Ninety-five percent of the height/weight proposals that contained no ethical problems (19 out of 20) were approved without complications, whereas only 60% of the two proposals that did contain problems or areas of special IRB consideration (12 out of 19 deception proposals and 10 out of 17 deception and debriefing proposals) were approved, x^2 (2, $N = 56$) = 3.78, $p < .05$.

For the two types of socially sensitive proposals (reverse discrimination proposals and discrimination proposals), even when they contained no problems, the approval rates usually did not reach the levels observed for the height/weight proposals, even when the latter did contain ethical problems. However, as can be seen in Table 1, the two types of socially sensitive proposals did differ from each other. In general, proposals dealing with reverse discrimination were significantly more likely to be rejected than were those purporting to investigate discrimination, $ps < .05$. This suggests either that IRB members perceived a greater risk to personnel officers in the reverse discrimination proposals than in the discrimination proposals (e.g., loss of jobs or litigation may have been perceived to be more probable in the event that a finding of reverse discrimination became public), or that there is a greater likelihood that liberal values are shared by IRB members (i.e., a conflict between the purported aim of the study to document reverse discrimination and IRB members' personal values regarding this issue). We tend to place more credence in the latter explanation, for two reasons: First, the personnel officers' welfare was rarely mentioned in the accompanying narratives as the reason for nonapproval; and second, the legal impact of discrimination is at least as great as, and possibly even greater than, that associated with reverse discrimination (the former is protected by federal legislation—Title 9 of the Civil Rights Act).[4] However, the main point is not whether liberal or conservative proposals fared better or worse: The data indicate that IRBs are reluctant to approve *any* socially sensitive proposal, vis-à-vis the same proposed treatment of human subjects couched in a politically neutral context, such as the height/weight one.[5]

Finally, 74% of the IRBs that participated provided some accompanying narrative to explain their decision. Usually this took the form of a copy of the minutes of the meeting or the individual comment sheets used by the reviewers. These were analyzed for clues to the IRB members' values. Table 2 shows the results of a content analysis of these accompanying narratives. The most frequent reason given for nonapproval of proposals that contained deception was, in fact, the presence of the deception. This also was true of proposals that contained both deception and a failure to debrief. Only 10% of the latter that were not approved mentioned the failure to debrief as the reason; the rest gave deception as the reason. This was equally true of the sensitive and nonsensitive proposals, and it suggests that the argument made against debriefing was considered persuasive or that debriefing was not seen as critical. Given the related findings of Smith and Berard (1982), we are inclined to favor the former explanation.

In the case of proposals that contained no ethical problems, there was a dramatic difference between the responses to the sensitive and nonsen-

---

[4] Other interpretations are also possible, though not very probable. One such interpretation might be that IRB members believed that there was overwhelming evidence for discrimination against women and minorities and that any effort to document reverse discrimination was bound to fail. Thus, any costs, no matter how mild, could not be offset by the benefit of new knowledge, because finding reverse discrimination was not even a remote possibility. Yet, even this interpretation involves a value statement, though not necessarily along liberal-conservative lines. Another interpretation, more difficult to assess, is that IRB members' "antennae" were raised by the socially sensitive proposals because of their potential societal impact. Thus, it could be that sensitive proposals are scrutinized to a degree not true of socially innocuous proposals. If this is true, there is still the matter of the differential outcomes of the two types of sensitive proposals: Both discrimination and reverse-discrimination proposals should have received intensive scrutiny because of their potential impact, yet the former were approved more often than the latter.

[5] Whether socially sensitive topics per se or only socially sensitive topics with "social agendas" are more likely to be rejected by IRBs than nonsensitive proposals cannot be determined from the present data. It would be interesting to have data regarding the fate of socially sensitive proposals (race and gender) that were couched in neutral language as well as "advocacy" language. It may be the case that IRB members perceived their personal values to be especially besieged by the overtly political nature of the present proposals in a manner that would not be the case if race and gender were studied in a seemingly more neutral manner.

TABLE 2
Content Analysis of 157 Returned Proposals

Type of criticism	Discrimination			Reverse discrimination			Height/weight		
	1	2	3	1	2	3	1	2	3
Deception	100	100	20	100	100	10	100	100	0
Debriefing	0	60	0	0	80	0	0	28	0
Methodological	25	20	70	22	20	60	14	0	0
Political implications	17	20	37	38	44	63	0	0	0
Value[a]	12	10	20	11	10	20	0	0	0

Note: Figures represent the proportions of nonapproved proposals in each category that were criticized on a particular ground; 1 = proposals containing deception; 2 = proposals containing deception and lacking debriefing; 3 = no violations. (Categories are not mutually exclusive; that is, a proposal could be criticized on more than one ground.)
[a]Trivial, unimportant research question.

sitive narratives: The tone of the latter was uniformly approving, whereas the former frequently contained types of complaints that were not listed in the other cases, though the alleged problems should have pertained to all of the proposals, for example, methodological weaknesses in the design (sample size too small, range of positions or background of fictional applicants too narrow to be informative, accompanying fictional vitae not sufficiently realistic, etc.). There were only two instances in which height/ weight proposals were criticized on methodological grounds, and in both cases the criticisms were viewed as minor and not sufficient grounds for nonapproval. Thus, the conclusion that can be drawn from the narratives for the proposals that did not contain ethically problematic procedures is that IRBs found the sensitive proposals to be socially objectionable, especially the reverse discrimination ones, and invoked whatever reasons were most convenient to justify their decisions to deny approval. When deception or lack of debriefing was part of the protocol, these ethical problems were given as the reason for the nonapproval. When no ethically problematic procedures were present, however, methodological objections were raised that had not been raised in the other cases. The following question is suggested by these results: Why were these methodological flaws usually not mentioned in the narratives accompanying the height/weight proposals and only infrequently mentioned in the sensitive proposals that contained violations?

In 25% of the discrimination proposals and nearly 45% of the reverse discrimination proposals, the narratives contained explicit political criticisms, for example, "The findings could set Affirmative Action back 20 years if it came out that women with weaker vitae were asked to interview more often for managerial positions than men with stronger vitae." Of interest is the general absence of concern for the welfare of the Fortune 500 personnel officers in these narratives. Only 2% of the narratives listed possible repercussions to the personnel officer (e.g., job termination or litigation) as a concern.

The IRBs used scientific criteria in the evaluation of a proposal for its treatment of human subjects in 46% of our sample. In these cases (all but two of which involved politically sensitive proposals), IRBs listed methodological flaws as reasons for nonapproval. Their reasoning was that in a cost–benefit analysis, a serious methodological flaw would preclude any scientific contribution from accruing, and therefore any costs to the subjects, if only their waste of time, could not be offset by benefits. Several IRBs explicitly stated in their narratives that they avoided making such judgments of a proposal's scientific value in the belief that such consideration was not within their purview or that it was undesirable to do so.[6]

IMPLICATIONS

What are we to make of these results? First, if anything is clear, it is that IRBs are extremely interesting and variable bodies. The same type of proposal involving the same level of violation often was approved at one institution but not at another; sometimes this occurred even when the two institutions were located in the same community. The IRBs involved in this study could not have used one single, objective set of criteria in their deliberations (unless these criteria were so vague as to lend themselves to opposite interpretations), because there was so much within-proposal variability. For instance, nearly half of each of the three discrimination proposals were approved, which means that the other half were not. This suggests that approval of a proposal, especially a socially sensitive proposal, could sometimes be a matter of luck, such as where one happened to be working when the proposal was submitted for human subjects review. Luck, according to this interpretation, includes such factors as being affiliated with an institution whose IRB members' values are congruent with the aims of the proposed research or whose members do not regard the scientific review of a proposal's merit to be desirable. (It is difficult to argue that the observed intraproposal variability was due to differences in local community standards, as the same proposal frequently was approved at one institution but not at another within the same community, for example, New York City.)

Another implication of the findings is that IRB deliberations reflect the sociopolitical ideologies of their members in ways not entirely congruent

---

[6] IRBs are permitted to engage in scientific reviews of proposed research under past and present DHHS guidelines.

with their federal mandate. The narrative accounts of IRB meetings revealed that a major reason for nonapproval of a socially sensitive proposal was the nature of its potential sociopolitical impact, especially when no ethically problematic procedures could be cited. The Code of Federal Regulations that governs IRB functioning states that

> The IRB should not consider possible long-range effects of applying knowledge gained in the research (for example, the possible effects of the research on public policy) as among those research risks that fall within the purview of its responsibility. ("Protection of Human Subjects," 1981, pt. 46.111)

Yet, it was clear that IRBs *did* consider that the sociopolitical consequences of the proposed research in their cost–benefit analyses. (It came as a surprise to us that so many IRBs stated their sociopolitical objections so openly in their reasons for nonapproval. Does this reveal their ignorance of federal regulations governing the responsibilities of IRBs?) One might wonder whether other IRBs also used sociopolitical criteria but did not state them because they were aware that it would be inappropriate. One indication that this could be the case can be inferred from the analysis of narratives. For both types of socially sensitive proposals, the nonapproval rates were the same regardless of the presence or absence of ethically problematic procedures. For deception proposals, the reason that was nearly always given to justify nonapproval was the use of deception itself (e.g., "The committee deems the use of deception as a serious violation and would insist on nondeceptive practices as a condition for approval"). Similarly, in the narratives of proposals involving deception *and* failure to debrief, the use of deception or the lack of debriefing was given as the reason for nonapproval. However, when a socially sensitive proposal did not contain any ethically problematic procedures, methodological reasons frequently were given to justify nonapproval (e.g., "The use of only Fortune 500 corporations was viewed as a limitation of your study as was the use of only one type of managerial position and the small range of background training"). Because we have no direct evidence that sociopolitical factors were operating in these nonapprovals, this hypothesis will remain only a plausibility until an experimentally sound test of it is provided. However, the fact that the nonapproval rate for politically sensitive proposals was unaffected by the presence of ethically problematic procedures does suggest that ethical problems were not the basis for nonapproval (even when they were cited), but were perhaps a convenient justification.

Another source of evidence for the plausibility of this position can be found in the differential approval rates of the two types of socially sensitive proposals themselves. Because the proposals were virtually identical in their treatment of personnel officers, any tendency to reject one more than another must be due to its sociopolitical nature. As we have suggested, the potential risks to subjects (personnel officers) were at least as great in the case of discrimination proposals as in the reverse discrimination proposals, yet the former were approved significantly more often than the latter. Furthermore, even though the height/weight proposals without violations were approved 95% of the time, the reverse discrimination proposals without violations were approved only approximately 40% of the time. The two types of proposals were similar in all respects except their relationship to a social policy issue that has received considerable debate in recent times.

An implication of the above interpretation is that the use of scientific criteria and standards in the evaluation of a proposal for its treatment of human subjects can be problematic. This follows from the fact that seemingly objective scientific criteria (such as a small sample size or poor control group) were invoked to reject socially sensitive proposals but were almost never mentioned in relation to the height/weight proposals. If anything is clear from the recent studies of peer review, it is that one cannot expect reviewers, who are presumably knowledgeable about an area, to agree about the scientific merits of research (see Peters & Ceci, 1982). It may be asking too much of a committee made up of diverse members of an institution and its surrounding community to make valid scientific judgments, given that experts cannot. Although the reasons behind the use of scientific criteria are understandable (see Reynolds, 1979, p. 269), the difficulty, it would seem, is that their use, under the guise of objective scientific standards, permits the rejection of proposals whose real offense might be their social and political distastefulness to IRB members. A better approach might be for IRBs to make specific recommendations to the researcher regarding the alleged methodological problems and invite a response before refusing to approve a proposal without substantial modifications. But even this procedure would, in light of the present findings, result in the disproportionate selection of socially sensitive proposals for reevaluation, thus lengthening their turnaround time and adding extra costs to the concerned investigator hoping to study topics of social significance. The long-term effect of such a policy could be to discourage socially important and applied research.

Recent outcries against the IRB process have assailed its increasingly bureaucratic nature (Pattullo, 1980), its unreliability (Eaton, 1983), its costliness (Cohen, 1982, 1983), its conservatism in judging risks to subjects (Smith & Berard, 1982), and its effect on researchers' choice of topics (de Sola Pool, 1979; Glynn, 1978; Seiler & Murtha, 1980). To this list we may add its variability and the apparent insertion of sociopolitical values into its deliberations. If sociopolitical considerations are being used to evaluate the merit of a proposal—and it appears to us that they might be—then this would seem to be in direct conflict with DHHS guidelines and, more important, with the "open and self-referencing" norms of science (Harnad, 1982; Merton, 1973; Ziman, 1980).[7] Although IRBs help ensure a level of protection that might otherwise be absent (see Veatch, 1979), it seems crucial that we learn more about their functioning in order to prevent them from becoming something they were never intended to be, namely, censorship committees.

REFERENCES

Asch, S. (1955). Opinions and social pressure. *Scientific American, 193,* 31–35.

Bradley, J. V. (1981). Pernicious publication practices. *Bulletin of the Psychonomic Society, 18,* 31–34.

Bradley, J. V. (1982). Editorial overkill. *Bulletin of the Psychonomic Society, 19,* 271–274.

Ceci, S. J., & Peters, D. (1982). Peer review: A study of reliability. *Change: The Magazine of Higher Learning, 14,* 44–48.

Ceci, S. J., & Peters, D. (1984). How "blind" is blind review? *American Psychologist, 39,* 1491–1494.

Chalkey, D. T. (1975, May 22). *Requirements for compliance with Part 46 of Title 45 of the Code of Federal Regulations as amended March 13, 1975.* Memorandum from the Director, Office for Protection from Research Risk. Bethesda, MD: National Institutes of Health.

Chubin, D., & Gillespie, G. (1984). *Funding success and failure: Cancer researchers rate NIH peer review.* Unpublished manuscript, Program on Science, Technology, and Society, Cornell University, Ithaca, NY.

Cicchetti, D. (1980). Reliability of reviews for *American Psychologist:* A biostatistical assessment of the data. *American Psychologist, 35,* 300–303.

Cicchetti, D. (1982). On peer review: We have met the enemy and he is us. *Behavioral and Brain Sciences, 5,* 204.

Cicchetti, D., & Eron, L. (1979). The reliability of manuscript reviewing for the

---

[7] The desirability of reviewing proposals for their social impact is not an issue here. The DHHS guidelines explicitly caution IRBs against doing so. Persuasive arguments can be and have been made that scientists should not be exempt from the usual laws of moral conduct, including taking responsibility for their actions (i.e. the applications of their research findings). The Nuremburg Code, which serves as a basis for many contemporary codes of professional conduct, casts doubt on the right of investigators to maintain with impunity that they are engaged in "basic" research and should not be held accountable for the political, social, or economic consequences of their research. ("If someone else develops my nuclear research into a catastrophic weapons system, that is not my problem.") On the other side of this controversy can be found the argument that science, in order to flourish, requires freedom from censorship, including the right to challenge dominant beliefs, pet theories, and values. An entire generation of genetics research was lost in the Soviet Union as a result of Lysenkoisim, and it has been argued that Italy lost its preeminent status in science during the Middle Ages because of the Catholic Church's censorship of Galileo. Although cogent cases can be made for and against the use of social criteria during IRB deliberations, the current guidelines unambiguously forbid them. To insert such criteria into the review process would seem to require a national consensus that was lacking during the original discussions that led to the creation of IRBs.

Journal of Abnormal Psychology. In *1979 Proceedings of the social statistics section* (pp. 596–600). Washington, DC: American Statistics Association.

Cohen, J. (1982). The cost of IRB reviews. In R. A. Greenwald, M. K. Ryan, & J. E. Mulvihill (Eds.), *Human subjects research: A handbook for institutional review boards* (pp. 39–47). New York: Plenum Press.

Cohen, J. (1983, August). *The financial costs of IRBs.* Paper presented at the 90th meeting of the American Psychological Association, Anaheim, CA.

Cole, S., Cole, J. R., & Simon, G. (1981). Chance and consensus in peer review. *Science, 214,* 881–886.

Crane, D. (1967). The gate-keepers of science: Some factors influencing the selection of articles for scientific journals. *American Sociologist, 32,* 195–201.

de Sola Pool, I. (1979). Analysis of HEW draft IRB Regulations of 8/14/79. *IRB Journal: A Review of Human Subjects Research, 8,* 187.

Doob, A. N. (1983). The reliability of ethical reviews: Is it desirable? *Canadian Psychologist, 24,* 269–270.

Eaton, W. O. (1983). The reliability of ethical reviews: Some initial empirical findings. *Canadian Psychologist, 24,* 14–18.

Glynn, K. (1978). *Regulations regarding the use of human subjects in research: Effects on investigator's ethical sensitivity, research practices, and research priorities.* Paper presented at the annual meeting of the American Sociological Association, San Francisco, CA.

Goodstein, L. D., & Brazis, K. L. (1970). Credibility of psychologists: An empirical study. *Psychological Reports, 27,* 835–838.

Gray, B. H., & Cook, R. A. (1980). The impact of IRBs on research. *Hastings Center Report, 10,* 36–41.

Harnad, S. (1982). Peer commentary on peer review. *Behavioral and Brain Sciences, 5,* 185–186.

Human research subjects. 46 *Fed. Reg.* 8366–8368, 8399 (1981).

Inglefinger, F. J. (1974). Peer review in biomedical publications. *American Journal of Medicine, 56,* 686–692.

Mahoney, M. J. (1977). Publication prejudices: An experimental study of confirmatory bias in the peer review system. *Cognitive Therapy and Research, 1,* 161–175.

Mahoney, M. J. (1979). Psychology of the scientist: An evaluative, review. *Social Studies of Science, 9,* 349–375.

Merton, R. K. (1973). *The sociology of science.* Chicago: University of Chicago Press.

Mitroff, I., & Chubin, D. (1979). Peer review at NSF: A dialectical policy analysis. *Social Studies of Science, 9,* 199–232.

National Commission on Research. (1980). *Review processes: Assessing the quality of research proposals.* Washington, DC: Author.

Pattullo, E. L. (1980). Who risks what in social research? *The Hastings Center Report, 10,* 15–18.

Peters, D., & Ceci, S. J. (1982). A naturalistic study of the peer review process in psychology: The fate of published articles, resubmitted. *Behavioral and Brain Sciences, 5,* 4–17.

Protection of Human Subjects. 45 C.F.R. pt. 46 (1981).

Reynolds, P. D. (1979). *Ethical dilemmas and social science research.* San Francisco: Jossey-Bass.

Reynolds, P. D. (1982). *Ethics and social science research.* Englewood Cliffs, NJ: Prentice-Hall.

Scarr, S., & Weber, B. L. (1978). The reliability of reviews for the *American Psychologist. American Psychologist, 33,* 935.

Seiler, L. M., & Murtha, J. M. (1980). Federal regulation of social research using human subjects: A critical assessment. *American Sociologist, 15,* 146–157.

Smith, A., & Berard, S. P. (1982). Why are human subjects less concerned about ethically problematic research than human subjects committees? *Journal of Applied Social Psychology, 12,* 209–221.

Smith, C. P. (1981). How (un)acceptable is research involving deception: *IRB: A Review of Human Subjects Research, 3,* 1–4.

Stark-Adamec, C., & Adamec, R. (1981). Breaking into the grant proposal market. *International Journal of Women's Studies, 4,* 105–117.

Title IX of the Civil Rights Act of 1964. 42 U.S.C. §1983.

Veatch, R. M. (1979, February). The National Commission on IRBs: An evolutionary approach. *The Hastings Center Report,* 22–28.

Watkins, M. W. (1979). Chance and interrater agreement on manuscripts. *American Psychologist, 34,* 796–797.

Whitehurst, G. J. (1984). Interrater agreement for journal manuscript reviews. *American Psychologist, 39,* 22–28.

Ziman, J. (1980). What is science? In E. D. Klemke, R. Hollinger, & A. D. Kline (Eds.), *Introductory readings in the philosophy of science* (pp. 162–186). Buffalo, NY: Prometheus Books.

35

CURRENT NIH PERSPECTIVES ON MISCONDUCT IN SCIENCE

MARY L. MIERS

Until recently it would have been highly unusual for a staff member of a federal agency to receive an invitation to prepare an article for a professional journal on the subject of misconduct in science. Although the scope and causes of such misconduct are not fully understood—and indeed, raise interesting questions for study—there is little doubt that the increased visibility of the aberrant scientist has colored both the public and professional view of the research enterprise (Brandt, 1983; Broad & Wade, 1982; Jackson & Prados, 1983; Kilbourne & Kilbourne, 1983; Relman, 1983; Schmaus, 1983; U.S. House of Representatives, 1981; Wigodsky, 1984). The impact of recent developments can be appreciated if one measures that form of significant social commentary, the editorial cartoon, a small collection of which now graces my bulletin board.

It is important to recall that fraud and misrepresentation of various kinds have always occurred in science. Although the popular concept of "pure" science emphasizes the quest for knowledge for its own sake, every

Reprinted from the *American Psychologist, 40*, 831-835. In the public domain.

scientist knows that the object of the quest is an exciting finding, and furthermore, the elucidation and publication of that finding in advance of one's colleagues. The temptation and opportunity to exploit the process have doubtless existed since the development of science as an organized activity, moderated by some combination of individual ethics, intellectual rigor, and the safeguards imposed by the processes of experimentation and publication. However, the sheer size of the research enterprise today and its dependence on public support present special dilemmas for both the patrons and practitioners of research when misconduct seems to have—or actually has—occurred.

Although fraud in science is not a new phenomenon, there is no question that the incidence of *reported* misconduct has increased dramatically. In the past three years, NIH has received an average of two reports per month of possible misconduct that appears to go beyond the traditional kinds of issues encountered in the fiscal and administrative management of grants, cooperative agreements, and contracts. About half of the reports have proven to be factual. Some of those reflected not fraudulent intent but some error in methodology or sloppy technique. Others appeared to be the result of the failure to develop and communicate appropriate policies and internal controls within academic and research institutions. The reports of misconduct cover a full range of behaviors. A few have involved possible egregious misuse of funds, but the majority are concerned with departures from accepted research practices, including fabrication, misrepresentation or selective reporting of results, inadequate attention to the rights of human subjects, and unacceptable treatment of laboratory animals.

Viewed against a denominator of more than 20,000 NIH awards active at any instant, these numbers are small, almost insignificant. They have, however, given rise to well-founded concerns about the efficacy of traditional practices often cited as safeguards against misconduct. Those practices include peer review of research proposed for funding or publication and replication of significant findings. Such safeguards are based on the assumption that individual investigators are honest and well intentioned, although they may make errors in methodology or theory. These procedures are not designed to detect clever, systematic cheating or research practices that are markedly at variance with what they are reported to be.

The realization that traditional safeguards of science cannot entirely prevent misconduct has been accompanied by increasing evidence that awardee institutions, funding agencies, and professional organizations are often ill prepared to deal with allegations or evidence of wrongdoing. Most funding agencies have access to some type of audit or investigative unit to pursue cases involving apparent misuse of funds or possible criminal activities. Recent trends such as the establishment of Offices of Inspector General throughout the federal government have underscored the importance of integrity in publicly funded programs of all kinds. Within the Department of Health and Human Services (DHHS), the Office for Protection from Research Risks (OPRR) has played an important role in detecting and dealing with failure to comply with requirements designed to protect the welfare of human subjects and animals, in addition to its role in developing and refining the needed policies and procedures.

The biomedical research community has been quick to recognize that the research institutions play a critical role in preventing, detecting, and dealing with misconduct in science. Professional organizations have traditionally assumed varying degrees of responsibility for the integrity of their members. Both the Association of American Medical Colleges (AAMC) and the Association of American Universities (AAU) have developed statements of principles and model procedures for the guidance of their member institutions (AAMC, 1982; AAU, 1982). Several institutions have developed their own guidelines or are in the process of doing so.

Until recently, NIH tended to treat reports of misconduct as isolated events, employing ad hoc procedures for each case on the assumption that the probability of encountering a similar incident was minimal. In the past few years, it has become clear that more explicit and predictable procedures are needed to enable the funding agencies to deal with some level of recurring activity involving allegations or evidence of misconduct. Of equal concern has been the lack of guidance to awardee institutions and investigators regarding their rights and responsibilities.

It is clear in retrospect that the lack of established policies and procedures led to false starts and inordinate delays in some cases. Nothing in previous NIH experience had prepared agency staff to deal with the conflicting demands of accountability and fiscal stewardship, on the one hand, and respect for civil liberties on the other. A more positive (and, one hopes, not too self-serving) assessment of recent NIH performance might conclude that the incremental approach taken in a series of investigations served to develop a body of knowledge and experience that could form the basis for development of more formalized procedures.

Although most of the recent attention has been centered on NIH, the problems posed by misconduct in science are not limited to that agency. In the fall of 1981, Secretary of Health and Human Services Richard S. Schweiker identified as a major management initiative the development of policies and procedures for dealing with misconduct in science. Early efforts undertaken by the research agencies included: (a) conducting regional seminars for investigators, academic officials, and institutional review board members regarding protection of human subjects and related regulations and policies; (b) discussing with members of NIH advisory councils and peer review groups their responsibilities related to misconduct in science and soliciting their views on approaches to be taken; (c) improving internal NIH procedures for identifying incoming grant applications and contract proposals from individuals or institutions under investigation or subject to postinvestigational sanctions; (d) modifying the coding and processing of competing grant applications to ensure that all requirements for protection of human subjects are met; and (e) developing a uniform procedure for documenting the results of agency staff review of annual progress reports.

NIH also undertook an intensive review of its policies and procedures to identify the need for improved guidance to agency staff and awardee investigators and institutions. This led to publication of a notice in the *NIH Guide for Grants and Contracts* in July 1982, inviting comments and suggestions. About two dozen responses were received. These were about evenly divided among those who believed firmer action was needed, those who suggested NIH was addressing a nonproblem and was proposing to repeal the Bill of Rights, and those who felt the situation was serious but under control. There was general agreement that the primary responsibility for preventing and dealing with misconduct rested with the academic institutions.

In August 1982, Assistant Secretary for Health Edward N. Brandt, Jr., directed NIH to take the lead in developing policies and procedures for all Public Health Service (PHS) research programs. This effort was not intended to override or replace the internal management controls of awardee institutions or the conditions imposed through routine grant and contract management practices. Rather, it was designed to deal with the special problems created by potentially serious breaches of the canons of science or conditions of the funding relationship. An interagency committee focused on the following broad types of misconduct: (a) serious deviations from accepted practices in the conduct or reporting of research, such as fabrication, falsification, or plagiarism; and (b) material failure to comply with federal requirements affecting specific aspects of the conduct of research, for example, protection of the welfare of human subjects and laboratory animals.

The committee has proposed a set of detailed policies and procedures for dealing with possible misconduct in research funded, regulated, or conducted by PHS. These documents were accepted by Brandt and his agency heads and were transmitted to appropriate offices in DHHS for review and approval. The latter process is nearly completed. It is expected that the documents will be made widely available for comment; and, where appropriate, some aspects will be incorporated into regulation. In brief, their coverage is as follows:

General Policies and Principles

This brief statement of policy is intended to underscore the commitment to integrity in all research funded, conducted, or regulated by the PHS.

Policies and Procedures For Awarding Agencies

This step-by-step guide for agency staff will cover the "life cycle" of an incident. It will outline procedures for evaluating the significance of allegations, conducting an investigation, taking interim administrative actions when appropriate, and imposing postinvestigational sanctions when warranted. It will emphasize the need to protect the rights of accused individuals and "whistle blowers" and to provide an adequate public record of the agencies' actions without violating the civil liberties of individuals. An important section of this document is a statement of expectations for awardee institutions that underscores the institutions' responsibility to take prompt and appropriate action when misconduct is known or suspected and to inform the funding agency when the matter is judged to be serious enough to warrant an investigation.

Policies and Procedures For Research Conducted By PHS

This document will provide guidance for agency research managers who may confront allegations or evidence of misconduct in an agency's intramural research program. It will embody many of the same principles enumerated above, adapted to take into account the employer–employee relationship, and will serve as the PHS internal counterpart of procedures now in place or being developed at many research institutions.

Policies and Procedures Affecting Research Regulated By PHS

This document is a compendium of regulatory procedures, primarily those of the Food and Drug Administration (FDA), with special attention to the interface of regulatory requirements and research funded or conducted by PHS. It differs from the preceding two documents in that it is primarily a distillation and summary of existing, well-known procedures used by the agencies to ensure the integrity of regulated research.

PHS ALERT System

As noted earlier, NIH has a mechanism in place for identifying incoming applications and proposals from individuals and institutions under investigation or subject to some sanction as the result of investigational findings. Because NIH has 14 different awarding components, some process was needed to ensure appropriate follow-up to completed investigations if an action were taken that would affect future funding. Similarly, although the fact that an investigation is ongoing does not preclude an award, there is a need for responsible NIH officials to consider all available information before a decision is made. This last document represents an effort to define the appropriate boundaries for sharing information among the various PHS agencies and to provide safeguards comparable to the strict confidentiality built into the NIH system when investigations are still underway. In addition to the public commentary planned for all these documents, a description of the proposed PHS ALERT will be published as a proposed major modification to the NIH ALERT, which is a system of records under the Privacy Act.

It may be of some interest to describe the approaches currently being used by NIH. In general, NIH staff share the concern, often expressed by representatives for the research community, that administrative solutions not create more problems than they solve. This agency has moved cautiously in an effort to develop sensible and equitable approaches based on precedent and the best advice available.

An early and critical step is distinguishing between frivolous or malicious allegations and those that may have some basis in fact. Although it is often difficult to make this distinction, it is generally possible to make a discreet, preliminary inquiry without compromising individual reputations or the integrity of research projects. NIH relies primarily on the awardee institutions to investigate, take actions when warranted, and provide agency staff with the information needed to make reasonable and equitable decisions regarding awards and pending applications. A typical incident would be handled in the following manner. When NIH staff become aware of allegations or other information suggesting misconduct may have occurred, the Office of Extramural Research and Training (OERT) is notified. Depending on what awards or pending applications are involved, one or more awarding units or investigative offices will participate in deciding what action should be taken. If there is general agreement that the allegation or report is plausible, the appropriate office will initiate an inquiry. Typically, this includes asking the institution and/or individual to respond. If the responses to the initial inquiry suggest that more fact-finding is necessary, an investigation will be undertaken. NIH does not conduct secret investigations, although in very rare instances a law enforcment agency may direct us to take no action because an investigation of possible criminal activity is underway.

It is not unusual to find that an active award or pending application is involved. This presents a very difficult problem. On the one hand, it is essential that agency staff not prejudge the outcome; at the same time, they are obligated to protect NIH interests based on the best information available at the time. When it appears that some interim action is necessary, every effort is made to minimize the effects of possibly premature decision. An awarding component may, for example, extend a current budget period for a few months—with or without funds—rather than make a new noncompeting award on the anniversary date. The process of investigation is a highly interactive one, designed to obtain the views of both the individuals suspected of misconduct and appropriate institutional officials. It is standard procedure to invite comments on a draft report and to change the report if warranted. Even if NIH does not change its findings, the affected parties may have their comments appended to the report as part of the record.

In cases in which misconduct is not established, NIH attempts to minimize any harmful results of an unsubstantiated allegation or suspicion. Specific actions may include a letter to employers, removal of interim restrictions on awards, or briefing of agency staff and peer reviewers who may have incomplete or incorrect information. If misconduct has been established, a range of actions may be called for, depending on the circumstances. As a first step, the final report, including comments and rebuttals, is shared with a group of senior staff charged with making a recommendation to the NIH director. This "decision group" includes representatives from the OERT, affected awarding units, the DHHS Office of General Counsel, and at least one senior official with no direct involvement in the matter. Sanctions could include special prior approval requirements, consideration of relevant findings in future review and award processes, suspension or termination of an active award, or a recommendation that the Secretary of DHHS initiate proceedings to debar the individual or institution from eligibility for funding for some period of time.

As a general rule, pending investigations are not considered in the review of applications for scientific merit. Occasionally, when there has been media publicity or rumor about a particular case, reviewers are informed of the known facts in an effort to avoid compromising the review. Another option is to defer the review, although that may not work to the advantage of the applicant.

A similar process obtains when the alleged misconduct involves an intramural scientist. In such instances, inquiries and investigations are the responsibility of intramural officials, and actions are taken in accordance with regulations affecting civil service or PHS commissioned corps staff. The Office of Extramural Research and Training may be consulted at any time during the investigation and is required to assess the significance of established misconduct as it may affect an individual's eligibility for extramural funding.

The full impact of recent events on the research enterprise will probably not be understood for some period of time. In some instances, the reputations of individuals or institutions have suffered, and there have been instances of damage to research projects. More subtle and potentially more serious effects could include an erosion in public confidence in science, as well as inhibition of collaborative relationships among individual scientists and groups.

On balance, the response of the research community can be viewed as a reaffirmation of traditional scientific practices and values. And NIH, after the initial shock wave, is accommodating to the task of dealing with possible misconduct as an infrequent but significant feature of the agency's role as the largest supporter of biomedical research.

One of the most striking features of this process of adaptation is the extent to which it has been self-directed. For the casual observer, the topic of misconduct in science brings to mind the publicity generated by one or more recent cases. Both the general and scientific presses have published fairly detailed accounts of these—notably, plagiarism and falsification of results by Vijay Soman, irregularities in consent documents and protocols carried out under Marc Straus, Martin Cline's use of recombinant DNA in human subjects without required approvals, and most recently, John Darsee's fabrication of research findings. These examples and others have prompted considerable discussion about the adequacy of actions taken by research institutions and funding agencies. It is noteworthy, however, that NIH has experienced remarkably little outside pressure related to either the details of general procedures or actions to be taken in specific cases. We view this as encouraging evidence of public confidence in the integrity the research enterprise, and we welcome the cooperation of the research community in maintaining that confidence.

REFERENCES

Association of American Medical Colleges. (1982). *The maintenance of high ethical standards in the conduct of research.* Washington, DC: Author.

Association of American Universities. (1982, April). *Report of the Association of American Universities Committee on Integrity of Research.* Washington, DC: Author.

Brandt, E. N., Jr. (1983). PHS perspectives on misconduct in science. *Public Health Reports, 98,* 136-139.

Broad, W. J., & Wade, N. (1982). *Betrayers of the truth: Fraud and deceit in the halls of science.* New York: Simon & Schuster.

Jackson, C. I., & Prados, J. W. (1983). Honor in science. *American Scientist, 71,* 462-465.

VII

PUBLICATION AND COMMUNICATION OF RESEARCH

Critical to the research process is the publication and communication of one's ideas, methods, and results. Preparing reports of planned or completed research is not merely a task of describing what one will do or has done. Rather, the task of communicating one's research is fundamentally related to the decision-making processes underlying methodology and design. The written work must make explicit the rationale for critical methodological decisions. Some of the many questions include who was selected as subjects and why, what constructs and measures were included, and why various comparison and control groups were included or omitted. The rationale for methodological facets and the impact of potential biases and design practices on the conclusions are critical. In this section, articles raise issues designed to enhance communication of research.

In the initial article, Brendan Maher (1978) provides a brief set of guidelines for article preparation developed during his years as a journal editor. The guidelines are designed to assist authors who prepare research reports to be submitted for publication. Several questions are presented that focus on various issues such as manuscript format, clarity of writing, and methodology. The article was included to bring these latter issues to the attention of authors. Questions pertaining to the rationale for various procedures, characteristics of various methods (e.g., selection of measures), and potential impact of biases convey the continued importance of methodological issues in preparing the written report.

In the article by Donald Fiske and Louis Fogg (1990), the process of reviewing manuscripts for journal publication is examined. A central focus of the article is the disagreement between reviewers who evaluate a given manuscript for publication and make recommendations to the editor. Although the lack of agreement between reviewers is of interest, the article is included here for another reason. A large number of articles and comments from reviewers were evaluated. From the evaluation, Fiske and Fogg coded the types of weaknesses cited by reviewers. The salient weaknesses serve as a further guide for preparing reports for publication.

The final article, E. R. Oetting (1986) discusses issues in relation to grant writing. The article is engaging because of its description of the process, including the many slings and arrows awaiting the person who applies for funding. The issue of obtaining a grant is beside the point. The article was included here because selected ideas pertain to the communication of planned research and methodological issues that arise. Central to research is a clear rationale for why a study is needed and how it will contribute to our knowledge. The rationale for methods and procedures is essential within the write-up of a proposal or article. Why were these subjects, constructs, measures, and data analyses selected? Integration of points from all features covered in previous sections of this book come to bear in the written communication of the research.

36

A READER'S, WRITER'S, AND REVIEWER'S GUIDE TO ASSESSING RESEARCH REPORTS IN CLINICAL PSYCHOLOGY

BRENDAN A. MAHER

TOPIC CONTENT

1. Is the article appropriate to this journal? Does it fall within the boundaries mandated in the masthead description?

STYLE

1. Does the manuscript conform to APA style in its major aspects?

Reprinted from the *Journal of Consulting and Clinical Psychology, 46*, 835–838. Copyright 1978 by the American Psychological Association.

INTRODUCTION

1. Is the introduction as brief as possible given the topic of the article?
2. Are all of the citations correct and necessary, or is there padding? Are important citations missing? Has the author been careful to cite prior reports contrary to the current hypothesis?
3. Is there an explicit hypothesis?
4. Has the *origin* of the hypothesis been made explicit?
5. Was the hypothesis *correctly* derived from the theory that has been cited? Are other, contrary hypotheses compatible with the same theory?
6. Is there an explicit rationale for the selection of measures, and was it derived logically from the hypothesis?

METHOD

1. Is the method so described that replication is possible without further information?
2. **Subjects:** Were they sampled randomly from the population to which the results will be generalized?
3. Under what circumstances was informed consent obtained?
4. Are there probable biases in sampling (e.g., volunteers, high refusal rates, institution population atypical for the country at large, etc.)?
5. What was the "set" given to subjects? Was there deception? Was there control for experimenter influence and expectancy effects?
6. How were subjects debriefed?
7. Were subjects (patients) led to believe that they were receiving "treatment"?
8. Were there special variables affecting the subjects, such as medication, fatigue, and threat that were not part of the experimental manipulation? In clinical samples, was "organicity" measured and/or eliminated?
9. **Controls:** Were there appropriate control groups? What was being controlled for?
10. When more than one measure was used, was the order counterbalanced? If so, were order effects actually analyzed statistically?
11. Was there a control task(s) to confirm specificity of results?
12. **Measures:** For both dependent and independent variable measures—was validity and reliability established and reported? When a measure is tailor-made for a study, this is

very important. When validities and reliabilities are already available in the literature, it is less important.

13. Is there adequate description of tasks, materials, apparatus, and so forth?
14. Is there discriminant validity of the measures?
15. Are distributions of scores on measures typical of scores that have been reported for similar samples in previous literature?
16. Are measures free from biases such as
    a. Social desirability?
    b. Yeasaying and naysaying?
    c. Correlations with general responsivity?
    d. Verbal ability, intelligence?
17. If measures are scored by observers using categories or codes, what is the interrater reliability?
18. Was administration and scoring of the measures done blind?
19. If short versions, foreign-language translations, and so forth, of common measures are used, has the validity and reliability of these been established?
20. In correlational designs, do the two measures have theoretical and/or methodological independence?

REPRESENTATIVE DESIGN

1. When the stimulus is a human (e.g., in clinical judgments of clients of differing race, sex, etc.), is there a *sample* of stimuli (e.g., more than one client of each race or each sex)?
2. When only one stimulus or a few human stimuli were used, was an adequate explanation of the failure to sample given?

STATISTICS

1. Were the statistics used with appropriate assumptions fulfilled by the data (e.g., normalcy of distributions for parametric techniques)? Where necessary, have scores been transformed appropriately?
2. Were tests of significance properly used and reported? For example, did the author use the p value of a correlation to justify conclusions when the actual size of the correlation suggests little common variance between two measures?
3. Have statistical significance levels been accompanied by an analysis of practical significance levels?
4. Has the author considered the effects of a limited range of scores, and so forth, in using correlations?

5. Is the basic statistical strategy that of a "fishing expedition"; that is, if many comparisons are made, were the obtained significance levels predicted in advance? Consider the number of significance levels as a function of the total number of comparisons made.

FACTOR ANALYTIC STATISTICS

1. Have the correlation and factor matrices been made available to the reviewers and to the readers through the National Auxiliary Publications Service or other methods?
2. Is it stated what was used for communalities and is the choice appropriate? Ones in the diagonals are especially undesirable when items are correlated as the variables.
3. Is the method of termination of factor extraction stated, and is it appropriate in this case?
4. Is the method of factor rotation stated, and is it appropriate in this case?
5. If items are used as variables, what are the proportions of yes and no responses for each variable?
6. Is the sample size given, and is it adequate?
7. Are there evidences of distortion in the final solution, such as single factors, excessively high communalities, obliqueness when an orthogonal solution is used, linearly dependent variables, or too many complex variables?
8. Are artificial factors evident because of inclusion of variables in the analysis that are alternate forms of each other?

FIGURES AND TABLES

1. Are the figures and tables (a) necessary and (b) self-explanatory? Large tables of nonsignificant differences, for example, should be eliminated if the few obtained significances can be reported in a sentence or two in the text. Could several tables be combined into a smaller number?
2. Are the axes of figures identified clearly?
3. Do graphs correspond logically to the textual argument of the article? (E.g., if the text states that a certain technique leads to an *increment* of mental health and the accompanying graph shows a *decline* in symptoms, the point is not as clear to the reader as it would be if the text or the graph were amended to achieve visual and verbal congruence.)

DISCUSSION AND CONCLUSION

1. Is the discussion properly confined to the findings or is it digressive, including new post hoc speculations?
2. Has the author explicitly considered and discussed viable alternative explanations of the findings?
3. Have nonsignificant trends in the data been promoted to "findings"?
4. Are the limits of the generalizations possible from the data made clear? Has the author identified his/her own methodological difficulties in the study?
5. Has the author "accepted" the null hypothesis?
6. Has the author considered the possible methodological bases for discrepancies between the results reported and other findings in the literature?

37

BUT THE REVIEWERS ARE MAKING DIFFERENT CRITICISMS OF MY PAPER! DIVERSITY AND UNIQUENESS IN REVIEWER COMMENTS

DONALD W. FISKE AND LOUIS FOGG

An author receiving the editor's letter about a submitted paper is apprehensive not only about the editor's decision but also about the paper's weaknesses as alleged by the editor and the reviewers. The knowledgeable author is little comforted by the fact that no more than 2% of initial submissions are accepted (Eichorn & VandenBos, 1985), although 20 to 40% of revised manuscripts are accepted.

But what do the reviewers and the editor say about the author's cherished paper? It is certain that most of the perceived weaknesses will surprise the author. Perhaps the receipt of such painful feedback would be more tolerable if the author knew more about the contents of reviews received by other authors.

A survey of reviewers' and editors' criticisms can also provide indirect evidence on the methodological sophistication of authors and of reviewers and editors. What types of defects are reported? What kinds predominate?

Reprinted from the *American Psychologist*, 45, 591–598. Copyright 1990 by the American Psychological Association. We are indebted to the Biomedical Research Support Program of the Division of Social Sciences, University of Chicago, for a grant that enabled this research to be started.

Are the improvements proposed by reviewers ones that a colleague might have suggested or ones known only to methodological specialists?

Most papers are sent out to two or more reviewers. Are multiple reviews replicative or independent? Although their wording may differ, are the reviews saying much the same thing about a given paper? Do reviewers agree on the editorial actions they recommend to editors?

Many articles have been written on the editorial process. Largely critical, they often propose changes. Yet almost nothing has been reported on the free-response comments of reviewers. Smigel and Ross (1970) presented reasons given by associate editors for recommending acceptance or rejection of submissions to one journal. Daft (1985) classified the major problems he had found in 111 of his own reviews. Agreements between reviewer recommendations have often been studied—the reported correlations converging around .3. Aside from some instances given by Smigel and Ross, and some general statements made by Spencer, Hartnett, and Mahoney (1986), we have found no comparisons of the specific comments made by reviewers of the same paper.

The editorial process has many stages, from the author's selection of the journal to which a paper is submitted to the editor's final decision about that paper. At an intermediate stage is the work of the reviewer, reading the paper one or more times, thinking about it, and writing a report giving a general recommendation, a list of weaknesses noted by that reviewer, and perhaps a sentence or two on the paper's strengths and contributions. This article considers just the products of that stage, as reported back to the editor and author: What irremediable errors did the author make in planning and executing the research? What corrigible faults are there in the exposition, the presentation of the research? Do the several reviews report the same errors and faults?

METHOD USED

We have studied the reviewers' reports and the editors' decision letters for 153 papers submitted for the first time to American Psychological Assocation (APA) journals in late 1985 or in 1986. (The project was approved by the APA Publications and Communications Board.) At our request, editors sent these materials from their files to a consulting editor for an APA journal who painstakingly deleted the names and institutions of all authors and reviewers. Sampling widely in the spectrum of APA journals, we encountered one editor who refused to assist us and two others whose reluctance was respected. The final list included seven journals or sections and 12 action editors: For five journals, separate sets of materials were obtained for an associate editor as well as the editor. We used materials on 7 to 16 papers per editor. The journals were these: *Developmental Psychology, Journal of Abnormal Psychology, Journal of Comparative Psychology, Journal of Experimental Psychology: Human Perception and Performance, Journal of Experimental Psychology: Learning, Memory, and Cognition, Journal of Personality and Social Psychology: Attitudes and Social Cognition,* and *Journal of Personality and Social Psychology: Personality Processes and Individual Differences.*

We were impressed by the amount of time and effort that reviewers put into their work. Some of the submitted reports ran three or four single-spaced pages, lending credence to statements that manuscripts had been reread several times.

Coding

Each review, consisting of the reviewer's report to the editor and author, together with any comment directed only to the editor, was searched for statements about weaknesses identified in the submitted manuscript. Each critical point was coded separately. In each review, the number of such points ranged from 0 to 37, with a mean of 8.6. The brevity of the two reviews with no criticisms suggests a rapid if not cursory reading of the paper.

Each point was coded into the category in the research process to which it referred. The categories form a rough temporal sequence, from prior conceptual formulation to interpretation, conclusions, and writing (see Table 1). In addition, the defect was coded as having occurred during the Planning and Execution of the research itself or later, during the Presentation, the preparation and writing of the submitted paper. We coded only weaknesses because reviewers focus on them; they make only broad statements—if any—about the positive features of papers.

The coding was a long and difficult task. After some practice coding and the development of a preliminary manual, each of us independently coded reports, and then we discussed our judgments and reached consensus on the final coding. The agreement between our independent judgments was only fair. After efforts to improve it had very limited success, we decided that, with the ambiguities in the reports and in the coding system, higher agreement was not feasible. Of all the segments identified as codable by either of us, we agreed on 79%. For 73% of the agreed-on points, we agreed on which of the 11 categories in the research was involved in the criticism (kappa = .69). Many disagreements involved adjacent categories

TABLE 1
Distribution of Weaknesses as Reported by Reviewers for APA
Journals by Percentages

Category	Weakness attributed to		
	Planning and execution	Presentation	Total
Conceptual: Pre-execution	4.9	10.3	15.2
Conceptual: Linkage to execution	3.0	2.0	5.1
Design	6.9	3.9	10.8
Procedures	6.0	6.3	12.3
Measurement	3.4	3.9	7.3
Statistical analyses	5.8	2.7	8.5
Results	4.1	9.1	13.2
Interpretations and conclusions		16.1	16.1
Editorial and writing		8.5	8.5
General	0.3	2.6	2.9
Total	34.4	65.4	99.8

Note: For 153 submitted papers, 3,477 weaknesses were coded from 402 reviews.

or steps. Agreement was 85% (kappa = .67) on whether the problem occurred in the Planning and Execution of the research or in the Presentation of the manuscript.

Because the critic's judgment of the seriousness of just a single defect can play a major role in the reviewer's or editor's overall evaluation of a paper, the reader may wonder why we did not code the severity of each point. We did have such a scale for points referring to the Planning and Execution of the research, and seriousness was implied in some subcategories for Presentation points. Our agreement, however, was lowest on this aspect of the coding. Although a reviewer would sometimes write that the paper should not be published because of one or two specified points, more commonly the reviewer did not weight the points, or at most classified them as major or minor. It must also be recognized (as a thoughtful reviewer has reminded us) that the same weakness may be judged as fatal or as troublesome but acceptable as a function of the substantive context and the research area. In a well-developed research area in which the nature of the appropriate controls is generally accepted, overlooking one control could make a paper unpublishable. In a new area or a socially important one, the omission of a reasonable control—especially an expensive one—might be tolerated.

Note also that a criticism can be serious in several diverse ways. A critical flaw in the design may (in the eyes of the reviewer) make the paper worthless. An omission or ambiguity in exposition may make the reviewer uncertain about the soundness of the research plan. Departing from current practice in a research area may cause the reviewer to infer that the author is not sufficiently qualified in background and experience to attempt such a research study. These several types of seriousness could not be captured readily in a single scale.

RESULTS

Loci and Weaknesses

Weaknesses were associated with activities in all the categories or stages of the research and with the presentation of all activities (see Table 1). Over all the reviews coded, the most frequent locus for weaknesses was in the Interpretations and Conclusions made after the research was completed. (This finding rebuts the proposal by Kupfersmid,1988, that editorial decisions be made without seeing the Results and Discussion sections of submitted papers.) The next most common type was in the presentation of the conceptual work that was done before the empirical research was started. After these come the categories in which most authors probably expect to receive criticisms: Results, Procedures, and Design. Note that the proportions for Presentation are large for the first two of these.

Of all criticisms, two thirds were coded as Presentation problems. Although this accumulation is due largely to defining the Interpretations and Conclusions stage as occurring subsequent to the research execution (along with the Editorial and Writing category), it is impressive that the reviewers saw as many problems in the presentation—exposition and description—as in the actual research activities (the categories in the first seven rows of Table 1). Moreover, these data slightly understate the actual frequencies of presentation problems because we had the convention of coding each type of minor problem, such as typographical errors and poor sentences, only the first time it was mentioned. Criticisms of presentation are corrigible. Many of them could have been prevented by more careful review by the authors themselves and also by frank critiquing from a number of colleagues.

Types of Weaknesses

But just what criticisms were made? How were the categories in Table 1 defined? Table 2 provides answers to these questions by showing the types of contents subsumed under each grouping. The labels for the subcategories are almost paraphrases of reviewer comments. The reviewer would write something similar to one of these headings and then, typically, specify more concretely the nature of the difficulty. Thus, the reviewer

TABLE 2
Classification of Weaknesses Reported by Reviewers for APA Journals

Category	No. of criticisms
Conceptual: Pre-execution	
Planning and execution	**39**
Does not seem to know current state of the field	7
Other poor scholarship	4
Poorly differentiated concepts or issues	5
Concepts poorly defined	3
Conceptual basis for study poor or incomplete	7
Other poor conceptualizing	3
Reviewer disagrees with author's statements	8
Presentation	**87**
A body of literature is slighted or left out	11
A reference or author is left out	5
Report of prior research is erroneous	8
References to the literature are out of date	2
Theoretical presentation incomplete, needs expansion	4
Omissions in Introduction	6
Concepts or issues not clearly described	6
Overall theoretical presentation poor or unclear	5
Conceptualizing is erroneous or poor	6
Introduction or theoretical discussion too long	10
Introduction is inadequate	4
Terminology in Introduction is incorrect, confusing, etc.	9
Other problems in writing of Introduction	5
Conceptual: Linkage to execution	
Planning and execution	**27**
Poor basic rationale for study	8
Experiment or task does not test the theory	9
Rationale does not justify the measure used	3
Measures are poorly chosen	3
Presentation	**18**
Conceptualization or hypotheses unclear	6
Rationale for experiment unclear	2
Predictions are not justified	2
Design	
Planning and execution	**61**
Design is defective, incomplete or inappropriate	9
Design should be within-subject (or within-group)	4
Variable, condition, or manipulation missing	4
Faulty procedure	3
Sample is too small	11
Sample is too restricted or not appropriate	4
Sample is poor or contaminated	5
Sample is too heterogeneous	3
No control or comparison group	4
Poor control group	6
Variables not controlled	5
Presentation	**25**
More information about subjects is needed	6
Explain selection or elimination of subjects	7

Table 2 (*continued*)

Category	No. of criticisms
Number of subjects is unclear	3
Design or experimental protocol unclear	5
Procedures	
Planning and execution	**58**
No or poor controls	5
Confounding, nonindependence, or lack of counterbalancing	11
Poor task	4
Poor instructions	3
Poor experimental procedures	8
Poor choice of stimuli	10
Manipulation defective or not checked	5
What are the processes in subjects	3
Effects of demand characteristics	3
Presentation	**45**
General lack of clarity	8
Procedural detail missing	12
Give justification for procedure	3
Clarify the stimuli	10
Were there order effects?	4
Measurement	
Planning and execution	**34**
Measure is indirect, superficial, not the best	11
Measure does not cover the construct	3
Potential bias in the measure	4
Problems with recall and self-report	4
Measure is not validated	6
Reliability poor or unknown	3
Presentation	**35**
Describe item characteristics, format	5
Explain development and scoring of measure	5
Describe administration of measures	3
Reliability or validity data not given or unclear	8
Statistical analyses	
Planning and execution	**48**
A statistical error is specified, and a better statistic is suggested or implied	9
A statistical error is specified, but no remedy is suggested	5
The statistical analysis is performed incorrectly	5
General, unspecified criticism of the analyses	6
A specified statistical analysis should be added	12
Some additional analysis is needed	5
Presentation	**23**
Rationale or justification for the analysis is faulty	14
Unclear how an analysis was done	5
A statistical procedure is described poorly	4
What data were used?	3
Statistical results are not given	3
Report of statistics is incorrect	3

Table 2 (*continued*)

Category	No. of criticisms
Results	
Planning and execution	**50**
Results are inconsistent	6
Results are inconclusive, incomplete	7
Results are puzzling, difficult to interpret, confounded	7
Results are weak	6
Results are chance	3
Results are obvious, expected, not surprising	6
Results replicate prior work	7
Results give little or no new information	8
Presentation	**63**
Unreported relationships	6
Other results not given	7
Tables and descriptive data are needed	7
Present the results more succinctly	8
Delete some tables or figures	4
Tables or figures need clarification	8
General presentation of results unclear	5
Specific clarifications are needed	6
Inconsistencies in presentation of results	5
Interpretations and conclusions	
Presentation[a]	**121**
Interpretations or conclusions are not warranted by the data	17
Statement is unacceptable, unconvincing	19
There are alternative interpretations	7
Findings or results are not interpreted or not explained	10
Their meaning or theoretical relevance is unclear or not shown	8
Their implications need to be worked out	6
Discuss or elaborate on a point	10
Discussion is too long	6
Discussion is generally poor or unclear	7
A specific point in the discussion is unclear	8
Inaccurate statement about the literature or does not know it	7
Prior literature should be cited or discussed	7
Methodological matters pertinent to findings or conclusions	10
Editorial and writing	
Presentation	**44**
Generally poor writing	10
Bad sentence	5
Poor or wrong word or phrase	5
Specific suggestions to improve writing	3
Paper is too long	6
Make it a short report	3
Citations missing, unclear, or inappropriate	4
Typographical errors	3
Not in APA format	2
General	
Planning, execution and presentation	**25**
Contribution is of little or no importance	8

Table 2 (continued)

Category	No. of criticisms
Paper is premature; not enough work or studies	3
Paper replicates previous research	2
Paper should be submitted elsewhere to a more appropriate (e.g., specialized) journal	4
Paper should be submitted to a less demanding journal	5

Note: For each cell, the items not accounted for by the stated category frequencies were placed in a "miscellaneous" category not listed here.
[a]Also included here are nine points originally coded as overinterpretations.

might devote several words, a sentence, a paragraph, or a whole single-spaced page to a difficulty that was coded as one point.

How was Table 2 produced? Forty papers were arbitrarily selected for analysis, 4 from each of 10 editor–journal sets. (At the request of one editor, materials from one journal were not included in this analysis.) For each of the subcategories in Table 1, all reviewer points about these papers were assembled and inspected. Types perceived by one of us were reviewed by the other, and the final types listed in Table 2 were derived by consensus. The number in the right-hand column gives the frequency of reviewer criticisms falling in the preceding grouping. A frequency of 39 means that there were 39 criticisms falling in, say, the Conceptual: Pre-execution, Planning and Execution subcategory. In this case, 39 of the 40 papers were likely to have received such a criticism, assuming that a given point about a paper is not made by more than one reviewer. This assumption was rarely violated (as shown subsequently). This estimation also neglects the fact that a paper with more reviewers, and hence more criticisms, would be more likely to have a criticism of a given type.

From inspection of Table 2, it is obvious that hundreds of different kinds of criticisms are made by reviewers. Even within the individual subcategories of the table, there are from 3 to 13 types. The fact that there are no types with large frequencies is purely a consequence of our approach to the categorizing: We wanted our types to be reasonably specific in order to maximize their potential usefulness to authors.

The types in Table 2 are empirical, being derived from the recorded examples. After the fact, it looks as though kinds of weaknesses, as opposed to contents, could profitably be classified as follows: something not done or omitted, something done incompletely, something done poorly, and something done wrong. That classification is applicable to Planning and Execution points as well as to Presentation points. For the latter, "done poorly" has two subtypes: The exposition can be either unclear or too long.

For the methodologist, the types in Table 2 suggest that the typical reviewer is aware of standard methodological considerations and also of the special problems in each given type of research. Most of the criticisms concerned methodological matters that are fairly well known and generally accepted; they were not arguments for specialized or unusual techniques lacking consensual endorsement nor were they objections to the failure to use methods only very recently developed and disseminated. Note, however, the frequencies of diverse conceptual problems in planning the research and the numerous criticisms of interpretations and conclusions.

We also coded each letter communicating the editor's decision to the author, using the same coding scheme as that for reviewer reports. These data were not subjected to intensive analysis for two reasons. First, editors varied greatly in the length of their letters: Some simply said, "Given these reviews, I must reject your paper," whereas others wrote two- or three-page independent reviews of papers before discussing the points made by reviewers. Also, the majority of points noted in editors' letters were restatements of reviewer points.

THE RELATIVE UNIQUENESS OF EACH REVIEW

In principle, the several reviewers for each paper could make the same or similar points, and that set of points might have little overlap with the set for another paper. Instead, as we coded, it became clear that reviewers were not making the same points—in fact, rarely did one reviewer make the same point as any other reviewer of that paper. To elucidate this perception, we made a number of exploratory analyses, using various criteria for a match or correspondence between points made by different reviewers. In no analysis did we find a suggestion of more than a quite minimal degree of overlap between a pair of reviews.

To demonstrate this state of affairs, we carried out an analysis using eight papers per editor (only seven were available in one case). For each paper, we compared two reviewers chosen a priori. We looked for instances in which the two reviewers had points coded in the same cell of the original coding scheme. Points in the same cell were in the same row (category) and the same column—one of three degrees of seriousness for Planning and Execution points or one of five types of inadequacy for Presentation (defective, unclear or incomplete, missing, excess length, and weak or other). Whenever the two reviewers made criticisms falling in the same cell, we went back to the original reports to see if the points were identical. For example, here are quotes from two reviewers making the same point: "On page 12 the author states that the relation between {X} and {Y} was not examined but Footnote 3 reports such an analysis," and "On p. 12, it says that the relation between {X} and {Y} will not be examined, but it is in Footnote 3." In contrast, here are two statements making similar but different points: "There seems to be no particular reason for interest in specific {items} so Tables {X and Y} are unnecessary," and "The discussion in places reiterates the results by listing . . . items showing significant effects. . . . Because the individual items are not derived from a tight rationale . . . these types of conclusions do not help the reader get the big picture of what happened in the study."

In order to evaluate the agreement between a pair of reviewers, we determined the level of agreement that might occur by chance. Two reviews of different papers can make the same point, such as not having enough subjects or having too lengthy a discussion section. We generated an estimate of chance agreement by comparing, systematically, one reviewer of each paper with one reviewer of the next paper in our set. Because the two papers had different content, the criteria for a match had to be relaxed a bit: For example, "Figure 1 is unclear" was judged to match "Figure 3 is confusing." Note also that some points can be made only about a specific paper: See the earlier example, "On page 12. . . ."

The results of this analysis are given in Table 3. For each of 95 papers, a pair of reviewers were compared. The number of possible correspondences, in which cells would have a point from each reviewer, is obtained from the smaller of the two reviewers' total numbers of points (e.g., if one made five points and the other nine, there could be no more than five correspondences). For reviews of the same paper, there were 585 possible correspondences. Among these, there were 156 instances of a point from each of the two reviews being coded into the same cell. Finally, among these, we judged that in 42 instances, the same point was being made by both reviewers. So, for these 95 papers, there were 42 instances in which the two reviewers made the same point—0.44 instances per pair of reviewers for a paper.

TABLE 3
Correspondences Between Points Made by Two Reviewers

Count	Same paper	Different papers
Number of pairs of reviewer reports compared	95	95
Maximum possible correspondences	585	538
Number of pairs of points similarly coded (same cell)	156	113
Number of exact matches: Same point is made by both reviewers	42	11

To estimate the rate of chance agreement, we carried out a similar analysis for pairs of reviews for different papers. There were 113 instances of a pair of points being coded into the same cell, but only 11 of these involved the same point (e.g., "How many did not agree to participate?" and "How many patients declined [to participate]?" So, at this level of analysis, some correspondences are found between the points made by a pair of reviewers, but similar matches sometimes occur in reports on different papers. In these data, out of 585 possibilities, there were only 31 matches beyond the number expected by chance.

To permit exact comparisons, the preceding analyses required strict criteria for matches. Perhaps those criteria were too strict. Given the modest reliability of the coding, it was possible that the same point made by two reviewers of a paper might have been coded into adjacent cells rather than the same cell (e.g., because of the point's different contexts in the two reports). An analysis testing this possibility included all possible pairs of reviewers (361 instead of 95). In this way, we identified 125 different points on which two or three reviewers agreed. Thus, this looser criterion for matching of points did not increase the low rate of occurrence of matches.

Of these 125 points, 51% concerned Planning and Execution—which had only 34% of all points. In contrast, for the same categories (Conceptual through Results), Presentation matters had 38% of all points but only 22% of the matches. (The greater proportion of agreed-on points for the Planning and Execution area is highly significant by chi-square.) Relatively high rates of correspondences were also found for the Editorial and Writing (e.g., "The paper is too long") and for the General (e.g., "The paper is not appropriate for this journal") categories.

Finally, it should be noted that when two reviewers make the same point about a paper, it does not necessarily mean that they have much the same overall impression about the paper. Comparing pairs of reviewers making the same point with pairs not making any common point, we found reviewers' overall recommendations to the editor showed similar disparities in both sets of pairs.

It was of course possible that even though reviewers reported different points, their general evaluations of papers agreed fairly well. As mentioned earlier, the prior literature did not encourage that hope. Nevertheless, we computed intraclass correlations for the several reviewers' overall recommendations to the editor. Using both the reviewer's checkmark on the brief multiple-choice item furnished by the editor and the general tone of the reviewer's broad qualitative appraisal (especially in any note directed to the editor alone), we coded each reviewer's recommendation onto a 15-point scale. That scale was developed from the alternatives in the items used by the several journals for obtaining reviewer overall judgments and from standard editor phrases in their letters to authors. The scaling of the statements and phrases was based on the judgments of 15 colleagues. Although the intraclass correlations varied from −.23 to .68 because each of the 12 samples per editor journal was small, the mean was .20—a little lower than other studies have found.

Not reported earlier were our analyses looking for differences between journals and between editors. The data are messy—several points per review, several reviews per paper, but not very many papers per editor. We focused primarily on profiles of category means: Did the reviewers for a given editor produce a profile of points per category (stage of the research) that differed from that for other editors? We applied our primary criterion: Were the results consistent? In our judgment, the answer was negative. For example, clusters of editors for the Planning and Execution side differed from those for the Presentation side. Similarity between areas covered by journals was not matched by correspondence between profiles. The editor and associate editor for the same journal might or might not fall into the same cluster. It was our impression that the basic unit was each editor and that editor's choice of reviewers.

DISCUSSION

It is possible that our failure to find consistency in those analyses comparing editors was due to the unreliability of our coding, but we do not believe that unreliability was a major factor. Because our data were pooled codings, they are more reliable than the figures given earlier. Typically, when one of us found that he had missed a point noted by the other, he would accept his oversight. Similarly, one of us would usually agree that the other's case for his coding was better than his own.

What are the possible effects of our limited coder reliability on the findings reported earlier? We believe that another pair of judges, using our coding manual, would generate data like those in Table 1. Similarly, they would find the same weaknesses we found, and so their table would look like our Table 2, with some differences in the frequencies and perhaps some variations in the locations of some subcategories. Finally, with more reliable coding, the number of exact matches in Table 3 would presumably be larger although the basic finding would remain intact. More generally, the relative independence of the comments made by separate reviewers would still be evident: Any author who has available the reviews for a submitted paper can confirm this finding by taking each point in one review and searching for its replication in another review.

As an anonymous reviewer of a prior draft of this article pointed out, one's interpretation of our findings depends on one's conception of the reviewers' role in the editorial process. The points we coded from each reviewer report included all the weaknesses noted by that reviewer, and hence provided the basis for the reviewer's overall judgment of the quality of the paper. But what does the editor want from each reviewer? Does an editor want merely the overall recommendation, with the comments of the reviewer being primarily for the edification of the author? It seems likely that most editors want to know what weaknesses each reviewer saw, as an aid to the editor's own evaluation of the quality of the paper. But each additional reviewer contributes one more list of weaknesses. Is an author's paper at greater risk of rejection with more reviewers? We cannot provide a clear answer because the number of reviewers is a multiply determined variable. The analysis of editors' decisions and their precursors must be left for a later article.

Saying that two reviewers typically do not agree does not necessarily mean that they disagree. An attempt to locate explicit disagreements turned up only a few instances in which one reviewer said a given aspect of the paper was satisfactory but another found a problem: For example, "As for the methods, they are clearly and sufficiently described," and "The methods presented are insufficient to reproduce the study in another lab." Of course, because the typical review devotes little space to positive statements about the paper, there are undoubtedly many hidden disagreements of this sort.

Given the low degree of manifested consensus between reviewers, it is reasonable to ask whether the reviewers' criticisms were appropriate. Although we cannot give a definitive answer to that question, we believe that they generally were. We very rarely saw any criticism that we were inclined to question, on the basis of internal or other evidence, such as the reviewer's stating that a statistical test had a particular assumption. Also, in instances in which we consulted the original manuscript, we found no reviewer criticisms with which we disagreed. (We obtained some censored manuscripts to see whether we could code more reliably with their aid. We could not.) Finally, it was very uncommon for an editor to indicate disagreement with a point made by a reviewer.

Our evidence for the relative independence or uniqueness of reviewer reports will not surprise many editors. (See Roediger, 1987, for a judicious discussion of this and other aspects of the editorial process.) Editors are familiar with such nonoverlap, and of course they pick reviewers with different kinds of expertise, reviewers who will be likely to emphasize different kinds of defects.

These data raise questions for editors and reviewers. First, given the limited agreement between reviewers and the sizable but finite population of weaknesses that can be identified for any one paper, are two reviews sufficient? Don't the editor and the author need to have a larger set of points called to their attention? Second, should editors ask reviewers to consider more explicitly the positive features of each paper? Perhaps a bipolar scale could be used to indicate the overall positive or negative balance between strengths and weaknesses. One question that editors and reviewers might (or perhaps do) ask themselves is this: Assuming that the authors prepared a revision that successfully dealt with the reported problems in exposition or presentation, would the remaining weaknesses outweigh the paper's potential positive contribution from its ideas and findings?

Everyone who has submitted manuscripts for publication knows that reviewers always can and do find some weaknesses to report. An author's aim should be to minimize the number of such reported defects, thereby reducing their negative influence on the overall evaluations of the paper by the editor and reviewers. One can only do so much alone. One needs to get a number of colleagues to help by reading one's paper as carefully and critically as possible. Scientific research is a community activity. As von Békésy (1960) reported in his own experience,

> Another way of dealing with {potential research} errors is to have friends who are willing to spend the time necessary to carry out a critical examination of the experimental design beforehand and the results after the experiments have been completed. An even better way is to have an enemy. An enemy is willing to devote a vast amount of time and brain power to ferreting out errors both large and small, and this without any compensation. The trouble is that really capable enemies are scarce; most of them are only ordinary. Another trouble with enemies is that they sometimes develop into friends and lose a good deal of their zeal. It was in this way that the writer lost his three best enemies. (pp. 8–9)

REFERENCES

Daft, R. L. (1985). Why I recommended that your manuscript be rejected and what you can do about it. In L. L. Cummings & P. J. Frost (Eds.), *Publishing in the organizational sciences* (pp. 193-204). Homewood, IL: Irwin.

Eichorn, D. H., & VandenBos, G. R. (1985). Dissemination of scientific and professional knowledge: Journal publication within the APA. *American Psychologist, 40*, 1309–1316.

Kupfersmid, J. (1988). Improving what is published: A model in search of an editor. *American Psychologist, 43*, 635–642.

Roediger, H. L. III. (1987). The role of journal editors in the scientific process. In D. N. Jackson & J. P. Rushton (Eds.), *Scientific excellence: Origins and assessment* (pp. 222–252). Newbury Park, CA: Sage.

Smigel, E. D., & Ross, H. L. (1970). Factors in the editorial decision. *American Sociologist, 5*, 19–21.

Spencer, N. J., Hartnett, J., & Mahoney, J. (1986). Problems with reviews in the standard editorial practice. *Journal of Social Behavior and Personality, 1*, 21–36.

von Békésy, G. (1960). *Experiments in hearing.* New York: McGraw-Hill.

38

TEN FATAL MISTAKES IN GRANT WRITING

E. R. OETTING

I have just stepped down as the Chair of the National Institute on Drug Abuse (NIDA) Initial Review Group for Epidemiology, Prevention, and Services Research. The massive title means only that I chaired the meetings of the group of scientists who reviewed the grant proposals that many psychologists and other scientists submitted: grants to study epidemiological, social, psychological, or treatment aspects of drug abuse. Our primary task was to decide whether the research had scientific merit. If, in our judgment, the proposed study was good science, we then assigned a priority score to the grant: a score showing how much we thought the research would contribute to scientific knowledge about drug abuse.

Those ratings were extremely important; they almost always determined whether a proposal could eventually be funded. While I was on the committee, not one single grant that the committee rejected was funded.

Reprinted from the *Professional Psychology: Research and Practice, 17,* 570–573. Copyright 1986 by the American Psychological Association.

Furthermore, more than 90% of the time, the proposals that were funded were selected from those that had the best priority numbers.

I do not want to discuss how to prepare a good grant proposal or even list all of the little things that can go wrong. There are excellent materials available elsewhere on how to write a grant (Gordon, 1978; Holtz, 1979; Lindholm, Marin, & Lopez, 1982). After participating in this review process for several years, however, I decided that there were a few very basic mistakes that people made, mistakes that almost always led to rejection of their proposals. I saw these same fatal flaws time and again at NIDA, and also when serving as a special reviewer for other agencies. Avoiding these errors might keep one from wasting a lot of time and effort in preparing a proposal that would have almost no chance of being funded.

MISTAKE 1: "LET'S GET A GRANT TO PAY FOR TREATMENT"

Careful reading of the goals of the grant and the budget reveals that the primary aim is to get more treatment staff or to fund treatment staff that have been cut by budget reductions. The research plan is weak, and the emphasis is on how much good will be done by providing service.

It is, of course, possible to provide service on a research grant, if it is an integral part of the research. A project, for example, could be conducted to test treatment effectiveness, if the research plan would actually allow determination of what kind of treatment worked, for whom it worked, and how well it worked. Many proposals, however, are dominated by service delivery and include only a sparse and patched-together research plan. They are often, but not always, submitted by a service agency, with a research plan added by an academic from a nearby institution. The goal is clearly to provide service, not to answer important questions about how and why treatment works. Even if the committee agrees that providing the service is laudable, they still must rate the project in terms of its contribution to science, and just providing service does not usually add much to knowledge.

MISTAKE 2: SIGNING UP FOR THE WRONG RACE

If you were a sprinter, fast but without much endurance, it would be a blatant error to sign up for a marathon. Despite this obvious principle, NIDA receives grant proposals from scientists that do not enable them to use their greatest strengths, and instead focus on areas in which they are relatively weak. I have deep sympathy for some of the personal and professional goals that lead to this error. One researcher, for example, applies for a grant to study an idea that is totally novel and does not fit into his or her past research. Another scientist is trying to use grant funds to retrain, to move into a different area of research. Still another scientist, highly skilled and experienced in psychological assessment, tries to be thorough and includes extensive physiological measures in the proposal despite minimal experience with physiological measurement.

In an ideal world, all of these behaviors should be encouraged. Unfortunately, given current conditions of funding, any of these proposals is likely to end up being rejected. A decade ago, when more grant funds were available, a proposal that was only reasonably good, or one that entailed considerable risk of failure, might have been funded. Today, a proposal has to be very strong to be funded, and that usually means that the risk of failure has to be low.

It is hard enough to design a tight and carefully controlled experiment when you already have considerable research experience in an area. When the idea is really new, creating innovative measurement techniques and experimental methods can be very difficult, and a proposal is likely to leave doubts in the minds of at least some members of the committee. Sadly, funding for research is tight enough so that even one or two committee members with doubts can be enough to put a priority score out of the funding range. The scientist who is trying to retrain or move into a new area, or the one who includes areas outside of his or her expertise, is at a real disadvantage: The proposal will be read by people who are already skilled and knowledgeable in that other area, and the proposal is likely to look unsophisticated and weak to those experts.

A strong consultant or a co-principal investigator (Co-PI) who is an expert in the new area could solve some of these problems. All too often, however, the consultant is an afterthought and was not deeply involved in writing the proposal or in designing the study, and the proposal remains weak. Investigators might be better off if they thought seriously about their strengths and considered how they might contribute to knowledge by using their existing talents, skills, and experience, while retraining or polishing new skills or innovative ideas until they can be winners.

MISTAKE 3: "TRUST ME—I'M AN EXPERT!"

The principal investigator does not provide details of how important tasks will be done, pointing only to a past record of solving similar problems. This may appear to be arrogance, but there is a good chance that it is not. Part of the problem that experienced researchers have is that they are excruciatingly familiar with a particular aspect of the problem or with a particular method. It is hard to remember that others may not have the same familiarity.

Being famous is definitely not enough to automatically get you a grant. No matter how "important" the scientist is, or how experienced, providing complete details in the grant proposal is essential. Proposals are not reviewed "blindly." In fact, part of the committee's task is to evaluate the credentials of the investigator and to judge whether the investigator is competent to complete the project and likely to succeed. Having a strong publication record can be an asset; the past record is important because it demonstrates that the principal investigator (PI) does have the capability to complete research and bring it to fruition. But in some ways, the committee expects more of an established scientist. An experienced researcher is expected to have a firm grasp of the literature and should have the ability to write a proposal in which he or she perfectly describes procedures, methods, and instrumentation. If the proposal is not excellent, the committee is likely to wonder why. Although committee members try to maintain complete objectivity, they are human and are likely to be more critical of the expert's proposal than if it came from a relative novice.

Sometimes young investigators feel that they are at a disadvantage, but this may not be entirely true. The new investigator, proposing a reasonably well-designed study, is often viewed with considerable sympathy. The risk with a new investigator may be somewhat higher, but in assigning a priority score, the committee may weigh the value of recruiting and encouraging a new scientist fairly heavily, particularly if the cost of the study is reasonable. When this weight is added to the perceived value of producing the study, a proposal may receive a very favorable priority number.

It is not only senior scientists who fail to provide enough detail. The single most frequent reason for rejecting a reasonably good proposal or approving it with a low priority number may be that it did not include enough detailed information.

MISTAKE 4: IGNORING THE "PINK SHEETS"

When your grant proposal is evaluated by the committee, you get feedback. The results of the review are printed on baby pink paper. If you really want to have your research funded, these "pink sheets" are more precious than rubies. They tell you, in detail, just what that committee saw as the strengths and the weaknesses of the proposal.

When you resubmit the proposal, the information on the pink sheets can be used to emphasize the strengths and to deal specifically and clearly with every weakness in the proposal. This may seem obvious, but many investigators do not resubmit, and others send the proposal back with only cosmetic changes and do not deal with the weaknesses that were clearly specified on the pink sheets. Dealing directly and effectively with every weakness does not guarantee that you will be funded, but ignoring a weakness or glossing over it does ensure that you will be rejected again.

Incidentally, a criticism of your proposal does not necessarily mean that you are "wrong." Your approach could be perfectly appropriate, but you need to communicate better, showing exactly why what you plan to do is the best way to do it. You do not have to refute the pink sheets; you can clarify, present the material from a different angle, or provide what is missing to make your point clear. Why are you doing it in this way? Why are you doing this project at all? A criticism on the pink sheets means that you have not convinced the committee.

The pink sheets may also show that you were approved, but with a poor priority. This means that the committee thought that your proposal had scientific merit and did not have any fatal flaws, but that you have not convinced the committee that the result, as you planned the study, would be highly valuable. The criticisms provide a good set of ideas about how you might modify your proposal, but you cannot just answer the questions. You need to rethink the proposal, clean it up, make it really relevant and important. In short, make it better science.

MISTAKE 5: "I'M GOING TO DEVELOP A SCALE"

When I see this statement on a proposal, I always hear Andy Hardy shouting, "Let's do a show!" Andy thought that doing a show was going to solve everyone's problems. In all too many grant proposals, "I will build a scale" is presented in the same way: as the solution to all of the project's problems.

Building a scale is usually listed as a supposedly minor part of the project. The author finds that there is no already tested method for assessing one or more of the variables that have to be measured. The answer is to build a scale. That would be fine, but the proposals that are likely to be rejected usually present "building a scale" as a simple solution to the problem. There may be a few short sentences mentioning that the scale will be tested for reliability, but the author provides no details to show that he or she is aware of the technical steps needed to construct a reliable and valid measure, or of how difficult the task really is.

Unless, for example, the author includes samples of items that may appear on the scale, the committee may find it difficult to even begin evaluating whether a scale will be able to take its place as an important part of the research. Experienced researchers and the members of the committee have a great deal of experience, know how hard it is to write good items, and are likely to want to see what kinds of items the author is capable of creating. Are they clear? Will the research subjects be able to read and understand them? Could they have more than one meaning? Do they relate to the construct being assessed?

The PI sometimes mentions testing the new scale for reliability but does not mention what will happen if the scale is not reliable. There is no pilot test, no opportunity for revision, and no alternative plans, simply an assumption that the scale will be reliable. The reviewer has no choice but to mark a proposal like this unfavorably because if the scale does not work, the research is usually of little or no value.

Constructing a reliable and valid scale is a very difficult, technically complex, and challenging task. If a new measure must be constructed for a study, the PI has to show in-depth awareness of the theoretical and practical problems involved, show knowledge about where and when things might go wrong, and show how adjustments and alterations can be made so that eventually an adequate measure will be produced. If the value of the research depends totally on the adequacy of a new scale that is yet to be constructed, it is essential to present at least pilot data showing that there is very good reason for believing that with a minimum of further work, a reliable and valid scale will be produced.

MISTAKE 6: "IF I 'TACK ON' DRUG ABUSE, NIDA WILL FUND MY RESEARCH"

This kind of proposal usually results when the principal investigator has a consistent and ongoing research program in an area other than drug abuse. Sometimes funding has been cut off by another agency; sometimes the scientist wants to expand research into new areas. The result is a proposal that can be very strong in those parts that deal with the investigator's true love and very superficial in the parts that link that research with drug abuse.

The committee has little choice but to reject the resulting proposal because it would usually contribute little to scientific knowledge about drug abuse. Rejection is often accompanied by real regret because drug use, like other human behaviors, is cross-linked to a very wide range of human problems and personal and social characteristics, because the investigator is often a very good researcher, and because the proposal sometimes presents interesting possibilities and ideas.

The solution is obvious: the scientist sending a proposal to NIDA has to recognize that drug use is as important to the proposed research as the rest of the study and warrants the same in-depth review of the literature and the same careful and sophisticated consideration as the other variables in the study. One approach might be to include a Co-PI or consultant who is experienced in research on drug abuse and who has a major involvement in preparing the proposal. Another is simply to do your homework: to truly study the literature in drug use as you would the literature related to your own initial field of interest.

MISTAKE 7: THE "NO-PROBLEM" PROBLEM

Suppose one proposed a study to examine drug use by high school superintendents, or another to provide expensive drug avoidance training for institutionalized handicapped youth. In neither of these situations is there any evidence that a real drug use problem exists, and in both of them there is fairly good reason to believe that there will be relatively minimal drug involvement. Neither study seems to attack a real problem.

Another kind of "no-problem" involves the hypothesis that is hardly worth testing: for example, "I am going to find out how the make of car that a person owns relates to drug use."

You could, of course, make a case that no one really knows whether high school superintendents have drug problems. They do have high-stress jobs and might be tempted to use drugs to relieve that stress. If no hard choices about research funding had to be made, an argument that high school superintendents are an important group and that people should know about their drug use might be cogent.

You might also draw up some inferences about what automobiles symbolize to people and how particular drugs match those symbols. You might also argue that people could learn something about Freudian theory from the relationship between cars and drugs. But research funds are severely limited. When there are obvious and serious drug problems, cogent and important theoretical hypotheses that need to be tested, and not enough funds to do the research that really needs to be done, a proposal to study a "non-problem" is likely to get short shrift.

The argument "little is known about . . . " is not a very good one. Little is known about making love in a canoe while standing up, but then again, why bother? If you really believe that what you want to study represents a serious problem, then you will probably have to do the pilot research to demonstrate that fact, and write a very persuasive section on significance of the research, before you will get funding.

MISTAKE 8: EXCUSES—EXPLAINING WHY THE STUDY CANNOT BE DONE RIGHT

"The administrators of the clinic would not agree to a control group." "Subjects in School D cannot be given saliva tests because the administration will not allow those tests." If you are writing a proposal, you have to remember that the purpose of the research grant program is to fund good research, not to fund your research. An excuse counts for nothing; it is only the quality of the research that will actually be done that counts. If a control group or a saliva test would be important to producing a good study, and if either one is not possible, then the study is not worth funding as it stands.

This is not to say that control groups or saliva tests or any other specific conditions are essential for good research. If, however, particular experimental conditions or methods would ordinarily be needed for a good research plan and cannot, for some reason, be provided, you have to present a strong case showing why they are not essential parts of your proposed study.

Failure to provide control conditions in treatment or prevention studies can be particularly serious. Although the reviewers know that they are difficult to construct and that it is hard to obtain approval for them, not having adequate comparisons or controls may not only damage the ability of the study to reach conclusions, but also suggests that the PI may not have real control over other essential conditions of the study. If administrators or staff feel the need to dictate conditions and do not understand or are not in sympathy with research goals and needs, it may be symptomatic of other potential problems. What other changes might be dictated by treatment staff or administration either before or during the course of the study that may negate the value of the research?

MISTAKE 9: USING INAPPROPRIATE TESTS OR MEASURES

I can list only a few of the many different ways that this mistake has been made:

1. Giving a test or scale developed on college students to 7th grade students, and not presenting any data showing that it is reliable or valid for that group;

2. Giving a test validated on one cultural group to another, with no recognition of the need to determine whether it is reliable or valid in that group;

3. Giving a test such as the Minnesota Multiphasic Personality Inventory to determine "adjustment difficulties" with no discussion of how it will be interpreted;

4. Stating that a particular test or measure will be used but providing no data on its reliability or validity, thus forcing the reviewer either to look it up or to guess at its suitability;

5. Listing tests or scales to be used with no mention of why they are being used;

6. Presenting a test or scale and claiming prior use in one's own research, but presenting no data from that prior use;

7. Presenting pilot data on a test, but data with internal inconsistencies that show that the data are inaccurate;

8. Picking a measure of a particular characteristic on the basis of the name of the test or trait, when examination of the test items would show that it would not enable one to assess what the investigator really wants to measure;

9. Giving so many tests or repeating tests so often that they are almost bound to be reactive and lead to inaccurate results;

10. Changing the method of test administration from written to oral without considering possible effects.

MISTAKE 10: THE CRITICAL MISTAKE THAT ONE NEVER SEES

A minister prayed again and again, asking to win the lottery in order to use the money for good works. Time and again the lottery went by and the minister did not win. Finally one night after a hard session of prayer, the minister asked, "Why don't you answer my prayers? I am a good man and I have promised to use the money for good works. Why won't you let me win the lottery?"

Suddenly a voice spoke from the heavens, "Buy a ticket!"

The biggest mistake of all is not to write a proposal. It is absolutely fatal. You cannot get funded without trying.

Writing a proposal and having it rejected is painful. You will invest a lot of work, and will almost undoubtedly invest considerable ego. Being rejected is no fun. But it is not necessarily a waste of time even then. There are secondary benefits that can be important. Writing a proposal makes you consider seriously the significance of what you are doing, forces you to review the recent literature, and encourages detailed planning of your next research efforts. The pink sheets provide feedback on your effort. The exercise sharpens your thinking and creativity, and will improve your work regardless of whether you are funded.

And there is always the chance that you can convince the committee that your ideas will really advance science. Then you will have money and time to invest in your research that you could not hope to get in any other way. Go ahead and "Buy a ticket!"

REFERENCES

Gordon, J. (1978). Research work book. A guide for initial planning of clinical, social, and behavioral research projects. *Journal of Family Practice, 7*(1), 145–160.

Holtz, H. (1979). *Government contracts, proposalmanship and winning strategies.* New York: Plenum.

Lindholm, K. J., Marin, G., & Lopez, R. E. (1982). *Proposal writing strategies* (Monograph No. 9). Los Angeles: University of California, Spanish Speaking Mental Health Research Center.

INDEX

power studies and, 390–391
psychiatric clinical research and, 540–541, 547, 547–548, 553
research publication system and, 419, 423
therapeutic, 560, 562, 586
within-subjects designs and, 160

Attenuation paradox, 209

Audiovisual records, 681–682

Bayesian methods, 268, 401–403, 409, 430, 432, 434

Behavioral science, 273, 419, 561–562, 565, 568, 637–645

Beta/1-beta, 319–321, 324, 389, 390, 396–397

Between-subjects design, 87, 157–167

Biases
exaggerated effects and, 125–126
experimenters and, 410
multitrait–multimethod designs and, 572
null hypothesis prejudices, 260, 407–436
randomization and, 545–546
response, 204, 210
reviewers and, 460–461
small group, 450
study effect meta-analysis and, 452
testing and, 191–192

Binomial distribution, 442

Binomial effect-size display, 303, 345

Biomedical research, 550, 562–563, 707

Bivariate data, 318

Bogardus social distance scale, 204

Box-score review, 441

Brandt, E. N., Jr., 708

Brief psychotherapy, 670–672

British empiricist philosophy, 295–296

Bryant, M. B., 452

Bunge, M., 24

Busse, T. V., 450–451

Campbell, D. T., 476–478

Cancer patients, 575

Canonical variates, 357

Carry-over effect, 163–164

Case studies
characteristics of, 477–478

individual and series, 476–477
small sample research and, 469–470, 475–533
uncontrolled, 477–478
valid inferences and, 475–489

Categorical variables, 447

Causality
alternative interventions and, 469–470
analysis and, 8–9
behavior and, 6–8
mentalistic concepts and, 11–14
modeling and, 259, 373–376
probability and, 293
therapeutic alliance and, 575
validity and, 265–266

Central tendency, 443, 462

Chamberlain, T., 577

Chance, doctrine of, 287

Change
analysis of, 471
ATIs and, 561
change design, 547
correlates of, 611–612, 616–617
cutoff point for, 634–636
incremental change, 608–612
index of (RC), 636–637
manipulation checks and, 572
meaningfulness and, 631–647
modeling individual growth, 607, 617–618
nonspecific factors in, 471
placebos and, 593–594
process of, 609–610
qualitative change, 608
quantitative change, 608–610, 628
rate of change, 561, 621–623
true change, 617

Chase, S., 13

Chemotherapy, 575

Children, research with, 367–384, 620–626

Chi-square, 370, 372, 378, 379

Chi-square test, 289–290

Chow, S. L., 270

Civil liberties, 707

Classical theory (CT), 233–240

Client-specific research, 33

Cluster analysis, 444, 456, 459

Effect size
ATIs and, 571, 575, 579
comparability and, 398–399
counseling psychology and, 337–348
correlation analysis and, 327
data analysis and, 452
frequency weighting and, 456
meta-analysis and, 443, 446–452
population and, 301–302, 390
power analysis, 390–396, 443
sampling error and, 461–462
statistics and, 329, 571
strength of results and, 301
unit of analysis and, 456
variations and, 455

Efficacy studies, 97–98, 585–589, 684

Efficiencies, interactions of, 560

Eligibility, 545

Elementism, 5, 9, 20

Empiricism, 6–8, 19, 27, 295–296, 440

Employment tests, 456–457

Endpoint design, 546–548

English Essay Test, 178

Environmental factors. *See* Context

Equated scores, 189

Equivalence, 93–97

Error. *See also* Biases; Validity
estimate of effect, 431–432
measurement, 181–182
methodological flaw, 269
modeling misspecification, 375–376, 382
statistical power, 571
Type I, 275, 299, 316, 240, 361–362, 426–429, 567
Type II, 275–276, 299–301, 389, 567–570
Type III, 567–570, 580
variance, 328, 548

ES. *See* Effect size

Ethics, 649–712
acute patients and, 676–677
animal research and, 663, 706
assessment techniques and, 660–661
audiovisual records and, 681–682
authority issues and, 672–673
clinical judgment and, 673–674
clinical trials design and, 672–679
collaborative trials and, 665–684

competence and, 653–654
confidentiality and, 649, 657
individual vs. collective responsibility, 679–683
informed consent and, 540, 545, 666–667, 680–681, 684
IRBS research proposals and, 691–699
management of ethical issues, 672–683
misconduct in science, 705–712
moral and legal standards of, 654–655
placebo controls and, 675–676
professional relationships and, 658–661
protocol failures and, 678–679
public statements and, 655–657
random assignment and, 674–675
recruitment of subjects and, 680
research issues in, 661–684, 706
research reports and, 435
research values and, 20–21
responsibility and, 649–653, 679–683
technology and, 682–683
terminations and, 678–679
welfare of the consumer and, 658

Ethnic groups, 191–192

Exaggerated effect bias, 125–126

Expectation, 271–275. *See also* Assumptions

Experimental design. *See* Design of experiments

Experimental method. *See* Methodology

Exploratory data analysis, 328–329, 355, 369, 553–554

External criterion methods, 205–206

External validity, 164–166, 568–569

Extraneous variables, 278–279

Facets, fixed vs. random, 245–246

Face validity, 551

Fact-finding, 29–30

Factor analysis, 846–847, 201–202, 369–373, 377–384, 720

Failure to comply, 708

Falsifiability, 7, 322, 708, 712

Falsificationist approach, 266–268, 576

Fears, 368–370, 372–374, 376–382

Heredity, 6–7, 576

Heterogeneity, 195, 478, 482, 544, 571

Hierarchically related models, 370

Hilgard, E. R., 27

Holism, 5–6, 9, 20

Homans, G. C., 27

Homogeneity, 452, 454–458, 461, 544

Huberty, C. J., 356

Hull, C. L., 18–19

Human rights, 661–663, 706

Human subjects committees, 687–702, 708–711

Hunter, F. L., 445

Hunter, J. E., 456–458, 462

Hybrid statistics, 390, 400–403

Hypotheses. *See also* Constructs; Theory
  alternatives to, 478, 482, 485–489, 576
  ambiguity in, 271–275
  Aptitude × Treatment interactions, 557, 577–579
  case studies and, 478, 482, 485–489
  clinical assessment, 368–376, 378–382
  confirmatory data analysis, 553–554
  constructs and, 368–373
  evaluation and, 257–259, 265–333
  focal, 411, 413–416, 422–424
  ideas in, 2
  inconsequentiality and, 270–274
  major vs. minor, 391, 395
  meta-analysis and, 325
  multiple hypotheses, 577
  noncongruence and, 274
  omnibus tests, 276
  personality and, 475
  psychotherapy research, 265–283
  rival, 576
  specificity and, 273–275
  structural modeling, 383
  targeting in, 71–73
  testing of, 2, 64–69, 70–73, 322–328, 383, 425–427, 435
  theoretical propositions in, 64–67, 70, 258
  two-point, 390, 402
  validity and, 257–259, 265–333

Hypothesized mediating variables, 572–573

Hypothetico-deductive systems, 18–19, 56

Ideas, 2, 42–45, 71–73

Ideologies, 699–700

Implications, statistical, 270–274

Inclusion standards, 460, 544–545

Incompetence, 409–410, 425

Incremental view of change, 615

Independent variables. *See* specific methods

Index of difficulty, 185

Indices, 420–423, 636–637

Individual differences, 546–547, 558

Inference, 34, 321–322, 330, 374, 475–489

Inflated Ns problem, 448, 449, 451

Informal narrative review, 459–460

Information–transmission index, 421–423

Informed consent, 540, 545, 666–667, 680–681, 684

Inheritance. *See* Genetics

Initial status, 611–612

Inpatient–outpatient contrast, 558

Institutional Review Boards (IRBS), 688–702
  costs of, 689–690
  criteria and standards in, 701
  criticisms of, 701–702
  extensiveness of, 689
  ideologies of members of, 700–701
  misconduct and, 706
  personal values and, 691–699
  reliability of, 690–691

Instructional psychology, 28, 563–565

Instruments. *See* Measurement

Integration, research and theory, 33–34, 440, 446, 449

Integrity, defined, 143

Interaction. *See also* Aptitude × Treatment interactions
  contrasts in, 558
  effects of, 308–309, 415, 428, 557–561, 564
  Heredity × Environment interactions, 576–577
  ordinal vs. disordinal, 559

Intercorrelation. *See* Correlation

Internal validity, 476, 478, 480, 483–489, 568

concepts in, 169
design and, 169–170, 242–243
direction of, 210
generalizability and, 242–243
hypothesis testing and, 72–74
individual change measures, 615–628
insensitivity in, 599
physical science vs. behavioral sciences, 173
psychiatric research and, 550–552
scale evaluation in, 170
treatment assessment and, 150, 444

Median power, 391, 395–396, 398–399

Memory, 50, 51

Mental concepts, 20

Merton, R. K., 27

Meta-analysis. *See also* specific forms
approximate data pooling, 454–458, 461
cluster analysis in, 445
coding, 220–222
combined probability method, 453–454, 462
defined, 261, 439–440
effect size–based, 327–328
Glassian, 446
history of, 440–445
hypothesis testing, 325
informal narrative review in, 459–463
meaningfulness and, 578
methodological flaws in, 448–452
MMPI in, 217–232
naming of, 305
null hypotheses, 442
quantitative, 301
study-effect (SEM), 443–444, 450–453, 462
validity generalization technique, 445
WAIS in, 217–232

Methodology. *See also* specific issues
case studies and, 477
ethics in research and, 649–712
flaws in, 260
hard vs. social sciences, 268
issues in, 85–167, 373
manipulation checks and, 572–573
meta-analysis and, 443–445, 459–463
methods section of reports, 718
modifications in meta-analysis, 454–455
power of studies and, 393–399

spirit in, 297–301
substance in, 306–309

Milgram, S., 132–134

Minnesota Multiphasic Personality Inventory (MMPI), 170, 217–232

Miscomputation, 410

Misconduct in science, 705–712

Misspecification, 375–376, 382

Mixed independent variables, 461

MMPI. *See* Minnesota Multiphasic Personality Inventory

Modalities, clinical research, 449

Modeling
analysis of change, 607–628
misspecification in, 375–376, 382
multiple hypotheses and, 271
research publication system, 414–426
structural equation and, 367–384

Moller, H., 39

Morals, 654–655

Multiple Analysis of Covariance (MANCOVA), 306

Multiple Analysis of Variance (MANOVA), 306

Multiple-choice tests, 176–177

Multiple factors, 470

Multiple hypotheses, 271

Multiple statistical tests, 274–276

Multiple working hypotheses, 577

Multisite research programs, 682–683

Multivariate analysis, 247–252, 259, 277, 351–363

Narrative review, 459–460

National Depression Collaborative Research Program, 570, 573, 575, 577

National Institutes of Health (NIH), 705–712

National Institute of Mental Health (NIMH), 570

Nature–nurture interaction, 9–10, 442

Neuropsychology, 620–626

Neyman-Pearson theory, 390, 400–403

Nomothetic span, 208

Noncongruence, 274

Nonexperimental variables, 375–376

psychiatric research and, 471, 547, 585–603

psychotherapy research and, 471, 585–603

standardization of, 595–596

Plagiarism, 708, 712

Plants, 429

Platt, J. R., 271

Point null hypothesis, 432–433

Polychloric correlations, 371, 378–380

Popper, K., 322, 576

Population standardized mean difference, 460

Positivism, 375

Post hoc analysis, 546

Posterior probability, 432–434. *See also* Bayesian methods

Post-test only design, 45

Potential, vs. performance, 10

Power
  analysis of, 260, 316, 325–326, 342, 348, 565
  defined, 258
  journal articles and, 413
  level of, 329
  psychiatric research and, 542–543, 546–547, 549–550
  significance testing and, 298–301, 303
  statistical, 260, 301, 361, 389–403, 550–551, 571
  of studies, 389–397, 400–402, 443
  tests and, 340, 550
  within-subjects design and, 159–160

Practice, within-subjects design and, 160–161

Practitioners, clinical, 68, 338, 373, 476–477, 558, 580

Prediction, 6, 205–206, 208, 345, 410, 413, 425

Prejudices. *See* Biases

PRELIS, 378

Presentations, graphic, 44–45, 318, 578, 720

Pretesting, 185

Principle of symmetry, 246

Prisoner's dilemma research, 28

Privacy Act, 710

Probable error, 289, 291

Process dynamics, 45–46

Product–moment correlation, 318, 338–340, 343–345, 377

Professional relationships, 658–660

Projectability, theory of, 30

Proposal preparation, 691–699

Protected *F* test, 353

Psychiatric clinical research
  biases in, 545–546
  data processing in, 552–554
  diagnostic systems in, 550
  difference scores and, 612–615
  inclusion/exclusion in, 544–545
  informed consent in, 540, 545, 680–681
  measurement in, 550–552
  patient reponse designs in, 546–547
  power in, 542–543, 546–547, 549–550
  random sampling in, 540, 545–546
  sensitivity in, 551–552
  statistics in, 546–554

Psycholinguists, 8–9

Psychology of Interpersonal Relation (Heider), 51

Psychology without concepts, 14–18

Psychometry, 17–18, 551. *See also* Measurement

Psychosocial therapies, 585–586, 592–594, 597

Psychotherapy and Behavior Change (Higgenbotham et al.), 571–572

Psychotherapy. *See* specific issues, modalities

Publication, 715–748. *See also* Informal narrative review
  ANOVA, 548
  APA Manual, 305
  grant writing, 716, 739–748
  journal editors and, 402
  journal reviews, 716, 723–733
  meta-analytic reviews, 459–463
  misconduct and, 706–708
  narrative reviews, 459–460
  null hypothesis bias and, 410
  public statements, 655–657
  research-publication system, 414–426, 429
  research reports, 717–720
  research results and, 435

ABOUT THE EDITOR

Alan E. Kazdin is professor of psychology and professor in the Child Study Center (child psychiatry) at Yale University. He is also director of the Yale Child Conduct Clinic, an outpatient treatment clinic for children and their families. He received his PhD at Northwestern University in 1970. Prior to coming to Yale, he was on the faculty at the Pennsylvania State University and the University of Pittsburgh School of Medicine.

Currently his work focuses on assessment, diagnosis, and treatment, particularly of antisocial behavior and depression in children, and on psychotherapy outcome. He has been the editor of the *Journal of Consulting and Clinical Psychology, Psychology Assessment*, and *Behavior Therapy*, a Fellow at the Center for Advanced Study in the Behavioral Sciences, and president of the Association for Advancement of Behavior Therapy. He is a Fellow of the American Psychological Association and editor of the Sage Book Series on developmental clinical psychology and psychiatry. Some of his other books in clinical psychology and methodology, design, and evaluation include: *Research Design in Clinical Psychology* (Macmillan Press), *Single-Case Research Designs: Methods for Clinical and Applied Settings* (Oxford University Press), *The Clinical Psychology Handbook* (with A. S. Bellack & M. Hersen; Pergamon Press), and *Advances in Clinical Child Psychology* (with B. B. Lahey; Plenum Press).